REGION-BUILDING

REGION-BUILDING

Volume I: The Global Proliferation of Regional Integration

Ludger Kühnhardt

Berghahn Books
New York • Oxford

Published in 2010 by

Berghahn Books
www.berghahnbooks.com

©2010 Ludger Kühnhardt

Library of Congress Cataloging-in-Publication Data
Kühnhardt, Ludger, 1958–
    Region-building / Ludger Kuhnhardt.
        p. cm.
    Includes bibliographical references and index.
    ISBN 978-1-84545-654-2 (hardback : alk. paper)
    1. Regionalism (International organization)   2. Globalization.   3. Regionalism—
European Union countries.   4. Regionalism—Europe.   I. Title.
    JZ5330.K64 2010
    341.24—dc22   2010008024

British Library Cataloguing in Publication Data
A catalogue record for this book is available from the British Library

Printed in the United States on acid-free paper

ISBN: 978-1-84545-654-2 Hardback

For Enikö Noemi, and for our children,
Victoria Elisabeth and Stephan Maximilian,
with love. They traveled with me through this
project and continue doing so in all other
ventures of our common life.

Contents

PART III | CONTEXT AND IMPLICATION

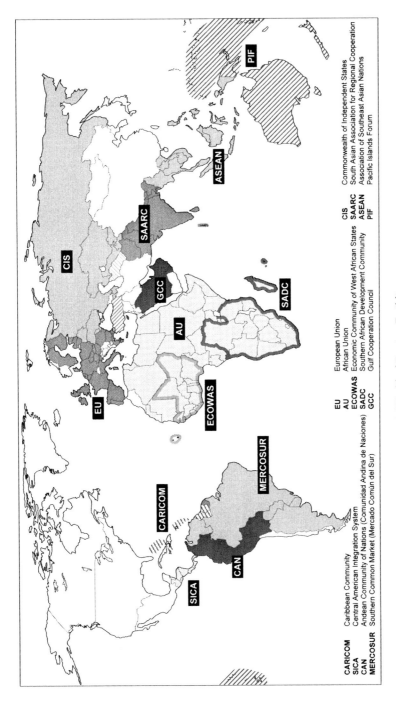

CARICOM	Caribbean Community
SICA	Central American Integration System
CAN	Andean Community of Nations (Comunidad Andina de Naciones)
MERCOSUR	Southern Common Market (Mercado Común del Sur)

EU	European Union
AU	African Union
ECOWAS	Economic Community of West African States
SADC	Southern African Development Community
GCC	Gulf Cooperation Council

CIS	Commonwealth of Independent States
SAARC	South Asian Association for Regional Cooperation
ASEAN	Association of Southeast Asian Nations
PIF	Pacific Islands Forum

A World of Region-Building

Abbreviations

—◉—

ACCP, Assembly of the Caribbean Community Parliamentarians

ACP, Africa, Caribbean, Pacific

AFTA, ASEAN Free Trade Area

APEC, Asia-Pacific Economic Cooperation

ASEAN, Association of Southeast Asian Nations

ASEM, Asia-Europe Meeting

ASEP Asia-Europe Parliamentary Meeting

AU, African Union

BCIE, Banco Centroamericano de Integración Económica
      (Central American Bank for Economic Integration)

CABEI, Central American Bank for Economic Integration

CACM, Central American Common Market

CAFTA, Central American Free Trade Agreement

CAN, Comunidad Andina de Naciones (Andean Community of Nations)

CARICOM, Caribbean Community

CARIFORUM (forum of the Caribbean member states of ACP)

CARIFTA, Caribbean Free Trade Agreement

CCJ, Caribbean Court of Justice

CEMAC, Communauté Économique et Monétaire d'Afrique Centrale (Central African Economic and Monetary Community)

CENTO, the Central Treaty Organization

CFA, French Community of Africa

CIS, Commonwealth of Independent States

COMESA, Common Market for Eastern and Southern Africa

CSCE, Conference on Security and Cooperation in Europe

CSME, Caribbean Single Market and Economy

EAC, East African Community

ECLA, Economic Commission for Latin America and the Caribbean

ECOWAS, Economic Community of West African States

ECSC, European Coal and Steel Community

EEC, European Economic Community

EFTA, European Free Trade Agreement

EPA, Economic Partnership Agreement

EU, European Union

EUPOL COPPS (EU Police Mission in the Palestinian Territories)

FAO, UN Food and Agricultural Organization

FTA, free trade agreement

FTAA, Free Trade Area of the Americas

GAFTA, Greater Arab Free Trade Area

GATT, General Agreement on Tariffs and Trade

GCC, Gulf Cooperation Council

LAFTA, Latin American Free Trade Agreement

LAIA, Latin American Integration Association

MERCOSUR, Mercado Común del Sur (Southern Common Market)

NAFTA, North American Free Trade Agreement

NATO, North Atlantic Treaty Organization

NEPAD, New Partnership for Africa's Development

OAU, Organization of African Unity

OECS, Organization of Eastern Caribbean States

PARLACEN (the Central American parliament)

PIF, Pacific Islands Forum

PTA, preferential trade agreement

SAARC, South Asian Association for Regional Cooperation

SADC, Southern African Development Community

SAFTA, South Asian Free Trade Area

SEATO, the Southeast Asian Treaty Organization

SICA, Sistema de la Integración Centroamericana (Central American Integration System)

SIECA, Secretaría de Integración Económica Centroamericana (Secretariat of the Central American System of Economic Integration)

STABEX, Stabilization of Export Earnings

UEMOA, Union Économique et Monétaire Ouest Africain (West African Economic and Monetary Union)

UNIFIL, United Nations Interim Force in Lebanon

WTO, World Trade Organization

INTRODUCTION

———‹(◉)›———

This study is about region-building and its role in today's world order. As any glance at a map reveals, regions constitute geographical realities around the world. But regions are also mental realities conceived and shaped by notions of culture, identity, and material interests. Regions are political, as their delineation and inner order are never developed without the influence of political norms and actions. Regions are markets, no matter whether these markets are integrated and shaped in a cooperative, competitive, or protectionist way. Regions are home to people and to their history. Regions might experience their future—and endure it—as objects of developments inside and outside the region. Whenever a region wants to determine its own destiny, it needs to shape the future by proactively building the region. Regions, however, are not natural personalities with a holistic identity. Regions consist of multitudes of actors and factors: individuals, social groups, economic resources and constellations, political institutions and structures of power, states and subregions, and private and public interactions. Beyond continents and hemispheres, regions are one of the cornerstones of our world.

Regions of all sizes, shapes and powers exist. But regions are not merely abstract and empty forms. They are shaped by their people, history, culture, economics, politics, and the relations among states and societies inside and outside a region. While this all may be self-evident, it is nonetheless worth bearing in mind. Furthermore, regions influence and are influenced by the agendas that define public life. The history of most regions in the world could be written as a history of struggles for resources, recognition, and power, but also as a history of missed opportunities and failed, often ultimately irreversible, efforts. However, the most positive form of writing about regions is to write about the way regions discover region-ness and build up commonality in order to serve their best interests, to bring their resources together, and to embark on a journey of mutual gain and benefit through cooperation and integration. When regions turn into a regional grouping, they begin to create new realities. Efforts in regional integration have become more or less a worldwide phenomenon.

By all accounts, the European experience in region-building under the framework of the European Union is the most advanced example of a regional grouping in today's world order. But by no means is it the only one. Across the globe, regional groupings have emerged that aim in their own way to advance common interests through the mutual gains of cooperation and integration. Much of the literature about these phenomena applies a rather loose definition of "region," "regional grouping," or "regional integration." But not every form of regional cooperation and integration is structurally identical. Efforts to form a common free trade area differ from efforts in a multifaceted project of region-building that includes political aspects, is joined by common institutions, and strives to achieve a regional community with a certain sense of belonging and identity.

This study adds to our understanding of regional integration efforts and hopes to raise it to a higher level empirically. In doing so, this study wishes to contribute to an understanding of regions above the state level that is to an understanding of region-building linked to the normative idea of good governance and democratic rule of law. No region-building effort across the globe, the main thesis of this study argues, can be deep, lasting, and legitimate without recognizing the norms of democratic accountability and rule of law as its cornerstone. The constituent members of a regional grouping need to be democracies at home in order to achieve deeper integration with partner countries abroad. Deep integration requires trust in the political, legal, and economic system of one's partners.

My study is divided into three parts. The first part—"Framing the Issue"—introduces the topic and its underlying theses. Chapter 1 formulates the necessary definitions that guide my study: globalization, regionalization, and integration are catchwords that can become meaningless if not properly defined. Objective criteria for defining these and related terms are limited. The chapter discusses the definitions that are most common in academic literature and then provides my own interpretation: I relate globalization, regionalization, and integration to the notions and roles of politics and the market. Understanding these respective spheres is essential for linking the key notions of political theory with the study of the empirical realities that shape regional groupings across the globe. I also discuss the fundamental difference between economic regionalism and community-building regionalism. I conclude that the North American Free Trade Agreement (NAFTA) and the European Union (EU) are two different concepts of regionalization. They are not each one's "other" but simply follow a different logic and aspiration. Community-oriented region-building as embodied in the European Union is, I conclude, the criterion for selecting the regional groupings studied in the empirical survey of my book.

Chapter 2 examines the meaning of the European integration experience for assessing and understanding the global proliferation of regional integration schemes. It is by no means a Euro-centric prejudice to introduce the European Union as a model for many non-European efforts in region-building. Across the world it is recognized that the European Union represents the most advanced scheme of region-building. It is certainly not perfect; it is not even complete. Nonetheless, the European integration experience has been emulated in other parts of the world. Often, it seems to be perceived as a speedy and easy "path to paradise." This would be an utterly erroneous misunderstanding of the ambition, role, and impact of the European Union. Efforts to copy and transpose European institutional mechanisms have often occurred without even reflecting upon the necessary preconditions that made those European experiences possible. The most fundamental precondition for successful integration in Europe has been the democratic nature of governance in all EU member states. This chapter discusses the meaning of democracy and regime cohesion in region-building. The European Union has proactively begun to promote regional integration across the globe as one of the mantras of its enhanced global posture. More research beyond the scope of my study is needed to better understand the real effects of this policy and the constraints originating in domestic constellations elsewhere and in competing global concepts of other internationally active actors.

The second part of this study—"A Global Survey"—gives an overview of those regional groupings across the world that aim at a political dimension of community-building. The regional groupings discussed in this study are based on institutionalized means of region-building, and one way or another they aim, according to their own treaties and political statements, at community-building. In most cases, initially this has only been a rhetorical claim. But in claiming institutionalized community-building, the regional groupings chosen for my study represent an ambition closer to the European integration experience than other regional groupings in the world, including NAFTA and Asia-Pacific Economic Cooperation (APEC). NAFTA and APEC represent a market-oriented economic approach to facilitating regional interactions and interdependencies. Since they do not claim to engage in politically driven community-building, they differ from the regional groupings discussed in this book and hence will not be included in more detail in my study.

The global survey chapters of my study follow the same structure and analytical pattern. In doing so, I hope to strengthen the basis for reasonable comparative work. Chapters 3, 4, 5, and 6 of the global survey follow the same design: basic facts, intrinsic motives and external pressures, performance, federators, transformations, role and interests of the European Union, prospects and obstacles. Chapters 7 and 8 follow the same structure but use contingent subheadings.

In Chapter 3, I introduce four efforts of region-building in Latin America and the Caribbean. The System of Central American Integration, the Andean Community of Nations, the Caribbean Community, and the Southern Common Market cover the continent from Tierra del Fuego ("Land of Fire") to the

Mexican and US borders. They are inspired by the historical dream of continental unification, which, since the conception of this vision, has not yet been accomplished. But these region-building efforts, each of them, can enjoy success only to the extent that they are precise in their pursuit of a genuine regional agenda, supported by the rule of law and consistent symmetry of national political norms.

Chapter 4 looks at the impossible effort to conceptualize Asia as one continent. Even more than Latin America, which culturally, or at least linguistically, is relatively homogenous, Asia is the most diverse religious, cultural, and ethnic space in the world. No one has ever seriously claimed to embark on continental unification there. However, in three of the Asian subcontinents, region-building has emerged. I analyze the Gulf Cooperation Council, the Association of Southeast Asian Association, and the South Asian Association of Regional Cooperation. Their degree of integration differs considerably, as do their respective preconditions and objectives. Yet these three regional groupings, which cover vast territories of Asia, are to this day the most visible and promising structures of community-building in Asia.

Chapter 5 initiates an effort to better understand Africa through the lens of the continent's integration efforts. In Africa, regionalism is equivalent to the hope of a renaissance of a continent largely perceived as the world's basket case. Since decolonization, Africa's independent states have been preserved by the Organization of African Unity. Since it was refounded as the African Union in 2002, regional integration and continent-wide cooperation have become a leitmotiv for a relaunched notion of statehood, accepting intervention as a means to strengthen security, development, and good governance. Among Africa's plethora of regional schemes of coordination, cooperation, and integration, two are most prominent in genuinely serving as engines for region-building on the continent: the Economic Community of West Africa and the South African Development Community are the most advanced schemes for regional cooperation in Africa, having gone beyond their original objective and demonstrated the ability to reinvent themselves under new conditions.

Chapter 6 looks at the youngest and so far weakest regional grouping, the Pacific Islands Forum. The small island nations of the vast Pacific Ocean have realized the limits of their resources in coping with the region's natural and economic limits. Preserving a viable form of statehood requires regional cooperation and integration. Advanced cooperation and partnership with the European Union is one important pillar in the Pacific islands' future. But in order to be accepted as a partner of the European Union for deep association, the Pacific Islands Forum must speed up its regional integration efforts. The Pacific Islands Forum has been the embryo of region-building in its region. Often this example is forgotten in Europe, since the Pacific region is so far away geographically and seems to be economically irrelevant for Europe. But in the Pacific, the idea of emulating the European Union is gaining remarkable ground.

Chapter 7 discusses the concept of regional integration as a means to manage the decline of the Soviet empire. Although often declared dead, the Eurasian effort of establishing a Commonwealth of Independent States (CIS) has not yet come to an end. Primarily, it must be understood as a means to organize the demise of the Soviet Union and prevent it from escalating into a multitude of local and regional conflicts beyond the ones that already absorb the world, most notably in Chechnya. The regional idea has tamed the potentially eruptive nature of the implosion following the dissolution of the Soviet Union. Although it was always highly unlikely that de-integration of the enforced Soviet unity would automatically lead to a democracy- and market-based model of positive integration, the Commonwealth of Independent States has played a laudable role in managing the geopolitical opening of Eurasia. The CIS was never aimed at supporting the growth of democratic governance in its constituent republics of the former Soviet Union. Not surprisingly, the biggest tension for the CIS arose when some of these republics embarked on the path of Western-oriented democratization while others reinforced authoritarian governance.

Chapter 8 focuses on the two most prominent regions in the world with the least visible efforts in region-building. In spite of all evident differences, Northeast Asia and the Broader Middle East have two features in common: they are defined by intensive geopolitical tension, and they lack regime cohesion—that is to say, shared democratic governance among their member states. Other regions in the world lack regime cohesion too, yet they have begun with region-building, at least in a minimal sense. A more relevant factor preventing region-building in Northeast Asia and in the Broader Middle East, obviously, is the geopolitical constellation in both these regions. As long as the current geopolitical constellation in these two regions prevails, partial security cooperation and even broader economic cooperation may occur, but regional integration, including a political component aimed at community-building, seems unlikely and even impossible.

The third part of my study—"Context and Implications"—draws conclusions and offers theoretical reflections based on this broad empirical survey. Chapter 9 assesses the proactive role of the European Union in supporting the worldwide development of regional integration. It is interesting to note that the European Union's claim to a stronger global presence is coupled with a normative quest for regional integration that is increasingly incorporated in the EU's foreign policy actions. Although the EU approaches lack coherence and their results are mixed, the European Union has clearly started a new relationship with many parts of the world, notably those that have been former European colonies. Yet the nascent process of promoting interregional relations with other regional groupings has become the focus of attention (and surprise) in some of the scholarly literature. More research will be necessary to precisely assess the effect of EU policies in promoting regional integration. We need to know in more detail to what extent, for which political actors, and under which circumstances the European integration experience serves as a model for conflict resolution and problem management in other parts of the world. EU policies in promoting regional integration do not explain any immediate causal links about the effects of these policies elsewhere.

EU policies in promoting regional integration are also constrained by competing concepts of other global actors. Chapter 10 focuses on the relationship between regional integration, world order–building, and the primacy of the global role of the United States. The United States is not part of any regional grouping in the definition of this study. It represents the traditional "old" European notion of the primacy of autonomous statehood as the ultimate expression of state sovereignty. As a federation and as a democracy, the US represents two essential features for the formulation of objectives and normative prerequisites of region-building. Yet the global proliferation of region-building has been perceived with ambivalence in the US. The global projection of US interests is not centered on the idea of region-building. It is not rare that region-building efforts are portrayed as a means to tame, if not to control, the global power of the United States. On the other hand, the rise of China poses a different set of challenges to the normative approach of the EU. China's interest in other regions is largely driven by economic interests without political conditioning. More research would be helpful to better understand how far this imposes constraints on EU policies by undermining some of its key normative conditions.

Region-building, the European Union would argue, can eventually succeed as a new and additional feature of world order only if it is democratic. Regionalism must be rooted in domestic democratic governance in order to build up political legitimacy and sufficient public trust in deeper integration. Regionalism must also develop political structures on the regional level that are compatible with the most fundamental notions of democratic trust to maintain legitimacy and sustainability. Democratic regionalism—such is the central hypothesis of my study, summarized in Chapter 11—is the precondition for region-building to make any lasting impact on world order and governance. Democratic region-building, properly implemented, is an open process with a stabilizing and broadening function for key notions of political theory and central features of international politics. Democratic region-building, I emphasize in summarizing my study, is precondition, tool, and objective of solid and legitimate regionalism that goes beyond functional measures of cooperation. It deserves further research to measure this argument.

The interest in studying the global proliferation of regional integration evolved in the course of my work as director at the Center for European Integration

Studies of Bonn University. Often, it seems to me, European integration is more appreciated the further away somebody is from the EU's daily battlegrounds. Whereas inside the European Union the progress of integration often coincides with doubts and crises about its path and depth, the European Union is mostly understood as rock-solid and successful by outside observers. My colleagues and I are often approached by non-European policy actors expressing their interest in learning about EU structures and possible ways to transfer them into their own region. Academic analysts outside Europe have become increasingly curious to discuss the implications of regional integration in Europe for their own regions. Postgraduate students applying for our Master of European Studies Program come from all four corners of the world, underlining the global interest in learning more about European integration, its impact, and its relevance for other regions and efforts of region-building.

My study is based on a systematic analysis of the documents of region-building and a wide array of fine scholarly writings on the different aspects of my study. I studied all documents available on the regional groupings presented in this study, and I am much indebted to all the authors I have mentioned in my text. Their texts have broadened my insights and perspective and helped me to reassess my own assumptions. This valuable service was also rendered by several colleagues with whom I had the pleasure of personally discussing several of my theses and parts of my empirical assessments. Likewise, I have benefited from extensive field research in all regional groupings and in the regions without integration that are analyzed in this study. Here, I was able to interview many experienced officials and local analysts. More than anything else, this field research has broadened my perspectives. It has helped me to get a better sense and a differentiated view of the regions discussed in this study. My personal experiences prevented me, I hope, from applying a Euro-centric or solely dry and theoretical perspective. I always tried to understand the historical background and intrinsic conditions, the potential and problems of each region. On this basis, I have tried to give life and differentiated meaning to the documents on regional integration that have been concluded across the globe. I am also grateful to the anonymous referees who have provided me with valuable comments. This helped me in a careful review of my study.

Most beneficial for writing the first draft of this study were the terms I had the pleasure of spending at Oxford's St. Antony's College. At the invitation of its European Studies Centre's director, Timothy Garton Ash, my friend for more than two decades, I immersed myself in the familiarity and global horizon, unique to St. Antony's College, where concentrated learning in a quasi-monastic environment meets with a permanent involvement in the affairs of the world. The rector of Bonn University, Matthias Winiger, granted me a sabbatical for which I am sincerely grateful. My work at Bonn University's Center for European Integration Studies gave me the inspiration for this study and provided the means to conduct field research that was essential to deepening my knowledge and sharpening my judgment on region-building across the world. Without the generous and supportive environment at Oxford and Bonn—which happen to be twin cities—I could not have completed this study.

I am grateful to all who made this book possible, most of all my family, to whom I dedicate this book. All responsibility for judgments and errors in this book or for any omissions of topics I should have considered remains, of course, with me.

Ludger Kühnhardt
Bonn, January 2010

PART I

FRAMING THE ISSUE

I

GLOBALIZATION, REGIONALISM, INTEGRATION

Politics and Identity in the Age of the Market

———⊶⟨◉⟩⊷———

Defining Region-ness

During the nineteenth and twentieth century, the world has experienced state-building on a massive scale. The number of recognized sovereign states around the globe has increased dramatically, from 55 in 1900 to 205 in 2010, 193 of them being UN member states. The project of nation-building has produced mixed results while the term was largely attributed to postcolonial efforts in Asia, Africa, and Latin America. Many sovereign states, without being home to coherent nations, have joined the global community after their respective colonizing powers had left. In the late twentieth century, the phenomenon has been experienced in post-communist Europe, too.

In the twenty-first century, the world is experiencing a new phenomenon: region-building. For a long time, subregions have been designed within nation-states and across their once rigid borders. Today, equally—and more—important are the processes of region-building among the states of the world. These processes have long-term implications, and not only for the order of the world. They are also influencing and transforming key notions of political theory and terminology. Multilevel governance pooled or shared sovereignty, supranationalism: this is some of the jargon associated with the European integration process that began more than five decades ago. Increasingly, these and related terms also provide a better understanding of long-term trends in other regions around the world. Region-building, in fact, has matured into a global phenomenon. It is not just about larger markets, although this is a logical implication of the theory of economies of scale. Region-building is also about establishing common institutions, joint norms, and legislation. Finally, region-building is a form and a function of the quest for identity, recognition, and difference. Region-building, as understood in this study, is about politically supported community-building. Region-building is the signature of the twenty-first century.

The rediscovery of regions as political units is as confusing as the academic effort of systematizing and interpreting the global trend. While the Cold War was a phenomenon with global outreach and clearly defined origin, region-building is a near-global phenomenon without clearly stratified roots. Confusion and ambivalence permeate all aspects of the phenomenon: the definition of regions is often vague; the meaning and objective of building a region has generated manifold approaches and even more interpretations; and integration is a controversial term, not only in the context of the European Union. The same applies for the relational context of integration, the definition of its base, meaning, and goal.

From a simple geographical point of view, the world is divided into continents. The Olympic rings represent the five corners of the world, all honored by female names: Europe, Asia, America, Africa, Australia. The notion of continents, which originated in Europe, is as much a construction as the global impact of the European formula for the nomenclature of continents. While continents can be considered the natural geographical areas of the world, by all other criteria continental regions are overly ambiguous and almost meaningless. Culture and history, ethnic composition and economic activities, and political orders and global projection turn continents into a multitude of identities and factors. The Cold War was a meaningful period in world history, one that seemed to transcend notions of culture and geography as hemispheres and continents fell under the purview of a bipolar global divide. To the extent that revolutions are the return from the artificial to the real, the dissolution of the Soviet empire, along with the failure of communism as an ideology, economic law, and inspiration for human progress, opened new avenues for the reassessment of the world in much more differentiated shades and colors. The hegemonic role of the United States did not give ultimate answers about the future structure and stability of the world. On the contrary, it provoked resentment. It generated the search for a new orientation with regard to the global management of public affairs.

The deciphering of the post–Cold War world has taken different forms. Most spectacular and controversial was Samuel P. Huntington's proposal to divide the world into seven civilizations: Western (including Israel), Latin American, African, Islamic, Sinic, Hindu, and Japanese.[1] The Harvard professor warned of the danger that these civilizations might clash, not least along their respective fault lines. His theories were debated with much emotion during the 1990s and into the early days of the twenty-first century. For our intents and purposes, it is not especially relevant whether or not Huntington's proposal to understand the key features of the post–Cold War world were properly understood or rejected as the author's recipe for triggering the very clash of civilizations he was warning of.

However, Huntington's understanding of the world as a collection of civilizations did pose a number of unanswered political, as well as cultural and geographical questions.

Regions as civilizations cannot be understood without clarifying their relationship to the states that constitute the political order of the world. Their respective interests, their meaning, and their objectives have to be related to the role of regions and the impact of civilizations. Likewise, in the age of economic and technological globalization, the role of the market has to be assessed. While the market is potentially borderless, the state is defined by strict borders and limits that constitute its autonomy and identity. Regions above the state are stepping stones to a global order, but they are not necessarily building blocks of globalization. Civilizations as expressions of culture and history have political meaning once they are related to the sphere of politics. Hence region-building is a phenomenon above the nation-state and below the global market. This is a rather static demarcation that gains substance only if it is related to the issues and objectives that constitute a region.

Regions are social constructs. They might be defined by natural factors such as geographic delineations, cultural divisions, and historical experience. Yet in reality, regions are more often efforts to transcend the effects of these patterns. Regions are meant to overcome geographic delineations in their implications for economic, social, and political interaction. They can represent cultural homogeneity, but it is more likely that they are efforts to overcome cultural divisions. They can be based on historical experiences in a region, but more often they are aimed at reconstructing a region against its historical experience of division, enmity, and conflict. The external dimension of region-building is important, for regions do not exist in a geographical and geopolitical vacuum. They are driven as much by external pressure as they are by projections of intra-regional aspiration. In all cases, constructivism cannot be denied. There would be no region-building without a social concept and a sociological or political construction.

Region-building is not equivalent to the work of architects and town planners. Regions are multidimensional realities. Their evolution is contingent and might happen against all currents of history, social engineering, and political planning. Yet they are planned phenomena and remain therefore processes without a static objective, ultimate end, or petrified structure. In its engineered character, region-building is comparable to state-building and nation-building. None of these guiding processes of political organization in the world can claim natural origins. States and nations are the product of historical processes, ideational concepts, and social constructions. They have never been static, although the longevity of states and the persistence of their claim to political primacy tend to suggest the opposite. States and nations, especially those that can look back on a long history, have undergone transformations. States and nations seem to perish only very seldom, even if their foundations have become weak and their objectives remain loose. The dissolution of states and the formation of nations have long been the object of academic interpretation. By contrast, regions and region-building are still young phenomena in the social sciences, as these realities of our world have only been of secondary importance so far. This will change in the course of the twenty-first century.

The global proliferation of efforts in region-building is undeniable. Regional integration, which is found worldwide, is a normative concept with a confusing array of conceptual ingredients. It is a dynamic reality with evolving structures, objectives, and results. It is a growing feature of academic interpretation that leaves room for a much deeper and wider occupation with the manifold aspects and implications of this peaceful proliferation. The European Union (EU) is usually considered to be the most elaborate structure of region-building in the world. Besides its role as a normative inspiration for other regions in the world, the European Union is actively pursuing the global promotion of regional integration as one of its political priorities. While more research is needed to better understand the real scope and effect of this EU policy, region-building clearly brings Europe back as a global power.

Region-building is a reaction to several major trends of the past century:

- It is a response to the flaws and failures of the unchallenged supremacy of the concept of autonomous statehood and the primacy of the nation-state. The notion of sovereign nation-states as the prime actors of international relations emerged with the Westphalian peace order following the end of the Thirty Years' War in Europe (1618–1648). The nation-state and sovereign statehood became the key features of the European state system. Following European colonialism and the subsequent decolonization between the early nineteenth and late twentieth centuries, the traditional European notions of sovereign statehood and the primacy of an order based on the concept of the nation-state spread across the globe. Europe encountered the limits of this traditional concept of political order in the aftermath of a second Thirty Years' War (1914–1945) and began with the construction of an integrated European order aimed at replacing the traditional European experiences with hegemony, balance of power, and autarkic state sovereignty. Following the processes of decolonization, it took the new states in other parts of the world several generations to recognize the limits of their statehood. While the state often could not provide what was expected by its growing citizenry, in many cases the nation was not a cohesive agent of promoting state order either. Helping the nation blossom did not really justify the state's protective power. Once the limits of sovereign statehood were recognized, more and more state actors in the southern hemisphere began to understand the significance and potential of region-building as a path to strengthen the state through its transformation and the cooperative effects of regional integration.

- As the bipolar order of the Cold War faded away, the global diversity of cultures gained new centrality. The uniqueness of each region and its people was increasingly recognized. The formation of regions gained new momentum, driven by the quest for cultural identity and economic well-being. Regional security, and to a lesser extent the hope for more stable and democratic governance, added to the growing trend of region-building. Several older regional organizations and integration schemes were revitalized on the basis of a new contractual foundation. The European Union became increasingly active in the promotion of regional integration and began to develop a coherent policy in this regard. Post–Cold War region-building was also a response to the leveling and unavoidable trend of globalization. Globalization, often understood as Americanization, was framed as the economic and technological extension of US geopolitical primacy. While a global market for consumer goods, services, and means of communication became increasingly evident across the earth, resistance to its leveling effects coincided with skepticism about, or rejection of, the primacy of the US as the only remaining superpower. Region-building was not inevitably an anti-American concept, but its possible effect was and can be understood as a global contribution to frame and tame American hegemony. Region-building was, and sometimes still is, driven by the desire to escape, or at least to tame, the forces and effects of economic globalization. Region-building can, however, also be regarded as anticipated globalization in one region, which has been said about the European Union and its achievement of a common market.
- Region-building contributes to a reassessment, and an at least partial reorganization, of internal relations and external interdependencies between the conditions and effects of statehood, development, and security. In the age of globalization, new opportunities and the fear of being marginalized are parallel experiences in many parts of the world. Region-building is considered to be a protective shield against the unfiltered effects of globalization and at the same time an instrument to shape the path of globalization in a region. The enormous diversity of regional structures and the inadequate precision in defining region-building and regionalism are not helpful in clarifying the scope, role, and effect of region-building in a simple and conclusive way. But there can be no doubt that region-building is more than the conclusion of the free trade agreements that have mushroomed across the world. Region-building is a variant of community-building. As such it includes social and political, at times also cultural, dimensions that go beyond the unquestionable logic of economic cooperation. Region-building is rooted in preconditions and generates effects beyond its original aspirations and objectives. All experience demonstrates that democratic governance and rule of law among the member states of a regional scheme are the main precondition to make regional integration work. There can be no successful region-building without regime cohesion in terms of democratic governance—this might be the ultimate conclusion to properly understand the potential and the limits of the global proliferation of region-building.

The term regionalism has been introduced in sociological theory, but it is often related to subregional constructions below the level of the nation-state. These might exist as cross–nation-state ties in accordance with the famous notion of Daniel Bell that the nation-state is too small to deal with the big questions of our time and too big to deal with the small ones. Regions below the nation-state are bigger than one's hometown and smaller than one's home country. They are certainly forged by common memory, historic experience, patterns of interaction and tradition, lifestyle, architecture, food and language, culture, and geographical proximity. Nations are considered to be state-protected sociological units with a high density of interaction, common will and purpose, and shared memory and destiny. Nation-states, finally, are perceived as best protecting a nation, securing its survival and strength, defining its role in the world, protecting its sovereignty, and struggling with its limits.

On the other end of the logical and sociological spectrum are the continents, constructions of Europe's first wave of globalization between the fifteenth and eighteenth century. During that period Europe itself was neither a clear-cut region nor a comprehensive continent in terms of its own nomenclature. Rather, it was a combination of ambitious, imperial, and clashing nation-states at the time when it exported the notion of continents as a category of world order. Europe's imperialism was followed by the global proliferation of the concept of statehood, ideally defined as nation-state. This was the consequence of Europe's withdrawal from world hegemony owing largely to internal European quarrels, exhaustion, and the replacement of Europe's global dominance by the fringe powers, the United States and the Soviet Union.[2]

Colonialism shaped postcolonial nationalism in most parts of the non-Western world. In a first wave, the emancipation of North America took place, followed by the independence of Latin America. The subsequent development of the nation-states in the New World facilitated the repetition and enforcement of European concepts of sovereignty, state autonomy, and nationalism. Neither the modern democratic character of the North American republics nor the cultural and religious homogeneity of Latin America helped to generate concepts and notions of postnational state regionalism in the two Americas. When Africa and Asia as well as Australia and Oceania gained independence from European (and partially American) colonial rule, they again copied the Western model of national sovereignty and state autonomy. Region-building and regional integration were only introduced at a later stage, driven by the European model and by the realization of the limits of formal, independent sovereignty. In the meantime, the European concept of regional integration has demonstrated its modernity and sustainability. With the end of the Cold War, the artificial division among many regions of the world was replaced by the rediscovery of historical proximity and common interests beyond all regional quarrels.

Defending parts of a region in the name of freedom and under the umbrella of American protection had already earlier helped to accomplish novel concepts of regional cooperation, as was the case in Southeast Asia and in the Gulf region. The Cold War partially facilitated such security regionalism. In many regions of the world, its effects were frozen boundaries and conflicts, but also the discovery of unique cultural and economic potentials. Along with the end of the Cold War and the beginning of the age of the globalized market, new space for regionalism came about on a global scale. The shift to economic regionalism, sometimes also labeled development regionalism, was consequential and partially successful. However, it could not answer all relevant questions regarding the preconditions of sustainable and community-building regionalism. Without recognition of the primacy of the rule of law and democratic governance in the member states of a region, all region-building efforts would sooner or later—or perhaps sooner than later—meet their limits. This does not suggest that democratic governance and rule of law are the natural, automatic, and sufficient engines for successful and sustainable region-building. But, as the European and other examples of regional integration show, region-building without solid roots in democratic governance and pluralistic civil societies among the member states and member societies of a regional grouping will remain highly limited in its scope of action and fragile in its trust-base.

Constitutive and Constructed Criteria

According to geographers, regions can be distinguished by their climatic (hydrological, ecological), physical (relating to physiology such as mountains, landlocked areas, etc.), and spatial (of space and places) features. Historians look at time; geographers at space. According to the insights of both disciplines, regional boundaries can be absolute, relative, or transitional. The space constituting a region can be formal or functional. The cultural aspect of regionalism includes anthropological, ethnical, cultural, religious, and political dimensions. The cultural landscape, a term coined in the 1920s in Berkeley by Carl Ortwin Sauer, is primarily the focus of cultural geography as a subdiscipline. It deals with population distribution and density, the development level of the economy, and center-periphery-relations in states.[3]

Regions inside continents are somewhat the antithesis to the idea that continents are the region complementing subregional entities below the level of the nation-state. Continents are geographic givens, territorially defined yet culturally undefined and highly diverse, and for the most part extremely pluralistic and not homogenous politically. There has yet to be a successful attempt to unite continents defined merely by geography. The United States of America is often quoted as the exception to this rule, but then there are also

Canada and Mexico, both federations themselves. Ethnic features or religious bonds proved to be as unhelpful as continental-wide political schemes driven by ideology or idealism. Neither the Council of Europe nor the Organization of American States or the Organization of African Unity has been able to grow into the most influential institution representing its region as a political unit. Realistic definitions of interests, goals, and applicable instruments have been more successful in advancing the idea of cooperation or even integration, yet this is usually at the expense of geographical homogeneity and cohesion. The European Union is the most visible example underlining this experience.

European integration can be understood as the transformation of parts of a continent into a regional political entity based on the rule of law, aimed at community-building, and projecting an increasing global presence. Whatever Europe was and is, it was very different before the establishment of the European Union, and it remains more than the European Union. For the philosopher Aristotle, Europe was a form in being; for the historian Arnold Toynbee it was an Asian peninsula. Throughout its long history, Europe has been a series of ideas, empires, and cultural and political layers. It never was what the European Union is today. Yet the European Union does not include the whole of Europe as understood by geography or culture. Europe has always been a continent in search of its order. As long as geography was the focal point for the definition of interests and borders, the European search for order was continuously insufficient. Often, it failed. The European Union is the expression of the common economic, legal, and political interests of its constituent parts. As such, it is not primarily defined by Europe's past—and often changing—identities. The European Union is the expression of an emerging political identity, of community-building under the conditions of a common market, the rule of European law, and the ever increasing influence of European political institutions.

This definition of Europe as a politically induced community-oriented process of region-building will be the criterion for the comparative character of this study. As much as the European Union has become the political form of the continent without representing the comprehensive idea of the whole of Europe, similar efforts in region-building can be identified across the globe. While the European Union is not identical to Europe, increasingly the EU defines the region covered by its membership as its unique continent. The Council of Europe helped to bolster the idea of Europe during the time of Europe's partition in the Cold War, serving as an instrument for countries striving to "return to Europe" after the end of totalitarian rule. It was and remains open to all European countries that do not want to join the European Union or are not eligible to join. While the European Union is trying to bridge the remaining geographic gaps on the map of Europe through a comprehensive enlargement policy and a neighborhood policy aimed at establishing rings of partnership around its borders, the Council of Europe has lost weight. Elsewhere in the world, other regions are increasingly emulated as a distant mirror of the European experience. The uncertainty about what constitutes a region has not disappeared in light of this almost worldwide trend.

Size and population, resources and performance, pattern of identity and projected power differ from region to region. Yet the regions that are discussed in this study are defined by one structural similarity: according to their own ambition, expressed in founding documents and further elaborated in treaties and texts, they want to create visible community-building and project common interests in clearly defined spheres, be they economic, security, or political. Initially, these may only be rhetorical claims. Even so, this makes them comparable with the European integration experience. Their ambitions distinguish them from other possible concepts of regional groupings, especially those pursued by NAFTA and APEC.

Region-building efforts in the world of the twenty-first century have been generating different typologies:

- Regions as markets: The most widely understood type of region is defined by the interactions of an increasingly open and interconnected market. Trade patterns, investment conditions, labor laws, consumer patterns, and production conditions are relevant in understanding the meaning and scope of a region as a market. Free trade agreements across the world aim at broadening markets through the means of liberalizing tariff and non-tariff conditions of market access.

- Regions as cultural entities: The cultural interrelatedness within a region is often understood as the expression of a coherent civilization. Issues of identity are often related to a focus on the role of "the other," that is to say the nonparticipant cultures of a region. Cultural coherence does not necessarily translate into a form of community-building that goes beyond intuitive cultural commonality. Latin America is an example of the ambivalence of the meaning of regions as cultural entities. Matters of cultural identity raise the issue of borders, of the sense of belonging, the meaning of memory and of commonality. It would be useful to add a reflection about the implications of culture for agenda-setting in a region.

- Regions as polities: Politically defined regions are social constructions. Based on prepolitical realities, they include cultural factors and historical memories. They are also dependent upon a political will that can translate material and essential aspects of a region into a sustainable political program and a wide array of objectives. They will best be served by legal foundations that can transcend single issue interests and transient conditions to arrive at a basis for a genuine community-building process. Regions as polities are driven by internal and external causes, push and pull factors, and experience and prospects. They are limited by the constructivist nature of their origin.

The most evident and simple definition of "region" harks back to the Latin "regio," which was considered to be an administrative area or a geographical area with similar features, while "regere" meant "to rule, to direct." Since their origin in the time of the Roman Empire, regions have had geographical as well as order-related connotations. In modern times, the main features of regions as discussed in the pertinent academic literature include geographical delineation, the regularity and intensity of interactions, a shared perception of the region and its meaning, and issues of agency, that is, matters of common action in a region.[4] The formula seems to be: geography and interaction and will and agents make a region. This formula, however, does not limit regions in their scope, nor does it provide answers to the necessary preconditions to make a region work. Finally, this formula does not explain the relationship between the constitutional and the constructed components of a region.

The components of a region can be constitutional or constructed. Among the constitutional components are factors of geography; interactions concerning culture, economics, infrastructure, and power relations; matters of memory; and ethnicity and its implications. Among the constructed components are political institutions, common law, common trade structures, common objectives, common experiences, and common perception from the outside and of others, common projection of material and essential aspects, and common security concerns.[5] "Definitional ambiguities," writes Peter Katzenstein, "are a striking characteristic of the international relations literature dealing with the issue of regionalism."[6] He distinguishes internal sociocultural factors and political factors external to a region as the two guiding perspectives in analytically dealing with international regionalism. Geographical proximity, international interactions, common bonds (such as ethnic, cultural, linguistic, social, and historical), and a sense of identity, sometimes accentuated by actions and attitudes of states external to a region, are the main aspects relevant for the study of region-building. Sociocultural behavior and political attitudes, political institutions, economic interdependence, and external behavior are relevant, too. The regularity and intensity of interactions, as well as shared perceptions of the regional subsystem as a distinctive framework for common action, are also relevant components for the study of regions.

Katzenstein defines a region as "a set of countries markedly interdependent over a wide range of different dimensions. This is often, but not always, indicated by a flow of socio-economic transactions and communications and high political salience that differentiates a group of countries from others." In order to advance a solid definition of a region, it is important to properly understand the term "region": Like all key terms of political theory, "region" is relational: a region has to be understood in relation to its own history, in relation to its neighboring geography, in relation to the understanding of motivations and sources of region-building, in relation to social linkages and priorities, and in relation to the global state-system. As a consequence of this relationality of regions, region-ness will necessarily find different expressions and interpretations. There simply is no standardized code for defining a region.

More helpful than searching for an artificially consensual definition of a region is the broadening of the analytical perspective, distinguishing between the form and function of a region. A set of queries can help in doing so:

- Motivation: How do push and pull factors relate to each other?
- Actors: How is the region-building effort related to the traditional state order and the perspectives of globalization?
- Objectives: What are the strengthening parts of a region that help build commonality, both affirmatively ("in favor of what?") and negatively ("against whom?")?
- Preconditions: What are the key conditions that make a region viable and the process of region-building sustainable?

Mostly, regions are analyzed in the context of their functional relevance. Security and development have become the most prominent spheres in which regional functions tend to be considered favorably even by skeptics of deeper integration of a region. But security and development are not static and one-dimensional matters. They require understanding of the unique context. Standards and criteria for understanding the potential and the limits of region-building and region-ness are critical. To assess the community-building process of a region, usually the applied criteria originate in the experience with the state. Economic and technological matters reflect a pluralistic approach, and policy matters are driven by the quest for order-building; societal issues must confront the reality of idiosyncratic diversity; efforts to achieve common interests need to understand the dynamics of constructivism; matters of finality of region-building will be confronted with the experience of history as an ongoing, infinite process; institutional approaches are rooted in the ambition to transform ideas into lasting realities; and the continuous questioning of integration priorities and challenges to region-building echoes the struggle between idealism and realism. Ultimately, one might understand a region with Rodrigo Tavares "as a cognitive construction that spills over state borders, based on territoriality, with a certain degree of singularity, socially molded by a body of different actors, and motivated by different (and sometimes contradictory) principles."[8]

In sum, regions are social realities that produce memory, meaning, and communication. Regionalism is the theory of the process of region-building. Neither social and political realities nor theoretical reflections can provide conclusive responses concerning the necessary conditions for a peaceful, viable, and lasting region-building experience. Internal pluralism and democracy in the member states of a regional grouping are essential for regenerating public legitimacy for region-building as a process. A minimal sense of shared destiny between the people and states pertinent to a regional grouping is necessary in order to generate sustainable perspectives. Common memories regarding the possible alternatives to region-building remain helpful, if not necessary, in order to revitalize the rationale of community-building in a regional grouping.

The concept of this study includes two hypotheses that have been of minor importance in other discussions of region-building: One relates to the procedural character of region-building. The other refers to the democratic precondition of community-building. An inherent tendency of social science literature seems to neglect the historical—that is, the genetic and evolutional—nature of political and sociological processes. To reconstruct realities by means of academic theories can generate fine exercises in logic. But they might miss important points that seem to be too simple because they are boringly real. Region-building has always been—and will always remain—a process with quantum leaps and backlashes, detours and unintended consequences. Regional groupings are the product of trial and error. They cannot be expected to come to imminent conclusion, and it would simply not be fair to judge declaratory norms by the sheer amount of paper they have been written on. Their unfolding in real life has to be studied with the patience that stems from applying a historical perspective. This must include the recognition of the subtle law of indirect transformation: neither an original regional grouping nor its initial objectives have ever remained unchanged in the course of the process of region-building.

Probably even more important is the application of normative criteria to better understand the nature of success and failure in region-building. Constructed political orders require trust among their actors as the essential basis for legitimacy and progress. It is unlikely that trust and legitimacy can grow beyond a certain point if regimes and governance structures are antagonistic or incomprehensive. The European experience in regional integration suggests that the creation of supranational law and governance is proportional to the degree of democratic rule and embedded rule of law inside all constituent member states of a regional grouping. The European integration experience therefore suggests that studies of the global proliferation of regional integration ought to pay more attention to the issue of regime cohesion among the member states of a regional grouping in order to better understand the necessary preconditions of its success.

The European integration experience can be defined as "democratic region-building." The term "democratic region-building" is coined in this study, fully recognizing the fact that more research has to be conducted to better understand its effects and constraints. Democratic region-building will remain a process with flaws and limits. But wherever regional groupings embark on the long path of regional integration, they will encounter fewer structural limits the more they can resort to the culture of democracy and the primacy of the rule of law among their constituent member states. This study proposes to consider democratic region-building as an additional normative reference point for further comparative regional integration studies. Democratic region-building has been tested in practice in Europe, and it is normatively conclusive as a potentially universal precondition and objective of the global proliferation of regional integration. This focus on democratic preconditions for successful regional integration requires an objective analysis of the deficits and obstacles to region-building in regions that try to achieve regionalism without first establishing a democratic foundation for it.

The Changing Nature of Region-Building

Since the end of the Cold War, regional integration has gained new momentum across the world. Old regional groupings have been revitalized. New avenues for region-building have been entered. Existing region-building efforts have been streamlined or reorganized. The European integration experience has gained worldwide attention, though it is by no means the only relevant integration scheme in the world. Efforts to increase free trade have found support all over the world. But free trade agreements are far from the only relevant approach to regionalism. This study focuses on community-building efforts that go beyond free trade arrangements. Free trade is an essential part of regionalism, and it can be the vehicle to launch a comprehensive region-building process. But it would be suboptimal to reduce regionalism and region-building to the economic dimension. With the emerging new world order, the notion of region-building has changed and, most importantly, broadened. The main features of this trend are as follows:

- The motivation for regional integration: region-building more than ever is understood as a development tool. Regional unity and social progress are functionally linked to successful, multidimensional, and sustainable cooperation, and eventually also integration. Growing prosperity and a better base for public welfare have been identified as objectives for regional cooperation and integration, not least in developing regions. Independence is no longer considered a singular and abstract goal. Independence can only remain meaningful if it generates prosperity and welfare. Regional cooperation and integration is no longer rejected in the name of abstract notions of sovereignty and non-interference. Rhetorically, the quest for sovereignty and autonomous statehood prevails as the dominant discourse in most parts of the world. In reality, however, the meaning of sovereignty has changed.
- It has become more content-oriented: sovereignty is where social progress adds to political recognition. This can only be achieved in a cooperative spirit with other countries and societies. It can mean a limitation of formal sovereignty for the sake of substantial progress in opportunities for people. Region-building is a possible counter-measure to variant forms of dependency that have prevailed after formal

sovereignty and independence were achieved. The European experience of successful integration has supported this change of paradigm in the southern hemisphere: if traditional European nation-states show their readiness to pool essential elements of their sovereignty—in monetary and security matters as well as through the process of multilevel governance—this might not be altogether without merit for consideration by new states elsewhere. Protectionist industrialization, for example in Latin America, has not been successful. While the main driving force of European regional integration—regional reconciliation after thirty years of belligerence and more than a century of nationalism—was largely meaningless in many other parts of the world, the idea of combining political recognition with developmental progress gained support in much of the southern hemisphere. Regions that have not at all embarked on efforts of region-building, notably in the Middle East and Northeast Asia, prove the effects of the prevalent divisiveness of geopolitical conflicts and regime asymmetries.

- Region-building as a means of empowerment: several state actors have realized that region-building could strengthen their international veto capacity, primarily in matters of global trade, and their regional actor capacity, primarily in matters of regional development. The effort of the European Union to be recognized as an equal partner in leadership by the United States has served as a source of inspiration—and caution—in other parts of the world. The regional groupings in Latin America, Africa, and Asia include the notion of regional empowerment as one of their objectives.

- Institutional tools of region-building: region-building as an institutional construct has been solidified during the past two decades. The link between welfare gains and necessary political instruments has been reconsidered. While during the first decades of independence and under the shadow of the requirements of the Cold War, formal sovereignty, non-interference into domestic affairs, and autarkic pursuit of policy goals marked a widespread pattern of state behavior. The reassessment of the meaning of sovereignty, of the value of cooperative governance, and of the legitimizing effect of democratic principles and rule of law has led to new conclusions about the value and possible effect of region-building. New insights have grown in understanding the relationship between cultural diversity and common political interests, procedural identity and stable means of cooperation, and legal predictability and socioeconomic progress.

- Regional groupings as building blocs of world order: globalization has become a catchall phrase to indicate the potential of economic liberalization and modernization through the expansion of market forces. In order to solidify the position of a region in the context of negotiations under the umbrella of the World Trade Organization, regional groupings have begun to mushroom. Basically they are meant to enhance free trade. Their membership is mainly defined by their presumed economic potential. Usually, further steps toward cooperation and integration are not intended. But the unintended consequence of cooperation in one area for other spheres of public life, including political governance and social interactions, has become increasingly evident. Different and competing concepts of world order have emerged. While the EU is promoting policies of regional integration, the US prefers bilateral economic ties with partner countries. Both are united in the promotion of democratic rule of law and human rights. China, in turn, is pursuing trade relations without political conditionality. More research would be helpful to better understand the implications and possible effects of these different conceptual and normative approaches. Regional groupings have not turned world order relations and power projections upside down. But they have added a new dimension to the international system.

One of the inescapable consequences of region-building is the transforming effect it has on its constituent actors. Intuitively, region-building is primarily understood as a means to strengthen one's own country and society. This has always been one pattern of regional integration in Europe, best analyzed by Andrew Moravscik.[9] It cannot come as a surprise that non-European integration efforts tend to follow this example. Meanwhile, integration comes with consequences, no matter how unintended they may be. The efforts of cooperation and integration on governance structures, on the evolution of legal systems and lawmaking, and on their meaning for the creation of common memories and identity-forming habits have been experienced in Europe at length. Eventually, non-European regional groupings cannot escape unintended consequences either.

Region-building transforms its constituent parts. This is an inevitable yet voluntary process. No country or society in the world is forced to join a regional grouping if it understands this membership as counterproductive to its inherent interests and its ability to pursue its interests autonomously. At some point, Albania was considered the most closed society in Europe. It was not opened by force, and no representative of the European Union has ever pressed Albania to prepare for membership in the EU. Albania's effort to reverse the tradition of autarkic statehood and embark on cooperative and integrative processes stemmed from a revision of the country's analysis of its interests, resources, and the possible cost-benefit effects of cooperation and integration.

Region-building transforms the political culture of its constituent parts and creates new habits as well as new structures. This metamorphosis does not tend to happen in quantum leaps. Instead, it happens slowly and silently. It implies the need to reassess the parameters of key issues of political theory, such as the notion and meaning of sovereignty, of statehood, and of integration gains. With region-building, the question of legitimacy enters a new sphere: it is no longer related to one's own political system alone. Legitimacy is projected into the realm of the partner states of a regional grouping. With or without purpose, this has implications for interstate relations and for the interpretation of one's own political system and culture. No member state of a regional grouping can ultimately escape the effects of actions (and non-actions) of and within its partner states. This broadening meaning of the basis for judging the legitimacy of a political system affects the very objective of regional integration. Regional integration is never only about objectively formulated goals. It is also about the absorption of the consequences of these goals

Two Contrasting Concepts: NAFTA and the EU

Region-building as a global phenomenon has followed two different and eventually circular stages. On the one hand, it has been a response to the combination of global war and dissolving colonialism, contending ideologies and the rise of globalization. In this respect, it followed the primacy of Europe in world affairs, Europe's self-destruction, and its integration-based rehabilitation. On the other hand, everywhere region-building has developed based on its unique internal history. Both trends are connected and form a single circle, mutually accelerating each other.

Structurally, European integration has followed a pattern similar to other trends of region-building: it has been driven by the internal European vision of a peacefully united continent. And it was pushed by the American support for a revitalized and democratic Western Europe that could serve as a strong bulwark against communist expansionism and Soviet hegemony. In past centuries, European ambitions for peaceful integration had always failed from within. After 1945, European integration was embarking on a successful path with the help of pressure from outside, fostering a peaceful transition from within. Over time, other regions responded to Europe's new beginning and its obvious success. They also responded by rejecting further European dominance as experienced during centuries of colonial rule. Only after its internal transformation did Europe's image begin to change in the wider world. Only then did Europe become a partner and even a model for region-building elsewhere.

It is interesting to note that the United States has both inspired and limited the evolution of global region-building. After World War II, and under the shadow of Soviet expansionism, the US favored the integration of Western European democracies and, most importantly, the reconciliation between France and the Federal Republic of Germany. The US attitude toward regional cooperation and integration in Europe was, however, ambivalent. While security in Europe and for Europe was a strategic interest of the US, the rise of Western Europe as an economic competitor to the US was not. The same was true with regard to other regions in the world: the US supported the establishment of the Organization of American States and even the beginning of Latin American regional economic integration. After Fidel Castro's revolutionary takeover in Cuba in 1959, the need for Western allies in Latin America was of prime interest to the US. To build up democratic partners that could succeed in economic integration and might even become relative competitors to the US was another matter. In Southeast Asia, the US favored the creation of ASEAN as an expression of security regionalism. It realized the economic potential of the "tiger states" of that region but never supported the deepening of their economic integration, let alone the political steps toward community-building and democratic region-building.

US efforts in promoting regional activities were ultimately functions of the larger East-West conflict. They did not translate into a genuine global strategy for the promotion of community-oriented region-building. Some of the regions in the world had begun to emulate European integration in the 1960s and embarked on a genuine strategy of deeper integration out of fear: they wanted to prevent the implications of a potentially protectionist Europe.[10] For the United States, the main concern during the Cold War remained the Soviet challenge. Too much integration among their allies, they thought, could encourage them to escape from the US security umbrella and search for a third way in world affairs.

Since the end of the Cold War, a new wave of region-building has spread across the world. In a colloquial way, scholars distinguish between "old" and "new" regionalism as if the end of the Cold War was some sort of a "watershed" in region-building. Before 1990, as the argument goes, regional economic integration was largely inward-oriented, import-substituting, and protectionist. Since then, and under the pressure of globalization, regional economic integration has become outward-oriented, favoring free trade and the establishment of larger trading blocs. The theoretical jargon that has developed to accompany this process is as confusing as the realities across the globe. The difficulties of conducting a meaningful comparison often originate in the reductionist perspective of seeing regional integration purely as an economic trend. However, region-building can only be fully understood as a multidimensional and potentially comprehensive approach in the transformation of interstate and intrasocietal relations in a region.

Two contrasting concepts of regional integration exist in today's world. In some parts of the world, economic integration is pursued without any intention of achieving a common legislation, joint institutions, or political decision-making processes. The less regulation and institutionalization, the better it is for free trade: such is the rationale of these regional groupings, most prominently represented by the North American Free Trade Agreement (NAFTA) and the Asia-Pacific Economic Cooperation (APEC). Many other free trade arrangements have emerged across the world, but NAFTA and APEC are the most visible and the most powerful. In other parts of the world, integration concepts go beyond the economic sphere. They include legal, political, and sometimes cultural components aimed at achieving community-building. The European Union is the most advanced model of this type of regional grouping. Other regional groupings, according to their founding documents and subsequent treaties and protocols, are heading in the same direction, albeit so far often more in rhetoric than in real terms.

These two concepts of regional integration are not conflictual, but neither are they complementary. It would be misleading to assume that NAFTA is the EU's "other" or that NAFTA and APEC would be permanently clashing competitors. The United States prefers a policy of deregulatory free trade with the least possible degree of integrationist or even legislatory arrangements. The European Union, in turn, has opted for a sophisticated, at times overly complicated and bureaucratic form of institutionalized and law-based community. These are different policy choices in reaction to different interpretations of one's regions identity.

With 31.1 percent (compared with the EU's share of 28.8 percent), NAFTA is the biggest contributor to the world's GDP. The North American Free Trade Agreement, in force since January 1994, has never stimulated any broad-based theoretical academic debate about its integrationist meaning. In fact, NAFTA by definition is no integration system, but can best be understood as "a complex intergovernmental network."[11] NAFTA is highly institutionalized as a network-based regulatory scheme, but is little integrationist. It includes a clear set of rules governing trade and investment, provisions to ensure the integrity of labor and environmental standards, and a dispute settlement mechanism. NAFTA is more an expression of the rise of economic issues and globalized economic liberalism in international relations than a new form of regional integration. However, in structure, ambition, and perspective, NAFTA by and large is the lens through which the United States perceives regional integration, including the European Union. NAFTA is the American model for region-building. One cannot but conclude, in the words of Alberta Sbragia, that NAFTA and the European Union are institutionally incompatible: "NAFTA is not the beginning of some kind of integration within the Americas analogous to the integration we have seen in Europe; rather it is a strategy designed to respond to specific challenges facing the United States in its external environment."[12]

Maybe due to these structural incompatibilities, the European Union has no coherent strategy for dealing with NAFTA. After the failed WTO summit in Cancun in 2003, both NAFTA and the EU rushed to conclude bilateral trade links with as many emerging markets as possible. Between NAFTA and the EU there clearly exists a commercial rivalry, at times appeased by cooperative activities. While in most other regions of the world the European Union feels dominant (and by and large is dominant in terms of its economic weight), with regard to the EU-NAFTA relationship, the European Union is somewhat elusive. Here the EU encounters the limits of inter-regionalism even before it has started with efforts to establish inter-regionalism.[13]

As for NAFTA, its key objective is clearly defined: the promotion of free trade. NAFTA promises win-win constellations for all three of its member states, the US, Canada and Mexico. In 1982, Europe received 20 percent of Mexico's exports. By 1999, this share had fallen to 3.1 percent. As for overall EU-Mexico trade, it dropped from 9 to 6 percent between 1993 and 2000, while Mexico-US trade has increased by 5 percent. In absolute terms the NAFTA effect on Mexico is even stronger: in 1982, Mexico sent 53 percent of its total trade to the US; in 1999 the figure had risen to 90 percent. As for Canada, 86 percent of its exports go to the United States.[14] Neither in terms of its goals or its policies is NAFTA integrationist. It is not aimed at pooling resources, let alone sovereignty titles. It is "born of the convergence of prag-matic self-interest among its members."[15] NAFTA is not a customs union and thus has no common external dimension. It has a secretariat, based in Mexico, but no institutional set equivalent to the European Union with its Commis-sion, Parliament, Court of Justice and Council. NAFTA cannot make propos-als of its own. It not only lacks institutional capacity, but it has also been de-signed not to prevent domination by the United States. Along with NAFTA, the US is involved in several other regional groupings whose loose aim is the promotion of preferential trade agreements, such as APEC. But none of them represents an evolving system of governance as the European Union does— and as do those regional groupings analyzed and compared in this study. The advantage for the US to be involved in several groupings aimed at promoting free trade is that it "gives [the US] leverage within the multilateral system dif-ferent from that enjoyed by the European Union."[16]

Like NAFTA—and the project of a pan-American Free Trade Zone—APEC does not represent regional integration as understood in this study. It is a single-issue, network-based cooperative instrument for promoting preferential trade ar-rangements among the dynamic economies around the Pacific Basin. It lacks the political ambition and community-building objective that are characteristic of regional groupings as discussed in this study. Accordingly, the European Union and its Asian partners have designed the Asia-Europe Meeting (ASEM) as a sort of responsive counter project to APEC. ASEM lacks clarity of purpose and sense of direction. This is not surprising, given the lack of precision as far as objectives, instruments, and institutional procedures of APEC—and of its echoing counter-part ASEM—are concerned.[17]

This study looks into the most important community-oriented regional groupings in today's world. The regional groupings discussed in the subsequent chapters are defined by political ambitions of region-building that go beyond the single-issue agenda of free trade regimes. No matter their rhetorical limita-tions, the regional groupings covered in this study have a political agenda and an ambition for community-building. Unlike NAFTA or APEC they are de facto or potentially promoting an evolving regional governance dimension.

Therefore, a deeper analysis of NAFTA and APEC is not included in the survey chapters of this study. The economic dimension of regional integration remains important, but what is genuinely new in the globalized world of the twenty-first century is the global proliferation of regional integration as a community-building process.

Region-Building through Peaceful Integration

A look back into the history of earlier (and mostly violent) region-building efforts reveals fundamental differences from the contemporary trend of democratic region-building as initiated by the European Union. The ancient Greeks under Alexander, the Roman Empire, the Chinese Qin Empire, and czarist Russia, but also France under Napoleon and Hitler's racist fury, are examples of military-driven efforts to create a region and form it according to the model of the imperial center. The industrial revolution and its technological foundation inspired a focus of cooperation on financial and trading matters: the idea of a customs union between Sweden and Norway (1874–1900), the many preferential trade arrangements in the Germanic center of Europe during the nineteenth century (Prussian Customs Union, Bavarian-Wuerttembergian Customs Union, German "Zollverein") and last but not least, the Latin Monetary Union of 1864 (France, Italy, Switzerland, and Belgium agreed to standardize the value of their coinage) were models of region-building along fiscal or trading lines. The European colonial empires were imperialistic spheres beyond the home region. It is telling that British imperialism began to crumble with the end of the British pound as the basis for the gold standard in 1931.

Interwar economic efforts like the Anglo-Soviet Trade Agreement of 1921 or the 1934 Rome Agreement between Italy, Austria, and Hungary, establishing a "Danubian bloc" to counterbalance the Little Entente, remained rather meaningless. Security structures established after World War II—such as NATO, Cento Pact, SEATO, Rio Pact, and Anzus—followed the logic of the Cold War. With the functional integration scheme introduced with the 1951 European Coal and Steel Community (ECSC), a new era was initiated for region-building in Europe and beyond. This precursor was followed by the 1957 Treaties of Rome and the founding of the European Economic Community. The most successful peaceful transformation of Europe started while the EEC itself underwent continuous transformations, which continue to this day as it has grown into the European Union.

The "new regionalism" outside Europe included the revitalization of old, or the creation of new, schemes of regional groupings in the aftermath of the Cold War and in reaction to globalization. At the same time, the European Union began to be perceived as a certain model for regional integration. The

EU started to project itself as an actor in the promotion of regional integration and inter-regionalism.[18] It remains uncomfortable to distinguish between "old" and "new" regionalism as if the two would mark two different historical eras. In reality, their paths are interrelated. Without the European experience, other regional groupings would not be able to identify a certain model they try to emulate. On the other hand, it took the European pressure through colonial times and the export of the European model of state sovereignty to accentuate the sense of marginalization and dependency in many parts of the world, which in turn became a driving force to pool resources and interests to stand up against Western dominance.

The term "generation" implies a generic nature in the evolution of social processes. Yet it seems appropriate to use the term "generations" of region-building in order to better understand the inner dynamics and interconnectedness of stages of region-building. Generations by definition are overlapping. They contribute to each other, enrich each other, and define each other against the past without being able to escape its consequences. In this sense, three generations of region-building may be distinguished in accordance with the studies of Fredrik Söderbaum and Luk van Langenhove:

- First generation: This included the creation of free trade areas and common markets, both in Europe and elsewhere. The phenomenon is still booming and developing beyond established regional groupings. In 2002, a total of 172 Regional Free Trade Agreements were reported to the GATT/World Trade Organization.[19]
- Second generation: Trade and the economy are not considered to be isolated from other aspects of social and political life. Justice, security, the environment, culture, identity, and governance may form part of the region-building process. The results are "more complex, comprehensive and political."[20] This pattern has spread widely across most regional groupings in the world, albeit without achieving global cohesion or global consent concerning the priorities.
- Third generation: This stage of region-building includes a stronger external orientation. Regions begin to play a more assertive and visible role in international affairs "on a series of fronts."[21] In the case of the European Union, one has to add that global relations already existed for individual member states of the current European Union during the age of colonialism. For them, this third generation is a return to the world stage in a different context and under completely transformed conditions.

These generations and their specific ingredients can overlap. The generational analogy does not imply a deterministic path dependency in the global promotion of region-building. The exact sequencing of "generations" of regional integration does not provide an eternal answer regarding the sustainability of a regional grouping. Integration can fail as often as it can surprise its skeptics.

"There is no scholarly agreement on what constitutes either integration or region"[22] writes Philomena Murray. She explains the most evident reason: "There is no single model of integration."[23] Surprisingly, the conceptualization of region-building often neglects the democracy factor. Implicitly, it may be mentioned as a social condition propitious for regional integration. But the findings of this study suggest a need to emphasize much more strongly the importance of democratic regime cohesion among member states of a regional grouping as a prime precondition for long-term success.

Andrew Hurrell has contributed helpful distinctions of different factors relevant for understanding regionalism. He suggests five factors as relevant for the solid establishment of regionalism as a theory dealing with region-building:[24]

- Societal integration, which implicitly might include a notion of democratic governance although Hurrell has not explicitly said so.
- Regional awareness and identity as expressions of a feeling of region-ness that may be helpful in defining and pursuing common interests and objectives.
- Interstate cooperation and agreements as implication of a mutual political will to apply societal integration and regional awareness by turning it into objective projects and goals.
- Regional economic integration and state-promoted removal of barriers as the often cited expression of the primacy of economic region-building through the means of negative integration, that is by dissolving barriers to integration.
- A consolidated bloc, which is usually a combination of the first four factors, although more factors ought to be added to better understand what a consolidated bloc is, including common political objectives, institutional provisions, and legal norms.

Based on such factors, theories of regionalism have evolved in the academic community. Once more, Andrew Hurrell was at the forefront of political scientists to systematize and summarize the inevitable cacophony that has emerged. He distinguishes three patterns of theories of regionalism:

- Systemic theories, such as neorealism, structural interdependence, and globalization theories.
- Regional theories, such as neofunctionalism, neoliberal institutionalism, and constructivism.
- Domestic theories, such as theories about state coherence and theories regarding regime types and democratization.

Other theoretical efforts followed and were elaborated along the line drawn by Hurrell. Finn Laursen and Fredrik Söderbaum and Timothy Shaw were helpful in giving readable overviews about the main theoretical reflections concerning region-building.[25] Most of these theories applied to assess global regionalism are rooted in the European integration experience—or more precisely, in the Europe-related theoretical discourse:

- Functionalism, focusing on the creation of a set of functional agencies that may socialize politicians, civil servants, and societies at large in order to adopt less nationalistic and autarkic attitudes.[26]
- Neofunctionalism, discussing how national interests may be achieved through functional spillover effects in the process of integration.[27]
- Liberal institutionalism, studying why states turn to institutions beyond the state in order to solve cooperation problems, establish liabilities, and reduce transaction costs.[28]
- Intergovernmentalism, understood as the process of political bargaining aimed at minimizing each participant's individual power while maximizing each other's welfare and security gains.[29]
- Regional economic integration theories, referring to a linear increase in economic interdependencies through a process of fixed stages (preferential trade area, free trade area, customs union, common market, economic and/or political union).[30]
- Neorealism, focusing on regional groupings that are formed predominantly by states reacting to an external, mostly security, threat.[31]
- Constructivism as a sociopsychological theory dealing with perceptions and images in international relations, including the effects of inter-regionalism or of transregionalism.[32]
- World order approaches, trying to integrate the different stages or "generations" of regionalism.[33]
- Global governance approaches, reflecting on the potential of organizing forms and processes of global governance beyond the functional activities in economic or financial matters.[34]

Methodologically, the theoretical work about globalization and its effects claims to introduce theories of postmodernism into the sphere of social sciences. It may be helpful in drawing attention to the contradictory and conflicting elements of "regionalization from below" related to the mechanisms of inspiration, arbitration, and conditionality of the International Monetary Fund and the World Trade Organization, or the global negotiations in the framework of its Doha Round.[35] But most promising in enhancing our understanding of region-building and regionalism remains empirical work. Empirical studies have produced valuable and enriching insights.[36]

More difficult than analyzing region-building and the different categories of regionalism is measuring regional integration. In trying to do so, the focus is shifting from "region" to "integration." This excludes the further study of most trade arrangements, as they emphasize economic liberalization in a region but not regional integration per se. According to Walter Mattli's insightful work, the following characteristics are typical for economic theories of regional integration:

- Reflection about welfare gains and losses.
- Little work on political choices and conditions.
- Often, the theories have a tendency to be static.[37]

The most widespread economic theory of integration deals with the perspective of establishing a customs union.[38] The underlying theoretical assumptions deal largely with markets for goods, the welfare implications of integration through trade creation, trade diversion, and the improvement of terms of trade. Theories about "optimal currency areas" have been developed since the 1960s.[39] These theories start with the assumption of exchange-rate rigidities that are useful if prices and wages are flexible. The concern of these theories is related to the conditions for efficient customs unions. Fiscal federalism is the most elaborate and sophisticated variant of economic theories of regional integration. Its main focus is on the interactions of markets and public goods. It discusses fiscal spillover as far as concerns the transfer of authority over the levels of decision making and the incentives to reallocate cross-border resources in supplying public goods. Fiscal federalism analyzes how market integration is likely to shape the provision of public goods in a region.[40]

Theories on regional integration related to the insights of political science are largely the product of discussing and analyzing the experience of European regional integration. Functionalism, neofunctionalism, intergovernmentalism, federalism, realism, and also the more contemporary approaches, such as multilevel governance, are united in one point: they are shifting the discourse from teleology to utility. They discuss what is useful in regional integration, not what is desirable.[41] Whether this is a sufficient methodology and norm to understand the intrinsic rationale of the global proliferation of regional integration will have to be discussed in more detail. Usually, theoretic approaches are limited by some evident shortcomings:

- They tend to be static.
- They tend to be one-dimensional.
- They tend to be fixed on material (market) or essentialistic (sovereignty and other norms) givens as a recurring point of reference.
- They show little empathy for or knowledge of regional integration efforts in the non-Western world.
- The focus on regions diminishes the differentiated recognition of all categories of integration.
- The focus on integration relativizes the differentiated understanding for all criteria that constitute a region.

Integration is not only about its genuine mechanisms. It is also about "adaptive behavior," as Mattli has put it.[42] Shifting expectations, changing priorities, perceptions, and value movements have to be taken into account. Regional integration may be generated by combining national interests and supranational activities in response to sectoral issues and decisions. In the end, region-building and integration formation are not about mechanisms and mechanics. They are a matter of governance, norms, and political culture. They are also about unintended consequences, political identities, external pressure, and informal benchmarking.

In this regard, the need to clarify the relationship between trading agreements (as a means to create a functional region) and community-building arrangements (as a means to create a system of functional integration and increasingly a structure of political life) has become vital. It is here that the normative quest for democratic region-building, the insight into the limits of other regional activities, and the methodological search for clarity meet. Regional integration does not work without success. Eventually, success may be the most important benchmark for measuring integration.

Measuring Integration

Recent efforts in regionalism studies include the search for criteria to measure the degree of integration. Mainly, the economic logic and a highly technical approach prevail. Economic logic is rooted in the assumption that integration is a process involving two or more national economies aimed at generating a free trade area. Economists such as Bela A. Balassa have introduced the concept according to which free trade is the precondition of a customs union, a customs union the precondition for a common market, and a common market the precondition for a comprehensive economic and potentially a political union.[43] The political logic of integration reflects on completely different categories and characteristics: choice, causes (conflicts), and goals (objectives) of integration; the role of leadership and of institutions (actors); the context of sovereignty; and the role of policy factors. Finally, the method of integration and the relationship of functions and paths are of relevance for political science–related analyses of regional integration. Measuring preconditions and effects of regional integration by traditional economic parameters is, as difficult as it is for the political science parameters, often underrated in regional integration literature.

It is difficult to objectively define quantifiable attributes to a regional grouping. Size, population, natural resources, market power, human development index, geopolitical presence—these are the classic criteria for measuring the development level and the power projection of countries in the world. To translate them into the sphere of regional groupings has never been done in a comprehensive way. In order to make sense, it would be necessary to link quantifiable attributes with intangible variables such as ideology, history, the context of security and economy, normative claims like those represented by the institutional makeup of a regional grouping, and power criteria reinforcing or limiting the objectives of a regional grouping. The prerequisites of measuring regional integration will have to be connected to the measuring of contextual conditions, such as the unintended consequences of a regional grouping and its activities, overlapping effects of region-building, and the consequences of crises and other catalytic events that may halt, spur, or detour region-building.

The next level of measuring integration criteria would have to focus on push and pull factors. These include the role of the internal drive (gradual, incremental, actor-factor-nexus, belated, contingent) and the role of the external impact (events, structural pressure, incentives, economic difficulties, market access, aid diversion, norm projection). These efforts may be related to the effort of measuring the outcome of integration. The usefulness of integration depends on economic gains or potential economic gains. It also touches on the degree to which integration may pay off for political and other community leaders. The timing of integration sequences might not follow a universal logic but rather is contingent on the specific context of a regional grouping. The need for integration-related institutions to be tangibly committed and continuously respected in pursuing objectively appreciated norms of integration is a universal factor. The matter of loyalty is invariably related to the outcome, the effects of integration. To frame "commitment institutions"[44] is a necessary precondition for overcoming theoretical obstacles of integration (the prisoner's dilemma) and for institutionalizing cooperation beyond contingent objectives. "Building capacity and community"[45] is the most critical step any regional grouping has to take before solidifying its claim to longevity. Stakeholders are the necessary precondition for a sustainable process of region-building: Without a solid constituency across a region, no regional grouping can turn from vague theory into lasting practice.

In assessing region-building, the set of criteria ought to be as broad as possible. At the same time, it is useful to standardize the analysis in order to gain comparable data. Values, norms, legal provisions, political choices, inevitable factors of political and economic nature, externalities and transaction costs, and incentives and cost-benefit analysis belong to a potentially long list of aspects useful for any measurement of region-building and the achievements of integration. Creation of a scientific system of indicators of regional integration will, however, remain a transient activity. After all, no regional grouping has ever been developed in response to a theoretical framework. No regional grouping has ever achieved eternal permanency and unalterable stability based on theoretical assumptions or objectives. Integration is about human activities and by that nature is contingent and ephemeral. Monitoring regional integration tends to be a vast field attractive to a certain species of social scientist.[46] But whether or not the effort to monitor regional groupings across the globe can generate more refined and universally applicable notions of integration concepts or exchangeable criteria for region-building may be questioned. Region-building is a universal phenomenon with local expressions.

It is with these theoretical criteria and coordinates that the following empirical studies are conducted. They recognize the global existence of region-building efforts. They owe their exposition to the historical method linked with both features of international relations theory and insights into the nature and effect of regional integration in Europe and elsewhere, and they are open to further reevaluation. Unlike other studies, the subsequent analysis also emphasizes failures of integration and assesses obstacles to region-building. This is important to better understand the gap between ambition and performance of region-building. Such a gap should, however, not come as a surprise. After all, region-building is work in progress everywhere across the globe.

Notes

1. Samuel P. Huntington, *The Clash of Civilizations and the Remaking of World Order* (New York: Simon and Schuster, 1993), 26.
2. See David B. Abernethy, *The Dynamics of Global Dominance: European Overseas Empires, 1415–1980* (New Haven: Yale University Press, 2000).
3. See Carl Ortwin Sauer, "The Morphology of Landscape," in *University of California Publications in Geography* 2 (1925): 19–54; Harm J. de Blij and Peter O. Muller (eds.), *Geography: Realms, Regions and Concepts* (Hoboken, NJ: Wiley Text Books, 2001), 2–31.
4. See Rodrigo Tavares, *The State of the Art of Regionalism: The Past, Present and Future of a Discipline*, UNU-CRIS e-working paper W-2004/10 (Bruges: United Nations University-CRIS, 2004), online at http://www.cris.unu.edu/fileadmin/workingpapers/WProdrigo%20tavares.pdf.
5. See Björn Hettne, Andras Inotai, and Osvaldo Sunkel (eds.), *The New Regionalism Series*, 5 vols. (London: Macmillan Press, 1999–2001); Peter Katzenstein, *A World of Regions: Asia and Europe in the American Imperium* (Ithaca: Cornell University Press, 2005).
6. Ibid., 129.
7. Ibid., 130. See also Bela A. Balassa, *The Theory of Economic Integration* (London: Allen and Unwin, 1962); Bruce M. Russett, *International Regions and the International System: A Study in Political Ecology* (Chicago: Rand McNally, 1968); Louis J. Cantori and Steven L. Spiegel, *The International Politics of Regions: A Comparative Approach* (Englewood Cliffs, NJ: Prentice-Hall, 1970); William R. Thompson, "The Regional Subsystem: A Conceptual Explication and a Propositional Inventory," in *International Studies Quarterly* 17, no.1 (1973): 89–117; Emanuel Adler and Michael Barnett, *Security Communities* (Cambridge: Cambridge University Press, 1998); Mario Telò (ed.), *European Union and New Regionalism: Regional Actors and Global Governance in a Post-Hegemonic Era* (Aldershot: Ashgate, 2001); Michael Schulz et al. (eds.), *Regionalization in a Globalizing World: A Comparative Perspective on Forms, Actors and Processes* (London and New York: Zed Books, 2001); Markus Perkmann and Sum Ngai-Ling (eds.), *Globalization, Regionalization and Cross-Border Regions* (Basingstoke and New York: Palgrave Macmillan, 2002); Morten Boas (ed.), *New Regionalism in the New Millennium* (New York: Palgrave Macmillan, 2003); Fredrik Söderbaum and Timothy Shaw (eds.), *Theories of New Regionalism: A Palgrave Reader* (Houndmills and New York: Palgrave Macmillan, 2003); Paul F. Diehl and Joseph Lepgold (eds.), *Regional Conflict Management*

(Lanham: Rowman and Littlefield, 2003); Luk van Langenhove, *Theorizing Regionhood*, UNU-CRIS e-working papers, W-2003/1 (Bruges: United Nations University—CRIS, 2003), online at http://www.cris.unu.edu/fileadmin/workingpapers/paper%20regionhood.pdf; Barry Buzan and Ole Waever (eds.), *Regions and Powers: The Structure of International Security* (Cambridge and New York: Cambridge University Press, 2003); James J. Hentz and Morten Boas (eds.), *New and Critical Security and Regionalism: Beyond the Nation-State* (Aldershot: Ashgate, 2003).

8. Tavares, *The State of the Art of Regionalism*, 5–6.

9. Andrew Moravcsik, *The Choice for Europe: Social Purpose and State Power from Messina to Maastricht* (Ithaca, NY: Cornell University Press, 1998).

10. See Walter Mattli, *The Logic of Regional Integration: Europe and Beyond* (Cambridge and New York: Cambridge University Press, 1999).

11. Alejandro Chanona, *Is there a Comparative Perspective between the European Union and NAFTA?* UNU/CRIS e-Occasional Papers, O-2003/5 (Bruges: United Nations University-CRIS, 2003); online at http://www.cris.unu.edu/fileadmin/workingpapers/Alejandro%20Chanona%20OP1.pdf; Francesco Duina, *The Social Construction of Free Trade: The European Union, NAFTA, and Mercosur* (Princeton: Princeton University Press, 2006).

12. Alberta Sbragia, "European Union and NAFTA," in Mario Telò (ed.), *European Union and New Regionalism: Regional Actors and Global Governance in a Post-Hegemonic Era* (Aldershot: Ashgate, 2001), 108.

13. See Vinod K. Aggarwal and Edward A. Fogarty, "The Limits of Interregionalism: The EU and North America," *Journal of European Integration* 27, no. 3 (2005): 327–346.

14. Ibid., 331–332.

15. Ibid., 333.

16. Sbragia, "European Union and NAFTA," 99.

17. Chin-Peng Chu, "Regionalism and Regional Integration in the Asia-Pacific and the European Union: Theoretical Discussion and Developmental Experience," in Christopher M. Dent and David W.F. Huang (eds.), *Northeast Asian Regionalism: Learning from the European Experience* (London: Routledge, 2002): 34–64.

18. See Fredrik Söderbaum and Luk van Langenhove, "The EU as a Global Actor and the Role of Interregionalism," in *Journal of European Integration* 27, no. 3 (2005): 249–262.

19. Ibid., 255.

20. Ibid., 255.

21. Ibid., 256.

22. Philomena Murray, "Toward a Research Agenda on the European Union as a Model of Regional Integration," in *Asia-Pacific Journal of EU Studies* 2, no. 1 (2004): 33–51, 40; see the interesting collection of essays from a host of regional groupings across the world by Ariane Koesler and Martin Zimmek (eds.), *Global Voices on Regional Integration*, ZEI Discussion Paper C 176 (Bonn: Center for European Integration Studies, 2007).

23. Murray, "Toward a Research Agenda," 35.

24. See Andrew Hurrell, "Regionalism in Theoretical Perspective," in Louise Fawcett and Andrew Hurrell (eds.), *Regionalism in World Politics: Regional Organization and International Order* (New York and Oxford: Oxford University Press, 1995): 122–168.

25. Söderbaum and Shaw, *Theories of New Regionalism: A Palgrave Reader*; Finn Laursen (ed.), *Comparative Regional Integration: Theoretical Perspectives* (Aldershot: Ashgate, 2003).

26. See David Mitrany, *A Working Peace System: An Argument for the Functional Development of International Organization* (London: Royal Institute of International Relations, 1943).

27. See Ernst B. Haas, *The Uniting of Europe: Political, Social and Economic Force, 1950–1957* (Stanford: Stanford University Press, 1958); Leon Lindberg, *The Political Dynamics of European Economic Integration* (Stanford: Stanford University Press, 1963).

28. See Robert Keohane, *After Hegemony* (Princeton: Princeton University Press, 1984); John Gerard Ruggie (ed.), *Multilateralism Matters: The Theory and Praxis of an International Form* (New York: Columbia University Press, 1993).

29. See Moravcsik, *The Choice for Europe*.

30. See Balassa, *Theory of Economic Integration*.

31. Kenneth Waltz, *Theory of International Politics* (Reading, MA: Addison-Wesley, 1979).

32. See Alexander Wendt, *Social Theory of International Politics* (Cambridge and New York: Cambridge University Press, 1999); Heiner Hänggi et al. (eds.), *Interregionalism and International Relations* (Abingdon and New York: Routledge, 2006).

33. See Gamble and Payne, *Regionalism and World Order*.

34. See Richard Falk, "Regionalism and World Order: The Changing Global Setting," in Söderbaum and Shaw (eds.), *Theories of New Regionalism: A Palgrave Reader*, 63–80.

35. See Boas, *New Regionalism in the New Millennium*.

36. See Hettne, Inotai, and Sunkel (eds.), *The New Regionalism Series*.

37. Mattli, *The Logic of Regional Integration*, 18.

38. The original thesis was developed by Jacob Viner, *The Customs Union Issue* (New York: Carnegie Endowment for International Peace, 1950).

39. See Robert Mundell, "A Theory of Optimal Currency Areas," *American Economic Review* 51, no. 4 (1961): 657–665.

40. See Alessandra Casella, "On Markets and Clubs: Economic and Political Integration of Regions with Unequal Productivity," *American Economic Review* 82, no. 2 (1992): 115–121.

41. See Mattli, *Logic of Regional Integration*, 23.

42. Ibid., 26.

43. See Balassa, *Theory of Economic Integration*.

44. Mattli, *Logic of Regional Integration*, 54.

45. Murray, "Toward a Research Agenda," 41.

46. See Philippe de Lombaerde and Luk van Langenhove, *Indicators of Regional Integration: Conceptual and Methodological Issues*, UNU-CRIS Occasional Papers, O-2004/15 (Bruges: United Nations University—CRIS, 2004), online at http://www.cris.unu.edu/fileadmin/workingpapers/OP%20IndicatorsPDL-LVL-2004.pdf.

EMULATING THE EUROPEAN UNION?

The Incomplete Model for Democratic Region-Building

───────⪥•◎•⪤───────

A Model for What?

When the European Economic Community (EEC) was founded in 1957 through the Treaties of Rome, nobody would have seriously thought of a global role for Europe. A thirty-year period of civil wars had left Europe in ruins. Moreover, the continent was divided and its Western part under heavy pressure from expansionist communist regimes under the totalitarian leadership of the Soviet Union. The Marshall Fund aid program of the United States and the creation of the North Atlantic Treaty Organization (NATO) had reversed American policies toward Europe: the US was to stay committed to Europe's recovery and security. Under the protective shield of the United States, France began an impressive revision of its policies toward defeated Germany. The former policies of fear, revenge, and security concerns were to be replaced by a strategy of hope, cooperation, and a new common beginning. The Schuman Plan of May 1950 will always be remembered as one of the most far-sighted strategic decisions of modern France. The postwar policies of the United States and of France were perceived as generous in West Germany and in other parts of Western Europe. They may have hardened the Soviet grip over Central and Eastern Europe. But they initiated an unprecedented new beginning for Europe, based on the notion of reconciliation and aimed at defending freedom and democracy through common policies and structures that eventually led to the continent's unification.

About five decades later, the world has completely changed. The Cold War division of Europe has ended, democratic governance has succeeded in most parts of Europe, and the Western part of the continent is enjoying unprecedented levels of mass affluence. The security umbrella with the United States continues formally, but it has undergone enormous transformations and encountered a serious adaptation crisis. Moreover, this crisis has been exacerbated by new asymmetric threats stemming from terrorist acts in Western cities, the war in Iraq, the pressure from failing or failed states, including illegal streams of migration, and the ever present and often escalating conflict in the Middle East. European integration, on the other hand, had achieved a landmark success with the introduction of a common currency in 2002. The introduction of the euro completed the creation of a common market and thus the initial period of functional economic integration. The project has not come to full fruition, with Great Britain, Denmark, and Sweden remaining outside the euro, at least for the time being, and with more new EU member states from Central and Southeastern Europe waiting to be accepted into the eurozone. Slovenia was the first of them to introduce the euro in 2007, followed by Malta and Cyprus in 2008, and Slovakia in 2009. Other countries will follow.

The enlargement of the European Union (EU) by ten new members in 2004 was meant to symbolize the end of the division of Europe. However, EU enlargement, and hence the process of continent-wide reconciliation, was still incomplete. Several countries of Southeastern Europe, Turkey included, were still waiting to be accepted as EU member states. The outbreak of four wars of Yugoslavian succession in the 1990s had confronted Europe with the first and very brutal outbreak of mass violence since 1945. The answer given by the countries of the European Union was helpless for a long time, yet far-reaching and appropriate in the end: A European perspective for all Southeastern European countries would be the only viable answer to overcome ethnic hatred and conflict, even if this would take another generation or more.

Self-doubts about the path of European integration in the age of globalization were spreading in the EU. The rejections of the first-ever European Constitution in referendums in France and in the Netherlands in 2005 were symptoms of deeper crises in integration and of Europe's place in the world. While the European Union was increasing its foreign policy presence with peacekeeping missions in more than a dozen places, many European citizens were afraid of becoming social and cultural victims of globalization and global changes. Migration, the future relationship with Islam and the Muslim world, and the uncertainties for the European welfare state, compounded by slow economic growth rates and an aging population amidst a sharp decrease in birthrates throughout Europe, attributed to a lamentable myopic attitude toward European integration. In light of such adversity, the European Union was confronted with the serious need of a thorough renaissance.

Most paradoxical was its mismatch with the overall global perception of Europe. In the United States, the global role of Europe was often criticized for being insufficient and parochial. But even in the US, it was realized that the management of most global affairs would require a European partner. Some analysts went even further and extolled the European Union as the new superpower, gradually replacing the United States.[1] This seemed exaggerated, and yet it indicated the central mismatch: the relationship between European integration as it is, and its global perception. Self-doubts stand side by side with overly high esteem, while frustration about crises in integration stands beside the appreciation of the success of integration. It is in this atmosphere and context that European integration has begun to be discussed as a model for other regions and regional groupings in the world.

This discussion originates in the doubtless success of European integration since its inception in 1957. By and large, institutional European unity has been achieved, while true "Europeans" remain a limited species across the EU. Yet from outside Europe, unity and harmony seem stronger than Europeans tend to feel it themselves. Security and affluence inside Europe, coupled with solid democracy, the rule of law, and the protection of human rights, comprise the image of Europe in the early twenty-first century. The colonial legacy and its inherent notion of exploitation have been overcome. This is also true with regard to the consequences of two world wars and the destruction stemming from this tragedy. Europe, in many parts of the world, has become a shining example of peace and affluence, as well as conflict management and the integration of different interests. Europe, without a doubt, is widely respected around the world. But is or can Europe be considered a model for other regions and their efforts in organizing public life?

It is imperative to define with more precision which aspects of European integration might be considered a model:

- Europe as a model of conflict resolution? European integration is usually lauded as the alternative to war and destruction on the continent. But it must be added that it took centuries of wars and a terrible degree of onslaughts before Europe was ready to revise its past ways of conflict resolution. Nobody can wish other regions to go through the ordeal of war and destruction on the scale that Europe underwent before embarking on the path toward regional integration. In this context, the role of the Franco-German relationship must be addressed critically. Its unique character and legacy most certainly cannot be found elsewhere. On the other hand, it does not seem to be a deterministic law of global politics that it takes the political far-sightedness of long-term archenemies to reverse the cause of a region. It might be useful to benefit from the engine of two strong regional partners, united in diversity or in real commonality. Indeed, there may not be other structural equivalents to the Franco-German relationship. But this might not mean that Europe's experience with conflict management and reconciliation is irrelevant for non-European regional groupings.

- Europe as an institutional model? European integration is strongly institutional and has always been driven by political elites inside the constitutional institutions of their respective countries. The high degree of institutionalization has become characteristic of the pursuit of European politics. Procedures and structures are often considered an essential factor in dealing with the integration issue. It is the intuitive reflex of the multilateral creed to assume that procedural politics, based on a highly complex degree of institutional provisions, by definition alleviate tension, encourage compromise, and support the development of mutually reinforcing perspectives, common interests, and joint actions. Traditionally, no non-European regional grouping has put so much emphasis on the role of institutions, yet the degree of emulation of Europe's integration institutions across the globe is astonishing. However, non-European regions have to develop their own institutional structure, capable of solving their specific problems. Simply copying the EU-institutional framework is not a feasible solution. In some cases, one might critically argue that this emphasis on institutional politics is a disguised form of paternalism. It would, however, be too simplistic to reduce the role of institutions in politics to that of pseudo-democratic elitism. Institutional structures and procedures turn ideas into lasting processes and prevent eruptive conflicts from escalating in uncontrollable ways. Institutional structures are, however, no natural guarantee for success and efficient outcome.

- Europe as a governance model? Closely linked with the European emphasis on—some say obsession with—institutional questions are the efforts to generate, shape, and refine the governance structures of the European Union. Multilevel governance has become a sophisticated topic for the academic discourse on EU integration. Primarily, however, it has grown into a complex web of horizontal and vertical modes of coordination and preparation of decision-making. Often, its ways and means appear secretive to the outsider. Yet they are a guarantee for stable policy processes with predictable developments and centered policy outcomes, thus preventing radical eruptions of arbitrary moods to take over the political process. In as much as governance structures can promote a predictable and long-term perspective in non-European integration schemes, their value is highly relevant for regional groupings outside Europe. How and to which degree European modes of governance can be emulated and transferred to non-European integration schemes, is a matter of empirical measurement.
- Europe as an economic model? Europe's unprecedented mass affluence after 1945 has become the focus of attention and fascination in many parts of the world. The European Union has achieved an economic outcome that is more or less equivalent to that of the United States, although levels of per capita income still differ in favor of the US. Among economists the debate continues as to what extent Europe's economic success since 1945 is due to European integration. Some critics argue that Europe's economy recovered in spite of European integration. In the early twenty-first century, the European Union is struggling hard to maintain and regenerate its competitiveness vis-à-vis the United States. Europe's slow growth rates have become a matter of concern. They are partially related to a saturated market that is aging and has much lower birthrates than other parts of the world. The link between European integration and European economic performance is defined by a wide set of unique aspects that do not exist in other parts of the world,

or are extremely difficult to emulate. Yet Europe as a successful integration model is largely understood as being a successfully integrated economy that other regional groupings envy and would like to copy.

- Europe as a social model? Inside Europe, several social models exist: an Anglo-Saxon, a Rhenanian, a Scandinavian, and a Mediterranean one. All of them contain strengths and weaknesses, and none of them can simply be transferred to the postcommunist new member states of the European Union in Central Europe. The welfare state is the natural sibling of the political nation-state in Europe. While the latter has been transformed as a consequence of European integration, the European welfare state has largely been exempted from this systematic transformation. Its flaws and limits keep the political systems of most EU member states busier than any other contemporary issue. It is difficult to argue that the European Union represents one social model. Furthermore, it will be even more difficult to convincingly suggest how and by which means this non-existing model might be emulated in other regional groupings. Social cohesion and solidarity have to find local answers. Regional socio-economic asymmetries will have to be dealt with inside any of the non-European regional groupings.[2] European experiences might serve as a laboratory in order to study the diversity of the species of social models. But the answers to genuine social and developmental problems in non-European regions have to be found there. In the end, European solutions such as the concept of the Development Fund and the Cohesion Fund might find applied variants outside Europe.

- Europe as a model in defining regional identity? The biggest challenge for Europe is the precise and consensual interpretation of a common European identity. It has been said that Europe was created, but Europeans have not yet been created. The rich resources of cultural traditions, so it seems, are sometimes more of a burden than a source of inspiration for Europe in its quest to formulate and define its identity. Europe is only in the early stages of beginning to realize the value of a common political culture, based on common memories, joint actions and institutions, and an increasing awareness of a common destiny and future. Such an approach resembles the usual American attitude when referring to political culture. Defining "identity" simultaneously as cultural and political remains the biggest unresolved intellectual quest for European integration. What sort of conclusion may be drawn from the European debates and reflections remains undefined. Some of the other regions in the world that have embarked on a process of region-building are home to very rich cultures, either homogeneous or diverse. Yet the political degree of identity formation through political values and institutions is still weak in all non-European regional groupings.

- Europe as a model of input and outcome legitimacy? The European Union is assessed among academics and in the political arena for its degree of legitimacy. Participation in the elections to the European Parliament is often mentioned as a key indicator for measuring input and output legitimacy of the European integration process. Applying these categories of legitimacy to non-European integration schemes would mean a more structural effort of comparing the European with non-European region-building efforts. Legitimacy, as a criterion to measure the quality and effect of regional integration, can draw theoretical insights from the European discourse. But it will be essential to primarily understand the preconditions, circumstances, and effects of non-European regional integration in their own right before imposing overly loaded theoretical concepts upon them. The problem with some European theoretical approaches is that they are not theoretical in a universal or universalizable sense. They are rather theoretical reflections on European integration realities. Hence, they might have a limited reach to measure and assess non-European regional integration experiences.

• Europe as a model for the sequencing logic of integration? European integration has begun with functional and sectoral integration efforts in the economic sphere. Although the rationale for regional integration in Europe was political—building peace and stability—and its rationale remained political over time—defining the global role of Europe—the sequencing of integration measures and tools was based in the logic of economic integration from negative (eliminating trade barriers) to positive integration (creating a customs union, then a common market, and finally a common currency). The broadening of the European integration project to genuinely political dimensions (direct election of a European Parliament, extension of qualified majority voting, developing a common defense and security policy) was sometimes understood as reflection of a genuine and universal path dependency. This absolute assessment of the extension of integration from the economic sphere to the political sphere might not be transferable to non-European integration schemes. Some of them have begun as an effort in security regionalism; others put priority on development measures. To assume a universally binding logic of sequencing integration processes might be a static and deterministic view that does not comply with empirical evidence.

• Europe as a model for casual (informal and contingent) inspiration? To understand European integration as a mirror through which to better see oneself might be the simplest and yet most effective way to raise the right set of questions for modeling non-European integration patterns. The European integration experience might be helpful not in finding certain absolute answers but in raising the right and rigid set of questions to better assess the conditions, circumstances, possible effects, and serious obstacles to regional integration elsewhere. European integration has never followed a fixed blueprint. It was shaped by its unique history and changed through its crises. It was transformed in its rationale, instruments, and objectives, and it underwent unintended consequences as far as goals, norms, and assets were concerned. Throughout its integration history, the European regional grouping that began in 1957 with the Treaties of Rome has developed and been strengthened through change, controversy, and crises. It would be surreal not to assume similar modes of life in any non-European integration context. It would also be unfair to judge non-European integration schemes by a "higher" and "purer" logic than the European integration project. As much as European integration was "at times sporadic, and at times sclerotic,"[3] the same pattern might be identified in assessing non-European integration schemes. None of them, in fact, could have done more than recognize a casual inspiration for emulating the European integration.

Philomena Murray must be credited for having outlined the first research agenda for comparative regionalism studies. She has suggested studying the following aspects in order to understand the meaning of European integration for non-European regional groupings:

- The reasons for joining or establishing a regional entity.
- The external factors that are similar to or different from the ones defining the EU.
- The difference of time scales.
- The adaptation to different circumstances and crises, such as World War II in the case of Europe and the currency crises of the 1990s in Asia.
- The perceived need for, and the benefits to, all members of a regional grouping.
- The willingness to engage in regionalism and to advance it in stages.
- The willingness to develop a specific model or pathway to integration.
- The agreement on market regulation and/or deregulation.
- The desire to engage with other regions in inter-regional dialogue.
- The desire to pursue an increase in intra-regional trade flows.

Murray also offered a list of preliminary factors on which the advancement of region-building depends:

- The importance of one issue binding all members of a regional grouping.
- The ability of all members of a regional grouping to carry out their objectives.
- The willingness of all members of a regional grouping to sincerely cooperate.
- The willingness to decide on the leadership issue within a regional grouping.
- The necessary clarification of the main actors in a regional grouping.
- The evidence of a desire for integration, from either the "top down" or the "bottom up."
- The evidence of shared goals, commonalities, and visions.
- The evidence of a lasting commitment to norms, governance, and regulatory mechanisms.
- The commitment to the global growth of regional actors.[4]

These lists surely can be extended, refined, and refocused. But they are a valuable contribution to initiate a new academic field: comparative regionalism. In the age of globalization, Europe needs to broaden its perspective, also in this context.[5] Important for advancing this field is a solid empirical basis. Theoretical frameworks do not help if the empirical evidence from the main regional groupings in the world is superficial or arbitrary. A systematic empirical revision of the main regional groupings is the necessary starting point to advance comparative regionalism as a subdiscipline of political science, covering aspects of international relations, governance matters, and issues of political theory. Comparative regionalism will also need to resort to the insights and findings of related disciplines such as economics, law, anthropology, and cultural studies. More research ought to be dedicated to the real impact of the European Union on other regions, their actors, and their structures.

Europe: Where Does It Come From? Where Might It Go?

In 1900, Europe represented one fourth of the world's population. By 2000, Europe's share had dropped to one eighth. In 2050, it will be down to one fifteenth of the world's population. Maybe even more remarkable is the fact that in 2050, one third of all Europeans will be above sixty-five years of age. An aging Europe with low birthrates in most countries and a shrinking share in the world economy has nevertheless gained enormous international attraction. For five centuries, Europe was a continent of migration. From the seafarers to the colonists, from adventurers to people escaping from hunger, oppression, and war, Europe has provided migrants that shaped the face of large parts of the "new world" in North and South America, South Africa, Australia, and New Zealand. Since the 1960s, the trend seems to have reversed and Europe has become a continent of immigration. People from all the four corners of the world come to Europe, many legally, many others illegally. Now it is they who are running away from hunger, oppression, and war. They want to join Europe, which is attractive for them as a safe haven and as a continent of peace and freedom, of affluence and tolerance.

Europeans might struggle with multicultural identities in many of their inner cities. Some Europeans might even be racist, and many of them clearly have mixed feelings about the role and future of Muslims in Europe. In a highly secularized Europe with strong Judeo-Christian traditions, the arrival of a new religion must create ambivalence, as the traditional leading religion of Europe is encountering a grave crisis. Muslims have surpassed Jews in Europe to become representatives of the second-largest religion in Europe after Christianity with its various denominations. No matter how many Europeans consider themselves nonreligious and secular these days, religion as a public issue has returned to Europe. Immigrants to Europe expect to enjoy Europe's tolerance. Indigenous Europeans who feel pressured by religious immigrants are afraid of intolerant Islamic fanaticism and terrorism in the name of Islam.

The face of Europe is changing in the early twenty-first century. European identity has never been more diverse, and yet its roots are incontestable. Europe's roots are Judeo-Christian as far as religious life, ethics and much of education, architecture, music, and culture are concerned. These roots were shaped by the Age of Enlightenment, the reasoning of law, and the primacy of human dignity and civil rights. In such a Europe of ambivalent and changing identities, European integration is strongly embedded. The norms of multilateral, supranational integration and cooperation have been enshrined in the spine of a Europe that used to project itself as a colonial power and dominating force in many regions of the world. The values of peace and nonviolent conflict management have been introduced as a new mantra into the souls of many in a Europe that destroyed itself and much of the world two generations ago.

The idea of European unity has had a long history. It never came into fruition under peaceful and voluntary conditions. It always failed when some leaders, nations, or ideological beliefs tried to impose it upon the other nations, countries, and thought patterns in Europe. Only under the pressure of total self-destruction after two world wars, under the benevolent pressure of the new American protector, and the expansionist pressure of the new Soviet-Russian foe did Western Europeans begin in earnest to shape a project of peaceful integration.

European integration was never a linear success story. It was almost the opposite. Most dramatic were several of the frequent crises *in* integration. One could argue that European integration has advanced through a steady chain of adaptation crises.[6] Nevertheless, none of them has escalated into a crisis *of* integration.

- Without World War II the speedy beginning of European integration would hardly have been conceivable. But the French initiative to begin with security integration failed in 1954, when the French National Assembly rejected the establishment of a European Defense Community, which ironically the French government had proposed and initiated itself two years earlier. Soon, the shock of this crisis found a reasonable reaction in the efforts that led to the formulation of the Treaties of Rome in 1957. European integration was to begin with economic regionalism.
- Two initiatives to carry the integration project further and into the sphere of political integration failed in the early 1960s when the Fouchet Plans were rejected as too ambitious by the then member states of the European Economic Community. It took until the mid 1980s to relaunch the idea of a political union. Gradually, qualified majority voting was introduced in the decision-making processes of the European Economic Community, now renamed the European Community (EC).
- The Werner Plan of 1971 was intended to pave the way for a comprehensive currency union by the end of that decade. An international currency crisis in the aftermath of the oil crisis derailed this ambitious project to complete the European common market. But the project did not die. It took several new monetary crises in the European Community and a very cautious, gradual new beginning to finally open the way for the key political decisions on monetary union in the late 1980s. By 2002, the euro was physically introduced with banknotes and coins.
- The pressure of adapting the institutions of European integration was felt on the occasion of every enlargement to new members. When the European Union, as it has been called since the Treaty of Maastricht (in force since 1993), took ten

new member states from Central and Eastern Europe on board in 2004, the effort to combine "widening" of the community with "deepening" of its integration substance ran into a new, deep crisis *in* integration. The proposal for the first-ever European Constitution (officially called Treaty Establishing a Constitution for Europe), prepared by a European Convention in 2002/2003 and signed by all EU member states in 2004, was rejected in referendums in France and in the Netherlands. Although eighteen of the twenty-seven EU member states had ratified the document, the Constitutional Treaty could not be implemented. The Reform Treaty of 2007 (officially: the Treaty of Lisbon) became a low-key version of the original Constitutional Treaty, aimed at enabling the EU to advance with necessary institutional improvements (including a regular co–decision-making process between the European Parliament and the European Council on most matters of EU legislation, a permanent President of the European Council, a stronger role for the High Representative of the Union for Foreign Affairs and Security Policy, and a better ordering of competencies between the EU institutions and the EU member states). In June 2008, the Treaty of Lisbon was rejected in a referendum in Ireland. Eventually, the positive result of a second referendum in Ireland in October 2009 paved the way for the ratification of this treaty by all EU member states. On December 1, 2009, the Reform Treaty came into force.

The European Union insists on being a law-based supranational entity. Historically speaking, EU democracy was to follow its legal beginnings. The *acquis communautaire*, the comprehensive body of EU norms and regulations, has evolved over time, as have EU institutions. Increasingly, they have been criticized for being insufficiently transparent, democratic, and accountable to the European citizenry. As long as the EU remains considerably undemocratized, EU citizenship, the critics argue, would be a mockery. Comparable to the national history of democracy, the rule of law—as enshrined in the increasing importance of the European Court of Justice—was only gradually followed by broader democratic participation.

In spite of many idiosyncrasies and a great deal of the academic literature in the field, the European integration process has always been able to eventually achieve a new constellation by which the widening of membership and the deepening of integration structures and policies are mutually reinforcing. Multilevel governance has developed gradually, and it has broadened the notion of identity in Europe. The traditional interpretation of identity as understood by national and cultural identity has often been transformed into a matter of diverging mentality. Yet Europe has not been freed from violence, as became evident during four wars of Yugoslavian succession in the 1990s, but also during socioethnic riots in the suburbs of Paris and political clashes in downtown Budapest in 2005. On the whole, however, Europeans have acquired multilevel identities, including a local, a regional, a national, and a European component of identity, along with the religious, professional, and habitual elements that constitute the integral human identity.

Among the other experiences of European integration is the successful yet complicated, and at times daunting, transformation of the rationale for integration. European integration started as a project of reconciliation within the continent. Before this rationale had come to full fruition, the end of the Cold War and the imminent division of Europe, along with the new realities of globalization, forced the European Union to address the issue of its global role and the implications of its increasing global presence. The European Union was oscillating between hope and fear, its member states and the citizenry across the EU often divided. It seemed to be much more comfortable to define European integration by its limits and the global role of the EU as purely that of a civilian power. Yet global realities were forcing the EU "to get its act together" internally and to broaden its horizon externally.

The European integration process never followed any blueprint. It was never exempt from liability for failures and shortcomings offered by the reality of integration-building. Yet the more strongly the EU became integrated, the more doubts about the irreversibility of its course were heard. And the more EU institutions were strengthened, the more the weakness of the creation of "Europeans" was felt. The more Europe was encountering self-doubts about its future strength, economic dynamism, and global projection, the more non-Europeans seemed to appreciate, even envy, European integration and its underlying success. These might well be understood as dialectical processes inevitable in such a complex and unprecedented context.

It is interesting to look back to the first text ever written about the link between European integration and its global perception and, maybe, emulation. When Ernst B. Haas, one of the founding fathers of European integration theory, published an article under the title "International Integration: The European and the Universal Process" in 1961, he could not have foreseen the evolution of almost half a century that was to follow until the publication of this study. He analyzed the European Economic Community and other emerging regional groupings as they were at that particular moment. Among his many stimulating lessons, one insight into the nature of evolving regional integration groupings deserves to be remembered particularly. "Policies made pursuant to an initial task and grant of power," Haas wrote with reference to spillover effects of integration, a concept that he had developed in conjuncture with the immediate developments of European integration after World War II, "can be made real only if the task itself is expanded."[7]

This thesis of Haas may find a distant echo in the survey chapters of this study. European integration has indeed expanded its tasks throughout its existence. One test case for non-European integration to succeed will be the degree of the ability of regional groupings to continuously expand their tasks, to renew and transform their rationale, and to overcome inevitable crises of and crises in integration through processes that help them to recover and emerge from crises strengthened and more dynamic than ever.

Different sets of criteria can be applied to assess regional integration groupings and their respective efforts in region-building. Among the most obvious are the following:

(1) Content pattern: It is useful to assess the pattern of the factual development of a regional grouping in time. It is also feasible to assess this development in its relation to its abstract potential or the challenges it is objectively confronted with. Finally, certain developments of issues can be assessed in their own right, such as the effect of a customs union on the expansion of regional trade.

(2) Mechanics pattern: It is useful to study the role and impact of certain engines of region-building and the effect of internal and external federators or federating issues. In this context, the role of treaties and other documents of integration becomes relevant. They initiate patterns of action even if their initial implementation is limited. Governance mechanisms are relevant in as much as they impact the institutional arrangements of a regional grouping and will increasingly be influenced by its effects. In this regard, the role and pattern of reform procedures, including treaty revisions and expansions, are of interest. Overall, the relation between economic developments and governance issues, including the security issue, remains an important matter throughout any longer-term academic assessment of comparative regional integration.

(3) External elements: This rubric includes questions of geopolitics, the effect of regional conflicts or neighborhood controversies, matters of economic competition, the role of norms, including norms of international law, and political theory, such as sovereignty or non-interference, in domestic affairs.

(4) Theoretical connotations: In most regional groupings, certain more or less focused debates occur concerning the norms in integration and the rationale of integration. Theoretical models of integration are being reflected among members of the political elites, and integration efforts are sometimes models rooted in more or less coherent theoretical assumptions.

(5) Criteria related to the effects of integration: In light of the experience of regional integration, its impact can be studied: on actors, on national factors and their revision, and on related social realities, often possibly with unintended consequences. This pattern of assessment includes reflection on priorities in integration and their potential redefinition as a consequence of integration effects.

(6) Effects of proactive EU policies: The European Union is actively promoting region-building across the world. Its strategies and policies are not always coherent, and their effectiveness varies. But a pattern has become evident and must be taken into consideration when assessing region-building elsewhere.

Structural comparisons between the European integration experience and non-European groupings need to include reflection on the functional understanding of integration in each grouping: what are the priorities, why, how is the process organized, what were and are its effects? The comparison includes an assessment of the driving forces of integration: the relationship between the political elite and the broader population; the relationship between economic and political factors and integration goals; and intrinsic goals and effects of external federators. The comparison must also include a study of the effects of integration failures that encompasses the role of institutions and their mandates.

Finally, those policies ought to be identified that were important in advancing European integration, as they might structurally be of particular relevance in a non-European context. Although this goes beyond the scope of this study, it may be suggested that such scholarly work could include issues of solidarity organized via reallocation of resources, including the work of a development fund or a cohesion scheme. The much-loathed EU agricultural policy, with its redistribution mechanisms and market interventions, might be more than outdated in the EU context and even morally discredited. It cannot, however, be excluded that similar patterns could be reinvented in the context of developing agricultural societies in the southern hemisphere.

Certainly difficult to assess, owing to lack of empirical material, is the matter of interest formation and memory building in non-European integration groupings. Empirical evidence is weak, and most of the scholarly literature has been occupied more with discussing and justifying theories than with studying the issue empirically. The political cultures of non-Western societies remain an under researched field, as do their decision-making mechanisms and processes. This has implications for the assessment of popular opinions in these regions about supranational community-building and the prospects of regional integration.

Mimicking Europe?

The general trend in comparative regional integration literature is the positivistic comparison: What else is necessary for model A to reach the level of model B? Much less attractive and potentially provocative, but equally important, is an honest reflection about obstacles to regional integration: What does not work at all, and why? At the top of a list of related questions must be the worry that the very idea of emulating the European integration experience is futile. Instead of translating the pattern of integration into a different context, there is the danger of simply mimicking European institutional arrangements without any sense of the European rootedness and the preconditions that might have made certain institutions and mechanisms work successfully in Europe.[8]

It would be based on overly static assumptions to believe that integration processes could be copied without taking into account the inner dynamic, the external and intrinsic preconditions, the role of actors, and the scope of their actions. Neither the geopolitical environment that generated European integration after 1945 nor the cultural patterns determining the European political history can be repeated in other regional circumstances. It is also difficult to conceive that the European experience of generating a common market would constitute a universal path dependency that could be emulated in other regions. Reference to the institutional plethora of European integration can be a useful hint to allude to the multidimensional character of regional integration. Institutional considerations might be necessary, yet not sufficient, aspects for enhancing region-building elsewhere. The federating factors and actors will, in all likelihood, be unique in each regional grouping.

This is the main reason why, in the last resort, the European Union's support of regional integration can only be limited. It can encourage the establishment of certain institutions. It can serve as a model for the development of institutional mechanisms and integration tools. It can also encourage projects that are aimed at supporting regional integration. But in the end, region-building has to be recognized and needs to grow within each region that aims at some form of regionalization. To negotiate biregional means of cooperation is a useful contribution to stability in world affairs. It adds to the structure of a world order that is often perceived as intrinsically anarchic. But again, external support for region-building, including support through biregional channels, is limited.

Having stated this, however, one must raise the question as to which measures and goals promote and support genuine, viable, community-oriented region-building. This question overlaps with reflection on the intrinsic aspects that might lend momentum to support for community-building through regional integration. As most of these concepts are rather new in the context of non-European regions—and they are not even properly rooted in Europe in spite of more than half a century of integration practice—early results and effects are unlikely. This should encourage analytical caution and judgmental restraint. It would be neither fair nor analytically appropriate to expect judgments to be passed on non-European region-building while these processes are only in their very early stages. Community-oriented region-building in the non-European context is, after all, an embryonic phenomenon.

The time line applied to measuring region-building in the non-European context must take this fact into account. It must also recognize the difficulty stemming from the past fixation on autonomous national sovereignty. For decades, the leadership of non-European countries, particularly those in the southern hemisphere, was conditioned by claims of autonomous statehood and sovereignty as the ultimate national goals. Nation-building was to be achieved through independent statehood. This was the mantra of the political leadership across the world, and it became the benchmark for measuring the legitimacy of their actions among their broader population. A revision of this ideology of sovereignty in favor of a cooperative and even integrative regional approach to the resolution of political conflicts and the maximization of welfare gains cannot happen overnight, and it cannot happen without confronting resentment and skepticism.

More helpful and appropriate than absolute judgments—mostly critical—about the limits or even failure of region-building in the context of non-European regions would be an emphasis on structural comparisons with the evolution of European integration experience. None of it occurred with laser-light speed. All of it was challenged one way or the other. Most of it came about in spite of—if not because of—daunting crises, frustrating backlash, and temporary stalemate. It would be helpful not to forget these European experiences when judging the young efforts of region-building in a non-European context.

It is imperative to recognize the local context of region-building. Conditions and challenges, priorities and actors, and factors and goals depend primarily on local and regional conditions. External pressure includes geopolitical factors and the widespread fear of being left out in the age of globalization. Such external factors contribute to regional reflections about the value of region-building and may even frame their scope. In the end, though, local constellations define the path, the pace, and the results of region-building. No process of regional integration has been without its unique idiosyncrasies. A region can be staged in spite of an original absence of common interests and shared governance norms. Membership in different regional groupings can overlap, including the possibility of membership in two or more regional groupings with different, even non-complementary objectives.

All regional integration experience could probably be written as a perpetual story of achievements under the law of unintended consequences. Different phases, time lines, and effects of region-building depend not only on the priorities and will of political actors, but also on external events and suddenly changing circumstances. None of this can be excluded when collecting empirical data about region-building across the world. Yet it is always important to keep in mind the main focus—namely, the novelty of global proliferation of region-building in the formation and evolution of world order.

It is a realistic assessment that the European integration experience is understood as a source of inspiration elsewhere. More detailed research would be helpful to better understand which actors in a non-European regional grouping do invoke, and under which conditions, which element of the European integration legacy in pursuing their genuine policy agenda. The institutional provisions of the European Union are often understood as a functional precondition for faster achievement of the promised goals of integration, namely peace and prosperity. Policy patterns and policy areas as they evolved in the European Union cannot simply be exported to other parts of the world, and no one is expected to attempt to do so. The policy agenda is different in each region. Policy formulations therefore must be designed according to the specific regional constellation. As for the goals of integration and the identification of the main institutional instruments for a regional grouping, the European Union can serve as a mirror.

Unfortunately, most comparative reflections about the mirror function of the EU are reduced to simply (and somewhat naively) underlining the ambition of region-building elsewhere. This attitude provokes the danger of reducing European integration to a mechanistic set of institutions. As long as they function, integration seems to work. This mechanistic understanding of integration would be as short-sighted as the notion that regional integration happens once communiqués and treaties of integration are signed and promulgated. In the European context, treaty revisions and policy communiqués intended to advance the integration process have always been a resume of de facto developments, achievements, and sociopolitical facts on the one hand, and normative patterns to advance a goal-oriented path of integration on the other.

For the development of regional integration outside Europe, it might be particularly useful to reflect on the application of criteria for measuring integration progress. Despite more than half a century of regional integration in Europe, common European interests have evolved only gradually and slowly—if at all. The most effective process in promoting the evolution and adaptation of a common European interest was the mechanism that was applied in bringing about the European currency, the euro, during the 1990s. France and Germany were in agreement about the overall idea of completing the European common market with a common currency. At times, open disputes broke out in the European Community as to whether a common currency should crown the process of completing the common market or ought to be understood as a complementary measure in advancing the common market. But most important was the fact that France and Germany, the two leading engines of currency integration, wanted to pursue this very goal for very different reasons. The Germans wanted to facilitate the operations of their export-oriented economy by introducing a common currency across the EC. The French wanted to participate in the strength of the German currency, the deutschemark, hoping to benefit the modernization and competitiveness of their economy. In the end, both partners struck a compromise: the goal of a common European currency was formulated and outlined in the Treaty of Maastricht based on the combination of a precise time line and a comprehensive catalogue of criteria.

Precise time lines and comprehensive catalogues of criteria are usually absent from regional integration efforts outside Europe. Instead of purely embarking on an institutional overdose and an obsession with the implications of certain measures of integration on sovereignty, non-European regional groupings would certainly be well advised to formulate their objectives and projects as specifically as possible. This ought to include precise time lines for projects to be achieved and catalogues of criteria to measure progress in this process. Instead of fearing too much regulation, the introduction of such measures of benchmarking integration achievements would probably cause the opposite. It would enhance transparency and strengthen the specific focus of an integration goal.

It cannot be denied that regional integration outside Europe is—at least partly—driven by the disincentives of fear. In some cases, integration measures are promoted out of fear of a region's further marginalization in the global economy. The increase in European integration has forced some other regions to respond with a new dynamic in their own regional ambition. Usually, they perceive integration achievements in Europe as the expression of an inward-looking strategy by Europe. Creating a common market might prove to be to the detriment of traditional non-European partner countries. Creating a more integrated political space might provide the European Union with instruments of power. If projected properly, they could limit the autonomous scope of action of certain other countries. Regional integration is therefore perceived as a logical means to strengthen individual scopes of action through cooperative and collective means of empowerment.

In analyzing region-building outside Europe, the existing academic literature is confronted with two challenges that usually limit the analytical value of most existing studies. Some of them focus their empirical approach on one regional grouping, or at best compare two of them. This provides for highly specialized and sophisticated, if not microscopic, insights into processes, considerations, objectives, actors, and other factors. It does not, however, necessarily help to enhance the level of comparative understanding of regionalism. Only a comprehensive assessment of all key regional groupings in today's world—as much as they extend beyond the goal of a preferential trade zone, apply institutional measures that contribute to an evolving governance structure, and are political in their objective to contribute to region- and community-building—can help accomplish this goal. The second impediment to comparative regionalism is the theoretical framework applied to the study of regional groupings. Some analysts resort to the set of theoretical notions and models usually used to analyze and shape the European integration process, which clearly is the most advanced in the world. While the analytical tools are sharp and tested, their applicability to completely different circumstances is problematic—and all the more so, if it is only linked to limited empirical material. Some analysts limit their theoretical tools to those offered by economists, often shaped and concluded in the context of the European integration experience. The comparative value of these theoretical tools might be analytically strong, yet it could be objectively weak in the absence of empirical substance.

The European Union as a "Developing Region"

The most interesting aspects for non-European efforts in region-building are based on the results of the European integration experience, which provides insights into key notions of political theory. At first sight, the evolution of European integration is related to the southern hemisphere only in negative terms. Europe's self-destruction in two world wars ended its supremacy over many of its long-time colonies. Decolonization meant the end of European hegemony. The quest for independence seemed to be invariably interwoven with the decline of Europe, notably its colonial powers. Independence in the "Third World" was closer to the idealism of the American dream of self-determination and freedom than to the European doctrines of past centuries. Unfortunately, in many newly independent countries the dream of self-determination was relegated to the foreign policy arena. The internal dimension of self-determination—that is to say, popular sovereignty under the rule of law and through democratic governance—was often neglected. Geopolitical calculations during the Cold War reduced the relevance of many newly independent countries in the southern hemisphere to the role of pawns on the chessboard of the bipolar struggle between the Western camp under US leadership and the communist camp under the dominance of the Soviet Union.

Only modest thought has been given so far to some interesting coincidences that might lead to a reassessment of the relationship between European integration and the regional development in non-European groupings. It has often been said that the combination of the Suez Crisis and the Soviet suppression of the Budapest uprising in 1956 made European integration possible, because these events directed the attention of every hesitant policy maker in Western Europe, and notably in France, toward the combined pressure of increasing Soviet aggression and expansionism and of the inevitable limits of the European powers' role in world affairs. The limit of their global power was echoed by the independence of many of their former colonies. It was, of course, a non-causal coincidence that the process of decolonization was almost brought to an end with the full and internationally recognized independence of Namibia in 1989, that is to say, in the very same year that the Cold War was laid to rest, the division of Europe was overcome, and European integration experienced a new boost with the launching of the policy process that led to the Treaty of Maastricht on monetary union two years later. Independence of the southern hemisphere was completed as European integration became more serious and deeper than ever.

This overlap of constellations may be more than just a parallelism in time. It might be understood also as a parallelism in stages of sovereignty. Only after all former colonies had gained their state-based independence was it possible for non-European efforts in region-building to gain a certain distance from the obsession with autonomous statehood and impermeable, almost sacrosanct sovereignty as the ultimate expression of freedom. Now, a new assessment of possible welfare advancements and security opportunities through region-building became possible. Europe was no longer the despised continent of imperialism and colonial oppression. As Europe became a continent of serious and deep experimental regional integration, it was increasingly perceived as a continent of hope and a model of a transformed region for other regions in transformation. Europe, one might say, began to be recognized as a developing world. No longer the static, inflexible, and intolerant embodiment of stubborn national pride and colonial primacy, Europe was increasingly understood as a laboratory for multilevel governance and multilayered identity. Recognized as a promoter of multicultural diversity and sincere multilateralism as the preferred instrument of conflict management, the European Union was beginning to become a laboratory for the world, even as it became a joint laboratory for Europeans themselves.

The metamorphosis of the nation-state made this secular trend of transformation possible. It is still in its beginning stages, and nobody can predict with certainty the final outcome and its effects—probably with new transformations. So far, the biggest difference between the European integration process and its echo in non-European regions relates to democratic governance. In Western Europe, the rule of law, democratic governance, and fervent commitment to the protection of human rights were at the heart of the integration process from its very beginning. The European Economic Community could never have started, and would certainly have ceased to exist before achieving serious results, if its founding members had not been democratic countries. The geopolitical revision of Europe's strategies for organizing the continent and balancing its power was a complex and multifaceted process. But it would be grossly insufficient not to recognize the democratic base inside the member countries of the European Economic Community as the first and most important precondition to make this process work and succeed.

Only after communist one-party rule had come to an end in Central and Eastern Europe did the question of possible EU membership of many of this region's countries become a serious matter. Only in 1993 did the EU define its Copenhagen Criteria for EU membership—the rule of law, a market economy, and respect for human rights and minorities—but in reality, the 1957 Treaties of Rome had already been the first application of the Copenhagen Criteria. The metamorphosis of the European nation-state was able to begin and has continued for more than half a century only because the protection of human rights, democratic governance, and the rule of law are at its root. Their primacy and the end of global hegemony as a concept for the projection of interests of single European countries are two sides of the same coin. The European Union cannot possibly reinstall the notion of hegemonic power projection as its global creed if it wants to adhere to its inner norms and democratic values. Therefore, the global promotion of region-building is only conceptually coherent for the European Union if the EU promotes democratic regionalism.

This inherent and irrevocable link between democratic rule and integration success is not always present in the context of non-European regional groupings. It would be utterly wrong to understand the European experience as a new effort in dominance. However, the history of emancipation must be written and read fully in order to benefit from it and draw lasting conclusions. Most of the former colonies in the "Third World" have successfully freed themselves from northern hegemony and colonial dominance. They have achieved equal status in the formal application of the ideology of state-based sovereignty. Often their statehood was but the first step in nation-building, and the limits of both processes were felt more than once. It would be simplistic to reduce all failures in nation-building, development achievements or any kind of regional security formation to the absence or weakness of democratic rule. But in light of the European integration and democratization experience, it certainly is a key factor that should no longer be overlooked.

This study is introducing the concept of democratic regionalism. It embodies the quintessence of the prior European experience: No democracy without eventual region-building, and no region-building without democracy in its constituent states. If post-1945 or pre-1990 Europe had wanted to reorganize the balance of power among its old and new nation-states and the system of mutually suspicious security formations without rooting these efforts in domestic democratic rule, it would have failed. Similarly, if Europe had stabilized and re-created democratic rule across the continent without revising the parameters of traditional interstate relations in Europe, it would have failed. Democratic regionalism was the double answer to the two main problems of organizing public life, politics, and statehood in Europe: It was the answer to the normative condition of legitimate rule in each country, and it was the answer to the strategic condition of legitimate power among the many countries of Europe. Democratic regionalism is the new feature of Europe.

In a paradoxical sense, the "new" Europe becomes increasingly linked with the "old" "Third World." While Europe's nation-states have undergone a thorough transformation since 1945, the European welfare systems have not been Europeanized yet. In fact, many would argue that they have not even been modernized and brought up to date with the socioeconomic and demographic challenges of the early twenty-first century. The European Union sees itself confronted with competitiveness issues vis-à-vis the United States as well as China and other emerging economic powers in the world. Its expensive welfare systems have come under pressure because of the aging European population and much cheaper production sites outside Europe that attract investments, which are then missing in Europe to modernize infrastructure, education, and the economy. The welfare systems of Europe are also confronted with the implications of migration, largely from poorer countries and very often from former European colonies. While the rising non-Western economies are demanding their share in the world economy, immigrants to Europe look for security and welfare gains that their own weak or failing home countries cannot provide them with.

This is not a matter of reversing the path of power or providing belated justice after a century of European global hegemony. But there clearly is a link between the transformation of the perception of Europe in the southern hemisphere, the pressure felt in Europe due to migration, the difficulties in adjusting welfare systems, strengthening European economic growth rates, including the demographic growth rate, and preparing the continent for competition in the age of globalization. Peace and democratic integration are not natural guarantees for preserving a privileged place for Europe in world affairs.

In fact, the deficits and shortcomings of democratic integration are felt more strongly than ever in the European Union. They are by and large the consequence of an incomplete democratic regionalism that has evolved under the roof of the European Union. Democratic regionalism has been achieved as far as the solidity of European national democracies is concerned, and it has been achieved as far as secure peace and stability on the European continent have been created. However, after the sad experiences in Southeastern Europe and the prevailing instability in the Caucasus, which is after all Europe's periphery, this statement can only be made with reservation. Moreover, democratic regionalism has not been fully achieved in the structures of the European Union itself. The parliamentarization of the European integration process has advanced remarkably. The role of the European Court of Justice as an engine of integration and defender of the primacy of community law has been recognized. The extension of policy areas covered by actions and decisions of the European Union has increased enormously. Nonetheless, the practical translation of the meaning of a European citizenship is still very deficient, and the social dimension of Europe is at best embryonic. Many analysts believe participatory democracy on the European level remains impossible.

Hence, the European Union remains an incomplete model for non-European region-building.[9] The EU's embryonic efforts to promote biregional relations with non-European regional groupings may eventually contribute to new links between domestic governance, region-building, and global governance. For the time being, permeable sovereignties are the most tangible effect of integration. They prevail in each relevant field of politics, from the environment to migration, from poverty alleviation to security. Any biregional agenda will have to be specified, focused, and advanced to gain meaning. It cannot increase its relevance and raise its level of recognition if it is merely a supplementary effort for the promotion of free global trade. It must become an instrument for the promotion of the free world.[10]

Democracy and the Limits of Region-Building

The role and relevance of democratic governance for region-building is evident if the European integration experience is honestly compared with other regional groupings that also strive for community-building. Democratic societies tend to promote democratic principles and rule of law across their borders. The legitimacy of their political regimes is trust-based and success-driven. Without trust among a solid majority of its people, a democratic form of governance will not prevail. Without success in the pursuit of the political choices and objectives of a society, democratic governance will lose trust. By their inherent nature, democratic governments tend to look beyond their borders.

The promotion of democratic rule and human rights has never been a coherent element in international relations. Different degrees of hypocrisy have been practiced. Conflicting priorities have clashed. Unequal instruments in the pursuit of policy goals have been registered. Yet it is one strategy to promote democratic rule, the primacy of law, and human rights in other corners of the world. And it is another strategy to bind one's own destiny to neighboring countries that are not guided by the same principles of governance, the rule of law, and human rights.

In the context of the European integration experience, the response to this dilemma has been unequivocal: membership in the European Economic Community, the European Community, or the European Union is subject to domestic democracy in each member state. Only after Southern European countries had returned to democratic rule was their European integration possible. Only after Central and Eastern European countries dissolved communist regimes and established democratic structures and rule of law-based constitutions were they accepted as EU member states. Whatever else had to be considered in order to join the European Union, one principle has always been clear: No integration without democratization.

Unfortunately, so far this insight has not found a prominent place in the analysis of regional integration outside Europe. Instead, it is usually economic theories and many technocratic arguments that are used to better understand the forces, obstacles, and limits of region-building in a non-European context. In doing so, actors have underrated the main normative perspective for successful region-building: coherence in democratic rule among member states of a regional grouping. How can one expect Pakistan and India to pool sovereignty if these two member states of the South Asian Association of Regional Cooperation position nuclear missiles against each other, one being under military rule, the other being a democracy? How can the Southern African Development Community turn into a political project if the authoritarian rule over Zimbabwe has no consequences for the country's membership in SADC? How can MERCOSUR possibly grow into a political union if the populist-authoritarian regime of Hugo Chávez in Venezuela joins a grouping that has come about only after Argentina and Brazil have overcome dictatorship and authoritarianism? How can ASEAN turn into a constitution-based community if the military regime in Myanmar is acceptable as an ASEAN member without conditionality regarding good governance? The conservative monarchies of the Arab Gulf were at least honest enough in one aspect: they have not accepted the Republic of Yemen as a member of the Gulf Cooperation Council, fully realizing the relevance of regime cohesion in the GCC—even if their perspective is the opposite of democratic regionalism.

Clearly, most non-European constellations of region-building do not embrace the concept of pooled sovereignty. In doing so, non-European actors in region-building should not be surprised about the limits of cooperation they will face over time. Democratic region-building, as the European experience has shown, is the most principled precondition for pooled sovereignty, which in turn is the most far-reaching precondition for successful community-building through regional integration. Democratic rule is no guarantee for successful region-building. It is not even necessary for democratic countries to join others in the pursuit of regional community-building, as shown by the examples of Switzerland, Norway, and Iceland in Europe itself. But whenever a regional grouping wants to achieve more than a minimalist agenda of trade promotion through deregulation and liberalization of trade barriers, it will need a degree of mutual trust that can only stem from symmetric governance patterns. The Arab Gulf states demonstrate that governance cohesion need not mean democracy. They are cooperating exactly because they are not democratic and want to protect their vested interests, including economic gains and regime stability, through cooperative means. But this constellation also shows its limits: for now, the Gulf Cooperation Council is an example of security regionalism. Democratic region-building is of a different nature.

Democratic region-building was always the quintessence of regional integration in Europe. Europe would only transform its state-system, went the rationale, if its constituent states would transform themselves into democracies. Constitutional monarchies could join ranks with strictly secular republics, but the basis of governance had to be democratic in order to contribute to a regional integration worth its name. Regional integration would not have succeeded only because the member states of the unique European experiment were democratic—democracies can fail their norms. But democracies were necessary to start the process of supranational, law-based order-building in Europe.

In light of the transforming effect of regional integration, one might hope for the transformation of governance structures even under the conditions of a constellation in which democracies join ranks with authoritarian states. Theoretically, this possibility may not be excluded, but practically, there have not been convincing examples yet. The transformation toward democracy, the rule of law, and the full recognition of human rights ought to come from within. Regional partners might support the process or help prevent an infant democracy from derailing and reverting to authoritarian rule. External pressure might help to open up authoritarian structures. But even then, as the case of Myanmar shows, the projection of external pressure is limited. Regional groupings that are weak in their commitment to democratic regionalism will be weak in influencing the democratization among any of their member states.

The application of the concept of democratic regionalism for judging the normative character of regional groupings does not originate in European arrogance or unjust Euro-centrism. To the contrary, it will help non-European regional groupings to better understand the dynamics and limits of region-building if they look at it through the lens of democratic regionalism. The whole world lives under state structures that originated in Europe. Many of the states of the world are weak, failing, or already failed. They often are suboptimal and have not met the expectations that enabled them to come about in the first instance. Overcoming the obstacles between state formation and state achievement is a complex and potentially painful process. It serves this process and its smooth unfolding if the European experience, in overcoming the limits of its own concept of the autarkic sovereign superiority of state-centered policy, can be appropriately applied to this process elsewhere in the world.

Democratic region-building is an experience and a norm for success. It is the response to the failures and deficits of order-building in Europe. It is also a response to the ideological excesses that accompanied the political and intellectual history of Europe during much of its modern existence. Combining democratic rule with regional integration has become Europe's response to Europe's disasters. No other region in the world should feel obliged to follow that path, but given that all regions in the world are living under state-centered conditions originating in Europe, they might want to consider the European experience as part of their own process for shaping the future.

The market and scientific progress may drive and define globalization. Regional economic cooperation and eventual integration can be the choice of countries. As we have seen, this concept may not aim at achieving political objectives and community-building. Yet even regional economic cooperation requires political and legal decisions aimed at regulating a free trade area. Clearly, region-building that goes beyond the concept of a free trade area also requires political framework decisions as far as its economic goals are concerned. As can be seen in the European case, establishing a customs union, a common market, or even a currency union remains a political choice and requires political decisions. The European common market is the result of complex political processes that interacted with interests of the private sector.

Sometimes it is believed that functional target dates for achieving integration objectives can substitute for political trust, democracy-driven social networks, and long-term private sector interests. The setting of target dates in regional economic integration—as well as in other policy areas—has functions other than announcing a specific objective. Target dates are also meant to focus the actions and thought patterns of relevant actors within a regional grouping, regardless of the precise implementation date. Target dates and stages of implementing a project of integration, such as a common external customs tariff, indicate a direction. It would be unfair to simply judge non-European integration efforts in a harsh way that would rarely be applied to the process of European integration, its history, pace, detours, and failures. The overall decision in favor of regional integration is the overriding consideration that can be detected in many regions of the world, and the consideration that needs to be recognized. The implementation of details and principles may be slower than expected, with more detours than hoped for and more frustration than idealism thinks acceptable. In the end, regional integration must be understood as a process in which, as a Spanish poet once said, the paths are being marked while walking. Failure and success in achieving target dates for specific integration projects cannot be the main criteria for measuring the depth of integration. Integration without trust among its actors remains a hollow technocratic form at best.

Eventually, every step toward market liberalization has to also be considered a political move. Matters of security, sense of ownership, democratic accountability, the role of stakeholders in region-building, and the issue of political will and direction are discussed today by most regional groupings worldwide. The renewal of several regional groupings during the 1990s was a remarkable sign of the broadened focus of regional integration. The interrelatedness between globalization-induced activities such as those under the umbrella of the World Trade Organization, and politically inspired developments like the evolution of the regional groupings aimed at community-building in Latin America, Africa, and even Asia, has become increasingly fluid.

Whether democratic region-building can be achieved in all regions of the world is an open issue. It is even a matter of debate whether democratic regionalism should be the ultimate objective of region-building. Normatively, it is in the interests of the European Union to advance this objective. The constraints and contradictions of this concept will become clearer the closer we look at them. Analytically, more than a grain of caution and doubt has to be added, given the very mixed empirical record of democratic region-building so far. Traditionally, regional integration was primarily understood as a concept for pooling economic interests. Preferential trade arrangements have mushroomed across the world, driven by the desire to harvest the fruits of globalization. At their root lies the hope to maximize affluence and welfare gains for one's own people, or even more specifically, for as many individuals as possible. Maximizing affluence and welfare gains in the age of globalization corresponds with the traditional dictum of utilitarianism: the greatest amount of good for the greatest amount of people, or maximizing the interests and benefits for the biggest possible number of people.

European integration does not deviate from this goal. It differs, however, in the approach taken to achieve its ends. Its means are mostly regulatory activities based on political decision-making and legislative acts. European integration, more than anything else, is a process of evolving law-based governance. In this it corresponds more with the performance of the classical state than with that of the liberal and open, yet at times anarchic, market, or any free trade area, no matter how successful it may be. European integration has never been free from market considerations. In fact, its proponents claim to frame the market in order to make it work better. They even claim to be building a political structure for the EU to give order to freedom aimed at protecting the weak parts of society while providing the stronger ones with the opportunity of pooled resources and a larger space for action and interaction.

In as much as regionalism means region-building, it is a process that terminologically reveals an engineering aspiration. It is the opposite of the voluntary and arbitrary freedom that defines the market. Yet the architects of European integration have always rejected the charge that they are curtailing the dynamics of the market and undermining its potential for human growth and freedom. A certain intrinsic conflict between order and freedom cannot be washed away by the most elegant possible interpretation of European integration. Region-building is a process of engineering social and political conditions. In as much as this is the antithesis of the free pursuit of the market, it is limiting its free evolution. But region-building in the European sense of the word has always been as much about solidarity as it was and is about freedom. It is not law-based for the sake of sophisticated legal hair-splitting; rather, its legal norms are intended to protect the weak, individually and socially, as far as their role in the overall European market and political process is concerned.

Such a sense of region-building has, so it seems, increasingly appealing components for developing countries. Yet they cannot presume to realize an order of solidarity that focuses only on distribution, protection, and cohesion. The developing regions of the world, as much as the European Union is an incomplete model for region-building, need to fully incorporate the values of an order of freedom. Without a democratic backbone, regional integration cannot achieve sustainable success. It might generate regional groupings that represent precisely defined interests of its members. It can contribute to the extension of the marketplace in the world and to a broader inclusion of more citizens than ever in its benefits. But it will always remain subject to the arbitrary actions of the strongest participants in this market if it is not framed by the primacy of law. These basic insights into the nature and character of separation of power and an order of freedom on any national level are no less relevant in the context of regional integration.

Region-Building and the Transatlantic Partnership

In a speech to the Canadian Parliament in Ottawa in February 2001, British Prime Minister Tony Blair made a plea for a political declaration of intent between the European Union and NAFTA. It is telling that this idea never materialized. Obviously, the incompatible structures of the European Union and

NAFTA do not provide sufficient ground for a structured strategic relationship. More realistic has been the suggestion to formulate a transatlantic treaty that could frame the multi-pillared reality of transatlantic relations between the United States and the European Union and its member states in a comprehensive way that includes security, economic, political, and community matters.[11] But neither has this idea materialized. The two largest markets in the world, the EU and the US, are "the cornerstone of the international economy."[12] They are also the key actors in the management of world affairs. Economically, they absorb 20 percent of each other's exports with a total trade of approximately $650 billion per year. In 2001, EU firms accounted for 60 percent of the stock of foreign direct investments in the US, an amount of approximately $870 billion, while the US owns approximately $630 billion worth of foreign direct investment in Europe. Much of this transatlantic exchange is intra-firm–based, indicating even a stronger bonding between the two economies.

After the Cold War ended, the former primacy of security and defense matters in transatlantic relations initially vanished, only to rebound in rather controversial ways in the aftermath of the terror attacks on the US on 11 September 2001. The subsequent "War on Terror," its interpretation, and its approach were most controversial with regard to the US-led invasion of Iraq in 2003.[13] However, transatlantic economic relations continued at a rapid pace. Reciprocal investments on both sides of the Atlantic Ocean increased even amidst the political controversies over Iraq.[14] Since the end of the Cold War, EU-US relations have increasingly focused on economic issues. The Transatlantic Declaration (1990), the New Transatlantic Agenda (1995) with its concepts of a transatlantic marketplace and the introduction of a Transatlantic Business Dialogue, and finally the Transatlantic Economic Partnership (1998) were elements of a deepened bilateral structure, giving a public and more political voice to the broad and active exchange among businesspeople and community leaders. Since 1990, the United States and the European Union have conducted regular annual summit meetings, as have the EU and Canada. The agenda has increasingly broadened and is shifting from bilateral matters to questions regarding the common management of global issues.

With several changes in European leadership positions and a new American administration, the time is ripe for a new transatlantic beginning. The EU and the US remain indispensable partners of the greatest importance to one another. Fundamental differences in the approaches of the two pillars of the Atlantic community may come up time and again. Often, they stem from different historical experiences and concepts of politics that yet are based on the same values. At the heart of different transatlantic perceptions seems to be the understanding of the concept of statehood and the notion of sovereignty. The European Union's concept of pooled sovereignty and multilevel governance remains alien to most US policy makers and analysts. In the eyes of some of them, Europe ought to be divided between "old" and "new" Europe, a distinction introduced during the Iraq

War dispute by then Defense Secretary Donald Rumsfeld. In the eyes of many Europeans, in turn, the United States, with its primacy on state sovereignty and selective multilateralism, is somewhat of an example of "old Europe," that is, the old Europe of the era of the Congress of Vienna: a country primarily pondering its global role in categories of balance of power, non-interference in its own or other's domestic affairs, autonomous sovereignty, and supremacy of statehood.

More than the member states of the European Union, the United States remains rooted in a concept of sovereignty that has by and large vanished in Europe. European integration has transformed the notion of sovereignty and reduced its emotional overture. Sovereignty has become a pragmatic concept. It is recognized that most attributes of sovereignty have become porous in a world of interdependence, innumerable transnational relations, and new realities that permeate all human boundaries. In fact, European integration has also transformed the notion of the territorial boundary. It is no longer perceived as a national bulwark against intrusion, territorial claims, or pressure from the other side. Borders inside the European Union delineate cultural and, most importantly, linguistic identities. Europe's nations are not dissolving in the process of European integration. They are protected by the respective states, which frame a certain cultural shield around the nations of Europe. This shield does not provide answers to the challenges of migration and the necessary Europeanization of the welfare state. But the shields of national borders in Europe have become permeable.

Among the majority of member states of the European Union, border controls have been dissolved. The physical experience of moving from one country to another has lost the formerly visible trappings of authority. Although no more than 1 percent of Europeans live in a country of the EU other than their own home country, the degree of interaction and travel—for business as well as for pleasure—has exponentially increased in Europe within the last generation. Some analysts even argue that "a generation Europe" has emerged.[15] Other, more skeptical analysts point out, as previously mentioned, that whereas Europe has been created, Europeans are still missing.

In the US one might almost conclude the opposite: Americans exist while the US still has to evolve. The strong spirit of patriotism and the fascination with the "American dream" are constitutive pillars of the US presence in the world. The American state is strong and projects its power and presence across the globe. But unlike the European state, it has not undergone the metamorphosis of more than half a century of regional integration. The US has not only been the unquestionable leader of the free world, it is also a "colossus" with ambivalent views on the value of multilateralism.[16] It lacks the experience and transforming effects that the membership in a regional grouping provides for the European states who are members of the EU.

On several occasions, the US and the EU have undergone contrasting experiences in the course of the first decade of the twenty-first century.[17] In doing so, they have clashed not over different norms, but over different interpretations of the same norms. Yet the transatlantic partners would be well advised to find common, or at least complementary, ground in dealing with the emerging role of regional groupings in world affairs. To perceive the role of regional groupings as mere participants in global trade negotiations will increasingly be insufficient. To judge regional groupings only by their economic weight or geopolitical power would underestimate the governance dimension of region-building. As the process of the global proliferation of regional integration continues, the US and the EU will have to respond to it in a more comprehensive and strategic way. For the time being, however, it is not clear whether their concepts of world order remain in competition with regard to the perception of political region-building and its promotion by the EU.

The United States and the European Union are the main pillars of the Western world. They incorporate and represent the principal values of democracy that have originated in Europe and in the US. Notwithstanding their long and daunting struggle against prevailing realities in Europe and in the US alike, they are the principal representatives of the democratic West. They share democratic values with other parts of the free world, but along with their economic prosperity, the United States and the European Union are the leaders of a viable global system that can manage the central challenges mankind is confronted with. Democratic regionalism can be understood as one component in the management of the global order. The United States needs to accept the trend toward region-building as a rational political process that can be much in line with its enlightened self-interests. For the European Union, the global proliferation of regional integration is not only a matter of rational insights into inevitable trends. The EU is also proactively supporting region-building and considers it in line with its own normative understanding of political, economic, and security developments in today's world. The EU should not try to promote regional integration as a means to contain the influence of the US.

The United States and the European Union are in a position to promote democratic regionalism together. While security regionalism might originate from the necessity of stabilizing a region, and development regionalism is presented as a facilitator of economic and social progress, only democratic regionalism can achieve human development, political freedom, and regional transformation all at once. Its promotion should be a common interest of the United States and the European Union. As the most affluent, most developed, and strongest federal units in the world, the EU and the US can share their unique experiences in democratic governance, inter-regional strategic partnership, and being home to the most affluent societies in the world. They ought to proactively contribute to overcoming those deficits in many other parts of the world that stem from insufficient state-building, excessively ideological interpretations of autonomous sovereignty, denigration of the value of democratic governance in the pursuit of prosperity, peace, and stability, and the fear of being marginalized in the age of globalization. The promotion of democratic region-building, not least in the geopolitically most troublesome regions of the world, could become one of the priority issues on the common agenda for the management of world affairs in the twenty-first century.

Notes

1. See, for example, Jeremy Rifkind, *The European Dream: How Europe's Vision of the Future is Quietly Eclipsing the American Dream* (Cambridge: Polity Press, 2004).
2. See Alessandra Casella, "On Markets and Clubs: Economic and Political Integration of Regions with Unequal Productivity," *American Economic Review* 82, no. 2 (1992): 115–121.
3. Philomena Murray, "Toward a Research Agenda on the European Union as a Model of Regional Integration," *Asia-Pacific Journal of EU Studies* 2, no. 1 (2004): 33–51, 39.
4. Ibid., 46–47.
5. See Cordula Janowski, *Globalization, Regional Integration and the EU: Pleading for a Broader Perspective*, ZEI Discussion Paper C 162 (Bonn: Center for European Integration Studies, 2006).
6. For a comprehensive history of European integration see Desmond Dinan, *Europe Recast: A History of European Union*, (Boulder, CO: Lynn Rieffer, 2004); see also Ludger Kühnhardt (ed.), *Crises in European Integration. Challenges and Responses, 1945–2005.* (Oxford and New York: Berghahn Books, 2009); Ludger Kühnhardt, *European Union—The Second Founding: The Changing Rationale of European Integration* (Baden-Baden: Nomos, 2008).
7. Ernst B. Haas, "International Integration: The European and the Universal Process," *International Organization* 15, no. 3 (1961): 366–392, 368; see also Ernst B. Haas, *The Uniting of Europe* (Stanford: Stanford University Press, 1958); Ernst B. Haas, *Beyond the Nation-State: Functionalism and International Organization* (Stanford: Stanford University Press, 1964).
8. Critically Sanoussi Bilal, *Can the EU be a model of regional integration? Risks and challenges for developing countries*, Paper presented at the CODESRIA-Global Studies Network (GSN), Second International Conference on 'Globalisation: Overcoming Exclusion, Strengthening Inclusion' (Dakar, Senegal, 29–31 August 2005), online at: http://www.ecdpm.org/Web_ECDPM/Web/Content/Download.nsf/0/52D667FD6C95057DC125719D004B65F6/$FILE/Bilal%20-1%20of%20RI%20Draft%20for%20comments.pdf.
9. On the prevailing federal vision of European integration and its comparison with the United States see Kalypso Nicolaidis and Robert Howse (eds.), *The Federal Vision: Legitimacy and Levels of Governance in the United States and in the European Union*, (New York: Oxford University Press, 2001); see also Ludger Kühnhardt, *Europäische Union und föderale Idee: Europapolitik in der Umbruchzeit* (Munich: C.H.Beck, 1993).
10. See Timothy Garton Ash, *Free World: Why a Crisis of the West Reveals the Opportunity of our Time* (London: Allen Lane 2004).
11. See Hans-Gert Pöttering and Ludger Kühnhardt, "EU-US: Plädoyer für einen Atlantischen Vertrag," *Integration* 26, no. 3 (2003): 244–250.
12. Vinod K. Aggarwal and Edward A. Fogarty, "The Limits of Interregionalism: The EU and North America," *Journal of European Integration* 27, no. 3 (2005): 329.
13. See Philipp H. Gordon and Jeremy Shapiro, *Allies at War: America, Europe and the Crisis over Iraq* (New York: MacGraw-Hill, 2004).
14. See Daniel S. Hamilton and Joseph P. Quinlan, *Partners in Prosperity: The Changing Geography of the Transatlantic Economy* (Washington, D.C.: Center for Transatlantic Relations, The Johns Hopkins University—SAIS, 2004); Daniel S. Hamilton and Joseph P. Quinlan, *The Transatlantic Economy 2005: Annual Survey of Jobs, Trade and Investment in between the United States and Europe* (Washington, D.C.: Center for Transatlantic Relations, The Johns Hopkins University—SAIS, 2006).

15. See T.R. Reid, *The United States of Europe: The New Superpower and the End of American Supremacy* (New York: Penguin Press, 2004), 205. He talks of a "Generation E," the new young, dynamic, and much-traveled Europeans.

16. See Niall Ferguson, *Colossus: The Price of America's Empire* (New York: Penguin Press, 2004).

17. See Ludger Kühnhardt, *Contrasting Transatlantic Interpretations: The EU and the US toward a Common Global Role* (Stockholm: Swedish Institute for European Policy Studies, 2003).

Part II

A GLOBAL SURVEY

3

LATIN AMERICA AND THE CARIBBEAN

Between Regional Identity and Continental Aspiration

―――◈―――

Central American Integration System
(Sistema de la Integración Centroamericana, SICA)

Basic Facts

It has been called "the most politically advanced integration process in the Americas."[1] Certainly, it is one of the least known. The Central American Integration System (SICA, abbreviated from its Spanish title Sistema de la Integración Centroamericana) is torn between the claim of supranational integration based on rule of law and political and economic union, on the one hand, and on the other the realities of dire poverty, structural impediments to development, and weak, if not fledgling, democracies in most of its member states. It is also burdened by a long history of failed integration in Central America and sometimes ridiculed by the likewise long history of unsuccessful attempts to fulfill the great Bolivarian dream of continental unity in all of Latin America. Yet the Central American Integration System has prevailed for half a century. In fact, it has been reinvented and strengthened substantially since the last decade of the twentieth century.

Among the 177 states on the Development Index of the United Nations Development Program, Central American countries rank between places 99 (Panama) and 121 (Guatemala).[2] The dilemma of being torn between poverty eradication and developing the roots of a democratic culture is tangible wherever one looks at the Latin American continent. Even so, there is a new trend, opinion polls indicate, of "a growing resilience" in democracy: in 2005, 62 percent of respondents across Latin America said that under no circumstances would they support a military coup.[3] It is against this background that advocates of regional integration in Central America see growing potential for stabilizing democracy and the rule of law at home, and cooperation and integration across the region. They understand the Central American Integration System as the expression of a regional constitution with supranational institutions based on an evolving community law.[4]

Although this claim echoes an overly optimistic perception of the current state of regional integration in Central America, policy actors and analysts are aware that they are struggling with the burden and image of a long history of failed integration in their region. Following independence from Spain in 1821 and the short-term annexation of the region by the Mexican Empire between 1821 and 1823, the short-lived Federal Republic of Central America (1824–1838) constitutes the proud model for the region to this day. In Francisco Morazán, the federation, also known as the United States of Central America, found its intellectual hero and martyr. Morazán, its most respected president, came from Honduras, the country that paradoxically initiated the dissolution of the federation by separating from it in 1838. Morazán was killed in Costa Rica in 1842.

Based on a genuine constitution and encompassing five provinces of the region, the Federal Republic of Central America, with its capital in San Salvador, was destroyed by peasant revolts and, still more, by local feudal interests. Seventeen failed efforts of integration were to follow in Central America, along with twenty free trade agreements between 1840 and 1940. Most memorable among these efforts was the creation of a Confederation of Central America in 1842, which did not last long either.

The construction of the Panama Canal (1902–1914) redesigned the geopolitical and geo-economic role of Central America. To this day, the potential of this secular revision of geography, space, and the notion of time to travel it, has not been properly discovered, interpreted, and emulated in the Central American region. In Latin America, a certain obsession prevails regarding the region's relationship with the United States. This focus has prevented Central America from looking in other directions and, among other things, from making full use of the Panama Canal. In a much stronger way, it could serve as a shared symbol of a joint identity that connects the region with the worlds eastward and westward. Neither links with China and the other booming regions of East Asia, nor Africa and the potential model of Central America for that continent's effort in reconciliation, democracy-based development, and rule of law–based integration are properly understood, let alone used in Central America's joint efforts to connect the region with the world. Instead, Central America for the most part looks only to the US—or at best to Europe, in order to balance the dominant northern neighbor. However, the role of the United States in Central America is not only that of a dominating economic power. Analogous to its contribution to the evolution of European integration after World War II, the United States supported regional integration in Central America as part of its Cold War strategy.

Based on the Doctrine of National Security, the United States supported the founding and initial development of the Central American Common Market (CACM) in 1960 with $100 million.[5] By 1963, the original General Treaty of Economic Integration in Central America (Tratado General de Integración Económica Centroamericana, signed on 13 December 1960) was ratified by Costa Rica, Honduras, Nicaragua, El Salvador, and Guatemala.[6] Original achievements were impressive: US investments increased threefold between 1960 and 1970 (from $1.6 million to $5 million) and intra-regional exports fourfold (from $30.9 million to $132.8 million). In 1979, intra-regional exports reached a peak of $1.8 billion. The goal of a common market with a customs union was always present, although never fully achieved. The creation of institutions such as the Secretariat of the Central American System of Economic Integration (SIECA), the Central American Bank for Economic Integration (CABEI), a Monetary Council, and the Central American Council of Economic Ministers as the highest political body reflected these ambitions. Yet the original effort for regional integration collapsed because of the ultimate "failure to transform the economic performance into genuine prosperity."[7] However, most institutions founded in the 1960s survived this breakdown during the next two to three decades.

The lack of democratic stability overshadowed improvements in the region's infrastructure. The construction of 5,000 kilometers (ca. 3,100 miles) of new roads and improved telecommunications, growth rates between 4 and 5.5 percent on average, and inflation below 3 to 4 percent on average could not prevent social and civil unrest. The outbreak of the "Soccer War" between Honduras and El Salvador on 14 July 1969 was a bad omen of things to come.[8] The radicalization of the Sandinista movement in Nicaragua in 1977 led to the ousting in 1979 of the country's dictator, Somoza, who was replaced by a Marxist regime of similar cruelty. Eight guerrilla movements operated in El Salvador, Honduras, and Guatemala during the 1970s. In the end, the civil wars in Central America killed 250,000 people and turned 2 million into refugees. As much as Marxist radicalism against feudal and authoritarian realities was a reflection of the region's unique radical conflicts and the effect of imported dimensions of the global East-West conflict, its consequences meant a "decada perdida," a lost decade, for regional integration in Central America.[9]

The terrible experience of a decade of civil war and anti-democratic terror cannot be overestimated in its effect on a new generation of leaders and representatives of civil society. Their quest for a new beginning of regional integration in Central America started with the will to end a legacy of war, violence, and destruction. Not unlike the European experience with World War II as a catalyst for reconciliation and integration, Central America encountered the cause and effect of the region's legacy of civil wars. It is interesting to note that the new beginning in Central America coincided with the discovery of the region by the European Community, whose initiative, which came to be known as the

San Jose Process, constituted an important element in the pacification process of Central America. This process was launched in 1984 by the then nine member states of the European Community, its candidate countries Spain and Portugal, and six Central American countries in the presence of the United Nations, the United States, and the Contadora Group, which consisted of Mexico, Colombia, Venezuela, and Panama. At more or less the same time, a local initiative supported the external efforts: upon the initiative of Oscar Arias and Marco Vinicio Cerezo Arévalo, the presidents of Costa Rica and Honduras, the indigenous Central American Esquipulas process solidified and advanced the external peace-brokering in 1986 and 1987. During the first meeting of all presidents of Central America on 2 October 1987, the Central American parliament PARLACEN was established as a consultative body, to be formally inaugurated in 1991. Despite its initial weakness, the regular meeting of a hundred representatives in one parliament, twenty from each Spanish-speaking Central American county, constituted a complete novelty in the region.

The genuine refounding of Central American integration culminated in the formal establishment of the Tegucigalpa Protocol (Protocolo de Reforma a la Carta de la Organización de Estados Centroamericanas) on 13 December 1991.[10] In conjunction with the Guatemala Protocol (Protocolo al Tratado General de Integración Económica Centroamericana) on 10 February 1993, these documents constituted the establishment of the Central American Integration System (Sistema de la Integración Centroamericana, SICA). The Guatemala Protocol (Article 1) described economic union as its final goal, but it was always evident that the underlying political ambition was based on common norms and intended to build a genuine regional community. The logo on SICA's flag demonstrates its political background and normative aspiration: it states "Peace, Liberty, Democracy, Development" as its guiding principles. Article 1 of the Tegucigalpa Protocol defined Central American integration as the expression of an economic-political community ("una comunidad economicopolitica") aspiring to the integration of the region.[11] The Tegucigalpa Protocol gave legal personality to the Central American Integration System (Article 29 and Article 30).

Following textual revisions and institutional innovations, SICA consists of the following bodies, supported by a wide array of technical institutions:

- The Secretary General (from 1 January 2005 to 31 December 2008, Aníbal Enrique Quiñónez Abarca) installed by the presidents of SICA member states and supported by a Secretariat based in San Salvador.
- Two annual presidential reunions, operating on the basis of a six-month ad tempore presidency and maintaining unanimity as its decision-making principle.
- A Council of Ministers (foreign ministers of SICA member states) as the political coordinating body.
- The Central American Court of Justice, based in Managua.

- The Central American Parliament, based in Guatemala City.
- The Central American System of Economic Integration (SIECA), with its own Secretary General and Secretariat, based in Guatemala City.
- The Central American Bank for Economic Integration (BCIE), based in Tegucigalpa.
- The Monetary Council, based in San Jose.

The SIECA structure of economic cooperation and integration has been fully incorporated into the Central American Integration System. Nevertheless, confusion about conflicting competencies and structures prevails. As part of the SICA system, Central American efforts to cooperate and integrate the region are organized in eight subsecretariats and fourteen independent regional institutions. The effort of promoting and strengthening regional integration in Central America is overly institutionalized but remains utterly underfinanced: the annual budget for SICA is $1.25 million, and for SIECA, $2.5 million, derived from membership contributions. Many regional integration projects depend upon external funding, largely provided by the European Union.[12]

The Central American Integration System consists of Costa Rica, Honduras, Guatemala, El Salvador, Nicaragua, Panama, and Belize, with the Dominican Republic as an associate member. Membership in SICA bodies varies, which adds confusion, incoherence, and a lack of authority to the entire process: The Central American parliament, PARLACEN, was inaugurated in 1991 with elected members from El Salvador, Guatemala, and Honduras. In 1997 Panama joined PARLACEN, in 1999 Nicaragua followed, while Costa Rica and Belize remain outside. Paradoxically, the Dominican Republic, which is not a member of SICA, joined PARLACEN in November 2007. The Central American Court of Justice started operating in 1994 with six judges from El Salvador, Nicaragua, and Honduras—which withdrew in 2004, demanding reforms in line with Honduran national interests before it would send judges again.[13] The other SICA member states signed the statute without ratifying it and hence have not joined in the Court's work.[14] Yet it cannot be denied that the idea of regional integration in Central America gained a new focus during the 1990s. The protocols dealing with the establishment of a regional Court of Justice (1992), and those on the importance of social integration (1995) and democratic security (1995), reflect the intellectual and political maturation of the process. They also indicate that regional integration in Central America extends far beyond the economic dimension, as important as this dimension is. Central American integration is understood by its actors as a normative program, politically induced and aimed at creating an ever-increasing sense of community across the region.

The evolution and interpretation of a community law for the 46.6 million citizens in SICA have only begun. Juridical interpretation in the region itself indicates that the process has gone beyond the hands of a few committed (or only self-serving) political actors. While the broader civil society is not yet significantly involved in the trend toward regional integration, the self-strengthening process of building a community of law has begun with its genuine normative interpretation. In its judgment of 27 November 2001, on a border dispute between Honduras and Nicaragua, the Central American Court of Justice stated that a material community with its own life ("vida propia") is evolving, represented by bodies with authentic judicial personality ("con personalidad juridical") that promote the realization of faculties of sovereignty in a joint and coordinated manner ("en forma conjunta y coordinada").[15]

Intrinsic Motives and External Pressures

(1) Central American integration efforts lingered for long decades in the shadow of the region's peripheral status in relation to the United States, Mexico, and the bigger countries in South America. They failed in a cascade of right-wing authoritarianism, social upheaval, radical Marxist ideology, and civil war. Past failures of regional integration in Central America must be understood as a consequence of failed democracy and failed social justice and cohesion. Therefore, the civil wars of the 1970s and 1980s initiated a new sense of urgency for a thorough reevaluation of social conditions, societal needs and claims, political duties, and regional perspectives. On average, per capita income in Central America decreased by 70 percent in the 1970s and 1980s. Poverty increased by 70 percent and 25 percent respectively in Guatemala and Costa Rica, considered the most advanced countries of the region. It began to dawn on a new generation of leaders in the region that only the rule of law and a regional investigation of causes and effects of the socioeconomic challenges could serve as an alternative. Democracy and the promotion of human rights became the normative driving force for regional cooperation and integration. At the beginning of a remaking of regional integration in Central America during the 1990s, the normative and moral quest for peace, human rights, and the rule of law stood as preconditions for justice and social inclusion.[16]

(2) Regional integration in Central America is highly ambitious when it comes to community-building. The Tegucigalpa Protocol mentions the desire to reconstruct a Central American Fatherland (Patria Centroamericana, Article 4). Although this is more a rhetorical contribution to an imaginary past, it indicates the potential emotional implication of the technocratic efforts undertaken by bureaucratic institutions. This grand rhetoric comes across as a regional variant of the overall dream of Latin American unity, ever present since the days of Simón Bolívar but to date meeting with failure in every attempt to implement it. The Latin American experience—and for that matter the Central American one—gives surprising evidence to the fact that cultural, linguistic, and religious coherence might be useful preconditions for building a regional identity.

Obviously, they are not sufficient causes and tools for identity formation. The dominating effects of national sovereignty, delineated borders, and formal state structures, based on notions of homogeneous nationhood, have imposed their lasting effect on supranational aspirations across Latin America. It is, however, relevant and encouraging that the domestic constitutions of most Central American countries provide ground for a transfer of sovereignty.[17]

- Costa Rica's 1948 constitution defines national democracy but grants the possibility to transfer or attribute competencies to a legal order intended to realize regional community-building objectives (Article 121.4).
- El Salvador's 1983 constitution provides for the possibility of engaging in the creation of bodies with supranational functions (Article 89).
- The 1985 Magna Carta of Guatemala recognizes the Central American community with the goal of exercising political union and economic union analogous to the old Central American Confederation of the nineteenth century (Article 150).
- Nicaragua's 1986 constitution establishes the principle to pursue privileged policies aimed at regional integration and the reconstruction of the Great Central American Fatherland (Gran Patria Centroamericana, Article 5).
- Honduras's 1982 constitution evokes the country's faith in restoring the Great Central American Fatherland (Gran Patria Centroamericana).
- Panama's 1972 constitution refers to the promotion of regional integration without being specific about the scope of a possible transfer of sovereignty to integrative bodies.
- Belize's 1981 constitution expresses the country's aspiration to join the Central American System of Economic Integration.

The empirical test of constitutional invocations shows a highly incoherent application among SICA member states. More than any other country of the region, Costa Rica originally supported the political revival of Central American integration in the 1980s and the formulation of the Tegucigalpa Protocol in 1991. The government of José Figueres Olsen ratified the Tegucigalpa Protocol, but in a strange twist declined to join the regional parliament and refused to sign the Statute of the Central American Court of Justice, the two most prominent expressions of supranationality in the region. Integration *à la carte* is not uniquely a European experience.

(3) The realization of a peripheral status in the age of globalization has led to a reevaluation of the region's leaders in politics, business, and academia. Fifty-one percent of all citizens of Central America live in poverty, 23 percent in extreme poverty. The dependency on the United States, often rhetorically cursed by politicians and intellectuals in the region, contributes partly to a resolution of this

situation: 18 percent of El Salvador's GDP originates in the earnings of migrant workers in the US ("remesas").[18] The need to diversify the regional economy and to modernize its society has been widely recognized. This coincides with a reassessment of the region's relationship with the US. After a series of bilateral negotiations, the Central American Free Trade Agreement (CAFTA) with the US came into force on 1 January 2006. The debate continues over whether or not this is a favorable scheme to attract more US investment and "help further reduce output volatility,"[19] and about the effect of CAFTA on regional integration under SICA: Will the latter be encouraged, as Europeans have traditionally hoped, or deviated from, as integration skeptics presume? It is beyond doubt that the preparation of CAFTA has done more for progress toward an internal Central American customs union and the creation of a common market than any other activity in the region during the past four decades. The increase in the region's manufacturing basis—which rose from 24 percent of its gross national product in 1994 to 34 percent in 2005—indicates that regional free trade with the US can serve as a complementary strategy for regional integration. In any case, the two are not mutually exclusive.

An open economy does not provide an automatism to consolidate democracy on the national level, balance the differences in speed and lack of cohesion of institutional commitment on the regional level, or transform bureaucratic quarrels among competing institutions and their overall attitude toward supra-nationality. But no matter how "contentious and convoluted"[20] the process remains, Central American regional integration has returned as a widely noticed issue on many agendas in the region. It is no longer a vision. It has begun to grow into a visible reality.

Performance

Strong and weak elements constitute the reality of Central American regional integration. On balance, they leave room for both optimistic and pessimistic assessments of the region's future. On the stronger side of regional integration performance in Central America are, inter alia, the following facts:

(1) The institutional makeup of Central American regional integration is strong, and almost too complex. Inter-institutional conflicts have not been resolved yet, and the dominant role of presidential summits remains as both a source of leadership and an obstacle to real progress amidst specific national obstacles. The Council of Ministers maintains unanimity in voting on relevant matters, while the principle of qualified majority voting can only be applied on procedural issues. Critics argue that SICA includes too many institutions that are often uncoordinated and even in competition with one another. Yet the institutional streamlining and progress associated with the Tegucigalpa Protocol of

1991 is promising and has certainly a long-term perspective, as represented by the installation of a regional parliament in 1991 and a regional Court of Justice in 1994, irrespective of their temporary deficiencies and shortcomings.

(2) The agreement on a common external tariff in 1995 has started the path toward a serious customs union and hence the precondition for a complete common market. While some tariffs were immediately eliminated, other tariffs fall under a long-term transition regime, including exceptions up until 2015. The most sensitive products—white corn for El Salvador, Guatemala, Honduras, and Nicaragua, potatoes and onions for Costa Rica—were exempted on principle from the tariff reduction scheme based on eight complicated baskets. In its negotiations with the region, the United States made sure to exclude sugar from its preferential trade agreements with Central America.

(3) Intra-regional trade in Central America has increased considerably. At 27.3 percent for exports and 12.8 percent for imports of its GDP, it is still much lower than the equivalent figures in the European Union, which are above 50 percent for both imports and exports. Central America's largest trading partner is the United States (37.4 percent exports, 41.9 percent imports), with the European Union considerably far behind (13.4 percent exports, 9.8 percent imports).[21] It is remarkable that the value of goods exported from Central America increased by 50 percent between 1995 and 2002, with the greatest increases in Costa Rica—which has become a production site for the computer manufacturer INTEL—and El Salvador.[22] The regional orientation of many companies in Central America is playing an increasing role in lobbying for further advancements in the area of free movement of persons, exports, and services.

(4) The region's project of a customs union has progressed and is beginning to gain momentum. In 1996, Guatemala and El Salvador decided to go ahead with the development of a customs union. Nicaragua and Honduras joined their effort in 2000; Costa Rica followed in 2002. While by the end of 2004 only Guatemala and El Salvador had achieved full customs union, it was remarkable that by then 98 percent of all 6,198 relevant titles were agreed upon by all members of the project. The borders between Guatemala, Honduras, Nicaragua, and El Salvador have become open for commerce and private travel. It cannot be denied, however, that some of the most sensitive areas of commerce are still under dispute, in particular agriculture, with fruits and sugar being most important for the total amount of trade in most SICA countries. Complete harmonization remains difficult because of different national tariffs and different interpretations of agreed customs tariffs. This should not surprise anybody conducting comparative work on the history of European integration.

(5) Projects promoting a regional infrastructure, such as the Plan Puebla-Panama, support the overall goal of Central American integration. The Plan Puebla-Panama was launched by the presidents of Central America and Mexico in 2001. It strives at building a region-wide highway—60 percent of the costs of

approximately $4.321 billion were guaranteed by 2006, underlining the usefulness of the regional bank BCIE—and energy interconnections that will facilitate trade, boost regional competitiveness, and help human resource development, as well as prevent natural disasters and promote tourism. It will, however, also have implications for competition between SICA and the southern part of Mexico.

(6) As for good governance, the record remains mixed. There have been sound improvements in human freedoms and civil rights across the region, but ambivalent governance performances in all SICA member states.[23] The very existence of the Central American Court of Justice must be considered a positive signal. It is the "embryo of a Community legal order" with an increasing potential to define the regional interest.[24] When the Central American Court of Justice ruled on a border dispute between Honduras and Nicaragua, it was not just about the border issue. The Court obviously wanted to create a precedent for reinterpreting the limits of national sovereignty in Central America and establish the primacy of community law. The ruling was not accepted by Honduras (which even withdrew from the Court) and was never implemented. But over time the Central American Court of Justice might still turn out to be a critical and powerful engine of supranational regional integration.[25]

On the weaker side of regional integration performance in Central America are, inter alia, the following aspects:

(1) The hesitation of Costa Rica and Panama to fully immerse themselves in the integration stream prevails. As much as both countries could be engines of further regional integration and development, they continue to look for options that would enable them to go it alone. Equally disturbing is the double membership of Belize in SICA and in the Caribbean Community CARICOM, while SICA remains undecided about the Dominican Republic's desire for full membership in SICA.

(2) Prevailing mistrust and pride among political actors limit their readiness to think in categories of shared sovereignty. This facilitates the continuous existence of political and economic protectionism in the region. It also has implications for the overall implementation of SICA decisions: between 1990 and 1999, 450 presidential decrees were promulgated, based on unanimous decision, but only 60 percent of them were implemented.[26]

(3) Integration à la carte is not only a matter of internal cohesion, but also of external credibility. The highly selective ratification and implementation of decisions, and the selective participation in certain organs of SICA, weakens the very concept of regional integration in Central America. It undermines the reputation of the process and the degree of trust in its potential. Costa Rica portrays itself as a democratic lighthouse in the region and continues to express

skepticism about the democratic maturity of its partners in SICA. Besides the inconsistent membership commitment of SICA members—Costa Rica and Belize do not participate in PARLACEN or the Central American Court of Justice; Panama and Honduras continue to prefer staying outside the Court of Justice—SICA member states continue to pursue bilateral free trade relations with other regions. Costa Rica even maintains bilateral free trade relations with CARICOM. During a SICA presidential summit on 15 December 2004 in El Salvador, efforts were initiated to achieve harmonized membership in SICA institutions in the foreseeable future. So far, Costa Rica and Panama's lack of readiness to contribute to regional solidarity limits the potential for conceptualizing a Central American equivalent to the European cohesion fund, that is, a regional mechanism for resource reallocation.

(4) Inter-institutional power struggles and conflicting interpretations of the primacy of national sovereignty slow down the potential dynamics of regional integration in Central America. Disputes over the claim to primacy of the Central American Court of Justice broke out again in April 2005 when the court ruled over competencies of Nicaragua's national institutions in a conflict between the country's president, Enrique Bolaños, and Nicaragua's Constitutional Court. The Constitutional Court of Nicaragua immediately rejected the Central American Court of Justice's decision in favor of President Bolaños and claimed the primacy of national constitutional law over SICA community law.

SICA's presidents practice a selective use of supranationality. But most ambivalent was their decision of 15 December 2004 to limit the number of judges on the Central American Court of Justice from two to one per country, reduce the time of their mandate from ten to six years, and redefine the court's competencies so that its right to judge national constitutional disputes—so far obligatory under Article 22f of the court's statute—should only be facultative in the future, thus supporting the return of the primacy of national law. The Central American Court of Justice remains dependent upon SICA's member states. They even have a highly mixed record as far as the payment of their shares for the court's budget is concerned. In a highly unusual public statement on 22 November 2004, the Central American Court of Justice demanded $1.5 million from Nicaragua and $650,000 from Honduras in membership fees after both countries had missed paying them for three and two consecutive years respectively. Nicaragua finally paid $500,000.

The budgetary structure of SICA remains highly intransparent. The annual budget is prepared by the Executive Committee of presidential appointees. SICA is said to have an annual budget of $1.2 million based on each member country contributing $200,000. SIECA has its own annual budget of $2.5 million equally based on member state fees. Payments of various member states are irregular. Beyond the financing of a basic institutional infrastructure and the personnel costs, most SICA projects are financed by donor countries.[27]

(5) The role of the Central American parliament, PARLACEN, installed as a body for the purpose of "proposal, analysis and recommendation,"[28] is far from being part of any relevant decision-making process in the region. Its shabby building in Guatemala City is indicative of the degree of respect it receives in the region. Yet it exists, and it is worth recalling the daunting and unappealing beginnings of the European Parliament to put the very existence of PARLACEN in a broader perspective. So far, proposals to install direct elections have not found favorable attention across the region. SICA members Costa Rica and Belize do not send deputies at all to PARLACEN, while the other countries are represented by twenty per country. Skepticism about PARLACEN's potential is continuously nurtured because certain politicians of the region have misused their immunity as PARLACEN deputies in order to avoid being prosecuted on pending corruption charges in their home states.

The Decree of the SICA Presidents from 15 December 2004 is intended to eliminate the structural deficits of PARLACEN. At the same time it tries to limit the potential powers of the regional parliament. Ending immunity might be a justifiable measure in individual cases but still would undermine a fundamental component of parliamentary authority. Curtailing the budget of PARLACEN would weaken it further, especially as its current budget is already extremely small.[29] Allowing politicians a double mandate, both in their national parliaments and in PARLACEN, could weaken the independent role of PARLACEN, but it should be recalled that the European Parliament stopped this highly ambivalent practice only in 2004. It would be more useful to abolish the automatic right of former national presidents and vice-presidents of SICA countries to become lifetime members of PARLACEN. In the past, such uses have contributed to the lack of legitimacy of PARLACEN in the region.[30]

(6) In spite of the existence of a SICA Consultative Committee representing twenty-six private organizations of the region, civil society so far has been largely absent from Central American integration. A sense of ownership has been as weak as SICA's information policy about its activities, ambitions and effects. When the region's president's decided in June 2005 to introduce a common passport, Costa Rica expressed reservations. The lack of political will to speak with one voice in the region is in part an effect of presidential democracy, particularly the overall inclination to focus on actors rather than on factors of integration through common projects. This considerably limits the ability of civil society to partake in regional integration-building.

(7) Obstacles to full implementation of free trade and a genuine customs union can be found in the specific interests of individual SICA member states and in their rather myopic fixation on national interests. This is particularly noteworthy when strategic national interests are concerned: the idea to pool them in order to strengthen the whole region currently has limited appeal to those who still tend to think they can maintain individual national strength without regional

partners. The individual rush toward bilateral relations with the United States, also driven by the hope of a better deal than the one that could stem from a regional approach, is another obstacle to comprehensive free trade, a customs union, and a common Central American market.

The strategic exceptions in regional free trade are noteworthy and relevant, not in numbers but in terms of their degree on the overall economy of the region: sugar for all SICA members, alcoholic drinks for Honduras, ethyl alcohol for Costa Rica and Honduras, roasted coffee for Costa Rica, non-roasted coffee for all SICA members, derivatives from oil and gas for Honduras.[31] As far as a Central American customs union is concerned, the challenge ahead is to make it compatible with CAFTA, the region's free trade agreement with the United States. Critics argue that the preference for Central American products to be traded primarily in the region "has been eroded"[32] by CAFTA. An institutional mechanism to monitor the relation between the effects of CAFTA and the goal of a complete and comprehensive customs union inside SICA is missing. This puts a heavy burden on SICA's ambition to modernize customs infrastructure with thirteen joint new border posts, in place since 2006. Small improvements can, however, carry a strong symbolic message: Nicaragua declared its readiness to eliminate the 35 percent "sovereignty tax" on wheat flour and other imports from neighboring Honduras, which it had imposed in the course of the border disputes between the neighbors in the late 1990s. But the very existence of such a "sovereignty tax" demonstrates how widespread the protectionist mood still is in the region.

(8) As for political integration, most noticeable in Central America is the absence of a common foreign policy in spite of all the rhetoric across the region about its need and desirability. Bilateral border disputes—such as those between Belize and Guatemala, Guatemala and Honduras, among all three against one another, and between Honduras and Nicaragua—are telling reflections of the prevailing status of national sovereignty. They also echo the economic fear of migration, such as in Belize against migrants from Guatemala and Honduras, or in Costa Rica against migrants from Nicaragua. In the absence of a political will for a genuine common foreign policy, the current weakness of the Central American Court of Justice is all the more regrettable. Properly developed and genuinely recognized across SICA, the Central American Court of Justice could serve as a comprehensive engine for further law-based regional integration.

Federators

Like other regions, Central America has experienced a complex path toward regional integration, with periods of stagnation and even regression, but also with a new focus, stronger commitment, and visible progress. Some of the forces that used to serve as regional federators can be detected in the region's integration history, while other federators—often untapped so far—are evident from the most superficial assessment of the region and its potential. Some of the past driving forces for Central America include:

- The effects of war, insecurity, and poverty in Central America have strengthened the appreciation for democratic government and the protection of human rights in the national context of each SICA member state. They have also inspired fresh reflection on regional security defined by social inclusion, economic cooperation, mutually reinforcing democratic governance, peace, and political predictability as sources and effects of a sustainable development that is more inclusive, more promising, and more in line with the limited potential of each of the countries in the region.
- The issue of size and geography has two dimensions in the context of Central American regional integration. Often, the small size of the region's countries has been a barrier to overcoming the protective myth of national independence and sovereignty. However, understanding the value added through regional integration is not only a matter of abstract reflections on sovereignty. Such an approach can be facilitated by the experience of an economy of scale that can break the cycle of weakness as long as each country strives to achieve development, affluence, and social inclusion on its own. The positive initial experiences with regional integration since the signing of the Tegucigalpa Protocol have broadened the understanding of the material usefulness of regional integration.
- The "peripheral-ness" of Central America and the burden of its dependency on the United States has always served as a driving force in the struggle for identity, autonomy, and integration. Without an economic base and without clearly defined political goals and projects, the vision of Central American unity must remain elusive. In a paradoxical way, the signing of the free trade agreement with the US (CAFTA) in 2003 by most countries of Central America (Costa Rica followed in 2004) has also supported the awareness of regional integration as a complementary strategy to tap the optimal potential of both processes. CAFTA has been implemented since 2006.
- Political leaders have been relevant in trying to formulate and implement concrete targets of regional cooperation and integration. In order to break the cycle of peripheral neglect, poverty and instability, and lack of peace and democracy, the initiatives taken by Costa Rican President Oscar Arias and Guatemalan President Marco Vinicio Cerezo Arévalo in 1986/1987 opened completely new horizons, both realistic and visionary.
- The common experience, coming from the close proximity of the nations of the region, is felt by the approximately 70 percent of all citizens of SICA countries who are said to have relatives in at least one of the neighboring states. Customs papers at border crossings have been standardized and represent a symbolic token of region-ness. Large infrastructure projects, such as those included in the Plan Puebla-Panama, indicate the broader context in which the future development of Central America could gain momentum.

- As in most other regional integration schemes across the world, SICA is both torn and driven by the multidimensional relationship between actors and factors in defining and advancing regional interests ("el intéres regional").[33] Actors in politics and business, academia, and the media contribute to the interpretation and reevaluation of a reality that imposes itself with its own weight upon the citizens of the region. The biggest unresolved question is that of a Central American equivalent of a coal and steel union and the role it played for European integration. Which resources and projects could irreversibly link conflicting interests and traditions in order to launch long-term value added? Answering this question will decisively impact the potential and prospect of regional integration in Central America in the years and decades ahead.

Transformations

The evolution of regional integration in Central America has never been linear. It has not been free of conflicts, setbacks, failures, and detours. Interesting are insights stemming from the regional integration history of almost six decades, largely accentuated by the fresh and incomplete experience since 1991, when the Tegucigalpa Protocol factually constituted the reinvention of regional integration in Central America. Most important was the adaptation and transformation of Central American integration aspirations in the context of the end of the Cold War. Originally, regional cooperation in Central America had the function of defending the strategic interests in the Western hemisphere against communist expansionism. The Cuban revolution of 1959 brought the issue from Europe and Asia to the doorstep of the United States. Keeping Central America in the Western camp became the overriding priority for the US. However, the link between Western loyalty and Western values—that is to say: democratic-political values as well as values of social solidarity and cohesion—was neglected. Authoritarian rule in Central America undermined the very basis of its claim to defend Western values. The Marxist revolution in Nicaragua represented an extreme counterreaction, reinforced by the sad and ugly civil wars in El Salvador, Guatemala, and, partially, Honduras.

Only with the end of the Cold War did Central America get a chance to redefine its identity and aspirations on the basis of genuine norms and honest goals as they ought to be represented by the Western world. Revitalized democracies helped to broaden the horizon toward a new assessment of the potential of regional integration beyond the obsession with national sovereignty and security. Security was redefined as a broad scheme encompassing civilian, economic, sociological, and environmental components. The institutional plethora, indicative of Central American efforts in cooperation and integration, began to be properly focused in so far as purpose, priorities, and instruments were concerned. Admittedly, none of this took place in a coherent manner free of contradictions and shortcomings. But a new beginning has been generated. Notions of national security were substituted by the much more advancing and inclusive, and at the same time democratic and integration-friendly, notion of democratic security espoused by SICA's Treaty on Democratic Security in Central America of 15 December 1995 (Tratado Marco de Seguridad Democratica en Centroamerica).[34]

The value of democratic symmetry among the countries in the region began to be understood as a source and incentive for economic integration and the aspiration of supranational community-building. The economic ideology of import substitution and isolation began to be replaced by a new sense of the value of openness, market liberalization, and integration. Although much of this happened too slowly and too late compared with the US and other Latin American regions, it has begun to happen. The invocation of the "golden" traditions of the regions became more realistic and went beyond finding consolation and pride in looking back to the glorious days of Mayan culture, the Guatemalan "capitanat," and the Vice-royalty of New Spain. Throughout the torn modern history of Central America, the idea of a "great fatherland" remained alive, even if only as a myth. The Tegucigalpa Protocol of 1991 invoked as the ultimate goal of Central American integration the resuscitation of the Central American Fatherland (Patria Centroamericana, Article 4). This might have sounded overly rhetorical and airy to outsiders, but to the citizens of SICA member states it activated the memory of a real future. It is therefore singularly consequential that the presidents of SICA member states were granted the privilege of contributing to the strengthening of regional identity. Although this is easier said than done and convincing contributions with transforming and lasting effects remain to be seen, the notion of SICA as a process of community-building resonates.

Role and Interests of the European Union

For the European Community, the civil wars in Central America during the 1980s constituted both a challenge and an opportunity. In the past, the European Community had not taken comprehensive interest in Central American developments. The threat of a Marxist takeover in a series of countries that traditionally belonged to the Western world enhanced sensitivities in Europe about the Marxist threat and its authoritarian-based root causes. Human rights advocates and geostrategists developed overlapping arguments concerning the relevance of Central American developments to Europe's own security and place in the world, including the authority of its normative claims to promote democracy and human rights. The imminent accession of Spain and Portugal to the European Community in 1986 added a new sensitivity to Latin America as a whole.

The San José Process began in 1984 and has continued ever since with annual meetings of the European (EU) leadership (since 1991) and the leaders of the countries that constitute SICA today. On 15 December 2004, the

European Union and SICA concluded an Agreement on Political Dialogue and Cooperation. Followed by an intensive process of evaluation of the Central American integration process, it was announced at the EU–Latin America Summit in Vienna in May 2006 and culminated in the EU's decision to initiate negotiations aimed at reaching an Association Agreement between SICA and the EU. The European Union had always insisted that such an Association Agreement would only be negotiated with SICA as a whole and not with individual member states on a bilateral basis. Instead, biregional relations are the goal.

The European Union is nourishing this process by supporting regional integration in Central America through a variety of highly focused projects. In 2006, the EU donated €10 million in support of a complex regional project intended to design and apply common Central American policies. In addition, €8 million was spent in support of the Central American customs union, €15 million went toward various activities of capacity-building, and €54 million was devoted to a program for developing border areas in Central America, traditionally neglected in socioeconomic terms and the source of border disputes among SICA member states.[35] There can be no doubt that the main intention of the European Union was and is political and normative. While the overall domestic economic product of SICA equals 1 percent of that of the United States, external trade of SICA with the European Union represents only 0.4 percent of the EU's total trade. In spite of traditional cultural ties with Spain, 30 percent of all trade with SICA passes through the port of Rotterdam, the biggest port in the European Union.

Prospects and Obstacles

After the euphoria of the 1960s, the lost decade of the 1970s, the period of gradual revival during the 1980s, and the recomposition of Central American regional integration during the 1990s, SICA finds itself both consolidating and deepening its efforts.[36] With the accession of Panama and Belize, the mechanism for expanding was handled successfully, although the issue of the Dominican Republic's possible membership is still pending. Resolving the unclear links between the free trade agreement with the US (CAFTA) and the prospects of regional integration under the framework of SICA are more complicated, it seems. SICA claims its plans for the region extend beyond 2010. The goals for its human development have been formulated in accordance with the Millennium Goals of the United Nations: 50 percent poverty reduction, 100 percent of population covered by basic health care, and 100 percent of rural areas with access to healthy and potable water.[37] SICA will need to strengthen the perception of its own role in achieving these honorable goals. The ever-lingering uncertainty about democratic stability in several SICA member states casts a shadow over this task. The same is true with regard to the impartiality of the rule of law, and, moreover, of community law, as long as corruption remains an all-pervasive fact of life and undermines the credibility of political actors, bureaucracies, and also regional business representatives.

An interesting new feature in assessing the future prospects of SICA is related to the rise of China and Asia's growing role in Central America. South Korean capital generates 66 percent of the textile industry in Guatemala, 15 percent in Honduras, and 25 percent in El Salvador. Throughout SICA, political relations with Taiwan are extremely close. Yet at the same time, imports from the People's Republic of China to the region are growing: from $45 million in 1994 to $22 billion in 2002.[38] As far as the manufacture of clothes ("maquila") in Central America is concerned, China is increasingly becoming a competitor for cheap labor. Labor costs in China are less than one fifth of labor costs in Mexico, and energy costs in China are half the price of those in Mexico. The same holds true for Central America's SICA countries, which have begun to experience the "China factor." Guatemala has already closed 10 percent of its "maquila" production because of Chinese competition. Since 2006, the former quota system for Chinese textile exports across the globe has been eliminated. Its medium-term effect on the Central American economy is no less relevant than the effect on any other part of the world. The integration of Central America will have to find common answers to the opportunities and implications of this phenomenon.

Most urgent, and not only in this context, is an overall assessment of costs and benefits of regional integration in Central America. In the 1980s, Paolo Cecchini undertook a study about the costs and benefits of European integration, which has become famous under his name as the Cecchini Report. SICA would be well advised to undertake a similar study in a comprehensive way. It would have to emphasize ways of making the equilibrium between advantages and liabilities of integration visible to the citizens of SICA. The potential is evident, since a bigger market and a more genuine political community will be more attractive for direct foreign investment. Critics argue that one of the costs of integration could be reduced trade with efficient firms outside the integration orbit.[39] Only a full-fledged economic union could generate the conditions for an optimum currency area, which is so far not feasible for SICA.[40]

Most important, however, will be the link between the national rule of law, democracy, and good governance on the one hand, and regional law-based integration driven by transparent decision-making and effective implementation on the other hand, together with sustainable peace, sound development, and social progress across Central America. In the end, and contrary to conventional wisdom, the key to sustainable, solid, and deep integration in Central America might not be economic. Instead, the key might well be the establishment of community law and the solid development of democratic regional institutions.

This challenge waits to be tackled by SICA and by all those honestly pursuing its cause.

Andean Community of Nations
(Comunidad Andina de Naciones, CAN)

Basic Facts

Simón Bolívar's great vision of creating an independent and united Latin America was only achieved in its first part. Decolonizing the continent south of the Rio Grande was a major historical achievement. It meant the application of Europe's own values—self-determination and democratic popular rule—in most European colonies. But Latin American independence in the early nineteenth century destroyed the unity of the continent under the Spanish and Portuguese crowns and led to the independence of a wide range of countries in reaction to the Napoleonic Wars in Europe. It preempted the dream of Latin American unity.

The oldest dividing line on the continent had been drawn with the Treaty of Tordesillas (7 June 1494). Upon the return of Christopher Columbus, Spain and Portugal exclusively divided any newly discovered world along the north-south meridian of 1,100 miles west of the Cape Verde Islands. The treaty, with enormous implications for the future of Latin America, was endorsed by the Spanish-born Pope Alexander VI, one of the most controversial renaissance pontiffs. With the Treaty of Tordesillas, the traditionally most remarkable division in Latin America was predestined, namely that between Portuguese-speaking Brazil and the other Spanish-speaking countries. Beside this, the cultural proximity between all the countries of Latin America is as tangible as it is between Portugal and Spain. Latin America is Catholic, and in spite of its ethnic composition—besides migration from Europe largely the result of slavery from Africa with elements of indigenous populations—is a rather coherent region. Defining its identity is much easier than it is in Africa or Asia—or even in Europe, for that matter. Yet Latin America never achieved unity. Instead, it followed the European path of disintegration in the name of parochial nationalism.

The deficit of Latin America is stunning: in spite of an apparently high degree of cultural identity among the political elites, political unity was never achieved. A series of independence movements and declarations in the early nineteenth century was followed by a series of failed efforts to unite what had been the Spanish and Portuguese colonial possessions. Simón Bolívar, the father of Venezuela's independence, but not that of the whole continent, started the effort of uniting the divided pieces of Latin America by organizing a conference in Panama in 1826 with the aim of promoting regional integration. It failed yet was followed by a number of other failed meetings: in Lima in 1847, in Santiago de Chile in

1856, 1864, in Lima again in 1877 and 1879, and in Montevideo in 1888 and 1889. Latin America bears testimony to the fact that cultural identity alone is not a panacea for overcoming political division. More than that, Latin America demonstrates that cultural identity alone cannot be the most decisive precondition for regional integration. More important are democratic governance, the rule of law, and political legitimacy that can generate trust and penetrate notions of sovereignty and seemingly impermeable borders set up during the age of national independence and state-building.

Surprisingly enough, the first serious efforts to create Latin American cooperation, integration, and unity began in the shadow of the continent's poverty after World War II. In 1960, Argentina, Brazil, Chile, Paraguay, Peru, Uruguay, Colombia, Ecuador, Venezuela, and Bolivia signed the Treaty of Montevideo. The Latin American Free Trade Association, which they created, was driven by the theoretical assumptions of Raúl Prebisch (1901–1986). This Argentinean economist, who headed the United Nation's Economic Commission for Latin America and the Caribbean, is known as the founder of the "dependencia-theory." He argued in favor of a consistent substitution of imports coupled with the development of a genuine, state-sponsored and state-protected industrialization. In the end, this approach to development did not succeed. It did not prevent a growing marginalization of Latin America in the world economy. It undermined democratic regimes and saw the rise of authoritarian, often military-backed regimes. It provoked Marxist counterreactions and, moreover, an increasing neglect of Latin America both in Europe and, to a lesser degree, in the United States. During the 1960s and 1970s, dependency theories served as self-consoling illusions in the region, but they could not truly impress the makers and shapers of the affluent societies in North America and Western Europe.

"Dependencia" theories projected an end to poverty and growing prosperity on the basis of the creation of an autonomous, indigenous common market in Latin America or any of its subregions. Following this logic, Bolivia, Ecuador, Colombia, Peru, and Chile signed the Cartagena Agreement on 26 May 1969,[41] and the Andean Pact (Pacto Andino) was born. In 1973, Venezuela became a full member of the Andean Pact (but left the Andean Community of Nations in 2006). In 1976 Chile withdrew its membership. The Pacto Andino was never more than an idiosyncratic effort of developmental integration. Intra-regional trade increased among its member states from 1.2 percent in 1970 to 2.5 percent in 1988.[42] The reasons were no less economic than political. The participating countries did not achieve a common external tariff, the precondition for establishing a genuine customs union. Peru wanted a maximum of 40 percent, Colombia 60 percent, and Ecuador and Venezuela 80 percent. The Lima Protocol of 1976 was the first effort to revise the deadline for tariff liberalization. With the Protocol of Arequipa on 21 April 1978, the decision was taken to postpone the implementation again until 31 December 1989. This was at least honest in acknowledging the reality. A common external tariff was never approved, and the liberalization of competitive goods was continuously postponed. Recession, hyperinflation, declining investment, rising unemployment, and galloping deficits in democratic governance were expressions of the real Andean community at the time. The effort to achieve centralized industrial development and to succeed in centralized investment policies was a failure altogether.

This does not mean that the Andean Pact did not begin to take institutional shape. The first regional integration institutions were established, and they became the basis for later improvement in the context of a factual refounding of the Andean community. The year 1969 saw the establishment of the Andean Commission with one plenipotentiary representative from each member state of the pact. The Junta, as it was called, was created along with a variety of advisory councils. In 1997, the Junta was turned into the Lima-based Andean Secretariat, giving it not only a more civilian name, but also a stronger profile. The Andean Development Corporation was founded in 1970. More successful were pragmatic operational efforts aimed at enhancing regional cooperation and serving the region in concrete terms. Most notable were the 1970 Andres Bello Agreement on Higher Education, inter alia establishing an Andean University with campuses across the Andean region, and the 1971 Hipólito Unanue Agreement on health projects, also across the region. In 1979, the gradual enhancement of the institutional design of Andean integration led to the establishment of an Andean Parliament. It is based in Bogota with delegate members and a mandate for consultation only. The Andean Council of Foreign Ministers and the Andean Court of Justice, based in Quito, were established in the same year, the latter having one judge from each member state and operational since 1983. The 1970s were a formative decade, followed by a transitory decade that blurred regional integration as the Andean region fell back into protectionism and military dictatorship in the 1980s.[43]

Andean developments during the 1980s oscillated between a hope for democracy and free trade on the one hand, and a return to protectionism, nationalism, and authoritarian rule on the other. Thereafter, the first signs of a gradual revision of the negative trends were promising: Bolivia returned to free trade in 1985; Colombia, Ecuador, Venezuela, and Peru followed in 1992, though without immediate effects on the ambition for regional free trade. Negotiations toward a custom union among these countries got bogged down, however, "because of major differences over the design of a common tariff, harmonization of export incentives, and the rules for negotiating free-trade agreements with third countries."[44] As for democracy, the decade 1985–1995 saw the return of several Andean countries to more or less stable democratic governments with respect for the rule of law and human rights. But it also brought the shocking resurrection of dictatorial powers by Peru's President Alberto Fujimori in 1992, followed by Venezuela's suspension of diplomatic relations with Peru. Fujimori retaliated by temporarily withdrawing

Peru from the Andean Pact, arguing that Venezuela and Colombia were subsidizing their export goods to Peru to the disadvantage of his country. In May 1994 Peru announced its willingness to gradually return to the activities of the Andean Pact. Without any effect on their governance structures, the five members of the Andean Pact "within a few weeks agreed to launch a customs union with a four-tier common external tariff on January 1, 1995."[45]

This speedy act of economic integration progress in a region with roughly a hundred million inhabitants (excluding Venezuela) did not coincide with the strengthening of the rule of law as its underlying base. The agreement on the external customs tariff included a 10 percent flat rate for most items and the elimination of most non-tariff barriers. Details were telling as far as the socio-economic realities in the Andean region were concerned: no external tariff at all was imposed on health and educational products, a 5 percent external tariff was announced for raw material and industrial inputs, a 10 to 15 percent tariff for intermediary products, a 20 percent tariff for final consumption goods, and a 40 percent tariff for assembled cars. Colombia and Venezuela reached exemptions for 230 of their products, with Ecuador attaining them for 400 items.[46] These idiosyncrasies made it impossible to immediately achieve comprehensive customs union. However, the biggest obstacle to properly implementing the Andean Integration System, as it began to be called in the mid 1990s, was the political dissonance in the region. A formal change of its name took place with the Act of Trujillo on 10 March 1996. The Pacto Andino was renamed Andean Community of Nations (Comunidad Andina de Naciones, CAN).[47] This indicated the aspiration of community-building beyond the creation of economic integration. But the strong institutional focus and the promising economic goal to achieve a full common market by 2005 could not hide the weak practice inside CAN's structures.

The dramatic political turnarounds in Argentina and Brazil in 1982/1983 had shed rays of hope across the Andean region. Democracy and the rule of law were on the rise in the two biggest Latin American countries. This was seen as a precursor of things to happen in the Andean region, too. More relevant for the Andean region were the creation of the Southern Market MERCOSUR in 1991 and the launching of a Free Trade Area of the Americas (FTAA) by the US administration under President Clinton in 1994. The Andean region could not stay outside if it did not want to fall completely into peripheral neglect and oblivion. The growing effects of transnational economic and societal bonds, the emerging realities of globalization, and finally, after 1990, the realization of beginning a new world order following the end of the Cold War all reached the Andean countries later than other parts of the hemisphere. But they arrived there nonetheless, and within a few years a new strategic design and institutional structure evolved, setting the process of regional integration in the Andean region on a "new trajectory."[48]

The Andean Community of Nations consists of the following organs and institutions:

- The Andean Presidential Council brings together the presidents of the Andean Community's member states as the highest regular body of CAN.
- The Andean Council of Foreign Ministers is the seat of regular political leadership.
- The Andean Commission is the main policy-making body, bringing together ministers or vice-ministers of CAN member states who are responsible for trade; together with the foreign ministers they share the legislative role of the Andean Community.
- The Andean Parliament, based in Bogota, is a deliberative body. Initially, its members were only drawn from each national parliament. Since then, direct elections have taken place in Ecuador and Peru, as well as in Venezuela before the country withdrew from CAN.
- The Andean Court of Justice, based in Quito, operates on the basis of an independent statute since 1996.
- The General Secretariat of the Andean Community, based in Lima, is the executive body of CAN. As of 2007 the secretary general is Freddy Ehlers, from Ecuador.
- Technical institutions complete the broad array of arrangements that are in place in the Andean Community. CAN is often criticized for not being effective enough. The Sucre Protocol of 25 June 1997 was another step toward the full liberalization of the Andean market, though the discrepancy between public declarations and daunting realities remains tangible. This is evident with regard to market liberalization and the declared goals of the Andean Community. It is certainly also true with regard to the full recognition of the link between stable, transparent, rule of law–based national democracies and a serious and respectable evolution of regional integration. In light of this undeniable deficiency, it is at least a promising sign that the Andean Community has explicitly expressed its commitment to democracy in a remarkable statement by the presidents of its member states on 7 August 1998. They underlined the commitment to democratic norms and consolidated rule of law as the main rationale of Andean integration.[49]

Intrinsic Motives and External Pressures

Andean regional integration is largely the result of external pressure due to internal failures, and internal accommodations due to external circumstances. This became evident with the realization that "dependencia" theories had failed to genuinely advance the socioeconomic realities in the Andean region. It was noticeable in the Andean Community's efforts to react to the debt crises of the 1980s and their negative effects on both the economy and prospects for democracy in the region. The belated character of Andean integration initiatives became again noteworthy in CAN's reaction to the original success of MER-COSUR, which challenged the much older integration scheme in the Andean region. The initial dynamics of MERCOSUR and the sheer size and weight of its main member states forced the Andean Community to honestly assess its short-comings and deficiencies. Finally, the initiation of NAFTA between Canada, the US, and Mexico, and the potential effects of the FTAA, promoted by the US, required the Andean Community to reevaluate its unique role in the world economy and in the geopolitical constellation of its hemisphere.

Performance

Although regional integration in the Andean Community remains weak and under permanent pressure to achieve even the most modest results, certain progress must be acknowledged:

(1) The creation of a free trade zone with a common external tariff—in spite of all its exceptions—that has gone down, on a regional average, from 33 percent in 1990 to 13.6 percent in 2000—is a positive achievement with useful implications for the economic prospects of the region.[50] Intra-regional trade grew from $1.3 billion (1990) to $2.8 billion (1993) and $4.7 billion (1995). This positive trend certainly was helpful in bringing the free trade area about and helped it to expand: by 1998, intra-regional trade had reached a volume of $5.3 billion. In terms of the overall foreign trade of the Andean region, the significance of these developments is noteworthy: intra-regional imports increased during the 1990s from 4.3 percent to 13.8 percent, and exports went from 6.7 percent to 11.5 percent.[51] Foreign investment increased ninefold between 1990 ($1.2 billion) and 1998 ($10.6 billion). Most foreign investment was attracted by Venezuela, Colombia, and Peru. Remarkable was the overall increase in investment originating in other Latin American countries. Peru's economic upswing was of particular significance during those years: after it had liberalized more than 50 percent of its trade, Peru finally joined the free trade zone in 2005.

(2) "Considerable progress"[52] has been made in the area of harmonizing economic and social policies across the Andean Community. This is attributed to the increased lawmaking competencies of the Andean institutions. In particular, the harmonization measures have included: the establishment of a legal framework; a revision of measures taken during the import-oriented period (Declaration 24 became famous for radically revising the conditions for foreign investors in the Andean Community, putting them on equal legal footing with nationals and eliminating most restrictions on the remittance of capital and profit); a common regime for the protection of intellectual property rights; and liberalization in transportation, air traffic in particular. While the original target date for a common market (1998) had to be postponed and not all its aspects had been

implemented as of 2007, considerable progress toward the full realization of a functioning Andean common market has been made.

(3) The elaborate institutional structure of the Andean Community lacks authority to implement supranationally binding decisions. In fact, implementing powers needed to reach out for supranational solutions have not yet been granted. The Quirama Declaration of 28 June 2003, however, was an important stepping stone in the direction of a political culture that can be favorable to supranational integration: for the first time in the vexed, and still short, history of Andean regional integration, a comprehensive agenda for the promotion of good governance was outlined in a document of the Andean Community. The Quirama Declaration includes an unequivocal commitment to human rights, the rule of law, and democracy as cornerstones of regional integration. It also includes explicit provisions to combat illegal drugs and to regulate labor migration, and it outlines the framework for the development of a common foreign policy.[53] Declaratory rhetoric has never been transformed into Andean realities. But the Quirama Declaration can serve as a solid point of reference for future assessments of political and executive leaders in the region. Almost unintentionally, this bears a supranational quality that is totally new to the Andean Community.

Among the weak or even worrisome aspects of regional integration efforts so far undertaken by the Andean Community are the following:

(1) A considerable set of institutional devices have been created without defining their competencies properly. One of the evident deficits concerns the absence of coordinated macro-policies, particularly regarding exchange-rate policies. The existence of an Andean Community Advisory Council composed of ministers of economy and finance, of central banks on the national level, and of high officials responsible for economic planning on both national and the community levels, has not been able to revise this lamentable deficit.

(2) Theoretically, the Andean Court of Justice, which has existed since 1979, could exert an important role in promoting community law and hence implant the principle of supranationality in the Andean region. As far as legal scholarship is concerned, the existence of the Andean Court of Justice has triggered preliminary interpretative studies trying to compare its supranational character and potential with the European Court of Justice.[54] It cannot be excluded that this normative interpretation will turn into effective legal practice over time. So far, however, the Court has not been very visible, to say the least.[55] Institutional weakness is also the main criticism addressed to the Andean Community Secretariat. While democracy is under regular, if not permanent pressure in some of the Andean Community member states, an unwavering and uncompromising performance of Andean Community organs dedicated to the preservation and development of

the rule of law is more than needed. This, however, has not happened. Lack of transparency on budgetary matters within the Andean Community is matched by the almost complete absence of the issue in the academic literature about the Andean Community, with the exception of a passing remark in one paper that a Presidential Council is formally responsible "for evaluating the budgetary performance of the General Secretariat."[56] The low-level civil war in Colombia, continuous upheavals in Ecuador, two coup attempts in Venezuela during the 1990s, and the country's national-socialist-populist regime under Hugo Chávez since 1998 have left the prospects for rule of law–based, unbiased, and effective democracy a largely unfulfilled dream in many parts of the Andean region. Under such national circumstances, it is almost a miracle that the Andean Community prevails at all. Diplomatic regionalism and a competency-emptied array of institutions of impressive scope and breadth seem to be the only achievable form of regional integration at this point. The imperative that national democracy and the rule of law are complementary conditions for the evolution of solid regional integration finds ample proof in the Andean region.

(3) The weak infrastructure in the Andean region prevents lively regional interactions. Remote and impoverished rural areas, marginalized indigenous populations, mountainous regions, poor administrative structures on the local and regional levels, insufficiently modernized economic structures, and deficits in education and in the promotion of human capital are but a few characteristics of a region in which weak integration corresponds with weak states. Comparing the situation of the Andean Community with that of Western Europe in 1957, one encounters an important difference. While multiple external factors were a strong motive to initiate European integration, a similar array of external factors exercising a certain degree of pressure to move forward with deeper integration is obviously not present, or at least is not felt strongly enough, in the Andean region.

Federators

By and large, Andean regional integration has always been a function of continental or global developments. But it also echoes the regional priorities, obstacles, and dynamics in terms of economics, politics, and leadership. Andean integration is caught between seemingly mutually contradicting trends. On the one hand, democratic governance and the rule of law remain overly fragile, weakening the set of preconditions necessary for the sustainable implementation of regional integration. The weakness of democratic governance is, however, one of the main arguments for the proponents of regional integration. They regard rule of law–based regional integration "as an insurance policy or a remedy for weak democratic governance and a fledgling rule of law.

The desire to shape an Andean political identity is present among the elites in the core countries of the Andean Community. It is weak among the larger public. At the same time, the geographical definition of the Andean Community has remained vague and transient. Why should Venezuela qualify as an Andean country? And why should Chile stay outside CAN? While it was convenient for the Andean Community to have Venezuela on board as the biggest oil producer in Latin America, the advantage of membership in the Andean Community for Venezuela was always less clear. The aggravated problems with democratic governance in Venezuela since the rise of populist authoritarianism under President Chávez in 1998 have added doubts about the wisdom of Venezuela's membership in the Andean Community. It was no surprise that the Andean Community reacted to the withdrawal of Venezuela from CAN membership in May 2006 by inviting Chile to join the Andean Community at Chile's earliest convenience. An agreement on associate membership of Chile was finalized on 20 September 2007. In parallel, the Andean Community invited Venezuela to return to CAN and reactivate its membership.

Democratic governance has often been a matter of concern not in Venezuela alone but in several member states of the Andean Community. The biggest challenge in this context is the proper handling of the relationship between the national quality of democratic governance and the prospects for regional integration. A democratic "normative" is only slowly emerging as a rationale for regional integration in the Andean Community. The recognition of a democratic rationale for regional integration could redefine the scope of regional integration, its claim, and its legitimacy. It is a compelling argument that regional integration can only work on the basis of mutual trust among democratic countries firmly rooted in the rule of law and guided by principles of good governance. But to transform this argument from a theoretical assessment of policy trends into the rationale of regional integration in the Andean Community is no easy and linear process. The general experience seems to be that countries with a weak democratic record tend to project hopes for stability into regional integration—if they do this at all—while countries with a strong democratic record tend to be cautious about binding their own destiny too much with the destiny of weak democracies (or more generally, weak states) in their neighborhood. Formal membership in a regional integration scheme that was established to generate processes of community-building beyond the minimalist fulfillment of limited policy goals or economic aspirations is no natural barrier against such behavior. The contemporary history of the Andean Community provides ample evidence.

Yet the Andean Community's experience also indicates that the reverse method might lead to achievements in regional integration, for achieving progress, in democratic rule at home and integration in the region alike, is not necessarily a function of national developments and their results. It can also be a cause of regional progress. Colombia and Venezuela agreed on dismantling all external tariffs and non-tariff barriers in 1992 on a bilateral basis, thus setting a precedent for the other Andean Community member states to reconsider their own rather protectionist attitudes. Colombia and Venezuela had concluded that it would not be in their interest to wait until the most underdeveloped economies of the Andean Community were ready for a comprehensive free trade area. They opted for "enforced cooperation" among the two biggest economies in the community, to borrow a term from the European integration experience. The other member states of the Andean Community could not abstain long: Bolivia joined the Andean Community's free trade arrangement in late 1992, Ecuador in 1993, Peru finally in 2005. Although different tariffs are still being applied by these countries, as shown above, the average external tariff for imports has declined substantially from a regional average of 33 percent in 1990 to 13.6 percent in 2006.

Transformations

Three transformations can be identified that have altered the initial aspiration of regional integration and the approach to its instruments.

(1)   The change of development theory from import-substituting industrialization to "open regionalism" and export-oriented diversification has taken place only with great difficulty. The assumption that state-protected monopolies could operate on bigger markets once regional integration was achieved was a miscalculation that reflected the overall parochialism of the initial analysis. Latin American industry needs to be competitive under the conditions of the world market if it is to maintain its role in the region. Therefore the change in the attitude toward the appropriate development strategy for the region has to go hand in hand with a comprehensive modernization of the economy and its underlying infrastructure, including human resources. Instead of protecting the region from external pressure, successful integration will require adequate responses and innovative actions in light of global challenges. This process has not been completed in the Andean Community, but it has become an integral part of the integration strategy of the region. Allan Wagner Tizón started out as secretary general of the Andean Community on 2 February 2004 with the program "Integration for Globalization." Such a perspective would have been unimaginable ten years earlier.

(2)   The lawmaking powers of the Andean Commission and other organs of the Andean Community are only slowly emerging. But their addition to the initial economic goals of regional integration as a means to protect the local economic development has began to transform the Andean Community from an economic project into a project of community formation. No matter how long it might take to achieve noticeable results in this regard, it must be recognized that the Andean Community is still a young integration scheme troubled by domestic instability in most of its member states. However, regional integration is increasingly understood as part of the solution. The recognition of democratic governance in each Andean Community member state as a crucial condition for sustainable progress in regional

integration is a serious step in the right direction. The Andean Community's additional protocol to the Cartagena Agreement, titled *Andean Community Commitment to Democracy* and promulgated in Porto, Portugal, on 27 October 1998, was initially nothing more than a rhetorical invocation, published under a certain pressure from the European Union.[57] It did not reflect unchallenged realities on the ground. Yet when elections were held in all member states of the Andean Community between December 2005 and November 2006, the Andean Community's democracy clause was both a threat to those who were inclined to play with the old illusion of populist authoritarianism, and a promise to those who recognized good governance and the rule of law on the national level as a precondition for, and necessary consequence of, any durable regional integration.

(3) The Andean Community has begun to broaden its political role by including the coordination of the region's foreign policy in its mandate. But without achieving immediate success through foreign policy coordination, the Andean Community increased the unpredictability of political judgments among its member states. The broadening of its political profile led to its inevitable politicization. Not having strengthened the community's bodies, the Andean Community has become more vulnerable to domestic political interests, conflicts, and constellations. Most dramatically, the consequence of this vacuum became apparent in April 2006, when Venezuela announced its withdrawal from CAN. President Hugo Chávez argued that the bilateral free trade agreements signed by Colombia and Peru with the United States had caused irreparable damage to the normative goals of the Andean Community. On 22 April 2006, he declared his country would renounce the Cartagena Agreement.

Worrisome was the fact that President Chávez, who has tried to portray himself as the "new Castro" of Latin America, had found a loyal supporter in the first indigenous president of Bolivia since the Spanish conquest. Evo Morales assumed his office on 22 January 2006 after winning the 2005 elections, backed by his party Movimiento al Socialismo. In mid May 2006, Bolivia took over the rotating presidency of the Andean Community for the period 2006/2007. CAN made considerable efforts to manage the deep crisis it was encountering. In September 2007 Chile became an associate member of CAN. Venezuela was invited to reconsider its withdrawal and rejoin the Andean Community. It was evident that both sides wanted to continue cooperation in mutually beneficial areas of economic development.

Role and Interests of the European Union

The European Union has limited economic interests in the Andean Community region. With 0.7 percent of the EU's total trade, the Andean Community ranks twenty-ninth among the economic partners of the European Union. For CAN, the situation is different: after the United States, the EU is the second largest trading partner of the Andean Community, representing 14.5 percent of the total trade of the Andean Community, 17.4 percent of its imports, and 12.8 percent of its exports. For CAN, the European Union is the biggest investor, contributing 25 percent of the total direct foreign investment in the region. Following privatization processes in the Andean Community, European investors made inroads in some of the strategic markets of the region, particularly telecommunications. In absolute terms, the increase in trade with the Andean Community also echoes this development: It grew from €9 billion in 1980 to €15 billion in 2004, an increase of 73 percent in fifteen years.

The European Community's relations with the Andean region began in the 1970s on the basis of bilateral trade-facilitating agreements on handicrafts signed with Ecuador, Bolivia, and Peru . The first biregional agreement was signed in 1993. On the basis of this Framework Cooperation Agreement the EU began to recognize the regional integration effort and potential in the Andean region. When the initial Framework Cooperation Agreement was stepped up on 15 December 2003 in Rome and transformed into a Political Dialogue and Cooperation Agreement, this reflected clearer focus on both sides: regional integration in the Andean Community had obviously become more solid and promising, while the European Union was ready to engage in a political dialogue with its Andean partner community, thus recognizing the political nature of Andean regional integration and a broadening of its own strategic interest in the Andean Community.

The European Union now began to integrate its relations with CAN into its overall strategy of upgraded relations with Latin America. The summit of the EU and all the Latin American countries in Guadalajara (Mexico) in May 2004 initiated a comprehensive evaluation of the integration process and its prospects in the Andean Community. In January 2005, the evaluation process began. The EU–Latin America summit in May 2006 in Vienna had intended to assess the result of the evaluation favorably. But only a few days earlier, on 22 April 2006, had come Venezuela's announcement of its withdrawal from membership in the Andean Community, followed by Bolivia's decision to nationalize its oil and gas industries. The European Union postponed the opening of association negotiations with the Andean Community until September 2007, when the first round of formal negotiations took place in Bogota.

These negotiations are aimed at supporting a variety of concrete measures by which the European Union has already promoted regional integration progress in the Andean Community in the past. Most noteworthy among them are the following measures:

- The EU has granted €1 million in institutional support to the Andean Secretariat in order to strengthen the capacity-building necessary for the development of common CAN policies.
- The EU has supported CAN customs modernization with €1.9 million.

- The EU has supported the development of more competitive structures in a common CAN market with €2 million and the enhancement of technical standards in the CAN economies with €2.3 million.
- The EU has facilitated the harmonization of statistical services in the Andean Community with €5 million.[58]

With the beginning of association negotiations, the European Union provided CAN with an additional €50 million in support of regional integration. The Andean Community follows its own logic of integration and is limited by its unique shortcomings. But it is remarkable how much the European integration experience serves as a point of reference for CAN activities. This includes the formal macroeconomic targets in CAN, which are inspired by the Maastricht criteria of the European Union, despite the weak performance in actual macroeconomic coordination in the Andean Community. CAN macroeconomic targets refer to single-digit inflation rates, a public sector deficit of not more than 3 percent of each member state's GDP, and a public debt ceiling of 50 percent of each member state's GDP. At least in theory, the European integration experience has become a model for CAN.

Prospects and Obstacles

The Andean Community surprised international observers and its own citizens alike when it announced direct elections for the Andean Parliament in 2006. The initial announcement was considered premature and overly ambitious, but direct elections took place after all in Ecuador, Peru, and (before leaving CAN) in Venezuela. Gradual implementation of community elements and a broader involvement of civil society are essential to enhance the legitimacy of the Andean Community. This need is increasingly recognized among the political elites in the region, especially with regard to the underperformance of the Andean Parliament and the Andean Community Secretariat. It is remarkable that the idea of direct elections to the Andean Parliament has begun to be accepted across the region. The direct election of Andean parliamentarians is more than a public relations operation. It echoes the genuine awareness in the region that some fundamental changes have to be introduced in order to make the Andean Community work. This is essential to regaining legitimacy for the very project of regional integration, its contribution to the region's development, and its prospects in the world of the twenty-first century. Waiving visa obligations for citizens of CAN member states traveling from one CAN member state to another—a practice in place since 2003—is certainly not enough to enhance popular recognition and legitimacy for the integration project. The use of a common Andean passport was decided in 2001 and has become practice in Ecuador, Peru, and (before leaving CAN in 2006) Venezuela. Bolivia and Colombia announced its introduction in 2006. But from a common passport, there is still a long way to go to substantiate the foundations of a common civil society.

The main dilemma for Andean regional integration goes beyond specific actions or aspects. It is the dilemma between the claim for Andean cohesion and the perception that neither geographical nor political nor economic logic points in the direction of immediate or intuitive harmonization. The consequence is a set of non-harmonized integration efforts. Only three member states of CAN share a complete customs union (2006). Colombia and Venezuela maintain special bilateral free trade agreements with Mexico. Since 2005, Bolivia, Ecuador, and Peru, together with Chile, have become associate members of the Southern Common Market (MERCOSUR). Venezuela joined MERCOSUR in December 2005 and left CAN in April 2006. This had strong negative consequences for CAN because Venezuela immediately withdrew its 20 percent of professionals from the CAN Secretariat. For an institution that is structurally short of human resources, this came as a particularly painful blow.

While the idea of regional integration has gained ground in the Andean region, its shape and prospect remains uncertain. Or, to be more specific, the relationship between economic and political integration remains in the dark, covered by the all-prevalent ambition to build a genuine community. This is unhelpful for coherent development of any of the existing regional processes. It would be even less helpful if this uncertainty were simply moved upward to a continental-wide level by a full merging of MERCOSUR and CAN.

This biggest of all questions can no longer go undetected on the radar screen of Latin American politics. Without resolving the essential discrepancies in political and economic terms, any rhetorical integration of Latin America as a whole (maybe excluding Central America and the Caribbean) will remain weak at best. The leaders in the region do not seem to be overly clear about their ultimate objectives and long-term goals. Interim steps and contradictory statements have therefore almost become the norm. In December 2004, CAN and MERCOSUR signed a cooperation agreement outlining the prospects for negotiations for future integration of the whole continent. On 7 July 2005 the four MERCOSUR countries Argentina, Brazil, Paraguay, and Uruguay became associate members of CAN by virtue of Economic Complementarity Agreements that CAN signed with each of the four countries. If the political goals of the integration terms are not clarified, even economic community–building will be impeded. Since a strong drive for community-building guides all integration ideas in Latin America, the region has to deepen its debate about integration and its final objectives, including the political dimension in particular. As long as different types of democracy exist in Latin America, this will be no easy task. In fact, it might turn out to be a more difficult task than the one stemming from the parallel existence of democracies and dictatorships in a region. Under such conditions, it is easy to draw a line and accept only democratic states as members of an integration scheme. But what could be done in the case of different, even contradicting forms of democracy—one representative, another populist; one pro-Western and pro-American, another anti-American; one emphasizing social, national, even indigenous and ethnic identities, another broadly pluralist, and a third authoritarian and guided? Latin America is politically as diverse as it seems to be culturally homogeneous. Even as it features numerous socio-economic commonalities, it fails to translate them into solid forms of pooled interests and deep integration.

Achieving cohesion in both dimensions of Andean integration—"deepening" and "widening," to use two classic terms from the European integration experience—is not only difficult because of the autonomous policy actions and economic interests of CAN's member states. The Andean Community is also under pressure "from above." The vision of a united Latin America, no matter how abstract, is a recurrent source of inspiration for new and most often unsustainable initiatives. The most recent one, formulated at a Latin American summit in Cuzco on 8 December 2004, was to achieve a South American Community of Nations with its own constitution by 2006.[59] Instead of solidifying what formally already exists, the political leaders of the continent found pleasure in embarking on a new vision. During a second summit on 30 September 2005 in Brasilia, they declared their intent to study all efforts to harmonize the existing asymmetries between the various regional integration systems in Latin America by March 2006. The idea of a Latin American constitution was not mentioned again, and it was not achieved by 2006.

Instead, the Andean Community entered an almost existential crisis when Venezuela's President Hugo Chávez announced on 22 April 2006 that his country would rescind its CAN membership. The bilateral free trade agreements between Colombia and Peru with the US, he argued, had undermined the aspirations and authority of CAN. They would reduce labor security and undermine labor rights, they would have negative effects on the future role of government's scope of action, and they would enhance the monopolization of capital in the region. President Chávez's charges were very much in line with his general anti-American rhetoric, and one might wonder whether the Andean Community might even benefit from Venezuela's withdrawal, under the current conditions of that country's politics. But at the time the withdrawal came as a blow to the Andean Community. And even if Chávez used the bilateral actions of Colombia and Peru only as a pretext, he had a point: bilateral negotiations certainly do not strengthen, but in fact undermine community-building in the Andean Community. One might even go so far as to say that the bilateral approach of the US in trade relations with Andean countries has undermined the potential for regional integration. Indeed, the US has never even considered negotiating a free trade agreement with the Andean Community as a whole. Keeping CAN weak might not be a proactive policy of the US, but this factual effect of US trade negotiations does not seem to bother policymakers in Washington.

Under the existing circumstances, it cannot come as a surprise that regional integration is often perceived as more of a liability than an asset among the citizens of the Andean Community and, in fact, also in the other Latin American regions. It is simply implausible to announce grand designs without providing answers as to how to build the foundation for a realistic development. The Andean Community has to find a genuine application of the European experience of combining a focused integration goal (the regional equivalent of coal and steel that played this initial role in Europe) with a realistic and binding time frame for the implementation of concrete goals and instruments in their support. The solution to this challenge will be the watershed for judging whether regionalism in the Andean Community is truly new or remains hidebound and unable to reform.[60] Common infrastructure projects, including energy security, and the advancement of human capital, including fundamental efforts to improve the educational standards in the region, must rank high on the list of priorities to bring the Andean Community into the world of globalization. As long as unilateral measures (or the prevention of them) remains a regular experience among CAN member states, the form under which the countries of the Andean region have began to organize their cooperation and integration remains too loose to translate into viable and crisis-resistant integration mechanisms. The form has been achieved; the function has to follow.

In developing the functions of real and concrete regional integration in the Andean Community, the political leaders of each of the CAN member states have to reevaluate the notion of national sovereignty and the concept of regional solidarity. They will not succeed in any of their common ambitions if they remain unwilling to substantially pool national resources in order to achieve a common value-added goal for the Andean region and its people. Their often grand rhetoric will also fail them if they do not strive for binding rules and mutually recognized norms that remain robust during times of challenge. As long as the member states of the Andean Community of Nations do not comply with common regional lawmaking and effective implementation of laws, all efforts to modernize the Andean region through the instruments of regional integration will remain futile, or at least feeble. Yet they do exist, and perhaps this is at present the best news in a broader historical context.

Basic Facts

Regional integration in the Caribbean has to struggle with certain facts of nature and with certain misperceptions that by their nature tend to be facts. The Caribbean islands are small in size and economic potential. Their populations are small, their economic output limited, their dependency on certain assets and on external partners enormous, and the expectations regarding their impact on world affairs low. By the nature of their structure, the potential for intra-regional trade is limited. They are vulnerable, yet they contribute to the good of their people and the world. It would be a misperception to assume that Caribbean efforts in regional integration are irrelevant, obsolete, or even nonexistent. Deducing regional integration qualities and potentials on the basis the gross domestic product of a region, the size of its population, or its potential for trouble in geopolitical matters would be a rather inappropriate assumption. Yet these criteria tend to be applied to the Caribbean, and also to the Pacific islands on the other side of the world.

The Caribbean islands were importers of slaves and sugar-producing colonies for most of their modern history. Today, they are usually best known as tourist destinations and regular victims of hurricanes. Regional integration ranks low as a feature in the perception of this region of the earth. Paradoxically, it is exactly because of the unique conditions in the Caribbean that regional integration has relevance for Caribbean island countries and is meaningful to them. The Caribbean Community (CARICOM) is formed of 15 million citizens, 8 million in Haiti alone, in fourteen countries with a combined GDP of $762 billion, translating into a per capita income of $3,126 (2001 figures). Each year the Caribbean countries welcome 30 million tourists, the single most important source of their revenues.[61] But the Caribbean is not merely beaches and sunshine. In many ways, CARICOM is the most advanced regional grouping next to the European Union.

The Caribbean Community is still transforming from a postcolonial identity to a new awareness of regional interaction and commonality. During past decades, the project of building viable independent states has absorbed all the available local resources of most small island nations. Their human resources are often too limited to instantly apply CARICOM decisions. The Caribbean countries are proud members of the global community and take UN membership as seriously as their own independence. Yet, two generations after most islands in the Caribbean gained formal independence, their economic well-being fares poorly compared with those Caribbean islands that are still dependencies of the US, Great Britain, and the Netherlands or are integral parts of France (and hence the EU), such as Martinique, Guadeloupe, and French Guiana. Economically, the case for independence has remained weak. Politically, it is irreversible. But as far as the adopted interpretation of sovereignty is concerned, time has turned Caribbean anti-colonialism into a somewhat sober reality, giving room to the honest distinction between real and rhetorical independence.

The readiness to pool resources and sovereignties might not originate in a choice "from the heart." But rational calculations about the best possible options to make real sovereignty lasting and meaningful are not bad guiding principles either. The awareness of these insights has grown in the Caribbean Community along with the understanding that identity of a region cannot be induced artificially through political institutions and economic projects. Yet the identity of the Caribbean Community is remarkably vivid and present across the region.

What is often lacking is the implementation of decisions, very often due to enormous limits in human resources in countries that are as small as Saint Kitts and Nevis with 47,318 inhabitants.

The original efforts to bring the tiny islands of the Caribbean together was an act of colonial benevolence, intended to prolong British supremacy and maybe even suzerainty over the English-speaking Caribbean. The British Caribbean Act of 1956 created the West Indies Federation. Under this act, ten Caribbean territories formed a federal government, headed by an executive governor general who was appointed by the United Kingdom. The West Indies Federation consisted of Antigua and Barbuda, Dominica, Barbados, Grenada, Jamaica, Montserrat, Saint Kitts-Nevis-Anguilla, Saint Lucia, Saint Vincent, and Trinidad and Tobago. It had a 10-member cabinet, a 44-member House of Representatives, and a 19-member Senate. The West Indies Federation immediately met with suspicion. It was short-lived and came to an end when Jamaica withdrew in 1962, claiming, as the biggest of the member territories of the West Indies Federation, that it could go it alone and would be better off pursuing the independent use of national sovereignty. The gradual independence of the other territories of the West Indies Federation was only a matter of time. Jamaica and Trinidad and Tobago gained independence in 1962, followed by Guyana and Barbados in 1966 and the other smaller islands after 1967. Independence was immediately seen as a limited way of guaranteeing the well-being of the new states in the Caribbean. A Caribbean Free Trade Agreement (CARIFTA) was concluded in 1968. It understood the European Free Trade Agreement (EFTA) as its model for liberalizing trade in the Caribbean and thus strengthening the economic dimension of independence.[62] The Caribbean Development Bank was created as an instrument of implementing the development philosophies of that time.

Genuine regional integration began in 1973. On 4 July 1973, the Treaty of Chaguaramas was signed in Trinidad, initially bringing Trinidad and Tobago, Barbados, and Guyana together under the roof of the Caribbean Community.[63] Within a year, Antigua and Barbuda, Belize, Dominica, Grenada, Montserrat, Saint Kitts and Nevis, Saint Lucia, and Saint Vincent and the Grenadines followed. The Treaty of Chaguaramas "substantially widened the remit of regional integration,"[64] embracing three new goals beyond the Caribbean Free Trade Agreement:

- Creating a Caribbean Single Market and Economy.
- Broadening functional cooperation in such fields as health, education, transport, and meteorology.
- Coordinating foreign policy among the independent Caribbean states.

CARICOM started with a clear commitment to political integration and community-building. It was ambitious and much more forward-looking than many other of the postcolonial integration devices in the world. The main driving force of Caribbean integration was the understanding that none of the small island nations would be able to retain factual sovereignty and achieve the development goals claimed as part and parcel of their quest for independence, unless the nations collaborated in the strongest possible way. Supranationality was not mentioned in the Treaty of Chaguaramas; rather, there was tacit consent among CARICOM members that cooperation among them would in fact make supranational solutions to common problems superfluous. But with the founding of the Caribbean Community, a new chapter in the history of the Caribbean islands had begun whose result nobody was able to anticipate at the moment of the signing of the Treaty of Chaguaramas.

The more the leaders of Caribbean Community member states insisted on maintaining full national sovereignty, the more it was evident that probably only the opposite was realistic. The genuine evolution of regional cooperation and integration can be driven by the justifiable desire to strengthen its constituent parts. But all experience indicates that in the process of regional integration-building, both the member states and the original integration design will change. The Caribbean was no exception to this rule. The composition of membership was interesting, as it included not only island nations, but also the littoral countries Belize and Guyana. All of them have one historic legacy in common: they are English-speaking former slave plantations, and they were formerly British colonies or dependencies. The Caribbean Community has grown considerably and now includes fourteen independent Caribbean countries, one dependent territory (Montserrat), and five associate members. Antigua and Barbuda, the Bahamas, Barbados, Belize, Dominica, Grenada, Guyana, Jamaica, Saint Kitts and Nevis, Saint Lucia, Saint Vincent and the Grenadines, Suriname, and Trinidad and Tobago are full CARICOM members, along with Haiti, which is the giant of CARICOM with 8.8 million citizens.

Because of its unique history, Haiti still oscillates between its strong sense of exceptionalism and its inevitable destiny as part of the Caribbean region. Haiti's membership was suspended between 2004 and 2006. Traditionally a troubled country with a high degree of poverty and political instability, Haiti experienced an internal coup against the elected President Préval. Subsequently, Haiti's interim government was not recognized by CARICOM. Reasonable free and fair elections took place in Haiti in February 2006, reinstalling President Préval and leading to a new parliament and reincorporation into CARICOM. Anguilla, Bermuda, Turks and Caicos, the British Virgin Islands, and the Cayman Islands are associate members of CARICOM. Aruba, Colombia, the Dominican Republic, Mexico, the Dutch Antilles, Puerto Rico, and Venezuela are observers, while special arrangements for market access have been made with Venezuela (1992) and Colombia (1994).

In 2005, the Dominican Republic applied for membership in CARICOM. It seems as if CARICOM's answer might take some time. Some of the tiny island nations are afraid of the membership of this regional giant, which accounts for 50 percent of the entire Caribbean economy. Others doubt that the Dominican Republic is ready, either administratively or in terms of its political culture, which links it with the Spanish-speaking regions of Latin America. In any case, compared with its modest beginnings, CARICOM has become a colorful realm that is not always fully consistent. The Bahamas and Haiti are members of CARICOM, but not of its Single Market and Economy. Belize maintains simultaneous membership in CARICOM and in the Central American System of Integration (SICA).

Region-building in the Caribbean is more complex than one might assume given the size of the area's countries. In many ways, the ultimate objectives of CARICOM were anticipated in the context of the Organization of Eastern Caribbean States (OECS). Founded by the Treaty of Basseterre on 18 June 1981, the OECS includes Anguilla, Antigua and Barbuda, the British Virgin Islands, Dominica, Grenada, Saint Kitts and Nevis, Montserrat, Saint Vincent and the Grenadines, and Saint Lucia as its members or associate members. The OECS figures as an associate institution of CARICOM.[65] Its Secretariat is located in Castries, Saint Lucia. Since 1983, the OECS—except for the British Virgin Islands—has created a monetary union with a single currency, the East Caribbean dollar, and a joint pool of foreign exchange reserves. The Eastern Caribbean Central Bank is the central monetary authority, deciding on the currency union's monetary policies. The Organization of Eastern Caribbean States maintains a more advanced monetary integration scheme than most other regional integration mechanisms outside Europe and includes the work of its Court of Justice. As the Eastern Caribbean dollar is pegged to the US dollar, it is not really an independent currency. The OECS is CARICOM in a nutshell, but at the same time—because of the size of its member states—it is limited in its power to project OECS experiences across CARICOM. In the end, though, OECS may provide the model for the final stage of a CARICOM Common Market and currency union.[66]

Formally, the Caribbean Single Market and Economy (CSME) went into effect on 1 January 2006. In reality, the final shape of the single market took more time, especially for sensitive issues such as freedom of movement. Most decisions had been taken and implemented by 2008. In order to compensate poorer member states for revenue losses in a common market, CARICOM is in the process of implementing a Regional Development Fund, modeled after its EU namesake. In spite of the lack of a common economic sphere and the gap between formal decisions and factual implementation, CARICOM can claim to represent the more comprehensive approach to regional integration in the Caribbean—both in terms of member states and in terms of issues and policies covered. The inspiration provided by the OECS must, however, be appreciated in the context of the regional dynamics.

The original CARICOM treaty established two separate entities, the Caribbean Community and the Caribbean Common Market. Its focus was on market integration, the provision of common services, joint actions aimed at increasing production, commitment to the differential treatment of less developed countries in the community, and the coordination of foreign policy. An elaborate institutional structure was created, whose mandate and competencies became a matter of gradual and continuous development:

- The Conference of Heads of Government serves as the supreme decision-making body. Based on the principle of unanimity, it has operated with "quasi-Cabinet Portfolios" since 2001.[67] In effect, this has enormously enhanced the direct involvement of member states and their political machineries in the process of regional integration.
- The Common Market Council is a ministerial body in charge of the Caribbean Common Market.
- The Conference of Ministers for Health symbolizes the technical cooperation among CARICOM member states in promoting common services and the well-being of all.
- Standing committees of ministers exist in the fields of education, labor, financial affairs, foreign affairs, agriculture, energy, mines and natural resources, industry, transportation, legal affairs, science and technology, and tourism.
- The CARICOM Secretariat with about 200 employees is based in Georgetown, Guyana. Secretary General Edwin Wilberforce Carrington has held his seat since 1992.
- Social groups, including the Caribbean Association of Industry and Commerce, the Caribbean Congress of Labor, the Caribbean Council of Customers, the University of the West Indies, and the Caribbean Law Institute, represent the wide array of civil society activities with a firm interest in regional integration.[68]

British membership in the European Economic Community in 1973 created enormous drawbacks for many of the Caribbean countries. The 1973 oil crises had even more disastrous effects on them. The worst of all the negative consequences was a trend to economic nationalism across the CARICOM region. Trinidad and Tobago, the only CARICOM country with oil and gas resources, began to look to oil-rich Venezuela for new partnership, neglecting CARICOM interests. Jamaica and Guyana intensified their respective bauxite production and increased taxes on this raw material, while Jamaica struck a deal with Venezuela on the construction of an aluminum processing firm, again neglecting the perspective of a common CARICOM approach. This Jamaican action led to the cancellation in 1974 of the first joint CARICOM production of aluminum, which had already been agreed upon.[69] While some CARICOM member states resorted to economic nationalism, others increased their ideological profile during the 1970s. In 1970 Guyana opted for "cooperative socialism"; in 1974 Jamaica advocated "democratic socialism"; and in 1979 Grenada had a revolutionary government under the leadership of Maurice Bishop. This coincided with Ronald Reagan's election to the US presidency. Reagan's Caribbean Basin Initiative of 1981 was part of a rollback strategy, escalating in the elimination of the revolutionary regime in Grenada in October 1983. An internal coup and a limited US intervention brought CARICOM into disarray over the question of what to do next. The fear of complete dissolution hovered over CARICOM. Even worse, CARICOM's Multilateral Clearing Facility, the instrument to facilitate intra-regional trade, broke apart. Intra-regional trade among CARICOM member states declined from $577 million in 1981 to $432.5 million in 1984.[70] CARICOM survived the oil crises and its aftermath, but only "at the cost of stagnation."[71]

As was the case in the context of the European integration experience, the Caribbean Community had to wait for new initiatives and a more propitious environment to catch up with its original goal and ultimate destiny. The small booklet "From CARIFTA to Caribbean Community", published in 1972 by the Caribbean Free Trade Association Secretariat (CARIFTA), remained the guiding star in the midst of this depressing downward spiral. This booklet laid out perspectives that remained valuable, although they could not be achieved immediately and were never to be achieved in easy and completely coherent ways:

• Common external tariff and a joint protection policy
• Harmonization of fiscal incentives
• Common foreign investment policy
• Rationalization of regional agriculture
• Regional industrial policy
• Cooperation in tourism, fiscal, and monetary affairs
• Common external commercial policy, especially toward the European Economic Community
• Coordination of foreign policy.[72]

In the end, it took until 1989 for CARICOM to turn its crisis into a new beginning. Only a few months before the fall of the Berlin Wall, the CARICOM heads of state met in Grand Anse (Grenada) in June 1989. After fifteen years of stagnation they gave the process of regional integration a new push, a second chance. Under the chairmanship of former Commonwealth Secretary General Sir Shridat Ramphal, they launched the work of the West Indies Commission. Its task was to make suggestions on how the Caribbean countries should react to the "challenges and responses presented by the changes on the global economy," as the Grand Anse Declaration put it.[73]

According to the Grand Anse Declaration, new initiatives were to happen with laser-light speed, compared with the past two decades. By the end of 1990, CARICOM nationals were to be allowed to travel the whole region without passports. At the same time, the Monetary Facility was reestablished. By January

1991, CARICOM was to have decided on a common external tariff, and by July 1991 it should have removed all trade barriers. An effective regional air and sea transport regime was to be in place by July 1992 and a comprehensive system for movement of capital by 1993. At the same time, an Assembly of Caribbean Parliamentarians and a judicial service commission should have begun to work.

The implementation of the ambitious relaunching of CARICOM was problematic and did not conform to the initial timetable. The joint external tariff was implemented initially only by Trinidad and Tobago, Jamaica, and Guyana. When a new target date was fixed in May 1991, only Barbados and Saint Vincent and the Grenadines had joined the first pioneering group. Actions were still required from Belize, Saint Kitts and Nevis, Antigua-Barbuda, Saint Lucia, and Montserrat. In reality, little progress was made, or few visible results achieved, regarding the other measures of a reinvigorated CARICOM. Nevertheless, there had been no precedent in CARICOM history for such a committed will to visible and speedy progress in thorough regional integration. Now, the will existed and was measured against its slow implementation.

The team reviewing the state of regional integration in the Caribbean analyzed the excessive deficits in the countries and in the CARICOM system itself. In a 1991 interim report, the West Indies Commission outlined its top proposals, which encouraged that year's CARICOM summit to convene study groups on the key issues of regional integration, each of them chaired by distinguished regional politicians: on a common currency, on the establishment of a Caribbean investment fund, on the free movement of labor, on intra-regional travel, and on the goal of implementing the Single Market and Economy by 1994. When the final report of the West Indies Commission was presented to the 1992 CARICOM Summit Meeting, it was not only the "most thorough and serious review of the region's condition" ever published.[74] It called for a "time of action" the political leaders of CARICOM should now embrace.

During their summit in July 1991, CARICOM heads of state and government had already decided on a revision of the Treaty of Chaguaramas. These revisions took the form of nine protocols to the original treaty: Protocol 1 on bodies, institutions, and procedures of the community; Protocol 2 regarding the right of establishment, right to provide services, and right to move capital by any CARICOM national in the community; Protocol 3 on a community industrial policy; Protocol 4 on trade liberalization; Protocol 5 on a community agricultural policy; Protocol 6 on a community transportation policy; Protocol 7 on special actions favoring disadvantaged countries, regions, and actors in CARICOM; Protocol 8 on dispute settlement; and Protocol 9 on rules of competition. All were incorporated as chapters within the revised treaty. This whole process took the remainder of the decade, and only in 2001 was the Revised Treaty of Chaguaramas approved by CARICOM's heads of state.[75] In form and effect, they altered the structure, ambitions, and prospects of regional integration in the Caribbean.

They reinitiated regional integration and gave it new profile and impact. Still, supranationality was not an issue.

In June 1990, US President George Bush launched the Enterprise for the Americas Initiative with the prospect of a free trade arrangement between CAR-ICOM countries and the United States. CARICOM member states knew that the US would prefer bilateral arrangements with individual Caribbean countries over a comprehensive free trade accord with CARICOM as a whole. Yet the perspective of participating in the dynamics and prosperity of the US as the leading locomotive of globalization resonated in the Caribbean Community. The Revised Treaty of Chaguaramas was not able to create immediate new realities and stimulate new dynamics and growth in the Caribbean economy. But it claimed to provide the political framework for future initiatives. Future political initiatives were needed to implement the main institutional innovations that were included in the Revised Treaty of Chaguaramas:

- CARICOM was established as one legal entity fusing the original Caribbean Community and the original Caribbean Common Market into one legal body, with the Common Market reconceptualized as the CARICOM Single Market and Economy (CSME).[76] In November 2007, the Caribbean Competition Commission was set up, financially supported by the European Union. This was the first genuine step in recent years toward finally realizing a genuine Caribbean Single Market no longer undermined by plantation interests or dominated by oligarchies of different kinds.
- The Caribbean Court of Justice (CCJ) was established to serve as replacement for the colonial Judicial Committee of the London-based Privy Council. The Caribbean Court of Justice began its operations on 16 April 2005 in Port of Spain. The CCJ has the potential to gain authority over time as an appellate court and a court with genuine jurisdiction in matters of the Caribbean Single Market.
- An Assembly of the Caribbean Community Parliamentarians (ACCP) was established to serve as a link between CARICOM actions and national parliaments in CARICOM member states. Its meetings have been held between rather long intervals, in 1994, 1996, 1999, 2000, 2002, and 2004.
- A Caribbean Regional Negotiating Machinery (RNM) was established to formulate regional strategies for external trade negotiations.
- The Common Market Council of Ministers was replaced by a CARICOM Community Council of Ministers, responsible for developing strategic planning and coordination of economic integration, functional cooperation, and external relations of CARICOM.
- A plethora of standing committees was replaced by and confined to four new councils intended to streamline CARICOM business: the Council on Finance and Planning, the Council on Trade and Economic Development, the Council on Foreign and Community Relations, and the Council on Human and Social Development.[77]

The Barbados-based Caribbean Development Bank supports the monetary objectives of the Caribbean Common Market.

Ever since the revision of the Treaty of Chaguaramas, CARICOM has remained what one analyst called "a hybrid creature" between Caribbean nationalism and Caribbean regionalism.[78] Another author describes CARICOM as being "in an advanced stage of transition" and involved in a "fundamental departure from the old dispensation."[79] These assessments refer to the broadening of CARICOM's perspective. Without a formal increase in supranational powers, CARICOM has embarked on a more serious effort to make regional integration a living reality. It has become more focused. The underlying political will cannot be denied any longer, and most importantly, the business conducted under the umbrella of CARICOM has become exponentially more serious. Yet CARICOM has not achieved any level of supranationality, although across the region the European Union is claimed to be the CARICOM model. The absence of a common economic space is often used as an excuse not to implement what has been decided. Local interests in preserving economic monopolies or protected segments of the economy seem difficult to thwart as long as debates over the costs of regional integration dominate the broad awareness of the benefits of regional integration. Nevertheless, CARICOM has taken roots in the Caribbean region, both among political elites and relevant citizens in CARICOM. This promising process has been equivalent to "reinventing CARICOM."[80]

The revitalization of CARICOM since the 1990s has been often slow and painful, always gradual, and never spectacular. But the core result of this process is nothing less than a factual refounding of the Caribbean Community and a much more solid projection of its underlying idea and prospect. The gradual institutional improvement of CARICOM and the enhanced will to achieve concrete results in regional integration reflect the unavoidable recognition of weak sovereignty on the part of the individual member states of CARICOM. For Caribbean countries, there simply is no alternative to the prospect of improved development and security through regional cooperation and subsequently integration. The recognition of the process of community-building among CARICOM citizens remains essential in order to achieve sustainable results for this political engineering.

The region needs further spurs to deeper integration if it wants to come fully into line with its rhetorical claims. Deeper integration, especially as far as the primacy of community law is concerned, remains essential in order to accommodate countries of different size and structure. Whether or not to accept the Dominican Republic as a CARICOM member state is not primarily a matter of the size of the Dominican Republic, but a matter of the weaker CARICOM states improving their performance and deepening their integration first. A common economic space between excessively asymmetric countries can work, as long as strict criteria for performance in a common market apply. CARICOM might want to reflect on its experience of digesting the memberships of Suriname and of Haiti. Membership of the Dominican Republic also raises issues of political culture and legal traditions. The bridging of the primarily anglophone and the Spanish-speaking Caribbean may also eventually provoke the matter of Cuba's possible membership in CARICOM. For the time being, the "Cuban question" has met with inconclusive answers. For example, Cuba belongs to the Association of Caribbean States, in existence since 1995 with twenty-five member states, "anchored in CARICOM, but open to the wider Caribbean region,"[81] which in the final analysis is no more than a diplomatic debating club. While Cuba belongs to the Association of Caribbean States, Puerto Rico and the US Virgin Islands do not. In some island states, the US and Cuba have diplomatic missions, in the meantime often joined by rather excessively large Chinese embassies.

CARICOM has begun to address issues of democratic governance. It has been intensively involved in contributing to the crisis of stability and democracy in Haiti, thus projecting the hope that it will never include Cuba unless proper rule of law and democratic governance prevail there. CARICOM will also have to address the matter of deeper integration for the sake of its current shape. As much as weak democracy will only generate weak and symbolic integration, weak sovereignties will continue to have difficulties generating strong integration. The only way out for the small and vulnerable Caribbean island countries is a substantial and much speedier development of functional forms of integration.

Highly important for CARICOM—as is the case in regional integration schemes elsewhere—is the further evolution of concrete integration conditions and projects. The Cricket World Tournament in 2007 was the occasion for introducing a common CARICOM visa regime. This may serve as an encouraging and stimulating precedent to look for other creative measures. With the establishment of the Caribbean Court of Justice, CARICOM has demonstrated the community's determination to gradually advance the goal of law-based integration. The CCJ will certainly take a reasonable period of time—and most probably undergo conflict, backlash, and crises—to stretch the borders for a genuine Caribbean community law whose primacy over national law is recognized by CARICOM member states. Initially, its jurisdiction was recognized only by Barbados and Guyana. Experience with the evolution of community law elsewhere shows that supranational community-building based on law is a process that requires time, patience, and the ability to handle frustration by turning it into an engine for progress.

The long-term goals of the Caribbean Court of Justice are precise, albeit for the time being only on paper: it wants to become a Court for Trade Disputes and the Supreme Appellate Court, finally replacing the Judicial Committee of the Privy Council in London. The CCJ is waiting for the first cases dealing with matters under the framework of the Caribbean Single Market. Only then can it develop its ambition to become an appellate court and a court of original jurisdiction. In another decade or so, the CCJ may truly impact Caribbean supranational integration, particularly in terms of strengthening the Caribbean Single Market. In support of this goal, a Competition Commission was established in Suriname in 2005. While this is a reasonable addition, at some point CARICOM must seriously reflect on the relationship between the increase in its structures and the effect on its outcome. The path CARICOM has taken is impressive. Patience will be needed in judging any concrete progress—after all, it has taken the European Court of Justice several decades to become fully accepted across the EU.

Basing Caribbean integration on the primacy of law and recognizing the need to root the very idea and meaning of regional integration in the hearts and minds of Caribbean citizens are obviously the two biggest challenges. CARICOM needs to respond to these challenges in order to gain stronger public legitimacy. CARICOM leaders recognized the necessities ahead when they decided on the introduction of a CARICOM passport. In January 2005, Suriname was the first CARICOM member state to issue the CARICOM passport, followed thereafter by Saint Vincent and the Grenadines and Saint Kitts and Nevis. The existence of a CARICOM passport underlines the dual existence of indigenous nationality and CARICOM citizenship as two interconnected and mutually reinforcing concepts. This is an important element in the further evolution of multilevel governance and shared sovereignty in the Caribbean.

Intrinsic Motives and External Pressures

The original motive of regional integration in the Caribbean was related to the period of late colonialism and was also transformed by this period. In moving from the status of an instrument of British claims to continuous presence and dominance in the West Indies, Caribbean integration became an expression of Caribbean self-determination and nationalism. External pressure was also one of the driving forces in regard to the economic constellation in the Caribbean. Small markets, the prevalence of colonial-type plantations focused on monocultures (namely sugar and bananas), and dependence on markets for the local raw materials, bauxite in particular, have been constituent features of the Caribbean economy. Political independence could not overcome economic dependencies. The contrast between formal sovereignty and a lack of economic sovereignty was felt more than ever after the Caribbean countries had gained political self-determination. The limits of human resources, the markets for production and distribution, and the small size and ecological vulnerability of the Caribbean countries became constant features of postcolonial worry. The effects of the oil crises added to the awareness of dependency. For a certain period of time, some Caribbean countries drew detrimental conclusions that were no remedy at all:

economic nationalism and political socialism were fatal paths into further isola-tion and impoverishment.

The prospect of open regional cooperation and eventual integration gained ground amidst a crisis of independence, when honest reflection was devoted to the objective potentials and limits of each of the independent states of the Carib-bean, including the Caribbean Community states on the shores of the Caribbean coastline. Belize, Suriname, and Guyana are quasi islands surrounded by jungle that disconnects them from their hinterlands. For them, their connections with the Caribbean island countries by sea have become the only bridges to the outer world. In CARICOM they have found partners to help them grow into a wider community.

The proximity of the Caribbean to the United States, and the dependency that stems from the fundamental power differentials between the US and the Caribbean nations, has served as a lasting external pressure investing Carib-bean integration concepts with a sense of priority. From the point of view of the US, the Caribbean is a sea of trouble as much as it is an area of potential for cooperation. Poverty, instability, and a lack of democratic participation gener-ate illegal migration and reduce the Caribbean's potential as a stable market and tourist destination. The United States' claim to take prime responsibility for regional developments has been enshrined in the region's consciousness and its policy parameters since the days of the Monroe Doctrine (2 December 1823). The North American Free Trade Agreement (NAFTA) between the US, Canada, and Mexico has been criticized as a modernized version of the Monroe Doctrine applied to the sphere of the globalized economy. The Ca-ribbean Basin Initiative and the Enterprise for the Americas Initiative were further expressions of the projection of American interests and values. Con-cern for Caribbean deficits and expectations of American cooperation with the area converged in these initiatives of subsequent US presidents. Their overall goal was not the promotion of Caribbean regional integration. Instead, the US was driven in its Caribbean initiatives—as in the case of other coop-eration initiatives with Latin American regions—by a claim to "hegemonic regionalism."[82] In order to become a viable partner for the US, the member states of CARICOM were advised to cooperate among themselves as closely as possible. In order not to become more dependent upon the US than necessary, they were advised to cooperate even more and pool their potential as much as possible.

Globalization and its effects have been felt in CARICOM countries not only by way of proximity to US spheres of interest. The People's Republic of China has increasingly begun to reach out to the Caribbean. Most CARICOM member states have replaced their diplomatic ties with Taiwan with ones with Beijing. Rather large Chinese embassies prevail across the region, and the economic pres-ence of China is becoming noticeable. In Grenada, China even built the stadium for the 2007 Cricket World Tournament, with several hundred Chinese workers on the spot day and night.

The same ambivalence of being torn between cooperation and self-determination—or to put it differently, of having external sources that strengthen intrinsic motives—defines CARICOM's relationship with Europe. In the beginning, the relationship was colonial. European sea powers had discovered and colonized the West Indies and organized the slavery and plantation economy in the pursuit of their interests. The process of decolonization will not come to full completion in the Caribbean unless the dependency status of several Caribbean islands is recognized as the self-determined expression of the genuine will of the local population. But even before decolonization had been completely terminated, Europe began to discover the Caribbean in a new light. In an interesting way, the two unequal regions embarked on a similar project: as Europe began its regional integration, so did the Caribbean.

As a first step in this new encounter of regional entities, both sides tried to overcome their colonial and postcolonial traumas. When European integration started in 1957, most of today's CARICOM member states were still colonies of European countries. In a surprising paradox, the European Community (as the European Union was called until 1993) and the Caribbean Community began to encounter each other as postcolonial regions. They started to perceive each other as regions with genuine ability for partnership and cooperation. A series of Lomé Conventions (beginning in 1975 and renewed every five years until they were replaced in 2000 by the Cotonou Agreement, which has a duration of twenty years) made this aspiration manifest. It put relations between the European Community and most of Europe's former colonies in the Caribbean, Africa, and the Pacific Ocean on a new footing.[83] The Lomé Conventions granted preferential market access and protection mechanisms for Caribbean raw materials to the partner countries of Europe in the region.

A long-standing dispute between the United States and the European Union brought this special preferential system to a halt. The US challenged the special preferential agreements between the EU and banana producers in the Caribbean, claiming that price distortion and quota systems between the EU and banana producers in former European colonies were detrimental to banana producers in other regions, notably those with investment and trade ties to the US. The World Trade Organization got involved as the arbiter of the "banana war" between the US and the EU. The first WTO panel to intervene between 1995 (immediately after GATT had been replaced by the more thorough WTO in that year) and 1997 marginalized the interests of the Caribbean banana producers by declaring the EU's banana regime inconsistent with WTO rules on free market competition. The EU revised its banana policy, inter alia abolishing the import license system that discriminated between banana producers in Lomé Convention partner countries and those operating on a dollar basis in cooperation with the US. The revised quota system, which came into force in 1999 and was intended to last until the end of 2004, remained unacceptable for Caribbean countries and the US alike.

A second WTO panel decided in 1999 to demand from the EU a further revision of its quota system of banana imports from the Lomé partner countries. It also forced the EU to accept sanctions, to be paid to the US, of a total of $191.4 million. "It is ironic," one analyst observed, "that after the second WTO panel the immediate result was not a liberalization of the EU's banana regime, but an increase in trade protectionism on the part of the US to punish the EU for its perceived intransigence, a move authorized by the WTO itself."[84] In early 2006, a system based only on tariffs came into force, ending the period of preferential banana relations between the EU and the Caribbean. American producers, who operate on bigger production sites than those available in the tiny Caribbean islands, are the main beneficiaries of the WTO-induced changes. In Honduras and Guatemala alone, the Chiquita corporation has 40,000 workers under contract.

For CARICOM, the experience in the banana dispute—followed by a similar fate of the region's sugar production and its past relations with the European Community—was eye-opening.[85] The independence of most of CARICOM's member states had coincided with Great Britain's entry into the European Community. Special relations through the Commonwealth continued nevertheless. Now, the constellation was different. The special relations with Europe were not capable of preventing the revision of trade preferences on which a substantial part of the Caribbean economy had been thriving. CARICOM was forced to speed up its genuine efforts for development, economic growth, and social progress. In political rhetoric, regional integration became the only option for broadening a market that was under genuine control of the region's people and countries. CARICOM was no longer an indirect insider of the European agricultural policy regime. More than ever before, CARICOM was forced to grow into a mature regional entity, making the best possible use of its own resources, no matter how limited they were. But the path from complaining to stocktaking, and from deciding new realities to implementing them, remains daunting in the Caribbean.

Performance

The overall record of regional integration in the Caribbean is as mixed as in any other regional scheme across the world. Because of the small size of CARICOM in terms of population and economy, the Caribbean regional integration history is often underestimated or simply forgotten. But in light of the difficulties of the region, as well as the serious and honest intentions of many of those committed to Caribbean regional integration, it is worth paying tribute to the efforts of CARICOM in their own right. Most impressive is the increasing sense of rootedness in a region-wide commitment to the idea and usefulness of regional integration in the political institutions of the region. The overall sense of being part of a Caribbean community is very advanced, though public awareness about concrete effects of regional integration and its benefits remains ambivalent. As part and parcel of the successes of Caribbean integration, one ought to mention:

(1) CARICOM has always had to struggle with the effects of external pressure, the frustration of internal failure, and the burden of lethargy in speedy decision-making. Yet the Caribbean Community has managed to reactivate itself and to revitalize and strengthen its goals and the instruments needed to achieve them. Pragmatic steps, such as the establishment of a Regional Negotiating Machinery in 1997, attest to CARICOM's ability to tackle concrete deficits in the region's development. Meanwhile, CARICOM has proved its capacity for finding compromises whenever reasonable arguments are put to the table. The gradual extension of CARICOM's agenda serves as a confirmation of the power of pragmatic reactions, particularly in times of integration crisis. But empirical evidence indicates that despite these successes, CARICOM might find itself weakened again once a crisis has vanished, and with it the need to maintain the high profile of a specific integration effort. This is the conclusion one must draw from the experience with the Regional Security System established in October 1982 by Barbados, Antigua, Saint Vincent and the Grenadines, Saint Lucia, and Dominica in reaction to the turmoil in Grenada. Although the Regional Security System might have had the potential to serve as an early warning mechanism for future crises or as a tool of crisis management and post-crisis management in different circumstances, it has not been further activated since the early 1980s.[86] One wonders what role it might have been able to play during the outbreak of new political unrest in Haiti in the 1990s, inter alia.

(2) Caribbean regional integration has begun as a parallel operation intended to achieve a common market while establishing a community-building design for the newly independent Caribbean states. These achievements have matured and are increasingly related to each other. With the revision of the Treaty of Chaguaramas, both "pillars" of Caribbean regional integration have been merged. Economic integration and the political process of community-building are understood as complementing each other. This process will continue as CARICOM evolves. Its coherent implementation requires first and foremost political leadership and "post-sovereignist" political will and input. For the time being, the feeling of Caribbean community-building among citizens and elites is more widespread than their readiness to embrace the implications of the Common Market. Bringing highly asymmetric and mostly very small economies under the umbrella of a Common Market is not immediately understood as a win-win situation in the Caribbean. The genuine CARICOM institutions have only limited means to reverse this course. Unlike its European model, CARICOM did not

start with a distinct commitment to supranationality. The principle of unanimity prevails as the main voting pattern in the Conference of Heads of Government. But it is a positive fact that, in so far as the other organs of CARICOM are concerned, the principle of unanimity was in reality abandoned with the revision of the Treaty of Chaguaramas in 2001.[87]

With the revised Treaty of Chaguaramas, the Council for Foreign and Community Relations (COFOR) was made a CARICOM organ. Formerly, it only ranked as an "institution" of CARICOM. The upgrading reflects the desire to develop common foreign policy propositions in a more focused and relevant way. This includes relations with the European Union, for which COFOR is responsible. The establishment of the Caribbean Court of Justice in 2005 is another indicator of a stronger commitment toward real integration.

These examples cannot, however, deny the weakness of CARICOM. Not unlike other regional integration schemes with a strong intergovernmental base, budget transparency in CARICOM is poorly developed. CARICOM recognizes a Budget Committee as a Community Council supporting body charged with examining the draft budget and work program of CARICOM's Secretariat, but further details about budgetary matters are difficult to obtain. It is understood that the CARICOM Conference of the Heads of Government defines the budget of the Caribbean Community.[88] Further details are absent from the official or academic literature on CARICOM. One academic paper explains that 49.1 percent of the CARICOM Secretariat budget for 1995 came from donor finances, 16.8 percent from member states contributions, and 17.4 percent from "external agencies."[89] The latest available information provides only a survey of the share of total member state contributions toward financing the CARICOM Secretariat without net figures and sources of origin.[90] It would certainly strengthen CARICOM's reputation if more precise and updated information were available on this important matter of the community's work.

(3) Although the revised Treaty of Chaguaramas underlines a growing priority for regional integration in the Caribbean, it remains undeniable that not all of CARICOM's member states have wholeheartedly embraced the regional agenda. Slow progress in the implementation of the Single Market and Economy on the part of some member states of CARICOM is one of the saddest expressions of this situation. On average, the common external tariff is fixed between 9.7 percent and 11.2 percent for imports into CARICOM. So far, this common external tariff has only been applied by Belize, Grenada, Saint Lucia, Guyana, and Jamaica. Local monopolists of all sorts resist the dissolution of their petit advantages. Governments in the region are often more scared by the costs of integration than they are able to communicate the benefits of integration. It is positive that intra-regional trade reached around 17.5 percent (2003 figure) after stagnation on a lower level during the 1990s. Given the non-complementary structure of most CARICOM economies, this is probably the highest degree

of intra-regional trade one can realistically expect. The enormous asymmetries among CARICOM economies remain a matter of concern for the Caribbean Community as a whole: Trinidad and Tobago represents 70 to 80 percent of all CARICOM exports and 15 percent of CARICOM imports.[91] The introduction of a regional development scheme and the balancing mechanisms of a value-added tax are meant to alleviate the situation.

Practically all CARICOM member states maintain some national measures restricting free trade and the comprehensive implementation of a common market in CARICOM. Import licenses are in place in Antigua, Barbados, Belize, Dominica, Grenada, Guyana, Jamaica, Montserrat, Saint Kitts and Nevis, Saint Vincent and the Grenadines, Saint Lucia, and Trinidad and Tobago. Quota regulations are practiced in Antigua, Saint Lucia, Saint Vincent and the Grenadines, Montserrat, and Trinidad and Tobago. Price controls are a feature of daily life in Antigua, Barbados, Belize, Dominica, Guyana, Saint Kitts and Nevis, Saint Lucia, and Saint Vincent and the Grenadines. Finally, import duties are applied in Dominica, Grenada, Jamaica, Saint Lucia, Saint Vincent and the Grenadines, and Trinidad and Tobago.[92]

In spite of the ideological rifts and violent conflicts in the 1980s, the comprehensive application of CARICOM standards for good governance have also remained weak. The idea of strengthening CARICOM's civil society by expressing its importance in a genuine charter has remained a mere idea. Common citizenship cannot be created via issuance of common passports alone; indeed, this process has so far been executed by only a very few CARICOM member states. CARICOM remains a limited effort in regional integration building because the scope of supranational developments, disconnected from national idiosyncrasies, remains limited. No example could better underline this deficit than the career of the bombastic resolution adopted by the CARICOM heads of state at their summit of 2–5 July 2003 under the title "Regional Governance and Integrated Development."[93] So far, lack of follow-up has kept this laudable paper from becoming a visible reality. In the absence of supranational mechanisms, CARICOM decisions continue to lack binding legal effect.

Federators

CARICOM developments follow a very unique pattern. They cannot be extrapolated from other regional integration experiences. One of the traditional assumptions in integration theory relates to the role of bigger states serving as engines for regional integration. Even better, so it is said, would be the combination of two states that are committed to regional integration, not the least as an expression of reconciliation with one another. The Franco-German experience in the context of European integration is often invoked, if only tacitly. CARICOM, however, has different features. Bigger member states with noticeable economic strength certainly exist: Trinidad and Tobago, Jamaica, Barbados, and Guyana account for 87 percent of the total population of CARICOM and 93 percent of the total production. The relationship among them is at times strained, at times cordial. As for relations between these four big elephants and the other many small or even micro-states of CARICOM, they cannot be said to be free of frictions and jealousy. Only upon realizing that they are all united under the pressure of small size and peripheral status in the world of the twenty-first century do CARICOM countries put their internal disputes aside. Even then, however, they carry the paradigm of sovereign autonomy and independence with them like a mantra.

It still serves a unifying purpose if CARICOM member states can invoke their colonial legacy to identify the original source of evil and backwardness in the Caribbean. Defining regional purposes in reaction to colonial legacies helps them to shy away from self-made problems and defects, and the ideological, or at least rhetorical, function of these invocations of historic injustice helps to rally skeptics of regional integration. But it does not resolve any real-world problems.

The banana shock of the 1990s helped to focus regional economic interests. The more the European Union curtailed its preferential relations with the banana producers in the Caribbean, the more banana producers started to define their own interests in a regional setting. When they had initially founded the Caribbean Banana Exports Association in 1988, relations between French and British interests, and those of their partners and satellites in the Caribbean, were marked by jarring disputes. But the more the European Union as a whole forced Caribbean banana producers to reassess their position in the world market and to redesign their access to the world market, the closer they became to one another.[94] It is not unthinkable that pressure on sugar production in the Caribbean might have a similar effect of strengthening the sense of common interests in CARICOM.

Sugar production on the small and often hilly farms of Caribbean islands was profitable for more than three hundred years. But in recent decades it was only able to compete with mechanized plantations in Latin America and elsewhere because of the preferential arrangements between the Caribbean producers and the EU. Similar to the development in banana production, the European Union had to phase out its preferential arrangements with Caribbean sugar producers. This brought about terrible challenges in some CARICOM member states. Guyana, the poorest of all Caribbean countries, is largely dependent upon its sugar production. By 2009, the European Union was to eliminate its fixed sugar price for producers and bring the sugar regime in line with world-market prices. Driven by the interests of producers in Brazil and Australia, Caribbean sugar production has come under threats similar to those faced by the banana producers a few years earlier.[95]

CARICOM economies are being forced to diversify and to enhance cooperation and integration. They have already achieved remarkable success: in 1985
services contributed to 29 percent of the CARICOM GDP; by 2004, the share of
services had gone up to 58 percent.[96] But no matter how much environmentally
friendly tourism the Caribbean might promote, including tourist management
and service schools, the limits of space remain natural barriers in the whole Caribbean Basin. The enormous brain drain that the Caribbean is experiencing
underlines the structural problem of the region's development. In some places,
such as Guyana, more citizens are living outside their home country than inside.
Remittances—for instance in Saint Lucia—constitute the most important revenue for their home country.

Transformations

Caribbean integration has turned from a late-colonial instrument of British interests to an anti-colonial instrument in support of decolonization to a postcolonial
mechanism for managing weak sovereignties. It has also outlived the normative
starting point according to which integration and the pooling of sovereignties
are zero-sum games and therefore unacceptable threats to sovereign states. Caribbean integration has become increasingly understood as the evolution of a
community relationship that has every potential to be a win-win constellation
for all participating member states and their societies. Technically convincing
solutions in support of this general insight might take time, remain contested,
and continue to be part of a long-term process. But the general attitude toward
regional integration has changed considerably. This is also visible with regard to
the attitude of some of those countries that have had the reputation of being
particularly reluctant to support regional integration in the Caribbean, such as
Jamaica. Jamaica has turned from a position of hesitance (1970s) and aggravation
during a period of destructive opposition (1980s) to an attitude of constructive
engagement and a driving force of Caribbean integration (1990s/early twenty-
first century).

The Caribbean outlook on matters related to identity, language, tradition,
culture, and ethnicity has broadened. What began as a Commonwealth Caribbean has been turned into a Caribbean Commonwealth.[97] The focus, previously
fixated on the English-speaking Caribbean, has been slightly expanded, although
the dominance of English is still present. In addition to the linguistic aspect,
there is also the continuous effect of British legal traditions and the orientation
of political and social elites toward Great Britain and the United States. The
massive brain drain in the region gravitates toward the former "mother countries," while the notion of freedom of movement within the Caribbean region
itself is a rather slowly developing concept. Caribbean societies and countries are
still in the process of refocusing their minds toward an indigenous and inclusive

Caribbean identity without limitations in the legal, economic, and political spheres. CARICOM does not provide this identity itself, as it is more about processes and less about normative goals. But it provides a new framework in which the quest for a genuine, modern, postcolonial, and integrative identity of the region can be pursued. The first steps in a long process have been taken.

Role and Interests of the European Union

The European Community began to discover the Caribbean in the course of its membership negotiations with Great Britain in the early 1970s. When Great Britain joined the EC on 1 January 1973, its Caribbean territories and dependencies and the former colonies with continuous special links to Great Britain were automatically associated with the EC. Article IV of the 1957 Treaties of Rome had set a precedent from which former French, Belgian and Dutch overseas territories and colonies had benefited. Now Great Britain insisted that its special links with the Caribbean were to be "communitarized." The most noticeable implication was the patronage of Caribbean banana and sugar production under the framework of five subsequent Lomé Conventions that the European Community (European Union since November 1993) conducted with many former European colonies in Africa and the Pacific, the Caribbean (ACP countries). The continuous struggle between this preferential trade relationship and the quest for liberalized, open world trade, under the auspices of first the General Agreement on Tariffs and Trade (GATT) and since 1995 the more institutionalized and rigid World Trade Organization (WTO), has forced the EU to finally change its policies vis-à-vis Caribbean producers, turning them factually "from insiders to outsiders."[98] The resentment is still strong in the Caribbean.

Originally—and due to its traditional focus on Great Britain—CARICOM saw the European Free Trade Area as a model for its own evolution. Much as Great Britain had to withdraw from the idea that EFTA could be the leading design for the new European architecture, CARICOM had to realize the primacy of the European Community that evolved into the European Union with the Treaty of Maastricht. Consequently, the European Union became a point of reference for CARICOM and in some ways the model for authentic Caribbean efforts to "deepen" and "widen" Caribbean regional integration.[99] As far as the institutional architecture and the evolution of policies in CARICOM are concerned, the European example is certainly echoed. In so far as the issue of widening is concerned, CARICOM has so far remained undecided on the issue of membership of the Dominican Republic. And it has never openly discussed possible prospects and implications of Cuban membership. In the meantime, it has by all means passed a critical threshold with the membership of Haiti and Suriname.

Annual trade between CARICOM and the European Union lingers around a total volume of €3 billion in imports and €3.5 billion in exports. While the European market is relevant for CARICOM products, bananas, rum, sugar, and aluminum in particular, CARICOM is of limited economic relevance for the European Union. Only 0.5 percent of the total imports of the EU originate in CARICOM, and 0.7 percent of its total exports, mainly industrial goods, go to CARICOM. The EU is focusing its development aid to the Caribbean on the development of regional integration in CARICOM: between 1976 and 2000, Europe contributed €353 million to the development of regional integration in the Caribbean, notably to facilitate business and trade, to improve education standards on the tertiary level, to ameliorate the transportation infrastructure, and to promote tourism, disaster preparedness, health standards, and drug control mechanisms in the region. In the period from 2001 to 2006, the European Union contributed €57 million to regional integration in the Caribbean. Skepticism is mounting in the EU as to whether this has truly contributed to sustainable region-building. Ownership and accountability are overdue in CARICOM: it needs to take the destiny of the region's development into its own hands. It remains to be seen whether the effects of Economic Partnership Agreements as negotiated with the EU have a cleansing and modernizing effect in the Caribbean.

As outlined in the 2000 Cotonou Agreement, political dialogue between the European Union and CARICOM takes place in joint institutions under the broader framework of EU relations with the ACP countries. CARICOM membership is not totally identical with the membership of Caribbean countries in the ACP group. By 1982, fifteen independent Caribbean countries had therefore established a forum of the Caribbean member states of ACP, CARIFORUM. It includes CARICOM, the Dominican Republic, and, since 2001, Cuba, the only Caribbean country so far without a cooperation agreement with the EU. The overall goal of CARIFORUM is the optimal coordination of the region's relations with the European Union. The Cotonou Agreement stated the goal of replacing the existing preferential trade relations between the EU and its ACP partners with several regional Economic Partnership Agreements (EPAs), intended to gradually introduce reciprocity in trade relations and make them compatible with the competition and liberalization rules of the WTO.

Since 2002, CARIFORUM has been negotiating such an Economic Partnership Agreement with the European Union. The EU's first effort was directed toward capacity-building in the partner countries. This was the least controversial aspect; other issues were much more controversial and significant. The Caribbean countries demanded a balance between their understanding of the EPA as a development tool and the EU's perception of the EPA as primarily an instrument in support of free trade. The new constituent base for Caribbean-EU relations, the Caribbean countries argued, ought to include a compensation mechanism for the loss of markets due to the opening of trade. The suggestion that a CAR-ICOM-wide value added tax be introduced was received with mixed reactions. Antigua even moved away from its initial practice of a value added tax in 2006 because the national tax base was considered to be too low.

The more realistic idea of a regional development fund inside CARICOM was designed to better react to the needs of vulnerable economies in the Caribbean. The EU introduced the notion of "interconnectivity" of the small islands in order to gradually support the evolution of a common economic sphere in the Caribbean. Deeper integration and the opening of the region into the global market would need to go hand in hand, should Caribbean integration reach a higher level.[100] By the end of 2007, the European Commission had initialed an EPA with fourteen CARICOM countries and the Dominican Republic under the somewhat confusing format of EU-CARIFORUM relations. Most ambivalent was the EU's declarative position to promote regional integration through its EPA negotiation: while CARICOM had established itself as the most advanced regional grouping in the Caribbean, the EU was negotiating the Caribbean Economic Partnership Agreement outside CARICOM. Beyond the finalization of the EPA negotiations in 2008 it remained controversial whether or not this latest tool for liberalization and free trade could genuinely support deeper regional integration in the Caribbean.

Prospects and Obstacles

The future development of CARICOM depends primarily on two factors: domestic developments in the individual CARICOM member states, and the readiness of CARICOM member states to gradually introduce elements of supranationality into their elaborate institutional structure without relying on external pressure and financing. Stable rule of law will remain a basic precondition for successful regional integration. Stronger public awareness and the inclusion of the civil society on the path toward integration are equally essential. The Cricket World Tournament 2007, which took place in five CARICOM member states, contributed more to the spirit of regional identity than many political meetings. Due to the massive structural differences between most CARICOM countries and the difficult infrastructure in the Caribbean, the evolution of a common economic sphere will remain a long and daunting process. Yet it is promising that initial serious steps have been taken to advance in this direction with the membership of twelve countries in the Caribbean Single Market and Economy since 2006. The idea of turning to a Caribbean Youth Parliament and gradually developing a directly elected CARICOM Parliament is intriguing. Efforts to integrate the region through better use of mass communication media, including a common television channel, have been discussed, though only in very limited ways. CARICOM could also benefit from reconsidering the possibility of making better use of its enormous diaspora. Several CARICOM member states are smaller than the number of their citizens living abroad. They may provide more input in the modernization and change toward regional integration.

Caribbean integration takes places in the shadow of the United States. The attitude of the United States to the region is linked with the perception of the US in the region, and hence also with the interpretation and perception of the kind of globalization it represents. The US is pursuing a form of regionalism that is primarily interested in the promotion of free trade. This collides with CARICOM's interest in developing its genuine integration mechanisms. It also collides with the EU's interest in seeing this happen in a favorable and sustainable way. The developments in the Andean Community should be a warning for CARICOM: as long as the region does not organize itself as one entity in trade negotiations with the US, or the European Union for that matter, it will weaken all member states without necessarily working for the long-term advantage of those who think they can go it alone and negotiate a bilateral agreement with the US.

The European Union is precluding this scenario as it insists on only negotiating with the region as an entity. The United States defines its actions by contingent circumstances and interests. These might not collide with regional integration, but they could. It is not clear in which direction the strategic perspective of the US for the future of its relations with Latin America and the Caribbean is focused. Will NAFTA, CAFTA, and a possible free trade agreement with CARICOM remain separate arrangements, or will they merge into the Free Trade Area of the Americas (FTAA) as intended by the Bush administration? An interesting aspect of this open question is the role the US ascribes to Puerto Rico and the US Virgin Islands. Even more relevant for the Caribbean would be the effect of regime change in Cuba. In 1993, and against explicit US interests, a joint CARICOM-Cuban commission was set up to promote bilateral trade, technical cooperation, and measures for environmental protection. This might be just the beginning of an historical rapprochement. But for the time being, neither Cuba nor CARICOM is prepared to consider any revolutionary change in Cuba and hence in the region.

The second important feature affecting the future of CARICOM is related to the internal development of its member states. Domestic weakness and integration stalemate have coincided in the past. Only under the pressure of further marginalization of the Caribbean could they be stopped. However, the Revised Treaty of Chaguaramas has not yet offered a solution to the weak implementation of CARICOM decisions. The weak implementation of CARICOM decisions remains one of the most fundamental flaws of CARICOM. This weakness is rooted in the structural dependency of CARICOM institutions on CARICOM member states. As long as Caribbean Community rules lack a certain degree of independence from the idiosyncratic considerations, interests, and moods of individual member states, CARICOM will remain as much a hostage to its member states as an instrument for serving them. What has been said about CARICOM in the 1980s is still valid twenty years later: "The failure of CARICOM to have a bigger development impact on the region is more attributable to weaknesses at the national level than to deficiencies in the economic integration instruments."[101] Or, to quote a UN-sponsored report of 2004 with more detailed reference to the problem of implementing rules of the Caribbean Common Market: "Intra-CARICOM trade is also affected by lack of compliance with commitments on the part of various member countries, some of which have not included the agreements regarding the formation of the customs union in their national legislations. Non-compliance is a problem in a considerable proportion of member countries."[102] In response to this situation, in November 2007 CARICOM initiated a Caribbean Competition Commission, largely financed by the European Union.

Most important for overcoming inertia would be the development of a much stronger sense of urgency.[103] Many CARICOM leaders still seem to think that they have an endless amount of time to position their region on the newly emerging map of globalization. They may believe that any pooling of sovereignty can be prevented whenever undermines their national pretensions and sources of pride. They need quicker, more energetic reactions to the new challenges of globalization so as to turn them into opportunities for their people, countries, and region as a whole. This would, however, require a stronger sense of urgency, authentic focus on regional integration that works, and readiness to reckon with its implications. The ways these implications can improve the living conditions and their preconditions in the Caribbean remain to be developed in reality. CARICOM has introduced regional integration. Now it must live up to its potential and turn it into a living reality.

Southern Common Market
(Mercado Común del Sur, MERCOSUR)

Basic Facts

The speed with which the Southern Common Market (Mercado Común del Sur, MERCOSUR, in Spanish; Mercado do Sul, MERCOSUL, in Portuguese) has become the shining star of regional integration efforts in Latin America is surprising. Founded only in 1991, MERCOSUR has become the embodiment of regional integration on the Latin American continent, clearly surpassing the other integration schemes there. It finds itself often on par with ASEAN to describe its respective role for their continents. This exuberance is not necessarily helpful in understanding the real nature of either of these two regional integration schemes.

It does not help full understanding of the overall context of Latin American regional integration efforts. Moreover, it does not do justice to MERCOSUR: as much as MERCOSUR was lauded initially, it was declared dead immediately during its first crisis. None of these interpretations truly depicts the contingent nature of MERCOSUR, its potential and flaws, and its path of evolution and progress through obstacles and crises. Its experiences are not new. They can be found in any other regional integration scheme across the world. But a careful examination of MERCOSUR is needed to understand how it developed during its first two decades, where its strength and weaknesses are located, and how further trends might develop.

The interest in MERCOSUR certainly stems from the fact that it includes the two biggest countries and economies of Latin America. Along with Argentina and Brazil, Uruguay and Paraguay are also member states. Venezuela's membership was approved in 2005, albeit amidst concern about the possible implications, bad and good. The oil resources of Venezuela are an attractive addition to the economic potential of MERCOSUR countries and their economic strategies. The populist-nationalist-socialist chauvinism and authoritarianism of Venezuela's President Hugo Chávez are cause for concern inside the other MERCOSUR countries and elsewhere. Have the old member states of MERCOSUR reflected on all of the implications of their decision to accept Venezuela's membership in MERCOSUR? Are they aware how much this could alter, if not even derail, the original MERCOSUR process? Is this perhaps their intention and goal? Can only an enlarged MERCOSUR preempt the US project of the Free Trade Area of the Americas, which has been rejected by many Latin American countries and heavily contested by some of its most outspoken governments?

MERCOSUR represents about half of Latin America's economic potential ($1.2 billion) and covers nearly 260 million citizens (including Venezuela's 25 million and with Brazil alone accounting for 190 million). Since Bolivia, Peru, Ecuador, and Colombia have become associate members, the prospects for MERCOSUR's widening seem to have grown substantially. Yet this perspective could turn out to be a curse rather than a blessing should it not go hand in hand with further clarifications regarding the political nature, the community-building ambition, and the overall context for economic integration, including preconditions and implications of a legal nature. European integration experience indicates that there is no natural law for pursuing regional integration. To begin with, a common market does not preclude political integration at a later stage, but it also does not lead automatically to political integration. It requires stocktaking and political decisions at every new corner turned in the integration process. This is not to say that integration might fail without incessant political input. But it indicates that political decisions of a strategic nature are required at every critical juncture in the integration process to redefine its objective, to formulate and focus its goals, and to help it stay on course. MERCOSUR is experiencing such a critical juncture toward the end of its second decade of existence.

The origins of regional integration in Latin America during the second half of the twentieth century were of a purely economic nature. The Economic Commission for Latin America and the Caribbean (ECLAC), founded in 1958, and the Latin American Integration Association (LAIA), founded in 1960—at the time of the first effort to establish regional integration schemes in Central America and in the Andean region—were as limited in their relevance as the Latin American Free Trade Agreement (LAFTA) of 1960. LAFTA was able to collect eleven member states, helped to increase regional trade, and was meant to eliminate tariff rates by 1973. It failed to implement the Common Schedule, a road map for gradually creating a common market for the whole Latin American continent. The overall approach was only economic, and the implementation effort was highly technical. The idea of achieving regional integration through trade expansion failed. The average share of intra-regional trade in LAFTA remained limited to, on average, 8.7 percent; after 1967, no relevant increase was noted.[104] Finally in 1973 the deadline for the completion of free trade was postponed to 1980, and the Common Schedule was suspended.

The idea of a common market always remained rhetorical in LAFTA. But after all, to give it some credit, it did introduce the idea of regional integration. After one and a half centuries of the primacy of national sovereignty, the breakthrough of this idea of regional cooperation and integration was almost as relevant as the fact itself. In any case, it paved the ground for a serious reconsideration of protectionist and nationalist acts of autonomy and opened the gate to a completely new way of thinking. Regional integration could certainly not be achieved overnight. European integration experience demonstrated that it had taken two world wars with terrible losses across the continent to spread the idea of integration over nationalism. It would not be realistic to expect anything different in the context of the biggest countries of Latin America, which have always been an echo of European developments and counterdevelopments.

In a way, what has been called a belated beginning was probably a revolutionary kick-start: the Treaty of Asuncion, signed on 26 March 1991, created MERCOSUR (Mercado Común del Sur), the Southern Common Market. No other regional scheme has gained global prominence in such a short period of time and with such global recognition as MERCOSUR. This was partly due to the fact that, Argentina and Brazil, the two biggest countries and economies of Latin America, had now embarked on the journey of regional integration. It was partially because Latin American integration efforts had failed time and again in the past, and many countries in the region were investing their last resource, hope, in this scheme. It was also because the time was ripe to constitute a serious beginning of regional integration in response to the overarching dominance of the United States in all aspects of world and regional economic and political affairs. MERCOSUR was considered to be a sign of hope and a promise of a different course of global order–building.

In a certain way, the founding of MERCOSUR was also a reaction to and a function of the Treaty of Maastricht, which accelerated European integration with the road map for a currency union. "We must reply to one integration with another," as the President of Uruguay was quoted as saying at the time, "to one increase of acquisitive power by internal enrichment by another, to inter-European cooperation by inter-Latin American cooperation."[105] It seemed as if the perception of Europe turning itself into a fortress stimulated "integration by fear" in Latin America. The danger of being increasingly marginalized in the world community had become a sort of obsession in Latin American policy-making circles. The Treaty of Asuncion was the first vocal answer to this self-assessment. But Argentina, Uruguay, Brazil, and Paraguay did not only come together because of external pressure. Equally imperative were internal changes inside these countries and in the relationship among them. The return to democracy in Brazil and Argentina, and a certain democratic consolidation in Uruguay and Paraguay, were absolutely decisive for beginning a project based on trust and the will to cooperate.

The Treaty of Asuncion outlined the four original objectives of MERCOSUR, which were economic in nature but unimaginable without a declared political will. These objectives remain crucial elements for a gradual process of community-building that might eventually go well beyond the economic sphere:[106]

- Liberalization of trade and complete elimination of custom duties and non-tariff barriers among the MERCOSUR member states.
- Introduction of a common external tariff by 1995, coupled with the right of exception in strategically relevant areas of the economy.
- Coordination of macro-economic policies.
- Sectoral agreements with strong commitments of MERCOSUR member states to harmonize their respective legislation.

Only three and a half years after the founding of MERCOSUR, the Protocol of Ouro Preto was signed by all MERCOSUR member states with the intention of substantially improving and advancing the perspectives of regional integration as outlined in the Treaty of Asuncion.[107] Four qualifications were of importance:

- The revision of the original treaty indicated that MERCOSUR ought to be understood as a dynamic process and could not be judged from a static interpretation of its origin.
- MERCOSUR was granted legal personality.
- A plan was designed to implement the external tariff of MERCOSUR by 1999/2000.

- The organizational structure of MERCOSUR was completed.

In fact, the organizational structure of MERCOSUR has remained weak and by no means comparable to the combination of intergovernmental and supranational elements that are significant for the European integration experience.

As for the economic goals of integration, toward the end of the first decade of the twenty-first century MERCOSUR has fallen short of its initial goals. While 90 percent of all goods can be traded freely, several strategically important products still have to be traded on the basis of a common external tariff ranging between zero and 20 percent, averaging 14 percent. Each government is permitted to exempt 300 products, including cars, sugar, telecommunications equipment, and capital goods. A vague target for convergence was set between 2004 and 2012. To look at the exemptions in detail is telling: MERCOSUR countries chose the most relevant strategic goods, which left the analysts wondering whether the intention of creating a customs union was serious at all:

- Argentina chose 232 products, including steel, chemicals, paper, and shoes.
- Brazil chose 175 products, including chemicals and petroleum derivates.
- Uruguay chose 212 products, including mill products, chemicals, paper, and shoes.
- Paraguay chose 210 products, including chemicals and agricultural products.[108]

Besides, MERCOSUR recognizes special regimes for capital goods, computing and telecommunications goods, and the automobile sector. The common customs code has not been adopted yet. While legally speaking MERCOSUR may claim to be a customs union, in fact it is neither a customs union nor a free trade area yet.

As far as the institutional structures of MERCOSUR are concerned, it has been criticized for being underinstitutionalized. A realistic assessment must come to the conclusion that the original institutional setup of MERCOSUR was the best possible one that could have been achieved at the time. It provides a basis on which to build in the years and decades to come.[109]

- MERCOSUR presidential summits are the most visible, symbolic, and powerful body to advance the course of regional integration.
- The MERCOSUR Common Market Council (Consejo del Mercado Común, CMC), the key decision-making body of MERCOSUR on matters of the evolution of a common market, consists of its ministers of foreign affairs and of economics.
- The Common Market Group (Grupo Mercado Común, GMC), consists of high officials from MERCOSUR member states and is authorized to pass directives with less binding character; the Common Market Council has delegated many of its responsibilities to this group, consisting of four incumbent members and four alternates for each MERCOSUR country's ministries for foreign affairs and economics.

- The MERCOSUR Secretariat, based in Montevideo, a semi-supranational, largely administrative and politically weak body. It is the only MERCOSUR institution with a communitary budget, contributed to by MERCOSUR member states. Since 2003 the MERCOSUR Secretariat is in the process of developing more qualities and strength as a technical institution, yet it is far away from exhibiting the role and power of the European Commission.
- The MERCOSUR Trade Commission (Comisión de Comerció del MERCOSUR, CCM), is responsible for supervising the implementation of the common trade policy of MERCOSUR as agreed to on the regional level.
- The initial Joint Parliamentary Commission (Comisión Parlamentaria Conjunta, CPC) consisted of 64 parliamentarians—16 per member state—delegated from the national parliaments. It was replaced in 2005 by the MERCOSUR Parliament with 18 delegated members from each MERCOSUR member state.
- The Economic and Social Consultative Forum (Foro Consultivo Económico-Social, FCES) is considered a "conveyor belt" for introducing the positions and perspectives of the organized labor partners into the deliberations of MERCOSUR's political bodies.

MERCOSUR institutions are lean, as far as the types of norms they can promulgate are concerned. The Common Market Council can exercise decisions, the Common Market Group resolutions, and the Trade Commission directives. Before the Permanent Court of Review was established in 2002, the Trade Commission was responsible for dealing with trade disputes. Between 1995 and 2004, a total of seventeen trade disputes were presented to the Trade Commission. They dealt with tariff and non-tariff restrictions, issues of alleged tax discrimination, the refusal to incorporate MERCOSUR norms into national legislation, export rights, and matters of sugar trade. With the Protocol of Olivos (18 February 2002), the core of a MERCOSUR Court of Justice was established. The MERCOSUR Permanent Court of Review strives for a unified interpretation of MERCOSUR regulations and norms. It is much too early to judge the effects and shortcomings of the Asuncion-based institution, yet it could become the nucleus of law-based development of regional integration in MERCOSUR. The MERCOSUR Permanent Court of Review is "without a doubt the greatest innovation of the Olivos Protocol."[110] The Court includes five arbitrators, four of whom can stay in their position for a maximum of six years while the fifth position, always held by a lawyer from one of the MERCOSUR member states, is to rotate every three years.

While the European Union and some other regional institutions, including the Central American Integration System, have been criticized for being too focused on institutional structures, MERCOSUR has been confronted with opposite charges. Some analysts have turned weakness into virtue. They have lauded the "institutional minimalism, its relative lack of legal complexity, and shared cultural background" as a source of strength in focusing on real achievements.[111] Instead of getting trapped in institutional inertia and exhausting decision-making mechanisms, MERCOSUR, one analyst argued, should be appreciated as "a study in bureaucratic minimalism."[112] MERCOSUR's lean structure would provide for more flexibility and its presidential diplomacy for less bureaucracy compared with other regional integration schemes.

The structure of decision making in MERCOSUR includes four instruments: decisions, recommendations, resolutions, and directives. The authority of decision making and normative scope in MERCOSUR stretched into the political realm after a failed coup in Paraguay in 1996: MERCOSUR reiterated an original provision of the Treaty of Asuncion according to which membership in MERCOSUR is conditional on democratic governance. MERCOSUR created the MERCOSUR Mechanism for Political Consultation and Coordination. It is defined by a "Democracy Clause" (in addition to a "Disarmament Clause"). In the absence of an intermediary consultative mechanism—leaving aside the provisions for high-level political meetings in times of a grave crisis of democracy in a MERCOSUR member state—this clause remains highly rhetorical and primarily dependent upon national politics.[113]

MERCOSUR is the product of turbulences in Latin America, and it has gone through turbulences itself in the course of the less than two decades of its existence. Felix Peña has distinguished three stages in the evolution of MERCOSUR: the founding period 1986–1991, the factual beginning of MERCOSUR and the escalation of its first serious crisis between 1991 and 1999, and a revival of MERCOSUR with new political impulses and the perspective of an eventual strengthening of MERCOSUR since 1999.[114]

Before the launching of MERCOSUR, Latin America had undergone enormous turbulence. During the 1970s, Brazil underwent a swift industrialization that made it the most competitive and productive country in Latin America's light and heavy industries, including cars, planes, and chemicals. Argentina was concentrating on its comparative advantages, mainly in the areas of processed meat, wheat, dairy products, and energy. Traditionally, Argentina had a reputation for being rather "pro–free trade," as expressed in the country's external tariff of 19 percent on average, while Brazil was known to be restrictive and protectionist with an average trade tariff of 39 percent. Paraguay was nominally restricted, but de facto liberal, not least because of the strong influence of smuggling.

The overall Latin American economic crisis between 1989 and 1993 hit Brazil and Argentina, the two biggest countries on the continent, hardest. In 1990, Argentina launched the Convertibility Plan, which pegged the country's currency, the peso, to a fixed parity with the dollar. This measure controlled inflation, improved the fiscal conditions, and increased confidence in the national currency. In 1989, the GDP in real prices between Argentina and Brazil had been 48 percent in favor of Argentina. By 1990, the gap had diminished to 5 percent. In 1991, the GDP gap was 10 percent in favor of Brazil. Inflation was the worst price Brazil had to pay: in 1993, the country faced inflation of 2,500 percent, Argentina of only 7.4 percent. A year later, in 1994, Brazil introduced the "Real Plan" with a new currency, the real, and pegged it immediately to the dollar. Inflation fell and Brazil's currency appreciated considerably against the Argentine peso. While the whole region had a large trade deficit in 1995, Brazil gained a trade surplus of $50 billion.

The economic constellation in Latin America must be seen in its political context. MERCOSUR started against the legacy of 150 years of mistrust between Brazil and Argentina. It was possible only after a century of authoritarian dictatorships in the southern part of the continent had obviously come to a close. In fact, only in the early 1980s had failed military dictatorships enabled a turnaround of the region to democracy. In the case of Argentina, this fundamental change was connected to the country's defeat in the Falklands War against Great Britain.

When MERCOSUR started, asymmetries between the partners were undeniable. Brazil represented 67 percent of the total exports of MERCOSUR, Argentina 31.5 percent, Uruguay and Paraguay together only 5.5 percent. Exchange rate fluctuations were enormous, market structures highly incoherent, and the inflation rates among MERCOSUR partners very different.[115] For the first fifteen years of its existence, MERCOSUR was struggling with the implementation of its original goals, new economic crises, and political changes of a rather substantial nature in its member states, not to mention the continuous effort to turn the project of MERCOSUR into its original ambition: the creation of a visible community in the southern cone of Latin America with an increasing political ambition and projection.

This happened, however, in a paradoxical way, after 9 December 2005, when Venezuela became a new member of MERCOSUR, a decision that was confirmed by the MERCOSUR summit in Cordoba in July 2006. Venezuela contributes energy, mainly oil, but also an unpredictable, authoritarian-populist and anti-US regime under President Hugo Chávez, who tries to portray himself as the new Simón Bolívar and the natural successor to Cuba's Fidel Castro. According to his vision, Latin America should be more socialist, more radical, and inherently anti-US. The widening of MERCOSUR membership has completely changed the nature of MERCOSUR. All of a sudden, the sober technical implementation of daunting economic norms and procedures no longer constitutes the center of MERCOSUR's efforts. Politics all of a sudden matters more than anything else. New skepticism has emerged about the wisdom of Venezuela's membership and the longer-term ambition of MERCOSUR to deepen integration.

It must be admitted, however, that the MERCOSUR summit that acknowledged Venezuela's controversial membership on 9 December 2005 also decided to establish the MERCOSUR Parliament. Its first meeting was held in December

2006 in Brasilia, with 90 representatives of the national parliaments of MERCOSUR's member states (18 representatives per country). The formal constituting session was held on 8 May 2007 in Montevideo, the designated seat of the MERCOSUR Parliament. In three stages, the MERCOSUR Parliament is intended to develop momentum, eventually leading to its direct and simultaneous election by all MERCOSUR citizens on one day in 2015 (MERCOSUR Citizen's Day).[116] To be taken seriously, the MERCOSUR Parliament will have to aim at gradually enhancing its competencies and its authority vis-à-vis MERCOSUR's member state governments.

The membership of Venezuela has had fundamental and unpredictable effects on the design and prospects of MERCOSUR. While for some, the anti-American attitude of Venezuela's President Hugo Chávez suggests that MERCOSUR could conceptualize itself as an alternative to the US-sponsored project of a Free Trade Area of the Americas, others are highly skeptical of whether MERCOSUR will even survive. Both in economic and in political terms they express worry about the inner cohesion of MERCOSUR. Others, finally, express optimism about the push Venezuela's membership might give to the idea of Latin American integration as a whole. They indicate as significant that Mexico too has expressed interest in joining MERCOSUR. Mexico's interest has been confined, however, to a concept of MERCOSUR as a Pan-American Free Trade Area, which Venezuela rejects fundamentally. It should be noted that the member states of the Andean Community of Nations (CAN), Bolivia, Colombia, Peru, and Ecuador, as well as Chile, have been associate members of MERCOSUR since 2004. It appears that MERCOSUR will live through the most defining years of its existence.

In terms of its objectives, its potential, and its instruments, it will have to deal with the relationship between "widening" and "deepening." MERCOSUR will be forced to come up with strategically important answers with long-term impact on its profile, ambition, and the way MERCOSUR is perceived. Most of all, with Venezuela as a member country, MERCOSUR will have to clarify whether it will be an instrument of regional integration or a tool for confronting the US. It spite of some concern, it seems as if Brazil, MERCOSUR's biggest country, will ensure that this alternative remains academic: Brazil simply cannot allow MERCOSUR to become mainly an anti-US instrument.

Intrinsic Motives and External Pressures

The failure of former development strategies was one of the main reasons for the emergence of MERCOSUR. State-induced, import-subsidized industrialization had led to industrialization in Latin America's biggest economies. But competitiveness was lacking, and subsequent stagnation was one of the consequences. Along with growing external debts and growing deficits throughout the 1980s, the political stability of the newly emerging democratic regimes was less than certain. Under the pressure of the escalating debt crisis, democracy began to be delegitimized as a tool for resolving the mushrooming problems of the biggest societies on the continent. Argentina needed to slow down its unilateral market opening to maintain control of the development. Brazil needed to introduce more flexibility in its trade policy in order to gain competitiveness. Under the pressure of these circumstances, a rapprochement between Brazil and Argentina became possible. In fact, it was the only solution for the domestic problems of both countries.

Two new ideas were floating around in the late 1980s: that regional integration could complement global integration into the world market and balance the US pressure under which Latin America usually operates, and that regional integration would strengthen the region and upgrade its global competitiveness.[117] The first results after the founding of MERCOSUR in 1991 were promising. In 1994, Brazil had resumed growth and was able to absorb Argentinian imports. Yet severe macroeconomic turbulences prevailed in MERCOSUR and undermined the initial hope for a new beginning through regional integration.

Regional integration in southern Latin America became possible only after the successful transition to democracy in the area. In Argentina, this cycle had begun in 1993 after its defeat in the Falklands War one year earlier. Brazil and Uruguay followed in 1985, Paraguay after the end of a decade of authoritarianism under General Alfredo Stroessner in 1989.[118] These developments were a turning point. They provided a new normative reference and an intellectual pull factor for the idea of regional integration. The Argentina-Brazil Integration Act of 1986 (Acta para la Integración Argentino-Brasilena) must be considered the embryo of MERCOSUR. It established a program for integration and cooperation and laid out the perspective for solidified integration. The specific and strong role of the two countries' presidents became evident for the first time and was evident on many occasions thereafter in top down-projects initiated by the heads of state of Brazil and Argentina. Factual economic interdependence was not considered to be a condition for regional integration in Latin America, but democratic governance was essential. The more democratic rule was to grow, the more trust among MERCOSUR partners was also to develop. The integration idea was, as can be seen from this point of view, highly political from the very outset. MERCOSUR was never substantially institutionalized, but it was always—and almost overly—politicized.[119]

Frustration about being increasingly marginalized in world affairs coincided with a convergence of economic policies across the region that considered aggregated trade a benefit for all. While global trade had increased by 9.7 percent between 1945 and 1972, Latin America's share in global trade had dropped from 13.5 percent to 4.4 percent (by 1975).[120] MERCOSUR integration was imperative in order to overcome the further decline of the region's role in the world and of the well-being of its citizens. Unfortunately, this obvious intrinsic motive and strong pull for regional integration did not prevent MERCOSUR member states from running into integration deadlock and failure. Brazil devalued its currency, the real, in 1999 without consulting its MERCOSUR partners. The devaluation had strong negative effects on Argentina because its goods lost much of their competitiveness when Brazilian goods became cheaper. Argentina reacted with retaliatory measures, which is unusual for partners in an integration project. Brazil withdrew its participation from MERCOSUR until Argentina's President Fernando De la Rúa had taken office at the end of 1999 and helped to ease the tension. In turn, Argentina's financial and economic crisis of 2002 was a disaster for the whole region and the MERCOSUR process. Argentina itself suspended MERCOSUR's common external tariff. Moreover, it lost much of its credibility as a viable economic partner. Only since 2003—with President Nestor Kirchner in office in Buenos Aires and Brazil's President Luiz Inácio Lula da Silva governing its neighboring state since October 2002—has MERCOSUR been rescued from agony and been given a new chance to revitalize its ambition and potential. In reality, nothing has substantially altered since Venezuela joined MERCOSUR in 2006.

Performance

Although MERCOSUR has not finally decided upon its political goals and ambitions, strong and weak points in its period of existence are noticeable. Among the positive experiences of MERCOSUR are:

(1) Intra-regional trade, a key indicator for economic integration, increased from 8.8 percent among the newly emerging MERCOSUR partners in 1990 to 20.5 percent in 2000—followed, however, by a sharp drop to 11.3 percent in 2002 as a consequence of the economic crisis in Argentina. In 2003, exports of MERCO-SUR partners to Argentina increased again by 90 percent, but the experience showed the volatility of the overall economic constellation in MERCOSUR.[121] Yet long-term benefits of regional integration have become evident across MERCOSUR, and "the growing potential for gains from regional exchange has created a powerful lobby in the private sector for deeper integration."[122] It is interesting to look in more detail at the importance of intra-regional trade for all MERCOSUR member states: for Argentina, intra-regional trade covers 36.2 percent of its total trade, for Brazil 17.1 percent, for Paraguay 60.9 percent, and for Uruguay 49.7 percent.[123] MERCOSUR confirms the hypothesis that regional integration depends upon the biggest actors in a region but is most beneficial for the smaller participants.

Much of MERCOSUR's intra-regional trade could also be described as inter-industry trade on a regional level. Companies are swapping products or components of products across the region. For 1995, the estimate of Argentina's share in inter-industry trade as part of its overall intra-regional trade was 50 percent; for Brazil it was 85 percent.[124] Regardless of such hairsplitting details (which are of no relevance for economists anyway), regional integration has turned out to be beneficial for the region's economy as it provides it with a larger market for production, labor, and consumption. The increase of intra-regional merger and acquisition operations indicates the same trend. Cross-border transactions during the first decade of MERCOSUR constituted 18 percent of all merger and acquisition operations in the region.

(2) In terms of MERCOSUR solidifying its reputation, it helped that foreign direct investment increased visibly during the first years of its existence. MERCOSUR's jump in foreign direct investment from $2.8 billion in 1990 to $32.5 billion in 1998 helped to put the subsequent effects of the Argentinean crisis into clearer perspective. The free movement of goods covers 90 percent of all intra-MERCOSUR trade of around 9,000 products. The exceptions are telling as far as national economic interests are concerned. While MERCOSUR was never free from disputes among its member states over free trade issues, the overall advantage of regional cooperation and integration has gradually helped to draw institutional conclusions for deeper integration. In 2002, with the signing of the Protocol of Olivos, MERCOSUR introduced a dispute settlement scheme and established the MERCOSUR Permanent Court of Review in Asuncion, along with a Mercosur Center for Promoting the Rule of Law. Although these structures have remained rather weak, they constitute the nucleus of a judiciary review component, which is helpful in strengthening the idea of a MERCOSUR Court of Justice and the overall acceptance of good governance under conditions of a solid rule of law. In 2003, Brazil was the last MERCOSUR member state to ratify the Protocol of Olivos.

(3) MERCOSUR leaders are aware of the fragility of democracy and the rule of law in their region. Since 1996, MERCOSUR partners have pressured Paraguay twice not to return to military rule. The presidential declaration concerning democratic rule in MERCOSUR cannot have any binding effect on those who might consider the idea of a coup d'état. But a certain moment of deterrence cannot be denied, while MERCOSUR as an institution is enhancing its credibility by linking the future of regional integration to that of democratic rule in the region.

MERCOSUR's failings are not few. The initial positive trend was immediately counterbalanced by the structural deficits of MERCOSUR. MERCOSUR rules do not constitute a community law *strictu sensu*.[125] The supremacy of national lawmaking prevails, and no judicial entity of a solid nature exists so far. This corresponds with the general lack of strong institutions in MERCOSUR and the unpredictability of political will, exacerbated by the absence of any supranational mechanism to maintain community-building efforts in moments of crisis and in terms of integration. The decision of the MERCOSUR summit of 9 December

2005 to establish the MERCOSUR Parliament after 2007 can be considered
a promising signal, although only real implementation of the idea—not realistic before 2011—will prove the sincerity of the political leadership across
MERCOSUR. To MERCOSUR's credit—and to put the Latin American integration experience into historical and comparative perspective—one must add
that European integration was not much more advanced following the two decades after the original Treaties of Rome. It will, however, not serve the cause of
regional integration in MERCOSUR to shy away from its inherent deficits by
only comparing MERCOSUR with the track record of the European integration
experience, which has been mixed indeed.

Just as lamentable as the absence of judiciary mechanisms and strong institutions is the weak implementation mechanism for decisions. It is an honest ges-
ture of the MERCOSUR Secretariat to publish the list of incorporated norms
on its Web page, but the simple fact that too many exceptions to free trade are
allowed in the first place has had problematic consequences over time. Instead
of decreasing gradually, non-tariff barriers increased from 285, at the time of
the Protocol of Ouro Preto in 1994, to 350 only five years later.[126] It must be
added that the record of transposing MERCOSUR decisions into national law
is even weaker than the system of secondary lawmaking itself: of 1,128 norms
issued by MERCOSUR's decision-making bodies between 1991 and 2000,
only 254 (34 percent) of them have been translated into domestic law in all four
MERCOSUR member states.[127] Even more uncomfortable for MERCOSUR
should be the prevailing lack of coordination of the macroeconomic policies
of its member states. MERCOSUR has established a Macroeconomic Monitor
Group that continuously reaffirms MERCOSUR's commitment to fiscal discipline and its stability targets, which echo the provisions of the EU (5 percent
inflation rate, with public debt dropping to 4 percent by 2010). But the overall
sensitivity among policy makers and even the public discourse in MERCOSUR
remains weak as far as the urgency and relevance of these criteria are concerned.

It can therefore come as no surprise that recurring proposals to establish a common currency in MERCOSUR are not really taken seriously across the community.
In May 2003, for instance, the Argentine government proposed the establishment
of a single currency between Brazil's real and its own peso and a new currency band
for future trade and tourism operations. Hardly any debate occurred over this idea.
Since then, a positive step in support of regional convergence has begun with the
creation of a MERCOSUR Convergence Fund of $100 million in support of the
less developed and weaker small MERCOSUR countries.

For the time being, MERCOSUR has been living under the shadow of failure.
Setbacks and crises since 1991 must lead to the conclusion that crises *of* integration remain as serious a problem for MERCOSUR as crises *in* integration.[128] In
the absence of a clearly defined political project, MERCOSUR seems to walk in-
crementally through crises and difficulties, making qualitative steps in economic

integration difficult. Optimists see the first projects of the MERCOSUR Convergence Fund (Fondo para la Convergencia Estructural del MERCOSUR) as a promising alternative path that was launched in 2007. All in all, however, the region remains overly entangled in bilateral trade relations, including the continuous debate about the advantages and shortcomings of the Free Trade Agreement of the Americas. MERCOSUR oscillates between a real hope, an imagined community, and a lasting expression of stagnation. As long as national interests are not properly bound together and each country tries to only benefit from its own potential rather than also adding the dimension of a common value added, MERCOSUR remains uncertain of itself. Argentina tends to look regularly across the Andean mountains to study the Chilean economic performance and hopes to benefit, as its Western neighbor does, from bilateral free trade agreements as the gateway to the global economy. Brazil, in turn, often follows a rather aggressive policy in order to prevent too much dependency on the MERCOSUR partners. It has explicitly rejected the idea of a MERCOSUR bank, opted against aid to Argentina when its partner was in the most depressing of crises, and opposed the cheap manufacture of clothes ("maquila") in Paraguay, the poorest and most vulnerable of all MERCOSUR partners.[129]

Like other regional integration schemes in Latin America, MERCOSUR provides analysts with no transparency about its institutional budget. Citizens' participation in MERCOSUR activities has been, at least so far, invisible, and the implementation of important infrastructure projects is overly slow. The plan for a highway between São Paulo and Buenos Aires is outlined for thirty-five years from 1995 until 2030, including the construction of a 28-mile bridge to Uruguay.[130] It cannot be denied that MERCOSUR lost focus in the late 1990s. It became too unspecific, too vague, and too politicized without becoming goal-oriented. Deplorable was the "scant interaction" between MERCOSUR's agenda and the national political and economic agendas.[131] Most troubling, however, was the inconclusive enlargement of MERCOSUR in December 2005. It remains to be seen how far Venezuela, under its radical President Hugo Chávez, will truly give a "Bolivarian" boost to MERCOSUR or will rather derail the integration process because of the political radicalization introduced by Chávez.

Federators

Improved relations between Argentina and Brazil in the mid 1980s, and a gradual convergence of political regimes in the region, helped to prepare for the Treaty of Asuncion (26 March 1991). Although Argentina and Brazil cover 80 percent of all MERCOSUR trade—out of which 60 percent is transacted via lorry trucks—the main reason for the rapprochement between the two big countries in Latin America was political. Argentina and Brazil became the engines of regional integration, but they became engines only once they had embraced democracy and the rule of law at home. MERCOSUR refers regularly to the European integration experience without explicitly outlining the similarities and differences.

Argentina and Brazil have only very cautiously begun to utilize their positions as the two biggest MERCOSUR countries for joint initiatives. In 2006, they launched a plan to bring academic studies in both countries closer and to harmonize curricula, degrees, and quality criteria aiming to bring about a MERCOSUR University. In light of the rapid speed of integration elsewhere, this seems to be a suboptimal contribution to turn MERCOSUR from a good project into a living reality that includes viable institutions, binding legal rules, and civil society involvement.

Whenever its path got stuck, the fear of complete marginalization has inspired MERCOSUR. Several times, the fear of marginalization has helped to overcome crises of, as well as crises in, MERCOSUR integration. The experience of crisis has been present in MERCOSUR since its founding days; indeed, the threat of crisis and the inspiration by crisis have often gone hand in hand and have sometimes even become indistinguishable. Most important, however, has been the fear of a return to authoritarian or military rule. MERCOSUR could never serve as a perfect insurance policy against the destruction of democracy, but it has developed its own political authority as an expression of postdictatorial conditions of governance in Latin America. Since Venezuela gained membership in 2005, this consensus has obviously eroded. The "Bolivarian radicalism" introduced by Venezuela into MERCOSUR sheds unavoidable light on the fragility and diversity of democratic models in Latin America in the early twenty-first century. None of the member states of MERCOSUR would accept being labeled as non-democratic. But all of them practice such different types of democracy that one can only wonder about the validity of using the term any longer in order to analyze political realities in the region. One might also start wondering about the democratic inspiration and claim of MERCOSUR.

Transformations

In spite of all shortcomings und uncertainties, some transformations that have occurred during the first one and half decades of MERCOSUR integration are remarkable, as they indicate this regional integration scheme's adaptability to new challenges and opportunities. Starting from cautious sectoral trade liberalization agreements in 1986, MERCOSUR began as a wide-ranging trade liberalization program in 1991. By then, the national objectives among the founding members of MERCOSUR had converged and liberalization of markets was considered the right path for dealing with the respective national problem of economic stagnation. Argentina came to this conclusion in 1989, Brazil in 1991. The main decisions to liberalize trade in the region were hence already taken before the formal initiation of MERCOSUR, a pattern not atypical for regional integration: only rarely do political decisions advance in concert with regional integration; more often it is likely that politicians choose the cautious way and formalize trends that have become evident.

After the negative growth rates between 1998 and 2002, a veritable sense of urgency grew in MERCOSUR. The changes of political leadership in the two biggest MERCOSUR countries between October 2002 and May 2005 helped to promote new impulses for regional integration as part of the solution. Immediately after assuming their respective offices, President Lula da Silva and President Kirchner announced explicit political projects in order to give new dynamics to the idea of regional integration. They prioritized regional integration, tried to boost serious market liberalization, and advanced political projects with long-term implications. In mid 2003, President Lula da Silva presented his "Target 2006 Plan," which included the proposition to create the MERCOSUR Parliament, a MERCOSUR citizenship, enhanced cultural cooperation among MERCOSUR countries, a common external negotiation structure, common measures for anti-dumping protection, and a MERCOSUR foreign policy. Argentina's President Kirchner proposed a MERCOSUR Monetary Institute as the foundation for the development of monetary union.

Many of these presidential propositions were included in the decisions of the IVth Extraordinary Meeting of the MERCOSUR Common Market Council on 6 October 2003. Further measures were added to these decisions aimed at solidifying the basis for a common market, such as the liberalization of services, the development of a regional capital market, the promotion of regional investment, and the evaluation of the basis for a common currency. As a first concrete step to strengthen MERCOSUR's institutional base, the MERCOSUR Committee of Permanent Representatives was established, drawing from a structurally similar experience in the European Union. In light of the usual time it takes to advance and implement European integration projects, one should not be surprised that the presidential initiatives in MERCOSUR were not immediately turned into reality. But they have become part of the MERCOSUR discourse and its decision-making process. As usual in MERCOSUR, it will take time to implement top-down decisions. Even though they seem to reflect consensus among political elites, connecting such decisions with the real development of the respective political systems and the societies behind them tends to take a long time. From the outside, one might get a wrong impression about the relevance and function of presidential initiatives in MERCOSUR countries. This also holds true for ambivalent decisions, such as the one of December 2005 to welcome Venezuela under its unpredictable and radical President Hugo Chávez as a new MERCOSUR member.

The improvement of the image of the Latin American region gave MERCO-SUR's political leaders after 2003 an additional incentive to develop a certain sense of ownership in the regional integration project. Argentina and Brazil had

successfully overcome internal crises and failure. They had hindered their partner country Paraguay from returning to military rule. Now they wanted to demonstrate the logic of democratic regionalism: their presidents introduced a set of
ideas and initiatives that indicated the long-term readiness to get involved and
stay committed to regional integration, even if no immediate implementation of
a "grand design" was likely.

In intervals, integration and cooperation in the MERCOSUR region echo
reference to a historical region. As much as this is plausible regarding the geographical location of the River Plate Basin—the area through which the Parana,
the Paraguay, and the Uruguay rivers flow along the borders of the core countries
forming MERCOSUR—this invocation of history is highly ambivalent. Between
1864 and 1870, the "War of Triple Alliance" between Argentina, Uruguay, and
Brazil prevented Paraguay from reaching the Atlantic Ocean. The war deci-
mated Paraguay's population by two thirds and led to the country's partition. For
the next hundred years after this war, no significant trade integration took place
in the region. Only since the 1960s has regional trade become a respectable idea
and a recognized asset again. Allusions to the region's history could, therefore,
only be interpreted as counterfactual invocations of the need to do better than
those who lived in the River Plate Basin a century earlier.

Role and Interests of the European Union

The European Economic Community began its cooperation with Argentina in
1963 through a Cooperation Agreement, and with Brazil in the context of a controversial debate about the country's right to the peaceful use of nuclear energy in
1965. This was followed by non-preferential trade agreements with Argentina in
1971, and Uruguay and Brazil in 1973. When Argentina and Great Britain went
to war over the Falkland Islands in 1982, the European Community imposed
collective sanctions against Argentina and condemned the Falkland occupation.
But EC unity on the matter did not last much longer than two weeks, although
all partners agreed in their preference for democratic rule across Latin America.

When Spain and Portugal joined the European Community in 1986, the outlook toward Latin America was enhanced. The establishment of MERCOSUR-
EU relations benefited from the growth in understanding, contact, and affinity.
The basis of this trend was not only cultural ties but also shared values, with
Latin America returning to democratic rule in the 1980s, and common interests, particularly the desire to improve economic cooperation as part of the
growing globalization. Immediately after MERCOSUR was founded in 1991,
an Inter-Institutional Cooperation Agreement between the MERCOSUR
Council and the European Union Commission was signed on 29 May 1992.
The EU Council summit in Essen in 1994 started the negotiation of an inter-
regional agreement with MERCOSUR, "a significant shift in policy" for the

EU.[132] The EU had seemingly found its beloved partner, if not potential alter ego, in Latin America.

On 15 December 1995, an Inter-regional Framework Cooperation Agreement was signed between the European Union and MERCOSUR. As clumsy and bureaucratic as this title sounded, it constituted a new dimension in the global projection of the European Union and its normative interests: the EU was expressing its proactive support for regional integration in MERCOSUR. The objective was to promote integration among democratic countries and encourage them to reflect on the European integration experience, if not to emulate and apply it. The EU-MERCOSUR agreement included a clause on political dialogue, underlining that the European Union was taking MERCOSUR seriously as a political partner in the common search for contributions to world order–building in the post–Cold War context.

With its support for regional integration in MERCOSUR the EU got involved, and not only in a declaratory way. In 2006, the following projects in support of regional integration in MERCOSUR received financial contributions from the European Union:

- Institutional support was given to various MERCOSUR bodies, including to its Secretariat (€900,000), the Joint Parliamentary Committee (€917,175), the Economic and Social Consultative Forum (€950,000) and the Permanent Dispute Settlement Court (€310,000).
- MERCOSUR's customs harmonization projects received EU support in the amount of €5.3 million.
- The development and harmonization of technical norms and standards in MERCOSUR was supported with €3,950,000, statistical harmonization with €4,135,000, and macroeconomic harmonization measures with €7,100,000.[133]

In 1999, MERCOSUR and the European Union entered into a new dimension of their relationship. They began to negotiate a Regional Association Agreement, meant to be the first of its kind in the world among two democratic economic and political communities above the nation-state level. The process of negotiation turned out to be a component of educative region-building. But soon, it also encountered the limits of each partner's readiness to give up specific interests for the sake of a global experiment.[134] In the autumn of 2005, the EU-MERCOSUR negotiations were temporarily suspended. After a year of soul-searching, their resumption in November 2006 was clouded by EU frustration over the lack of commitment by its MERCOSUR partners. No result was expected before a successful conclusion of the Doha Round on world trade.

The main impulse behind the enhanced cooperation and structured process of biregional architecture-building is political. From a purely economic point of view, MERCOSUR is not overly important to the European Union. While 50.9

percent of all EU exports to Latin America go to MERCOSUR—a significant increase from 34 percent in 1990—and MERCOSUR receives two thirds of all EU investments in Latin America (compared with 40 percent in 1990), the overall European investment in MERCOSUR constitutes no more than 3.51 percent of the total EU outward foreign direct investment. MERCOSUR represents 2.8 percent of total EU imports and 1.8 percent of total EU exports (2003 figures). Although investment and trade have increased since the founding of MERCOSUR, the main interest of the European Union in Latin America, and in MERCOSUR in particular, is strategic.

It is not only driven by competition with the United States, although this dimension can never be underestimated in the triangular relationship between the old world and the two continents of the new world.[135] The European Union is certainly aware that its direct investment in MERCOSUR increased fivefold alone during the first decade of MERCOSUR's existence, while the share of the US in direct investment to the MERCOSUR region decreased from 51 to 40 percent.[136] The more the United States focused on the implementation of NAFTA with its partners Canada and Mexico, the more the European Union revitalized its economic ties to the other regions of Latin America. The competitive nature of the transatlantic triangle needs to be taken into account. Yet the European Union, going beyond a simplistic component of competitiveness, tends to be careful not to embark on relations with Latin America as a function of anti-(North) Americanism. The European Union is promoting regional integration and multilateralism as one of the cornerstones of its role in the world. Sometimes, as critics argue, it seems as if the EU is promoting regional integration as a value in itself without giving due attention to the current problems of a certain country or region. This criticism is debatable. In any case, regional architecture-building has to be understood as a genuine and normative EU foreign policy goal, intended to diversify and multiply the regional actors and global factors of stability. The EU's role and interest in MERCOSUR and its development is a case in point of this strategic orientation.

Prospects and Obstacles

MERCOSUR's biggest deficit is the uncertainty about the political profile and prospect of the integration scheme. Since its inception in 1991, MERCOSUR has projected itself as a contribution to community-building by economic means. But community-building cannot take place without political regulations and aspirations. For many years, consensus about democratic rule as the basic cornerstone of MERCOSUR has provided one partial answer. This foundation of MERCOSUR has been assessed and tested favorably. It is not to say that MERCOSUR will forever be risk-averse or that its member states could never fall back into one form of authoritarian rule or another. The inclusion of Venezuela in December

2005 has again, through the back door of community enlargement, focused attention on this issue. The democratic credibility and authority of MERCO-SUR will be weakened, not least because of the enormous diversity of concepts and realities of democratic rule practiced in the region. MERCOSUR will always project itself as a community of democratic regimes under the rule of law. In reality, however, MERCOSUR has become a community held together by completely divergent, if not mutually exclusive, concepts of democracy and overly problematic interpretations of the rule of law. Authoritarian populism, parliamentary democracy, leanings toward economic socialism, and notions of politico-economic equality have defused the comprehensive understanding and the application of democratic rule in MERCOSUR. Its diversity has helped MERCOSUR to maintain unity because, at least so far, the purpose and objective of this unity has not yet been properly defined.

This is the real challenge for MERCOSUR: defining community-goals, gradually providing the appropriate instruments, and consistently organizing a political will and the mechanisms to properly implement them. MERCOSUR will need to move ahead and grow from the ambition of a common market into a broad political community—or it will remain in danger of becoming a victim of stagnation, inertia, and a new form of marginalization. MERCOSUR's member states have felt the effect of being at the periphery of their continent, "the Western world," and the global economy. If MERCOSUR were to continue only as a creeping effort to establish a common market, it would undermine its own potential as a community of political profile. But MERCOSUR must ultimately become explicit about its ambition. Will it become an economic alternative to the Free Trade Agreement of the Americas and therefore political, as an anti-US economic forum? Does it aspire to be the nucleus of pan–Latin American integration, following the Bolivarian dream and remaining revolutionary in spirit but rhetorical in action? MERCOSUR must address the question of whether it wants to be more of a movement or gradually become a rather stable institutionalized political community. Looking at the European integration experience, it is only fair to say that a comprehensive answer to these questions and related queries might take years, if not decades. Certainly Europe, in the sixth decade of integration, is still in the process of searching.

One lesson, however, should by now have been learned by all MERCOSUR member states: none of them can go it alone and return to economic and political protectionism. Brazil is two and half times larger than Argentina and three times larger than the whole Andean Community (CAN). Although the "rest" of MERCOSUR has only 39 percent of Brazil's population and 44 percent of Brazil's GDP, it is unlikely that Brazil will be able to resolve its own domestic problems and the social marginalization of many of its citizens in particular. After all, per capita income in Brazil is only 37 percent of MERCOSUR's average.[137] To understand that regional integration is a win-win situation for all participating countries and societies might not be the most attractive political idea floating in Latin America, but this idea is developing. While Latin American countries are beginning to understand the limits of national sovereignty in its economic and social context, and even in its political reality, they will need more time to overcome the intuitive reference to the gigantean dreams of continental integration whenever they refer to the vision of regional integration. As much as Bolivar failed in his own time, continental integration driven by rhetoric, anti-US attitudes, and myopic parochialism would fail today. Instead of resorting to the allusion of a viable and fully integrated Latin American Community, the political leaders of the continent would be well advised to improve and sustain the existing structures of regional integration.

As for MERCOSUR, a reassessment is warranted of the potential and prospect for using a market economy as a tool to advance political community-building. MERCOSUR must jump to develop into a real common market, or it will fail to even make the best out of its existing potential. The prospect of a common currency might still be far away, but it is interesting to note that the debate about this goal has begun after all. Some optimists consider the creation of a common MERCOSUR currency feasible by 2015.[138] Considering the European integration experience, one should probably view this notion with more caution. From the Treaties of Rome to the full introduction of the euro, forty-five years elapsed. MERCOSUR will reach that age in 2036. Should it by then operate on the basis of a single currency, it would be a tremendous success story, still unthinkable for most analysts and political actors before the completion of the second decade of MERCOSUR's existence. For the time being, the skeptics see "dollarization" as a legitimate, and perhaps inevitable, alternative to monetary integration in MERCOSUR.[139]

The prospect of a common MERCOSUR currency is not altogether absurd. Debate in the region about a currency union began with a newspaper article on 8 April 1997 in the Brazilian newspaper *Estado de Sao Paulo*. It summarized an academic argument in favor of MERCOSUR currency union advanced by Fabio Giambiagi, an economist. The subsequent political career of the idea was striking. After the article had been mentioned by Argentina's then President Carlos Menem in a press interview of 27 April 1997, it was included on the MERCOSUR diplomatic agenda. In June 1998, the Argentinean government organized an international seminar dealing with the idea and its potential for realization. Among MERCOSUR officials, the idea of a MERCOSUR currency union was discussed informally.

Giambiagi's argument was straightforward. The Free Trade Agreement between MERCOSUR and the US is a challenge for MERCOSUR to harmonize internally. Incomplete integration would lead to permanent inconsistencies, a lack of credibility, asymmetric shock effects, and finally the undermining of MERCOSUR's market cohesion. Success would be a matter of applying the right logic for the necessary steps to reach the goal, but one market would need one currency. Among the necessary preconditions for a currency union mentioned by Giambiagi were: freedom of labor, a high level of intra-regional trade, labor market flexibility, macroeconomic convergence, and a clear timetable to implement a work agenda. One regional bank would reduce MERCOSUR's exchange rate risk. Should MERCOSUR achieve a currency union, based on a completed customs union and the necessary macroeconomic and statistical harmonization, it would be highly advantageous compared with the alternative, that is, "dollarization" of MERCOSUR. "Dollarization" would not be able to absorb real shocks stemming from the economic conditions in MERCOSUR, it would not provide a lender of last resort, and it would lack the political support to make it a lastingly beneficial prospect for MERCOSUR.[140]

Meanwhile, the development of a MERCOSUR community law has been a vision in MERCOSUR for a long time. Some believe that a community law already exists and simply ought to be deepened and developed over time.[141] Others refer to the constitutional limits in MERCOSUR member states when it comes to a transfer of sovereignty to a supranational entity. Paraguay's 1992 constitution and Argentine's 1994 constitution grant international treaties supremacy over national law and establish the readiness to delegate powers to supranational organizations. Brazil and Uruguay do not have constitutional provisions that would allow the transfer of sovereignty to supranational law or institutions.[142]

Two disputes between Argentina and Brazil in the late 1990s helped to give some impulse to the arbitration setting in MERCOSUR. The issue was whether or not a communication from the Brazilian Foreign Commerce Secretariat was unduly restricting cross-border trade through a series of classification schemes. Argentina, the plaintiff in these cases, which came to be known as LAUDO I and LAUDO II, claimed that 61 percent of its exports were impacted in an unfair way by the Brazilian scheme, thus undermining the very logic of MERCOSUR. The MERCOSUR arbitration panel debated whether or not this case was a violation of the Treaty of Asuncion. It came to the somewhat Solomon-like conclusion that Brazil was not guilty, but was nevertheless obliged to eliminate trade restrictions that might exist in violation of the Treaty of Asuncion.[143] One is reminded of the gradual evolution of European community law during the 1960s: At the time of the *Van Gend en Loos* case, it was in no way certain that the European Court of Justice could ever claim, let alone exercise, primacy over national jurisdiction. This 1963 case led to the conclusion of the European Court of Justice that Article 12 of the Treaty of the European Economic Community had direct effects on citizens and therefore created individual rights that national courts must protect, and that, should the national courts not protect these rights in an appropriate way, the citizens ought to have the right to rely on the ruling of the European Court of Justice. Who can exclude that the evolution of community law in MERCOSUR might take a path similar to that of Europe, where the Court of Justice has increasingly become an engine and guarantee for deeper integration?

MERCOSUR's dispute resolution mechanism has become institutionalized with the establishment of the MERCOSUR Permanent Court of Review in Asuncion. This court remains oriented "around the resolution of disputes through adjudication rather than negotiation."[144] Based on the Protocol of Olivos (18 February 2002), the MERCOSUR Permanent Court of Review is the nucleus of institutionalized community-law evolution.[145] One cannot expect it to be of a miraculous nature. But it would also be unfair to renounce its potential before it has even properly begun to work or become able to broaden its sphere of action.[146] The mechanism for implementing secondary law in MERCOSUR has to be strengthened, probably by some sort of monitoring. MERCOSUR must advance in the area of its rules relevant for trading in services if it aims to establish a viable common market. In the area of sanitary and phytosanitary matters, one analyst has argued, 37 norms exist, "but they do not really harmonize anything; they amount to little more than a list of measures."[147] The main deficit of MERCOSUR is related to the strong role of presidents in the national political systems. They serve as the embodiment of sovereignty and tend to be more vocal and powerful than established norms of law. As much as this is an inherent problem of democratic governance in Latin America, it is also an obstacle to swift progress in creating supranationality in MERCOSUR in those fields that are critical for its success: politics and lawmaking.

MERCOSUR is in need of a new agenda and focus. The paradox is that at this time, such an agenda could only be provided by its member state presidents, who have limited aspirations for MERCOSUR if it implies a reduction in their own role and power. A stronger involvement of national parliaments and an upgrading of the functions of the Parliamentary Assembly of MERCOSUR, increased powers of the Common Market Council, a reinforced role of MERCOSUR's Secretariat, initiatives to make better use of the private sector and to enhance the participation of civil society, a common project with broad public appeal, and last but not least, the formulation of a new constitutional treaty for MERCOSUR: this list of proposals to deepen regional integration in MERCOSUR and to turn simmering integration activities into a vibrant integration reality underlines the potential of MERCOSUR. As long as its political leaders do not grasp the opportunity, they are the biggest obstacle to real regional integration in MERCOSUR.

Notes

1. Giannis F. Papageorgiou, *The Regional Integration Process of Central America*, The Federalist Debate: Papers for Federalists in Europe and in the World, no. 3 (Turin: The Einstein Center for International Studies, 2001), 26.
2. Bernd Gallep, "Der zentralamerikanische Integrationsprozess: Probleme und Scheinprobleme," *KAS-Auslandsinformationen* 10 (2005), 30.

3. The Economist, 29 October 2005, 63.
4. H. Roberto Herrera Cáceres, *Imperio del Derecho y Desarrollo de los Pueblos* (Tegucigalpa: Litografía Lopez, 2003); Enrique Ulate Chacón, "Naturaleza Juridica de las Comunidades Europeas y la Comunidad Centroamericana," in Arnoldo Rubio Ríos (ed.), *Estudios Europeos y Integración Regional* (San Juan: Universidad Nacional, 2005), 119–164.
5. Arnoldo Rubio Ríos, "El Mercado Común Centroamericano, la Integración y la Union Europea: Tres Ejes complementarios?" in Rubio Ríos, *Estudios Europeos y Integración Regional*, 171.
6. Central American Economic Integration Secretariat (SIECA), *General Treaty on Central American Economic Integration* (13.12.1960), online at: http://www.sieca.org.gt/site/VisorDocs.aspx?l DDOC=CacheING/17990000000005/17990000000005.swf.
7. Papageorgiou, "The Regional Integration Process of Central America," 27.
8. In June 1969, Honduras had begun to reverse its tolerance policy against the 300,000 campesinos from El Salvador living in Honduras. When the team of Honduras lost a soccer game in El Salvador (the semifinal qualification for the world soccer tournament) and Honduran fans were beaten, Honduras stepped up the expulsion of the campesinos on its soil. Eventually El Salvador attacked its neighbor but lost, after a war of only a hundred hours, leaving several thousand people dead on both sides. More than 100,000 people became refugees, and half of El Salvador's oil refining and storage facilities were destroyed. See for details William Durham, *Scarcity and Survival in Central America: Ecological Origins of the Soccer War* (Stanford: Stanford University Press, 1979).
9. Rubio Ríos, "El Mercado Común Centroamericano," 173.
10. Central American Integration System (SICA), *Tegucigalpa Protocol to the Charter of the Organization of Central American States* (13.12.1991), online at: http://www.sica.int/busqueda/centro%20de%20 documentaci%C3%B3n.aspx?IdItem=372&IdCat=8&IdEnt=1.
11. See Ulate Chacón, "Naturaleza Juridica," 144.
12. See Shelton Nicholls et al., "Open Regionalism and Institutional Development among Smaller Integration Schemes of CARICOM, the Andean Community and the Central American Market," in Viktor Bulmer-Thomas (ed.), *Regional Integration in Latin America and the Caribbean* (London: University of London Institute of Latin American Studies, 2001), 141–164, especially 149–152; Bernd Gallep, "Der zentralamerikanische Integrationsprozess," 62.
13. Central American Court of Justice (CACJ), *Convention on the Statute of the Central American Court of Justice* (10.12.1992), in United Nations Treaty Series, Vol. 1821, No. I-31191 (New York: United Nations, 1994), 292–303, online at: http://untreaty.un.org/unts/60001_120000/29/32/00057577 .pdf.
14. For details see Martin Zimmek, *Integrationsprozesse in Lateinamerika: Aktuelle Herausforderungen in Mittelamerika und der Andenregion*, ZEI Discussion Paper C 153 (Bonn: Center for European Integration Studies, 2005).
15. Cited in Ulate Chacón, "Naturaleza Juridica," 149.
16. See Herrera Cáceres, *Imperio del Derecho*, 365.
17. For an in-depth analysis see Ulate Chacón, "Naturaleza Juridica," 119–164, especially 126–134.
18. See Juan José Taccone and Uziel Nogueira (eds.), *Central American Report No.2* (Buenos Aires: Institute for the Integration of Latin America and the Caribbean, 2004), 4, online at: http://www. iadb.org/intal/aplicaciones/uploads/publicaciones/i-Central_American_Report_2.pdf.
19. Ayhan M. Kose and Alessandro Rebucci, "How Might CAFTA Change Macroeconomic Fluctuations in Central America? Lessons from NAFTA," *Journal of Asian Economics* 16, no. 1 (2005): 77–104, 89.
20. Rafael Sánchez, "Rebuilding the Central American Bloc in the 1990s: An Intergovernmentalist Approach to Integration," in Finn Laursen (ed.), *Comparative Regional Integration: Theoretical Perspectives* (Aldershot: Ashgate, 2003), 31–52, 39.
21. See Edgar Chamorro Marin, *La Perspectiva Economica de la Integración Centroamericana* (Guatemala City: SIECA, 2005), 14.

22. See Taccone and Nogueira, *Central American Report 2004*, 10.

23. For details see Gallep, "Der zentralamerikanische Integrationsprozess," 46.

24. Papageorgiou, "The Regional Integration Process of Central America," 28; see also Herrera Cáceres, *Imperio del Derecho*, 52.

25. Sánchez, "Rebuilding the Central American Bloc," 45.

26. See Alvaro de la Ossa, *Der zentralamerikanische Integrationsprozess: Ende einer Entwicklungsalternative*, IBERO-Analysen 6 (Berlin: Ibero-Amerikanisches Institut Stiftung Preußischer Kulturbesitz, 2000), 17, online at: http://www.iai.spk-berlin.de/fileadmin/dokumentenbibliothek/Ibero-Analysen/Ibero-Analysen%20Heft%206.pdf .

27. See Nicholls et al., "Open Regionalism," 162–167; Gallep, "Der zentralamerikanische Integrationsprozess," 62.

28. Nicholls et al., "Open Regionalism," 158.

29. According to PARLACEN President Fabio Gadea in personal conversation, Managua, 22 September 2005.

30. Particularly spectacular were the cases of former Nicaraguan President Arnoldo Aleman and former Guatemalan President Alfonso Portillo. In the end PARLACEN membership could not protect Aleman from being sentenced in 2003 to twenty years of house arrest and a fine of $17 million on charges of corruption. Portillo fled in 2004 to Mexico, from where he was not extradited.

31. Chamorro Marin, *La Perspectiva Economica*, 9.

32. Taccone and Nogueira, *Central American Report 2004*, 41.

33. Herrera Cáceres, *Imperio del Derecho*, 53.

34. Ibid., 91–130; Central American Integration System (SICA), *Framework Treaty on Democratic Security in Central America* (15.12.1995), online at: http://untreaty.un.org/unts/120001_144071/22/9/00018606.pdf.

35. For details see the home page of the European Commission under http://www.ec.europa.eu.

36. For details of this interpretation see Rubio Ríos, "El Mercado Comun Centroamericano," 178–182.

37. See Taccone and Nogueira, *Central American Report 2004*, 27.

38. See Mechthild Minkner-Bünjer, "Zentralamerikas 'China(alb)träume': Herausforderungen und Zukunftsaussichten," *Brennpunkt Lateinamerika* 17 (2005), 199.

39. See Robert Devlin and Ricardo Ffrench-Davis, *Toward an Evaluation of Regional Integration in Latin America in the 1990s*, INTAL/ITD Working Paper 2 (Buenos Aires: Institute for the Integration of Latin America and the Caribbean, 1998).

40. See Markus Rodlauer and Alfred Schipke (eds.), *Central America: Global Integration and Regional Cooperation* (Washington, D.C.: International Monetary Fund, 2005).

Andean Community of Nations (Comunidad Andina de Naciones, CAN)

41. Andean Community (CAN), *Andean Subregional Integration Agreement (Cartagena Agreement)* (26.05.1969), online at: http://www.comunidadandina.org/ingles/treaties/trea/ande_trie1.htm.

42. See Walter Mattli, *The Logic of Regional Integration: Europe and Beyond* (Cambridge and New York: Cambridge University Press, 1999), 148.

43. See Claudia Mutschler, "Comparative International Experience: Latin America," in Christopher Clapham et al. (eds.), *Regional Integration in Southern Africa: Comparative International Perspectives* (Johannesburg: South African Institute of International Affairs, 2001), 137–165; Shelton Nicholls et al., "Open Regionalism and Institutional Developments among the Smaller Integration Schemes of CARICOM, the Andean Community and the Central American Common Market," in Victor Bulmer-Thomas (ed.), *Regional Integration in Latin America and the Caribbean* (London: University of London Institute of Latin American Studies, 2001), 141–164.

44. Mattli, *The Logic of Regional Integration*, 157.

45. Ibid., 157.

46. See Mutschler, "Comparative International Experience," 144.
47. Andean Community (CAN), *Trujillo Act* (10.03.1996), online at: http://www.un.org/documents/ga/docs/51/plenary/a51–87.htm.
48. See Mutschler, "Comparative International Experience," 143.
49. Andean Community (CAN), Presidential Summit, *Declaration about Democracy and Integration* (07.08.1998), online at: http://www.comunidadandina.org/ingles/documentos/documents/Preistate-08–07–98.htm.
50. See Mutschler, "Comparative International Experience," 146.
51. See Germán Creamer, "Open Regionalism in the Andean Community: A Trade Flow Analysis," *World Trade Review* 2, no. 1 (2003): 101–118.
52. Mutschler, "Comparative International Experience," 146; see also Miguel E. Cárdenas and Christian Arnold, *La Experiencia de la Unión Europea y sus Anécdotas para la "Comunidad Andina de Naciones"*, ZEI Discussion Paper C 145 (Bonn: Center for European Integration Studies, 2005).
53. Andean Community (CAN), Presidential Summit, *Quirama Declaration* (28.06.2003), online at: http://www.comunidadandina.org/ingles/documentos/documents/Quirama.htm.
54. See Rodrigo Javier Garrón Bozo, *Derecho Comunitario: Principes, Fuentes y Sistema Jurisdiccional de la Comunidad Andina de Naciones y la Union Europea* (La Paz: Edicion Cima, 2004).
55. Andean Community (CAN), *Treaty creating the Court of Justice of the Cartagena Agreement* (10.03.1996), online at: http://www.comunidadandina.org/ingles/treaties/trea/ande_trie2.htm.
56. Nicholls et al., "Open Regionalism," 155.
57. Andean Community (CAN), *Additional Protocol to the Cartagena Agreement (Andean Community Commitment to Democracy)* (27.10.1998), online at: http://www.comunidadandina.org/ingles/normativa/democracy.htm.
58. For details see the homepage of the European Union, online at: http://europa.eu.
59. On the context and prospects see Mary Turck, *South American Community of Nations* (Minneapolis: Resource Center of the Americas, 2005).
60. See Robert Devlin and Antoni Estevadeordal, *What's New in the New Regionalism in the Americas?* INTAL/ITD Working Paper 2 (Buenos Aires: Institute for the Integration of Latin America and the Caribbean, 2001).

Caribbean Community (CARICOM)

61. See Edwin Laurent, *Understanding International Trade: The Trading System from the Perspective of the Eastern Caribbean* (Castries: Organization of Eastern Caribbean States, 2006), 51.
62. See Anthony Payne and Paul Sutton, *Charting Caribbean Development* (Gainesville: University Press of Florida, 2001), 173–203.
63. Caribbean Community (CARICOM), *Treaty Establishing the Caribbean Community* (04.07.1973), online at: http://www.caricom.org/jsp/community/original_treaty-text.pdf.
64. Duke Pollard (ed.), *The CARICOM System: Basic Instruments* (Kingston: The Caribbean Law Publishing Company, 2003), 173.
65. Other associate institutions of CARICOM are the Caribbean Development Bank (CDB), University of Guyana (UG), University of the West Indies (UWI), Caribbean Law Institute, and Caribbean Law Institute Centre. Affiliated institutions of CARICOM are the Caribbean Disaster Emergence Response Agency (CDERA), Caribbean Meteorological Institute (CMI), Caribbean Meteorological Organization (CMO), Caribbean Environmental Health Institute (CEHI), Caribbean Agricultural Research and Development Institute (CARDI), Caribbean Regional Centre for the Education and Training of Animal Health and Veterinary Public Health Assistants (REPAHA), Association of Caribbean Community Parliamentarians (ACCP), Caribbean Centre for Developmental Administration (CARICAD), and Caribbean Food and Nutrition Institute (CFNI); see Anneke Jessen and Christopher Vignoles,

CARICOM Report No. 2 (Buenos Aires: Institute for the Integration of Latin America and the Caribbean, 2005), 45.

66. See Len Ishmael, The OECS Model of Integration in the Context of Caribbean Regionalism (Castries: Organization of Eastern Caribbean States, 2006).

67. Ibid., 38. The responsibilities are as following: Antigua and Barbuda, services; the Bahamas, tourism; Barbados, the Single Market and Economy, including monetary union; Belize and Montserrat, sustainable development; Dominica, labor; Grenada, science and technology; Guyana, agriculture, agricultural diversification and food security; Jamaica, external negotiations; Haiti, transport; Saint Lucia, justice and governance; Saint Kitts and Nevis, health; Saint Vincent and the Grenadines, bananas; Suriname, community and cultural cooperation; Trinidad and Tobago, security.

68. See Shelton Nicholls et al., "Open Regionalism and Institutional Development among Smaller Integration Schemes of CARICOM, the Andean Community and the Central American Market," in Viktor Bulmer-Thomas (ed.), Regional Integration in Latin America and the Caribbean (London: University of London Institute of Latin American Studies, 2001), 158–160.

69. Payne and Sutton, Charting Caribbean Development, 183.

70. Ibid., 191.

71. Ibid., 185.

72. Caribbean Free Trade Association Secretariat (ed.), From CARIFTA to Caribbean Community (Georgetown: CARIFTA, 1972).

73. Quoted in Payne and Sutton, Charting Caribbean Development, 194. The full text can be found online at http://www.jis.gov.jm/special-relations/CARICOMNew/grandAnse.pdf.

74. Ibid., 196.

75. Caribbean Community (CARICOM), The Revised Treaty of Chaguaramas Establishing the Caribbean Community including the CARICOM Single Market and Economy (05.07.2001), online at: http://www.caricom.org/jsp/community/revised_treaty-text.pdf.

76. On the context of the development of the Caribbean Single Market and Economy (CSME), also in its relation with the "Eastern Caribbean Currency Union," see Samuel Itam et al., Developments and Challenges in the Caribbean Region (Washington, D.C.: International Monetary Fund, 2000), 18–22.

77. See Nicholls et al., "Open Regionalism," 159; Pollard, The CARICOM System, 20–26.

78. Payne and Sutton, Charting Caribbean Development, 174.

79. Pollard, The CARICOM System, 4 and 22.

80. See Kenneth O. Hall (ed.), Re-Inventing CARICOM: The Road to a New Integration (Kingston: Ian Randle, 2003).

81. Payne and Sutton, Charting Caribbean Development, 197.

82. W. Andrew Axline, "Free Trade in the Americas and Sub-Regional Integration in Central America and the Caribbean," Canadian Journal of Development Studies 21, no. 1 (2000): 31–53, 33; see also Anneke Jessen and Ennio Rodriguez, The Caribbean Community: Facing the Challenges of Regional and Global Integration (Buenos Aires: Institute for the Integration of Latin America and the Caribbean, 1999).

83. On the context see Stephen R. Hurt, "Co-operation and Coercion? The Cotonou Agreement between the European Union and ACP States and the End of the Lomé Convention," Third World Quarterly 24, no. 1 (2003): 161–176.

84. Peter Clegg, "From Insiders to Outsiders: Caribbean Banana Interests in the New International Trading Framework," in Stephen J.H. Dearden (ed.), The European Union and the Commonwealth Caribbean (Aldershot: Ashgate, 2002), 105.

85. See Laurent, Understanding International Trade, 36–49.

86. See Payne and Sutton, Charting Caribbean Development, 193.

87. Pollard, The CARICOM System, 25.

88. Nicholls et al., "Open Regionalism," 159.

89. Ibid.
90. See Jessen and Vignoles, CARICOM Report No. 2, 41. According to this report, the share of total member state contributions (for 2002) toward financing the CARICOM Secretariat is as follows: Trinidad and Tobago 25.00%, Jamaica 22.78%, Barbados 10.74%, the Bahamas 9.80%, Guyana 7.009%, Suriname 7.00%, Haiti 3.00%, Belize 2.89%, Antigua and Barbuda 1.77%, Dominica 1.77%, Grenada 1.77%, Saint Kitts and Nevis 1.77%, Saint Lucia 1.77%, Saint Vincent and the Grenadines 1.77%, Montserrat 0.35%.
91. See Economic Commission for Latin America and the Caribbean (ed.), Latin America and the Caribbean in the World Economy 2002–2003 (Santiago: United Nations Publications, 2004), 98.
92. Ibid., 101.
93. Caribbean Community (CARICOM), The Rose Hall Declaration on Regional Governance and Integrated Development (04.07.2003), online at: http://www.caricomlaw.org/docs/rosehalldeclaration.htm.
94. See Clegg, "From Insiders to Outsiders," 79–113.
95. See "The Caribbean: Living and Dying on History and Artificial Economic Sweeteners," The Economist, 24 September 2005: 61–62.
96. See Ishmael, The OECS Model of Integration, 8.
97. Payne and Sutton, Charting Caribbean Development, 197.
98. Clegg, "From Insiders to Outsiders," 79–113.
99. Payne and Sutton, Charting Caribbean Development, 199.
100. For a Caribbean perspective see Laurent, Understanding International Trade, 21–29.
101. Excerpt from the report of a group of experts appointed by the Common Council of Ministers titled The Caribbean Community in the 1980s, published by the CARICOM Secretariat in 1980, quoted in Pollard, The CARICOM System, 15.
102. Economic Commission for Latin America and the Caribbean, Latin America and the Caribbean in the World Economy 2002–2003, 100.
103. See also Jean Grugel and Anthony J. Payne, "Regional Responses in the Caribbean Basin," in Björn Hettne et al. (eds.), National Perspectives on the new Regionalism in the South. The New Regionalism Series: vol. 3 (London: Macmillan 2000): 198–220.

Southern Common Market (Mercado Común del Sur, MERCOSUR)

104. See Walter Mattli, The Logic of Regional Integration: Europe and Beyond (Cambridge and New York: Cambridge University Press, 1999), 142.
105. Cited ibid., 140.
106. Southern Common Market (MERCOSUR), Southern Common Market (MERCOSUR) Agreement (26.03.1991), online at: http://www.worldtradelaw.net/fta/agreements/mercosurfta.pdf.
107. Southern Common Market (MERCOSUR), Protocol of Ouro Preto (17.12.1994), online at: http://www.sice.oas.org/Trade/MRCSR/Ourop/ourop_e.asp.
108. See Mattli, The Logic of Regional Integration, 105.
109. See Celina Pena and Ricardo Rozemberg, Mercosur: A Different Approach to Institutional Development, FOCAL Policy Paper 6 (2005), online at: http://www.focal.ca/pdf/mercosur.pdf.
110. Ibid., 11.
111. Jorge Guira, MERCOSUR: Trade and Investment amid Financial Crisis (London: and New York: Kluwer Law International, 2003), 140.
112. Ibid., 65.
113. See Samuel Pinheiro Guimaraes, "The International Political Role of MERCOSUL II," in Helio Jaguaribe and Alvaro Vasconcelos (eds.), The European Union, Mercosul and the New World Order (London and Portland: Frank Cass, 2003), 121; see also Anna Hallberg, Regional Integration in Latin America: The Mercosur Experience (Stockholm: Latinamerika-Institutet, 2000).

114. Felix Peña, *Civil Society, Transparency and Legitimacy in Integration Processes and Trade Negotiations: MERCOSUR's Experience and Lessons for the Negotiations with the European Union*, Chaire Mercosur de Sciences Po Discussion Paper 1 (2003), online at: http://www.felixpena.com.ar/index.php?contenido=wpapers&wpagno=documentos/2003-09-eng.
115. See Guira, MERCOSUR, 144.
116. See Common Market of the South (MERCOSUR), *Constitutive Protocol of the Parliament of the MERCOSUR* (09.12.2005), translation author, for the original document in Spanish see http://www.mercosursocialsolidario.org/images/stories/oficial/documentos/protocolo_constitutivo_mercosur.pdf.
117. See Heinz G. Preusse, *The New American Regionalism* (Cheltenham: Edward Elgar, 2004), 134–185.
118. See Guira, MERCOSUR, 57.
119. See Andrés Malamud, "Presidentialism and MERCOSUR: A Hidden Cause for a Successful Experience," in Finn Laursen (ed.), *Comparative Regional Integration: Theoretical Perspectives* (Aldershot: Ashgate, 2003), 69.
120. See Guira, MERCOSUR, 98.
121. See Economic Commission for Latin America and the Caribbean (ed.), *Latin America and the Caribbean in the World Economy, 2002–2003* (Santiago de Chile: United Nations Publications, 2004), 75.
122. Mattli, *The Logic of Regional Integration*, 159.
123. See Guira, MERCOSUR, 144.
124. See Mattli, *The Logic of Regional Integration*, 159.
125. See Ricardo Andrés Markwald, "Mercosul: Beyond 2000," in Jaguaribe and Vasconcelos (eds.), *The European Union, Mercosul and the New World Order*, 91–92.
126. See Fabio Giambiagi, "Why does Monetary Union Make Sense in the Long Run?" in Philip Arestis and Luiz Fernando de Paula (eds.), *Monetary Union in South America: Lessons from the EMU* (Cheltenham and Northampton: Edward Elgar, 2003), 63.
127. See Pedro da Motta Veiga, *Mercosur: In Search of a New Agenda. Mercosur's Institutionalization Agenda: The Challenges of a Project in Crisis*, INTAL Working Paper, SITI, 06E (Buenos Aires: Institute for Integration in Latin America and the Caribbean, 2004), 14, online at: http://www.iadb.org/intal/aplicaciones/uploads/publicaciones/i_IECI_WP_06e_daMottaVeiga.pdf.
128. See Preusse, *The New American Regionalism*, 182.
129. See Markwald, "Mercosul: Beyond 2000," 89.
130. See Guira, MERCOSUR, 132.
131. Da Motta Veiga, *Mercosur's Institutionalization Agenda*, 12.
132. Hazel Smith, "Actually Existing Foreign Policy—or Not? The EU in Latin and Central America," in John Petersen and Helene Sjursen (eds.), *A Common Foreign Policy for Europe? Competing Visions of the CFSP* (London and New York: Routledge 1998), 161.
133. For detailed figures see the EU Commission's homepage at http://www.ec.europa.eu.
134. See Paolo Giordano, *The External Dimension of the Mercosur: Prospects for North-South Integration with the European Union* (London: Royal Institute for International Affairs, 2002), online at: http://www.iadb.org/intal/aplicaciones/uploads/publicaciones/i_INTALITDSTA_OP_19_2003_Giordano.pdf; Felix Peña and Ramón Torrent (eds.), *Hacia Una Nueva Etapa en las Relaciones Unión Europea-América Latina: Un Diagnóstico Inicial* (Barcelona: Universidad de Barcelona (Observatorio de Relaciones Unión Europea-América Latina), 2005); Philippe de Lombaerde, Shigeru Kochi, and José Briceño Ruiz (eds.), *Del regionalismo latinoamericano a la integración interregional* (Madrid: Fundación Carolina, 2008).
135. See José Magone, *Challenging the Monroe Doctrine? The Relations between the European Union and MERCOSUR* (Hull: University of Hull, 2002), online at: http://www.psa.ac.uk/journals/pdf/5/2002/magone.pdf.
136. See Guira, MERCOSUR, 159.

137. See Markwald, "Mercosul: Beyond 2000," 73.

138. See Giambiagi, "Why Does Monetary Union Make Sense in the Long Run?" 39–66.

139. See Philippe de Lombaerde and Liliana Lizarazo, *La problématique de l'intégration monétaire en Amérique Latine et dans les Caraïbes*, UNU-CRIS Occasional Papers, 0–2004/13 (Bruges: United Nations University-CRIS, 2004); online at: http://www.cris.unu.edu/fileadmin/workingpapers/OP%20De%20Lombaerde%20LizarazoProbl%E9 matiqueIntMonAL2003.pdf.

140. Giambiagi, "Why Does Monetary Union Make Sense in the Long Run?" 39–66.

141. See Roberto Ruiz Diaz Labrano, *Mercosur, Integración y Derecho* (Buenos Aires: Ciudadargentina, 1998).

142. See Pena and Rozemberg, "A Different Approach to Institutional Development," 6.

143. See Guira, MERCOSUR, 88–95.

144. Ibid., 83.

145. Common Market of the South (MERCOSUR), *The Protocol of Olivos* (18.02.2002), online at: http://www.sice.oas.org/Trade/MRCSR/olivos/polivos_p.asp.

146. See Pena and Rozemberg, "A Different Approach to Institutional Development."

147. Andrew Crawley, *MERCOSUR: In Search of a New Agenda. Rapporteur's Report* (Buenos Aires: Institute for the Integration of Latin America and the Caribbean, 2004), online at: http://idb-docs.iadb.org/wsdocs/getdocument.aspx?docnum=548062.

4

ASIA

Regional Integration in a Continent That Isn't

—=≡:⦿:≡=—

Association of Southeast Asian Nations (ASEAN)

Basic Facts

The Bangkok Declaration of 8 August 1967 was clear and unambiguous: "The Association represents the collective will of the nations of the region to bind themselves together in friendship and cooperation, and through joint efforts and sacrifices, secure for their people and for posterity the blessings of peace, freedom, and prosperity."[1] The founding document of the Association of Southeast Asian Nations (ASEAN) declared cooperation in "common interest areas" as its main objective. Three main purposes for the founding of a regional architecture in Southeast Asia were outlined:

- To bring about regional peace and stability.
- To abide by law and respect the principle of justice.
- To accelerate economic growth, social progress, and cultural development.

Partnership in Southeast Asia was driven by geopolitical pressure. The establishment of the People's Republic of China in 1949 had introduced the East-West conflict to Asia. The presence of the Soviet Union might otherwise only have been felt in a peripheral way in Southeast Asia. This was certainly the case as long as Western colonial powers were present in the region. But the emergence of communist China, the Korean War, and the partition of the Korean peninsula, followed by the French defeat in Dien Bien Phu and the subsequent partition of Vietnam, made the whole region vulnerable. The retreat of Western colonial powers coincided with these developments, which escalated during the 1960s with the all-out warfare in Indochina. The "rest" of Southeast Asia had to look for new security guarantees while it began to embark on the path toward rapid, successful economic modernization. When Thailand, Malaysia, Singapore, Indonesia, and the Philippines came together in 1967 to establish ASEAN, the success story of the countries later known as the "little tigers" had barely begun. Intra-regional trade was around 15 percent, a significant figure compared with other regions in the world.

So far, the structures of ASEAN have remained weak and intergovernmental. A strong sense of rootedness has not developed across the region. ASEAN remains a bureaucratic operation, its visibility largely a function of political summits. ASEAN has developed without the rigid and multidimensional institutional framework known from the European integration experience. ASEAN leaders claim this deficit to be a genuine virtue given the political culture of their region. ASEAN's Treaty of Amity and Cooperation, signed on 24 February 1976, underlined the dilemma that was and remains structurally constitutive for ASEAN: whereas cooperation and integration are appreciated in the interest of commonly defined goals, mutual respect for independence, sovereignty, equality, territorial integrity, and national identity have to be safeguarded by all means. It was a statement directed not only against communist countries with the potential to turn expansionist, but also, equally, toward anybody inside ASEAN with second thoughts about any of the existing borders or even states. Each country's right to exist and the upholding of the principle of non-interference in domestic affairs were always as important as the desire to cooperate. ASEAN pledged not to threaten any other country with the use of force, announcing that its future cooperation would remain in effect and that any dispute in the region ought to be settled peacefully.[2] ASEAN has not overcome the strong feeling of the virtue of national independence. Unwillingness to give up national powers to any sort of supranational body is still considered to be in line with the overall political culture of Southeast Asia. The focus on consensual policies rather than on strong decision-making and rhetorical institutionalism remains a strong feature of ASEAN.

In the meantime, ASEAN represents 530 million citizens in ten countries with a combined GDP of $737 billion and a joint trade volume of $720 billion (2007). Membership has grown considerably: Brunei joined on 8 January 1984, Vietnam on 28 July 1995, Laos and Burma (Myanmar) on 23 July 1997, and Cambodia on 30 April 1999. Timor Leste, the youngest of Asia's countries, applied for ASEAN membership in 2006 and is expected to achieve it by 2010.

The institutional structure of ASEAN has often been described as insufficient. Partly updated by the ASEAN Charter of 2007, it is as follows:

- The ASEAN Summit comprises the heads of state or government and is the supreme decision-making body in ASEAN.

- The ASEAN Coordinating Council, the foreign ministers' meeting of ASEAN, comes together two times per year.
- ASEAN community councils are sectoral ministerial meetings in each of the three pillars of the ASEAN Community, i.e., the political-security, sociocultural, and economic communities.
- ASEAN sectoral ministerial bodies consist of senior government officials of each member state in the relevant policy field.
- A Committee of Permanent Representatives to ASEAN and ASEAN national secretariats in each member state guarantee an efficient transfer of information between member states and the ASEAN institutions.
- The ASEAN Secretariat, based in Jakarta, is headed by a secretary general (from 2008 to 2012 Dr. Surin Pitsuwan, a former foreign minister of Thailand), "mandated to initiate, advise, coordinate and implement ASEAN activities."[3]
- Specialized ASEAN bodies include the ASEAN University Network, ASEAN-EU Management Centre, ASEAN Centre for Energy, ASEAN Agricultural Resource Centre, ASEAN Earthquake Information Centre, ASEAN Regional Centre for Biodiversity Conservation, and ASEAN Timber Technology Centre.

Although ASEAN's institutional development has always been cautious and incremental, visible progress to deepen institutional integration is under way, if only most recently. It took ASEAN ten years to establish a general secretariat. The ASEAN Secretariat has grown into a full structure with 177 employees (including the gardeners; no more than 55 employees are professionals with integration expertise), and the annual budget is $9 million ($900,000 per member state). The officials at the ASEAN Secretariat wish to be considered the vanguard of regional integration in ASEAN, similar to the original aspiration of the European Commission, although in reality they are still far away from the EU Commission's competencies. As the ASEAN Secretariat is not a supranational structure, proposals originating in the ASEAN Secretariat are difficult to influence political decision-making processes inside ASEAN. The lack of institutional capacity remains an important obstacle for deeper integration in ASEAN.

One of the most remarkable success stories of ASEAN took place in 1984, when ASEAN established the ASEAN Regional Forum, the first Asian intra-regional structure to deal with security matters. Since 2004, the ASEAN Secretariat has included a unit dealing with the matters of the ASEAN Regional Forum, thus indicating a potential path of enhanced activity of ASEAN in the field of foreign and security matters. The possibility of developing some sort of an ASEAN peacekeeping unit has been discussed, albeit without imminent success. Remarkable was the 2003 decision of ASEAN's Bali summit to grow into an ASEAN Community. By 2020, the ASEAN Community shall be based on a structure of three pillars: politics, sociocultural matters, and economics, including a common regional market. ASEAN's Kuala Lumpur summit on 12 December

2005 passed a Declaration on the Establishment of the ASEAN Charter. At the ASEAN summit celebrating the fortieth anniversary of its founding, the ASEAN Charter was signed on 20 November 2007.[4] This remarkable step toward the gradual process of establishing an ASEAN constitution is intended "to facilitate community-building toward an ASEAN Community and beyond."[5] An Eminent Persons Group had been called upon to formulate the ASEAN Charter, which needed to be consensual in order to ever be implemented. Eventually, ASEAN's political leaders watered down several of the proposals of the Eminent Persons Group. The newly established Human Rights Body may remain toothless, as qualified majority voting could remain a taboo in ASEAN.

No matter what its flaws are, the ASEAN Charter was an innovative step, given ASEAN's traditional reluctance to engage in any sort of institutionalization. ASEAN would remain intergovernmental although, for the first time, it was granted the status of a legal personality. The creation of a rotating chairman of ASEAN for the duration of one year and the establishment of a more coherent structure went beyond the economic calculus. With the introduction of an ASEAN flag, hymn, emblem, motto ("One Vision, one Identity, one Community") and ASEAN Day (8 August), ASEAN focused on its identity more clearly than ever. Dispute settlement mechanisms, however, remain vague. The price of regional territorial cohesion became evident when ASEAN's reluctance to criticize the military regime in Myanmar overshadowed the media coverage of the signing of the ASEAN Charter.

When ASEAN started as a security scheme in the 1960s, reflecting regional awareness, a common threat perception, and readiness to cooperate, nobody could have anticipated the enormous economic progress to be achieved within only one generation. The economic success became the real basis for regional cooperation and integration. It gave the most convincing answer to the all-out threat, felt by the entire region, of being invaded by expansionist communist regimes during the later part of the 1970s. Ever since its beginning, ASEAN has preferred to be a loose intergovernmental scheme with a functional focus: security through prosperity. This overall goal was never translated into a treaty-based structure or a political union.

ASEAN's movement toward the signing of the ASEAN Charter echoed an incremental and successful experience with the dialectics of deepening and widening ties. Over a period of four decades, ASEAN had become territorially inclusive by granting membership to practically all of the countries of Southeast Asia. This process accelerated the dilemma posed by the reluctance of most ASEAN member states to deepen integration. ASEAN enlargement occurred in parallel to the geopolitical reconciliation in the region amidst ongoing asymmetries in governance and regime structures. The enlarged ASEAN has to accommodate extremely diverse political regimes, which limits the readiness of each of them to transfer sovereignty to the regional level. The creation of the ASEAN Regional

Forum in 1984 was the expression of a realistic broadening of ASEAN's policy perspective. The ASEAN Regional Forum is the logical consequence of the security integration that was at the center of the original ASEAN threat assessment and rationale. In other words, the original security integration has been superseded by the logic of economic development and cooperation. This, however, always functioned as an expression of the desire to strengthen the region and hence its security by economic means.

In light of these experiences, it must be understood as a sign of rational analysis that ASEAN embarked on a new phase of its existence directed toward community building. Many observers raise questions about this ambition. They refer to the unresolved issue of how ASEAN will ultimately reply to the hegemonic position of China. They also doubt ASEAN political leaders' seriousness about eventually pooling resources and sovereignty beyond minimal necessities. Yet the notion of an ASEAN Community must mean more to ASEAN policy makers than the formulation of an idealistic concept or the superficial echo of European processes of deepened treaty-based integration. The very idea of community-building in ASEAN has to be considered a genuine reflection of the desire of ASEAN's political leadership to advance the process of cooperation and integration. For the time being, the manageable projects and precise timetables that would ensure the eventual realization of an ASEAN Community are missing. The ASEAN Secretariat has suggested on several occasions that the inclusion of the private sector and civil society in the ASEAN process be more energetically promoted. The achievements of the first decades of ASEAN can only be safeguarded and advanced if the loose association of Southeast Asian nations nurtures a stronger sense of ownership across the region. Only such a renewal of ASEAN's rationale through deepened integration would increase the notion of region-ness in Southeast Asia. In light of globalization pressure, ASEAN will have to make unpopular choices in the years ahead if it wants to live up to the rather positive reputation it enjoys worldwide.

Intrinsic Motives and External Pressures

Like the European Union, ASEAN came into existence not in spite of conflicts in its region but because of them. However, ASEAN member states were not involved in a legacy of conflict that had to be reconciled. The original members of ASEAN were threatened by conflicts in the rest of the region and their potential spillover. Potentially aggressive communism, escalating military confrontation, and massive refugee movements exported the tensions and dysfunctional realities of their home countries across the borders of the region. Amidst these dire conditions, the creation of the Association of Southeast Asian Nations was an expression of self-defense. It soon turned into a framework for unprecedented economic modernization. Achieving growth and relative affluence over the course of less than a generation turned ASEAN from a shield of anti-communist self-defense and deterrence into a magnetic force attracting the other countries of the region, whose processes of postconflict stabilization became increasingly tied to the prospect of membership in ASEAN. As much as ASEAN was a magnet of intuitive normative character, it did not project normative standards as a demand and requirement on its neighbors. Torn between the hope of contributing to regional stability and the awareness that stability would require regime symmetry among democratic nations, ASEAN kept its own process of institutionalization fluid.

The term "Southeast Asia" did not appear before World War II and the emerging Cold War, but the historical roots of region-ness in Southeast Asia reach farther back. Identity formation and interactions between the people and countries of the region evolved in the shadow of the two gigantic countries and cultures in its vicinity, India and China. Their cultural influence in Southeast Asia was coupled with trade influence. Yet a genuine political culture in Southeast Asia evolved on the basis of what has been called the "mandala system of a circle of kings." The core of this political culture was a system in which a king was able to exert influence and to claim loyalty over allies and vassals. Various Southeast Asian kingdoms practiced this mandala system, including Pagan between the eleventh and thirteenth centuries, Angkor between the ninth and fifteenth centuries, and Ayutthya between the fourteenth and eighteenth centuries. Traditionally, statehood in Southeast Asia was primarily defined not by geography and territorial claims, but by political loyalties and the ability to mobilize people for a common cause.[6] This influence continues to this day.

Disagreements and conflicts in traditional Southeast Asian societies were seldom over territory, but rather over matters of status and behavior. Not much has changed to this day. Weak territoriality and loose central authority have often been regular features of political systems in the region with "overlapping sovereignties, patrimonial authority, and vaguely definable and continuously shifting territorial boundaries."[7] The maritime links in Southeast Asia were helpful in promoting regional trade even in precolonial times. Trade created regions, and it remained stronger between them than it ever became with the Western colonial powers. One of the interesting features of Southeast Asian interactions was overlapping jurisdictions coupled with cosmopolitan ethnic realities. Chinese merchants became present across Southeast Asia.

The colonial period and its aftermath introduced a political centralization following the notion of the sovereign Western state. National frontiers were drawn in line with the model of the European nation state. At the same time, the disconnecting effects of legal systems and colonial languages became pervasive across the region. American, Dutch, British, French, Portuguese, and at times also German and Japanese colonial ambitions put their mark on Southeast Asia and its constituent parts. Only anti-colonial nationalism created a common bond in the region, which was loosened again under the driving force of individual nations pursuing economic modernization. As diverse as the struggles for independence in Southeast Asia were, the nationalism that drove them was an expression of unity against the colonial powers. Similar though the independent states of Southeast Asia may have looked after the defeat of colonialism, the struggle for economic independence and social progress turned them into natural competitors. The ideological rift between Western-oriented modernization and anti-Western communism added to the antagonisms in the region. But in spite of all differences, the non-communist countries of Southeast Asia and China always remained united in their quest to overcome Western dominance in Asia.

The Japanese occupation of Southeast Asia had one ironic consequence: it was only then that the different leaders of Southeast Asian national movements met among themselves. A meeting in Tokyo in November 1943 brought Philippine's President José P. Laurel, Burma's Prime Minister Ba Maw, and Prince Wan Waithayakon of Thailand together. Paradoxically, Japanese occupation destroyed the legacy of colonial partition in Southeast Asia. But while different national trends emerged across the region after 1945, a sense of strategic region-ness had been born. In 1945, the anti-Japanese allies had established the Southeast Asian Command, encompassing Burma, Malaya, and Singapore with headquarters in Kandy, Sri Lanka. The Southeast Asian Command, with British, American, Australian, and Dutch participation, was headed by British General Sir Archibald Wavell. It shifted from combat operations to the management of a military government. It was dissolved in 1946, in the midst of the bloody national revolution in Indonesia against the return of Dutch colonial power. This struggle ended with Indonesia's independence in 1949. For the first time in history, the term "Southeast Asia" had been applied to a political structure. It was a response to regional security needs and the quest for political stability.

Cultural and strategic interdependence formed the notion of a Southeast Asian political region as a balancing factor between geopolitical giants. In light of persistent postwar conflicts, critics compared the region to the Balkans in Europe.[8] But the introduction of quarrels of a type so well known in Europe for centuries could not undermine the concept of region-ness. Disputes among Southeast Asian countries, such as the Indonesian confrontation, the Philippine opposition against the founding of Malaysia, and Singapore's expulsion from Malaysia, began to resemble the well-known interstate rivalries in Europe. The claim to national sovereignty was both a force against colonial dominance and an outcome of interstate rivalries among newly established states. It was only the common threat from external forces (the fear of communist expansion) that generated a sense of common destiny in the region. Ultimately, the quest for regional security and the claim to stabilized national independence were combined and found their response in ASEAN.

This development coincided with US strategic interests in stabilizing Southeast Asia. The first effort was purely strategic, when the Southeast Asian Treaty Organization (SEATO) was founded in 1954. The United States, Australia, New Zealand, Korea, South Vietnam, Thailand, and the Philippines were members of this strategic umbrella organization. After the fall of Dien Bien Phu, the emergence of a Southeast Asian equivalent to NATO was more than the natural interest of the United States. But SEATO became a victim of America's defeat in Vietnam. In 1977, after the US withdrawal from Indochina, SEATO was dissolved.

The Indochina wars had generated local and geopolitical divisions, and yet, in a paradoxical way, they facilitated regional integration and the evolution of ASEAN. ASEAN was founded in 1967, and after the Paris Peace Agreements of 1975 and the subsequent withdrawal of the United States from Indochina, it was able to flourish more than ever before. It was a security buffer that turned into an economic powerhouse, thus providing the best rationale and legitimacy for its security claims.

ASEAN's focus on economic development and modernization became an unintended tool for strengthening the region and upholding its independence. Between the 1970s and the 1990s, ASEAN's share of world trade increased from 4.2 percent of imports and 4.9 percent of exports to 6.7 percent of imports and 8.3 percent of exports. Japan's direct investments in ASEAN increased fivefold during these years. Intra-regional investment remained small, but nevertheless it more than doubled during the 1990s alone, from $12 billion to $26 billion. Even in face of the end of the Cold War and the Asian financial crisis of the 1990s, ASEAN's rise to modernity was not stopped. Between 2003 and 2004, the total of ASEAN's exports increased by more than 21 percent, from $456.7 billion to $555.1 billion, within one year. At the same time, imports jumped from $388.7 billion to $492.8 billion, an increase of 26.7 percent. As for foreign direct investment, the decline was reversed, and ASEAN saw an increase of 22 percent in 2004 alone, rising to a total of $25.1 billion.[9]

The readjustment after the end of the Cold War was a difficult time for Southeast Asia, but it brought a myriad of new opportunities. The room for strategic maneuvering within the region increased. This was reflected in the smooth and speedy enlargement of ASEAN, for which ASEAN had to pay the price of slowing down the potential for deeper integration. During the 1990s, the former enemies Vietnam, Laos, and Cambodia joined ASEAN. So did Burma, renamed Myanmar, whose democratic record has been particularly bad, so much so that it became a global concern. Meanwhile the fledgling and embryonic democracies in Indochina remained a regional worry. The absence of system cohesion imposed a strong limitation on ASEAN's ambition to advance regional integration. In light of the ambivalent experience of past enlargements, it was no surprise that Timor Leste's application in 2006 did not meet with enthusiastic reactions among other ASEAN member states.

The financial crisis of the 1990s raised global skepticism about the limits of ASEAN's modernization. Eventually, ASEAN revamped economically during the early twenty-first century. It was also able to create a certain balance between its original security-based regionalism and a renewed development-oriented regionalism. To solidify both, it became consequential that ASEAN should begin the path toward a genuine constitutional system, reflecting the overarching objectives of the integration process.[10] The ASEAN Charter of 2007 is a logical step in the region's future. Initially, ASEAN was the product of the division of the region. Over time, it has become an engine for its integration and a magnetic force on the path toward modernization. ASEAN has so far failed at establishing new standards for linking integration, modernization, and democracy, but its very existence has become a symbol of the integrating potential of Southeast Asia's interrelatedness.

Performance

ASEAN has been characterized as a model of "soft regionalism."[11] The weak institutionalization of ASEAN should, however, not be misperceived as simply a sign of weakness. Strength and limits of regional integration in Southeast Asia originate in the political culture of the region, the interests and possibilities of the countries involved, and the idiosyncrasies stemming from internal and external impediments. Among the strong features of ASEAN's performance, it is worth mentioning the following:

(1) Initially, ASEAN was conceptualized as a security and deterrence umbrella organization without a defense pact. Different strategic interests made such a pact impossible, Thailand and the Philippines being pro-Western, Indonesia emphasizing its non-aligned status, and Singapore and Malaysia initially struggling over the very right to exist. Yet the bonds that united these countries against communism and its potential expansion were stronger than strategic and political differences. In fact, politics was soon transcended by emphasis on the economic potential of ASEAN. ASEAN as a region of economic success did grow into ASEAN as a region in search of cultural proximity and community-building. Successful economic development strengthened the security of the region and broadened the perspective toward community-building there. At the same time, ASEAN has opened its original security agenda and developed it further. The ASEAN Regional Forum has grown into the first Asian security structure as ASEAN is preparing to increasingly manage low-key conflicts in the region using its own means.[12]

(2) ASEAN has often been criticized as being overly consensus-oriented and too lenient toward infringements on democratic principles. While ASEAN has always had a clear record of anti-communism, its attitude toward the limitations of the

democracy practiced among its own member states has been more ambivalent. ASEAN has gone through a mixed and somewhat surprising development. On the one hand, it embraced the postcommunist countries of Indochina, whose democratic record so far has been weak at best. On the other hand, ASEAN has begun to exercise critique and impose limited sanctions against Myanmar, whose human rights record has been so sharply criticized by ASEAN's Western partners. In July 2005, Myanmar was forced to renounce its upcoming chairmanship of ASEAN, due in 2006, because of its democratic deficits. While ASEAN countries still prefer not to debate democratic deficits among their member states in the presence of Western partners, among themselves they have increased awareness and action aimed at improving governance and democracy in all of ASEAN. Even so, during the 2007 escalation of human rights-related protests in Myanmar, China seemed to exercise more influence in persuading the regime in Myanmar to practice restraint than did ASEAN. As a consequence, the Western media coverage of the signing of the ASEAN Charter in November 2007 was focused more on ASEAN's failure to condemn Myanmar's military regime than on the possible potential of the first ever ASEAN human rights body, which was to be launched with the implementation of the ASEAN Charter.

The "ASEAN way" concept of soft regionalism is consent-driven, based on weak institutionalization, and aimed at strengthening the autonomy and independence of each of its member states and the region as a whole. With this approach, ASEAN worked through the times of the Indochina conflicts, managed to enlarge after the end of the Cold War, and enabled ASEAN partner countries to prioritize economic growth as their common interest and as a shield to emphasize their common security interest. In spite of competitive economic structures, ASEAN member states understood their cooperation as a way to mutually gain political and security benefits through economic modernization and gradual community-building. The more the community-building advances, the more ASEAN needs to come to terms with normative issues that require reasonably symmetric orientations and answers.

During the 1970s and 1980s, ASEAN's anti-communist stance and its sensitivity toward insurgency movements of all sorts constituted a strong catalyst for its own development. Some spillover effects of insurgencies originated among partner countries and were a "source of interstate tension."[13] Refugees from Indonesia's province Aceh fled to Malaysia in 1990. More troubling: Moro separatists in the Philippine island of Mindanao received support from Malaysia's predominantly Muslim state of Sabah. Yet conflicts among ASEAN member states never undermined ASEAN as such. ASEAN regionalism continued to be an expression of its member states' common interests, which included "the need of the postcolonial elite to ensure regime survival."[14]

(3) ASEAN's economic performance is impressive. All in all, three different stages can be distinguished: a) rehabilitation and reconstruction of the export-oriented

agricultural economy created during colonialism, b) import-substituting industrialization, driven by economic nationalism, c) export-oriented industrialization since the late 1970s, with Singapore being the pioneer since the mid
1960s, even before ASEAN formally began. ASEAN thus intensified national
trends but did not necessarily invent them. But ASEAN also triggered genuine
achievements, most importantly the increase in intra-regional trade and the
development of a free trade area. Around 1970, intra-regional trade constituted
around 15 percent of all ASEAN trade. Mostly competitive economies began
to join forces with the intention of creating a single production area with a free
flow of goods, services, investment, and capital.

By the early 1990s, intra-regional trade had grown to 25 percent; the differences, however, were evident between Indonesia's 6 percent and Singapore's 30
percent. Free trade was expanding in Southeast Asia throughout these years. According to World Bank statistics, Thailand and the Philippines were considered
poor countries in 1975 with a per capita GDP of less than $520. Indonesia was
among the poorest countries of the world with less than $265 per capita. Only
Singapore and Malaysia were above the global average with $2,450 and $760 respectively. With an average growth rate of 5.6 percent during the 1960s and 7.1
percent during the 1970s, all of ASEAN made a big leap forward. After ASEAN
had recovered from the Asian financial crisis in the late 1990s and had absorbed
the organization's expansion to several postcommunist countries, economic
growth in ASEAN bounced back. In 2005, according to the president of the
Asian Development Bank, the growth rate was back to 5.4 percent on average.[15]

Japanese production networks in Southeast Asia strengthened the overall
goals of economic modernization in ASEAN. The association became part of
the Japanese production system of "flying geese" and thus increased its export-
orientation further. The enormous economic modernization in ASEAN countries called for enhanced free trade. In 1994, the goal was set for AFTA, the
ASEAN Free Trade Area. The ambition was to achieve trade tariffs between
zero and 5 percent by 2008. But enlargement to the poor Indochinese countries
introduced new difficulties into ASEAN. Laos, the poorest of the new member
countries, entered ASEAN with a per capita GDP of $320. AFTA had to be
reconsidered, yet it was not given up. In fact, the achievement of its goals was
accelerated after 2003, when the poorest latecomers to ASEAN set target dates:
Vietnam for 2006, Laos and Myanmar for 2008, and Cambodia for 2010.[16] Subsequently these target dates were revised again, and they are now set for the old
member states until 2010 and for the new members Laos, Cambodia, Myanmar,
and Vietnam until 2015.

AFTA, modeled on the European Single Market, is still struggling to
eliminate the many exceptions to free trade, especially those for certain agricultural goods like rice. Between ASEAN member states, not all tariffs have
been scrapped yet. Some of them have just been lowered to below 5 percent.

ASEAN cannot be considered a customs union because it was formed under a common effective preferential tariff agreement, which means that each member state can still impose its own tariffs on imports from outside ASEAN. ASEAN is only aiming now to eventually achieve a common external preferential tariff. Its member states are still debating the inherent limits of regional cooperation and the effects of integration. A comprehensive cost-benefit analysis of regional economic integration as compared to global free trade schemes could become inevitable for ASEAN.

(4) Although ASEAN originated in external security threats to its founding members, it hardly developed a comprehensive security strategy, objective, or instrument during its first decades. Only after the end of the Cold War did ASEAN begin to boost its security profile. Declaring passive neutrality in regional conflicts, ASEAN had defined itself in 1971 as a Zone of Peace, Freedom and Neutrality. This reflected Indonesia's desire to emphasize the region's principal responsibility for ensuring regional stability without getting involved in the massive conflicts in Indochina. It also reflected fear of the impact of increased insurgency and guerrilla warfare in and beyond the Indochinese theatre. The overall pressure of the conflicts at its borders never translated into a comprehensive defense pact for ASEAN. When the Cold War was over, and with it the Indochinese conflicts, ASEAN was able to begin to genuinely expand its horizon toward matters of foreign and security policy. The ASEAN Regional Forum, founded in 1994, is to this day the only security-related body in any regional integration scheme outside of Europe.

The ASEAN's general reluctance to move from rhetoric to action in matters of peacekeeping gradually disappeared. The UN Transitional Authority in Cambodia in 1992/1993 did not see any ASEAN involvement. Even with the ASEAN Regional Forum in place, for the time being ASEAN remains a reluctant observer of security matters in its region and the region's periphery. A case in point was ASEAN's attitude toward the conflict in East Timor. Once Indonesia had taken over control in East Timor, following the retreat of the Portuguese colonial power in 1975, a low-level conflict simmered in the territory. It escalated in 1998 after the fall of Indonesia's President Suharto, which generated a strong shift toward democracy in Indonesia. Under UN supervision the people of East Timor were able to decide in May 1999 between independence and special autonomy within Indonesia: 78.5 percent voted for independence. Indonesia's forces were unwilling to accept the result, and violence and destruction escalated. Only an international intervention under Australia's leadership and authorized by the United Nations was able to return peace to East Timor. Most supportive of INTERFRET (International Force East Timor) were the democracies in ASEAN, notably Thailand and the Philippines. Under their initiative, ASEAN embraced the concept of "enhanced interaction" in July 1998. But in light of the overall concern about sovereignty and the concern that intervention in the affairs of one of its member states could backfire, ASEAN forbore to take any serious position, let alone action, in the immediate East Timor question. The idea of creating a comprehensive ASEAN peacekeeping force did not materialize.

After East Timor had gained independence on 20 May 2002, the United Nations established a mission of support (UNMISET) in Timor Leste, as the country is officially called since independence. First with a Japanese and then with an Indian head of mission, the operation also included force commanders from Thailand, Singapore, and Malaysia stationed in Timor Leste. Although they did not represent ASEAN as such, their presence demonstrated that individual ASEAN countries had become ready to get involved in peacekeeping and postconflict reconstruction and had overcome past reluctance.[17] The disastrous tsunami that hit Southeast Asia on 26 December 2004 had integrating effects as well: after a peace accord between the Indonesian government and the Free Aceh movement was brokered on 15 August 2005 in Helsinki, together with the European Union, five ASEAN countries became involved in the subsequent Aceh Monitoring Mission. Their mandate was the decommissioning of armaments from the former Aceh rebels and the relocation of illegal military and police forces. The Aceh mission was successfully concluded by the end of 2006. Even in the absence of a genuine ASEAN peacekeeping structure, the Aceh mission became an interesting example of how advanced joint security police projects between the European Union and ASEAN can work. As slow as this process was for both the EU and ASEAN, the increasing political character of ASEAN might eventually become a new regional reality.

The path toward an ASEAN Charter underlines this trend. It started with the decision taken at the ASEAN's summit of 15 December 2005 in Kuala Lumpur on a Declaration on the Establishment of the ASEAN Charter. The process, the declaration stated, is aimed "to facilitate community building"[18] and should be seen in the larger context of regional integration across the globe. Once completed, the ASEAN Charter "will codify all ASEAN norms, rules, and values and reaffirm the ASEAN agreements signed and other instruments adopted before the establishment of the ASEAN charter."[19] The signing of the ASEAN Charter at the ASEAN Summit at Singapore on 20 November 2007 opened a new chapter in the gradual and often reluctant path toward institutionalizing and codifying ASEAN.

The reference to Asian values in the 2005 declaration recalled a vexing debate of the 1980s and early 1990s. At that time, Singapore's Prime Minister Lee Kwan Yew and Malaysia's Prime Minister Mahatir Mohammed were promoting "Asian values" in contrast to the Westernization of their region. They were criticized for misusing the normative debate to exculpate their governance mode of enlightened authoritarianism within a guided democracy. The ideological function of this debate in bringing the region closer together and opening avenues for a new beginning between Southeast Asia and China has remained somewhat inconsequential. It has remained a variant of constructed community-building torn between the desire "to fortify regional independence in a deeper sense"[20] and to nourish an identity of interdependence among the partner countries of the region.

Among the particularly weak aspects of ASEAN's performance during the first decades of its existence have been the following:

(1) While ASEAN was initially driven by an overarching security threat, it could not develop a comprehensive defense pact. This shortcoming was the result of the ASEAN member states' unwillingness to compromise on national sovereignty, but also of their differences of opinion on geopolitical matters, mainly in so far as the role of the United States in the region is concerned. The defense of autonomy in matters of national sovereignty was exacerbated by the asymmetries in regime and governance structures among ASEAN member states. While they were united against communism and insurgency that might have undermined national independence and territorial integrity, they were overly sensitive about allowing any sort of interference in their respective domestic affairs. Several bilateral defense agreements made reference to the principle of non-extradition, limiting any serious cross-regional activity against government or government-protected corruption. The different human rights records and levels of democratic governance among ASEAN member states led to the mutual exclusion of criticism by any of the regional partners. The coups in Indonesia in 1965 and Thailand in 1976, as well as the imposition of martial law in the Philippines in 1972, indicated instability stemming from weak democracy and rule of law. Only by excluding normative issues like governance performance and human rights records could ASEAN members maintain consensus among themselves. However, in doing so, they limited their objective of becoming a strong and irreversible security community. They also hindered the speedy realization of a law-based common market. Nevertheless, the experience of economic cooperation softened the rigid rejection of pooled sovereignty as long as it was functional and did not limit political autonomy. Over time, ASEAN came to realize the overlapping and permeating effects of cooperation and integration in so far as the implications for autarkic notions of state sovereignty are concerned.

For a long time, ASEAN's elite-driven regionalism was intended to support the survival of the region's regime. This was evidently helpful for safeguarding the independence and territorial integrity of ASEAN member states. It had ambivalent consequences for the societies and individuals promoting human rights and democracy across Southeast Asia. Disputes with ASEAN's Western partners were an inevitable consequence. The inherent skepticism toward certain ASEAN regimes and their benign authoritarianism, no matter how limited, did little to promote ASEAN's legitimacy and popularity in the region's societies. Only the economic success of ASEAN led many to appreciate it as an engine for development.

(2) ASEAN's economic contribution to the rise of the region's "little tigers" has been debated and sometimes questioned. The impressive growth rates of most ASEAN member states are undeniable. But it is less clear how much of this development can be directly related to the existence of ASEAN. It is astonishing how little research in ASEAN is done on ASEAN's work and its effects. Most intra-regional trade remains confined to trade between Singapore and Malaysia and between Malaysia and Indonesia. Largely in reaction to the oil crisis of the 1970s, 65 percent of all intra-ASEAN trade has been identified as fuel trade. While fuel prices spiraled, trade with industrial products of local origin did not increase in any meaningful way in ASEAN.[21]

The Asian financial crisis of 1997/1998 found ASEAN rather unprepared and unfocused. Instead of recognizing the involvement of European banks and the EU in support of the IMF-coordinated rescue package for Thailand and Indonesia, some of the political leaders in ASEAN member states criticized the EU for being too focused on its own integration.[22] However, the Asian financial crisis also triggered cautious reflections in the ASEAN region about the need for improved currency cooperation. Some optimists even introduced the prospect of an ASEAN currency union. In theory, important factors for judging the optimal feasibility of a currency area are the level of industrialization in core countries of a potential currency union, the ability to manage currency volatilities, the increase in macroeconomic symmetries, the structures of exports, and the degree of a deepened regional capital market. ASEAN, concluded one analyst, would be "about as close" as the European Union in meeting the criteria of an optimum currency area.[23] The fact remains that political leaders in ASEAN remain much less enthusiastic about the idea of a currency union than European political leaders ever were before the launch of the euro.

Federators

The growing sense of region-ness in Southeast Asia has become noticeable among the societies of ASEAN member states. In the late 1990s, from among 28.6 million tourists to the ASEAN region, 11.2 million, that is to say almost 40 percent, came from within ASEAN. This figure has been increasing ever since. Intra-regional tourism contributes to the understanding of cultural and psychological commonalities in the region. Growing regional tourism is a product of the economic development in ASEAN and hence an expression of regional pride. Whether or not it can translate into further projects of functional integration—economic, political, or cultural—is a matter of discussion.

ASEAN is certainly less unknown in its own region than it was twenty years ago. Yet a solid sense of ownership has not developed, civil society involvement in ASEAN has remained extremely weak, and even the commitment of the private sector to ASEAN is surprisingly limited. During the period of geopolitical security threats, ASEAN was a project driven by elites and in the interests of the elites in power. It became a more popular expression of regional cooperation and integration with the effects of market development and pride in the rapid modernization of the region. In the meantime, four decades after its original founding, ASEAN remains a project largely driven by diplomatic elites and identified with by political leaders. ASEAN requires a noticeable broadening of its stakeholders if it is to succeed in achieving its hopes for developing political and community-building functions.

The role of crises in increasing regional awareness, and as a basis for intensified focus on regional integration instruments, cannot be overestimated. Without the geopolitical crisis of the Cold War and the fragility of the new nation-states in Southeast Asia, ASEAN would not have been conceived and created. Adaptation to crises in the Southeast Asian integration process were expressions of the overarching crisis of integration, that is, the cautiousness and slow pace in moving integration forward at all. With the broadening of ASEAN's scope and the widening of ASEAN's membership, external crises became not only crises *of* integration, but crises *in* integration. As such, they were able to contribute to the gradual development and an ever renewed focus of the integration objectives. External security threats, bilateral territorial disputes, insurgency movements, governance crises and crises in democracy, and finally the adaptation crises after enlarging ASEAN to include Indochina and to Myanmar, and the effects of the financial crisis of the late 1990s, were elements in a series of crises that ultimately strengthened and focused the objectives of ASEAN. Without the history of integration crises in ASEAN, the ASEAN Charter would have been inconceivable.

The biggest uncertainty for the future development of ASEAN concerns the role of China and its relationship with ASEAN. On 14 December 2005—immediately following ASEAN's regular annual summit—the first ever East Asian Summit took place. ASEAN leaders met with their counterparts from China, Japan, and Korea, but also from New Zealand, Australia, and Russia, as observers. The European Union, ASEAN's traditional partner, was not present. According to the chairman's statement, the vague goal discussed at the East Asia Summit was the establishment of an East Asian region as part of an evolving regional architecture.[24] The statement could not have been more imprecise. ASEAN has not decided how best to position Southeast Asia in the age of a rising Chinese world-power. Together with China, Japan, and Korea, ASEAN holds regular meetings in a format called ASEAN Plus Three. But this formula too can only be a transitory design. ASEAN still needs to find its proper role beyond its own region. It will be able to play the role of a regional balancer; but to do so it will need to deepen integration first.

Transformations

ASEAN has been continuously confronted with the effects of internal crises as part of the rationale for its existence. Immediately after ASEAN was created in August 1967, the Philippines and Malaysia clashed over the territory of Sabah, claimed by the Philippines. Until the end of 1969, the threat of ASEAN's complete breakdown and dissolution loomed over the region. With diplomatic ties between the Philippines and Malaysia severed, Thailand's and Indonesia's offers of good offices failed. Malaysia did not accept that the issue was brought up at ASEAN meetings. In mid 1969, representatives of the Philippines and Malaysia met for the first time in eight months. Only gradually did the tension ease and ASEAN become able to return to its normal business. However, this first serious conflict among ASEAN member states was not only a bad experience; it also had a positive component. In hindsight, it is now recognized that the dissolution of tensions without violence "gave ASEAN a new confidence and sense of purpose."[25] The territorial dispute did not find a real solution at the time, but ASEAN was able to avoid a dangerous escalation and conflict.

The relationship between regional security, territorial integrity, the claim to national sovereignty, and the pursuit of national interests has been on the ASEAN horizon ever since. In November 1971, ASEAN foreign ministers adopted the concept of a Zone of Peace, Freedom and Neutrality in Southeast Asia, which however never translated into any visible action. But ASEAN found gradual strength in cautious and pragmatic regional responses to imminent conflicts and crises.[26] This again became evident during the 1980s, when maritime borders were disputed across the region. Making reference to the provisions of the UN-sponsored Law of the Sea Convention, signed in 1982 and in force since 1994, fifteen maritime border disputes broke out in the South China Sea during the 1980s, six of them between ASEAN member states. Malaysia found itself in dispute with every other ASEAN partner country.[27] Fortunately, none of these border disputes escalated beyond diplomatic measures.

The withdrawal of the United States from Indochina in 1975 confronted ASEAN with new strategic requirements. Its original rationale had been one of deterrence against communist expansionism. Without the security umbrella of the US, ASEAN fell short of introducing a regional military arrangement. Rejecting the idea of a regional military pact, an ASEAN summit in February 1976 in Bali instead defined a comprehensive development concept for the entire region. The Declaration of ASEAN Accord underlined the vision of an

ASIA | 177

all-inclusive Southeast Asia region. While deterrence had guided the original rationale for ASEAN, ASEAN now began to project itself as the engine for the creation of an all-inclusive and harmonious region. The primacy of security matters was increasingly replaced by the aspiration of economic modernization. ASEAN leaders understood the economic success of their countries as the best possible security guarantee vis-à-vis their communist neighbors. They also understood that it was economic modernization and prosperity, rather than the democratic political nature of the region, that constituted the best magnetic force to gradually draw their communist neighbors toward a common regional affiliation.

ASEAN remained well aware of the dangers and limits of this approach to regional divisions and conflicts. After the Paris Accords on Cambodia were signed, ASEAN "made significant headway in reshaping its identity toward its long-held but nominal goal of a regional economic grouping, thereby expanding beyond its de facto security and political raison d'être."[28] Both the security dilemma of defending against potential communist expansion without forming a military pact, and the governance dichotomy of wishing to preserve regional aspirations amidst fundamentally different or even antagonistic political and economic regimes prevailed for many years. ASEAN achieved enormous economic progress, but had to be overly cautious as far as security and governance matters were concerned. Vietnam's Communist foreign minister visited ASEAN countries in the winter of 1977/1978, calling on ASEAN to promote peace through independence and neutrality. He knew too well that ASEAN's motto was "Peace, Freedom and Neutrality." ASEAN did not embrace his siren song. Cambodia's Khmer Rouge regime was more ideological and rejected the idea of regional cooperation from the outset. Vietnam's invasion of Cambodia in December 1978 terminated the hope for a rapprochement between ASEAN and Vietnam, at least for the time being. No matter what Vietnam's arguments for invasion were, ASEAN opposed Vietnam's succeeding in a fait accompli that undermined the principle of territorial integrity of a neighboring country. Withdrawal from Cambodia became the precondition for improvement of ASEAN's relations with Vietnam.

ASEAN remained highly interested in the search for peace process solutions to the conflicts in Indochina. It became an active participant of the peace process that evolved during the 1980s and supported the Final Act of the Paris Conference of 23 October 1991. Vietnam's withdrawal from Cambodia opened new avenues for relaunching the prospect for pan-regionalism in Southeast Asia. The beginning of Vietnam's economic liberalization in 1987 had already had immediate effects on trade with ASEAN, which increased sixfold within the first three years. The first visit of the Vietnamese chairman of the Council of Ministers to ASEAN countries was reciprocated by visits of the prime ministers of Thailand and Malaysia to Vietnam in 1992. It only took until 28 July 1995 for Vietnam to become a member of ASEAN, followed by the other countries of Indochina. The strategic division of Southeast Asia had been resolved. The asymmetries in governance and regime realities among the countries of the region continued. This ambivalence was ultimately outpaced by hope for the long-term effects of imminent economic modernization and market liberalization in Indochina and followed the earlier success stories of other countries of the region. But the absence of robust governance and democracy standards remained a liability for ASEAN.

The end of the Cold War had one geopolitical implication for ASEAN. While deterrence within the region of Southeast Asia was no longer the main concern of its member states, the relationship between Southeast Asia and Northeast Asia became an issue of increasing importance. ASEAN's relationship with China became enormously important, leaving ASEAN uncertain as to how to position itself strategically. The larger picture included ASEAN's relationship with the emerging Asia-Pacific Economic Cooperation (APEC) group and the positioning of ASEAN within the framework of the Asia-Europe Meeting (ASEM). Whereas the European Union and ASEAN had traditionally considered each other preferential partners, the broadening of the construction of a lasting Asian regional architecture and its connection with the United States on the one hand, and Europe on the other hand, had lasting implications for ASEAN and its regional role. At the same time, APEC weakened and strengthened ASEAN as a regional balancer and stabilizer.

Role and Interests of the European Union

The European Union is the second largest export market for ASEAN and the third largest trading partner after Japan and the United States. The volume of EU exports from ASEAN is more than $39 billion, while imports from ASEAN stand above $66 billion (2003 figures). As for the European Union, the total is not overly relevant: ASEAN represents 2 percent of EU exports and 3 percent of total imports. ASEAN's main importance for the European Union is strategic and political. Political relations between ASEAN and the European Community began in 1978, and annual meetings of the foreign ministers have taken place ever since. When all twenty-five EU foreign ministers and the commissioner for external relations of the EU met with their counterparts for the fifteenth time in Jakarta in March 2005, the occasion was particularly moving. In the wake of the tragic tsunami that had killed more than 300,000 people on 26 December 2004, the EU massively upgraded its aid to ASEAN and committed itself to working with ASEAN in improving climate forecasting and ecological security in the region. Out of a tragedy, so it seems, a new priority in ASEAN-EU relations was born. Soon thereafter, in December 2005, the EU and ASEAN celebrated the twenty-fifth anniversary of their relations. Alongside political and economic aspects, a human dimension had been added to this biregional relationship.

Since the Asian financial crisis of 1997/1998 came to an end, direct European investment in ASEAN has again increased. It is interesting to note that Singapore is attracting more European direct investment than all other ASEAN countries combined. As for the total, ASEAN is the fourth largest recipient of European direct investment outside Europe. Trade relations with the countries of Indochina doubled in the decade between 1990 and 2000. It is also noteworthy that trade services have increased between the EU and ASEAN. Lately, however, the enormous boom in China has worked to the detriment of investments in ASEAN.

For the European Community (European Union since 1993) ASEAN has always been a preferential, though not always easy, partner.[29] Since its beginning, the idea of regional integration in Southeast Asia has met with great support in Europe. In 1980, a Cooperation Agreement between the then European Community (EC) and ASEAN was signed. The EC's main policy objectives included concern for governance issues and the issue of human rights in Southeast Asia. It therefore did not come as a surprise that the European Union was not willing to extend the Cooperation Agreement to Myanmar once this country joined ASEAN in 1997. Myanmar membership in ASEAN reduced the reputation of ASEAN in Europe a great deal. Nobel Prize Winner Aung San Suu Kyi, the leader of Myanmar's democratic opposition, became a symbol for the freedom struggle in her home country. In a rare development between biregional partners, a meeting of the ASEAN-EU Joint Cooperative Council was suspended in November 1997 because ASEAN found it unacceptable to downgrade the role of Myanmar to that of passive presence as the EU had demanded.

The vexing Myanmar question has overshadowed EU-ASEAN relations even further. An annual foreign ministers' meeting between ASEAN and the EU, scheduled for March 1999 in Berlin, was canceled. Some EU member states—in particular Great Britain and Denmark—refused to accept the attendance of representatives from Myanmar at this summit. In May 1999, the EU-ASEAN Joint Cooperation Committee met for the first time in two years. The road remained rough. When the EU-ASEAN Ministerial Summit was held in Vientiane in December 2000, only three of then fifteen EU foreign ministers attended. While Laos and Cambodia signed the 1980 Cooperation Agreement with the EU, Myanmar was excluded from doing so.[30]

Entanglements between ASEAN and the EU were the price ASEAN had to pay for its enlargement without governance conditions. During a meeting of EU and ASEAN foreign ministers in Nuremberg in March 2007, both sides agreed on a joint agenda in their cooperation against terrorism, trafficking of human beings and drugs, piracy, arms trade, and cyberspace crime. On Myanmar, the EU conditioned its position of isolating the regime in Yangon by allowing Myanmar's foreign minister to attend the meeting, while both sides reiterated their deep concern about the insufficient degree of democratic reforms and political progress in Myanmar. The presence of the Myanmar representative at the Nuremberg meeting was ironic because it only underlined the EU's inability to make any difference inside Myanmar with its policy of selective sanctions. Since a military takeover in Thailand in late 2006, the EU-ASEAN relationship had become even more complex, Thailand being and remaining a cornerstone of EU policy in Southeast Asia. ASEAN got stuck in the dilemma between regional geographic inclusivity and normative ambitions on governance matters.

The European Union set out its main policy objectives in dealing with Southeast Asia in July 2003. A Communication of the EU Commission ("A New Partnership with Southeast Asia") stated the main interests of the EU:[31]

- Supporting regional stability and the fight against terrorism.
- Promoting human rights, democratic principles, and good governance.
- Advancing justice and supporting the most important issues in home affairs.
- Injecting new dynamism into regional trade and the investment relations between the two regions.
- Supporting the least prosperous countries of Southeast Asia.
- Introducing a set of special dialogue activities, particularly among representatives of civil society.

The European Union has often identified ASEAN as its preferred Asian partner grouping. Yet compared to its efforts among other partner regions in Africa, the Caribbean, and the Pacific, the EU has been less proactive in promoting deeper integration in ASEAN. In light of the economic interests of the EU in ASEAN, this is somewhat astonishing. In order to strengthen the political character of ASEAN, the European Union has always supported the development of the ASEAN Regional Forum. Founded in 1994, the ASEAN Regional Forum is essentially a dialogue forum bringing together the ten ASEAN countries and fourteen partners, including the European Union. The EU has continuously favored stronger institutionalization of the ASEAN Regional Forum. So far, this strategic interest of the European Union has not received the enthusiasm it might have hoped for in ASEAN. By now, a special unit dealing with matters related to the work of the ASEAN Regional Forum has been established at the Secretariat of ASEAN in Jakarta.

With the Asia-Europe Meeting, another dimension of biregional cooperation has been introduced between the EU and ASEAN, along with its three most important neighbors, China, Japan, and Korea. Biannual meetings of the heads of state and government have been held since 1996. During the 2006 ASEM summit in Helsinki, ASEM was enlarged to include India, Pakistan, and Mongolia, thus raising questions about the original focus of its work. Basically, ASEM is a dialogue platform, sometimes considered to be a balancing factor for Asia-Pacific Economic Cooperation, although without APEC's matter-of-fact economic agenda, which aims at promoting free trade in the dynamic Asia-Pacific region. So far, ASEM has fallen short of developing a coherent agenda and set of objectives.[32] Another biannual dialogue platform was established between the European Union and ASEAN in 2002 with the Asia-Europe Parliamentary Meeting (ASEP). Cohesion and coherence in EU-ASEAN relations have suffered with the rise of China and the undecided constellation in regional architecture potentially emerging from China's future role for and in its region. The question about convergence or divergence of regional integration trends in Europe and in East Asia has gained new and unpredictable dimensions.[33] For the time being, the weak institutionalization of ASEAN has also weakened EU efforts to influence integration trends in Southeast Asia.

Prospects and Obstacles

Paradoxically, modernization-driven nationalism was helpful in bringing about a first wave of region-ness in Southeast Asia. In spite of its inherent competitive character, the development strategies of the market economies in Southeast Asia served as an instrument for turning anti-colonial emotions into a new and promising regional strategy. But Southeast Asia's modernization-driven nationalism has not been too helpful in promoting stronger institutional schemes aimed at supporting, framing, and guiding the economic processes in the region. While ASEAN was conceived as a means of deterring communist expansionism in Southeast Asia, it did not bring about a concrete military pact. In fact, the military dimension in ASEAN could even invoke tensions among ASEAN members themselves. Arms procurement among ASEAN member states has always been accompanied by suspicion in the region. It has always been understood that sophisticated weaponry would not only serve to deter the communist countries in the wider region but could also be used in interstate conventional warfare among ASEAN states.[34]

A real dilemma for ASEAN has been—from its very beginning and carrying into its fifth decade of existence—inconclusiveness about the role and relevance of democratic governance for regional integration. In order to not get entangled in interfering in the domestic affairs of its member countries, ASEAN has fallen short of thoroughly analyzing the link between solidified democratic governance and deepened regional integration. As a consequence, ASEAN state practices could become obstacles to its integration progress. As long as the rule of law is weak inside ASEAN member states, it cannot unfold its full potential as a foundation of regional integration within the ASEAN community as a whole.

The limits on democracy, human rights, and the rule of law in "old" and "new" ASEAN member states have often found more concern outside ASEAN than anywhere in the region. The idea of a community law has remained weak in ASEAN, at least so far. The limits of democratic transformation in Indochina have been overshadowed by satisfaction over the resolution of the geopolitical tensions and divisions in the region. Only in the case of Myanmar has the strict position of the European Union triggered genuine reactions from within ASEAN. As of now, the EU has not been able to turn domestic affairs in Myanmar around with its selective sanctions, which thus have only made the regime in Yangon even more parochial. While the EU was absent in Myanmar, the military regime of Myanmar had a free hand in developing a strategic balance, in order to cope with the rising geopolitical aspirations of China and India, in the spheres of energy resources, possible transportation lines, and a huge market hitherto untapped in Myanmar.

Although ASEAN is always careful to save face for all parties involved, Myanmar's democratic deficit has led ASEAN to define limits for non-democratic behavior inside the association for the first time. Whether this was due to external pressure or internal insights, whether it was simply a matter of image or in a deeper sense one of democratic conviction, whether it was the consequence of Myanmar being a weak member of ASEAN, or whether it was the fact that right-wing military regimes have become more tainted in the world than left-wing populist authoritarian regimes is subject to contrasting attitudes and perceptions. But there cannot be any doubt that ASEAN is no longer able to simply shy away from addressing the nexus between solid democratic governance inside ASEAN member states and comprehensive and sustainable success in pursuing the objectives of regional integration. Economic modernization during the past decades has certainly prepared Southeast Asia reasonably well for coping with the challenges and opportunities of globalization. Law-based regional integration and democratic governance need to be understood in their interdependence as a set of preconditions and consequences if economic globalization is to bring lasting success to ASEAN. In order to turn ASEAN from an elite operation into a people's project across Southeast Asia, a sense of ownership has to emerge within ASEAN societies.

Among the untapped potentials of regional integration in Southeast Asia, the opportunities for subregional cooperation have not yet gained sufficient attention. Some of the more obvious "growth triangles" have been identified as embodiments of "micro-regionalism" in Southeast Asia. These "growth triangles" include the Singapore-Johor-Riau Triangle; the Indonesia-Malaysia-Thailand Growth Triangle; the East ASEAN Growth Triangle, including Sabah, Sarawak, Labuan, North Sulawesi, East and West Kalimantan, Mindanao, and Brunei; and the Growth Triangle of Mainland Southeast Asia, including Laos, Thailand, Myanmar, and the Chinese province Yunan. In these "growth triangles," joint management of natural resources and modernization of infrastructure can trigger sustainable economic development. This might possibly be followed by or coupled with the evolution of joint institutions for organizing, distributing, and multiplying public goods. Thus the "growth triangles" of Southeast Asia pose a challenge to the state-centric region-ness concept usually applied in ASEAN.[35]

The most interesting aspect of "microregionalism" in Southeast Asia can be found in the Mekong River Basin. Since ASEAN's enlargement between 1995 and 1999, the relevance of the Mekong River Basin has increased. It is home to 40 percent of ASEAN's total population. Since the beginning of the economic transformation in the communist countries of Indochina in the mid 1980s, foreign direct investment in the region has increased substantially. Other ASEAN countries are the main source of these foreign direct investments. In Cambodia the figure is 80 percent, 73 percent of which originates in Malaysia; in Laos 44 percent of foreign direct investment originates in ASEAN. Foreign investment in the Mekong River Basin is mainly targeted at infrastructure measures and the financing of development schemes.[36]

In 1995, the Mekong River Commission was established. Its secretariat is located in Phnom Penh. The Mekong River Commission is understood as a platform for regional resource management. To improve the reasonable and equitable use of the Mekong waters, a Mekong Basin Development Plan was developed in 1996.[37] A whole set of institutions has been established (inter alia, the ASEAN Mekong Fund, The Mekong Development Bank, and the ASEAN Mekong Basin Development Cooperation) with the aim of improving infrastructure, human resources, and the standard of living in the Mekong River Basin. In 1994, the first ever bridge between Thailand and Laos was opened, built as part of the regional development scheme with Australian development aid. The Mekong River Basin cooperation could become a win-win situation: while the poor Indochinese countries will obviously benefit from river regulations, dam projects, and agricultural development, the same is also true for Thailand, where 35 million people depend on rice production. The country also needs energy and fresh water, not least in the poorer regions of Northeastern Thailand. While experts in the region are primarily focusing on the technical, social, and ecological aspects of their endeavor, the first strategic objectives for the overall regional development and its integration potential are reflected in the capitals of the main countries in the region, mainly Bangkok and Hanoi.

The original activities in developing the Mekong River Basin date back to the founding of the Mekong Committee in 1957, which soon became a victim of the tensions in Indochina. Only after the end of the geopolitical divisions in the region did a new beginning for the idea of the Mekong as an engine of regional development and integration become feasible. The establishment of the Mekong River Commission in 1995 was its logical consequence. With a Council, a Joint Committee, and the Secretariat in Phnom Penh, the Mekong River Commission has taken organizational form. The commission's work began in 1995 with nine-ty-seven joint projects, mainly aimed at confidence-building.[38]

The Mekong River Commission's long-term prospects remain unknown today, yet one cannot help but look back to the long-term role of the Rhine Navigation Act of 1868, the first multilateral treaty to provide free passage on the Rhine River. It was signed in Mannheim by all Rhine riparian countries, Baden, Bavaria, Hesse, Nassau, France, the Netherlands, and Prussia. The Rhine Navigation Act was a precursor of the modern concept of European integration, long superseded by the European Union when its revised version was signed in 1999 by Switzerland, Germany, France, the Netherlands, and Belgium. It cannot be excluded that over time the Mekong River Commission may play a similar role in Indochina.

The main question in any speculation about the prospects of Mekong River Basin integration is: Will the Mekong River integration be engulfed in the wider ASEAN cooperation and integration? Or will it eventually serve as a vehicle for the projection of China's interests in Southeast Asia? China, where the Mekong River has its source, is a member of the Mekong River Commission. China's huge energy demand has triggered Beijing's interest in any pos-sible access to available resources, water included. A proposal for financing the Singapore-Beijing-Trans-Asia project, one of the infrastructure measures related to the development of the Greater Mekong River Basin, has been submitted to the Asia Development Bank. In the end, the Mekong River Basin might indeed become an engine for regional integration in Southeast Asia, much as coal and steel did in Europe during the 1950s. Pooling the access and management of strategic resources of a region to provide fresh water and energy can indeed be an issue of the first order.

The ultimate question related to such a vision of the Mekong as an engine for integration is of a geopolitical nature: In the end, some observers ask with irony, who will join whom? Will ASEAN link with China or China with ASEAN? To answer this question favorably in its own interest, ASEAN will have to achieve nothing less than reinventing itself, its objective, structures, and instruments. At some point in the not too distant future, ASEAN might find itself confronted with a choice: to truly institutionalize itself politically or "to be swallowed" up in its scope of action by China. ASEAN cannot influence the rise of China, and it can hardly tame its effects. The concept of ASEAN Plus Three is nothing but a transient solution, as inconclusive as the formula ASEAN Minus X for domestic decision-making among ASEAN member states has been. For the time being, the geopolitical constellation in Southeast Asia is in undecided limbo. Its actors, to their own displeasure, may be forced to decide between the primacy of re-gional integration coupled with the acceptance of a certain peripheral status vis-à-vis China on the one hand, and on the other the temptation to ride the waves of the emerging Chinese giant by trading regional autonomy for the protection of

China—a China that until recently was ASEAN's main and seemingly irreconcilable adversary and a unifying stimulus because of this.

ASEAN will have to connect the idea of region-ness with the emerging civil societies and, in particular, with the private sector. It is a paradox that the booming economies of Southeast Asia have not yet discovered regional integration as being in their genuine interest. Their activities are not linked to the political and diplomatic processes in ASEAN. The constituency for private sector–based initiatives toward deeper integration has remained weak across ASEAN. Federalizing factors, such as the ASEAN Secretariat, have been too weak to substantially impact the regional trend. ASEAN needs to initiate a regional equivalent to the once overly lauded European Cecchini Report about costs and benefits of integration, and especially about the costs of non-integration. ASEAN will also have to confront the constraints of its overly limited institutionalization. Tools such as an ASEAN equivalent of Eurobarometer, sometimes already discussed as ASEAN-Barometer, could help nurture, support, and tap region-wide public opinion on relevant matters of public interest.

ASEAN cannot become the European Union. It should not try to rhetorically and institutionally copy the EU as long as the internal political culture of Southeast Asia follows a different set of priorities. ASEAN has carefully studied the many dimensions of the European integration experience, for better or worse. Its main problem remains the reluctance of its political leadership to substantially advance deeper integration rooted in a stronger sense of ownership among ASEAN's citizens. The high reputation of ASEAN may justify this reluctance, which runs counter to the positive image of ASEAN. For the time being, ASEAN leaders seem to accept the paradox of high symbolic reputation and low factual integration.

Gulf Cooperation Council (GCC)

Basic Facts

The Gulf Cooperation Council (GCC)—which uses this name along with the more formal term Cooperation Council for the Arab States of the Gulf—is one of the paradoxical regional architectures. Originally a security scheme of the smaller Arab Gulf countries, it has never grown into a comprehensive defense pact. Representing the leading oil and gas producers of the world, it has nevertheless to cope with the implications of rentier societies that are facing enormous problems. Established with the intention of maintaining "regime stability"[39] among the conservative Arab monarchies of the Gulf region, it has to manage the evolution toward political pluralism and the tensions originating in the dilemma posed by Western-oriented modernization and Islamic traditionalism.

Finally, the Gulf Cooperation Council is torn between membership cohesion on the basis of its traditional regimes and the "pull" factors stemming from possible enlargement to include countries of a different regime nature with strong geopolitical implications for the future of the GCC. The Gulf Cooperation Council is caught between several simultaneously competing forces: achieving economic and currency union, promoting enlargements without undermining stability, coping with internal governance transformations, and last but not least, redefining its rationale amidst fundamental geopolitical changes in the region and beyond.

The Gulf Cooperation Council has become an element of stability in a region of tremendous upheavals, transitions, and uncertainties. When it was founded in 1981, the GCC was considered a protective shield against external pressure on the traditions of Arab Gulf monarchies. In fact, it was also a protective shield for the very modern, and very Western, nationalism that has evolved in that region, as it has everywhere else in the non-Western world: with the end of Western colonial or semi-colonial dominance, the modern national state and its legitimizing and constituting categories of sovereignty had to be protected against potential threats to its legitimacy and territorial integrity. In a dialectical twist, the GCC was seemingly created to protect overly non-Western, if not outright anti-Western conservatism, in the Persian Gulf. In reality, however, it began as an instrument for protecting what was the most modern and Western element in Persian Gulf politics: the integrity and territorial preservation of the nation-state.

The claim to sovereignty had reached most of the Persian Gulf region in a rather belated way. Saudi Arabia has been an independent kingdom since 1932, but the small Gulf countries were only created within the last generation after Great Britain withdrew from the region East of Aden. Oman became independent in 1952, Kuwait in 1961, and the Trucial States in 1971, dividing immediately into the United Arab Emirates, Qatar, and Bahrain. Yemen embarked on the most complicated history after the Arab Republic of Yemen became independent in 1962 and the People's Republic of South Yemen in 1967. The status of semi-sovereign protectorates was replaced by full-fledged independent states claiming their rights on the international scene. The rising conflicts among the bigger powers in the region turned into a challenge to their independence. The concept of regional cooperation and integration was born out of the fear of again losing independent statehood and national sovereignty—this time not to aggressive Western imperialism, but to power claims in the region, among Arab and non-Arab Muslim states.

Gradually, the concept of regional security for new and seemingly weak states grew into the prospect of combining the forces of economic development of the region. The original political goal of independence was transformed by the security analysis into the functional goal of economic cooperation. This, in turn, inevitably affected both the security constellation of the region and the domestic political agenda of each participating country. A pattern of mutually reinforcing cooperation elements and unintended integration consequences evolved. The constellation under which the GCC operates contains both important elements of unpredictability and promising components regarding the near-mid and the longer-term future of the Gulf region. In the shadow of its domestic regimes, and even more so of an unstable geopolitical environment, the Gulf Cooperation Council has become an engine of transformation that is also transforming itself.

The economic resources in the Persian Gulf region are impressive, and yet they do not naturally guarantee stability and prosperity. Saudi Arabia, Kuwait, Qatar, and the United Arab Emirates own 42 percent of all global oil reserves; Bahrain and Oman own 23 percent of all global gas reserves. Among the GCC member states, the distribution of oil and gas is very uneven: Saudi Arabia and the United Arab Emirates hold 98 percent of the total GCC oil resources. Qatar, with the third largest gas reserves worldwide after Russia and Iran, holds 44 percent of all GCC gas resources. The limits of the natural resources of the Gulf countries have become a matter of growing concern as the economies of the Gulf States need to diversify. In Kuwait and in the United Arab Emirates, oil will reportedly last for a hundred years. Gas in Qatar might last for eighty years and in Bahrain for ninety years, according to current estimates.

The Gulf States have built their modernization around the industry of oil and gas. Of the total exports from Gulf States, oil and gas products account for 65 percent. More than 50 percent of these exports go to Japan, China, and South Korea. Only 11 percent go to the European Union and 12 percent to the United States. Because of its global strategic importance, the energy resources of the Gulf region loom very large on the radar screens of geopolitical and geo-economic discourses across the world. The dependency of the world economy on the Gulf region is beyond any doubt. Yet the Gulf States are not themselves larger than life. With a population equivalent to Canada, their GDP is half that of Canada, or half of the combined GDP of Belgium, the Netherlands, and Luxembourg. The search for unity, cooperation, and integration in the Gulf region is also a function of necessary self-enhancement and self-help in a volatile region.

In stark contrast to the geopolitical volatility of the Gulf region stands the conservative continuity in the structures of power since the days of independence. The ruling families have not changed in the Gulf monarchies, no matter the different titles they carry: the Al Saud family in Saudi Arabia, the Al Khalifa family in Bahrain, the Al Nahayyan family in the United Arab Emirates, the Al Sabah family in Kuwait, the Qaboos family in Oman, and the Al Thani family in Qatar embody stability and loyalty in the Arab Gulf region. At the same time, they are part of the problem for those concerned with pluralism and governance based on democratic processes for the transfer of power, transparency, and critical revision in current affairs. The issue of governance and especially the deficit in democracy in the Arab world has been a taboo for too long. In the shadow of Western dependency on Arab oil, human rights have been a secondary consideration for many years. Only the resurgence of radical Islam, embodied in the horrible terrorism associated with the attacks on the United States on 11 September 2001, raised questions about the very structures of politics and power in Arab countries. The relationship between closed societies, a lack of pluralism, and the Islamic radicalization that threatened not only Western countries but also some of the pro-Western though overly conservative and undemocratic Arab regimes, has became a more widespread issue of concern and analysis.

"Of all the impediments to an Arab renaissance," the United Nations–sponsored Arab Human Development Report stated in 2005, "political restrictions on human development are the most stubborn."[40] The awareness of necessary reforms and international pressure has begun to show effects in even the most conservative and traditional Arab Gulf countries:

- In Qatar, a consultative assembly (Majlis-ash-Shura) has existed since the days of independence in 1971. The emir of Qatar has often been outspoken in favor of political reforms, but the first central municipal elections were held only in 1999. Women have been allowed to vote, although none have been elected. In 2003, a new constitution was approved by a referendum and promulgated by the emir in 2004. The right of the emir to appoint 15 out of 45 members of the Majlis-ash-Shura was confirmed, while the other 30 members are directly elected. Qatar is proud of its first National Committee of Human Rights and even more so of the fact that the television station Al Jazeera has been based in Qatar since 1996.
- In Kuwait, which has had a permanent constitution since 1961, the national assembly met from 1961 until 1976, when it was dissolved by the then emir. Ever since, governments have been appointed by the emir and dominated by the ruling Al Sabah family. Reestablished in 1981, Kuwait's parliament has been deeply divided between reform-minded and conservative representatives. It has been very reluctant to broaden the base for liberties and pluralism, and in 1999 a law to introduce voting rights for women was rejected by parliament. Finally, however, in April 2006, women in Kuwait were allowed to vote for the first time in local elections, followed by active and passive voting rights for women in Kuwait's national elections in June 2006. Under its 1997 constitution, Kuwait is a constitutional hereditary monarchy.
- In Bahrain, a new charter acknowledging the right of political association was issued in 2001 and approved by referendum. In May 2002, municipal elections took place with a clear victory for the conservative Shi'a groups. In October 2002, the same groups boycotted the election for the House of Deputies, which was meant to revitalize parliamentary life in Bahrain, suspended since 1975. In another problematic move, the head of the Bahrain Centre for Human Rights, Abdul Hadi Al Khawaja, was arrested in 2004 after calling for the resignation of Prime Minister Sheikh Khalifa Bin Salman Al Khalifa, and the Bahrain Centre for Human Rights was closed.[41]

- In Oman, a consultative council (Majlis-ash-Shura) has existed since 1991. Initially, its members were selected by a two tier-system in which qualified electors chose candidates in a limited system of suffrage; before that the Sultan appointed them. Over time, the active electorate has expanded. In October 2003, the first election to the Majlis-ash-Shura took place on the basis of universal suffrage, including the right of Omani women to vote. However, the Majlis-ash-Shura retains a purely consultative function.
- In Saudi Arabia, a consultative assembly (Majlis-ash-Shura) was installed by the then king in 1992. Albeit very slowly, a progressive opening for debates that are more political and relevant for a stable and reform-oriented future of the conservative Islamic kingdom has been noticeable since then. Between 2001 and 2005, four National Dialogues have taken place, making the political debate in Saudi Arabia slightly less dull than before. In the meantime, sessions of the Majlis-ash-Shura are televised. Women, who have no political rights in Saudi Arabia, were appointed to the police force for the first time in 2005.
- The United Arab Emirates is the only Gulf state without any representative body. As a first step toward parliamentary democracy, half of the Federal National Council was elected in December 2006; the other half remains appointed by the ruler of the United Arab Emirates, Sultan Khalifa bin Zayed Al Nahayan. The sultan has promised to eventually establish a constitutive assembly.

Based on these recent trends, the actual conservatism of the Arab Gulf states remains unchallenged. Political parties do not exist in any of them. Freedom of the press remains curtailed, Kuwait having more or less the most acceptable level of free press. The UN-sponsored *Arab Human Development Report* has identified across intellectual debates in the Arab world a trend toward combining "the principles of freedom and justice with the additional principle of social and economic development."[42] Dominance of the conservative dynasties remains the point of departure for any reasonable and thorough reform in the Arab Gulf states. It is against this background that the development of the Gulf Cooperation Council has to be understood and measured.

Ever since its founding in 1981, the GCC's primary concern has been regime legitimacy. External threats had made cooperation among the conservative dynasties in the Gulf region imperative. The Soviet invasion of Afghanistan in 1979, ending with Moscow's defeat in 1986, the Iranian revolution of 1979, in which the shah was ousted by the theocratic Shi'a regime under Ayatollah Khomeini, and the Iraqi invasion of Iran in September 1980, followed by eight years of a protracted war that paralyzed the whole region, dramatically affected the threat perception in the Gulf region. The region's trouble came closer to the Gulf countries when armed radicals seized the Grand Mosque in Mecca in 1979 and when in Bahrain a coup by radical Shi'a representing the country's minority failed in 1981. Between 1982 and 1987 various conflicts with Iranian radicals broke out in Saudi Arabia. In 1985 an assassination attempt took place against the emir of Kuwait. It failed, but it was evident that it was intended to undermine stability in the Gulf region. Kuwait and its neighbors started to fear that the radicalization in Iran could spill over to their countries. As a share of the population, Shi'a make up 80 percent in Qatar, 72 percent in Bahrain, and 5 percent in Saudi Arabia.[43]

Already in 1976, at the initiative of Sultan Qaboos of Oman, the foreign ministers of Iran, Iraq, Kuwait, Bahrain, Qatar, the United Arab Emirates, Saudi Arabia, and Oman met in Muscat to discuss the Omani proposal for the establishment of a regional security and defense policy. In the same year, Sheikh Jaber al Ahmad al Sabah, prime minister and later the emir of Kuwait, proposed the establishment of a Gulf union with the objective of realizing full economic, political, education, and foreign policy cooperation. These original initiatives and the overall geopolitical constellation paved the way for a fruitful Gulf cooperation.

The immediate reactions to the rise of Shi'a radicalism—including the Saudi Arabian government's measure to drain swimming pools and prohibit pictures of women in newspapers, and Kuwait's efforts to render the school curricula more conservative—were sociological and obviously insufficient. Protecting the Arab monarchies of the Gulf required more political attention. In February 1981, the foreign ministers of Bahrain, the United Arab Emirates, Qatar, Kuwait, Oman, and Saudi Arabia met in Riyadh and decided to establish the Gulf Cooperation Council. On 25 May 1981, the Cooperation Council Charter was signed in Abu Dhabi by the region's six heads of state.[44] On 11 November 1981, the signing of the GCC Unified Economic Agreement followed.[45]

The GCC Charter, consisting of its preamble and twenty-two articles, defines its ultimate aim: "to achieve unity between them,"[46] that is, the founding member states. The main objectives of the Gulf Cooperation Council were outlined as follows:

- Promote effective coordination, integration, and cooperation between member states in all fields in order to achieve unity.
- Deepen and strengthen relations, links, and scopes of cooperation between their peoples.
- Promote similar regulations in the fields of economy, finance, commerce, customs, communications, education, culture, social affairs, health in particular, information, tourism, legislation, and administrative affairs.
- Stimulate scientific and technological progress.

The GCC Charter explicitly outlined a minimalist program as far as political integration was concerned. The somewhat bombastic term "unity" was not intended to undermine and unravel the concept of state sovereignty. This was obviously a paradox in the context of Arab and Muslims countries, which tend to be torn between the goal of unity in the name of Islam and the defense of the states' principles, which obviously divide them. If taken seriously, the mechanisms for collective decision-making in a truly unitary GCC would have meant a threat to the very regimes that formed the GCC.[47] The Arab League founded in 1945 had continuously failed to resolve the dilemma between Arab unity and the preservation of national sovereignty. The GCC could only be pragmatic, functional, and limited in its scope if it wanted to become successful and gain respect. The result was a combination of increasingly growing economic integration with weak security cooperation.[48]

The Gulf Cooperation Council maintains a limited set of institutions, which grew as the GCC was developing. Most relevant are:

- The GCC Supreme Council: meeting twice a year, the summit of the heads of state of the GCC countries decides on the basis of unanimity on relevant matters, but has agreed (according to Articles 7 and 8 of the GCC Charter) to respect qualified majority voting on procedural matters.
- The GCC Ministerial Council: the foreign ministers' meeting of the GCC is the effective working group, supported by expert-level committees.
- The Economic Cooperation Committee: the finance ministers of the GCC have grown into an increasingly important role as economic integration has advanced.
- The Committee of Monetary Agencies and Central Bank Governors: this body has become crucial since the GCC decided to seriously prepare for the implementation of a comprehensive monetary union.
- The GCC General Secretariat: based in Riyadh, the General Secretariat, currently headed by the GCC Secretary General Sheikh Abdul-Rahman bin Hamad Al-Attiyah, has been described as "the engine room of the GCC ship."[49] The General Secretariat launches studies, coordinates meetings, and continuously claims the need for an increase in real executive powers.
- The Commission for Settlement of Disputes: attached to the Supreme Council and legitimized under Article 6 of the GCC Charter, the commission works on an ad hoc basis as a mediating body. In 1993, a GCC Commercial Arbitration Center was added.

The work of the Gulf Cooperation Council is supported by a wide array of specialized committees. The GCC has never been able to deny that its main constituent bodies are members of an "exclusive club of traditional and benevolent autocracies."[50] To their credit, though, they have consistently acted as "a force of moderation, conciliation, and mediation."[51] This is important not only as a geopolitical fact: the GCC member states have also grown to learn the usefulness, in fact the inevitable necessity of, pooling resources. The Unified Economic Agreement of the GCC was no immediate technical blueprint for a common market.

But it underlined the inclusion of the economic dimension into the whole rationale of the process of Gulf cooperation and integration. It outlined the economic goals, which, as described in the preamble of the Unified Economic Agreement, are "to coordinate and unify their economic, financial and monetary policies, as well as their commercial and industrial legislation."[52] Since 2002, the GCC has been working on a Common Patent Law. By 2003, a GCC Customs Union was in place.

Article 2 of the Unified Economic Agreement paved the way for increased trade among GCC member states. Products and natural resources of national origin in one of the GCC member states should be exempted from any customs duties in another member state. The agreement defined a product of national origin as a one whose value added inside the GCC is not less than 40 percent of the final value of the product. Tax exemption and mutual recognition of rules of origin were considered an important technical element in the development of a customs union. The same was true with regard to a uniform minimum customs tariff for third-country products. The unified tariff of between 4 and 20 percent for imported goods was intended to take effect as early as 1983, but at the time only Kuwait and Bahrain had complied with the provisions of the agreement. It took the other GCC member states much longer to overcome not just their procedural problems, but at times their outright vested interests.

The Unified Economic Agreement emphasized the need for coordinated developments in the movement of capital and citizens, technical cooperation, transportation, communications, and financial and monetary matters. These specific aspects were understood as highly important in the preparation of a possible GCC monetary union. Last but not least, the Unified Economic Agreement outlined the need to create a joint negotiation force of the GCC for dealing with third parties—an interesting dimension for future relations with other partners, including the European Union, and for a strengthened role of the GCC in the context of the World Trade Organization.

The Unified Economic Agreement was lauded as "the backbone of the GCC and its activities, the basic foundation on which all the rest of the GCC's cooperation and integrative endeavors are built."[53] In 2001, it was revised and replaced by a new and comprehensive economic agreement. Under certain pressure, after the introduction of the euro and in light of globalization, the Gulf Cooperation Council saw itself forced to intensify and focus its economic integration. Now, rhetoric was translated into real action: it took only two years, until 2003, for the GCC to achieve "the complete elimination of intra-regional customs duties, an accomplishment with few parallels in the history of Third World regionalism."[54] Finally, the external tariff came down to between 4 to 20 percent, depending on the product. De facto, all GCC currencies were pegged to the dollar. The common market, scheduled for 2007, was understood not as a technical process in itself, but as an important instrument in order to achieve full monetary union with a common currency by 2010. During the days of the British protectorate, the Gulf ports had used the Indian rupee. The common Gulf currency, whose criteria are by and large modeled after the European Monetary Union, shall be called Khaleej Dinar.

Intrinsic Motives and External Pressures

It does not seem evident when looking through the lens of politics of oil, but except for Saudi Arabia and Oman, the Arab Gulf states have to be understood in their role as small and rather weak states among bigger powers and amidst world strategic conflicts. The threat perception in the Arab Gulf states was focused and sharpened by their security considerations following the Islamic revolution in Iran and the Soviet invasion of Afghanistan. The freedom of navigation in the Gulf was, rightly so, their main concern, as it is the precondition for any predictable oil transport. The neutrality in the region's conflicts was sometimes disputed among the Gulf States, but in the end there was no real alternative, given their size and dependencies. The goal of binding security considerations together and strengthening each of them by way of improved cooperation and a possible integration of security instruments was rational.

The Arab Gulf states are linked with all other Arab countries through a common religion and language. The idea to rebuild the Arab *umma* has been a constant theme among Arabs, but it continues to be in conflict with the dividing force of the modern state. Under pressure from Shi'ite radicalism in Iran that had the potential to spread into the whole Arab peninsula, and from internal criticism of an overly strong Westernization in so far as a modern lifestyle and consumerism are concerned, the Arab Gulf states began to discover the need to enhance the stability of their political regimes. Commonalities had to be identified in order to justify each of the Gulf regimes. Paradoxically, the evolution of commonalities framed, advanced, and facilitated internal development within the regimes of the Gulf region. The advancement of a regional architecture became an instrument for the improvement of governance structures and the slow opening of the conservative Gulf societies toward pluralism.

Economic considerations were the obvious engine to advance the notion of region-building. The member states of the GCC harbor 45.9 percent of the world's oil reserves and produce 16.4 percent of the world's oil. Yet this fortune is also a curse, since 80 to 95 percent of all GDP of the Gulf States is oil-based and hence they are enormously dependent on one or two single commodities. The Gulf states are increasingly aware of the fact that oil is not just a weapon they can use in the world economy but also a weapon that can be turned against them as alternative energies are promoted more and more, especially in light of the undeniable limits of oil and gas resources in the Gulf region and elsewhere. Stable markets and prices are therefore as much in the interest of the Gulf states as they are in the interest of the consumers of oil and gas. The reciprocity between secure demand and secure supply binds both of them. It still leaves the Gulf States with the need to diversify their economies as they gradually enter the post-oil era.

The motivation for regional cooperation and integration was also rooted in food and labor dependencies. When the Gulf Cooperation Council started its existence, around 35 percent of the total labor force in GCC member states was made up of foreigners. Four million of them came from Arab countries or were Palestinian refugees, and more than one million came from South and Southeast Asia. The presence of a cheap foreign workforce always aroused great ambivalence in the Gulf. On the one hand, cheap labor was guaranteed. On the other hand, the rentier state mentality had a negative impact on the work ethic and mentality of Arab Gulf citizens.[55] Once they were confronted with the limits of their power and affected by economic slowdown, many of them did not know how to handle a situation in which Gulf Arabs were obliged to work to make a basic living. The more the complexity of labor relations in the GCC countries increased, the stronger the regional cooperation and integration became. GCC member states insisted that freedom of movement under the framework of a customs union and common market among GCC countries would not apply to non-GCC citizens. Due to the need for labor mobility among GCC member states, the matter of a common visa and a common migration policy arose.

The initial rationale for Gulf cooperation and integration was security. The founding of the GCC was not directed against any other country, and the GCC member states ensured all powers in the wider region that their cooperation was not based on any sort of hostility, but rather on caution and defense. The GCC, Saudi Arabia's then King Khaled bin Abdullaziz said in 1981, "is concerned with the common good of the region and will in no way, directly or indirectly, be hostile to anyone." The GCC, as the king underlined, did not see itself as a military bloc, but as "a fraternal group seeking the welfare and stability as well as the security of our people."[57] Initially, the logic of a common defense strategy did not translate into a formal defense alliance. Over time, the notion of security broadened and the concept of GCC defense started to include the economy. This concept ultimately stretched further, although very hesitantly and under external pressure, to begin to include matters of good governance. The Gulf Cooperation Council, founded in order to protect its member states from external pressure, became a framework for better coping with various internal threats to the secure development of the region, since they are rooted in the traditional regimes, if not archaic forms of governance, that have defined the Gulf region for so long.

Performance

Since its creation in 1981, the GCC has acquired continuous media presence in the Gulf region and beyond. Enhanced reputation can serve as an element in community-building and should not be underestimated. In empirical terms, among the strong points of the GCC record, the following can be identified so far.

The Gulf Cooperation Council has been able to exercise a geopolitical role in stabilizing the small states in the Gulf region. By and large, the GCC has been able to keep the Strait of Hormuz open for oil transport. The fact that 40 percent of all world oil passes through the Strait of Hormuz indicates the importance of this contribution to a functioning world economy. Keeping the Strait of Hormuz open to oil transport has been a joint interest of all GCC member states. In 1983, the GCC formally provided a grant of $1.8 billion to Oman to increase its capacities to counter possible attacks on the Strait of Hormuz.

The GCC member states' dependency on free navigation in the Persian Gulf indicates the intrinsic link between strategic considerations and the importance of economic security in and for the Gulf region. Although it took until 2003 to finally complete a GCC customs union, the economic harmonization activities had always been directed toward the achievement of a common market. Joint regulations and a unified external tariff (between 4 and 20 percent) made sense only if they were understood as an instrument for advancing the idea of a common market. It took twenty years to move from the establishment of a unified external tariff in 1983 to a completed customs union in 2003.

But the process itself has always been part of the success. It increased the understanding of a common interest among GCC member states in moving forward: from recognizing freedom of labor and capital movement (1984) to permitting all GCC nationals to engage in retail trade (1986) and later in wholesale trade (1990) in all other GCC countries. The establishment of the Gulf Investment Corporation in 1982 indicated the intention to promote the development of productive sectors across the GCC. The Kuwait-based Gulf Investment Corporation became involved, among other examples, in the modernization of the aluminum industry in Bahrain, the establishment of the National Wire Drawing and Products Corporation in Jubail, and the aircraft modification center at Riyadh's King Khaled airport. In 1985, the idea of a common market was taken a step further with the installation of the GCC Specification and Measures Organization, expanding a formerly Saudi Arabian system of harmonizing and standardizing norms throughout the GCC in spheres ranging from electrical appliances to environmental protection. Many other technical and specialized agencies got involved in the promotion of the conditions for a common market.

In macroeconomic terms, the improvements became measurable: during the first decade of the GCC's existence, intra-regional trade increased from 3 to 9 percent.[58] Intra-regional trade in the Gulf region has never become stronger. It differs markedly from intra-regional trade in Europe because of the export orientation of the energy-rich Gulf countries. The economic structure of the Gulf States limits intra-regional trade. On the other hand, regional cooperation does not necessarily imply increased intra-regional trade if it only happens at the cost of less trade with outside regions. In fact, the GCC objective of a monetary union will help to strengthen the GCC countries' links with countries outside of the Gulf region, even if it cannot substantially impact intra-regional trade.

Cooperation under the GCC umbrella has reached all economic activities and the infrastructure in GCC countries. Water, land utilization, and a common farming policy were discussed for the first time in 1984 in order to advance agricultural integration and strengthen food security. In order to provide the best possible environment for GCC commerce, all intra-GCC trade barriers were removed, at least in principle, in 1983, along with the introduction of a unified external tariff. Unified telephone tariffs were introduced by 1984, followed by standardized rates for water and electricity.

More difficult was the diversification of the Gulf economies in order to prepare the region for the post-oil era. During the first years of the existence of the GCC, agricultural imports increased by 26.8 percent, while the increase in the domestic agricultural production was minimal. However, some progress was beginning to evolve: by 1991, the growth rate in GCC agriculture had reached a figure of 7 percent.[59] The United Arab Emirates was the first to achieve a stronger share in its non-oil sector: in 1991, its share increased from 33 to 50 percent. During the next twenty years, new concepts of industrialization and modernization circulated in the Gulf region, including the idea of a railway link to Europe. Air and marine transportation have been standardized and harmonized. Oil- and gas-based industries (petrochemicals) and metal processing industries (aluminum and copper refining and smelting), but also consumer industries (food, bakeries, printing presses) and a common electricity grid, indicated improvements during these years of a "new industrialization wave,"[60] driven by increased availability of natural gas and the growing export of liquefied fuel. Saudi Arabia's stock market index rose by 76 percent in 2003 and by 88 percent in 2004. While a growing GCC bourgeoisie can be identified, the investment commitment of the most affluent Arabs in their own region remained restrained. Saudi Arabians alone have invested between $800 billion and $1 trillion abroad, mostly in the US and in Europe, while their home country and its GCC partners are looking for more investment, particularly since the image of Arab countries has deteriorated following the terrorist attacks in the US on 11 September 2001.

At the end of 2001, the Gulf Cooperation Council decided to go beyond the ongoing transformation in the region with the introduction of a common currency in 2010. This project, it was immediately assumed, "will likely strengthen the environment for non-oil economic growth and create employment opportunities for a rapidly growing national labor force."[61] The period 2005 to 2010 is dedicated to the full implementation of the criteria necessary for introducing the Gulf currency union. Political consensus has been achieved. Following the experience of the creation of a European currency union, the GCC needs a strong, credible, and independent central bank. The GCC has defined convergence criteria equivalent to those that led to the introduction of the euro: 3 percent budget deficit, public debt of less than 60 percent of a country's GDP, and an average inflation of no more than 2 percent. It will require the promotion of more intra-regional trade and reinforced surveillance over fiscal policies to make the GCC currency sustainable. Eventually, the GCC will need a harmonized, if not integrated, macroeconomic policy. The procedure toward a GCC currency is remarkable indeed. It demonstrates the GCC's potential and the ambition, along with the urgent need to take economic integration in the Gulf region more seriously. In 2007, Oman declared it would prepare for the currency union without immediately joining it in 2010. The internal diversification of its economy was to take priority over the Sultanate's joining a common regional currency.

Among the evidently weak aspects of the development of the Gulf Cooperation Council, one cannot fail to recognize the following.

(1) The strategic and military ambition of the GCC has remained unclear and inconclusive. Based on the original threat assessment that led to the founding of the GCC, and following two joint maneuvers of the GCC member states ("Peninsula Shield"), a small Rapid Deployment Force was created in 1985, consisting of two brigades of Saudi Arabian and Kuwaiti soldiers. The Supreme Council of the GCC adopted a common security cooperation agreement in 1987 but never turned it into a collective security alliance. Efforts to create a joint military industry have never materialized. Instead, the policy of separate procurement policies prevails, the US being the main supplier in Saudi Arabia and in Kuwait, the United Arab Emirates procuring French and Russian equipment, and Oman relying on British supply.[62]

Existing border disputes among GCC member states—such as the one between Bahrain and Qatar and the one between Qatar and Saudi Arabia— have not been resolved through the channels of the GCC. Moreover, the GCC member states have at times practiced highly astonishing separate approaches to regional crises. Out of fear of provoking Iran, the United Arab Emirates and Oman, for example, refused to participate in GCC military exercises sponsored by Saudi Arabia. Throughout the Iran-Iraq War (1980–1988), Oman's role in regional security matters was ambivalent as it tried to share the control of the Straits of Hormuz with Iran, the main target of GCC deterrence. The role of the United Arab Emirates was even more ambivalent, receiving a new Iranian ambassador in 1982 amidst the war with Iraq and, according to critics, starting "quiet payments to Iran."[63] The common apprehension toward Iran's aggressive revolutionary policies never translated into a thoroughly united GCC approach toward Iran. After Iran attacked oil tankers in the Persian Gulf in 1984, the GCC finally started a joint initiative and presented a common resolution to the

United Nations. The UN Security Council adopted this text, calling for free navigation in the Gulf.

The GCC's failure to prevent Iraq's invasion of Kuwait in 1990 remains another grave indication for the limited security relevance of the GCC, despite security being its original rationale. The costs of this failure were high: Kuwait lost two thirds of its financial reserves. For Saudi Arabia, the invasion and its aftermath were beneficial. Saudi Arabia became the largest oil producer in the world, developed its strategic partnership with the US (which was to last unchallenged until 2001/2002), and initiated a new opening in relations with Iran, helping to move the whole GCC to abandon preferential relations with Iraq and form a bloc against Iraq and the regime of Saddam Hussein.

Connected with the strategic orientation of the original rationale of the GCC was the growing dependency on US interests in the Gulf region. This dependency grew from a welcome source of protection into a liability and source of uneasiness. In 1981, US military bases were opened in Bahrain, Saudi Arabia, and Oman. In reaction to the occupation of Kuwait by Iraq in 1990, US "friendly forces" stepped up their presence in Saudi Arabia and Bahrain and were also deployed in the United Arab Emirates. When the Iraq crisis escalated again following the terrorist attacks on the US in 2001, Saudi Arabia came under increasing pressure from conservative religious circles condemning the presence of US troops on its holy soil. All US troops had to leave, and their new headquarters were established in Qatar, from where they coordinated the controversial attack on Iraq in 2003. To date, the US Central Command in the Middle East (CENTCOM) remains stationed in Qatar.

(2) Cultural homogeneity among the people of the Arab peninsula can be helpful in resolving conflicts, as was the case between Oman and Yemen in 1993. Often, however, the relations among the different people and tribes exhibit a certain trend to exclusion, exceptionalism, and parochialism. The dominance of Saudi Arabia and the rigid Wahabi interpretation of Islam is a recurring theme in the Gulf region. Most ambivalent in terms of ethnicity and population structures is the overall makeup of the population and its economic consequences. Less than 50 percent of the GCC work force is indigenous. Vocational training structures are largely absent for the local population. It came as a shocking awakening to many when the unemployment figure of GCC citizens registered at 13.5 percent in 2005. The Arab rentier societies were experiencing a serious social problem and were forced to increase their modernization and social openness if they were to prevent an implosion.

The expulsion of 350,000 Palestinians from Kuwait and more than a million Yemenite people from Saudi Arabia in the early 1990s was indicative of possible reactions to the demographic problems in the Gulf region. As long as demography and investment were not brought into a new balance—Saudi Arabia was investing 80 percent of its oil revenues in the US instead of using the bulk of this money for the necessary improvements in its own country—something remained essentially wrong and dangerous in the domestic development of Arab Gulf societies. The dependency on oil remained high in most GCC member states, and the volatility of oil prices did not help to alleviate this situation. Intra-regional trade has not substantially increased. The concern about domestic stability in the Gulf States has grown in the West after the terrorist attacks of 9/11 and has not been helpful in improving the image of the whole region.

(3) The deficit in democratic governance must therefore be described as the biggest obstacle to further regional integration. It is paradoxical that the Gulf region represents a high degree of regime cohesion, which explains the first successful steps toward cooperation and integration under external pressure, driven by the desire to generate economic win-win situations. But the regime cohesion in the Gulf region is also the biggest liability to the prospects of regional integration, because it is cohesion without democracy. Under the impact of Western pressure, and fearful of falling victim to radical Islamic trends from within their societies, the Gulf monarchies have begun to reform and liberalize their political and social systems. To many, these changes are insufficient and cosmetic. Others are more hopeful, knowing that the Gulf monarchies have no alternative but to thoroughly modernize and liberalize if they want to preserve their hereditary powers in the long run, albeit in a reformed way.

Gulf cooperation and integration have a paradoxical consequence. On the one hand they are limited by the nature of the regimes that have brought the GCC into existence. On the other hand, it is the very promise of integration that can serve as a framework to help manage the inevitable regime transformations in GCC member states. The whole project of the GCC operates in the shadow of the struggle between benevolent authoritarianism and pluralistic governance. The focus on economic cooperation and integration in the Gulf region has underlined the region's awareness of its limits. The prospect of a currency union is therefore linked in a surprising way to the debate about the limits of human and political freedom in the Arab Gulf. As the need to instigate and manage regime transformations has become inevitable, the very prospect of a currency union for the whole region serves as a counterweight to more myopic worries about losing identity and stability. Regional integration, according to the message of the project of currency union, can serve as a new framework for identity and stability of more pluralistic and open societies in the member states of the GCC. It is an intrinsic political and almost a cultural approach linked to a genuine economic and fiscal program.

Federators

Cultural and religious commonality and geographical proximity have helped to conceptualize the GCC. Geographical proximity was understood not as the expression of cultural commonality but as a geography subject to a common threat. The leading regional powers in the wider neighborhood—Iran and Iraq in particular—were negative federators. They helped to shape a sense of region-ness among the traditional monarchies of the Arab peninsula because of the threat they pose. The relationship toward Saudi Arabia, however, has always remained ambivalent. Saudi Arabia shares its conservative regime with the small states along the Persian Gulf. Yet its dominating tendency, coupled with its religious role as the protector of the most holy places of Islam, has at times made the small countries along the Persian Gulf uncomfortable. The knowledge that Saudi Arabia could always try to exert an overly strong influence over its partners hinders their readiness to join ranks with it.

Common threat perceptions helped conceive the Gulf Cooperation Council as a security scheme, although it has never really succeeded in this original conception. Instead, Gulf cooperation and integration only began to take shape with the shift of priorities from security to economics, legitimized in part by common economic and fiscal circumstances. The process of economic cooperation and integration was not simplified, but over time the technical process of promoting a common market produced results, including weakened resistance to implementing the original goals of a customs union. The shifting paradigm of Gulf integration opened new avenues, also in terms of understanding the very notion and meaning of security in the region.

Inside the Gulf region, the understanding of the usefulness of regional integration has not grown with sufficient speed and scope. But the strategic decision to introduce a common currency in the GCC will have a lasting impact beyond the economy and the financial sector. It could become a defining moment and finally turn the GCC into a successful federating force.

Transformations

In 1971, the Dubai Accord outlined the plan to create a federation for the whole region. National independence of the United Arab Emirates, Bahrain, and Qatar was a blow to this unifying plan. National self-determination was a stronger force than immediate federation, and the quest for autonomous sovereignty prevailed over the rational advantage of pooled sovereignty. In the end, national sovereignty turned out to be a detour from the road leading to the original concept of joint forces. The concern for regional security became a new, more functional and pragmatic argument for reconsidering the usefulness of cooperation and integration in the Gulf region. The original proposal for Gulf cooperation, as articulated by the sultan of Oman and the emir of Kuwait, resulted from reconsideration of the conditions and potential of the small independent Gulf states as denizens of a volatile region.

A second transformation concerns the relationship between regional security and regime stability. Originally, the proposal for Gulf cooperation and integration was driven by the understanding of a purely military concept of security and stability. It did not lead to the logical consequence—that is to say, to a defense alliance—and attitudes have remained ambivalent. On the one hand, the GCC member states were not in a position to completely alienate those regional powers they were leery of. On the other hand, inner cohesion was not strong enough to pool the resources in fear of undermining national sovereignty. Yet the GCC countries had to understand the limits of this formal independence. It was significant that finally the economic aspects of integration took the lead in moving the GCC forward and legitimized its existence. They turned the GCC from an unfinished regional security alliance into an undeclared program of regional economic integration.

Role and Interests of the European Union

The first initiative to establish relations with the European Community (since 1993: European Union) came from the Gulf Cooperation Council. In June 1984, the EC decided to impose a 13.5 percent tariff on Saudi methanol exports. In 1986 the EC tariffs expanded to include additional petrochemical products. Article 7 of the Unified Economic Agreement outlines the terms for joint negotiations of the GCC with third parties. This provision was activated for the first time in 1986: in order to convince the EC to reduce its tariffs on GCC products, the GCC threatened to retaliate by raising tariffs on EC exports to GCC countries.[64] The ironic background of the European attitude becomes evident only when this issue is set in a broader strategic context. The EC should have recognized that without access to industrialized markets, the GCC countries would never be in a position to successfully diversify their economies, which again was and remains so very much in the interests of the West as a key to stabilizing the GCC countries.

It took until 1990 for an economic agreement to be concluded between the GCC and the European Community, whereupon the EC opened the Western European market to GCC petrochemical products. "The Saudi-led efforts within the GCC for reciprocal security, i.e. security of the oil supply in return for security of demand, ran counter to the EC's proposed $3 a barrel carbon tax."[65] This debate came to an end after the invasion of Kuwait by Iraq in August 1990. Oil did not become a real weapon, while all GCC countries were weakened as a consequence of the invasion of one of them.

In 1989, the relations between the Gulf Cooperation Council and the European Community were formalized through a Cooperation Agreement intended to promote economic and political cooperation. The agreement ensures regular ministerial meetings between the GCC and the EU. Seventeen of these meetings took place before 2007. Negotiations for a free trade agreement between the GCC and the EC started in 1990 but have not yet succeeded. In 2001, they were relaunched after the GCC had effectively embarked on a path to a comprehensive customs union. The EU had always insisted that it would negotiate a free trade agreement, or any other agreement, only after substantial steps for deepened integration had been taken in the GCC. The EU also insisted that it would only negotiate with the GCC as a whole and not with individual member states.

The GCC is the EU's fifth largest export market. Machinery and transport materials, such as power generation plants, railway locomotives, aircraft, and mechanical appliances make up 51 percent of EU exports to the Gulf region. In turn, 69 percent of all EU fuel imports come from GCC countries. The EU maintains a regular expert dialogue with the GCC on energy matters. In 2004, the EU defined the relationship with the GCC as a strategic partnership. Given the proliferation of this term, it has not gained any immediate substantive meaning, and it was not evident from the EU proposition how it could become one.

The relationship between the EU and the GCC has always been a secondary consideration to the EU's Euro-Mediterranean Partnership. Started in 1995, the Euro-Mediterranean Partnership—better known as the Barcelona Process—has brought together all EU member states and all littoral states of the southern shores of the Mediterranean, including Israel, plus Jordan. This exceptional format has a number of flaws and has been described as an asymmetric partnership. It follows its own agenda, logic, and objectives. Neither the Gulf Cooperation Council nor its member states have played any relevant role in past deliberations of the Euro-Mediterranean Partnership. After more than a decade of existence, the Euro-Mediterranean Partnership has been critically analyzed in its potential and deficits.[66] Its transformation into the Union for the Mediterranean in July 2008 was no more than a semantic move, at least initially. In any case, the concept of a Euro-Mediterranean sphere differs logically from the goal of establishing a partnership between the EU and the GCC. The GCC countries criticize the EU for neglecting them, but the EU considers the GCC a strategic partner and recognizes the authenticity of the GCC. As for the EU's partner countries on the southern shores of the Mediterranean, they are far from being defined as a region with their own unique and jointly shared identity and the potential for genuine community-building.[67]

There is no biregional free trade agreement between the EU and the GCC, although it would certainly be in the interest of both sides. They would also benefit from a more focused and regular political and security dialogue. This would have to include questions of good governance as well as the need to strengthen human resources in the Arab Gulf states. A biregional relationship between the EU and the GCC has not yet properly begun.

Prospects and Obstacles

Domestic disputes in most of its member states over the development of governance and regime orientation are the main uncertainty that looms over the future of the GCC. It is not regional cooperation and integration as such, but rather domestic preconditions that pose a challenge to the prospects for the GCC. The Shi'ite factor has been mentioned, an issue related to the long-term projection of Iranian interests in the region. The attempted coup in Bahrain in 1981, a series of riots in Saudi Arabia in the early 1980s, agitation in Kuwait, and the attempt to kill the emir in 1985 were the first signs of tensions allegedly orchestrated in Teheran. Since the regime change brought about by war in Iraq in 2003, the geopolitical implications of the developments in Iraq, the relations between Iran and Iraq, and the repercussions of these relations on world politics have had increased resonance in the GCC countries. Their outcome is unclear at this point in time. But the external developments have direct and indirect effects on the discourse about advancing pluralism and democratization in the Arab Gulf countries. Since 9/11, the parameters of these discourses have changed. Acts of terrorism by totalitarian Islamic fanatics have caused numerous victims and terrible damage; not only in material terms but also as far as the image of Arab countries in the West and the very stability of Arab countries are concerned. With the publication of the Arab Human Development Reports between 2002 and 2005, the discourse has become more rational and forward-looking. It has been carried into the Arab world itself, where it has begun contributing to the inevitable modernization and transformation of the regimes governing most countries in the area.

The struggle between modernization, pluralism, and the future role of Islam in the identity of the societies and regimes in the Arab Gulf has become more complicated than ever with the outbreak of new waves of terrorism and the ambivalent attitude toward the United States and its role in the region. Analysts often neglect to note the importance of understanding the dynamics of these debates in the context of the overall socioeconomic development in the Gulf area. Since the 1990s, most GCC countries have experienced a combination of rapidly growing populations (3.2 percent on average during the 1990s), limited job opportunities for those pushing into the labor market, and a factual decline in the respective GDP. Qatar (500,000 citizens) with a GDP per capita of $31,396, the United Arab Emirates (3.1 million) with a GDP per capita of $28,216, Kuwait (2.2 million) with a GDP per capita of $18,720, Bahrain (700,000) with a GDP per capita of $11,946, and even Saudi Arabia (21 million) with a GDP per capita of $9,236 and Oman (2.4 million) with a GDP per capita of $8,497, number among the richest—or at least, richer—countries of the world. Yet the relationship between economic status, expectations, and radical politicization, let alone a radical quest for religious identity, cannot be measured in GDP categories alone. Around 40 percent of the GCC population is younger than fifteen, the quality of education is mediocre in most GCC countries, and the decline in per capita GDP has been most dramatic in Saudi Arabia, coupled with a lack of investment by Saudis in their own country. The implications of these trends pose questions of a different and somewhat worrying nature.

It is here that the absence of a substantial public debate about the future of politics in the GCC countries becomes relevant. Accountability of the political leadership, matters of representation, succession in power, broadened public inclusion in the reflection about the region's future, and by and large the issue of self-criticism are questions linked to the political stability and long-term legitimacy of the GCC regimes. Because people in Arab Gulf societies do not feel that they have any meaningful influence on the political life in their community, "political apathy and negativism pervade in Arab society."[68] This is a strong liability to the future evolution of GCC integration and its rootedness in the hearts and minds of the region's people. Whether or not democratization in the Arab world will enhance the popular recognition of GCC integration is the key challenge to this integration scheme, which so far has been driven by the ruling elites only.

The issue is even made more complicated by the implications of possible enlargement of the existing GCC membership. At times, possible membership of Iraq in the GCC is discussed. Some long-term reflection has even been given to the idea of Iran joining the GCC at some point in time. No external consideration is more pressing for the GCC countries than the freedom of navigation in the Persian Gulf. Every eight minutes, a supertanker passes the Strait of Hormuz. Cautious policies toward Iran and Iraq are a vital element of any foreign policy in the GCC. Yet there is a lot of room for maneuver between a cautious policy of containment and a proactive policy of GCC enlargement. The GCC will have to find the right approach as it continues to deepen its economic integration. This cannot happen without implications for its foreign policy profile in the wider region.

The question of the relationship between the GCC and Yemen remains vexing. Since 2006, membership negotiations have been under way, intended to lead to Yemen's full GCC membership by 2016. Whether or not Yemen might join the GCC is not just a matter of enlargement of the integration scheme and the genuine arguments related to enlargement. The potential membership of Yemen in the Gulf Cooperation Council is ultimately a matter of regime cohesion, but—in a paradoxical way—it is also a test case for reform pressure exerted by the concept of regional integration. Not only would Yemen have to change to join the GCC, but the GCC member states would also have to change to accept Yemen as a member.

So far, membership in the GCC has been equivalent to representing a conservative, traditional Arab monarchy. Yemen, however, has been a republic ever since it became an independent country. Moreover, the country has gone through a history of civil war, division, communist rule in one part of Yemen, and the unification of the two Yemens with highly mixed experiences and new traumas. Yemen was unified on 22 May 1990. Its population of 15 million citizens outnumbers that of Saudi Arabia (12 million) and every other Gulf state. More importantly, Yemen hosts a very coherent local populace, very different from the Arab Gulf states with their strong communities of expatriates. After a civil war in 1993/1994, Yemen became a socialist republic, soon embarking on the general socialist path of transformation but maintaining many features of a socialist-populist and republican-authoritarian state. The contrast with the rest of the countries on the Arab peninsula could hardly be more striking. Yemen is also the poorest country, and often the argument of economic asymmetry is used by skeptics among current GCC member states to keep Yemen at bay. In the final analysis, the main preoccupation is related to the regime governing in Sanaa.

Should Yemen ever be seriously considered for membership in the Gulf Cooperation Council, it would clearly indicate a fundamental shift in the character of the regimes that constitute the GCC so far. At least in terms of recognizing pluralism and regime diversity, this decision would be the most substantial the current GCC member states could possibly take. For this reason it has not yet happened and is rather unlikely to happen in the near future. A certain accommodation between Yemen and the GCC is evident, but it has not gone beyond technical forms of cooperation and political contacts. A weak and poor Yemen seems to be in the myopic interest of some in the GCC, notably Saudi Arabia. In the long run, however, Yemen's accession to the GCC could strengthen the whole regional scheme as much as it would pose a financial burden. After all, Yemen is more than a basket case: it is also a huge market.

The key to closing the existing "credibility gap" in GCC integration[69] depends on the degree of solid and sustainable economic integration that the GCC is likely to achieve over the next few years. The implementation of a common GCC currency in 2010 will only work if the political commitment of all participating countries remains as high as possible. Since 2002, a Monetary Union Unit has been attached to the GCC General Secretariat in Riyadh. The GCC Customs Union Committee, which has supervised the customs union since 2003, has remained intergovernmental. In the face of the global financial crisis, the GCC decided to accelerate the process of introducing a common Gulf currency. A GCC summit on 30 December 2008 paved the way for the establishment in late 2009 of a Monetary Council, understood to be the precursor of a Gulf central bank. The Monetary Council is intended to be the Gulf equivalent to the European Monetary Institute, which was the forerunner of the European Central Bank. Strengthened focus and seriousness in pursuing this most important project of regional integration is noticeable in the Gulf region.

Convergence criteria and implementation guidelines for the GCC monetary union have been developed. The convergence among GCC economies is reasonably high. The inflation rate in the GCC rarely exceeds 5 percent. On average, between 1990 and 2005 growth rates have been between 2.1 percent (Kuwait) and 9.1 percent (Qatar). So far, however, the GCC lacks an effective dispute settlement mechanism. Also absent is a truly supranational set of monetary institutions. The independent and supranational Monetary Council will be essential for the successful launch of the GCC currency, "notwithstanding the variety of approaches that can be followed concerning the division of labor between a supranational monetary institution and national central banks in other areas, such as the analysis, implementation and communication of monetary and exchange rate policy."[70]

The revised Economic Agreement between the GCC states of 31 December 2001 speaks to development integration as a key rationale for the Gulf Cooperation Council. Currency unification is understood as one of the preconditions for successful development integration in the Gulf region. The implementation of the monetary union itself depends upon a specified timetable and further requirements outlined in detail in the Revised Economic Agreement. "These include the achievement of a high level of harmonization between Member States in all economic policies, especially fiscal and monetary policies, banking legislation, setting criteria to approximate rates of economic performance related to fiscal and monetary stability, such as rates of budgetary deficit, indebtedness, and price levels."[71] One cannot deny that the Gulf Cooperation Council has decided to take its visions seriously and to make full use of its potential. Now, the world waits for the delivery.

South Asian Association for Regional Cooperation (SAARC)

Basic Facts

For the time being, it is not altogether clear whether SAARC has strong ambitions or merely acknowledges restricted powers as its true purpose. However, it would be unfair to judge the South Asian Association for Regional Cooperation by the degree of power it has accrued, without taking into account the short period of time since its creation in 1985. It could also be said that the most remarkable fact about SAARC is its existence as such. Given the geopolitical tensions in South Asia, the regime differences among the participating countries, and the insurmountable socioeconomic cleavages and cultural differences in the region, the existence of the only architecture of regionalism in South Asia is far from normal. Yet SAARC exists—and that might be the main message. It attests to the global proliferation of regional integration, at least as a theoretical concept and surely also as an appealing idea and slowly evolving reality in the most complex and difficult regions of the world. The South Asian Association for Regional Cooperation invokes all possible arguments about why regional integration does not work or could not possibly work in a particular environment. Yet SAARC has been established, and after two decades of existence it appears to have finally begun to turn vision into reality, ideas into practice, theory into application.

The South Asian Association for Regional Cooperation is home to 1.5 billion people, almost 25 percent of the world population. At roughly $600 billion, the GDP of the eight member states of SAARC represents no more than 1.9 percent of the world's economic output. SAARC holds 1 percent of global trade and is home to 40 percent of the world's very poor people. SAARC membership includes India, Pakistan, Nepal, Bhutan, Bangladesh, Sri Lanka, the Maldives, and—since 2007—Afghanistan.

According to its founding charter of 8 December 1985, SAARC's objectives are, inter alia:

- to promote the welfare of the peoples of South Asia and to improve their quality of life;
- to accelerate economic growth, social progress and cultural development in the region and to provide all individuals the opportunity to live in dignity and to realize their full potential;
- to promote and strengthen collective self-reliance among the countries of South Asia;
- to contribute to mutual trust, understanding and appreciation of one another's problems;
- to promote active collaboration and mutual assistance in the economic, social, cultural, technical and scientific fields.[72]

SAARC is the product of a genuine South Asian evolution from colonialism to independence and from autarkic, at times belligerent, nationalism to the understanding of regional cooperation and integration as a win-win situation for all countries and people in the area. SAARC is a contradictory project. It is not the result of natural harmony and the desire for cooperation. It cannot claim precedents or a history of continuity and invocation of the value of regionalism. Its underlying sense of region-ness is more the reflection of geographic proximity than of cultural cohesion and traditional collaboration. The world of South Asia is arguably the most diverse, polyphonic, and vibrant religious and cultural zone in the world. It appears as if only notions of federalism can translate the cultural diversity of the region into a reasonable political construction. India's genuine federalism may serve as a model for the region at large.

South Asia is among the most diverse and fascinating regions of the globe. Modern South Asia has been shaped by British colonialism and the struggle against it. The struggle for independence was polarizing, and not only with respect to the region's relationship with Great Britain. British tactics of divide and rule triggered conflicting nationalisms among the people of South Asia as well. While the Indian Congress Party opposed British colonial rule without striving for the revitalization of Hindu rule, the majority population in what was to become Pakistan ("Land of the Pure") was fighting for a Muslim state, largely directed against the continuous presence of Hindus among them. Once the British declared their departure from the Indian subcontinent in 1947, secular nationalism and theological nationalism clashed with each other immediately. The subsequent partition of British India and an atrocious war left more than a million people dead. Four million Muslims had to leave India, and seven million Hindus and Sikhs had to leave Pakistan. The war, which left Kashmir divided, was fought over the conflicting anti-colonial concepts of two local social elites. The formation of India and Pakistan—originally consisting of East and West Pakistan divided by the large India—did not calm the antagonisms. In fact, both countries continued to be a source of bilateral conflicts. Two more wars between India and Pakistan broke out in 1965 and in 1971, leading to the creation of Bangladesh in 1972. Ten million Hindu refugees from Bangladesh to India speak of the terrible human suffering that had again dragged the subcontinent into bloodshed.

When trade relations between India and Pakistan resumed in 1974, the prospect for gradual, incremental reconciliation was overshadowed by the Cold War and its specific Asian dimension. India had gone a long way from the original pan-Asianism it shared with China at the time of independence. After the annexation of Tibet in 1959, India cut relations with China, having always understood Tibet as a part of the Hindu-Buddhist cultural sphere. Sympathy for the US and its democratic ideals was always balanced by mutual suspicion between New Delhi and Washington over India's non-aligned and potentially Soviet-friendly foreign policy during the Cold War. Pakistan was no less predictable as a Western client state during the Cold War. In 1979 it withdrew from CENTO, the Central Treaty Organization, which had existed since 1959. The Soviet invasion of Afghanistan in December 1979 strengthened Pakistan's importance in the calculations of the West, the US in particular. Pakistan became the center of refugee policy toward Afghanistan and itself the hotbed of turbulences between pro-Western forces and increasingly radicalizing Islamic traditionalists. The Carter Doctrine of 1980, with its plea for independent security structures in Asia, remained without effect. Rather, domestic turbulences dominated the development of South Asia, limiting regional security and any predictable approach to a coherent policy of cooperation.

In 1980, Bangladesh's President Zia ur-Rahman proposed multilateral cooperation in South Asia. On 30 May 1981, he was assassinated. A country torn by war, natural disaster, overpopulation, and poverty was left in stagnation. Zia's message had been clear: he was looking for ways for the small states in the region to balance the power of India. Suspicious and apprehensive, India feared that the idea of regional security might be sponsored by Western interests trying to limit India's scope of action. India preferred bilateral relations in its region and did not want to limit its scope of action due to any sort of collective regional pressure. The domestic panorama in India was also highly confusing, if not chaotic.

Traditionally claiming to be the biggest democracy on earth, India's record was tainted when Prime Minister Indira Gandhi declared a state of emergency in June 1975 that lasted for nineteen bitter months. It goes to the credit of India's democratic instincts and institutions that martial law was brought down by the legal system of India. Indira Gandhi was ousted from office in free and largely fair elections in 1977, only to be reelected as India's prime minister in early 1980. On 31 October 1984 she was assassinated, following the storming of the Golden Temple of the Sikhs in Amritsar. Sikh radicals had gone so far as to claim secession from India when Indira Gandhi ordered the storming amidst mounting tensions in India over the degree of autonomy for the Sikhs, a religious minority. Thus, she was killed in an act of revenge. Religious-ethnic conflicts in India, traditionally labeled "communal riots," remain a stark pattern in the sociological fabric of this country that is itself a world of cultural and socioeconomic diversity.

Given this background and context, the initiative to launch a multilateral structure of regional cooperation was quite a surprise. The idea to create some sort of security arrangement was driven by three considerations:

- Enhancing regional security.
- Overcoming regional tensions and making better use of regional possibilities.
- Recognizing the democratic and peaceful potential of South Asia.

The first-ever meeting of South Asian foreign secretaries meeting took place in Sri Lanka's capital, Colombo, in 1981. Sri Lanka itself was suffering from aggravated tensions due to the ethnic quarrels between the Singhalese majority and the country's Tamil minority. The tensions, which escalated into a full civil war in the early 1980s, undermined the image of a peaceful, predominantly Buddhist, consensual and democratic society. With a diplomatic initiative aimed at establishing a structure of regional cooperation, Sri Lanka hoped to defuse some of the tension it was suffering from, assuming that the Tamil rebels in the north of the island's territory were receiving support across the Palk Straits from Tamil Nadu.

The initial Sri Lankan proposal was cautious and limited. Sri Lanka's government knew that it could not do too much too soon to conceptualize any meaningful regional scheme in and for South Asia. It identified five possible areas of regional cooperation: agriculture, telecommunications, rural development, meteorology, matters of health, and demography. Technical cooperation was the only realistic approach for the region to begin a new path in the relationship between its states. This would be the best way, Sri Lanka argued, to depoliticize the regional constellation and infuse a reasonable alternative into the agenda of mistrust, struggle, and tension in South Asia.

In 1982, India's foreign secretary handed over a draft for a Treaty of Peace, Friendship and Cooperation to his Pakistani colleague. This was a sign of bilateral efforts to normalize relations. A possible reconciliation between the two highly antagonistic powers on the Indian subcontinent would have given tremendous hope to the whole region. In 1983, the first-ever South Asian foreign ministers' meeting took place. Subsequently, the path toward a comprehensive regional scheme of cooperation emerged. The South Asian Association for Regional Cooperation (SAARC) was founded during a summit meeting of heads of state and government on 8 December 1985 in Dhaka.

SAARC had no chance of a speedy and simple development. The conflicts in the region were too grave, and the mutual recriminations and suspicions too entrenched. It was indicative that at the fringes of the third SAARC summit in 1988 in Islamabad, India and Pakistan signed three agreements of an altogether extremely different nature: to prohibit an attack against nuclear installations, to intensify cultural cooperation, and to prevent double taxation. The discovery of region-ness occurred amidst hopes of cultural exchange, the struggle with bureaucratic obstacles to further economic interaction, and the looming threat of nuclear annihilation. Normally, this is not a constellation in which regional trust and a spirit of cooperation can be expected to grow.[73]

The bilateral conflicts in South Asia, the hijacking of the region by the logic of the Cold War, and its inner tensions between the pride of cultural continuity and the frustration of its peripheral status in the contemporary world economy contributed to the need for a general reassessment of the region, its role, and its potential. The natural boundaries of South Asia, its ecological and geographical features, even its sense of a shared sociocultural commonality in diversity and the awareness of a shared political history of colonial suppression and subsequent economic consequences, helped to create the seeds of a new understanding of the meaning of region-ness in South Asia. In the final analysis, even the primacy of the region's obsession with security matters, mistrust, and deterrence contributed to an overly mixed bag of experiences and perceptions that help explain why SAARC was made possible and yet could not really work.

A little more than a decade after SAARC had been founded, one of its first secretary generals, Kant K. Bhargava, an Indian civil servant, was bitterly critical: "SAARC has hardly progressed beyond signs and symbols."[74] In light of the enormous contradictions and tensions in South Asia, and given the short period of time for judging with objective clarity, SAARC probably did not do so poorly. After all, it was undeniable that the ground had been laid for a long-term experiment in regional cooperation, and possibly integration, in South Asia. This introduced a completely new dimension into the postcolonial world of nation-state realities and idiosyncrasies. The regional perspective was both a postcolonial and a postnationalistic one. It would have to be reconciled with the strong reality of nation-state sovereignty in South Asia. But nation-state sovereignty has been as much as a protective shield against new external dominance as it has been an experience in the limits of coping with new challenges to statehood, identity, and better prospects for economic well-being.

SAARC has been able to establish a set of bodies completely new to the region's experience with the formation and execution of politics and interactions between its countries. SAARC's founding charter stressed the consensus among its member states, according to which controversial bilateral or regional issues were not to be addressed in the SAARC context. Decisions were to be taken unanimously. In other words, SAARC started as the incarnation of the lowest common denominator. It could only succeed if all member states were ready to agree. This implied that SAARC would need to pursue a non-political approach. Yet one could not dismiss the idea that technical cooperation might in the end be more promising to a changing political environment in South Asia than any openly political approach. In fact, non-political cooperation could turn out to be the best possible politics for South Asia. The very existence of a regional institutional structure was already a strong message. It was a long-term program for incremental contributions toward changing atmosphere, environment, procedure, and outcome for South Asian politics and economic performance.

The SAARC structure set up in the founding charter of 1985 is as follows:

- SAARC summits of heads of state and government are to be held on an annual basis.
- SAARC's Standing Committee of Foreign Secretaries, meeting regularly, is mandated to monitor and coordinate SAARC's programs of action.
- SAARC's Council of Ministers, consisting of the foreign secretaries of all SAARC member states, receives the regular progress reports of the Standing Committee and discusses their implications during two annual meetings.
- SAARC's Committee on Economic Cooperation brings together the secretaries of commerce of SAARC member states.
- The SAARC Secretariat, located in Kathmandu (Secretary General Lyonpo Chenkyab Dorji of Bhutan served between 2005 and 2008), serves as a technical coordination office.
- Technical committees and special institutions pursue continuous work along the line of SAARC's overall agenda. Most notable are the SAARC Documentation Centre in New Delhi, the SAARC Agricultural Information Centre in Dhaka, the SAARC Meteorological Research Centre in Dhaka; the SAARC Tuberculosis Centre in Kathmandu, and the SAARC Human Resources Development Centre in Islamabad.
- A SAARC Arbitration Council was established in 2005.

While ASEAN grew beyond the reality of its structure thanks to the impulse of rapid economic growth, and while the GCC did not need to evolve any more rapidly because of the innate cohesion among its member states, SAARC could only evolve through slow but steady steps and pragmatic activities. Its innate diversity and potential for conflict made SAARC an impossible combination of deterrence and cooperation, reform and non-intervention, a reconfirmation of the imperative of state-based autonomy and an affirmation of the need to move member states forward into a sphere of cooperation.

Until the 1990s, SAARC remained a technical body. Only in the 1990s did it begin to understand economic integration as one of its possible priorities. Under the pressure of globalization and the dire need to enhance economic reforms as a tool of development in South Asia, SAARC reconceptualized its ambition and focus. In 1993, the SAARC Council of Ministers signed the SAARC Preferential Trade Arrangement (SAPTA),[75] which was to become operational by 1995. The agreement outlined three rounds of preferential trade tariff cuts among SAARC member states in 1995, 1997, and 1998 respectively. The goal—to create a South Asian Economic Union—was too advanced for the instruments and preconditions it would have needed to take to become an immediate reality. Without achieving the goals of SAPTA, SAARC embarked on a new and even more ambitious idea in 1997: the SAARC summit in Male decided to create a South Asian Free Trade Area (SAFTA) by 2001.

In the beginning, nothing happened. In fact, South Asia went closer to the brink of nuclear war than to the implementation of the free trade agreement. The SAARC summit of 1999 was canceled because of Pakistan and India's bitter consternation about each other's nuclear tests, exacerbated by the military takeover in Pakistan. The world began to discuss the threat of an imminent escalation of South Asia's conflicts into a nuclear confrontation between India and Pakistan. It took until 2002 for SAARC to hold another summit meeting. And it took until 2004 for SAARC to launch a new beginning of its original ambition. The SAARC summit in Islamabad in January 2004 reached an agreement to implement the South Asian Free Trade Area by 2006.[76]

South Asia, the region with "the lowest intra-regional exports share in the world,"[77] has begun to wake up. Economists were quick to outline the shortcomings of the region, not least its lack of trade complementarity. South Asia is less important than many other regions in terms of its contribution to global trade, investment, and growth. The data base in South Asia is poor, for the degree of illegal trade is high and the published data on trade relations do not necessarily reflect the real picture of the trade structure in the region. Given the high degree of non-tariff barriers to trade, the idea of a South Asian Free Trade Area was not enthusiastically welcomed by many economists. Yet the political leaders in SAARC had to react to the rapid growth in East Asia and the overall impact of globalization on their region. A substantial increase in economic modernization and reform was more than urgent, lest South Asia fall behind the rest of the world permanently.

The political tensions in the region, intrinsically linked to the contrasting governance practices across South Asia, are the biggest obstacle to improved conditions in South Asia. It is estimated that trade between India and Pakistan is 70 percent lower than could be expected between two otherwise similar economies. The quest for national autonomy has been an inherent element in the history of nation-building in South Asia. The region has not been helped in the same speed and manner as the Southeast Asian "little tigers." Only in recent years has India begun to refocus its neighborhood policies by becoming more generous (regarding compensation matter with Bangladesh over garment industries and trade deficit), less fearful (as far as Pakistan's military regime is concerned), less interventionist (with regard to Sri Lanka) and more subtle in promoting the region (toward Nepal, Bhutan, and the Maldives).

In a paradoxical way, terrorism has become a unifying force across South Asia. It has also helped to reconnect its conflicting main powers to the US. Pakistan, irrespective of its poor democratic record, has been an ambivalent US ally since the days of the Soviet invasion of Afghanistan. India was a suspicious ally of the US and a neglected partner of Europe for a long time, in spite of its strong democratic record and geopolitical importance. For a long time, the legendary Indian "arrogance" concerning the all-pervasive presence of poverty has not been helpful in recognizing India as central partner of the West. Meanwhile, the rise of China and the simultaneous rise of India have contributed to the rediscovery of India in the West. Terrorism, experienced as a threat to both the West and South Asia, has had the double effect of revitalizing links with the West and bringing the region closer together again. The terrorist attack on the Indian parliament in December 2001, several spectacular terrorist attacks in Kashmir, and Afghan Taliban fighters' infiltration of Pakistan have forced SAARC to strengthen its security profile. Following SAARC's Regional Convention on Suppression of Terrorism of 4 November 1987,[78] an additional protocol, signed at the SAARC summit on 6 January 2004 in Islamabad, underlined the mutual agreement that terrorism is a threat to all countries and that no double standards in fighting terrorism should apply in South Asia.[79]

The new wave of realism spreading throughout South Asia culminated in a landmark agreement by SAARC member states to finally and genuinely set up the free trade area they had contemplated for years. On 1 December 2005, the decision to expand free trade in South Asia was finalized. Following the original signing of the agreement on a free trade area in 2004, the implementation was agreed upon. It will take another ten years—until 2016—until the SAARC Free Trade Area is fully realized, but at last the phased tariff liberalization program for turning SAFTA into reality has been agreed to by all SAARC member states. This could give the very idea of regional cooperation and subsequently integration in South Asia a thorough boost. It could turn the lofty idea of regionalism into an economic reality that in turn would have an impact on political relations, too.

Intrinsic Motives und External Pressures

South Asia's great cultural and political past is sometimes invoked as an element in promoting region-ness. Some in India dare to consider contemporary region-building as a quest for the reunification of the entire subcontinent, divided since the days of colonialism and the Great Game over Central Asia. They even refer to the natural Central Asian ties of India, meanwhile recognizing that India's Look East policy is driven more by contemporary competition with China over the access to energy resources, markets, and technologies. The Empire of Ashoka in the third century B.C. included most of the area that is today covered by Pakistan, India, Afghanistan, Nepal, and Bangladesh. Ashoka brought about his empire by force and exercised a regime of hardship. He is said to have then converted to Buddhism and become a peace-loving, benevolent ruler, supporting virtues in public life and a social order based on the Buddhist concept of inner conquest through dharma. The idea of expansion and imperial rule was legitimized as an instrument for promoting basic understanding of the norms and values of life as enshrined in the spiritual traditions of the subcontinent.

This concept had only a limited universal claim, and it remained regional in its political application. It is hard to imagine how Ashoka could be understood as a precursor of either political or religious unification in South Asia. But he belongs among the great leaders who helped shape a sense of region-ness defined by a cultural patterns and political memory. In the course of its long history, and following its original Hindu traditions, South Asia has experienced deep reform movements that have transformed Hinduism and were themselves transformed by its resilience. Buddhism and Sikhism, as well as the Zoroastrian tradition, Islam, Christianity, and in small numbers Judaism, have reached the shores of the Indian subcontinent. Culture remains the trademark of South Asian identity, and it is a culture of diversity and transformation. In a certain sense, this is relevant to the formation of a diverse order of political and economic cooperation. Still, it does not provide for it naturally.

The dominance of India as a cultural power is demonstrated by its ability to absorb, transform, and maintain the traditions that have constituted it through time immemorial. While it remains difficult to link these traditions to the contemporary challenges of politics, economics, and regionalism in South Asia, a certain cultural undercurrent—a sense of belonging—is undeniable in South Asia. It motivates those who rationally promote regional cooperation and integration in the age of globalization, impelled especially by the challenge of the rise of China. It also limits their action, as cultural memory is poorly applicable to the agenda of modern politics and economics. The inclusion of Afghanistan has introduced a failing state to SAARC, adding another serious problem to the region's agenda, which is already burdened by internal upheavals in Nepal and Sri Lanka and democratic deficits in Pakistan, Bangladesh, and the Maldives. In the meantime, the Buddhist kingdom of Bhutan has been embarking on a cautious path toward constitutional democracy and parliamentary monarchy.

Instead of invoking common cultural bonds, it is more useful for South Asia to start relating region-ness to the pressing socioeconomic agenda of the subcontinent and its neighborhood. Security and development concerns are intertwined and have given rise to extended notions of regionalism. Iran has applied for observer status in SAARC, indicating the projection of SAARC beyond its immediate region. The security obstacles prevalent in South Asia cannot be resolved without taking into consideration the regime question, that is, the discrepancies between the region's governance systems. South Asian governance structures are highly relevant to the agenda of development and the instruments considered important for implementing it. The stage of development in South Asia, in turn, is directly related to the security constellation of the region and beyond. This is true as far as ecological, demographic, and social matters are concerned. It is also true with regard to the South Asian security apparatus, including the lamentable arms race in the region.

A counterfactual approach has driven the motivation and achievement for regional cooperation in South Asia: because of security limits and development obstacles, the potential for cooperation and integration has been discovered as part of a possible solution to the current limits of the region. Regional cooperation, let alone regional integration, has never been enthusiastically embraced by any social or political group in South Asia. No South Asian intellectual stream of federalism exists. Yet insight into the limits of autarkic pursuit of national sovereignty has forced the political elites in South Asia to broaden their horizons. Region-ness might not be a much loved concept, but key actors have realized that it is a useful, supportive, and instrumental one. Under the pressure of the intrinsic cycle of conflict, tension, and poverty, South Asia cannot avoid reevaluating development strategies and the notion of statehood and sovereignty. Because of its grand cultural heritage, the Indian subcontinent, and Indian society in particular, has a tendency toward self-centeredness and myopic pride. It has taken some time and many painful realizations of peripheral neglect by others in the modern world to draw honest and thorough conclusions regarding the limits of national sovereignty and the usefulness of a more cooperative approach to its own region. India's dominant role as the central country of South Asia has made the evolution of any form of region-ness more difficult than in many other parts of the world. The Maldives, Bhutan, and Nepal cannot but look with awe and ambiguity on their gigantic neighbor. They need cooperation with India as alternative to strangulation by India, or—maybe even worse—to complete neglect by India.

These preconditions and circumstances were not propitious for an early discovery and speedy application of the concept of region-ness in South Asia. The
decision by the governing elites in all countries of the region to launch the South
Asian Association of Regional Cooperation must be considered courageous, if
not visionary. Pressured by limited progress across the region in all areas relevant
for the well-being of its people and the strength of its states, and by globalization
with its iron law of peripheral neglect as a means of punishment for those not
following its rules, South Asia became "one of the last regions to wake up to the
challenge of the new regionalism."[80]

Entrenched in regional security conflicts, nationalist obsessions, and ethnic
tensions, and furthermore embroiled in burning domestic agendas complicated
by issues of governance, socioeconomic problems, and matters of identity, the
South Asian countries have found it difficult to supersede the primacy of a national, autarkic search for solutions so much ingrained in the concept of national
independence and sovereign statehood. Only upon realizing that the cross-border effects of regional tensions and conflicts outweigh any ability to find domestic
solutions based on autarkic interpretations of the causes and effects of dominant
societal concerns, did the political elites in South Asia prepare themselves for
serious reflection on the potential of regional integration. Region-ness was slowly
discovered as a tool to overcome the limits of the respective national agendas
and the flaws inevitably linked to them. As much as the risks of secession and
civil war have always been cross-border phenomena in South Asia, so too do
the socioeconomic issues loom large in a region with the highest share of rural
poverty in all of Asia.

For a long time, it was not recognized that matters of governance had a limiting effect on the region's tension-oriented agenda or even a paralyzing effect on
the failed national agendas. Milder or stronger forms of authoritarianism were
understood as inherently inevitable tactics of survival. In reality, autocratic or
military solutions to sociological, ethnic, and economic cleavages turned out to
be counterproductive. Even though they managed to provide for short-term stability (and control of the people), they undermined their own logic by failing
to deliver dynamics as a necessary attribute of successful stability. The state became petrified while the society turned uncomfortable, nervous, and aggressive.
Economic reforms were absent or introduced too slowly, while at the same time
the vast agenda of ethnic or territorial tensions in the region obstructed resolution of the social deficits and obstacles to economic progress. Gradually, political
elites across South Asia could no longer avoid acknowledging that their prime
obsession with territorial, ethnic, and "communal" matters contributed little to
any positive development and, worse, aggravated the region's problems and overriding stagnation. The stigma of being the "basket case" of Asia was no longer
confined to Bangladesh, once characterized thus for its combination of ecological
disasters, political chaos, and horrific poverty. India, for all its pride and grandeur,

was increasingly considered to be another loser of globalization while failing in the fight to alleviate poverty. Something fundamental had to happen in order to overcome the region's inertia, including that of its dominating power.

It was significant that the states around India, smaller but possessing a certain weight of their own, were particularly active in conceptualizing the idea of a regional architecture for South Asia. The initial impulses from Bangladesh are noteworthy. With the initiative of its late President Zia ur-Rahman, the former East Pakistan was not only demonstrating the usual interest smaller countries take in regional cooperation and integration as a curb on the independent scope of action of the biggest actors in the region. It also sent a message of mediation, if not reconciliation, to India and Pakistan. South Asian region-building began against all obstacles, facing realistic skepticism and a lack of understanding of its potential. But it did begin, only to be moved forward by the unavoidable pressure represented by globalization. In the meantime, social forces, including the business community and various cross-regional activities, constituted a second push toward more effective and sustainable region-building with the prospect of concrete results for the people of South Asia.

Performance

The South Asian Association for Regional Cooperation has only begun. It has begun despite the obstacles and the realities of the region. It has begun without the mega-shock of World War II that brought Germany and France together. It has begun without the personal commitment of overly enlightened leaders. It has begun against all odds in the era of post-independence and its obsession with national sovereignty. And it has already survived crises that were more than capable of extinguishing the flickering light of region-ness in South Asia. SAARC is still there.[81]

Informal and formal components of regionalism have been activated to ensure that this process continues. Between the 1988 agreement, the non-attack of nuclear facilities, and the many ties between technical experts sharing experience and expertise on many levels, SAARC has grown into its own "chemistry," its own networking and intuitive procedures. The agreement in 1993 on the South Asian Preferential Trading Arrangement was certainly not baseless, although it remained overly optimistic in its timelines. Initially, SAARC failed to achieve an agreement on a South Asian Free Trade Area in 2001. But the eventual conclusion of such an agreement in late 2005 was not so bad, given the overall record and constellation of past ways and means in South Asia.

The deficits and limits of SAARC in its current form are evident. Most problematic is the fact that its ultimate purpose remains undecided. Security matters initiated SAARC, but they have also "frozen" its real performance from the very beginning. SAARC's contribution to the de-escalation of regional tensions has been lauded, but it is not without hesitation that one can accept that this is directly attributable to SAARC. Officially, political dialogue and debate are not allowed under the SAARC charter. But meetings of politicians are by their nature political. SAARC summits therefore have a strong symbolic content—and all too often not much more meaning.

In this sense, SAARC has been, or at least has grown into, a thoroughly political role. Given its lack of a mandate to play a political role, one must remain cautious about the long-term transformational effect of these sequences involving big politics in the overall SAARC process. In many other fields of foreign policy, the differences in opinion and interest among SAARC member states have remained rather strong. Consensual attitudes on the vexing matter of terrorism have not necessary spilled over into the gradual evolution of a comprehensive and coherent common approach on matters of foreign policy and strategy.

This caveat holds also true for the economic sphere. It certainly is to SAARC's credit that the agenda of economic cooperation and integration has been advanced. But in the field of economics, the enormous discrepancies in size and potential of the South Asian economies simply cannot be transposed into the lofty sphere of partnership discourses. India represents 76 percent of the total SAARC population and the total SAARC GDP. The share of intra-regional trade has remained low, with 5.3 percent of exports and 4.8 percent of imports (2005). Whether SAPTA and SAFTA can provide space and potential to enhance intra-regional trade remains to be seen. Critics argue that it should be the other way around: only growing shares of intra-regional trade justify the design of a viable development of preferential trade and free trade areas.

Functional economic cooperation can play a useful role in enhancing community-building in a region—and it is contributing to this process in South Asia. Yet the promotion of transnational networks has largely remained a rhetorical exercise in SAARC. This is particularly true if poverty alleviation is taken as the means for measuring success. More than 500 million people in the region continue to live in poverty, according to UN criteria. This represents 44 percent of the global total. SAARC has declared the period from 2006 to 2015 the SAARC Decade of Poverty Alleviation. This decision, taken at the SAARC summit on 13 November 2005 in Dhaka, has also brought about the establishment of a SAARC Poverty Alleviation Fund. For the first time in the history of SAARC, the nucleus of a regional reallocation mechanism has been established, following the UN-sponsored work of a South Asian Poverty Alleviation Program that was operational during the 1990s.[82]

One of the key issues in advancing sustainable development in South Asia is the better use of science and technology in the region. The scientific talents of South Asians are legendary, yet the region has not sufficiently benefited from its own talents. SAARC has identified the potential and the need in this area, where "unstructured information patterns need to be tailored in order to serve the developmental cause."[83] The 1997 SAARC summit had resolved to advance a SAARC-driven audio-visual exchange program and promoted the idea of satellite television for villages to promote educational programs in support of rural development. With the 850 million people in its member states, SAARC represents the highest number of rural citizens in any region of the world. Some 400 million of them are illiterate. The educational use of audio-visual media would therefore be the most obvious tool to promote knowledge, particularly in the fields of health, nutrition, and agriculture. As early as 1974, the Indian Space Research Organization beamed programs into hundreds of villages with the help of a satellite loaned from NASA. Neither at that time, nor later under the umbrella of SAARC, did any serious follow-up occur. In SAARC, the idea of a Regional Communications Satellite, SAARSAT, was launched. But the SAARC Technical Committee for Science and Technology never really started working, and the peaceful use of space technology, including satellite technology, has not yet reached the promising goals it has the potential to achieve in South Asia.[84]

This deficit is not only the responsibility of SAARC, but largely the result of insufficient priorities and inadequate focus on the part of SAARC's member state governments. Their performance is a reflection of the genuine quality and legitimacy of their governance structures and regime profiles. For instance, some SAARC member states, notably Pakistan and Bangladesh, have a strong record of too much military involvement in the national political life. Nepal's monarchy has come under increasing pressure from radical, Maoist rebels demanding an end to authoritarian rule in the Himalayan kingdom. Its neighbor Bhutan has opted for soft development, slow adaptation to globalization and its implications, and efforts to avoid any resolute modernization. The Maldives suffer from economic dissatisfaction coupled with tendencies toward increasing authoritarianism (on the part of its government). Sri Lanka has encountered many difficulties in trying to return from the horrors of civil war to the memories of peaceful and consensual democracy. Finally, while India has managed to pursue a positive track record of democratic life and the rule of law, the price of this has been a lack of economic reforms and modernizing transformation. To the exent that South Asia's countries are democracies, they have been labeled "crisis-ridden muddling-through democracies."[85]

Moreover, they have not always been clear in their commitment to regional cooperation and integration. Pakistan sometimes tends to prefer to look more to West Asia, and by virtue of being neighbor to the troubling areas west of its borders, it has been dragged more into the "War on Terror" than into the region-building to its east. Whether or not SAARC membership will make any difference for Afghanistan remains to be seen. Sri Lanka has tried, in vain, to join ASEAN. India continuously tries to connect with ASEM, ASEAN, and APEC and their respective agendas of global free trade. SAARC has largely remained an intergovernmental operation without being able to rely on full and uncompromising governmental commitment across the region. For the time being, the involvement of civil society has been a non-issue in SAARC. The year 2006 was declared the South Asia Tourist Year—a symbolic act with limited significance for the economic growth potential of the region. A comprehensive assessment of the role of SAARC societies for the future of community-building in South Asia remains to be done.

At the same time, SAARC will need to reconsider its institutional structures. In order to achieve the economic goals outlined in SAFTA and SAPTA, SAARC requires at least minimal macroeconomic harmonization and coordinated policies. How this can be achieved without a sufficient set of reasonably independent institutions in place remains a mystery. It might be appropriate to give SAARC the benefit of the doubt and put the necessary institutional and mental evolution into the context of a time span that is defined by a greater urgency than is usually the case in the Western world. In light of the mentality and political culture in South Asia, one would certainly be well advised to assume drawbacks resulting from the region's notion of time and urgency.

Therefore, it must be applauded that the 2005 SAARC summit decided on an Agreement on the Establishment of a SAARC Arbitration Council.[86] Whether or not this arbitration council might develop over time into a South Asian equivalent of the European Court of Justice cannot be predicted. Certainly, it is a promising beginning for promoting the idea of the rule of law as an underlying principle of cooperation and integration. Initially, the work of the arbitration council will be confined to matters regarding the implementation of the South Asian Free Trade Area. If its mandate turns out to be strong enough to truly wield the powers necessary to implement the political agreement on SAFTA, this in itself would already be a spectacular success. The region's sensitivity to interference in matters of national sovereignty is enormous. Yet the will to succeed in economic cooperation cannot be realized without accepting its consequences, the primacy of supranational law in particular.

Federators

Diversity has long served as a natural source of federalism in South Asia. But it has never generated a genuine political movement or intellectual contribution to promote the idea of federalism under the conditions of postcolonial nation-states proud to have gained independence, deeply involved in state-formation and nation-building, overly ambitious to demonstrate their potential for autonomous decision-making in the most relevant issues of state, and yet permanently confronted with the limits of statehood.

It is among the paradoxical realities of SAARC that from its very beginning it incorporated the parameters of the global conflict structure of the Cold War.

Unlike other regional schemes in the Cold War era, SAARC was not built to deter external factors and forces related to the Cold War. Rather, SAARC incorporated both sides of the Cold War and thus became "polytheistic" in its attitude toward "good" and "evil." Sometimes it looked like a secular and political version of Hindu symbolism, which is particularly gifted in balancing contradictions. "Considering the India-Pakistan rivalry and the weak economic ties in the region, it is rather surprising that the seven states have been able to cooperate at all."[87] For some, it might be in line with the logic of this surprise that SAARC incorporated Afghanistan as its eighth member state before establishing a more solid base for the deepening of the processes it launched throughout its first two decades. More importantly, Afghanistan was included in SAARC before security was reestablished at the Hindukush, following the regime change enforced in 2001 with the fall of the radical Taliban regime. Optimists would argue that SAARC membership in itself will help to stabilize Afghanistan.

Upon the end of the Cold War, SAARC's unique and idiosyncratic interpretation of security regionalism—defined as mutually controlled suspicion, not as mutually enhanced protection—was replaced by the aspiration of economic regionalism. This was advanced by the opening of India's economy to the world market. This enormously successful process began in 1991 under the government of Prime Minister Narasimha Rao and his very able finance minister, Manmohan Singh, a Sikh who became the first non-Hindu prime minister of India in 2004. In the early 1990s, India was suffering from a tremendous national budget deficit and a shortfall in currency reserves, coupled with the stagnation of its economy. Until he was toppled in 1996, Prime Minister Rao promoted rigid economic liberalization. The results were impressive, with annual average growth rates of 5.5 percent for a whole decade.

Initially, the Indian elite remained divided between economic and political calculations. While the proponents of the former advocated a strong and proactive inclusion of India in the world economy under the conditions of globalization, the proponents of the latter were protecting the old national paradigm of autarky, self-reliance, and the sensitive pride of never letting any other political body touch the parameters of India's sovereignty. Applying sociological ambivalence, India was itself the biggest obstacle for overcoming the position of a "reluctant policy maker" in SAARC.[88] SAARC's future success will largely depend upon India's readiness to overcome this attitude and project itself as a willing engine for the promotion of regional cooperation and integration in South Asia.

Transformations

SAARC has gone from being almost a caricature of regional architecture to forming the viable nucleus of a security community. It has also begun to transform from a failed or at least limited security community into an emerging economic cooperation and integration community in the 1990s and the first decade of the twenty-first century. Whether or not the pressure and opportunity of globalization, and the potential and burden of rural poverty in South Asia, can be transformed into a new development strategy that encompasses security matters and is able to overcome the traditional postcolonial ideologies of national sovereignty remains the most precarious test-case for the third decade of SAARC.

It would be a most impressive transformation if SAARC were able to overcome the traumatic legacies of colonialism, postcolonial conflicts, independence obsessions, and postcolonial nationalism by the logic of regional cooperation and integration. There is probably no other way for SAARC than to follow the success model of other regional architectures: to begin with the economy and to make integration real and deep. The prospect of a free trade area in South Asia is the first realistic step in this direction. If successful and properly implemented, it cannot remain without consequence for the character of policy articulation, policy formulation, and decision making in South Asia. In fact, it cannot remain without consequence for the very notion of statehood and management of the nation-state in South Asia.

Role and Interests of the European Union

As the European Union is interested in promoting regional integration elsewhere, it reacted favorably when SAARC was established. But the conditions under which SAARC started operation in 1985 were not optimal for the evolution of a serious integration scheme. Leaving the obstacles aside and emphasizing the potential more than the problems, the European Union and SAARC have engaged in a dialogue extending beyond the economic sphere. Only 2.2 percent of EU external trade is with the SAARC member states. Yet the European Union has identified several fields of interest in which to engage with SAARC and to exert influence in favor of the consolidation process of South Asian integration:

- The EU is keen to support South Asian integration "through its economic influence," although that seems to be as limited as the effect of the influence claimed.
- The EU wants to encourage South Asian integration by "dealing with diversity" in South Asia.
- The EU offers to share with SAARC its own historical experience in integration.
- The EU, finally, has declared its interest in SAARC-related crisis management.[89]

Unsurprisingly, the EU also hoped to project its political concept of biregional relations onto South Asia. But so far, not very much has been achieved. This is a function and consequence of the limited way in which SAARC has developed into a stable political partner of the EU. In 1994, the EU and SAARC began regular ministerial meetings, but these ended in 1999. It is significant that the EU signed a partnership agreement with India in 1995 but has not done so with any other SAARC member state or with SAARC as a whole.

In 1996, only a Memorandum of Understanding was signed between the European Commission and the SAARC Secretariat, opening the way for technical assistance from the EU. Although this memorandum was explicit in its non-political character, the implementation did not develop well. SAARC and its structures simply remained too weak to grow into a solid, predictable partner able to deliver and certain of its own interests, objectives, and applicable instruments. In light of the overall political constellation in South Asia, it would not be fair or reasonable to extend and project the current stage of EU-SAARC relations—or to project the current stage of SAARC development—into the future. SAARC can develop as much as its member states remain open to developments. But the EU seems to approach these potential developments with caution. While the EU is negotiating association agreements with other regional partners in the world, the EU has only very modest expectations of SAARC at this point in time. The EU has expressed its interest in harmonizing standards, facilitating trade, raising awareness about the benefits of regional integration in South Asia, and contributing to the networking of the business communities in both regions. As disillusioning as this stage is, progress against all odds should not be ruled out once SAARC gains momentum beyond the experience of the first two decades of its existence.

Perspectives and Obstacles

Like all other regional integration schemes in the world, SAARC has, finally, embarked on a free trade agenda. Recognition of economic interdependence has come to underpin SAARC policies aimed at nurturing community-building in South Asia. SAARC will increasingly have to address the relationship between development issues and security matters if it wants to advance a cohesive rationale for its future existence.

In spite of its beginnings and transformations, SAARC also remains an embryonic security community with the potential to contribute to crisis management in South Asia. SAARC still has "a long way to go before a regional approach to conflict resolution can be adopted."[90] But it has begun to play a growing role in the management of regional and bilateral conflicts in South Asia. Its very existence has helped to reduce tensions between India and Pakistan. The will to cooperate regionally cannot be reconciled with continued tensions and conflicts in the region. In a way, SAARC is a reflection of a more advanced concept of region-ness than it seems to project. Compared with other regional architectures, and facing the challenges that prevail in South Asia, SAARC seems to be an embryonic architecture of regionalism at best. But this perception could also be turned upside down: in light of the enormous political pressures, socioeconomic burden, ethnic and religious difficulties, and geopolitical tensions, SAARC is much more advanced than ought to be expected in the context of South Asia. SAARC might well turn out to be the underrated engine of silent transformations in the region. By transforming regional conflicts, SAARC has transformed itself already. Although this process has been rather silent, it has happened. It can be assumed that the process of "regional conflict transformation" through the medium of SAARC will continue.[91] Conflict management opens room for comparison with the experiences of other Asian regional integration schemes, such as ASEAN. The relationship between conflict management and the benefits for subregional cooperation has also gained attention in SAARC.[92] This is unsurprising in light of various intra-group conflicts in SAARC, such as the Indo-Pakistan dispute over Kashmir, the Bangladesh-India dispute over the sharing of the Ganges River, the tensions and ethnic conflicts between Singhalese and Tamil populations in Sri Lanka, and ethnic tensions in the Chittagong Hill Tracts in the border areas between Bangladesh and Myanmar, a member of ASEAN.

SAARC's agenda will continue to grow in the years ahead. It will obviously extend beyond the original security paradigm, and even beyond the logic of economic integration. The SAARC Social Charter of 2004 is a first diplomatic step toward recognizing the fight against poverty in South Asia as a common obligation. Issues like population growth, the provision of basic health care and primary education, and the incredible gap between rural poverty and urban affluence, but likewise the effects of asymmetric urbanization and forced migration on the social cohesion of the cities of South Asia, indicate the broad spectrum of relevant challenges for the emerging community-building in South Asia.[93] The sense of shared agendas is a new experience in South Asia. SAARC has contributed to the evolution of this awareness to the degree that it anticipates a partial answer: regional agendas require regional solutions. At least, they require common regional approaches in the search for answers. The most pressing test case of the meaning of this concept will be the fate of Afghanistan. In the years ahead SAARC needs to help Afghanistan stabilize peace, rebuild a functioning state, and establish reasonable democratic governance without opium-driven corruption. This tall order is no longer merely a concern for Afghanistan itself. SAARC membership has linked the destiny of Afghanistan with that of SAARC in a new and almost courageous way that remains, however, unpredictable for the foreseeable future.

Engaging in a much more forthcoming way in the debate on good governance in South Asia will be essential if SAARC sincerely wants to transform itself from an intergovernmental body of diplomatic cooperation into a mechanism for regional community-building. Such a development cannot be expected as long as discrepancies prevail among the nature of political regimes in SAARC and their respective governance performances. At some point, SAARC must confront the fact that only democratic regimes generate sufficient trust to embark on the journey of community-building beyond diplomatic rhetoric and political symbolism.

A second structural obstacle to advancing SAARC's full potential as a regional architecture lies in the dominance of India. Basic facts are unalterable as far as the size, population, and economic ambitions of India are concerned. This situation is a fact of life. It is up to India to realize what its SAARC partners already understand: regional integration, if conducted properly, is a win-win situation for all constituent parts. The biggest partners might be inclined to try to go it alone. But they must learn that even the biggest is not strong enough if the overall region is put in a global context. The smaller partners, in turn, need to appreciate that the leadership engine of a partner as big as India can serve to their benefit if the overall structure of a regional architecture is designed along federal lines. Given the member states' differences in size, population, and economic power, South Asian federalism would probably always be asymmetric federalism. But in South Asia there is still much to discover: for all intents and purposes, regional integration has only begun. Its instrumental consequences have been limited so far, but its unintended consequences deserve more credit than has been given to them. SAARC has put its mark on "conflict transformation in the region" and the "transformation of the structure of national identities."[94] These processes have not been completed, let alone concluded with unequivocal success. But neither process can remain incomplete any longer.

Notes

1. Association of Southeast Asian Nations (ASEAN), *The ASEAN-Declaration (Bangkok-Declaration)* (08.08.1967), online at: http://www.aseansec.org/1629.htm.
2. Association of Southeast Asian Nations (ASEAN), *Treaty of Amity and Cooperation in Southeast Asia* (24.02.1976), online at: http://www.aseansec.org/1654.htm.
3. See ASEAN homepage under http://www.aseansec.org; and *Charter of the Association of Southeast Asian Nations* (20.11.2007), online at: http://www.aseansec.org/21069.pdf.
4. Association of Southeast Asian Nations (ASEAN), *Charter of the Association of Southeast Asian Nations* (20.11.2007), online at: http://www.aseansec.org/21069.pdf.
5. Association of Southeast Asian Nations (ASEAN), *Kuala Lumpur Declaration on the Establishment of the ASEAN Charter* (12.12.2005), online at: http://www.aseansec.org/18031.htm.; see also Axel Schmidt, "Die ASEAN-Charter: Die Quadratur des Kreises oder der Scheideweg für die Region?" *FES-Kurzberichte aus der internationalen Entwicklungszusammenarbeit* 11 (2005), online at: http://library.fes.de/pdf-files/iez/03175.pdf.
6. See O.W. Wolters, *History, Culture and Religion in Southeast Asian Perspectives* (Ithaca: Cornell University Press, 1999).
7. Amitav Acharya, *The Quest for Identity: International Relations of Southeast Asia* (Oxford: Oxford University Press, 2000), 27; see also Gerald Tan, *ASEAN Economic Development and Cooperation* (Singapore: Eastern Universities Press, 2003); Linda Low, *ASEAN Economic Co-Operation and Challenges* (Singapore: Institute of Southeast Asian Studies, 2004).

8. See C.A. Fisher, "Southeast Asia: The Balkans of the Orient? A Study in Continuity and Change," *Geography* 47 (1962): 347–367.
9. See http://www.aseansec.org/19230.htm.
10. See Joakim Öjendal, "South East Asia at a Constant Crossroads: An Ambiguous 'New Region'",in Michael Schulz et al. (eds.), *Regionalization in a Globalizing World: A Comparative Perspective on Forms, Actors and Processes* (London: Zed Books, 2001), 147–172; see also Estrella D. Solidum, *The Politics of ASEAN: An Introduction to Southeast Asian Regionalism* (Singapore: Eastern Universities Press, 2003).
11. Acharya, *The Quest for Identity*, 128.
12. See Alvestad Erling, *The ASEAN Regional Forum: A Catalyst for Change?* (Oslo: The University of Oslo, 2001).
13. Ibid., 137.
14. Ibid., 140.
15. See Haruhiko Kuroda, "ASEAN Economic Outlook and Policy Issues" (2008), online at: http://www.adb.org/Documents/Speeches/2008/ms2008018.asp
16. See Nattapong Thongpakde, "Impact and Implications of ASEAN Enlargement on Trade," in Carolyn L. Gates and Mya Than (eds.), *ASEAN Enlargement: Impacts and Implications* (Singapore: Institute of Southeast Asian Studies, 2001), 45–79.
17. See Derek McDougall, "Humanitarian Intervention and Peacekeeping as Issues for Asia-Pacific Security," in James H. Hentz and Morten Boas (eds.), *New and Critical Security and Regionalism: Beyond the Nation-State* (Aldershot: Ashgate, 2003), 33–53.
18. Association of Southeast Asian Nations (ASEAN), *Kuala Lumpur Declaration on the Establishment of the ASEAN Charter* (12.12.2005), online at: http://www.aseansec.org/18031.htm.
19. Ibid.
20. Öjendal, "South East Asia at a Constant Crossroads," 154.
21. Acharya, *The Quest for Identity*, 97.
22. See Chin Kin Wah, "ASEAN's Engagement with the EU and the US in the 21st Century: Political and Strategic Dimension," in K.S. Nathan (ed.), *The European Union, United States and ASEAN: Challenges and Prospects for Cooperative Engagement in the 21st Century* (London: ASEAN Academic Press, 2002), 88.
23. See Michael G. Plummer, "The EU and ASEAN: Real Integration and Lessons in Financial Cooperation," *The World Economy* 25, no. 10 (2002): 1469–1500; also: Tamim Bayoumi et al., *On Regional Monetary Arrangements for ASEAN* (London: Centre for Economic Policy Research, 2000).
24. Association of Southeast Asian Nations (ASEAN), *Chairman's Statement of the First East Asian Summit* (Kuala Lumpur, 14.12.2005), online at: http://www.aseansec.org/18104.htm.
25. Achariya, *The Quest for Identity*, 92.
26. For the larger context, see Tran Van Hoa and Charles Harvie (eds.), *New Asian Regionalism: Responses to Globalisation and Crises* (Basingstoke: Macmillan, 2003).
27. Achariya, *The Quest for Identity*, 137.
28. Carolyn L. Gates and Mya Than, "ASEAN Enlargement," in Gates and Than, *ASEAN Enlargement*, 5.
29. See Jürgen Rüland, *ASEAN and the European Union: A Bumpy International Relationship*, ZEI Discussion Paper C 95 (Bonn: Centre for European Integration Studies, 2001); Alfredo C. Robles, Jr., "The Association of Southeast Asian Nations (ASEAN) and the European Union: Limited Interregionalism," in Heiner Hänggi et al. (eds.), *Interregionalism and International Relations* (Abingdon and New York: Routledge, 2006), 97–112.
30. See Chin Kin Wah, "ASEAN's Engagement with the EU and the US," 87.
31. European Commission (EC), "A New Partnership with South East Asia" (June 2003), online at: http://www.ec.Europa.eu/external_relations/library/publications/09_sea_en.pdf.

32. See K.S. Nathan, "The ASEM Process and Cooperative Engagement in the 21st Century: Challenges and Responses," in K.S. Nathan (ed.), *The European Union, United States and ASEAN*, 347–368.

33. See Bertrand Fort and Douglas Webber (eds.), *Regional Integration in East Asia and Europe: Convergence or Divergence?* (London and New York: Routledge, 2006).

34. Achariya, *The Quest for Identity*, 137.

35. Ibid., 153.

36. See Nick J. Freeman, "ASEAN Enlargement and Foreign Direct Investment," in Gates and Than, *ASEAN Enlargement*, 80–101.

37. Mya Than and George Abonyi, "The Greater Mekong Subregion: Co-Operation in Infrastructure and Finance," in Gates and Than, *ASEAN Enlargement*, 128–163.

38. See Joakim Öjendal, "Regional Hydropolitics in Mainland South East Asia: A New Deal for a New Era?" in Björn, Andras Inotai, and Osvaldo Sunkel (eds.), *The New Regionalism and the Future of Security and Development, The New Regionalism Series: vol. 4* (London: Macmillan, 2000), 176–209.

39. Scott Cooper and Brock Taylor, "Power and Regionalism: Explaining Regional Cooperation in the Persian Gulf," in Finn Laursen (ed.), *Comparative Regional Integration: Theoretical Perspectives* (Aldershot: Ashgate, 2003), 108.

40. United Nations Development Programme (ed.), *Arab Human Development Report 2004: Toward Freedom in the Arab World* (New York: UNDP Bureau for Arab States, 2005), 4.

41. See Giacomo Luciani and Felix Neugart (eds.), *The EU and the GCC: A New Partnership* (Munich and Gütersloh: Centrum für angewandte Politikforschung and Bertelsmann Stiftung, 2005), 11.

42. United Nations Development Programme, *Arab Human Development Report 2004*, 61.

43. Cooper and Taylor, "Power and Regionalism," 114.

44. Cooperation Council for the Arab States of the Gulf (GCC), *The Cooperation Council—Charter* (25.05.1981), online at: http://www.gccsg.org/eng/index.php?action=Sec-Show&ID=1.

45. Cooperation Council for the Arab States of the Gulf (GCC), *The Unified Economic Agreement between the Countries of the Gulf Cooperation Council* (11.11.1981), online at: http://www.worldtradelaw.net/fta/agreements/gccfta.pdf.

46. Cooperation Council for the Arab States of the Gulf (GCC), *The Cooperation Council—Charter* (25.05.1981), GCC Charter Article 4, cited in GCC, online at: http://www.gccsg.org/eng/index.php?action=Sec-Show&ID=1.

47. See Erik R. Peterson, *The Gulf Cooperation Council: Search for Unity in a Dynamic Region* (Boulder: Westview Press, 1988); Charles Tripp, "Regional Organizations in the Arab Middle East," in Louise Fawcett and Andrew Hurrell (eds.), *Regionalism in World Politics: Regional Organization and International Order* (New York: Oxford University Press, 1995), 283–308.

48. See Emile A. Nakleh, *The Gulf Cooperation Council: Policies, Problems and Prospects* (New York/Westport/London: Praeger, 1986); Cooper and Taylor, "Power and Regionalism," 107.

49. John Christie, "History and Development of the Gulf Cooperation Council: A Brief Overview," in John A. Sandwick (ed.), *The Gulf Cooperation Council: Moderation and Stability in an Interdependent World* (Boulder: Westview Press, 1987), 12.

50. Ibid., 13.

51. Ibid., 14.

52. Cooperation Council for the Arab States of the Gulf (GCC), *The Unified Economic Agreement between the Countries of the Gulf Cooperation Council* (11.11.1981), online at: http://www.worldtradelaw.net/fta/agreements/gccfta.pdf.

53. Christie, "History and Development of the Gulf Cooperation Council," 20.

54. Cooper and Taylor, "Power and Regionalism," 111.

55. See Nakleh, *The Gulf Cooperation Council*, 30.

56. Cited in Peterson, *The Gulf Cooperation Council*, 201.

57. Ibid.

58. See Cooper and Taylor, "Power and Regionalism," 111.

59. See Hassan Hamdan Al-Alkim, *The GCC States in an Unstable World: Foreign Policy Dilemmas of Small States* (London: Saqi Books, 1994), 69.

60. Luciani and Neugart, *The EU and the GCC*, 15.

61. Ugo Fasano and Andrea Schaechter (eds.), *Monetary Union Among the Member Countries of the Gulf Cooperation Council* (Washington, D.C.: International Monetary Fund, 2003): iv; on the same topic see also Michael Sturm and Siegfried Nikolaus, *Regional Monetary Integration in the Member States of the Gulf Cooperation Council* (Frankfurt: European Central Bank, 2003); Daniel Hanna, *A New Fiscal Framework for GCC Countries Ahead of Monetary Union*, International Economic Programme Briefing Paper 06/02 (London: Chatham House, 2006).

62. For more details see Uzi Rabi, "The Dynamics of the Gulf Cooperation Council (GCC): The Ceaseless Quest for Regional Security in a Changing Region," *Orient* 45, no. 2 (2004): 281–295.

63. Al-Alkim, *The GCC States in an Unstable World*, 106.

64. Nakleh, *The Gulf Cooperation Council*, 28.

65. Al-Alkim, *The GCC States in an Unstable World*, 67.

66. See Andreas Marchetti (ed.), *Ten Years Euro-Mediterranean Partnership: Defining European Interests for the Next Decade*, ZEI Discussion Paper C 154 (Bonn: Centre for European Integration Studies, 2005); Thomas Demmelhuber, *The Euro-Mediterranean Space as an Imagined (Geo-) Political, Economic and Cultural Entity*, ZEI Discussion Paper C 170 (Bonn: Centre for European Integration Studies, 2006).

67. It is noteworthy that some GCC countries have a very pragmatic attitude toward the Middle East conflict that overshadows so much of the Euro-Mediterranean Partnership. Qatar has even established formal trade relations with Israel and has agreed on the opening of an Israeli trade mission in Qatar.

68: Nakleh, *The Gulf Cooperation Council*, 86.

69. Ibid., 104.

70. Sturm and Nikolaus, *Regional Monetary Integration*, 64.

71. Cooperation Council for the Arab States of the Gulf (GCC), *The Economic Agreement between the Countries of the Gulf Cooperation Council (Revised)* (31.12.2001), 11, online at: http://www.worldtradelaw.net/fta/agreements/gccfta.pdf.

South Asian Association for Regional Cooperation (SAARC)

72. Quoted from South Asian Association for Regional Cooperation (SAARC), *Charter of the South Asian Association for Regional Cooperation* (08.12.1985), 1, online at: http://www.saarc-sec.org/data/docs/charter.pdf.

73. See Bent D. Jorgensen, "South Asia: An Anxious Journey Toward Regionalization?" in Michael Schulz et al. (eds.), *Regionalization in a Globalizing World: A Comparative Perspective on Forms, Actors and Processes* (London and New York: Zed Books, 2001), 125–146.

74. Kant K. Bhargava, *EU-SAARC: Comparisons and Prospects of Cooperation*, ZEI Discussion Paper C 15 (Bonn: Center for European Integration Studies, 1998), 7.

75. South Asian Association for Regional Cooperation (SAARC), *Agreement on SAARC Preferential Trading Arrangement (SAPTA)* (11.04.1993), online at: http://www.saarc-sec.org/data/agenda/economic/sapta/sapta.pdf.

76. South Asian Association for Regional Cooperation (SAARC), *Agreement on South Asian Free Trade Area (SAFTA)* (06.01.2004), online at: http://www.saarc-sec.org/data/agenda/economic/safta/SAFTA%20AGREEMENT.pdf.

77. Jayatilleke S. Bandara and Wusheng Yu, "How Desirable is the South Asian Free Trade Area? A Qualitative Economic Assessment," *The World Economy* 26, no. 9 (2003), 1296.

78. South Asian Association for Regional Cooperation (SAARC), *Regional Convention on Suppression of Terrorism* (04.11.1987), online at: http://treaties.un.org/doc/db/Terrorism/Conv18-english.pdf.

79. South Asian Association for Regional Cooperation (SAARC), *Additional Protocol to the Regional Convention on Suppression of Terrorism* (06.01.2004), online at: http://www.satp.org/satporgtp/southasia/documents/papers/SAARC_pak.htm.

80. Björn Hettne, "Security Regionalism in Europe and South Asia," in James J. Hentz and Morten Boas (eds.), *New and Critical Security and Regionalism: Beyond the Nation-State* (Aldershot: Ashgate, 2003), 159.

81. For a good overview on all aspects of SAARC activities in its early stages see B.C. Upreti (ed.), *SAARC: Dynamics of Regional Cooperation in South Asia*, 2 vols.(New Delhi: Kalinga Publications, 2000); M. H. Syed (ed.), *SAARC: Challenges Ahead* (New Delhi: Kilaso Books, 2003).

82. Thirteenth South Asian Association for Regional Cooperation (SAARC) Summit, *Dhaka Declaration*, (13.11.2005), online at: http://www.saarc-sec.org/main.php?id=159&t=7.1.

83. L.L. Mehrotra, "SAARC and the Information Revolution," in Eric Gonsalves and Nancy Jetly (eds.), *The Dynamics of South Asia: Regional Cooperation and SAARC* (Delhi: Sage Publications, 1999), 135.

84. See P.J. Lavakare, "Science and Technology in SAARC: Aspiration, Achievements and Hopes," in Gonsalves and Jetly, *The Dynamics of South Asia*, 157–170.

85. Hettne, "Security Regionalism in Europe and South Asia," 160.

86. South Asian Association for Regional Cooperation (SAARC), *Agreement for Establishment of SAARC Arbitration Council* (13.11.2005), online at: http://www.slmfa.gov.lk/saarc/images/agreements/saarc_arbitration_council%20_2005.

87. Jorgensen, "South Asia," 139.

88. See S.D. Muni, "India in SAARC: A Reluctant Policy Maker," in Björn Hettne et al. (eds.), *National Perspectives on the New Regionalism in the South. The New Regionalism Series: vol. 3* (London: Macmillan Press, 2000), 108–131.

89. European Commission (EC), *The EU & South Asian Association of Regional Co-Operation (SAARC)*, online at: http://www.ec.Europa.eu/comm/external_relations/saarc/intro/index.htm.

90. Hettne, "Security Regionalism in Europe and South Asia," 160.

91. See Masud Hossain, *Regional Conflict Transformation: A Reinterpretation of South Asian Association for Regional Co-operation (SAARC)* (Helsinki: Institute of Development Studies, 2002).

92. See A.K.M. Abdus Sabur and Mohammed Humayun Kabir, *Conflict Management and Sub-Regional Co-operation in ASEAN: Relevance for SAARC* (Dhaka: Academic Press, 2000).

93. See South Asian Association for Regional Cooperation (SAARC), *Social Charter* (04.01.2004), online at: http://www.saarc-sec.org/main.php?id=13.; K. Radhakrishna Murthy, "The Pace, Patterns and Problems of Urbanisation in the SAARC Countries," in K.C. Reddy and T. Nirmala Devi (eds.), *Regional Cooperation in South Asia: New Dimensions* (New Delhi: Kanishka Publishers, 2002), 106–139; R. Venkata Rao, "Strategic Implications of Forced Migration in SAARC Countries: The Need for Pan South Asian Approach," in Reddy and Devi, *Regional Cooperation in South Asia*, 140–146.

94. Hossain, *Regional Conflict Transformation*, 138–148.

5

AFRICA

Renaissance through Region-Building?

━━━◉━━━

The African Union (AU)

Basic Facts

Since 1950, world economic production has more than quadrupled and global trade has risen seventeen-fold. The only continent by and large unaffected by this enormous socioeconomic progress has been Africa. Even worse, on the whole Africa has suffered a stark deterioration in living standards. Its 850 million people (770 million in sub-Saharan Africa) in fifty-three countries produce a GDP of $1.5 trillion (by comparison, the EU GDP is $456 trillion), which translates into a per capita income of $1,842 (EU: $24,249). Thirty-three African countries are low-income countries with a GDP per capita below $905. Only 2.7 percent of world trade originates in Africa, and only 3.3 percent of global investment is done there. Even Africa's mineral resources are more often a curse than a blessing, being considered a development trap as they generate monopolist dependencies. With 2.3 percent population growth and, at best, economic growth rates of 3 to 4 percent, sub-Saharan Africa remains the slowest-developing region in the world.[1]

After the 1960s and the end of European colonialism, Africa experienced a wave of state-building. On the rhetorical and ideological level, this was paralleled by pan-Africanism. Pan-Africanism had started in the early twentieth century in the United States and the Caribbean, inspired by the writings of Marcus Garvey, W.E.B. Du Bois, and others. Its normative ideals were a driving force behind the creation of the Organization of African Unity (OAU). Its founding charter of 1963 echoed the idea of jointly managing the continental affairs of the emerging independent African states.[2] The founding of the OAU was the consequence of the work of regional groupings such as the Casablanca Group, the Brazzaville Group, and the Monrovia Group. All colonial federations, except for Nigeria, were dissolved into single states, often without genuine nations at their root. The vision of a United Africa was supported by the first generation of political leaders: Kwameh Nkrumah, Jomo Kenyatta, Leopold Sedar Senghor, Sekou Touré, Julius Nyerere, and Emperor Haile Selassie. Yet they could not overcome the paradox that independence in Africa was only gained on the basis and along the model of the colonial nation-state.[3] The inevitable primacy of national independence and claims of sovereignty across Africa undermined any realistic prospect of a continental union. The OAU was weak, except for its commitment to safeguarding all borders as they were drawn by the colonial powers upon their departure from Africa.

The priority of state-building took place at the expense of other tasks. Sufficient focus on the preconditions of economic well-being and the maximization of welfare gains was neglected. So was the domestic political context. Poor economic performances were increasingly coupled with bad governance, neo-authoritarian dictatorships, and ethnic conflicts exacerbating the overall depressing human rights record in most African countries. Under these conditions, the history of regional or even continental integration in Africa remained weak. The understanding of "regional integration as stepping stone to integration in the multilateral trading system"[4] was incoherent. Parochial state-building, legitimized by national development ideologies, prevailed.

At the same time, a confusing set of regional intergovernmental agreements mushroomed across Africa. By 2005, five countries of sub-Saharan Africa belonged to one regional agreement, twenty-seven were members of two, and eighteen countries were members of three or more regional systems. The objectives of these different regional architectures are not always clear, and their instruments remain weak and ineffectual. Most often, membership in one or another regional structure is considered a means to maximize the allocation of external development aid. Africa engages in a "resource-driven regionalism."[5] The overlap of memberships also reflects the competing nature of norms and the lack of clarity about goals. All in all, experts have counted more than a dozen regional or subregional economic communities with overlapping membership and mandates. Their dissolution is as rare as real success.

The dissolution of the East African Community (EAC) in 1977, after ten years of promising existence, was the honest recognition of deep ideological rifts between the governments of Tanzania and Kenya and their disputes over the fair distribution of costs and benefits. In other regional systems, the absence of this honesty was glossed over by stark rhetoric of brotherhood. In the East African case, a new beginning was undertaken in 1999, aimed at creating a common market and a political federation for 90 million people. Political conditions in East Africa had changed substantially. The ideological rifts of the 1970s had disappeared. During the 1990s and following economic reforms, Uganda had average growth rates of 4 percent and Tanzania of 7 percent, compared with a 2 percent growth rate in Kenya. The two new member states, Burundi and Rwanda, bring with them the horrible experience of Africa's worst genocide during the 1990s. With their membership, the new East African Community has defined peace and stability, rightly so, as its overriding rationale. Agreement to reach a customs union was established in 2004. Even monetary union by the five countries constituting the new East African Community seems "viable,"[6] and they have set 2010 as their target date. A regional parliamentary assembly and a regional court of justice have been installed.

In other parts of the African continent, the same emphasis on regime symmetry—that is, a mutual recognition that region-building can only succeed as democratic regionalism—has been gaining ground only slowly. For the time being, the overriding impression is one of regionalization without integration. "The multiplicity of overlapping and largely similar arrangements, a notorious phenomenon in Africa, actually dissipates effort and energy," one analyst wrote.[7] At least ten regional economic communities claim to be of relevance in advancing the goal of an African Economic Community: The Arab Maghreb Union (AMU), the Economic Community of West African States (ECOWAS), the Economic Community of Central African States (ECCAS), the Common Market for East and Southern Africa (COMESA), the Southern African Development Community (SADC), the Intergovernmental Authority for Development (IGAD), the Community of Sahelo-Saharan States (CEN-SAD), the Central African Customs and Economic Union (UDEAC), the Economic Community of the Great Lake Countries (CEPGL), and the South African Customs Union (SACU). But so far, none of these groupings has been able to fully bridge the gap between aspiration and reality.

The end of the Cold War had its effects on Africa. In the aftermath of the dissolution of the Soviet Union, Yugoslavia, and the German Democratic Republic, the first concern of the OAU was to prevent the breakdown of African national borders. Eritrea gained independence in 1993 by seceding from Ethiopia, but this creation of a new African state was understood as a return to the borders that had existed before the Italian colonial intervention in 1936. Otherwise, Africa's borders have remained intact. Yet with the search for a new world order, a general revision of the relationship between the goal of continental unity, the multitude of regional integration schemes, the relationship between the logic of economic development and good governance, and the impact of globalization on the development of the African continent became inevitable. Africa could no longer shy away from the widely spread critique that its development models had been too decoupled from politics and governance structures on the national level. Four decades into independent statehood, it was no longer persuasive to blame the former colonial powers for Africa's depressing realities. Africa had to recognize that its deficits—including its deficits in regional integration—result largely from problems of political commitment, coupled with weak rule of law, democratic deficits, and organizational deficiencies, including an enormous lack of human resources and organizational capacities.[8]

A general overhaul of governance structures, regional integration schemes, and the pan-African vision of the OAU were imperative. On the continental level, the necessary reform process began with the signing of the Treaty of Abuja (Treaty Establishing the African Economic Community) on 3 January 1991 during the annual OAU summit. The Treaty of Abuja (in force since May 1994)[9] formulates the goal of creating an African Economic Community by 2028. The existing regional cooperation and integration schemes were considered building blocks for this larger goal "in order to foster the economic, social and cultural integration" of Africa.[10] Constructivism had reached Africa. Regionalism as gradual community-building finally began to take root on the African continent. The Treaty of Abuja suggested the creation of an African Union with a Pan-African Parliament over a period of six phases, the final stages to be reached at latest in 2034. In its institutional approach, the Treaty of Abuja was trying to emulate the European Union. Africa could not make use of the preconditions that have shaped the European integration process. The Treaty of Abuja did not grant new functions or powers to the OAU to better enable it to implement its noble goals. But the treaty did already allude to most of the ingredients soon to be found in the Constitutive Act of the African Union.

Decades of postcolonial talk about integration in Africa had produced many lofty goals without practical effect, "as if it were some kind of exorcism against their own impotence."[11] Idealistic invocations of a return of "the original African soul" in order to pave the way for a continental integration remained fruitless. On the other hand, Africa had to learn the unpleasant truth that "grafted states are inherently artificial and unstable."[12] Unlike in Africa, the integration processes in Latin America coincided with structural reform processes, both in economic and political terms. Africa would definitely have to discover this unavoidable obligation, too. Whether or not Africa might be able to achieve economic union as anticipated by 2028 or 2034 will not only be a matter of sophisticated structures and programs; it will primarily depend upon the preconditions that have to be met in order to make any integration scheme meaningful. "The ability and willingness of African governments to create the appropriate environment conducive to economic cooperation on the continent"[13] will depend on the degree of self-critical behavior as far as the economic structures and the mechanisms of governance are concerned.

Economic growth in sub-Saharan Africa took a dramatic turn after independence: it dropped from 1.5 percent on average during the 1960s to 0.7 percent on average during the 1970s and then rose to 1.2 percent on average during the 1980s. The escalation of civil wars and civil unrest, coupled with continuous realities of authoritarianism and clan-based regimes defined more by corruption than by any reasonable sense of the public good, made a new beginning in Africa and for Africa imperative, should the continent hope to retreat from the abyss. As far as the role of regional cooperation and integration as a development tool is concerned, two departures are noticeable since the early 1990s:

- On the regional level, the existing regional integration systems experienced a general overhaul with strong emphasis on economic development and functional deepening, including in the sphere of security and parliamentary representation.
- On the continental level, the goal of African unity became more politicized and institutionalized while being broadened through mechanisms of functional deepening; simultaneously the limits of autonomous claims to national sovereignty as the highest goal of statehood were increasingly recognized and the notion of protecting human rights through preventive and, if necessary, interventionist measures gained ground over the stereotypical claim of non-interference in domestic affairs of individual African countries by fellow countries or any continental actor.

At the initiative of Libya's leader Muammar Gaddafi—clearly no symbol or guarantor of democratic regionalism—the summit meeting of the OAU in Sirte ended with a declaration on 9 September 1999 aiming at the merger of the OAU with a newly conceptualized African Union. Another OAU meeting in Tripoli on 2 June 2000 certified the relationship between the OAU and a new African Union, the Pan-African Parliament and the African Economic Union. Now it was decided to turn the OAU into the African Union. The Lomé Summit of the OAU adopted the Constitutive Act of the African Union on 12 July 2000. Until the OAU summit in Lusaka in July 2001, fifty OAU member states had ratified the Constitutive Act, which then came into force.[14] Except for Morocco all countries of Africa have joined the new institution. The African Union started with three principle objectives:

- Unity and solidarity of Africa
- Reassuring the sovereignty, territorial integrity, and independence of the AU's member states
- Emphasizing accelerated political and socioeconomic integration of the continent.

The African Union established a complex and comprehensive set of institutions. Not all of the seventeen institutions outlined in the Constitutive Act of the African Union came into immediate force or were able to begin with successful actions. But the structure of the African Union looks impressive:

- The supreme body is the AU President's Assembly (Article 7), which meets once a year and takes decisions by consensus or two-thirds majority on substantial matters and by a simple majority on procedural matters. The AU is presided over on an annual rotating basis by one of the continent's heads of state (in 2008, it was Jakaya Mrisho Kikwete of Tanzania).

- The AU Executive Council consists of the foreign ministers of the African Union and decides on regular matters from foreign trade to communications and foreign policy.
- The Pan-African Parliament, located in Midrand, is composed of representatives from across the continent.
- The AU Commission, based in Addis Ababa, is composed of ten commissioners (its president since 2007 is Jean Ping of Gabon). Its secretariat is responsible for coordinating the activities and meetings of the African Union.
- The AU Permanent Representatives Committee (Article 3) is composed of nominated permanent representatives of the member state governments. It prepares the work of the Executive Council.
- The African Court of Justice is in the process of being established, building on the experience and structures of the African Court on Human and People's Rights based in Arusha. Its eleven judges were elected in 2006 by the Executive Council of the African Union. The African Commission on Human and People's Rights, based in Banjul, reports to the AU President's Assembly.
- The AU Peace and Security Council is designed to be responsible for monitoring and intervening in conflicts and is intended to have an AU peacekeeping force at its disposal. The Peace and Security Council was formally launched in Addis Ababa on 25 May 2004 and received initial EU support of €250 million for its peacekeeping facility. The Peace and Security Council is complemented by a Panel of the Wise, a Continental Early Warning System, a Military Staff Committee, and an African Standby Force operational as of 2010. It can install special envoys and can resort to the resources of an AU Peace Fund for its operations.
- The AU Economic, Social and Cultural Council, mandated with an advisory role, is composed of representatives from professions and civil society.
- Financial institutions of the AU include the African Central Bank, the African Monetary Fund and the African Investment Bank.

Article 30 of the Constitutive Act of the African Union defines the procedure for suspending membership in the AU in clear words: "Governments which shall come to power through unconstitutional means shall not be allowed to participate in the activities of the Union."[15] Article 4d stipulates the goal of a common defense policy. These are but the most prominent differences between the OAU and the AU: the African Union differs "in its greater ambition: it proposes accelerated movement toward a single political and economic unit across the whole continent."[16] It was almost inevitable that the AU would fall short of living up to this ambition. Soon it was nicknamed the "Aspirational Union," and critics argued that it was "the expression of an end-goal of a future process rather than the organic fruition of existing economic and political ties."[17] The creation of the African Union was not debated in any national parliament or civil society. Only one year after its foundation, member states were already more than $50 million in arrears in their dues to the AU. Worse was the fact that the African Union did not seem to have much influence over the issue of economic reform, so urgently needed in Africa. Its necessity is shown by one telling figure: if Africa increased its share of world exports by just 1 percent, the net financial inflow would be $70 billion, an amount seven times higher than the current level of aid flowing into Africa.[18] All in all, if the African Union were taken seriously by its own member states, they could "contribute to a stronger continental authority."[19]

The main challenge for the African Union is the consolidation of its revamped and newly created institutions. The lack of human resources will pose capacity problems for many years, if not decades to come. Effectiveness of the AU needs to be measured realistically. Wherever possible, it must be judged by its ability to deliver concrete results. To gradually bridge the gap between renewed visions, consolidated institutions, and well-formulated declarations on the one hand, and the wide array of implementation challenges on the other, remains the main test for African leaders wishing to overcome their credibility deficit.

Intrinsic Motives and External Pressures

The African Union is the consequence of the failure of OAU and pan-African rhetoric, the product of adaptational pressure exerted by the increasing marginalization of the African continent, and the expression of hopes of achieving development progress, security, and a better governance record by emulating the institutional design of the European Union. The change of rationale from OAU to AU is rooted in the recognition of the limits of sovereign statehood and the false promise of parochial development nationalism that were constitutive for the first generation of postcolonial African states. Anti-colonial pan-Africanism was unable to fulfill any material promise attached to the notion of sovereign independence. In matters of security and human development, Africa has experienced decades of gradual, later of accelerated, decline. Weak, often failing or failed states had to look for other vehicles to link their interests, share their problems, and learn jointly from rather unpleasant experiences.

Complaining about the colonial legacy did not suffice to explain or justify the development deficits and increasing marginalization of most African states. The backwardness of Africa's human development could no longer be covered up by the friendly language of United Nations documents or the vibrating rhetoric of ideological grand designs. Pragmatic realism about the requisite preconditions for turning the wheel of Africa's contemporary history had become highly necessary. This must not exclude the plans for African unity. But only through functional developments, based on stronger institutions and the gradual introduction of binding supranational legislation, could African unity make any meaningful sense.

The inclination to formally emulate and copy the institutional arrangements of the European Union created immediate misgivings about the seriousness of the transformation from OAU to AU. Without the basis of European experiences, it seemed unlikely that the African Union would be able to apply the dynamics that had grown in European integration over several decades. The institutions of European integration had developed gradually and always with consideration of the realistically possible next level of integration. One could only wonder whether the African Union could achieve an equivalent set of integration architecture with the stroke of one treaty. Compared with the rhetorical overstretch of past decades, Africa seemed to have overextend itself institutionally. The African Union started where the European Union had arrived after five decades of an often daunting progress. Nonetheless, the new beginning of African integration deserves the benefit of the doubt.

Performance

Since the formal start of its existence on 9 August 2002 at the Durban summit, the African Union has not had enough time to develop a comprehensive profile and record. Yet some preliminary assessments can already be made, judging both the strong and the weak points of its performance. It was not surprising that the then African Secretary General of the United Nations, Kofi Annan, accompanied the first steps of the African Union with a word of caution. But it goes to the AU's credit that it includes one key innovation compared with the OAU: the ability to intervene in internal affairs. Although an explicit reference to combating corruption was deleted from the draft of the Constitutive Act of the African Union,[20] and although Article 4g reaffirms adherence to the principle of non-interference in domestic affairs, Article 4h indicates a virtual quantum leap in African affairs. It concedes the right of the AU "to intervene in a Member State pursuant to a decision of the Assembly in respect of grave circumstances, namely: war crimes, genocide and crimes against humanity."[21] In light of Africa's past failures, one cannot but recognize this shift "toward increased collective continental responsibility."[22] Beyond the AU's Constitutive Act of 2001, the Solemn Declaration on a Common African Defense and Security Policy was promulgated on 28 February 2004, reinforcing the new focus. Africa was moving "from non-intervention to non-indifference."[23]

(1) The recalibration of the institutions that stood at the center of the transformation from the OAU to the AU very much followed the structure of the European Union. This is flattering to many in the EU, but it does not indicate any factual result. The AU's structure will have to be judged on the basis of the

performance of its institutions. The institutional reorientation might help to strengthen the actual focus and power of the AU, but only time will tell. The OAU Secretariat has become the AU Commission, the Council of Ministers has become the Executive Council of the AU, and the Assembly of Heads of States remains under the same title, while the former OAU Bureau has become the Peace and Security Council. The African Court on Human and People's Rights, formally launched in January 2004, and the Pan-African Parliament, convened for the first time in March 2004, are brand-new experiences for Africa.

However, the arrangement of the AU Parliament indicates its inherent weakness. Each country—from Nigeria with its 137 million inhabitants to São Tomé and Príncipe with 181,000 inhabitants—can send five representatives. Although federalism based on state equality is always beneficial for the smaller constituent parts, over time the grave discrepancy will be hard to maintain in Africa. As long as the AU Parliament has no real powers and operates on the basis of an unclear agenda, the strict equality of representation is meaningless and hence not problematic. But the more the parliament evolves into an expression of African democracy—which is not unlikely under reasonably positive circumstances—the more it will have to reconsider the "equality" of representation, that is, whether it is based on equality of the member states or on representation proportionate to population. It will also have to decide on the recruitment mechanism: shall its members be directly elected, or always be nominated by each national parliament? Most important, the AU Parliament will need to follow the model of the European Parliament to struggle for the gradual development of genuine AU legislation, eventually based on co-decision mechanisms between the Pan-African Parliament and the AU member states.

(2) The most remarkable development in the African Union is the recognition of the incipient potential for intervention in grave cases of violations of human rights and other basic principles enshrined in the AU's Constitutive Act.[24] The African Union Mission in Burundi (AMIB), launched in 2003, was the first, rather easy operation executed by AU member states. In 2003/2004, AMIB "succeeded in deescalating a potentially volatile situation."[25] In 2004, the UN considered the situation in Burundi sufficiently stable to establish a UN peacekeeping operation there, replacing AMIB.

The first hard test case for the boosted security ambition of the African Union was the Darfur crisis, which began to escalate in 2003. It took the AU by surprise, much in the way that the European Union was stunned and unprepared upon the outbreak of the Yugoslavian Wars of Succession in 1991. The ethnic strife in Darfur, a region the size of France, left 180,000 people dead, 1.8 million people displaced within Darfur, and 200,000 refugees fleeing into Chad. On 8 April 2004 in N'djamena, the African Union was able to broker a first cease-fire agreement among the warring factions. Initially, with European Union support of €92 million, 2,400 AU peacekeepers were deployed in Darfur. Their number increased to 7,730 in September 2005, based on a broadened mandate to protect civilians under imminent threat. However, the warring factions in Darfur continued their struggle. The Darfur crisis was too big for the African Union to manage on its own through its Mission in Sudan (AMIS).

The AU's incessant efforts to broker a lasting peace deal failed, as did all interim agreements that were time and again violated. As of mid 2006, the demand for a more robust UN-led peacekeeping mission became stronger and stronger. By the end of August 2006, the United Nations had decided to bring the AU peacekeeping force under its command. In December 2006 Sudan's Islamic government continued to delay the introduction of any solid and robust external peacekeeping force. Eventually, it was ready to accept further peace negotiations on Darfur under the umbrella of the United Nations and the African Union. Finally, on 31 July 2007, the UN Security Council paved the way for the deployment of 26,000 soldiers and policemen under UN mandate, merging with the AU peacekeeping forces into one hybrid peace force in Darfur (UNAMID). The Sudanese government continued to resist this international operation, while the terrible humanitarian crisis in Darfur did not leave the world untouched.

In the meantime, the African Union had already been exposed to the next challenge. In March 2007, the first batch of peacekeeping soldiers under the auspices of the African Union was deployed in Somalia. The African Union Mission to Somalia (AMISOM) was authorized by the United Nations and aimed at including 8,000 soldiers. By 2008 it had accumulated no more than 1,200 men and lacked the commitment of several AU member states that, in light of the ongoing uncertainty and lack of security in Somalia, preferred to train Somalian soldiers in their respective home country. Those who had gone into Somalia were mandated to help the Somali interim government in bringing political stability to this most tragically impoverished country at the Horn of Africa, destroyed by three decades of regional and civil wars.

For the African Union, the enormous expectation that it manage the stabilization and possible rehabilitation of failed states was almost beyond imagination. The AU's peacekeeping obligations came almost too early, as it was only in the early stages of consolidating its new structures and gradually projecting its ambitions and capabilities. Unlike the EU, the African Union was not allowed to grow gradually (and merely diplomatically) to maturity. In a way, it had to act before its time. In spite of enormous difficulties in Darfur, Somalia, and elsewhere, the first peacekeeping operations of the African Union and thus its first direct interventions in a local conflict on the continent were a promising sign for the gradual rehabilitation of Africa and the credibility of its political leadership. Almost inevitably, postconflict reconstruction became a growing demand on the AU's Peace and Security Council. It will need to continuously build its reputation by cooperating with the United Nations and the European Union as its main international partners.

By 2010, the African Union intends to install an African Standby Force made up of five regional brigades with a total of 15,000 soldiers. The main implementation problem is related to the chain of command and decision-making procedures. For the time being, the African Union's Peace and Security Council—designed after the UN Security Council—has no power to unilaterally endorse or even enforce any peacekeeping operation. This is but one of the continuous "discrepancies between institution-building agendas and implementation ambition" on the African continent.[26]

(3) The economic performance of Africa is the dominant focus of global concern about the continent's future. The ability to implement the New Partnership for Africa's Development (NEPAD) under the umbrella of the African Union will hence be the single most important test of the credibility of regional cooperation and integration in Africa.[27] NEPAD does not simply represent "an endorsement of the normative tenets of new regionalism."[28] It is a unique initiative in the African context, since it includes the possibility of peer review in matters of good governance as the necessary precondition for a successful economic performance. NEPAD commits all African states to trade liberalization and investment-friendly strategies. The objective of a 7 percent annual growth rate is to be achieved through the diversification of production, the enticement of new investment, and an increase in external aid. By 2015, Africa's poverty is to be reduced by half.

The strategy for NEPAD arose from a mandate given to the heads of state of Algeria, Egypt, Senegal, Nigeria, and South Africa by the OAU in 2001. NEPAD was bringing together several strategic concepts for an African renaissance:

- The Millennium Partnership for Africa, initiated by South Africa's President Thabo Mbeki, Nigeria's President Olusegun Obasanjo, and Algeria's President Abdulaziz Bouteflika.
- The OMEGA initiative by Senegal's President Abdoulaye Wade.
- The Compact for African Recovery, drafted by K.Y. Amoako for the United Nations Economic Commission for Africa.

Based on the principles of good governance and African ownership in the process, they were asked to develop a strategy aimed at eradicating poverty, enhancing regional cooperation and integration, and improving capacity-building in African societies. The concept of a political governance peer review "has not been tried anywhere else in the world"[29] and will remain a demanding guiding principle of NEPAD. For the first time, the peer review of an African country's governance performance took place in 2005 in Ghana, Kenya, Rwanda, and Mauritius. On a voluntary basis, seventeen African governments have currently agreed to participate in the African peer review mechanism. It will certainly take a decade or so before the quality and effect of this unique element in the modernization strategy of Africa can be objectively assessed. The criteria and mechanisms of the peer review will require continuous adaptation and improvement.[30] For the time being, skeptics tend to believe that in reality the possible effects of the peer review will be watered down. The mechanism as such is unique and would be a remarkable step toward self-critical and accountable governance on any continent.

Doubt and skepticism have accompanied NEPAD from its inception. Only a few of the most advanced African countries, it was argued, could possibly meet the growth standards. Between 1991 and 2000, the African growth rate on average was never more than 2.1 percent. As population growth on average was 2.8 percent during the last decade of the twentieth century, in real terms the economic growth rate was negative. NEPAD's objective of 7 percent growth rates by 2015 would require an increase in domestic savings from 19 to 33 percent. In the course of less than one decade, it was inconceivable that this could happen as long as more than a third of Africans continue to struggle with a living standard based on the daily spending of one dollar. This is three times the average poverty levels of all other developing countries. Half of the world's children without regular formal education live in Africa. In light of such statistics, any African strategy that does not link economic development to political governance will be received with a certain dose of skepticism.

In fact, few of the ingredients of NEPAD are new and original—and maybe this is one of its strengths. Africa at this point in time does not need grand new rhetorical paradigms. What is needed across the continent is a pragmatic application of lessons learned from past failures "and a replication and broader application of existing best practices."[31] NEPAD, whose executive secretariat is based in South Africa, is now called a "mandated initiative" of the African Union, although the institutional interface between the African Union and NEPAD is not altogether clear yet. NEPAD's implementation committee reports to the African Union Summit, but there is no genuine AU control of the operations or evaluation of the effects of NEPAD's work by the AU. The AU Secretariat is represented in NEPAD through its steering committee. But the matter of accountability has not been completely resolved.

(4) Among the weak aspects of the construction of the African Union remains the possible set of mechanisms that could enable the AU to generate loyalty and commitment. This is not only a matter of rhetoric and political principle. It is also reflected in the degree of financial commitment the member states of the AU are ready to make to its common institution. The 2003 budget of the AU was designed for $43 million. Over the year only $12 million of this budget was collected from the AU member states. Of the 2004 budget of $43 million, only $26 million was provided by AU member states. The 2005 budget quadrupled to $158 million—approved, as in the earlier years, by consensus in the AU's

Executive Council—of which $75 million was earmarked for peace and security affairs and $63 million for administrative costs. AU member states were to pay $63 million of this budget, while $95 million was expected to be paid by Western partners of the AU.

Federators

So far, the African Union is a top-down project. It was brought about on the initiative of the leaders of Africa's nation-states, who were accepting the continental aspiration of Libya's Muammar Gaddafi. Hardly any of the other African heads of state was prepared to recognize the leadership of the eccentric Libyan head of state, but they all appreciated his initiative, hoping to benefit from a spectacular success that could help the whole continent to overcome its marginalization. What is good for the whole of Africa, most presidents calculated, is good for one's own country. For most of them, African integration was understood not a value in itself but as a service to each country's national well-being. The insight into the peripheral decline of Africa forced them to accept the limits of autarkic sovereignty and the ideological exaggeration of the value of autonomous statehood. The national sources for strengthening the state are not strong enough. Possibly, African cooperation and integration can serve a purpose akin to a bypass operation for a patient with a weak heart.

The need to couple new economic approaches—sustainable development, market liberalization, inclusion in the globalized economy—with the prospects of security and political community-building was mirrored in the European integration experience. In its hope to emulate the European model, the African Union has generated new optimism for top-down induced regional integration. However, the AU's founders did not study the differences between their situation and the background of the European experience in any detail. The desire to achieve affluence, stability, and progress was more attractive and, in fact, seductive than the sober assessment of the missing preconditions and inevitable requirements for the European experience to be repeated in any recognizable manner.

This may explain why some African leaders have become overly unrealistic, carrying the process of African unity since 2005 into the orbit of the vision of one single African government. Libyan leader Muammar Gaddafi and Senegal's President Abdoulaye Wade surprised many of their peers when they proposed discussing concrete plans for an African government aimed at realizing the United States of Africa by 2015. The subsequent debate between African federalists and gradualists was as fascinating as it turned out to be premature. For the time being, only the constitutions of Senegal (Article 89), Mali (Article 117) and Burkina Faso (Article 146) include the right to seize national sovereignty to the African level.[32] In 2005, the AU Assembly agreed to introduce ministerial portfolios in the AU Commission. Nigeria's President Olusegun Obasanjo presented a comprehensive study on the path toward the United States of Africa to the 2006 AU Assembly.[33] The 2007 AU Assembly, held in Accra from 1 to 3 July, experienced a "grand debate" among the continent's leaders, followed by divergent interpretations of the Accra Declaration, on which they all agreed.[34] After forty-one heads of state and government had spoken in Accra, it was evident that the gradualists were in the majority. But the idea to deepen African integration had been firmly established on the political agenda of the AU. This in itself contains the potential for future federal steps. It would be too simple to declare the vision of an AU governance structure a non-starter. It was rather remarkable that AU leaders had embarked on such a public debate at all. Thus they contributed to updating the vision of African unity and transforming it from postcolonial rhetoric into the parlance of contemporary multilevel governance as it has evolved in the context of European integration. Constructivism, however, would also haunt Africa with its inevitable idiosyncrasies and unexpected detours.

Admore Mupoki Kambudzi, the secretary of the AU Peace and Security Council, joined the camp of African integration constructionists by suggesting that supranational institutions could be established in three stages of ten years each until 2038. But a "collective/continental sovereign political and economic superstructure,"[35] while a courageous vision, proved to be more of a ringing concept to eventually bring reality into balance with conceptual visions. To use the language of the Obasanjo Report of 2006: it was time for Africa to end its over-dependency and the under-exploitation of the continent's potential.[36] The rhetoric of the debate about "finalité politique"—a rhetoric that in its European context always had the purpose to define today's focus by looking into future defining moments—has reached region-building. As such, a debate can serve as a federator by generating the organizing idea of its time.

Transformations

The Organization of African Unity's replacement by the African Union represents the change from decolonization to globalization. The new beginning in 2002 marks an effort to link the continent-wide vision of unity with the evolution of real integration and community-building. The planned African Economic Community will be achieved by 2028 only if its evolution is coupled with the necessary preconditions for such a scheme. Africa is increasingly realizing the importance of security regionalism. It also strives for development regionalism. But both will become and remain solid and sustainable projects only if Africa can transform its regional organizations into a form of democratic regionalism. This requires continent-wide ownership in democratic rule, peaceful resolution of conflicts, inclusive development strategies, and eventually, pan-African legislation.

The new emphasis on security introduced with the Constitutive Act of the African Union opens the door for a critical reflection on the meaning and limits of sovereignty as the embodiment of the quest for state autonomy. The founding of the African Union was an indirect recognition of the transformation of the notion of sovereignty. The AU is beginning to turn away from a mantra of the independence movements toward a more rational and sober claim for human rights and democracy-based development. The diverse national interests of the African states can be preserved only if security and peace prevail across the continent. This, however, depends upon domestic socioeconomic conditions and the degree of political ownership in the social and economic processes. Democratic governance will thus need to become the main rationale of African integration—which sounds like a revolutionary transformation indeed, if compared to the radical anti-Western and, often, anti-democratic rhetoric of the first generation of African freedom fighters. The power of realism and a new generation of leaders have been able to introduce a dimension of pragmatism and political revision to the African agenda. Whether this process can succeed is a matter of speculation. But it is only fair to exercise patience, rather than expecting every necessary implementation to occur over too short a period of time. African realism must be matched with realism about the African potential.

The plethora of integration efforts and regional schemes in Africa has not helped to focus priorities, modes of responsibility, or the best possible ways of assessing the effects and causes of their multiple activities. The intrinsic obstacles to African development cannot be dissolved by a new set of declarations and institutions. But institutional inflation still seems to be a more sober approach to Africa's development agenda than the excessive ideological platitudes of past declaratory battles. The observance of democratic governance has to be placed at the core of the rationale for regional integration in Africa. The Constitutive Act of the African Union is the first indicator of a new disposition. The application and recalibration of a wide range of necessary policy strategies and policy details on the AU member-state level will remain the most daunting task. The instruments available to the African Union have only a limited scope in executing the necessary transformation in its member states. Comparing the African situation with that of the European Union, it is fair to say that one cannot possibly expect the AU to be better, more consequential, or more powerful than its European model.

The African Union has begun the clearly overwhelming process of rationalizing the different regional integration activities across the continent. It has counted about 200 organizations aimed at achieving Africa's integration. In the meantime, the AU has reduced the number of regional schemes it officially recognizes as anchor communities to eight. In a process of rationalizing the efforts of integration and region-building in Africa, the following groupings are now recognized as building blocks for further integration: the Economic Community of West African States (ECOWAS, headquartered in Abuja), the Community of Sahelo-Saharan States (CEN-SAD, headquartered in Tripoli), the Common

Market for Eastern and Southern Africa (COMESA, headquartered in Lusaka), the Economic Community of Central African States (ECCAS, headquartered in Libreville), the Inter-Governmental Authority for Development (IGAD, headquartered in Djibouti), the Arab Maghreb Union (UMA, headquartered in Rabat), the Southern African Development Community (SADC, headquartered in Gaborone), and the East African Community (EAC, headquartered in Arusha). Formally, Article 88 of the Abuja Treaty discusses the provisions for establishing relations between the African Economic Community and the different regional groupings. In reality, the process of synergy-building only began with preliminary assessments of the overall situation during a first conference of the African Ministers of Economic Cooperation held in Ouagadougou on 30–31 March 2006.

The quest for a rationalization of regional economic communities in Africa has become a matter of priority for the African Union. Overlapping membership in two regional groupings, for instance, renders separate external tariffs of each of the two groupings impossible—or requires immediate joint tariff harmonization of the two groupings. Increased linkages between the AU and the strongest regional groupings—called anchor communities—are imperative to advance the overall African Economic Community.[37]

Role and Interests of the European Union

For decades, the European relationship with Africa has been overshadowed by the legacy of colonialism and postcolonialism. When the European Economic Community (EEC) was founded in 1957, France, Belgium, and the Netherlands requested special relationships with their former and ongoing colonies. Colonialism, after all, was ongoing at the time: Algeria as an integral part of the French Republic was a founding member of the European Economic Community. Belgium maintained its colonial control over Congo. The Netherlands had lost its Southeast Asian colonial empire at the end of World War II, but special relations with Indonesia prevailed, and Suriname continued to be a Dutch colony. France refused to open up its African markets to its EEC partners. Although its colonial ambitions had come under increasing pressure during the escalation of the Algerian war of independence, France insisted on including special relationships with overseas interests in the founding treaties of the European Economic Community. The Treaties of Rome granted a five-year trial period for the commercial and financial association of French, Belgian, and Dutch overseas territories. Article 131 and Article 136 created a de facto free trade area between the European Economic Community and its associated areas. The most visible immediate outcome was the availability of new European outlets for African tropical fruits. More long-term was the effect of the development fund established by the Treaties of Rome to improve the infrastructure in the southern hemisphere. This was the beginning of a European development policy.[38]

In 1963, the relationship between the European Economic Community and eighteen associated states in Africa plus Madagascar was renewed through the Yaoundé Convention, named after the capital of Cameroon, where the agreement was signed. It provided commercial advantages and financial aid to Africa. In force since 1 July 1964, its successor—the Yaoundé II Convention—followed in 1969. The quest for a new beginning between the now European Community and many of its former colonies was increasingly linked to the struggle for a new world economic order. In response to the continuous demands from the southern hemisphere, the European Community offered a comprehensive scheme of partnership and preferential cooperation for Europe's most desperate former colonies. In 1975, the European Community and forty-six countries of Africa, the Caribbean, and the Pacific signed the Lomé Convention. Further Lomé Conventions followed at intervals of five years. Lomé IV, signed in 1990, included seventy-seven countries. Unlike the first three Lomé Conventions, the last Lomé Agreement lasted for ten years and included a midterm review. It covered 638 million people in the southern hemisphere.

The Lomé Conventions introduced several innovations and improvements in North-South relations:

- On principle, trade was conducted on a non-reciprocal basis. The EC partner states—called ACP states (ACP stands for Africa, Caribbean, Pacific)—were exempted from the GATT multi-fiber agreement, which placed restrictions on textile exports from developing countries to industrial markets. When GATT was replaced by the World Trade Organization in 1993, this principle came under increasing pressure from countries and regions not participating in this non-reciprocal trade privilege.
- In a spirit of partnership and cooperation, the European Community unilaterally exempted certain ACP products from customs levies and import taxes.
- The most innovative component of the Lomé Convention was the stabilization mechanism for raw materials: A fund was created by the EC to provide for stabilizing capital for raw materials from the partner countries if the price for their raw materials fell below a certain threshold or in case of an excessively bad harvest. This STABEX system constituted a resource transfer to the ACP budgets.

The Lomé Conventions were not free of problems. Most widely discussed were the following issues:

- The STABEX mechanism only pertained to a few ACP countries with substantial raw materials relevant to the European economy. Its effect undermined the incentive of ACP countries to produce full manufactured products. Instead of encouraging them to diversify their economies, their focus on traditional raw materials was strengthened.

- Key agricultural products of the ACP countries, like bananas, beef, rice, and sugar, were excluded from the Lomé Conventions, although it was here that many ACP countries had comparative cost advantages over their European partners.
- Industrial cooperation was systematically excluded from the EC's cooperation with the ACP countries.

On 23 June 2000, a new long-term approach in the relationship between the European Union and its ACP partners, including Africa, began. The Cotonou Agreement was signed between the EU and 15 Caribbean, 14 Pacific, and all 48 sub-Saharan countries. Africa provides 95 percent of the total ACP population and gets 80 percent of all support funds defined by the Cotonou Agreement. This agreement replaced the Lomé IV Convention and is intended to last for twenty years. Its main features are the following:

- The Cotonou Agreement emphasizes political dialogue with a strengthened inclusion of civil society.
- In terms of economic cooperation, it replaced preferential relations with the principle of reciprocity as requested by the WTO, but this was potentially to the disadvantage of several EU partner countries in Africa. By 2008, new regional Economic Partnership Agreements were to be negotiated with each of the ACP regions.
- The ACP countries are no longer exempted from the WTO multi-fiber agreements with their restrictions on textile exports from developing countries to industrialized markets. This is extremely relevant for some African countries: 58 percent of total exports from Lesotho and 39 percent of total exports from Mozambique are in textiles.
- Several preferential elements of the Lomé Convention favored agricultural activities in countries producing beef (Botswana, Namibia, Zimbabwe), sugar (Tanzania, Mauritius, Malawi, Swaziland) and the economies of the land-locked African countries. They have been discontinued by the Cotonou Convention.

The main reason for the fundamental shift from preferential trade arrangements to the principle of reciprocity was a ruling of the WTO dispute settlement body, according to which the provisions of the Lomé Convention were unfair because they gave preference to banana exporters in the Caribbean and in other countries with special relations to Europe. The Cotonou Agreement stipulates the principle of reciprocity in free trade. To comply with its logic, the Cotonou Agreement divided the ACP countries into different regional groupings. The subsequent negotiation of Economic Partnership Agreements left it to the African countries to decide which configuration they wished to negotiate under with the EU. Eventually, between 2002 and 2008, the EU negotiated EPAs with the following groupings in Africa:

1. West Africa: all ECOWAS member states plus Mauritania.
2. Central Africa: all CEMAC member states plus São Tomé and Príncipe and the Democratic Republic of the Congo.
3. Eastern and Southern Africa: all COMESA member states except Angola, the Democratic Republic of the Congo, Egypt, Libya, and Swaziland.
4. SADC minus all SACU member states, including South Africa as an observer, plus Angola, Mozambique, and Tanzania.[39]

The share of ACP countries' trade with the European Union has declined, from 6.7 percent in 1976 to 2.8 percent in 1999. Based on the Cotonou Agreement, the European Union granted its ACP partners direct aid of €13.8 billion during the period 2000 to 2006. The amount increased to €22.6 billion for the period 2007–2013. This aid was and is part of the European Development Fund; it does not come from the general EU budget.

The European Union is hoping for fundamental positive effects in good governance and democracy-based rule of law in the ACP regions, Africa in particular. The Cotonou Agreement introduced a strong element of conditionality related to performance in human rights and good governance, including issues such as the degree of military spending, the fight against corruption, and the elimination of drug production.

The Cotonou Agreement introduced new dimensions and conflicts—such as migration and the complex agenda of conflict prevention—into the European Union's dialogue with its ACP partners.

Because of the regional differentiation that was introduced with the Cotonou Agreement and intensified by negotiating Economic Partnership Agreements, the normative support of regional integration by the European Union leads de facto to a multilayered relationship and concentric or overlapping, but no longer synchronized, circles in the relationship between the European Union and its African ACP partners. The same is true as far as EPA negotiations with the EU's Caribbean and the Pacific ACP partners are concerned. It remains a matter of dispute whether or not the EPAs will effectively be able to generate deeper and sustainable regional integration in Africa, the Caribbean, and the Pacific. As for the EU's relation with Africa, the main priority above all, evident with or without improved regional integration, is to break the cycle of underdevelopment rooted in poor economic and political performance.

The establishment of the African Union has opened a new dimension for Africa's relationship with the European Union. This remains an evolving relationship, structured by a first wave of formal meetings at the highest levels. After the first AU-EU ministerial meeting in Burkina Faso on 28 November 2002 (the current EU troika being represented by a Danish state secretary, Commissioner Poul Nielson, and Italy's foreign minister), then EU Commission President Romano Prodi delivered an address to the African Union summit in Maputo on 11

July 2003, followed by a meeting with the complete African Union Commission in Brussels on 24 March 2004. A planned AU-EU summit in Lisbon, scheduled for 4–5 April 2004, was canceled. Yet the diplomatic process continued: in 2006, the sixth EU-AU ministerial meeting took place in Vienna.

In December 2005, the European Union adopted an EU-AU strategy aimed at a "strategic partnership" between the two regions. The inflation of the term "strategic partnership" during recent years has not enhanced the credibility of this type of declaratory policy. So far, relations between the EU and the AU have been weak and fragmented. The European Union provides 60 percent of all aid to Africa, and EU investments in Africa increased from $1.5 to $2.7 billion during the first years of the twenty-first century. In the absence of a clearly defined regional partner, the European Union has remained cautious about projecting its support, interest, and ambition in and for Africa in overly stark terms. The EU-AU relationship will have to mature from the focus on aid to a stronger emphasis on politics and economic cooperation in the service of aiding Africa's development.[40] The opening of an EU Delegation (Embassy) at the seat of the African Union in Addis Ababa in late 2007 was understood as a clear message that the EU has begun to take the AU seriously.

The EU needs to continuously overcome its marginalized perception of the role and relevance of Africa. The newly expressed seriousness in dealing with Africa needs to be translated into a comprehensive political strategy. This political strategy needs to include those aspects of African development that are a security concern or outright threat to Europe—including illegal emigration—and those aspects of Africa's realities that provide promising opportunities in the age of globalization—including, most importantly, the human potential of Africa. The EU will more than ever emphasize that Africa bears the primary responsibility for the resolution of its problems.

As a first step to building a biregional relationship, the European Union has decided to focus its strategic support for the development of the African Union. Initially, this included the EU's support for the following projects:

- €2 million for general support of the institutionalized development of the African Union.
- €10 million to assist the peace and security agenda of the African Union.
- €25 million in 2003/2004 to support AU-led peacekeeping operations in Burundi (2,800 troops from South Africa, Ethiopia, and Mozambique).
- €0.4 million in support of capacity-building in matters of regional trade and economic integration.
- €2 million in support of the governance agenda of the African Union.[41]

The intensity of further EU-AU relations will be a criterion for measuring the mutual seriousness in a new beginning. The more the concept and approach of the African Union are rooted in real activities and achievements, the more it is likely that the European Union will broaden its approach toward biregional cooperation schemes. It is most likely that the EU will remain cautious and multidimensional for some time. Besides supporting the development of the African Union—without being naïvely optimistic about its prospects—the EU will continue cooperation with the leading region-building schemes on the African continent, notably with ECOWAS and SADC.

The path of evolution of internal developments and their interaction with the African Union, with the purely monetary integration schemes in UEMOA and CEMAC, and with the least sophisticated regional groupings in other parts of the continent, remains to be seen. The African Union has begun to promote the rationalization of the plethora of regional activities across the continent. ECOWAS and SADC clearly must be considered the two strongest anchor communities leading and advancing this process.

Prospects and Obstacles

The dream of pan-Africanism originated in the age of the colonial dominance of Africa. The failure of pan-Africanism became evident in the postcolonial era of single-state independence across Africa. Much has been said about misperceiving the artificiality of African regional integration by way of basing institutional comparisons with the European integration experience on wrong or superficial analogies (such as the one assuming that integration would automatically bring about affluence, while it can even be the other way around, at least for some time). Yet it is interesting that Africa as a whole and its most dynamic regions have embarked on a new stage of conceptualizing the relationship between independence, economic development, governance, and cooperation. Obviously, many of the European preconditions are absent in Africa and in its regions. But across Africa, the European model of the autonomous state dominates the political landscape. State-based independence does not bring about democracy, and it is no panacea for real sovereignty in any meaningful sense. These experiences have been learned in Africa, often the hard way.

It is here that the recalibration of political and economic trends in Africa begins by considering the possibilities for advances in integration.[42] In the age of globalization, the African fear of complete marginalization has hit even the elites, who might not have cared at all, in the first decades following independence, about the link between political self-determination and popular self-determination. Being in power or wanting to attain the helm of national power—which in Africa more than anywhere else implies access to limited resources—was often more of a driving force than the desire to truly embed democracy or achieve social development through the eradication of poverty. The pressure of civil unrest stemming from poverty, in socioeconomic as well as in participatory-political terms, has now reached the elites across Africa. Their rhetoric has become inclusive in the battle cry for human rights and freedoms and the vision of the Millennium Goals of the United Nations. They might not yet deliver—and perhaps they are limited by the constraints of African conditions, even if their intentions are honest and serious. But the existence of a declaratory will to region-building will have long-term effects on Africa's political deliberations and development.

The rhetorical quest for an "African Renaissance," originally expressed by South Africa's President Thabo Mbeki,[43] will take time to achieve. Unlike the Renaissance in Europe, the African one is meant to be a political project with a top-down approach. This might limit its scope and effect from the outset. In the original European Renaissance, the overall positive atmosphere was supported and promoted by artists and other intellectuals who were able to engage the whole society. Over time, politics followed, not always to the advantage of the original Renaissance spirit. But one lesson can be directly learned and transposed to the African context: there will never be any effective Renaissance, no matter how it is defined, without a strong sense of ownership by the people whose aspiration needs to be awakened.

When the OAU summit of 9–11 July 2001 in Lusaka merged the various papers and concepts for a revitalization of Africa and turned them into one New African Initiative, this clearly was a laudable beginning. It is notable that this was a precursor of the transformation from the Organization of African Unity itself into the African Union less than a year later. The New African Initiative claimed that "African peoples have begun to demonstrate their refusal to accept poor economic and political leadership."[44] As ambitious as this statement was, it was certainly new and promising in comparison to the many political platitudes that had previously emerged from postcolonial Africa. The New African Initiative emphasized that peace, security, democracy, good governance, and human rights are intrinsically linked to economic management and social development. For the first time in a genuine African document, they were recognized as vital preconditions for sustainable development (paragraph 53.1). Likewise, regional cooperation and economic integration were declared preconditions for sustainable African development (paragraph 53.2). The New African Initiative mentioned the following priority areas for urgent action:

- Infrastructure
- Information and communication technology
- Health
- Education
- Culture
- Agriculture
- Diversification of production and exports.

The Constitutive Act of the African Union introduced a new political framework for Africa's development prospects. UN Secretary General Kofi Annan added a sober and realistic tone to the celebration of the African leaders: "This historic effort," he said, "will require leadership, courage, and a willingness to depart from the ways of the past."[45] The New African Initiative was ambivalent on the question of how to define and fight corruption. It was also not explicit about the instruments necessary to promote good governance. Demanding "effective measures," as the initiative called for, was noble but not enough. The fact that the Constitutive Act of the African Union deleted explicit reference to the fight against corruption was not a good sign of sincerity or of the political will of African leaders to take their own norms seriously. As long as a strict enforcement strategy is missing, the invocation of good governance, the rule of law, and a commitment to human rights remains rhetorical.

Still under the auspices of the OAU, the New African Initiative was developed into the New Partnership for Africa's Development. Under this title, the project of revitalizing Africa was brought to the attention of the G8 summit in July 2001 in Geneva, endorsed by the World Bank and International Monetary Fund thereafter, and finally approved by the OAU heads of state in October 2001 in Abuja. Upon the commencement of the African Union in 2002, NEPAD became a mandated initiative of the AU.

The goals of NEPAD are as rational as they are unchallengeable on paper:

• Economic growth and increased employment
• Reduction in poverty and inequality
• Increased productivity diversification
• Enhanced international competitiveness
• Increased African integration.

Three fields of action were identified as the priority needs for Africa, and it will be here that the theoretical goals will have to stand the test of reality:

• Promoting peace, security, democracy and political governance as the most important preconditions for sustainable development.
• Bridging the infrastructure gap and improving human resources across the continent.
• Mobilizing resources, including capital flows and market access.

In order to ensure a continuous and coherent implementation of the NEPAD goals, a NEPAD Heads of State and Government Implementation Committee was installed. It reports annually to the African Union Summit. But beyond this, its right to intervene and correct any problematic patterns in any AU member state has remained vague and weak. Most deplorable is many African societies' insufficient attraction of direct foreign investment. Beyond the traditional investment in primary commodities, Africa has not been able to attract enough direct foreign capital to substantially improve its infrastructure and lay the ground for self-sustaining economic growth rates. The most recent increase has come in Chinese investment—largely in areas of strategic interest for China, with its enormous hunger for resources—and remains an ambivalent gift for many African regions.

The most astonishing reference to the European integration project that began to be discussed in academic circles following the establishment of NEPAD and the African Union was the prospect of a single currency for Africa.[46] The idea is not purely academic any more: in August 2003, the Association of African Central Bank Governors announced that it would work toward a single African currency and a common central bank by 2021. As much as this prospect seems far-fetched for most experts on current African affairs, it has reached the African agenda nevertheless. The African Central Bank governors have expressed their interest in a successful launching of the euro and declared their intent to jointly remedy the existing domestic weakness in most African countries. The experience with the CFA franc might, however, send an ambivalent and distorted message to Africa. In Western and Central Africa, monetary union works without being linked to trade integration and policy coordination. It would almost certainly be a self-delusion if the African Central Bank governors assumed that this experience could be replicated on the continental level. For UEMOA und CEMAC France serves as a type of back-up country. The African Union has no "France" backing its actions.

In addition to the normative goal of achieving monetary union, the announcement of this ambitious objective served tactical purposes. The idea to gradually expand the existing monetary unions in West and Central Africa to the whole continent, as one analysis of the potential of African monetary union states, "could be used as a means of inducing countries to improve their policies."[47] But it is unclear whether and how this most ambitious hallmark of the European integration experience can be replicated in Africa.

The establishment of the Pan-African Parliament is another ambitious example of African efforts to advance institutionalized region-building. In the European context, this effort would have been labeled "deepening," though for Africa it also means a thematic "widening" of the initial region-building effort. As the African Union was immediately launched by practically all African countries—except for Morocco because of the country's ongoing occupation of Western Sahara—the meaning of "widening" never had geographic relevance in Africa. "Widening" always referred thematically to a pattern that in Europe was understood as "deepening." The idea to establish a Pan-African Parliament was immediately confronted with the question of how serious, substantial, and ultimately powerful an African legislature and eventual pan-African legislation might be. In theory, the main issue was related to the matter of proportionality in representation: should the Seychelles get one member in the African Parliament, and if the Parliament were organized on the basis of equal representation, then it would require 5,137 members in total to be properly egalitarian in its structure. Nigeria would get 810 members, Ethiopia 418, and Egypt 401. Should the African Parliament rather be organized on the basis of equality, with a maximum number of 400 representatives, 207 of them—that is to say, more than 50 percent—would be reserved for Nigeria, Egypt, the Democratic Republic of Congo, South Africa, Tanzania, and Sudan.[48]

The reality began differently. On 18 March 2004, 202 legislators from forty-one countries were sworn in by Mozambiquan President Joaquim Chissano, the current chairman of the African Union. Gertrude Mongella from Tanzania was elected as the first president of the African Parliament, opening its inaugural session in September 2004 at its temporary seat on Gallagher Estate in Johannesburg. As of 2010, the African Parliament will find its permanent seat in Pretoria, as if "to exorcise the last ghosts" in this former symbolic city of Afrikaaner culture and white dominance over the African continent. The members of the African Parliament were selected from national parliaments. Mozambiquan President Chissano solemnly declared that the whole world "shall be watching to see what added value this organ is going to contribute to our plan of building a strong and prosperous African Union."[49] The Parliament's President Gertrude Mongella described the inauguration as "a sign of democratic maturity in Africa."[50]

As paradoxical as it sounds, the real test case for the democratic maturity and integration potential of Africa rests with its individual states. Their deficits in democratic rule of law, socioeconomic development, and human capacity-building have defined the overall negative, if not disastrous, image of Africa since the end of colonialism. It would be magnificent if the African states were able to overcome the worst of these deficits through the inspiration they gain from the prospect of region-building and continental integration. But, as Kofi Annan has reminded Africa, the experience of the past few decades teaches us to be cautious and reasonable.

During the 1990s and the first years of the twenty-first century, multiparty elections have been held in most African countries. A number of peaceful regime changes have occurred, such as in Zambia, Senegal, Benin, Congo, Guinea Bissau, and Cape Verde. But critics claim that only the development in Cape Verde "has been associated with systemic change—where, in other words, elections have helped to reduce neo-patrimonialism."[51] Botswana also receives some of the best marks for substantial reforms and real transformation.

It would not serve the future of Africa if democratization remained a purely formal process. Critics fear that democratization—like the structural economic adjustments often demanded by the international community—could be hijacked by the existing political and social elites. "Willy-nilly," one analyst wrote, "they began to implement structural adjustment—not primarily because they were convinced of its importance but simply because it was the price to pay for continued assistance."[52] As much as this assessment is probably too generalized, it also misses one point that might turn out to be important. African elites might succeed in restraining the prospects for democratization and the demands of structural adjustment. But it cannot be excluded that the mechanism also works the other way around and that they themselves could be restrained over time by the forces of democracy they unleashed and the structural adjustments they were forced to initiate. Revolutions notoriously devour their own children, and transformations might transform both their subject and their object.

An interesting question has to be raised regarding the relationship between the African Union and region-groupings in certain parts of Africa. There are different ways to understand this relationship and its possible evolution:

- They might be complementary and encourage each other. Sometimes, the African Union itself refers to the "spaghetti bowl" of overlapping memberships in regional groupings. The overlap in regional groupings has not helped to focus priorities or rationalize resources.[53]
- The African Union might serve as the normative umbrella while the operational work of deep integration and region-building takes places in the regions, most successfully in those with the best potential and strongest record.
- The most advanced regional schemes of cooperation and integration serve as building blocks for the dream of pan-African integration. The African Union defines them as rooted anchor communities.
- A sectoral approach might be favored, promoting sector-specific cooperation and integration, notwithstanding existing institutional links and loyalties. This approach might serve certain dominating interests without stimulating the need for an inclusive and evolutionary development if African integration should serve more than some sectors or countries.

Most advanced in comprehensive efforts in region-building are ECOWAS and SADC, which also cover the broadest geographic space. They aspire to link economic and political cooperation, an effort in which they are joined by the refounded East African Community (EAC). UEMOA and CEMAC are the most advanced in monetary integration, but they have become neither a common market nor in any significant way a functional tool that could be used to promote political cooperation and integration among their respective member states. In order to focus its priorities, Namibia left COMESA in 2004. Tanzania has also left COMESA, but remains a member of both SADC and the newly aspiring EAC.[54]

After its dissolution in 1976, the East African Community was refounded in 1996 between Kenya, Tanzania, and Uganda, beginning with the establishment of a new secretariat. The treaty of formal refoundation took effect in 2000.[55] Since then, all three East African countries have undergone enormous internal transformations. Their development levels have come closer to each other. Private sector involvement can be seen. By the end of 2006, Rwanda and Burundi were accepted as additional members of the EAC. Although its ambition seems to be more moderate than that of the original EAC, one should not underestimate the economic and possibly the political potential of a renewed and consolidated East African Community. With 18 percent of intra-regional trade, the EAC is already far ahead of other African regions that are trying to engage in serious intra-regional trade but still struggling with the absence of complementarity in their economies. The refounding of the EAC was also the occasion for establishing an East African Legislative Assembly and an East African Court of Justice, based in Arusha.[56]

The ultimate challenge for African region-building will not be answered by rhetoric, actions, programs, or projects. The ultimate benchmark will be the degree and quality of democratic regionalism, encompassing security regionalism and development regionalism—in other words, the democratic quality of its individual states. This is the paradox of the challenge ahead for postindependence and postcrisis Africa: Africa will need to overcome the parochial fixation on state sovereignty and build up a common record of shared gains through cooperation and ownership. In order to do so, however, Africa will need to emphasize the democratic modernization of its state structures, the governance mechanisms in its individual states, and socioeconomic performance across the continent, all of which is imperative to give democratic region-building a common sign of identity and destiny a real chance.

It is conceivable that the African Union will eventually evolve into something similar to the Council of Europe, a regional organization with guiding principles and facilitating powers for the continent. Thus, the African Union would give credence to the spirit of African unity by promoting common norms and causes. The AU will extend its scope of action according to the requirements of the continent but also in strict accordance with the readiness and national interests of its member states. Introducing majority voting in AU institutions, for example, seems unrealistic at this point in time. But it cannot be excluded that over time, the African Union will gain momentum based on gradual and lasting success. Its main problem for now is the uncertain degree of political commitment of many member-state governments that are not ready yet to establish the difficult path toward the primacy of some sort of African community law. Only through solid democratic rule in its member states can the African Union turn from an instrument of security regionalism and a hope for development regionalism into a plausible expression of democratic regionalism. The African continent deserves such a future.

The Economic Community of West African States (ECOWAS)

Basic Facts

The most noteworthy of all African regional integration schemes is ECOWAS. The Economic Community of West African States was founded on 25 May 1975 by fifteen states representing 500 ethnic groups: Burkina Faso, Benin, Ivory Coast, Guinea, Mali, Mauritania (which left ECOWAS in 2002), Niger, Senegal, Togo, Gambia, Ghana, Liberia, Nigeria, Sierra Leone, Cape Verde, and Guinea-Bissau. The original ECOWAS treaty was aimed at gradually achieving a customs union in three stages by 1990.[57] During the first two years, no increase in duties was envisaged. Within the next eight years the member states agreed to overcome differences in customs tariffs, and during the final five years the customs union was to be completed. The founding treaty of ECOWAS introduced a regional mechanism for dispute settlements and the coordination of monetary policies. It established a fund to compensate the poorest and least developed member states. Article 27 promised to remove all obstacles to the freedom of travel and residence, and Chapter IV introduced community citizenship. Among the functional and sectoral perspectives for integration was the agreement on joint agricultural training programs, the harmonization of economic and fiscal policies, the vision to move from the harmonization of mineral-resource policies to common mineral and energy policies, and a community fund to compensate for losses suffered as a result of the application of the ECOWAS treaty.

Since its beginning, the institutional arrangement of ECOWAS has been elaborate:

- The ECOWAS Supreme Authority, the meeting of heads of state and government, was to meet twice per year.
- The ECOWAS Council of Ministers consists of the foreign ministers and was also to meet twice a year.
- The ECOWAS Executive Secretariat (renamed the ECOWAS Commission in 2007 and headed from 2002 until 2010 by Dr. Mohamed Ibn Chambas from Ghana) was based in Abuja.
- A Tribunal was established.

In 1993, an elaborate treaty revision was made with the following main changes and additions:[58]

- The ECOWAS Parliament was established (duration of legislation is four years).
- The Tribunal was turned into the ECOWAS Court of Justice (judges being appointed for four years).
- The ECOWAS Economic and Social Council was established.
- The ECOWAS Bank for Investment and Development (EBID) was established as the central coordinating financial instrument.

A wide set of technical commissions operate in support of the ECOWAS agenda. Among them are the

- Food and Agriculture Commission
- Industry, Science, Technology and Energy Commission
- Transport, Communication and Tourism Commission
- Environment and Natural Resources Commission
- Trade, Customs, Taxation, Statistics, Money and Payments Commission
- Political, Judicial, Legal Affairs, Regional Security and Immigration Commission
- Human Resources, Information, Social and Cultural Affairs Commission
- Administration and Finances Commission.

In June 2006, a remarkable decision was taken by the 30th ECOWAS Head of States' Summit to transform the ECOWAS Secretariat into the ECOWAS Commission in January 2007. The analogy to the European Union is obvious. The ECOWAS Commission now consists of a president, a vice-president, and seven commissioners. Following a rotating schedule, the first positions were given to representatives of Ghana, Niger, Mali, Senegal, Sierra Leone, Ivory Coast, Togo, Burkina Faso, and Nigeria, with clearly defined portfolios (Administration and Finance; Agriculture, Environment and Water Resources; Human Development and Gender; Infrastructure; Macro-Economic Policy; Political Affairs, Peace and Security; Trade, Customs and Free Movement). ECOWAS was emulating the European Union more than ever. This emulation of EU institutions included the reform of the ECOWAS Parliament in 2006. Whereas in the past, obligations taken on by member states had been subject to lengthy ratifications of protocols and conventions, in the future decisions will be more binding with immediate effects. Preparations for the first direct election of the ECOWAS Parliament are under way. In spite of procedural reforms, the main problem of ECOWAS remains capacity-building beyond the ambitious doubling of ECOWAS Commission civil servants from 200 to 400.

The biggest achievement of ECOWAS, so far, is its very creation. While more than half of the countries in West Africa were French colonies before independence, English-speaking Nigeria, with more than 130 million citizens, is home to half of Western Africa's population and produces more than half of West Africa's GDP. To bring these two different groupings together, and thus to overcome ethnic and colonial legacies in the region, was a rare achievement. French West Africa (L'Afrique Occidentale Française, AOF) was a centralized empire of eight colonies aiming at assimilation through horizontal integration with France. In turn, British colonial policies, in West Africa as elsewhere, were based on indirect rule. Colonialism integrated the region as a primary export producer, but the differences remained startling.

The founding of ECOWAS was the first-ever effort to reconcile "French" and "British" Africa. In French-speaking West Africa, ECOWAS still has to struggle with the suspicion that it is an instrument of Nigerian hegemony. In 2004, ECOWAS began planning the realization of a common currency, the "Eco", aiming for implementation by 2009. In 1984, the French-speaking countries of the region strengthened their monetary ties with France and created the West African Economic and Monetary Union (Union Économique et Monétaire Ouest Africaine, UEMOA). For them, this continuation of postcolonial preferential relations with the former colonial center paid off. While intra-ECOWAS trade was never more than 6 percent, intra-UEMOA trade represents 10 to 12 percent of the total trade of UEMOA member countries.[59]

With this ambition, ECOWAS faces the need to resolve the competing realities of monetary cooperation in West Africa, which are determined by monetary arrangements among former French colonies in West and Central Africa. Two developments must be mentioned:

- The original West African Customs and Economic Union (Union Douanière et Économique de l'Afrique de l'Ouest, UDEAO) was renamed the West African Economic Community (Communauté Économique de l'Afrique de l'Ouest, CEAO) in 1972, which in turn became the West African Monetary and Economic Union (Union Économique et Monétaire Ouest Africaine, UEMOA) in 1994. In 1975 CEAO had agreed to join ECOWAS (and accepted the provisions of the Lomé Convention of the same year) on the condition that its member states be allowed to maintain their own structure and ties with France.[60]
- In Central Africa, the original Central African Customs and Economic Union (Union Douanière et Économique de l'Afrique Centrale, UEDAC), founded in 1966, was renamed Central African Economic and Monetary Community (Communauté Économique et Monétaire d'Afrique Centrale, CEMAC) in 1994.[61]

CEMAC and its Bank of Central African States with seven participating member states had a different genesis than UEMOA but led to the same effect: both currency unions operate on a parallel basis and issue separate currencies, freely convertible through the interbanking system. Together they are called the CFA franc zone, named after the French African Communities (Communautés Françaises d'Afrique, CFA). The CFA, originally created by France in 1945 as Colonies Françaises d'Afrique, was reorganized in 1958. The trade of the CFA zone with the European Union constitutes almost 50 percent of total African trade.

The creation of the two CFA franc zones in West Africa and in Central Africa helps the former French colonies of these regions to better manage the economic implications of their independence. The CFA franc maintains the regions' links and dependencies with France. The original idea of the monetary unions among former French colonies was to establish regional integration through harmonization of regulatory mechanisms and politics. Budgetary and fiscal surveillance were considered the first step. The ultimate goal was complete economic union—a free trade zone by 2000 and the creation of a common stock market. These ambitions of regional economic integration clashed with the ideology of autonomous sovereignty. No member state of the CFA franc zone was willing to substantially engage in any form of shared sovereignty. More than anything else, Nigeria's rise in economic power during the 1980s—due to its oil revenues—challenged the French-speaking countries in the region. In light of their revenue losses, a massive currency devaluation became inevitable in1994.[62]

Today, Burkina Faso, Benin, Ivory Coast, Guinea Bissau, Mali, Niger, Senegal, and Togo (UEMOA), as well as Gabon, Cameroon, Congo-Brazzaville, the Central African Republic, Chad, and Guinea-Equatorial (CEMAC) use the CFA franc. The Comoros is an associate member of CEMAC, with the Comorian franc pegged to the CFA franc. Hence, 100 million people in fourteen countries use the CFA franc. The confusing realities surrounding the CFA franc were intensified by various changes in the labeling of the regions' monetary unions and their different links with the euro.

In 1991, ECOWAS decided to become the prime economic community in West Africa. However, this proud declaration could not prevent the UEMOA from being established by the francophone member states of ECOWAS.[63] Despite all diplomatic declarations at the time, ECOWAS had produced a "competing body" from within.[64] ECOWAS has never been able to establish a cohesive link with the two working monetary integration schemes of the franc zone that make West and Central Africa very particular. The West African Economic and Monetary Union and the Bank of Central African States are the only expressions of real integration in West and Central Africa "whose grounding in reality goes beyond the marginal incantation of summit Declarations."[65] The full implementation of monetary union in the absence of a deep economic union will remain a burning issue on the ECOWAS agenda for more years to come.

The introduction of the euro in 2002 has come as a new challenge for the CFA franc zone and ECOWAS alike. Because the stability of the CFA franc system is guaranteed by France, the CFA franc had to be pegged to the euro. This required common decisions in the EU: the EU recognized that the French Central

Bank—which also prints the CFA franc notes—guarantees the convertibility of the CFA franc into euro (1 euro = 655 CFA francs). Thus these two CFA franc monetary unions, which are the only working systems of monetary integration in Africa, remain tightly connected to the French Central Bank. This link is not welcomed by the European Central Bank and has been increasingly criticized inside ECOWAS. Although the CFA franc is understood as a strong incentive to harmonize macroeconomic policies and regional integration in West Africa, its effects have been limited. Discussions about the free convertibility of the CFA remain inconclusive. The CFA franc member states can claim export gains due to reduced prices, but they may lose price stability as a consequence.

A common customs union of the UEMOA countries with Nigeria and Ghana has been discussed regularly in ECOWAS. Lately, though, this discussion has been replaced by the political decision to introduce a common currency for the whole of ECOWAS. ECOWAS could indeed benefit from the comprehensive inclusion of the CFA franc zone with its reasonably good economic growth rates, low inflation, and improved economic stability. In reaction to the introduction of the euro by the European Union, ECOWAS launched a monetary union of its own, the first stage of which started in 2004, aimed at leading to the West African "Eco". In 2007, it became a matter of internal dispute in ECOWAS whether it would make more sense to introduce a common currency for the non-CFA countries first before bringing both regions together, or to immediately introduce a monetary union for the whole of ECOWAS. Meanwhile, the international link of an ECOWAS currency became subject to another political controversy: while Nigeria's strong currency was originally pegged to the US dollar, the CFA franc was pegged to the French franc and later to the euro. The discussion about the long-term effect of pegging the future "Eco" to either of the two global currencies has not yet produced conclusive answers.[66]

The monetary future of West and Central Africa is ultimately dependent upon security and good governance in the region. The internal political crisis in the Ivory Coast in 2002 had a huge negative effect on the CFA franc monetary union because the Ivory Coast produces 40 percent of the GDP of all UEMOA member states. Market regionalization in West Africa has been difficult from the beginning of ECOWAS. Informal trading activities such as smuggling are widely spread in the region, which is known to be home to one of "the most mobile people in Africa."[67] State-centered efforts to generate regionalism have led to an inflation of institutions without meaning, mandate, or effect. West Africa can count 40 to 70 intergovernmental organizations operating on its territory. Nobody knows how to distinguish their functions and measure their real effects.

At the same time, regional integration efforts in West Africa have been "over-politicized,"[68] or in other words, have fallen victim to the sad and often poor state of politics in the region. Postcolonial politics has brought about a great deal of frustration in the region with the quality of governance, the state of human rights, and the honesty of politics in general. Between 1971 and 1990, West Africa experienced 21 attempted coups, 31 successful coups, and 54 plots—more than 55 percent of Africa's total political upheavals for that period. Several states of the region hardly deserve to be called functioning. Personalized and corrupt regimes have added to the insecurity in the region as they have often contributed to the privatization of the state's police power with the creation of personalized semiarmies. It was therefore more than necessary that the revision of the ECOWAS treaty broaden the objectives for regionalism in West Africa from developmental regionalism to security regionalism. However, democratic region-building has not yet become an uncontested ECOWAS priority. The 2001 ECOWAS Protocol on Democracy and Good Governance is but a first step in the right direction.

Intrinsic Motives and External Pressures

West Africa is the youngest region in the world: 45 percent of its population is under fifteen years of age, compared with 28 percent in Brazil, 33 percent in India, 34 percent in Malaysia, and only 15 percent in the industrialized world. In 1975, when ECOWAS was founded, it had a population of 120 million. In 2005 it was estimated at 265 million and projected to increase to 430 million by 2020. But while the population has tripled since independence, the per capita production in West Africa has remained constant—a steady path toward the impoverishment of many.

Although ECOWAS is largely perceived as an economic integration program, its beginning was highly political and inherently driven by security considerations: it was formed in reaction to the devastating Nigerian civil war (1967–1970) following the 1966 military coup in West Africa's largest country. In spite of its local oil resources, Nigeria had to look to its neighbors for cooperation if its recovery is to have any meaningful success. It was no intuitive affinity that brought English- and French-speaking countries in West Africa together. Former French West Africa had maintained strong postcolonial ties with France, and its denizens remain suspicious of Nigeria's possible hegemonic ambitions. After the departure of General de Gaulle from the French political scene in 1969, some of the ties between French-speaking West Africa and France came under increasing criticism. Although the special role of the franc zone with its West African Economic and Monetary Union remained a unique element in the architecture of the region, several former French colonies demanded a revision of the monetary and defense agreements that bound them bilaterally with France. The European Economic Community, interested in bridging the gap between French- and English-speaking West Africa, wanted to enhance trade between the region and Europe through a joint structure. The signing of the first Lomé Convention on 28 February 1975 opened the European market for African products through certain preferential treatment. The joint African negotiation with the EEC led many African states to appreciate the value of united action and integration aspirations among African countries. ECOWAS thus became almost a by-product of, and a follow-up measure to, the Lomé Convention negotiations.

The original idea for a West African Economic and Monetary Community coincided with proposals by the United Nations Commission for West Africa (ECA), launched during a West African political summit in Monrovia in 1968. It took several years for West African countries to come together, incidentally overlapping with the signing of the first Lomé Convention. On 25 May 1975 they signed among themselves the ECOWAS founding treaty, bringing together diverse potential and views of many joint problems. Most countries in the region are cash-crop economies, earning much of their foreign exchange through the export of a few primary products. Their mineral-rich soil makes capital-intensive exploitation operations necessary. Huge infrastructural deficits, inter alia in transportation and communication, add to the natural fate of the land-locked countries in the region.[69]

The extension of the ECOWAS mandate, particularly with regard to security and defense policy, and the broadening of its political perspective, particularly through the establishment of the ECOWAS Parliament, conveyed conflicting messages. On the one hand, these measures indicated progress in the understanding of integration and its application. On the other hand, they could not hide the limited success in the sphere of economic integration and the feeble state of governance in many West African countries. The civil war in Liberia 1989/1990 became a turning point in awareness among the region's leaders of the relationship between domestic rule of law and regional security. Yet without economic progress and economic integration, declaratory efforts in governance matters and security-related issues alike remain fruitless.

The development of ECOWAS and its restructuring during the 1990s and since 2006 have to be seen in the larger context of the development of Third World regionalism. It is often argued, simplistically, that this was and is an evolution from "old" to "new" regionalism. This terminology is largely meaningless if not properly substantiated. As for ECOWAS, it is more pertinent to describe its evolution as the logical extension of its normative origins. Preserving peace and making use of the potential of cooperation and integration were intrinsically linked to ideas that stood at the beginning of West African regionalism. The original strategy chosen did not succeed. It failed to prevent new conflicts in the region, and it failed to successfully position the region in the emerging era of globalization. Under the pressure of internal failure and external marginalization, ECOWAS "had to make the transition from its exclusive, protectionist, inward-looking regionalism to an outward and open regionalism into the global economy."[70] Security regionalism became the necessary precondition to make this transition meaningful. In focusing on security matters, ECOWAS member states have had to accept the permeability of state sovereignty and reject the dogma of non-interference.

It is beyond any doubt that the vulnerability of West Africa cannot be transcended by the "magical" restructuring of institutions. But the revision and extension of ECOWAS's rationale laid the foundation for a more realistic and comprehensive approach to region-building in West Africa. To achieve the goals of economic regionalism, ECOWAS has had to embark on the creation of security regionalism. In order to achieve and maintain both, it will have to embark on the sustainable creation of democratic regionalism.

Performance

The development of ECOWAS can be distinguished by three phases. The first period, 1975 until 1990, was defined by economic priorities. The second phase, between 1990 and 2006, was shaped by security priorities. The third phase began with the revamping of ECOWAS institutions in 2006. It is defined by a new politicization and the eventual achievement of more integrative and holistic approaches to region-building. In all, though, the main current running through all periods of region-building in West Africa is obvious: it exists to serve the region and its people. As elsewhere in the world, the track record of ECOWAS combines both shortfalls and strengths.

(1) Upon the establishment of ECOWAS, the initial emphasis was on the ways and means to create more regional trade, to improve the regional infrastructure, to enhance agricultural cooperation, and to enable visa-free travel for citizens of ECOWAS, including their right to reside and settle in all other ECOWAS countries. When the ECOWAS founding treaty was signed in Lagos, it was understood as a supportive element of South-South cooperation for the Lomé Convention between the European Community and its main partners in the Caribbean, the Pacific, and Africa. The overarching objective was the creation of a common market, thus emulating the parallel task of the European Community. While the EU went beyond customs union to a common currency in 2002, ECOWAS never succeeded in achieving the first substantial step toward customs union, a common external tariff.

The West African Clearing House was established in 1975 with the mandate of a specialized institution managing the financial affairs of international trade for all ECOWAS member states. Later, the Clearing House became the West African Monetary Agency, aimed at helping to create a single monetary zone with one currency finally replacing the CFA franc and all other nine inconvertible currencies in ECOWAS. But the ECOWAS strategists had chosen the wrong sequence of events. A common currency could not work in the absence of sufficient intra-regional trade and a norm-based common market. In

1988, only 4.9 percent of all trade in ECOWAS was intra-regional. In 1983, ECOWAS had explicitly stated its goal to adopt a single monetary zone by 1994. In light of a realistic assessment of the situation, the date was postponed in 1992 to the year 2000, which again did not bring the expected achievements. Now ECOWAS has announced its goal to achieve full monetary union and a single currency, the "Eco", by 2009. A general problem of ECOWAS's mechanical path has become evident: the artificial emulation of European integration will not work by simply copying European timetables and ambitions. Deeper preconditions for successful regional integration first have to be met.

In 1986 ECOWAS introduced visa-free travel and the right of free residence, which has been widely applied across ECOWAS. But well into the 1990s, not a single ECOWAS member state was using the harmonized immigration and emigration forms, and only five of sixteen member states distributed the ECOWAS travel card. In the meantime, the first ECOWAS passports have been issued. The long list of shortcomings in implementing ECOWAS objectives adds to the general impression that while ECOWAS is good at announcing goals, including the goal of a common external tariff, in truth these goals have had to be continuously revised and in the end have never been properly applied. Except for several intra-regional infrastructure projects—such as the Trans-Sahelian Highway, a Coastal Highway, and the West African portion of the Pan-African Telecommunication Network that now links all countries in the region—ECOWAS has not succeeded in macroeconomic coordination and hence has never achieved its ultimate economic objectives.[71]

(2) On paper, forty intergovernmental organizations exist in West Africa. Their presence is larger than their achievements. No genuine community spirit has developed in the course of any of their activities, and the degree of significant effects is debatable. Some of the leaders, including a former secretary general of ECOWAS, have openly complained about a lack of serious integration-oriented and developmental culture in the region.72 Some structures, such as the Mano River Union (MRU) between Guinea, Liberia, and Sierra Leone, are functional. Others, and in particular the two monetary unions UEMOA and CEMAC, overlap with ECOWAS and challenge its claim of exclusivity and integration leadership. Yet if one looks at the comprehensive picture of regional cooperation and integration architectures in West Africa, ECOWAS scores the highest.

ECOWAS chose "institutional expansion" as a means to fight its possible marginalization when it underwent a comprehensive treaty revision in 1993 and the reforms of 2006.[73] The revised ECOWAS treaty came into force on 23 August 1995. It claims that ECOWAS is the only economic community in the region. Moreover, it understands itself as a community that is granted a supranational status by its member states in order to strengthen the community institutions and to make community decisions directly enforceable in the ECOWAS region. Once decisions have been signed by the ECOWAS heads of states, they automatically become law after ninety days without further national ratification. But to get to common political agreements can take a terribly long time. In order to facilitate the process of decision-making and, moreover, of decision-implementing, the revised ECOWAS treaty enhances the powers of community institutions. By adopting new legal mechanisms, ECOWAS decisions can be directly applicable in member states without going through the daunting process of ratifications across ECOWAS. In 1996, the community Tribunal was replaced by the ECOWAS Court of Justice with seven judges. The Economic and Social Council and, most importantly, the West African Parliament based in Abuja, were established by Articles 6 and 13. These developments, along with the 2006 recalibration of the ECOWAS Commission, have enhanced the potential for supra-nationality in ECOWAS.

The ECOWAS Parliament started its work in 2000 "in the midst of an already existing and ever since evolving political and institutional framework that can be considered as the emerging subregional security architecture."[74] The parliament consists of 115 seats. Each member state has a minimum of 5 seats. Nigeria was granted 35 seats, Ghana 8, Ivory Coast 7. Burkina Faso, Guinea, Mali, Niger, and Senegal have 6 seats each. Benin, Cape Verde, Gambia, Guinea Bissau, Liberia, Sierra Leone, and Togo have 5 seats each. The original 5 seats reserved for Mauritania remain empty as Mauritania left ECOWAS in 2001, orienting itself more toward the Arab–North African region and hoping to be included in the Euro-Mediterranean Partnership (Barcelona Process).

For the time being, the members of the ECOWAS Parliament are selected from their respective national parliaments and serve a five-year term. The Parliament and its thirteen committees are mandated with consultative powers pertaining to the objective of creating an economic union in the region. They are also mandated to look into matters of human rights. Since its inception, the ECOWAS Parliament has played a certain mediating role through fact-finding missions. Notable was the mission in the Ivory Coast crisis in 2002, after a mutiny had broken out there. Most important was the ECOWAS mission as part of the final process to terminate the bloody Liberian civil war that ended in 2003 with a cease-fire. The ECOWAS engagement "created conditions for the exit of Charles Taylor from Liberia."[75] In 2006, Liberia's former president was imprisoned and extradited to the International Court of Justice in The Hague, while in the meantime, Liberia elected Ellen Johnson-Sirleaf as the first female head of state in Africa.

The oversight powers of the initial ECOWAS Parliament clearly limited its scope of action as a full-fledged legislature. However, the historical evolution of parliaments has never been much different. Be it on the level of the state or in the context of European integration, the role of parliaments was always strengthened gradually and through conflicts with the executive. In light of this, the very existence of the ECOWAS Parliament is a remarkable first step in a

presumably long march toward the full parliamentarization of ECOWAS. At
the end of its second legislature, in 2010, the ECOWAS Parliament will decide
on direct elections based on universal suffrage. Like all federal institutions, the
ECOWAS Parliament is reflecting on its future electoral law and the division
of seats granted to extremely diverse member states. The high illiteracy rate in
West Africa remains the biggest obstacle preventing ECOWAS politicians from
connecting with the citizens of the region through solid political parties. But
together with the ECOWAS Court of Justice and the ECOWAS Commission,
the ECOWAS Parliament is advancing the notion of multilevel governance in
West Africa.

The revised ECOWAS treaty states that the community will acquire an autonomous source of financing through the taxation of third-country imports—a
startling parallel to the EEC integration history. Since 1975, only Burkina Faso,
the Ivory Coast, and Togo have regularly contributed to the ECOWAS budget. In
1991, the ECOWAS heads of state decided to adopt automatic sanctions against
defaulting member states, but this rhetorical decision did not really change the
situation. During the year the revised treaty was negotiated, only $12 million
of the $50 million in expected membership fees reached the ECOWAS Secre-
tariat. Whether the revised financing mechanism will truly affect the solidity
of ECOWAS finances and strengthen the sense of ownership in ECOWAS is
unclear. Ten years later, the financial commitments of ECOWAS member states
are still a secretive and non-transparent issue. In principle, the contributions to
the ECOWAS budget are based on a coefficient of GDP and per capita income.
The annual commitment of ECOWAS member states, unfortunately, has never
reached more than 50 percent of what each country ought to pay.[76] The overall
budget structure of ECOWAS remains something of a mystery, as in many other
regional groupings.

(3) Among the promising innovations of the revised ECOWAS treaty is the
strengthened mechanism for conflict prevention and the resolution of conflicts
within or between member states of ECOWAS. The original 1975 ECOWAS
treaty did not include matters of foreign policy and defense, but gradually, and
driven by events in the region, ECOWAS has broadened its perspective.[77] Significant steps were the signing of the ECOWAS Protocol on Non-Aggression
in 1978, the ECOWAS Protocol on Mutual Assistance in Matters of Defense
in 1981, the ECOWAS Declaration of Political Principles in 1991, and eventually, the ECOWAS Protocol on the Mechanism for Conflict Prevention, Management, Resolution, Peacekeeping and Security in 1999. Although none of
these documents was ever fully implemented, they increased the sensitivity in
ECOWAS for necessary regional cooperation in security matters. The taboo on
interference in the domestic affairs of another African country was broken in
the face of gross violations of human rights. Political tensions among ECOWAS
member states might have been prevented with a more proactive and speedier

security action by ECOWAS. But the outbreak of civil war in several ECOWAS member states sharpened the need to change the sense of perspective and priorities in ECOWAS. As of the 1990s, security matters had to be taken seriously as a key issue in order for economic or political developments eventually to come to fruition in West Africa.

The Liberian Civil War in 1989/1990 was a turning point.[78] To increase ECOWAS's relevance, activities in the sphere of defense and security became a matter of "self-preservation."[79] In an extremely chaotic way, the Liberian Civil War which escalated between 1980 and 2005 in several stages was linked to regional political leaders: William Tolbert, Liberia's president, was the son-in-law of Félix Houphouët-Boigny,[80] the president of the Ivory Coast. Tolbert was killed by Sergeant Doe, who in turn was attacked by Charles Taylor. Taylor soon occupied 80 percent of the territory of Liberia. Tolbert's widow then married President Campaore of Burkina Faso, who was explicitly against an ECOWAS monitoring mission in Liberia to end that country's internal violence and politics of gross nepotism.

After it became evident that the United States would land in Liberia only to evacuate its own citizens, ECOWAS was the last hope the neighboring countries of Liberia could resort to. An ad hoc mediation and peacekeeping mission was established and, in a way, rescued not only Liberia but mainly ECOWAS— which in turn changed its priorities. In August 1990, ECOWAS established the ECOWAS cease-fire monitoring group ECOMOG and began to deploy peacekeeping soldiers in Liberia. Nigeria, which had pushed for the peacekeeping mission to take place as soon as possible, contributed 80 percent of the budget and the largest group of soldiers: 9,000 compared to 1,600 from Senegal, 1,500 from Ghana, 600 from Guinea, 700 from Sierra Leone, 150 from Gambia, and 6 from Mali. Eventually, Burkina Faso, the Ivory Coast, Niger, and Togo were also willing to participate with small contingents.

Nigeria's dynamic interest in the first ECOWAS peacekeeping operation immediately provoked criticism. It was suspected that Nigeria, under President Ibrahim Babangida, would claim supremacy in ECOWAS. But it could not be denied that a regional peacekeeping operation was more logical than one with outside personnel, although at some point soldiers from Tanzania and Uganda contributed to the mission in Liberia. From an integration point of view, ECOMOG attested to the ability of functional spillover in an African context: by taking on additional tasks, ECOWAS was able to prove its usefulness and thus managed to intensify its integrative potential. After its moderate economic performance, it was imperative for ECOWAS to present some form of success or fall into oblivion. The economies of most ECOWAS member states were crippled during the 1990s by structural adjustment programs of the World Bank and the IMF, bad internal governance, and an overall poor performance of the region's leadership. Even Nigeria lost oil revenues. Only the four biggest ECOWAS member states were engaged in any substantial form of intra-regional trade. It was against this background that ECOMOG raised the reputation of ECOWAS exponentially and instilled new hope in the goal for a comprehensive regional integration approach in West Africa. The Liberia peacekeeping mission from 1990 to 1997 was followed by one in Sierra Leone (1997–1999) and one in Guinea Bissau (1998–1999).[81]

While the Liberia mission was mandated to restore peace, ECOMOG's presence in Sierra Leone was replaced by a mission under UN auspices (UN-AMSIL) once it had achieved its objectives. After the overthrow of the lawful government of President Ahmed Tejan Kabbah, ECOMOG reinstated the constitutional order in Sierra Leone in February 1998 and brokered a final settlement between the government and rebel groups in September 1999.[82] In Guinea-Bissau parts of the armed forces had organized a rebellion in June 1998. ECOWAS decided to restore the constitutional order and keep the elected president of Guinea Bissau, Joao Bernardo Vieira, in office; eventually he was killed in March 2009 by his internal rival. Despite numerous cease-fire arrangements he was finally overthrown, with consequences for ECOWAS peacekeeping.

The ad hoc character of ECOWAS peacekeeping operations has changed. In 1999, ECOMOG was replaced by the decision to create a 6,500-man ECOWAS Stand-By Force until 2010. While it exists, this program is considered to be one of the five components of the African Union Rapid Deployment Force. Although conceptual clarity is lacking with regard to the link between military, humanitarian, and disaster-control missions, the force is developing. It is also one of the few examples across the globe that has brought practical and noticeable US support to a regional grouping. A military advisor from the United States is even working in the ECOWAS Commission. Furthermore, the ECOWAS security experience served as an example for the Southern African Development Community: in 1996, SADC created an Organ for Defense, Politics and Security under the SADC Secretariat, which was further upgraded in 2001.[83]

(4) Private-sector participation, particularly through cross-border investments, cooperation in science, technology and information, and the physical integration of the region through improved infrastructure, is also among the priorities of ECOWAS. Although a wide array of civil society groupings exists in West Africa, the involvement of private business in the process of region-building has been too slow so far. For the time being, ECOWAS remains a top-down operation, largely driven by the dynamics of its most committed leaders. As was the case in Europe, the ECOWAS Commission plays a pivotal role in this process. Increasingly, the ECOWAS Parliament is a promising expression of the potential for broadening the legitimacy of regional integration. Yet there is ample room to enhance the sense of

ownership through community-building efforts. ECOWAS, so far, remains an elite-driven project.

Federators

ECOWAS came about as the brainchild of the United Nations' regional concepts, European special relations with former colonies, and the progress-driven aspiration to speedy development and affluence in West Africa. The reconciliation between the English- and French-speaking countries of Western Africa succeeded partially. The reaction to Nigeria's aspiration to regional leadership was to bring all countries of the region together under one regional scheme. Initially, cross-linguistic leadership of Nigeria and Togo even had an important role in bringing about ECOWAS. Regional integration was a means by which to overcome mutually felt external dependency and to prevent indigenous regional hegemony. Yet Nigeria remains the strongest of all players in the region. It was not another country of similar weight but regional integration that was understood to be the counterbalancing force that would tame Nigeria, the giant of West Africa. Nigeria itself was and remains committed to collaboration with its different and diverse smaller neighbors to the benefit of all. Nigeria is also convinced that it has a primus inter pares role to play.

The dream of integration as a speedy path to development and affluence inspired West African leaders even in the face of setbacks. But the most effective test of reality came with the outbreak of violence in the region. Refocusing ECOWAS by introducing security regionalism was not only a mechanism to escape the frustrating work and limited success of development regionalism. The evolution of security regionalism was forced upon ECOWAS by reality and the events that shape it. In an indirect way, the recognition of security obligations in and for the region made ECOWAS aware of certain national preconditions for stability and tangible development in the region. Without peace, there can be no success. But beyond peace, good governance and democratic rule have to be achieved in order to pave the way for lasting region-building and economic integration with a social dimension.

The prospects for democratic regionalism in West Africa, as in other parts of Africa, remain ambivalent. The intellectual insight into its necessity is recognized in a growing body of proclamatory documents. But taking the challenge of democratic regionalism seriously would require the acceptance of limits on power by those who hold it. Security regionalism might affect the concept of sovereignty and autonomy, which remains, by and large, only a theoretical one. Democratic regionalism would definitely impact and limit the execution of power and put it under the primacy of law, transparency, and accountability. This is not only a theoretical matter. For many of the leaders of Africa's states, this is a matter of personal power and freedom for those who enjoy it. Democratic regionalism, therefore, has had limited success so far in becoming de facto a recognized engine for region-building in West Africa.

Transformations

ECOWAS had to recognize the deficiency posed for its long-term economic integration planning by the absence of peace and stability in the region. Upon the outbreak of the Civil War in Liberia in 1989/1990, Western Africa was confronted with the return of violence of dimensions unknown since the Biafra secession between 1967 and 1970. It is therefore not surprising that Nigeria was particularly interested in transforming ECOWAS from a relatively weak economic community into a more robust and successful security community under Nigerian leadership. In all of its depressing character, the Liberian Civil War was an opportunity to reinvigorate ECOWAS and strengthen its legitimacy in the region and its reputation beyond West Africa.

The Liberian crisis was a turning point for the obsession with non-interference in domestic affairs. The violent escalation was unacceptable and had to be stopped by Africans through regional means. The potential for failure, in the face of the magnitude of the challenge and ECOWAS's lack of preparedness, was acknowledged. But the effort had to be made in order to justify the rationale for regional cooperation itself, and for seeking integration. ECOWAS was poised to mature through crises. This was obvious when domestic crises in Ivory Coast, Togo, Guinea-Bissau, Niger and Guinea confronted ECOWAS with severe governance failures in a number of member states throughout the first decade of the 21st century.

The process of economic region-building must follow, if ECOWAS is to succeed. State-centered economic planning has turned out to be disastrous across the region. National planning in West Africa has largely undermined the hope for regional integration. A new beginning with more market-oriented policies and macroeconomic planning will not come about naturally. It will have to be initiated through ECOWAS channels, which in turn will always be only as strong as the member states permit. ECOWAS will have to cut through this vicious circle of the dependency of its region-building ambitions on state-centered structures of decision-making. The political goal of a common West African currency will be only a first step in a long-term process. ECOWAS will need to create—if only gradually—a supranational mechanism for economic policy-making. Otherwise, the potential and necessity for region-building in West Africa will remain a hostage to failing nation-states. The definition of a regional public good ought to be at the center of the discourse.

Role and Interests of the European Union

The European Union started regular political summits with ECOWAS in October 2000. The regular meetings bring together the rotating ECOWAS leadership and the rotating EU leadership in the "troika" format. The European Union does not maintain structured and detailed relations with ECOWAS yet. The scope of cooperation is defined by the EU's Regional Indicative Program, which considers the region of Western Africa an important element in the overall development of Africa. The EU is West Africa's leading partner in development cooperation and trade. The topic of an economic partnership agreement in accordance with the Cotonou Agreement has been on the agenda ever since the beginning of the regular ministerial meetings between ECOWAS and the EU.

The European Union supports the conflict management activities of ECOWAS. It has regularly expressed concern about the degree of arms trade and proliferation in West Africa. For the EU, the support of peace-building and conflict prevention in West Africa is "an ongoing learning process."[84] ECOWAS has developed its peacekeeping concept in response to conflicts in Liberia, Sierra Leone, Guinea-Bissau, and the Ivory Coast. Although capacities remain limited and some of the results are controversial, ECOWAS can claim to have succeeded in transforming itself from a purely regional economic organization into one also focusing on conflict resolution and concern for regional peace. The comprehensive peacekeeping strategies of ECOWAS have found the interest of the EU with its focus on conflict prevention and peace-building. The EU has begun to develop more sophisticated and differentiated strategies regarding early warning mechanisms and the possible array of political conditions and sanctions. The Cotonou Agreement of 2000 emphasizes the political dialogue with the EU partner states in Africa, the Caribbean, and the Pacific. The EU aims to support "structural stability" and "local ownership."[85] In the area of conflict prevention, including the burning problem of trade with "blood diamonds," the EU has discovered that West Africa is a necessary region of concern, interest, and commitment.

In the sphere of economic integration in West Africa, the European Union supports harmonization of the activities of ECOWAS and UEMOA. Since 2005, the issue of illegal migration from West Africa to Europe has also entered the agenda of the EU-ECOWAS ministerial summits. Especially Guinea-Bissau has been identified as "a new passing point for illegal immigration and drug-trafficking."[86] But human trafficking in general, including female prostitution and the search by qualified male labor for better-paid jobs in the EU, has become part of the joint agenda. In the first decade of the twenty-first century, the overriding debate among political elites in the EU and in ECOWAS has centered on the conclusion of Economic Partnership Agreements and their potential impact on region-building and on the regional achievements of the Millennium Goals of the United Nations.

Prospects and Obstacles

ECOWAS is one of the eight regional economic communities recognized by the African Union. But ECOWAS must also respond to the overall African question of how the effectiveness of regional integration across the continent and in its regions can be improved. Overlapping mandates and memberships in different organizations undermine the effective commitment of countries. Of the African states belonging to one regional integration scheme, 95 percent also belong to another regional integration scheme. This inflation of memberships and institutions inhibits a country's commitment to any one institution and its readiness to fully engage in any given region-building project. There are always second thoughts, including the annual financial commitments to the budget of a regional scheme.

In order to achieve an African Economic Community by 2028, as outlined in the Treaty of Abuja, ECOWAS, as one of the most stable regional institutions in Africa, has to rationalize its activities, optimize its focus, and redefine its priorities. Whether this implies the merger of ECOWAS with UEMOA—and how to do this, in practice—remains an open question. The monetary union project would certainly gain global recognition if achieved. In any case, ECOWAS cannot possibly claim to be the strongest regional scheme in West Africa without eventually resolving the burning social questions.

It remains a grave challenge for ECOWAS to incorporate and absorb the monetary union of West Africa and turn it into one single West African currency. This will inevitably require a thorough debate about the issue of sovereignty in West and Central Africa. ECOWAS can serve as the anchor community in such a process only if it is able to convey trust, confidence, and a sense of guidance and leadership fully recognized in all possible aspects by the member states of UEMOA. For Africa, ECOWAS's success in this operation will entail a unique variation of the European experience with the dialectics of "deepening" and "widening." A sensitive and controversial debate about national sovereignty and the merits of pooled resources and shared sovereignty is inevitable.

Only pragmatic successes and patient gradualism can ever produce such a constellation. ECOWAS's decision to launch its own genuine regional monetary initiative might be interpreted as a first cautious but calculated effort in such a direction. Along with abstract reflections on the value of an African monetary union, ECOWAS created the West African Monetary Zone in July 2005. This decision aims at an eventual merger with the West African Economic and Monetary Association UEMOA and the creation of a single West African currency by 2010. Regardless of whether this deadline can be met, the goal is ambitious and promising. As for obstacles, the lack of fiscal discipline in the region, particularly in Nigeria, pops to mind. But the absence to date of a genuine debate in ECOWAS about sovereignty, and of a cost-benefit-analysis of a comprehensive West—and perhaps also Central—African monetary union, is proving a similarly serious impediment.

The practical challenge for ECOWAS, in pushing forward the debate about its leadership in the project of a regional currency, is the necessary expansion of

intra-regional trade and in fact of trade diversification in general. Most sub-Saharan trade is with Europe. The monostructure of export trade has to be broken
and gradually reversed. The African countries face a complicated dilemma: the
greater the extent of processing raw materials, the higher the barriers in Europe
will be, due to quota systems and technical and sanitary regulations. So far, they
do not know how to circumvent the era of industrialization and move immediately from agriculture-based societies into the service societies of globalization in
the twenty-first century.

ECOWAS is sometimes confronted with the question of whether it can turn
into a success story analogous to that of the "Asian tigers" of the 1970s and 1980s.
Such comparisons and analogies are rather dubious. As long as West Africa's
prospects for achieving the Millennium Goals by halving poverty by 2015 look
unpromising, ECOWAS is trapped by the gap between elite ambitions and social
realities. ECOWAS, in the words of Commission President Ibn Chambas, is one
of those regions "that is most unlikely to have reduced poverty by 2015 at current average growth rates of GDP of 4 to 4.5 % and population average growth
rates of 3.5%. To significantly make an impact on the pervasive and excruciating
poverty in our region, we need to be growing our economies by 7% of the GDP
and upwards."[87]

Each region-building effort in the world follows its own logic and set of plans.
ECOWAS is no different. Its flaws and potentials are no reflection of any other region's legacy. The more they evolve as a genuine story of region-building and integration, the less they will serve as a model even for other regions in Africa. The
real question is whether ECOWAS can succeed over time. To measure success in
this context, one ought to put the main emphasis on consistency and coherence.
It is not so much the absolute success of a region-building effort, measured by
realizing a certain abstract finality, nor the mere economic success of integration,
measured in GDP outcome and intra-trade statistics, that defines success. Instead,
region-building and integration have to be measured against the background of a
region's history, its potential, its limits, and the overall context in which the region is situated. Seen through this lens, ECOWAS has not performed so poorly in
its first three decades of existence. Its very existence, transformed through crises
and broadened in ambition, is an encouraging sign for a region still in turmoil.
Under such circumstances, every element of hope is welcome. ECOWAS plays
this role for West Africa. In the end, the test of maturation will be defined by the
degree of democratic regionalism it can eventually initiate.

Democratic regionalism is no end in itself, and it is not enough as a comprehensive objective of region-building. But democratic rule is a prerequisite
for trust, which is a prerequisite for the readiness of countries to pool and share
aspects of their national sovereignty with others. The prospect of mutual gain
through integration needs to be justified by concrete success. In Europe, the
coal and steel industries served a perfect role for bringing contrasting interests

together under the umbrella of a supranational integration scheme that became possible only because the founding members of the EEC shared the same democratic norms. ECOWAS will need to define the West African equivalent of coal and steel. For the time being, legitimate security interests and development aspirations are uniting the countries of West Africa.

But in such broad terms, the objectives of a joint approach to shared sovereignty are not likely to work. ECOWAS needs to define spheres of common interest and achieve supranationality. The breakthrough of the concept of qualified majority voting may be a realistic step in that necessary direction. Concrete and pragmatic spheres of collaboration have to be identified. Energy and migration might serve that role, or agro-industry and water could take on the function. Whatever it is, there is no iron law that enforces upon ECOWAS—or any other aspiring region-builder in the world—the need to follow the European approach and experience. The member states of ECOWAS still have all formal prerogative rights to go their own way. Region-building requires more trust and solidarity, as well as the transfer of powers. For now, one might conclude that the effort is the goal. The paths are being shaped along the way. ECOWAS has the potential to be the shining star of a new African reality. Whether ECOWAS will go further and deepen its region-building aspiration remains to be seen. It lies in its own hands, which is the only statement about Africa's self-determination that one can possibly make in the age of globalization.

Basic Facts

Sometimes, the evolution of region-ness in Southern Africa is already linked to the arrival of Europeans in the late fourteenth and early fifteenth century. With their arrival the struggle for land and resources, labor and power in Southern Africa took a new course. Local kingdoms were destroyed, and colonization by Europeans began. Since the 1870s–1880s, the discovery of strategic minerals such as gold and diamonds and of energy resources such as coal has contributed to the perception of Southern Africa as one region. The "scramble for Africa" among British, Boers, Portuguese, and Germans, largely over access to and control of Southern Africa and its natural resources, strengthened the importance of the region, albeit in a paradoxical way. Cecil Rhodes established the British South Africa Company, thus adding to the understanding of a colonial variant of region-ness. Much later, the struggle against white minority rule and apartheid helped to build up a sense of common destiny in the twentieth century.

The region was hardly ever free from internal and intra-state conflicts. The territorial disputes between Namibia and Botswana over the Chobe River, massive civil wars in Angola, Mozambique, and the Democratic Republic of Congo, low-density conflicts in Lesotho and Zimbabwe, and criminal violence in South Africa have contributed to a rather bleak picture that was aggravated by an overall economic decline during the 1990s. With the end of the South Africa's apartheid regime in 1994, a new reality began to appear in Southern Africa. The heterogeneity of Southern Africa's state formation, governance structures, and socioeconomic development is enormous. Strong and reasonably successful states such as South Africa, Botswana, Namibia, the Seychelles, and Mauritius stand next to failing states such as the Democratic Republic of Congo and, increasingly, Zimbabwe. Multiparty systems are neighbors to authoritarian one-party states, personal dictatorships, and more or less constitutional monarchies.

Life expectancy is 72.2 years in the Seychelles, 50.9 years in South Africa, and 38.2 years in Swaziland. The HIV virus afflicts an estimated 12 million South Africans, almost half of all African victims of the pandemic.[88] As for the level of socioeconomic development, Southern Africa could not be more asymmetric. The GDP per capita income varies from $16,652 in the Seychelles, $11,192 in South Africa, $12,027 in Mauritius, $9,945 in Botswana, and $7,418 in Namibia all the way down to $943 in Zambia, $646 in the Democratic Republic of Congo, and $570 in Malawi.

The Southern African Development Community (SADC) was originally created as a tool of the anti-apartheid struggle. Over time, it has turned into the promise of an inclusive development scheme for the region. The original Southern African Development Coordinating Conference (SADCC) was founded in July 1979 by Zambia, Zimbabwe, Angola, Mozambique, Madagascar, Tanzania, Malawi, Lesotho, Botswana, and Swaziland in order to reduce their dependency on South Africa and to promote Southern African regional development among majority-ruled countries. After the end of apartheid in South Africa, SADCC underwent a serious period of revision. South Africa's GDP was four times that of all SADCC member states combined. A membership of South Africa would therefore raise concerns about the hegemony of one big country. On the other hand, the economic potential of South Africa could also serve as an engine for the other countries of the region, now liberated from absorbing many of their valuable and limited resources in the anti-apartheid struggle.

Against this background, region-building in Southern Africa found its name and direction: in 1992, SADCC was refounded as the South African Development Community (SADC) in Windhoek.[89] Namibia became its latest member, followed by South Africa in 1994, Mauritius in 1995, and the Democratic Republic of Congo and the Seychelles in 1997 (the Seychelles then withdrew between 2004 and 2007). Today (2008), SADC membership stands at fifteen countries with a total of 240 million inhabitants.

More than half of SADC member states are also members of the Common Market for Eastern and Southern Africa (COMESA, composed of Madagascar, the Democratic Republic of Congo, Angola, Malawi, Mauritius, Swaziland, Zambia, and Zimbabwe, along with Burundi, the Comoros, Djibouti, Egypt, Eritrea, Ethiopia, Kenya, Libya, Rwanda, the Seychelles, Sudan, and Uganda).

This generates problems of institutional overlap between SADC and COMESA, which was founded in 1981. COMESA, once only a preferential trade area, has turned its sights to the ambition of creating a common market.[90] COMESA's goals include enabling the free movement of goods, services, capital, and persons, improving transport and communications networks, strengthening the private sector, facilitating customs and payment systems, increasing intra-regional trade through tariff and non-tariff concessions, and searching for common rules of origin for products eligible for preferential treatment. In October 2000, nine of COMESA's twenty member states achieved a free trade area. COMESA aimed for a comprehensive customs union by 2008 and for a currency union by 2025. This process, which will continue to be both daunting and challenging, is supported by a wide set of institutions: the Trade and Development Commission based in Nairobi, the Clearing House in Harare, the Association of Commercial Banks in Harare, the Leather Institute in Addis Ababa, the Re-Insurance Company in Nairobi, and the Court of Justice of COMESA in Khartoum have been fully operational since 1998. The overall COMESA GDP of 374 million people is $33 billion. At the same time, the 34 million people of South Africa alone have a GDP of $79 billion. More than anything else, this fact demonstrates the power equation between COMESA and SADC.

As for SADC, its structures were overhauled in 2001. They now include:

- The SADC Executive Secretariat, based in Gaborone (headed by Dr. Tomaz Augusto Salomao)
- The annual SADC Summit of Presidents
- The SADC Council of Ministers
- The SADC Standing Committee of Officials
- The SADC Organ on Politics, Defense and Security
- The SADC Tribunal.

The basis for SADC's work is a Regional Indicative Strategic Development Plan that aims at implementation by 2015. The plan defines SADC's priorities as the promotion of sustainable and equitable economic growth, the promotion of common political values and systems transmitted through institutions that are democratic, legitimate, and effective, and the consolidation and maintenance of peace, democracy, and security. Specifics are as absent as any clear-cut timetable or set of criteria. The expansive rhetoric does not immediately translate into trust, as far as the ability to implement these noble goals is concerned. But it is to SADC's credit that the goals of development, security, and democracy have been applied to a regional context. While the strong South African rand has become the factual common currency in SADC, the goals of democracy, development, and security can only be achieved and maintained if all member states of SADC develop a sense of ownership in these objectives.

SADC's Organ on Politics, Defense and Security Cooperation began its life in 1996 in loose connection with SADC and then was fully incorporated into the SADC structure in 2001. It is the "first comprehensive attempt to build a regional collective mechanism for responding to peace and security issues"[91] in Southern Africa. The SADC Organ on Politics, Defense and Security Cooperation is lauded for conceptualizing security "from a multidimensional perspective embracing human, environmental and societal security."[92] The SADC summit on 8 August 2001 in Blantyre adopted the SADC Protocol on Politics, Defense and Security Cooperation, which commits the SADC organ to contributing to peace and security in its region but also states the primacy of the United Nations in the maintenance of international peace.[93]

The 2001 SADC reforms not only concerned the role of the Organ on Politics, Defense and Security Cooperation, but included an overhaul of the structure of the SADC Secretariat in Gaborone. Until 2006, four main departments dealing with the key activities of SADC were built up in the Secretariat in order to give it more leverage. Decision-making processes and coordination remain difficult in SADC, given diverging interests among its member states on many issues. As a paradoxical consequence, the overall reputation of SADC has suffered at a moment when the full potential of SADC has just become evident.[94]

Intrinsic Motives and External Pressures

More than any other region-building effort in Africa, the Southern African Development Community should be sensitive to democratic governance as a precondition for successful development and security in the region. SADC originated in the struggle against apartheid in South Africa and hence was deeply defined by its normative cause, the quest for protection of human rights and majority rule under law. The limits of weak states, the benefits of economic liberalization and integration, and finally the positive impact of the transformed South Africa as an engine for the whole region had to be translated into a new rationale for the region-building process. The turn from liberation to integration could not automatically bring about the necessary preconditions for the success of this transformation. Strong interdependence in the region, a remarkable supply of mineral resources, and a well-developed infrastructure, including railway lines, harbors, and roads, all constituted a number of advantages. But it remained necessary for SADC to include concrete projects in the overall rationale—and not the other way around.

Projects alone might not lead to integration and region-building. Although it was right to identify, for example, the Maputo Corridor as a link between South Africa's Mpumalanga Province and Mozambique, the Lesotho Highland Water Scheme as a joint water resource for Lesotho and South Africa, and other corridor projects across the Kalahari and from Zambia to the Indian Ocean, these

subregional activities will not automatically translate into Southern African regional integration. They could support the process and might serve as its engine,
but they cannot substitute for the necessary political decision about the overall
objectives and priorities of region-building in Southern Africa.

The biggest challenge for SADC comes from the Common Market for Southern Africa. COMESA, with the overlapping membership of eight SADC member countries, is focusing on trade integration and aims to establish a fully developed model of economic integration. SADC, in turn, is seen as an expression of
functional project cooperation hoping for spillover effects toward deepened integration. COMESA and SADC, as it stands, are two different approaches to "development integration."[95] While SADC has a stronger political reputation and
ambition, COMESA could challenge it as the more comprehensive economic
approach. In theory, at least, its objectives are linked to a coherent timetable:

- Full utilization of the clearing house's payments mechanism (1992–1996),
- Limited currency convertibility and an informal exchange rate union (1997–2000),
- Fixed exchange rate fluctuating within a given margin (2000–2024),
- Central banks remaining independent but monetary policy coordinated by a com-
  mon monetary institution (2000–2024), and
- Issue of a common currency by the common monetary authority (2025 and beyond).[96]

However, the implementation of this ambitious program has always been slower
than expectations. And since the end of apartheid in South Africa and its membership in SADC in 1994, the balance of power has changed in favor of SADC.
COMESA has not been able to properly achieve its objective of a customs union.
With twenty member states, COMESA is the biggest regional economic grouping in Africa, but it has not been able to turn size into advantage—in fact, it has
even diminished in size. The original participation of Somalia became unrealistic
when the country was stricken by complete state failure and breakdown. Lesotho
and Mozambique left COMESA in 1997, Tanzania in 2000, and Namibia in 2004.
SADC, and its new hegemon South Africa, became an inescapable pull factor for
the wider region. COMESA, however, has no natural "anchor country."[97] Egypt
may seem a likely candidate on the surface, but it is structurally incompatible with
the prevailing conditions in the other member states.

The overlapping membership in SADC and COMESA has hence generated
"conflicting commitments to two differently planned customs and monetary
unions."[98] The effect has become visible even with respect to the reliability of the
annual membership contributions paid to the respective budgets of COMESA
and SADC. SADC's budget is based on equal annual contributions of its member states, taking into account population and economic power. These contributions have never been sufficient to finance any sizeable regional development
plan beyond the very operation of SADC's institutions. All in all, the actual

commitment of SADC member states has been suboptimal: on average, SADC member states have allegedly never paid more than fifty percent of their dues. Exact figures are unavailable.[99]

SADC is not a natural success story. As is the case with other region-building efforts in Africa, SADC's aspirations are in conflict with the sociological fact, to put it in the terminology of one academic analyst, "that rent-seeking and the nature of African statehood block effective regionalism."[100] The overall criticism can be summarized by the term "shadow regionalism." Political elites, the argument goes, are involved in personally enriching trans-state activities, including a parallel economy. Sheltered by the façade of state authority, they pursue their personal business and exploit the institutions and mechanisms of regional integration to accumulate the interests of "important support groups of the patrimonial regime and sometimes for the state apparatus itself."[101]

It can indeed be argued that SADC combines elements of actual and formal regionalism with aspects of "shadow regionalism" and informal economic regionalism, including small business and trade activities, often exercised by women, in border regions. But it would be unfair to SADC to reduce its existence simply to its flaws. The intrinsic motive of turning South Africa from an enemy country into a welcome benign hegemon is a remarkable achievement. The emerging prospects of SADC have been recognized by the African Union and need to be followed up, under the pressures and opportunities of globalization. Like other region-building activities in developing areas, SADC has not been able to properly connect with the people in the region. Or to put it more precisely, the sense of ownership that is essential for any regional architecture to grow roots of legitimacy and authority has remained underdeveloped. It should be a limited consolation to add that this problem is not exclusively that of SADC. One would only have to look to the European Union to find a similar complaint. It seems to be the fate of region-building to have to start as a top-down, elite-driven project. It will be the long-term challenge of democratic region-building to reverse this order and balance the roles of the relevant actors. This caveat will always hover over Southern African region-building, which claimed such strong democratic credentials at its beginning.

Performance

The Southern African Development Community is aiming for "a common future within a regional community."[102] The biggest challenge in this context is psychological, given the original purpose of Southern African cooperation under SADC. During the time of apartheid in South Africa, enmity to white minority rule in the strongest country of the region brought its northern neighbors together. At the end of apartheid, as the revised SADC treaty signed in Windhoek in 1993 states, enmity had to be transformed into inclusive cooperation recognizing a certain leadership of the former enemy, South Africa. SADC met this politico-psychological challenge and succeeded in turning the former front-line states into a community with South Africa. From an economic point of view, this challenge was exacerbated by the need to transform SADC's "dirigiste import substitution industrialization"[103] with the laws of market liberalization and open regionalism. This had to be coupled with an equitable distribution of costs and benefits, meaning that no country in the region would be allowed to pursue cost-advantage strategies at the expense of its partners in SADC. The first positive trends became visible during the 1990s, mainly because of the rapid increase in South African trade with the region. Between 1990 and 1994 South African trade with Swaziland increased by 11 percent, with Botswana by 18.6 percent, with Namibia by 40 percent, and with Lesotho by 57 percent.[104] By 1995, intra-regional trade made up 35 percent of the total trade of SADC, quite a remarkable figure compared to most other regional economic initiatives among developing countries. Further progress became possible: the SADC trade protocol of 2000 defined the goal of achieving customs-free intra-regional trade area by 2008 for 85 percent of all goods and by 2012 for the remaining 15 percent.[105]

Technically, Southern Africa was able to benefit from the Southern African Customs Union (SACU), the oldest agreement of its kind on the African continent. It came into force on 1 March 1970 between South Africa, Botswana, Lesotho, Namibia, and Swaziland, replacing the Customs Union Agreement of 1910, the oldest customs union in the world. In 2002, a reappraisal took place in light of the end of apartheid, reconfirming the status of a customs union and de facto recognizing the South African rand as the common currency for all SACU member states.[106] While Botswana, Lesotho, Namibia, and Swaziland issue their own currencies, their economic and monetary policies are aligned with those of South Africa. Its currency, the rand, is allowed to freely circulate in these neighboring countries, which makes the SACU zone a precursor for any tangible economic union in SADC.

Monetary union "is an implicit objective"[107] of SADC. The disparities among the economies of SADC member states are enormous, and their degree of interaction is limited. While Mauritius and the Seychelles have benefited enormously from tourism in the Indian Ocean region, South Africa maintains the strongest economy and best-developed infrastructure. On the other end of the spectrum, Malawi, Mozambique, and Tanzania have annual per capita incomes slightly above $600. Zimbabwe, formerly a prosperous country, has suffered enormous decline since its government embarked on a dubious authoritarian course. Angola and the Democratic Republic of Congo have been shaken by many years of civil war. New oil wealth in Angola has not yet helped to reduce widespread poverty.

The lack of convergence of the SADC economies and the low degree of complementary intra-regional trade among SADC member states has led analysts to conclude "that southern Africa is not yet ready for regional monetary integration.

Premature attempts at monetary integration could have political costs, since a failed attempt at monetary integration can generate political disagreements and recriminations that weaken prospects for coordination in trade, infrastructural development, defense and law enforcement."[108] But it remains noteworthy that the logic of monetary union and its political calculus reached SADC no more than a decade after it came into existence. The successful monetary union in the European Union and the global pull factors of region-building have resonated in Southern Africa. Now time is needed to let the potential grow.

Following the development in ECOWAS after 1990 (i.e., the establishment of its first peacekeeping force ECOMOG after the Liberian civil war), SADC created its Organ for Politics, Defense and Security Cooperation in 1996. Since its links with the SADC Secretariat were formalized in 2001, its authority has grown.[109] In 2003, the Organ for Politics, Defense and Security Cooperation was followed by the (non-binding) SADC Charter on Principles and Guidelines Governing Democratic Elections, whereupon SADC established a regional Electoral Observation Mission.[110] The Southern African Development Community has begun to express public understanding for the unalterable link between security in the region and democratic governance in each of its member states. Southern African political elites have increasingly realized that regional integration can only work if it is rooted in peace, security, and the rule of law of a democratic regional community.

The first years of this effort were rough and reflected conceptual problems as well as the conflicting interests and regime realities in the region. Conceptually, SADC member states have had great difficulty making up their minds on whether they wanted to establish a regional collective security regime along the lines of the Organization of Security and Cooperation in Europe or a mutual defense pact. In the end, they opted for a regional collective security body. Immediately, it ran into the usual problems of collective security: it can maintain security but cannot produce it. In the absence of mutual trust and escalating conflicts, a collective security system must almost inevitably run into controversy and stagnation. The SADC Organ on Politics, Defense and Security Cooperation experienced this prevailing law of politics over the conflicts in the Democratic Republic of Congo, one of its member states.

The former Zaire had been suffering under the exploitative rule of Mobutu Sese Seko, who had privatized the state in the pursuit of his personal interests. In 1997 he was ousted from power after thirty years of dictatorship and replaced by the government of Laurent Kabila, the leader of the main liberation force, the Alliance of Democratic Forces for the Liberation of Congo-Zaire. Soon, however, a new civil war broke out, in the course of which large parts of Congo were occupied by troops from Rwanda and Uganda who were less interested in peace than in access to and control of the mineral-rich regions of Congo. In 1998, Kabila called on SADC to support his government with an interventionist force.

Nelson Mandela, then South Africa's president and pro tempore the chairman of SADC, was not against a SADC peacekeeping intervention but insisted it had to operate under a UN mandate. By coincidence, Robert Mugabe, the increasingly authoritarian president of Zimbabwe, was pro tempore chairman of SADC's Organ on Politics, Defense and Security Cooperation. He organized a rather secretive meeting from which Mandela was excluded. Zimbabwe, Angola, and Namibia declared their readiness to intervene in Congo in the name of SADC. So they did, but their claim was never authorized by SADC. In fact, this operation greatly discredited the SADC peacekeeping authority.[111] Zimbabwe sent 600 peacekeepers in August 1998 but to no avail. Retrospectively, it was claimed that SADC's preventive diplomacy in the Congo conflict, though inconsistent, played an "initial peacekeeping and conflict stabilization role" that made the UN peacekeeping operation possible.[112]

The conflict in the Democratic Republic of Congo escalated beyond the control of any African force and led to "Africa's first continental war."[113] The signing of the Lusaka Peace Agreement in July 1999 was supported by SADC. In January 2001, President Kabila was killed and replaced by his son, Joseph Kabila, who "initiated a fundamental foreign policy shift."[114] The withdrawal of all foreign troops from Congo was followed by the deployment of the United Nations Mission to the Congo (MONUC) under a UN Security Council mandate of February 2000. When the Final Act of the Inter-Congolese Political Dialogue was signed in April 2003, around 3.5 million people were reported dead in the Democratic Republic of Congo, 3.4 million were internally displaced, and between 350,000 and 600,000 had escaped as refugees to neighboring countries. The first democratic election in Congo in decades was supervised by EU peacekeeping troops in July 2006. It was time for SADC to draw appropriate conclusions from its limited initial success in peacekeeping and conflict management. There was further controversy and disagreement surrounding SADC after another limited intervention had taken place in Lesotho in 1998, with the full support of South Africa. Diverging interests and the inherent clashes between democratic multilateralists and authoritarian interventionists among SADC member states has added to the mixed record of SADC's regional security efforts. A new outbreak of violence in the Democratic Republic of Congo in the autumn of 2008 challenged SADC more than ever to initiate peace-enforcing and peacekeeping measures in its most troubling member state.

The most ambitious project for democratic region-building so far began in 2005 when the SADC Parliamentary Forum was established and the first ten members of the SADC Tribunal were sworn in.[115] The SADC treaty defines the Parliamentary Forum as a "regional interparliamentary body" (Article O). Thirteen SADC member state parliaments send three delegates each. For the time being Madagascar has not joined the Parliamentary Forum, which sees its priorities in supporting good governance and observing the democratic process in SADC member states.

Headquartered in Windhoek, the Parliamentary Forum is a deliberative body with two meetings per year. Upon becoming a comprehensive regional political structure, SADC will recognize the Parliamentary Forum as its legislative body, according to the SADC treaty. For the time being, SADC is confronted with issues of democratic governance in several of its member states: Angola's last pluralistic election was held in 1992, the Democratic Republic of Congo went through its very first democratic election in 2006, and Swaziland remains an absolute monarchy.

The partially overlapping relationship between SADC and COMESA requires clarification. Since South Africa joined SADC in 1994, the Southern African Development Community seems to have become the unchallenged leader in regional community-building. COMESA has not achieved real progress in intra-regional trade, not least because its member states lack tradable goods of international quality. Prohibitive transportation costs and a lack of export credit guarantees add to COMESA's shortcomings. In the meantime, Tanzania, Mozambique, and Lesotho have renounced their membership in COMESA, while Kenya and Zimbabwe are perceived as dominating the other COMESA members. COMESA maintains its regional clearinghouse in Harare, which houses local currencies for trade transactions, enabling trade partners to safeguard foreign exchange. COMESA traveler's checks can be obtained with local currency, which allows regional interactions without resorting to the use of the US dollar as often must be done in other regions of the world. Since 1995, the COMESA Bank for Trade and Development has operated from Bujumbura. Since the launching of its free trade agreement in 2000 with the participation of Djibouti, Egypt, Kenya, Madagascar, Sudan, Mauritius, Zambia, and Zimbabwe, certain hopes have been placed on COMESA. All in all, however, its plans for a common market in Southern and Eastern Africa have remained more declaratory than real.

On the other hand, SADC has remained under-focused, under-institutionalized, and largely dominated by national bureaucracies. In order to fully use its potential and implement its plans for a common market with dimensions of a political community, SADC will have to mature in terms of political leadership and its capability to project political will and establish viable and visible projects. The high dependency on South Africa's economy is a blessing and a curse for all SADC partners. Falling export prices for South African raw materials, the emergence of substitute products, and intensified competition among sellers of ore in other regions of the world have put South Africa's strength under strain. Politically, South Africa has not really made up its mind on how far it might eventually want to go with regional integration.

Although Southern Africa maintains a wide array of associations, most notably through its Christian churches and trade unions, grassroots-level support for regional integration has remained weak. The SADC Chamber of Commerce, founded in 1999, is part of the idea to better link public and private sectors in the region. These efforts are confronted with a more general African deficit, namely the absence of a human rights culture and democratic practices, which has "done more to kill the spirit of entrepreneurship and productivity than the perceived lack of resources in many parts of Africa," as one analyst argues.[116] Any possible regional integration largely takes the form of top-down, government-induced programs. And in any case, it cannot be substituted for bad governance and economic mismanagement on the national level. Therefore, governance deficits, including the controversies related to the increasing authoritarianism in Zimbabwe and endemic corruption in various SADC member states, are a serious concern in Southern Africa. When they are considered alongside high transaction costs and general underdevelopment, deficits in infrastructure, competitiveness, productivity, and work ethic, and an overall shortage of human capacities on all levels across the region, it is clear that SADC is unlikely to be a natural success. Its member states will have to work hard to make it one.

Federators

The main driving force for region-building in Southern Africa originates in the role of South Africa in, against, and for the region. Being by far the most developed country in all of Africa, South Africa's role on the continent and in its own region will always be ambivalent, oscillating between that of an encouraging model and the source of envy and jealousy. During its decades of white minority rule, South Africa was a negative unifier. But since the end of apartheid and the start of its voluntary participation in region-building efforts, it has become a positive unifier for Southern Africa as a whole. As an enemy, South Africa was an easy oratorical target for ideological politics across its borders. This had no reasonable effect on the developmental path in the other countries of the region, but it helped to rally like-minded opposition and boost emotional politics. With the end of apartheid and its peaceful resolution, South Africa has become a recognized partner and even a moral leader for its region.[117]

This is no small blessing, as the region's dependency on South Africa is enormous. Estimates assume two to three million illegal immigrants from neighboring countries in South Africa. The enormous economic and resource dependency of the neighboring countries has helped to enforce a certain convergence of macroeconomic policies across SADC through structural adjustment programs that are in line with the interests of South Africa. South Africa also exerts political pressure on its neighbors to comply with democratic principles. For example, Lesotho's King Letsie III, in office since 1996, was forced to rescind the nonconstitutional dissolution of his country's parliament in 1998. As long as South Africa's role and reputation is recognized, its role as a positive hegemon might work and be accepted. But in the absence of solid legal SADC provisions with immediate effect for all its member states, a certain dimension of arbitrariness remains linked to South Africa's benign hegemony.

SACU, the oldest formally existing customs union in the world, played an interesting role as an engine of integration in Southern Africa. SACU represents the only real integrated economic zone in Africa, and it has been a fully integrated market since its inception. It survived apartheid, albeit only on paper. Statistics on trade flows among SACU member states are unavailable, but it is certain that the international stigmatization of the white minority rule did not prevent local cross-ethnic and cross-border trade from happening. De facto, all relevant activities of the customs union were in the hands of South African experts. Once apartheid ended, the constellation began to change. Over several years, a new SACU agreement was negotiated. Finalized in October 2002, it introduced a certain stable institutional structure into SACU for the first time. The basic principles of a fair distribution of customs levies and the need to include mechanisms of solidarity were introduced in favor of the poorest countries of the region, which are not able to maintain a customs policy on their own. SACU was thus revitalized, but it still could not resolve the main structural problems, including the overlap of membership in different integration schemes and the limited power to implement SACU or SADC decisions.

Transformations

The South African Development Community has succeeded in completely transforming its raison d'être. It turned from an instrument in the anti-apartheid struggle into a region-building scheme that includes democratic South Africa as not only a partner and member but in many ways a leader and hegemon. Meanwhile, although SADC has begun to transform itself "from a project cooperation instrument to an ambitious trade and functional integration project,"[118] this process has not been concluded. As a consequence, the relationship between SADC and COMESA remains ambiguous.

SADC's legitimacy as an engine of democratic regionalism will depend on its ability to be recognized in this role by all its member states. In 2000, SADC exerted strong pressure on the leader of Mozambique's rebel group, Renamo Dlakhama, to fully respect the democratic elections in Mozambique and to properly participate. It succeeded, and Renamo gained 60 of 250 seats in the 2004 elections. But engaging a former rebel group in the process of democratic politics is a long way from a situation in which SADC would be in a position to criticize a member state government for undemocratic behavior. SADC might feasibly consider adopting a regional variant of the African Union's mechanism of governance monitoring.

Role and Interests of the European Union

The European Union does not maintain structured and detailed relations with SADC. It considers the region important in the overall development of Africa and defines its priorities of cooperation, as usual, through its Regional Indicative Program. A special relationship exists with South Africa. In March 1999, the European Union concluded a free trade agreement with South Africa that outlines the path for a substantial removal of all custom duties over a period of ten years. The EU has declared its readiness to remove custom duties for 95 percent of all imports from South Africa, while South Africa, in turn, has declared its readiness to remove custom duties for 80 percent of its imports from Europe.

Both South Africa's SADC partners and the member states of COMESA have been rather suspicious of South Africa and its preferential bilateral deal with the EU, which does not alleviate the fear of domination of the region by South Africa. The European Union, in turn, has emphasized the potential for the whole of SADC that stems from its focused bilateral relationship with the biggest and most powerful country in the region. Vision and reality are defining the EU-SADC relationship.[119]

Prospects and Obstacles

All in all, Southern Africa has by far the strongest economic potential on the whole continent. Despite a certain decline in the colonial infrastructure, the region still has a reasonably developed infrastructure. The highest degree of minerals—oil, diamonds, gold, ore, copper, and uranium—in all Africa is located in its southern cone. But only South Africa itself is recognized as an emerging market. It generates almost 25 percent of the continent's GDP. On the other hand, several SADC countries suffer more than other regions in Africa from monostructure in their exports: oil accounts for 90 percent of Angola's exports, copper for 85 percent of Zambia's, diamonds for 78 percent of Botswana's, tobacco for 55 percent of Malawi's, coffee for 50 percent of Tanzania's, and prawns for 42 percent of Mozambique's.[120]

One of the consequences of the economic disparities in Southern Africa is continuous labor migration in the region. South Africa is so attractive to migrants from neighboring countries that it can no longer control the influx. A similar situation exists in some of the strongest economies of Western Africa, notably Nigeria, the Ivory Coast, and Ghana. The consequences of these trends are twofold. On the one hand, relatively skilled workers are leaving their home countries, where their skills are urgently needed. On the other hand, lawless behavior, and in reaction to it xenophobia, is on the rise in the recipient countries. Freedom of movement as part of a regional common market is still a challenging concept in Southern Africa, as it is in other regions of the continent. The more solid the increase in private investment is, the greater the likelihood becomes of a reasonable integration of migrant laborers. Otherwise, labor migration is likely to circumvent legal channels, largely via smuggling.

Meanwhile, SADC is confronted with the ambiguities and unresolved issues of relationship and competition that link it with COMESA. Although COMESA's overall approach is less comprehensive and has not stood the remarkable test of transformation that SADC underwent with and after the end of apartheid, the focus on free trade makes COMESA more coherent in the pursuit of its objectives. Several COMESA member states were on opposing sides in the two Congo Wars (of 1996–1997 and 1998–2003), the largest military conflict in modern African history. The 1998 war between Ethiopia and Eritrea has inflicted lasting damage on the level of trust and credibility among COMESA member states. Finally, the poorer countries of COMESA are afraid that free trade—the overall mantra of its existence—would accelerate deindustrialization because 60 percent of all manufactured goods of sub-Saharan Africa and Egypt come from South Africa. To make matters worse, Madagascar, Zimbabwe, and Kenya are the lowest-ranking countries in the World Economic Forum's African Competitiveness Report.[121] The reductionist focus on economic free trade and cooperation has not served Southern and Eastern African goals of integration and region-building well.

The SADC decision of 2008 to establish a customs union for its 170 million citizens by 2010, with common external tariffs, a common market by 2015, and a currency union by 2018, has been met with much skepticism inside and outside the region. Yet this most ambitious integration project ever is the only possible prospect for SADC to gradually turn rhetoric integration into real and deep integration. Since the beginning of 2008, twelve of SADC's fourteen member states have gradually reduced tariffs on 85 percent of their traded goods. Intra-regional trade must tangibly increase if the effect of these decisions is to be recognized. So far, Angola and the Democratic Republic of Congo do not even participate in the free trade project of SADC, to which they belong, too.

In the sphere of functional integration, SADC's first priority must be to improve the region's energy situation and the modernization of its transportation and communication facilities. Despite many documents produced by SADC, its member state governments, and the international donor community, Southern Africa—and, in fact, the whole African continent—is still confronted with a depressing deficit in so far as these essential technical preconditions for any viable region-building and sustainable integration are concerned.[122] One central issue for the prospects of region-building in Southern Africa relates to the most precious commodity in the region: water. It is a key to sustainable development and in an indirect way a key to stable democratic regionalism. "Without sustainable economic growth," one analyst wrote, "nascent democracies in Malawi, Lesotho, Zambia, Mozambique and Namibia might falter."[123] Without regular access to sufficient water and energy, one might add, they will surely falter. Certain facts underline this problem, whose resolution could become an engine for necessary and useful cooperation and integration in order to enhance mutual gains:

- Wood fuel is the main source of energy for cooking and nighttime home heating in 95 percent of all SADC and 50 percent of South African households. All countries of the broader region, except Tanzania and Zimbabwe, face a wood shortage.

• Hydropower accounts for two-thirds of all electricity in Southern Africa, with Zambia and Zimbabwe depending on hydropower for 80 percent of their electricity needs. In South Africa, hydropower generates only 1 percent of the country's energy, while 82 percent is produced by local coal. Thermal generating plants exist only in Botswana and Zimbabwe.

Experts talk of the "power of water," looking at the fifteen major river basins in the SADC region, eleven of which are watercourses shared by two or more countries. Seven of these basins are subject to some form of agreement and institutional arrangements for cooperation, development, and management of water resources. Such arrangements include the Zambezi River Authority, the Songwe River Boundary Stabilization Agreements, the Cunene River Basin Management, the Epupa Hydropower Scheme, the Okavango Commission, a mechanism for managing the river basins of the Inkomati and Maputo and their tributaries, agreements on the Limpopo and Inkomati Rivers, and multilateral cooperation on the Highlands Water Project. It is uncertain whether any of these river management projects will be able to have a transforming effect on the region.

Most promising, certainly, is the potential of the Zambezi, the fourth largest river in Africa. Shared by eight countries, a third of whose total population lives within the Zambezi River basin, the Zambezi might grow into a role similar to the Rhine River in the history of supranational cooperation in Europe and, potentially, the Mekong River in its supranational potential for cooperation and integration in Southeast Asia. For the time being, the Zambezi has become an energy provider for its riparian states. Four hydropower projects attest to the uniting potential of the Zambezi: in Kariba at the Zimbabwean-Zambian border, at the Cabora Bassa Dam in Mozambique, at the Kafue Gorge in Zambia, and in Nkula on the Shire River in Malawi.[124] SADC's Zambezi River Action Plan of 1977 was a beginning to exploit the river and its adjacent streams as a web of energy for the transformation of the region's economies. A follow-up, however, has so far not emerged.

The Southern African region is engaging increasingly in "micro-regionalism,"[125] that is to say, in subregional cooperation projects across the borders of SADC member states. The most promising example—often cited as a model for other possible cross-border "micro-region-building" processes—is the Maputo Development Corridor, a project that links South Africa and Mozambique across their respective borders. The governments of the two countries, as well as the domestic and international private sectors, are involved in what is technically labeled a "Spatial Development Initiative," "the best known and arguably most successful"[126] of its kind. The Maputo Development Corridor is a complex development scheme aimed at improving infrastructure and the conditions for socioeconomic development through regional economic integration, especially trade, "within a holistic, participatory and environmentally sustainable approach to development."[127]

All in all, a realistic appraisal of SADC must concede that the region does not fully embrace the logic of security regionalism or, especially, of democratic regionalism, its preconditions, and its consequences. Any economic integration that is intended to be profound requires political trust among its constituent parts. Practically, this is only possible on the basis of a solid democratic rule of law across all SADC member states. Based on regime symmetry, a transfer of power and authority to some elements of supranational institutions would have to follow. Only on such a basis is a lasting stability conceivable in the relationship between the dominating South Africa and the many much smaller, poorer, and dependent SADC member states. Without some form of transfer of sovereignty to autonomous SADC institutions, SADC cooperation will remain at the mercy of South Africa's will. Given the importance and power of South Africa, this might be the fate of SADC in any event—at least for the foreseeable decades. But in order to alleviate the imbalance in the relationship between South Africa and its partner countries, SADC needs some form of structurally consolidated institutional integration.

This, however, depends largely on the readiness of political leaders in the region to work together closely. Personal animosities, structural differences based on national interests and regime character, and economic disparities have often impeded a closer cooperation and a regional perspective. Democratic consolidation will be the main factor in changing attitudes. The organizational future of the Southern African Development Community is inextricably linked to the democratic quality of political life in each of its member states. SADC itself cannot generate stronger democracies. But it could set benchmarks without alienating the very national leaders it depends upon for its success. There is no simple and clear-cut solution to this paradox in SADC or anywhere else in the world.

SADC is a very young regional concept, and it would be a good first step forward if the genuine SADC institutions could be strengthened. This includes the need to strengthen the authority of the SADC Secretariat and the role of its secretary general. Normally, the secretary general is not recognized as an equal by the respective ministers of SADC member states. But it would be altogether unfair and unhistorical to judge SADC's potential and future merely by the short period of its experience since 1994. In the second decade of its existence, the European Economic Community was light-years away from, for example, qualified majority voting, a directly elected parliament, a coherent foreign policy, or a common currency. One cannot possibly expect SADC to be better than its model within such a limited time span.

It is true that the consistent success story of European integration is largely related to the original inception of an independent supranational European Commission. But no law of politics—let alone any law of nature—stipulates that regional integration must begin with a supranational commission in order for it to gain momentum and for its institutions to gain authority. SADC has opted for a different sequencing of deepening and widening. Given the daunting history of divisive controversy in Southern Africa over the legacy of colonial rule and apartheid, it is remarkable that SADC has managed to begin as a geographically comprehensive operation. Clearly there is a price to pay in terms of the depth of integration, for it began with almost the widest possible—and hence most divergent possible—membership. Yet there is also great virtue to this approach, in that it leaves no doubt about the willingness of all participating countries to engage in region-building. How to do it successfully and sustain this success is a different matter. But to look beyond the fragile state and beyond old ideological rivalries and prevailing socioeconomic discrepancies is a genuine sign of maturity. It does not equal the highly emotional talk of African brotherhood that was heard at the cradle of initial pan-Africanism. It is institution-related and by definition procedural. Hence, SADC region-building is rational and deserves to be considered promising.

SADC needs to regularly monitor the implementation of decisions, once they are taken by its institutions. Sometimes the target dates for achieving certain integration milestones seem to be highly unrealistic. More often, the absence of any monitoring of the proper implementation of the sequencing steps of a decision is the bigger and more widespread deficit. "Matching ambitions with resources" is a challenge for all region-building efforts on the African continent.[128] Ensuring that region-building in Africa is appreciated as one of "the anchoring ideals of African unity"[129] requires solid and sustainable implementation of the standards and objectives set by the authorities responsible in each of the leading integration initiatives on the continent. Whether a sophisticated academic mechanism with indexes to measure integration success can facilitate this process is debatable.[130] It is, however, astonishing that the existing attempts to offer such indexes are purely dominated by economic and monetary calculations. Without a genuine inclusion of governance as a category by which to measure the solidity and viability of region-building, the whole effort will remain insufficient and academic. As is the case everywhere in the world, community-building is not a phenomenon whose essence can be conveyed by statistics. Legitimacy as a political category will be more important in judging the degree of ownership in the idea of region-building in Africa.

Democratic regionalism may mature in Southern Africa and could even inspire other regions of the continent to follow its path. Its success will remain contingent on which functional priorities a given region sets in order to practically advance the process of region-building and integration. Prioritizing energy and infrastructure, especially with respect to transportation and communications, is the most logical solution. But the functional attempts to enhance the integration of the African economies, and hence societies, will enjoy little success if they are not based in an understanding of the importance of the idea of ownership in the process. This is not only a matter of material ownership, energy safety, and improved transportation means, as important as these are. It is also a matter of measuring the quality of human development, including health, housing, nutrition, education, and decent salaries. Ultimately, it is a political matter that can only succeed if and when human rights are safeguarded, the rule of law is established, and good governance has turned from a noble concept into a reality extending across the continent and in its anchoring regions.

Notes

1. See Daniel Bach, "The Global Politics of Regionalism: Africa," in Mary Farrell et al. (eds.), *Global Politics of Regionalism: Theory and Practice* (London: Pluto Press, 2005), 171–186; World Bank (ed.), *World Development Report 2006*, online at: http://www.siteresources.worldbank.org/ INTWDR2006/Resources/477383–1127230817535/082136412X.pdf.
2. African Union (AU), *Charter of the Organization of African Unity (OAU)* (25.05.1963), online at: http://www.africa-union.org/root/au/Documents/Treaties/text/OAU_Charter_1963.pdf.
3. See Ludger Kühnhardt, *Stufen der Souveränität: Staatsverständnis und Selbstbestimmung in der "Dritten Welt"* (Bonn: Bouvier, 1992).
4. Pascal Lamy, "The Challenge of Integrating Africa into the World Economy," in Christopher Clapham, et al. (eds.), *Regional Integration in Southern Africa: Comparative International Perspectives* (Johannesburg: South African Institute of International Affairs, 2001), 15; for a broader analysis see Economic Commission for Africa (ed.), *Assessing Regional Integration in Africa* (Addis Ababa: Economic Commission for Africa, 2004), online at: http://www.uneca.org/aria1.
5. Bach, "The Global Politics of Regionalism," 183.
6. Paul R. Masson and Catherine Pattillo, *The Monetary Geography of Africa* (Washington, D.C.: Brookings Institution Press, 2005), 146.
7. Fantu Cheru, *African Renaissance: Roadmaps to the Challenge of Globalization* (London and New York: Zed Books, 2002), 128.
8. See Daniel Bach, "Institutional Crisis and the Search for New Models," in Réal Lavergne (ed.), *Regional Integration and Cooperation in West Africa: A Multidimensional Perspective* (Trenton and Asmara: Africa World Press, 1997), 77–101; see also Piero Pennetta, *Le Organizzazioni Internazionali dei Paesi in Via di Svipullo: Le Organizzazioni Economiche Regionali Africane* (Bari: Cacucci Editore, 1998); Tesfaye Dinka and Walter Kennes, *Africa's Regional Integration Arrangements: History and Challenges*, ECDPM Discussion Paper No. 74 (Maastricht: European Centre for Development Policy, 2007), 13–15.
9. African Union (AU), *Treaty Establishing the African Economic Community* (03.06.1991), online at: http://www.africa-union.org/root/au/Documents/Treaties/Text/AEC_Treaty_1991.pdf.
10. Manelisi Genge, "Formation of the African Union, African Economic Community and the Pan-African Parliament," in Manelisi Genge et al. (eds.), *African Union and a Pan-African Parliament* (Pretoria: African Institute of South Africa, 2000), 2.
11. Stanislas Adotevi, "Cultural Dimensions of Economic and Political Integration in Africa," in Lavergne, *Regional Integration and Cooperation in West Africa*, 66.
12. Ibid., 69.
13. Cheru, *African Renaissance*, 122.
14. African Union (AU), *The Constitutive Act* (11.07.2000), online at: http://www.africa-union.org/ root/au/AboutAU/Constitutive_Act_en.htm.; see for an interpretation Henning Melber, *The New African Initiative and the African Union. A Preliminary Assessment and Documentation*, Current African Issues No. 25 (Uppsala: Nordiska Afrikainstitutet, 2001), online at: http://www.nai.uu.se/ publications/download.html?91–7106–486–9.pdf?id=24670.

15. African Union, *The Constitutive Act* (11.07.2000), Article 30.
16. Alex de Waal, "What's New in the New Partnership for Africa's Development?" *International Affairs* 78, no. 3 (2002): 463–475, 467.
17. Ibid., 468.
18. Ibid., 470.
19. Melber, *The New African Initiative and the African Union*, 7.
20. Ibid., 8.
21. African Union (AU), *The Constitutive Act* (11.07.2000), Article 4h.
22. Melber, *The New African Initiative and the African Union*, 9.
23. Paul D. Williams, "From Non-Intervention to Non-Indifference: The Origins and Development of the African Union's Security Culture," *African Affairs* 106 (2007): 253–279, 253; see also African Union (AU), *Solemn Declaration on a Common African Defence and Security Policy* (28.02.2004), online at: http://www.africa-union.org/root/AU/Documents/Treaties/text/Non%20Aggression%20Common%20Defence%20Pact.pdf.
24. See David J. Francis, *Uniting Africa: Building Regional Peace and Security Systems* (Ashgate: Aldershot 2006), 117–137.
25. Timothy Murithi, *Institutionalising Pan-Africanism: Transforming African Union Values and Principles into Policy and Practice*, ISS Paper 143 (Thswane/Pretoria: Institute for Security Studies, 2007), 4.
26. Bach, "The Global Politics of Regionalism," 181.
27. See Organization of African Unity (OAU),"*A New African Initiative merger of the Millennium Partnership for the African Recovery Programme (MAP) and Omega Plan (11.07.2001)*", in Henning Melber, *The New African Initiative and the African Union. A Preliminary Assessment and Documentation*. Current African Issues no. 25 (Uppsala: Nordiska Afrikainstitutet, 2001): App. I. Online at: http://www.polity.org.za/html/govdocs/misc/mapomega.html?rebookmark=1 and http://www.nai.uu.se/publications/download.html/91–7106–486–9.pdf?id=24670.
28. Bach, "The Global Politics of Regionalism," 177.
29. De Waal, "What's New in the New Partnership for Africa Development?", 472.
30. See Steven Grudz, "Peace, Security and the African Peer Review Mechanism: Are the Tools up to the Task?" *African Security Review* 16, no. 3 (2007): 54–66.
31. Ibid., 465; see also Keith Gottschalk and Siegmar Schmidt, "The African Union and the New Partnership for Africa's Development: Strong Institutions for Weak States?" *International Politics and Society*, no. 4 (2004): 138–158.
32. See Delphine Lecoutre, *Vers Un Gouvernement de l'Union Africaine? Maximalistes vs. Gradualistes*, IIS Paper 147 (Thswane/Pretoria: Institute for Security Studies, 2007), 4.
33. For details see Kathryn Sturman, *New Growth on Deep Rocks? Prospects for an African Union Government*, IIS Paper 146 (Thswane/Pretoria: Institute for Security Studies, 2007), 7–9.
34. See Delphine Lecoutre, "Reflections on the 2007 Grand Debate on a Union Government for Africa," in Timothy Murithi (ed.), *Towards a Union Government for Africa* (Thswane/Pretoria: Institute for Security Studies, 2007), 45–59.
35. Admore Mupoki Kambudzi, "Portrayal of a Possible Path to a Single Government for Africa," in Murithi, *Towards a Union Government for Africa*, 25.
36. Cited in Timothy Murithi, *Institutionalising Pan-Africanism*, 13.
37. For a detailed survey of the possible scenarios see African Union (AU), *Rationalization of the Regional Economic Communities (REGs): Review of the Abuja Treaty and Adoption of Minimum Integration Programme* (Addis Ababa: African Union Commission, 2007).
38. See Mir A. Ferdowsi (ed.), *Vom Enthusiasmus zur Ernüchterung? Die Entwicklungspolitik der Europäischen Union* (Munich: Forschungsstelle Dritte Welt, 1999).
39. See Françoise Moreau, "The Cotonou Agreement: New Orientations," *The Courier* 9 (2000): 6–10; Siegmar Schmidt, "Aktuelle Aspekte der EU-Entwicklungspolitik: Aufbruch zu neuen

Ufern?" *Aus Politik und Zeitgeschichte* B 19–20 (2002): 29–38; Stephen R. Hurt, "Co-Operation and Coercion? The Cotonou Agreement between the European Union and ACP States and the End of the Lomé Convention," *Third World Quarterly* 24, no. 1 (2003): 161–176; Olufemi Babarinde and Gerrit Faber, "From Lomé to Cotonou: Business as Usual?" *European Foreign Affairs Review* 9, no. 1 (2004): 27–47.

40. See Ludger Kühnhardt, *African Regional Integration and the Role of the European Union*, ZEI Discussion Paper C 184 (Bonn: Center for European Integration Studies, 2008).

41. See http://www.Europa.eu.un.org and http://www.Europa.eu.int/scadplus/leg/en/lvb/r12106.htm; see also Alexandra Krause, "The European Union's Africa Policy: The Commission as Policy Entrepreneur in the CFSP," *European Foreign Affairs Review* 8, no. 1 (2003): 221–237.

42. See Christopher Clapham, "The Changing World of Regional Integration in Africa," in Clapham et al., *Regional Integration in Southern Africa*, 59–69; Lawrence O.C. Agubuzu, *From the OAU to AU: The Challenges of African Unity and Development in the Twenty-First Century* (Lagos: Nigerian Institute of International Affairs, 2004); Dinka and Kennes, "Africa's Regional Integration Arrangements," 20–24.

43. Thabo Mbeki, *The African Renaissance, South Africa and the World*, Speech at the United Nations University, 9 April 1998, online at: http://www.unu.edu/unupress/mbeki.html.

44. Cited in Melber, *The New African Initiative and the African Union*, 5.

45. Cited ibid., 7.

46. See Paul Masson and Catherine Pattillo, "A Single Currency for Africa?" *Finance & Development* 12 (2004), 8–15.

47. Ibid., 9.

48. See Steven P. Rule, "Option for the Composition of a Pan-African Parliament," in Manelisi Genge et al., *African Union and Pan-African Parliament*, 30–37.

49. See Gumisai Mutume, "Pan African Parliament now a Reality: 'A Sign of Democratic Maturity'," *African Recovery* 18, no. 1 (2004): 19, online at: http://www.un.org/ecosocdev/geninfo/afrec/vol18no1/181africa.htm.

50. Ibid.

51. Patrick Chabal, "The Quest of Good Governance in Africa: Is NEPAD the Answer?" *International Affairs* 78, no. 3 (2002): 447–462, 456.

52. Ibid., 457.

53. See African Union (AU), *Consolidated Report: Consultative Meetings of Accra and Lusaka. CAMEI/Consol Report (1), 27–28 March 2006* (Ouagadougou: 2006), online at: http://www.iss.co.za/dynamic/administration/file_manager/file_links/CAMEIREPMAR06.PDF?link_id=4057&slink_id=8497&link_type=12&slink_type=13&tmpl_id=3.; see also Dinka and Kennes, "Africa's Regional Integration Arrangements," 16.

54. Rolf Hofmeier, "Regionale Kooperation und Integration," in Mir A. Ferdowsi (ed.), *Afrika—Ein verlorener Kontinent?* (Munich: Wilhelm Fink, 2004), 216.

55. See http://www.eac.int/treaty.htm.

56. For details see http://www.eac.int.; see also Dinka and Kennes, "Africa's Regional Integration Arrangements," 10.

57. Economic Community of West African States (ECOWAS), *Treaty of the Economic Community of West African States (ECOWAS)* (28.05.1975), online at: http://www.unhcr.org/cgi-bin/texis/vtx/refworld/rwmain?docid=49217f4c2&page=search.

58. Economic Community of West African States (ECOWAS), *Treaty of ECOWAS (Revised)* (24.07.1993), online at: http://www.comm.ecowas.int/sec/index.php?id=treaty&lang=en.

59. See Frederik Söderbaum, "Turbulent Regionalization in West Africa," in Michael Schulz et al. (eds.), *Regionalization in a Globalizing World: A Comparative Perspective on Forms, Actors and Processes* (London: Zed Books, 2001), 73.

60. See Ibrahim A. Gambari, *Political And Comparative Dimensions of Regional Integration: The Case of ECOWAS* (Atlantic Highlands, NJ and London: Humanities Press International, 1991), 47.

61. Economic and Monetary Community of Central Africa (CEMAC), *Traité instituant la Communauté Economique et Monétaire de l'Afrique Centrale(CEMAC)* (16.03.1994), online at: http://www.izf.net/affiche_oscar.php?num_page=2389.

62. See Bach, "Institutional Crisis and the Search for New Models", 77–101.

63. West African Economic and Monetary Union (UEMOA), *Traité de l'union économique et monétaire Ouest Africaine (UEMOA)* (10.01.1994), online at: http://www.banque-france.fr/fr/Eurosys/telechar/zonefr/uemoa001.pdf.

64. Abbas Bundu, "ECOWAS and the Future of Regional Integration in West Africa," in Lavergne, *Regional Integration and Cooperation in West Africa*, 35.

65. Adotevi, "Cultural Dimensions of Economic and Political Integration in Africa," 70.

66. See Michael T. Hadjimichael and Michel Galy, *The CFA Franc Zone and the EMU* (Washington, D.C.: International Monetary Fund, 1997); Jacqueline Irving, "Varied Impact on Africa Expected from New European Currency," *Africa Recovery* 12, no. 4 (1999), online at: http://www.un.org/ecosocdev/geninfo/afrec/vol12no4/euro.htm.

67. Adebayo Olukoshi, *West Africa's Political Economy in the Next Millennium: Retrospect and Prospect*, CODESRIA Monograph Series 2/2001 (Dakar: Council for the Development of Social Science Research in Africa, 2001), 4, online at: http://www.codesria.org/Links/Publications/monographs/Adebayo_Olukoshi.pdf.

68. Fredrik Söderbaum, "The Role of the Regional Factor in West Africa," in Björn Hettne et al. (eds.), *The New Regionalism and the Future of Security and Development. The New Regionalism Series vol. 4* (London: Macmillan, 2000), 135.

69. See Gambari, *Political And Comparative Dimensions of Regional Integration*, 22–27.

70. David J. Francis, *The Politics of Economic Regionalism: Sierra Leone in ECOWAS* (Ashgate: Aldershot, 2001), 71.

71. Gambari, *Political And Comparative Dimensions of Regional Integration*, 32–50.

72. See Bundu, "ECOWAS and the Future of Regional Integration in West Africa," 29.

73. Bach, "The Global Politics of Regionalism", 180.

74. Jens-U. Hettmann and Fatima Kyari Mohammed, *Opportunities and Challenges of Parliamentary Oversight of the Security Sector in West Africa: The Regional Level* (Bonn: Friedrich-Ebert-Stiftung, 2005), online at: http://www.fes.de/in_afrika/documents/SB_ECOWAS_Parl_1_1105_001.pdf.

75. Ibid., 9.

76. See Stefan Mair, "Die regionale Integration und Kooperation in Afrika südlich der Sahara," *Aus Politik und Zeitgeschichte* 52, nos.13/14 (2002): 15–23, online at: http://www.bpb.de/files/NDVA5B.pdf.

77. See Francis, *The Politics of Economic Regionalism*, 39–61. Francis, *Uniting Africa: Building Regional Peace and Security Systems*, 139–179; Bastien Nivet, *Security by proxy? The EU and (sub-)regional organizations: the case of ECOWAS* (Paris: European Union Institute for Security Studies, 2006).

78. For background see Peter M. Dennis and M. Leann Brown, "The ECOWAS: From Regional Economic Organization to Regional Peacekeeper," in Finn Laursen (eds.), *Comparative Regional Integration: Theoretical Perspectives* (Aldershot: Ashgate, 2003), 229–249.

79. Ibid., 242.

80. Ibid., 232.

81. For a critical account see Clement E. Adibe, "Muddling Through: An Analysis of the ECOWAS Experience in Conflict Management in West Africa," in Liisa Laakso (ed.), *Regional Integration for Conflict Prevention and Peace Building in Africa: Europe, SADC and ECOWAS* (Helsinki: University of Helsinki, 2002), 103–169.

82. On the general implication of ECOWAS membership on Sierra Leone see Francis, *The Politics of Economic Integration*.

83. See Bach, "The Global Politics of Regionalism," 181.

84. Marie V. Gibert, *Monitoring A Region in Crisis: The European Union in West Africa*, Chaillot Paper No. 96 (Paris: European Union Institute for Security Studies, 2007), 41.

85. Ibid., 34 and 36.

86. Ibid., 15.

87. Mohammed Ibn Chambas, *The ECOWAS Agenda: Promoting Good Governance, Peace, Stability and Sustainable Development* (Lagos: Nigerian Institute of International Affairs, 2005), 19.

88. See Francis, *Uniting Africa: Building Regional Peace and Security Systems*, 184; United Nations Development Programme (ed.), *Human Development Report 2006, Beyond Scarcity: Power, Poverty and the Global Water Crisis* (New York: United Nations Development Programme, 2006), 283–286.

89. Southern African Development Community (SADC), *Consolidated Text of the Treaty of the Southern African Development Community* (17.08.1992), online at: http://www.sadc.int/index/browse/page/120.

90. Common Market for Eastern and Southern Africa, *The COMESA Treaty* (08.12.1994), online at: http://about.comesa.int/attachments/comesa_treaty_en.pdf.

91. Francis, *Uniting Africa*, 192.

92. Ibid.; for a critical assessment of its initial phase see Laurie Nathan, "'Organ Failure': A Review of the SADC Organ on Politics, Defence and Security," in Liisa Laakso (ed.), *Regional Integration for Conflict Prevention and Peace Building in Africa: Europe, SADC and ECOWAS*, 62–102.

93. Southern African Development Community (SADC), *Protocol on Politics, Defence and Security Cooperation* (14.08.2001), online at: http://www.sadc.int/index/browse/page/157.

94. See Hofmeier, "Regionale Kooperation und Integration," 215; on the potential of SADC see also Ariane Koesler, *The Southern African Development Community and its Relations to the European Union: Deepening Integration in Southern Africa?* ZEI Discussion Paper C 169 (Bonn: Centre for European Integration Studies, 2007).

95. Cheru, *African Renaissance*, 126.

96. Masson and Pattillo, *The Monetary Geography of Africa*, 139.

97. Ibid., 145.

98. Ibid., 140; see also Padamja Khandelwal, *COMESA and SADC: Prospects and Challenges for Regional Trade Integration*, IMF Working Paper 04/227 (Washington, D.C.: International Monetary Fund, 2004).

99. See Mair, "Die regionale Integration und Kooperation in Afrika südlich der Sahara"; Martin Adelmann, *Regionale Kooperation im südlichen Afrika* (Freiburg: Arnold-Bergstraesser-Institut, 2003).

100. Fredrik Söderbaum, *The Political Economy of Regionalism: The Case of Southern Africa* (Basingstoke: Palgrave Macmillan, 2004), 103.

101. Ibid., 105.

102. http://www.sadcreview.com.

103. Söderbaum, *The Political Economy of Regionalism*, 70.

104. Ibid., 78.

105. Cheru, *African Renaissance*, 141.

106. See Bach, "The Global Politics of Regionalism," 181.

107. Masson and Pattillo, *The Monetary Geography of Africa*, 113.

108. Ibid., 128.

109. See L.M. Fisher and Naison Ngoma, *The SADC Organ: Challenges in the New Millennium*, Institute for Security Studies Occasional Paper 114 (2005), online at: http http://www.iss.co.za/index.php?link_id=3&slink_id=388&link_type=12&slink_type=12&tmpl_id=3.

110. Southern African Development Community (SADC), *Principles and Guidelines Governing Democratic Elections* (19.08.2004), online at: http://www.sadc.int.

111. Francis, *Uniting Africa*, 196–199.

112. Ibid., 209.

113. Ibid., 199.
114. Ibid., 203.
115. See http://www.sadcpf.org.
116. Cheru, *African Renaissance*, 129.
117. See Bertil Odén, "The Southern Africa Region and the Regional Hegemon," in Björn Hettne et al. (eds.), *National Perspectives in the New Regionalism in the South. The New Regionalism Series vol. 3* (London: Macmillan, 2000), 242–264; idem, "Regionalization in Southern Africa: The Role of the Dominant," in Schulz et al. (eds.), *Regionalization in a Globalizing World*, 82–99.
118. Odén, "The Southern Africa Region and the Regional Hegemon," 255.
119. See Heribert Weiland, "The European Union and Southern Africa: Interregionalism between Vision and Reality," in Heiner Hänggi et al. (eds.), *Interregionalism and International Relations* (Abingdon and New York: Routledge, 2006), 185–198.
120. See Cheru, *African Renaissance*, 132.
121. Ibid., 147.
122. For details of the potential and the gap with present efforts, see Economic Commission for Africa (ed.), *Assessing Regional Integration in Africa*. (Addis Ababa: Economic Commission for Africa, 2004), online at: http://www.uneca.org/aria1., 131–193.
123. Larry A. Swatuk, "Power and Water: The Coming Order in Southern Africa," in Hettne, *The New Regionalism and the Future of Security and Development*, 217.
124. Ibid., 234–235.
125. See Fredrik Söderbaum and Ian Taylor, "Understanding the Dynamics of Micro-Regionalism in Southern Africa," in Fredrik Söderbaum and Ian Taylor (eds.), *Regionalism and Uneven Development in Southern Africa: The Case of the Maputo Development Corridor* (Aldershot: Ashgate, 2003), 1.
126. Daniel Tevera and Admos Chimhowu, "Situating the Maputo Corridor: A Regional Perspective," in Söderbaum and Taylor, *Regionalism and Uneven Development in Southern Africa*, 35.
127. Fredrik Söderbaum and Ian Taylor, "The Role of the State," in Söderbaum and Taylor, *Regionalism and Uneven Development in Southern Africa*, 43.
128. Economic Commission for Africa (ed.), *Assessing Regional Integration in Africa*. (Addis Ababa: Economic Commission for Africa, 2004), online at: http://www.uneca.org/aria1, 4.
129. Ibid., 1.
130. Ibid., 227–249.

6

PRE-INTEGRATION IN THE PACIFIC OCEAN

Pacific Islands Forum (PIF)

Basic Facts

It may seem as if the concept of sovereignty could not have any other meaning for the island countries in the Pacific Ocean than to maintain member state status in the United Nations. More than a dozen tiny states, often consisting of several hundred islands and atolls, stretch over a huge territory bigger than the European Union. The tyranny of distance is coupled with demographic limitations. In each of the Pacific island countries in the waters between Australia, China, the United States, and the Pacific coast of Latin America, small numbers of people are living on such scarce resources as nature has given them. Around 70 percent of Pacific island citizens live in subsistence economies, though barter trade does lift them to a standard of living above poverty (defined by the United Nations as daily per capita spending of $0.55). Yet all the small island countries in the Pacific value their sovereignty and take pride in forming modern nations under extremely difficult conditions.

The question of ownership in the Pacific Ocean has been formally answered by granting independence to most territories in the Pacific. Membership in the United Nations has become the most visible expression of their claim to sovereignty. The borders of the Pacific island states are delineated by geopolitical considerations. What began with the age of Western imperialism—including its American dimension—ended with the age of decolonization. Economic discrepancies between the independent countries of the Pacific and those territories still under direct or indirect external rule are startling: the independent Pacific countries have an average per capita income of $1,229, while those islands that remain associated with the United States or New Zealand have a per capita income of $2,187. The territories with continuous dependency upon France and the US enjoy a per capita income of $22,615, eighteen times greater than that of the citizens of independent Pacific Island nations.

All of the territories of the Pacific are defined by similar geographic, demographic, and economic features. They have small populations, and their territories stretch across vast waters and include many, often hundreds, of islands and archipelagos, most of which are uninhabited. The conditions for any economic activity beyond fishing and subsistence agriculture are limited by nature, size, and distance, leading economists to talk of dis-economies of scale. Moreover, all territories in the Pacific are exposed to natural calamities. Some of the Pacific territories have a sad record of typhoons and cyclones. Most recently, some have been declared the paramount victims of global warming and climate change. Tuvalu could become the first country on earth to be extinguished because of flooding due to global warming.

Courageous seafarers from Southeast Asia discovered the waters and islands of Melanesia, Micronesia, and Polynesia more than three thousand years ago. They had settled well into the island environment, culture, and lifestyle when Europeans appeared on the horizon. Vasco Núñez de Balboa, coming from Panama, coined the term "South Sea" in 1513. Alonso de Salasar was the first European to sight today's Marshall Islands in 1526. Since Ferdinand Magellan became the first to cross the waters that he called the "Pacific Ocean" in 1522, this vast region has been truly exposed to European, and subsequently American, interests and discoveries. Alvaro de Mendana y Neyra discovered parts of the Solomon Islands in 1568, and Pedro Fernandez de Quiros reached today's Vanuatu in 1606; both had started their journey in Peru. James Cook embarked on the first of his three Pacific voyages in 1769, in the course of which he discovered what would be named the Cook Islands, as well as Tahiti and New Zealand. In 1843 France began the colonization of Tahiti, and in 1874 Great Britain started to colonize the islands of Fiji.

Ambitions in the Pacific included the Japanese presence in the region, which began with the first Japanese settler on Truk Island in Micronesia in 1892. More than ever, the Spanish-American War of 1898 projected intra-Western power struggles for hegemony into the Pacific area. Guam changed its owner and became a non-incorporated US territory, which it remains to this day. With the decline of the Spaniards, Germans appeared on the scene to claim their share of a place under the sun. Between 1985 and 1899 Samoa and several islands in Micronesia and Melanesia became German colonies. The Bismarck archipelago in the North of New Guinea, as well as parts of the Solomon Islands, the Carolines (Yap), Palau, Nauru, parts of the Marshall Islands (Jaluit), and Saipan in the Northern Marianas, were eventually included in German New Guinea, administered from Herbertshöhe, today's Kokopo, on New Britain.

With the outbreak of World War I, German possessions were immediately occupied by Japan and Australia. In 1919, German New Guinea became a League of Nations Mandate under Japanese administration and Western Samoa a League of Nations Mandate under New Zealand administration. In 1922, the Japanese established a Pacific Islands Agency in Koror on Palau. The Japanese attack on Pearl Harbor in December 1941 turned the Pacific region into a battlefield, which gradually paved the way to the independence of most Pacific islands. Following the gruesome battles of Midway and Guadalcanal in 1942 and the battle of Saipan in the Northern Mariana Islands in 1944, the path was forged to Japan's defeat. With the end of World War II, the Pacific territories formerly occupied by Japan in the course of the empire's expansion became United Nations Trust Territories under US administration. The American testing of nuclear bombs and the hydrogen bomb on Bikini Atoll in 1946 on the one hand, and the French testing of nuclear devices on Mururoa Atoll since 1966 on the other, symbolized the continuous peripheral exploitation of the region by external powers: the Pacific's remoteness from Western shores made it a suitable destination for exports of possible negative health effects of the testings.

In 1962, a chain reaction of decolonization and independence in the Pacific began when Western Samoa became a sovereign state under the name of Samoa, followed by Nauru (13,000 inhabitants) in 1968, Fiji (893,354 inhabitants) in 1970, Papua New Guinea (5,545,268 inhabitants) in 1975, the Solomon Islands (538,032 inhabitants) and Tuvalu (11,468 inhabitants) in 1978, Kiribati (103,000 inhabitants) and the Marshall Islands (59,071 inhabitants) in 1979, Vanuatu (205,754 inhabitants) in 1980, the Federated States of Micronesia (108,105 inhabitants) in 1986, and Palau (20,303 inhabitants) in 1994. The hereditary Kingdom of Tonga (112,422 inhabitants) had always been a special case: a British protectorate after 1899, it joined the United Nations in 1999.

The Pacific as a region includes two giants, both with one foot in the Pacific and one foot in Europe and the US. Australia and New Zealand had been Western settler colonies since the eighteenth century before they eventually became players in the struggle for Pacific hegemony in the twentieth century. In 1901 Australia had become independent from Great Britain, which transferred ownership over New Guinea to Australia in 1908. Australia (20.4 million inhabitants), a former British dominion, continues to recognize the British monarchy but terminated all constitutional competencies of Great Britain in 1986 (via the Australia Act). New Zealand (4.1 million inhabitants), which after World War I was the de facto colonial power over Samoa, gained full independence from Great Britain in 1948. Like many Pacific island nations it belongs to the Commonwealth of Nations and maintains the British monarch as its head of state. To this day, New Zealand claims the ultimate political control over Tokelau, Niue, and the Cook Islands. Other non-independent territories in the Pacific include New Caledonia, Wallis and Futuna, and French Polynesia (under French control), Pitcairn (under British control), Easter Island (under Chilean control), American Samoa, Guam, the Northern Mariana Islands, Midway, Baker Islands, Jarvis

Islands, Howland Islands (under US control), and, of course, Hawaii, which has been a US state since 1959.[1]

Among the regional idiosyncrasies is the division of the territory of New Guinea. While Papua New Guinea comprises 65 percent of the population of the Pacific region, the Western part of the island of New Guinea belongs to Indonesia and, as such, is part of ASEAN. Timor Leste, one of the youngest countries in the world, is considered to belong both to the Pacific region and to Southeast Asia. Officially, Timor Leste has applied for membership in ASEAN, while unofficially it wants to benefit from special EU arrangements in support of the peripheral Pacific island nations.

Ocean makes up 98 percent of the Pacific area, a territory larger than all of the landmasses of the world together. Together, the islands in the Pacific are home to 7.7 million people, and if Australia and New Zealand are included the total reaches 32.2 million people. The population of the Pacific islands is young, with 60 percent under age twenty-five. In recognition of their similarities and regional proximity, the Pacific countries and territories have embarked on a complex journey toward region-building. Sixteen of the Pacific countries and territories are members of the Pacific Islands Forum (PIF): Australia, the Cook Islands, the Federated States of Micronesia, Fiji, Kiribati, Nauru, New Zealand, Niue, Palau, Papua New Guinea, the Marshall Islands, Samoa, the Solomon Islands, Tonga, Tuvalu, and Vanuatu. They claim to represent the "Pacific Way," a term coined in the 1970s by the first prime minister of independent Fiji, Ratu Sir Kamisese Mara. He argued that the "Pacific Way" was different from Western ways of conflict resolution: nobody would be left out, decision-making would always be consensual, and the norm of non-interference would be strongly recognized. For the time being, the Pacific Islands Forum remains an embryonic expression of region-building.

Pacific region-ness was initially rooted in the colonial past of the area. Immediately following the end of World War II, the South Pacific Health Service and South Pacific Air Transport Council were created in 1946 as joint US-British-Australian projects. In 1947, France, the United States, the Netherlands, Great Britain, Australia, and New Zealand organized the South Seas Conference. It was on this occasion that the South Pacific Commission was created, based in the Australian Foreign Ministry and "designed to provide technical advice on economic and social issues."[2] The South Pacific Commission organized triennial meetings of a body of representatives of the Pacific islands administering powers, the South Pacific Conference. It was an instrument of benign semi-colonial dominance. Consequently, when Samoa became independent in 1964, the raison d'être of the South Pacific Commission was put into question. Eventually, the issue was whether Samoa would have more leeway inside or outside the South Pacific Commission. Over time, the issue changed and referred to the inevitable presence of Australia and New Zealand: would they commit themselves to Pacific cooperation and eventual integration, or would they remain undecided at best, hegemonic in their aspirations at worst?

In 1965, Fiji's Prime Minister Ratu Sir Kamisese Mara organized the Lae meeting, the first concerted effort by Pacific islanders to protest against the structures of the South Pacific Commission. For the critics, these structures ensured the ongoing dominance of the region by the colonial or former colonial powers. At the initiative of Sir Kamisese Mara, the Pacific Islands Producers Association (PIPA) was founded in 1965. Composed of Fiji, Tonga, and Samoa, it was the first self-determined structure of indigenous Pacific cooperation. It became a platform for a unified position among the member countries in order to negotiate the prices of common agricultural goods. This was to become the nucleus of authentic economic cooperation among Pacific island nations. The real effects remained limited.

Between 1971 and 1999, a precursor to the Pacific Islands Forum was in effect: the South Pacific Forum. Founded in Wellington on 5–7 August 1971, it remained a structure largely dominated by New Zealand, much as the South Pacific Commission was defined by the strong role of Australia. The South Pacific Forum was by and large a confidence-building measure. It was never institutionalized and had neither a legal personality nor a formal voting structure. Decision-making among its members was done by consensus. No issue was off the table, while all matters of common concern were discussed in a semi-formal manner. The Cook Islands, Nauru, Fiji, Tonga, and Samoa were founding countries along with Australia and New Zealand, although Australia and New Zealand were only observers until they became full members in 1972. Australia and New Zealand remained the main sources of funding for the South Pacific Forum, each of them providing over a third of the budget. Collectively, the island states contributed to less than one third of the budget. The South Pacific Forum never had a founding treaty. Over time, the seven founding members were joined by nine other members, eventually including almost all future members of the Pacific Islands Forum.

In 1972, the South Pacific Bureau for Economic Cooperation (SPEC) was set up under the auspices of the South Pacific Forum to develop some form of institutionalized economic cooperation in order "to enhance the export capacity of the islands states."[3] In 1975, the SPEC was transformed into the Secretariat of the Forum, which in 1988 was renamed the South Pacific Forum Secretariat, located in Suva on Fiji. The Secretariat was headed by a director, later renamed secretary general. This position was mandated for three yeas and was renewable. About two dozen staff members were employed to assist the Secretariat. Unlike the situation in other more established regional schemes, the budget of the Secretariat of the forum was very transparent: in 1988, it was $919,000, with Australia and New Zealand each providing 37 percent of the financing, Fiji, Nauru, Tonga, Samoa, Papua New Guinea, the Solomon Islands, Micronesia, Vanuatu, and the Marshall Islands each providing 2.4 percent, and the Cook Islands, Niue,

Kiribati, and Tuvalu each contributing 1 percent.[4] A second functional structure developed in 1980 when the South Pacific Regional Trade and Cooperation Agreement (SPARTECA) was opened, "an early attempt to adapt to the shifting forces of economic globalization."[5]

The South Pacific Forum engaged in functional and technical forms of cooperation aimed at sharpening Pacific region-ness. In 1974, a Pacific Islands News Service was established. In 1977, the forum countries founded the Pacific Forum Line, a corporate joint venture headquartered in Apia with the goal of establishing regular shipping services between all member states of the forum. Member states who contributed ships to the Pacific Forum Line were also members of its board of directors. Eventually New Zealand, Tonga, Fiji, Samoa, Papua New Guinea, and Nauru found themselves in this role. Their ships could be chartered for a regional shipping line; in other words, national ships could be leased to the Pacific Forum Line. The same structure was chosen after failed attempts to establish a regional airline: Air Pacific broke down after Fiji had taken over its planes and turned them into a national airline. This troubling experience of inadequate distribution of benefits did not repeat itself in the shipping sector. Still, until 1985 the Pacific Forum Line was unable to announce a profit.[6]

Efforts in the education sector produced mixed results, too. After Papua New Guinea had founded its national university in 1965, the Suva-based University of the South Pacific was established in 1968. It did not properly develop into a truly regional institution in line with the original ambition. In 2000, the Council of the University of the South Pacific put forward recommendations to create a distinctively pan-Pacific identity for the university.

Intrinsic Motives and External Pressures

One of the few relevant commodities of the Pacific region is tuna fishing. It was, therefore, logical to focus on regional expectations for this sector. In 1979, the Forum Fisheries Agency was established in Honiara "to serve as the chief negotiating body between forum members and Distant Water Fishing Nations on licensing agreements to fish in the large and tuna-rich Exclusive Economic Zones (EEZs) of the forum nations."[7] Fishery in the Pacific is a business with an estimated annual volume of $850 million.

Most political and visible outside the Pacific was the signing of the South Pacific Nuclear Free Zone Treaty in 1985. It was a matter of debate whether this treaty was more driven by Australia's interest in eliminating French nuclear testing from the region or by a genuine awareness of regional foreign policy interests. Eventually all forum members except Tonga signed the treaty, sending a strong message to the global superpowers regarding the small Pacific nations' interests in safeguarding their living conditions. The same approach was repeated at the

Earth Summit in Rio de Janeiro in 1992, with strong statements from the forum concerning climate change and its impact on the Pacific.[8]

The thirtieth forum summit, held in Koror on Palau on 3–5 October 1999, was a turning point for region-building in the Pacific. The South Pacific Forum was renamed the Pacific Islands Forum, broadening its perspective and membership to the north of the equator and indicating the political will of its constituent members to revamp the basis for regional cooperation and eventual integration in the Pacific. The subsequent agreement to establish the Pacific Islands Secretariat was signed on 30 October 2000 in Tarawa[9] and was then replaced by a new constitutive treaty at the thirty-sixth forum summit on 27 October 2005 in Madang. This Agreement Establishing the Pacific Islands Forum sets forth the objectives, possibly for years to come: "The purpose of the Forum is to strengthen regional cooperation and integration, including through the pooling of regional resources of governance and the alignment of policies, in order to further Forum members' shared goals of economic growth, sustainable development, good governance and security"[10] (Article II). The ultimate vision is a region "where people can all lead free and worthwhile lives." The Pacific Islands Forum considers itself "an international organization in its own right."[11] It distinguishes between membership, associate membership, and observer status. The Pacific Islands Forum pretends to be rather apolitical, which is a deliberate way to avoid addressing the two most delicate issues the PIF is confronted with: vulnerable island countries' sensitivity about retaining formal sovereignty, and the ambivalent status of Australia and New Zealand vis-à-vis the small PIF member states. This is clearly more than a matter of small and big countries joining a regional grouping. It is a matter of identity torn between the claim to equality among states and the realization of quasi-hegemonic potential by the two indispensable countries that literally keep the PIF alive, at least financially.

Beside the Pacific Forum Secretariat and the annual leaders' summit, a forum officials' committee was introduced as an Executive Committee. The PIF remains a deliberative body that excludes controversial issues and is short of legally binding mechanisms that would help to implement decisions. This can be problematic for the realization of development goals as well as for decisions on security matters. It is worthwhile to note that across the region, government officials dealing with PIF matters are creating a formal and informal network that can be compared to the elite-driven beginnings of European integration. The main engine behind the Pacific Islands Forum remains Australia, as indicated by the fact that an Australian was able to become its secretary general (Greg Unwin from 2004 until 2008). Australia and New Zealand each provide a third of the PIF budget. By and large, the constructive involvement of New Zealand and Australia in the Pacific Islands Forum cannot be questioned. They have become recognized as Pacific countries, while their own attitude toward the Pacific islands region has also broadened. They still keep one foot beyond the region but have begun to accept the islands' presence in the Pacific, just as the Pacific island states have accepted the presence of Australia and New Zealand. One telling practical indicator is the increase in the number of Pacific migrants to New Zealand, from 3,600 in 1951 to more than a quarter million today. This human dimension has contributed to a change in outlook in New Zealand.[12] To a lesser extent, the awareness of proximity to the Pacific has also grown in Australia, although it still faces the dilemma of being often perceived as big brother while it tries to play the constructive role of a simple partner country.[13]

The Pacific Islands Forum has begun to transform the structures of the former South Pacific Forum into more viable institutions of regional cooperation. When the South Pacific Forum created the South Pacific Organization Coordinating Committee in 1988, it was charged with improving harmonization and collaboration among the economic areas in the region. In 1999, the Pacific Islands Forum changed this clumsy name into the Council of Regional Organizations in the Pacific (CROP). CROP was turned into an umbrella organization for a wide array of functional institutions of regional cooperation. Among them are

- The Pacific Community, formerly known as the South Pacific Commission
- The Forum Fisheries Agency (FFA)
- The South Pacific Regional Environment Program (SPRET), de facto active since 1983
- The South Pacific Applied Geo-Science Commission (SOPAC)
- The Pacific Islands Development Program (PIDP)
- The South Pacific Tourism Organization (SPTO)
- The University of the South Pacific (USP)
- The Fiji School of Medicine
- The South Pacific Board for Educational Assessment (SPBEA)
- The Forum Secretariat, which acts also as CROP's permanent chair and provides secretarial support.

The variety of activities organized on a regional level indicates the increased awareness of the importance of regional solutions to matters of common concern in the Pacific. Although the broader civil society is still absent from Pacific region-building, on the level of government officials the Pacific Islands Forum is gaining momentum as an actor promoting Pacific cooperation and eventual integration. In the meantime, each PIF summit is confronted with the issue of creating more legal cohesion between the different functional bodies and the primacy of the PIF Secretariat. In the end, the quality of the mentioned organizations' performance will decide the degree of support they receive in coming under the legal roof of the PIF Secretariat. But there cannot be any doubt that their very existence contributes to the forming of a regional consciousness. Meanwhile, the ultimate test case for the PIF to claim primacy in Pacific region-building lies in its ability to eventually legally incorporate the functional agencies of the region.

Performance

In 2001, the Pacific Islands Forum introduced new mechanisms to advance economic cooperation. This was done under Australian pressure in response to the European Union's Agreement with the EU partner countries in the Caribbean, Africa, and the Pacific (Cotonou Agreement). Australia, unwilling to lose its own position in the Pacific, was advancing its genuine interests in the region. Except for Vanuatu, all PIF members signed the Pacific Agreement on Closer Economic Relations (PACER), followed by the Pacific Island Countries Trade Agreement (PICTA).[14] PACER is an umbrella agreement that provides the framework for PIF-wide negotiations on a free-trade arrangement no later than 2011. PACER provides for cooperation among the PIF member states on trade facilitation schemes and financial and technical assistance, including in the areas of trade promotion, capacity building, and structural adjustment. PIF-wide free trade is obviously in the interests of Australia. In theory, the PACER agreement allows all PIF member states to negotiate a free trade agreement at their own pace and without external pressure. In reality, this sovereignty-friendly promise of PACER was undermined as early as 2002, when the PIF member states jointly (with the exception of Australia and New Zealand) began negotiations for a free trade agreement with the European Union as stipulated in the Cotonou Agreement of 2000.[15]

It does not seem exaggerated to say that a certain "scramble for the Pacific" is under way between Australia and the EU. It remains to be seen whether the Pacific region will effectively develop sustainable integration through the Pacific Islands Forum. Conflicting approaches are evident: while Australia is a member of the PIF, it operates at its own will when preferring multilateral actions or bilateral arrangements with individual Pacific island countries. The European Union, on the other hand, claims to promote regional integration through its trade negotiations but does discriminate against a coherent support of the PIF by not including Australia and New Zealand in its Economic Partnership Agreement with the region.

The Pacific Island Countries Trade Agreement (PICTA) took effect in 2003. It focuses on the free trade of goods and pursues the goal of trade liberalization over a period of eight years up to 2010 for the developing countries of the region and over a period of ten years for the smaller island countries and the poorest countries of the region. The most sensitive industries can be protected in each country until 2016. PICTA does not exclude a later extension of liberalization to the fields of services and investment. The European Union perceived PICTA as a stepping stone for its own negotiation of a regional EPA with the island countries. While Australia and New Zealand were left out of the negotiations that started in 2002, they are particularly keen on seeing PICTA and PACER succeed. Motivated by their own interests in the region, they seek to legitimize their regional trade liberalization policies as genuine expressions of local efforts by the small Pacific island states "to ride the waves of economic globalization without being swept away."[16] Even in the poorest and most remote Pacific Island States, globalization has become an all-pervasive catch-word.

Trade liberalization efforts in the Pacific are a matter of continuous discussion surrounding the relationship between globalization, national autonomy, and the social consequences of free trade—much as in other regions of the world. The small and poor Pacific countries' dependency on customs duties is a particular problem. In the absence of genuine domestic tax structures (given that 70 percent or more of any island population lives on barter trade in a subsistence economy), customs duties represent a high degree of total tax revenues in the Pacific: 64 percent for Kiribati, 57 percent for Vanuatu, and 46 percent for Tuvalu, just to name a few examples. Giving up these monopolist mechanisms of resource allocation would conflict with vested interests of local governments and their clientele.

Along with a new constituent treaty of the Pacific Islands Forum, the Agreement Establishing the Pacific Islands Forum, the thirty-sixth PIF summit on 25–27 October 2005 in Madang (Papua New Guinea) endorsed the Pacific Plan. The Pacific Plan outlines the long-term objectives of the Pacific Islands Forum, presenting a wideranging long-term concept for the PIF's potential future development. According to the Pacific Plan, the PIF aims

- to enhance and stimulate economic growth;
- to promote sustainable development;
- to enhance good governance;
- to provide and increase security for all Pacific countries.

The Pacific Plan is the first comprehensive outline of region-building ambitions under the umbrella of the PIF. On principle, the Pacific Plan is non-political, technical, and aware of sovereignty implications. "Regionalism under the Pacific Plan," it states, "does not imply any limitation on national sovereignty. It is not intended to replace any national programs, only to support and complement them."[17] The defensive character of this statement is telling. On the one hand, the Pacific island countries are aware of limitation of their sovereignty. On the other hand, their national pride is as strong as their desire to improve their real living conditions. The declaratory commitment to national sovereignty and autonomy is therefore coupled with concrete and realistic proposals for pragmatic and functional cooperation. Over time this cooperation, if successful, will transform the very notion and explicit character of national sovereignty and nationhood. At the moment, the Pacific Plan has no meaning for island country citizens. Even many of the officials know about it only through the media coverage of PIF summit meetings. But the Pacific Plan is gradually becoming a point of reference for government officials across the region. With its gradual implementation, the Pacific region may not be able to escape the universal experience of other schemes of regional cooperation and integration: integration affects and transforms domestic structures.

The Pacific Plan presents very detailed discussions of different models of regionalism and regional cooperation. It argues in favor of the view that regionalism is a way to strengthen the national sovereignty of all participating countries. It does not, however, show awareness of the dialectics of regionalism as far as its ability to transform the participating political and socioeconomic systems is concerned. Regional integration is discussed as a way of lowering market barriers between countries. Its implications for norm-giving, agenda setting, and the transformation of legal and political structures still seems to be a distant idea for the Pacific. But there cannot be any doubt that this transformation will occur one day, provided the PIF governments will take their own rhetoric seriously.

The Pacific Plan introduces a wide-ranging set of concrete proposals for cooperation and, potentially, for integration. So far they are mainly technical in nature, well-meaning and driven toward improved socioeconomic developments in the area. The proposals still lack concrete implementation mechanisms, but it is interesting to note that the Pacific Plan presents reflections on the use of market tests, subsidiarity tests, and sovereignty tests to assess the usefulness of concrete cooperation and integration measures. These "tests" are introduced as criteria to judge any progress and advantage of future integration in the Pacific region. That is, the Pacific Plan introduces benchmarking mechanisms before any action or structure can possibly be benchmarked.

The list of short-term cooperation activities is practical and reasonable. It includes maritime and aviation security cooperation, trade facilitation and enhanced private-sector involvement, the creation of a Pacific ombudsman, issues of financial regulation, gender issues, customs and revenue service issues, and education matters. The long-term goal, with the help of the Pacific Plan, "is to move progressively toward a comprehensive framework agreement amongst all Forum members that includes trade (and services) and economic cooperation."[18] These words might still be vague and the details unclear and the issue of political will is the ultimate test case for turning words into reality. But in spite of all its flaws, the Pacific Plan has introduced the idea of a common market as a tool to region-building (and region-building as a vehicle to enhance the living conditions and opportunities of the people and countries in the region) to the leadership of the most remote and tiny island nations of the Pacific.

External pressure on the islands region is the ultimate driving force behind Pacific efforts in region-building. But it is remarkable that the smallest and most remote countries in the world have embarked on the long, possibly daunting and never predestined journey of regional cooperation and integration. The Pacific Plan calls for "strong partnerships"[19] helping to implement its initiatives. It outlines the possible work of a Pacific Plan action committee, the rationale of a Pacific Plan fund, and the need for a monitoring and evaluation framework. Regardless of the Pacific rhetoric on national sovereignty, the Pacific Plan suggests the need to revise the traditional and static notion of autarkic statehood that prevails among most political elites in the region. It introduces the concept of region-building, even while being unaware or suspicious of its ramifications.

The Pacific Plan wants to be judged as a "living document."[20] It will remain a point of reference that may or may not force the political leaders in the Pacific to comply with their own self-declared objectives. With the Pacific Plan, the concept of development-driven region-building is to be gradually introduced in the Pacific: "As stronger national cooperation and integration is a means to support national development objectives, the development and implementation of national policies and strategies on regionalism are an important strategic objective of the Pacific Plan . . . Implementation of the Plan in the first instance will be the responsibility of the PIF Secretariat."[21] These are clear words, after all. It remains imperative that the competencies of the PIF Secretariat be outlined in more detail, even if the PIF Secretariat will not become a regional equivalent to the European Commission with explicit supranational authority. For the time being, the PIF Secretariat itself will remain its main promoting agency, hoping that political leaders and physical realities in the region support its gradual expansion as the engine of deeper cooperation and integration. Initial discussions in the region have addressed the potential and limits of a gradual development of PIF legislation and norm-building.

For the time being, the main effect of PIF work may be the growing networking between government officials across PIF member states. In preparing PIF summits and related business, leading government officials of all PIF member states get acquainted with their neighboring states. This is a new dimension to their life. Increasingly, they can discover the challenges and opportunities of cooperation that they face in common. One of the effects of intra-regional human exchanges is the realization that stronger national institutional structures and development results are a precondition for deeper regional integration.

The lack of human capacities across the region remains a strong obstacle to broadening ownership in the work of the Pacific Islands Forum. It will remain a top-down operation. But its non-institutionalized means of consultation and cooperation may eventually lay the foundation for deeper functional integration. The PIF is becoming more professional and serious about itself. Since the 2005 PIF treaty, the fusion of the Pacific Islands Forum and the PIF Secretariat is a permanent matter of deliberation. With this process, the question of institutional integration has gained a new legal and political dimension: officials in the governments across the vast Pacific basin are studying the advantages and disadvantages of functional integration. These discussions add a new dimension to the political life in the Pacific. In indirect ways, they are equivalent to a cost-benefit analysis of regional integration.

Federators

Size, limited resources, small populations, and peripheral geography are unalterable obstacles to regional cooperation and integration in many poor, land- or sea-locked countries across the world. The situation in the Pacific is especially difficult. Under the geographical conditions of the Pacific, awareness of regional cooperation benefits can only grow gradually. Likewise, a genuine rationale for Pacific regional integration can grow only step by step. The Pacific Islands Forum will need time to define any sort of economic and political finality in its region-building effort. This should not come as a surprise, for not even the European Union has completed this task in its more than five decades of existence. But the PIF is becoming the main reference point for reflections on the relationship between national sovereignty, region-ness, welfare gains, and security enhancement in the Pacific region.

Demographic factors add to the pressure on the Pacific island countries to cooperate. Young people are demanding better education and access to the job market. If their home countries do not provide them with sustainable prospects, their emigration is inevitable. Because of the economic conditions in most Pacific island nations, more Polynesians live in Australia and New Zealand than in all of Polynesia together. Sydney and Auckland have become the biggest Polynesian cities in the world. Increasingly, Melanesians too are beginning to move to Australia and New Zealand. However, most Melanesian migrants live in the United States. The limited economic potential in the Pacific island states serves as a strong push factor. Even regional integration may only contribute to relative changes: given the natural conditions, even under the scheme of a common market, the logic of economies of scale may not necessarily work in the Pacific region. Economists talk of the Pacific dis-economies of isolation. It is telling that the rapid growth in East Asia has not reached the Pacific island nations. Even more indicative of the Pacific condition is the fact that APEC, the Asia-Pacific Economic Cooperation among the Pacific Ocean rim countries, has no place for the member states of the Pacific Islands Forum, except for Papua New Guinea, leaving the core of the Pacific Ocean disconnected from the notion of Asia-Pacific cooperation and growth-driven development. Literally, planes between East Asia and North America, and ships between Australia and Southeast Asia and the Panama Canal, pass the Pacific island countries without direct contact or involvement. Remittances sent by migrant workers to their home countries are often the only positive feature of the economic boom surrounding, yet not affecting, the Pacific island countries.

Frustration over post-independence marginalization is strong in the Pacific. Genuine failures to combine services and production more intensively add to the objective sense of peripheral neglect. The original expectations stimulated by the founding in 1946 of the South Pacific Health Service and the South Pacific Air Transport Council were not fulfilled.[22] About two dozen regional organizations and institutions have been founded in the South Pacific since then, but many are overlapping, remain inconclusive, and lack clear focus. All of them, though highly technical, are in need of a larger rationale. The underdeveloped sense of urgency among political leaders remains a daunting problem across the Pacific island nations.

Against this background, proponents of regional integration advise solid and sustainable regionalization under the Pacific Islands Forum. Regional functional cooperation and eventual integration could be the only prospect for many countries. Functional cooperation—in health care, education, air and sea transportation, disaster prevention, and common global trade policies—seems logical. It may, however, work better on subregional levels than on the overall PIF level. For the time being, a big gap prevails between strategic deliberations about the future of the Pacific and real living conditions on most islands in the region. The life of most people in the Pacific centers on family, clan, and village. Even nation-building has remained a rather lose concept in many places. The Pacific has meaning as a marker of identity, but it has no meaning yet as a perspective for common approaches to enhance living standards and opportunities.

Moreover, the consensual and deliberative approach of the PIF's work echoes the political culture of the region: it is not driven by long-term planning and decision-making. As former Cook Island Premier Sir Albert Henry put it back in 1975: "Nobody gets left out."[23] The recognition of equality of Pacific cultures and people is a valuable attribute of interaction in this part of the world. This does not mean that the Pacific region is free of conflicts and security concerns. Meanwhile, the overall effort to maintain "the Pacific Way" of peaceful conflict resolution and consensual deliberation among PIF member states falls short of properly addressing the matters of governance that might present an obstacle to sustainable development and regional cooperation. The burning issue of lack of human resources and administrative capacities adds to the regional obstacles.

The PIF addresses security issues and matters of security cooperation in a very cautious manner. This sensitivity is indicative of a proneness to getting trapped in the web of claims and pride related to national sovereignty. Yet awareness is growing that domestic tensions can negatively impact the overall region. Logically, tensions in the region ought to be tackled by joint efforts in the region. In 1980, a secessionist movement within Vanuatu was suppressed by military force exercised by Papua New Guinea with logistical help from Australia. When Fiji was shaken by a coup d'état in 1987, the then South Pacific Forum did not act. Shortly thereafter, in 1989, the region was confronted with an uprising on the island of Bougainville in Papua New Guinea. The conflict began when social issues in Bougainville—related to the fair distribution of earnings from the local copper mine—erupted, followed by violence. Estimates of fatalities vary widely between 12,000 and 50,000, but were certainly in the range of one tenth of the island's population. In proportion to the island's population, the Bougainville civil war was one of the worst civil wars in the world, yet it remained very much unnoticed. Eventually, New Zealand led efforts at "regional self help" with major peacekeeping operations from 1997 onward, after the fighting on the island had ended. The truce was monitored by a New Zealand force, including Maori soldiers and additional soldiers from various Pacific islands. This was the first experience of inter-regional peacekeeping in the Pacific.[24]

The Honiara Declaration on Law Enforcement issued by the South Pacific Forum in 1992 was the first joint statement of Pacific island countries to deal with transnational crime, including money laundering and drug trafficking that were affecting the whole region. In 1997, the Aitutaki Declaration on Regional Security Cooperation also addressed the need for regional collaboration in the fight against environmental disasters. Finally, the 2000 Biketawa Declaration broadened the security focus in its effort to develop guidelines for regional assistance on internal security matters. Bearing in mind the Fiji coup of 1987, this declaration of the Pacific Islands Forum came about at the insistence of New Zealand and Australia. For a long time, they had pressed for a self-binding commitment by their fellow PIF member countries to accept guidelines of common concern, including those of good governance, equality of all under the law, human rights, peaceful transition of political power, and respect for indigenous values. With the Biketawa Declaration, the PIF embarked on a gradual redefinition of the notion of non-interference in domestic affairs. In the long run, went the optimistic interpretation, the Biketawa Declaration could mark a promising turning point in the overall understanding of sovereignty and the effects of regional actions and failures among the political leadership in PIF member states.

Critics have argued that the Biketawa Declaration at best provides a regional umbrella for possible intervention by Australia and New Zealand. The Honiara Agreement for a cease-fire in Bougainville had indeed been brokered by the Commonwealth and not by the Pacific island countries. And when a new armed conflict broke out in Bougainville in 2000, it was again Australia and New Zealand that intervened, not the Pacific Islands Forum. Civil unrest in the Solomon Islands in 2006 was likewise not a matter of concern for the PIF. Yet the issue of domestic governance and regional stability has reached the PIF agenda. This marks the first departure from past rhetoric of non-interference, despite immediate factual implications.

The main unresolved issue for the PIF concerns its rationale: the ultimate purpose and the projection of its ambition have never been discussed in detail. Neither a definition of sovereignty nor the purpose of region-ness has been discussed by PIF leaders. Most important, they tend to avoid an open discussion about the role of Australia, without which the PIF could not exist physically. At the same time, Australia's dominating presence in the Pacific and its interests beyond the Pacific islands make Australia somewhat ambivalent about committing to regional multilateralism. The continuous vestiges of European colonial rule in the Pacific Ocean remain another sensitive matter. It seems as if the PIF member states are beginning to accept and accommodate the prevailing overseas territories, mainly those of France and New Zealand, by factually incorporating them into the PIF work structures.

The slow pace of Pacific integration seems to coincide with the self-perception of the "Pacific Way" among Pacific island nations. PIF's former Secretary General Noel Levi is cited as saying: "Here in the Pacific, we take our time."[25] Thus the Pacific Islands Forum ought to be given the time it needs to discover a practicable balance between the "Pacific Way" as a philosophy of regional identity and the need to focus on the rationale of its institutional development as a reflection of authentic region-ness. How far this region-ness goes—in terms of deepened integration and regarding its institutional design—will be a matter of gradual development. But it must be noted that this process has begun.

Transformations

The Pacific Islands Forum cannot resort to a natural rationale that would bind divergent interests by turning them into the prospect of a common future. Nor has the PIF managed to come up with a team of natural leading nations other than Australia and New Zealand. Among the island countries, Papua New Guinea and Fiji often claim the role of leadership. This is logical in terms of size, population, and resources, but other PIF member states are not necessarily enthusiastic supporters of the claim. Sometimes the bigger Melanesian countries are torn between their ambition to lead the PIF and their claim to counterbalance Australia's and New Zealand's dominant position. Papua New Guinea represents 65 percent of the island people of the region, and Fiji claims primacy over most other islands. But both countries are dwarfed economically, and in terms of political strength, by Australia and New Zealand.

Still, the potential of this constellation has been a matter of constant reflection in Melanesia. Cultural identity is stronger in Melanesia than in most other regions of the Pacific. This was a factor in the birth of the Melanesian Spearhead Group, which began as an informal cooperation when the prime ministers of Papua New Guinea, the Solomon Islands, and Vanuatu first came together in 1986. At that time, they were united in strong anti-colonial, and more so, anti-French rhetoric as they expressed their opposition to nuclear testing in the Pacific. Initially, the Melanesian Spearhead Group lacked medium-term purpose and geographical scope. When Fiji tried to join the group in 1988 to boost its stance in economic negotiations with the European Community, the other countries declined the request.

Since 2006, the Melanesian Spearhead Group has claimed to be revitalized. Since 2008 it has operated a secretariat in Vanuatu, thus initiating a certain formality for the group. With 80 percent of the Pacific population and a similar share of the Pacific economy, the Melanesian group could become an engine for the region as a whole. Its efforts to install free trade by lowering and eventually eliminating tariff barriers is more advanced than any of these trends under the PIF. The Melanesian Spearhead Group may also counterbalance Australian and EU interests. It is sometimes speculated that the Melanesian Spearhead Group could eventually even replace the Pacific Islands Forum or render it superfluous. More likely is the development of a Melanesian subregion in the PIF and thus the application of the principle of variable geometry.

In the meantime, it seems likely that external pressure will be the driving force to bring the countries of the Pacific closer to each other. This holds true for any subregional as well as for any comprehensive regional activity. The pressure of globalization is coupled with alarm at the effects of climate change on the very survival of some Pacific island countries. The evolving worldwide rise of the sea level will hit the Pacific Ocean the hardest. Tuvalu may vanish completely from the face of the earth. Environmental concerns and the extreme limits of economic activities across the Pacific have increased emigration from the islands. The advantages of remittances sent by migrant workers in support of their families clashes with the dire effects of brain drain, especially among the skilled and professional groups of society, which are typically small in numbers in the first place.

Most serious are the effects of global warming and the continuous threat posed by natural disasters. The conflict between possible gains of independent autarky on the one hand, and pooling and sharing resources and sovereignty on the other hand, is no longer merely a theoretical political matter in the Pacific region. For some of the island countries, it has become a matter of survival. The pooling of regional resources and, if possible, the activation of regional solidarity have become increasingly essential for several of the poor Pacific island countries. This insight has spread across the region, but it has not yet found a visible, let alone sustainable, application in the region's realities.

The agenda of good governance is another pressure on Pacific Islands Forum members. It interlocks domestic developments with the regional consciousness. On several occasions, the establishment of a Pacific human rights commission has been contemplated, so far without consequence. The prospect of common legislation on routine matters has been discussed, too. Common legislation by the PIF on issues related to aviation, shipping, customs, quarantine and hygiene, technical standards, and administrative procedures would be equivalent to the creation of a wide-reaching supranational law. Political opposition to such a move will remain strong among the island countries as well as in Australia and New Zealand. In the island countries, the claim to national sovereignty is strong, and the memory of the anti-colonial struggle for independence remains part of the region's collective memory. Moreover, should a regional community law evolve; it would have to address different legal traditions. While the Federated States of Micronesia, Palau, and the Marshall Islands have legal systems similar to US law and have lawyers trained in the US only, British legal traditions dominate most other parts of the region. A special case is Vanuatu, formerly a British-French condominium, where French and British legal traditions exist side by side. Obviously, the French legal system is in place in all of France's overseas territories (French Polynesia, New Caledonia, Wallis and Futuna).

For the time being, most PIF member states tend to favor the view that they need to strengthen domestic sovereignty in order to prepare for regional integration. This is certainly a more realistic position than the one that hopes for regional integration as a mechanism for rescuing weak or failing states. On the other hand, the argument favoring stronger sovereignty could also be abused to prevent regional functional and political integration from happening at all. However, it seems that the Pacific region is not involved in such a tactical game but rather is genuinely in search of the right balance between nation-building and region-building. A supranational Pacific Islands Forum law is most likely to evolve at a much later stage in the development of both processes. A joint battle cry for regional autonomy and independence could one day bring the Pacific island countries together, should they opt for a common approach to cope with the effects of globalization, demographic and resource scarcity, climate change, and peripheral neglect. This would require most of their respective leadership to transform the mental parameters that were framed during the age of decolonization into appropriate mental parameters for the age of globalization. While decolonization was fought in the name of the Western notion of sovereign statehood, the challenges and opportunities of globalization may eventually only be met through region-building based on good governance and functional economic cooperation. It will take time to advance this type of reasoning in the PIF, but it should not be excluded as an unintended consequence of the innovations that have been agreed upon so far to strengthen its profile.

As for the Pacific Plan, it remains to be seen whether it can develop into a master plan for deeper integration in the Pacific Islands Forum. The key to its success will depend on the degree of ownership its projects can generate among the people of the PIF member states. For the time being, no widely spread sense of ownership in Pacific cooperation and region-building is noticeable in the region. The Pacific Plan is part of an ongoing process of turning the challenges of the Pacific region into viable and successful region-building. Its references to economic growth, sustainable development, good governance, and security will remain rhetorical codes unless the often daunting realities in the small island nations of the Pacific are transformed through its functional projects.[26]

A new wave of reasoning about independence and sovereignty under the umbrella of regional cooperation and integration will not be an easy task in the Pacific Ocean. On the political side, it would require the development of more visible regional political structures, probably including a Pacific parliamentary assembly and the installation of permanent representatives of the PIF member states at the seat of its Secretariat in Suva. Advancing national independence through a more independent region and strengthening national sovereignty by pooling regional sovereignty—these concepts went through a long period of incubation and eventual application in Europe. One cannot expect the Pacific island countries to simply copy European structures or realize the integration paradigm faster than Europe. But eventually, why should it be denied that the Pacific Islands Forum will write its own chapter in the evolution of a constellation of mutual gains and benefits through region-building? In practical terms, the question to be answered by the PIF concerns the balance between the equitable distribution of possible gains through regional solutions and the recognition of new supranational regulatory and redistribution mechanisms in order to accommodate the poorer countries and regions, facilitate sustainable economic developments, and make a persuasive case for regional solutions with reference to practical successes. This agenda is not very different from the challenges posed to any other regional grouping around the world.

Pacific region-building would have to advance in practically all socioeconomic and political sectors: from statistics to education, from environmental protection to migration issues, from matters of good, transparent, and accountable governance to the liberalization of markets, from the potential of a regional police force to a regional nurse training institute—the list is endless. For the Pacific Islands Forum, the test of credibility in the years and, presumably, decades to come lies in the actions it takes—or fails to take—to implement as many as possible of these and other ideas. Only if successful examples of regional cooperation are set will the idea of Pacific integration take root among the people of the region. The successful development of regionalism could give the Pacific Islands Forum a legitimacy that its current diplomatic operations will most likely not gain.

There is no easy recipe for turning frustration over the peripheral place of most of the Pacific island countries in the age of globalization into a viable political agenda of region-building and regional integration. The interests of Australia and New Zealand play a mixed role in each relevant step forward. Genuine resources of the region that could be projected as tools of an enhanced cooperation are critically limited. Turning the challenges of its peripheral and vulnerable status into opportunities that can enhance the dignity of life of its citizens—this should probably be the guiding principle of all PIF efforts ahead. There is no alternative, if the PIF is to achieve its goal, namely to give all Pacific people the chance for "free and worthwhile lives," as the PIF leaders aptly formulated it in the 2005 Agreement Establishing the Pacific Islands Forum.[27] Socioeconomic success, political stability under the rule of law, and a strong degree of cultural identity—these are the benchmarks by which to judge all efforts to turn this dream into a Pacific-wide reality.

Role and Interests of the European Union

The European Union has continuously declared its genuine interest in the promotion of Pacific regional cooperation and integration. The EU is pursuing this normative interest with a broad, yet not always coherent, set of policy instruments. The European Union may not serve as a blueprint for the Pacific Islands Forum, but it is its strongest external advocate. Judging by trade relations, the member states of the PIF are not important for the European Union. The EU imports goods in the volume of €530 million from PIF countries, largely palm oil, sugar, copper, and coffee. The EU exports goods to PIF member states in the volume of €210 million, chiefly transport goods, machinery, metals, and chemical products (2002 figures). Of the total regional trade in the PIF, 66 percent is covered by Papua New Guinea, Fiji, and the Marshall Islands. EU development aid toward the Pacific island countries is focused on the promotion of regional solutions. The EU tries to administer its key projects through the PIF Secretariat, even as it maintains bilateral development aid programs with all countries of the region. Among the most prominent examples of the EU's support for regional cooperation and integration since 1992 are:

- A Regional Plan for the preparation of negotiations on the Economic Partnership Agreement, including studies, technical expertise, and coordination meetings (€1.2 million),
- Support for the PIF Representation in Geneva at the seat of the World Trade Organization (€260,000),
- Payment of costs of the negotiation of the Economic Partnership Agreement (€4 million),
- General support for regional economic cooperation (€9.2 million).

The EU considers the PIF Secretariat the Regional Authorizing Officer for cooperation with and implementation of projects under the European Development Fund. Wherever possible, the European Union claims to promote and support measures to strengthen region-building in the Pacific under the umbrella of the Pacific Islands Forum.

Following four Lomé Conventions with its partners in the Caribbean, Africa, and the Pacific region (ACP countries), the European Union and its partners concluded the Cotonou Agreement in 2000, under which the Pacific region is considered one of the EU's preferential regions. As outlined in the agreement, the European Union launched negotiations with its Cotonou partners on a specific Regional Economic Partnership Agreement. These various negotiations began gradually in 2002 and were to conclude by 2008. The Lomé mechanism of preferential trade agreements, the EU argued, had to be replaced by a new economic partnership, largely a code word for mutually recognized free trade. The EU stated that it was forced to pursue these negotiations because of World Trade Organization (WTO) provisions. Article XXIV of the General Agreement on Tariffs and Trade (GATT) provides the framework of the content defining Regional Free Trade Agreements: elimination of tariffs, liberalization of investment, competition, procurement, data collection, and intellectual property rights are the main issues of relevance. The European Union considered the Pacific Island Countries Trade Agreement (PICTA) to be a good basis for concluding a sub-agreement with the Pacific region. In reality, its main purpose was political: to promote multilateralism and to expand the presence of the EU in the region.

On 10 September 2004, the European Union and the Pacific ACP countries (the Cook Islands, the Federated States of Micronesia, Fiji, Kiribati, the Marshall Islands, Nauru, Niue, Palau, Papua New Guinea, Samoa, the Solomon Islands, Tonga, Tuvalu, and Vanuatu) started their specific negotiations on the Regional EPA. These negotiations were accompanied by controversial debates in the Pacific, but little interest—if any—in Europe. Since the group of Pacific ACP countries is not identical to the membership of the Pacific Islands Forum, it was immediately questionable how far the EPA negotiation could realistically promote region-building in the Pacific. The island countries had mixed opinions about the whole approach, although most of them agreed that it would be to their advantage to coordinate their negotiating position on a regional level. The EPA approach was criticized for being too abstract about abstract gains in combination with an abstract content, given the extremely limited trade potential of many Pacific island countries.

Australia felt that under EU pressure it would have to go ahead with its own negotiation of a new preferential trade agreement with the Pacific island countries (PICTA II). The European Union, for its part, has been unable to resolve the two main dilemmas it is confronted with in dealing with the Pacific. On the one hand, the EU wants to promote regional integration even though EPA negotiations did not recognize the Pacific Islands Forum as the EU's genuine partner, thus undermining the potential authority of the PIF as the main and unquestionable representative of the region. On the other hand, it was difficult to believe that concluding a free trade agreement between the EU, one of the leading economies, and a region as weak as the Pacific ACP countries could work as an instant win-win situation for both sides. The limited trade potential of the Pacific was consistent with the region's limited relevance to the EU's trade record. Skeptics were concerned that a virtual trade partnership would end in what Martin Holland has called "imagined interregionalism."[28]

Sustainable development, integration of the Pacific into the world economy, poverty eradication, and instruments for development—these are the main and noble goals of EU-Pacific cooperation. The European Union was represented at the opening of the negotiations in Nadi by the then EU Commissioner for Trade Pascal Lamy and the then EU Commissioner for Development Aid Poul Nielson. The Pacific Islands nations were represented by PIF personalities, Prime Minister of Fiji Laisenia Qarase, Deputy Prime Minister of Samoa Misa Telefoni, representing the Pacific group of ACP countries, PIF Secretary General Greg Urwin, PIF Trade Officials, members of the regional Pacific ACP negotiating team, and the trade ministers of the Pacific ACP countries. One of the main problems preventing a stronger rooting of the idea of regional integration in the Pacific is the limited human capacity in the administrative, political, and private-sector structures of the region. While in each of the tiny Pacific island countries only a few government officials and political leaders are involved in PIF activities—and were involved in trade negotiations with the EU—a trickle-down effect is still missing. Nobody is to blame for this, but it indicates the limited scope of strategic planning and coherent action in the Pacific island region so far. By the end of 2007, the EU had initialed an interim EPA with Papua New Guinea and the Fiji Islands. All other Pacific ACP countries were invited to conclude a similar agreement in the course of 2008, the WTO deadline, in order to avoid trade disruptions that might arise from the termination of preferential conditions granted to them under the Cotonou Agreement.

The EU aims at reaching separate free trade agreements with Australia, New Zealand, and the Melanesian Spearhead Group. The EU presence in the Pacific region is suffering from the general deficit of the EU's global role: as strong as the EU is in global trade, and as sophisticated as it is in global development matters, its political profile is not as proactive and coherent as it ought to be. It confuses partners, EU representatives, and observers alike. Most importantly, it limits the overall normative ambition of the EU policy of promoting region-building even in regions as far from Europe and as weak and vulnerable as the Pacific.

Prospects and Obstacles

If the EU truly wishes to promote region-building among the Pacific island countries, it must include Australia and New Zealand in its strategic planning. It must also come to terms with the continuous overseas presence of its member state France (and to a lesser degree, Great Britain, which, along with France and the Netherlands, is still widely present in the Caribbean). Balancing national sovereignty and the desire to strengthen the role of all participating countries through cooperation is a similar concern in both world regions. The same holds true for the quest for good governance and the fear of interference in domestic affairs, for the desire for regional identity and the external pressure to pool resources and harmonize socioeconomic conditions. The Pacific Volunteer Service launched by the United Nations Development Program in the 1980s was short-lived, yet it indicated the need and the potential for strengthened citizens' involvement in the process of enhancing region-ness. The Pacific Writer's Prize and the Festival of Pacific Arts, the South Pacific Games, the Pacific Conference of Churches under the World Council of Churches, the Pacific Foundation for the Advancement of Women, and the Pacific Islands Association of Non-Governmental Organizations are likewise contributing to this awareness.

Identity formation in the Pacific is not intuitively directed at economic and political regionalism. The traditional orientations of the people and cultures in the Pacific Ocean differ. Micronesians are traditionally oriented toward the United States and have never looked south of the Equator. All travel in Micronesia, including dozens of flights per week, is in the east-west direction. Micronesians from Kiribati, Nauru, Guam, and the Northern Mariana Islands maintain a Council of Micronesian Chief Executives as one expression of their distinctness. Melanesians, as well as Polynesians, prefer to look toward their respective south, that is to say, to Australia and New Zealand. A special position is held by the French territories in the South Pacific. Largely funded by France, a Polynesian Community was established in 1987, headquartered in Rarotonga. Although France's main EU partner, Germany, was ready to help financially, the whole effort collapsed. As an alternative, a Small Islands States Summit was launched at the initiative of the prime minister of the Cook Islands, but it had no sustainable success.

Regardless of their traditional loyalty or feelings, all island countries in the vast Pacific Ocean are confronted with a structurally similar set of problems: small populations and lack of human resources in all spheres of modern life; negative growth rates on average in spite of high levels of remittances by migrant workers and external aid input; resource depletion and loss of biodiversity; natural disasters; decline in health and education standards; institutional deficiencies and partial breakdown of law and order; inequalities and concern about human security; lack of entrepreneurial skills coupled with continued high population growth.

Regionalism in the Pacific obviously must mean more than a rigid application of institutional mechanisms. A genuine commitment to public affairs has not even reached the national level in many Pacific countries, where the people's main loyalty is to their family, their village, their clan, their island. Promoting ownership in region-building is a detached, academic concept. Yet this concept has its merits, over time at the village level too. The "Pacific Way" toward region-ness seems to have only begun. Combining and complementing identity with regional cooperation will generate unique results. The material character of regional cooperation and integration under the umbrella of the Pacific Islands Forum—with a certain idiosyncratic contribution of Australia and New Zealand—is promising. Yet it must undergo a slow and challenging process before becoming noticeable across the world. Spectacular results can hardly be expected, given the potential of the Pacific island countries.

Negotiations for an economic agreement with the European Union have not really boosted the sense of urgency and the understanding of the rationale of region-building across the Pacific. In the past, region-building was considered with skepticism. Australia's and New Zealand's rather critical attitudes toward the European Union support this skepticism. It is often described as a resentment of infringement upon national sovereignty and independent statehood. Regional integration and multilateralism are not perceived as elements necessary for modernization, development success, or strong statehood. Among Pacific island leaders this view is gradually giving way to awareness that region-building is a tool for strengthening national identity in the age of globalization. Instead of losing, the member states of the Pacific Islands Forum may be gaining from cooperating with each other. As elsewhere in the world, a cost-benefit analysis of regional—or even of subregional—cooperation is still missing in the Pacific. It should be undertaken urgently in order to support the objectives of the Pacific Plan. The discourse on regional integration is altogether a new stream of thought around the Pacific Ocean. Pre-integration has reached the wide spaces of the small islands of the Pacific and its partners in Oceania. Whether it will build up speed and momentum remains to be seen.

Notes

1. On the history of the Pacific with background material to all its territories see K.R. Howe et al. (eds.), *Tides of History: The Pacific Islands in the Twentieth Century* (Honolulu: University of Hawaii Press, 1994); Brij Lal and Kate Fortune (eds.), *The Pacific Islands: An Encyclopedia* (Honolulu: University of Hawaii Press, 2000).
2. Eric Shibuya, "The Problems and Potential of the Pacific Islands Forum," in Jim Rolfe (ed.), *The Asia-Pacific: A Region in Transition* (Honolulu: Asia-Pacific Center for Security Studies, 2004), 103, online at: http://www.apcss.org/Publications/Edited%20Volumes/RegionalFinal%20chapters/Chapter7Shibuya.pdf.
3. Ibid., 105.
4. See Michael Haas, *The Pacific Way: Regional Cooperation in the South Pacific* (New York and Westview, CT: Praeger, 1989), 9.
5. Shibuya, "The Problems and Potential of the Pacific Islands Forum," 105.
6. Ibid., 107.
7. Ibid., 106.
8. See also Ron Crocombe, *The South Pacific* (Suva: University of the South Pacific, 2001).
9. Pacific Islands Forum (PIF), *Agreement Establishing the Pacific Islands Forum Secretariat* (30.10.2000), online at: http://www.forumsec.org/userfiles/file/2000%20Secretariat%20Agreement(1).pdf.

10. Pacific Islands Forum (PIF), *Agreement Establishing the Pacific Islands Forum* (08.11.2005), Article II, online at: http://www.forumsec.org.fj/_resources/article/files/Forum%20Agreement%202005.pdf.

11. Ibid., Preamble.

12. See Jim Rolfe, "New Zealand and the South Pacific," *Revue Juridique Polynesienne* 1 (2001): 157–169.

13. See Rosaleen Smith et al., "Big Brother? Australia's Image in the South Pacific," *Australian Journal of International Affairs* 51, no. 1 (1997): 37–52.

14. Pacific Islands Forum (PIF), *Pacific Island Countries Trade Agreement (PICTA)* (18.08.2001), online at: http://www.forumsec.org.fj/_resources/article/files/PICTA%20-%20endorse%20&%20sign(18–8-01).pdf.; PIF, *Pacific Agreement on Closer Economic Relations (PACER)* (18.08.2001), online at: http://www.forumsec.org.fj/_resources/article/files/PACER%20-%20endorse%20&%20sign(18–8-01).pdf.

15. For a critical assessment of PACER see Jane Kelsey, *A People's Guide to PACER: The Implications for the Pacific Islands of the Pacific Agreement on Closer Economic Relations (PACER)* (Suva: Pacific Network on Globalisation, 2004).

16. Shibuya, "The Problems and Potential of the Pacific Islands Forum," 113.

17. Pacific Islands Forum (PIF), *The Pacific Plan* (28.10.2005), online at: http://www.forumsec.org.fj/org/_resources/main/files/Pacific%20Plan%20at%20Oct202005%20text.pdf., 4.

18. Ibid., 9.

19. Ibid., 10.

20. Ibid., 39.

21. Ibid., 38.

22. See Haas, *The Pacific Way*, 20.

23. Cited ibid., 11.

24. See Jim Rolfe, "Peacekeeping the Pacific Way in Bougainville," *International Peacekeeping* 8, no. 4 (2001): 38–55.

25. Cited in Shibuya, "The Problems and Potential of the Pacific Islands Forum," 114.

26. See also Asian Development Bank—Commonwealth Secretariat (eds.), *Toward a New Pacific Regionalism: Joint Report to the Pacific Islands Forum Secretariat* (Manila: Asian Development Bank, 2005).

27. Pacific Islands Forum PIF), *Agreement Establishing the Pacific Islands Forum* (08.11.2005), Preamble, online at: http://www.forumsec.org/_resources/article/files/Forum%20Agreement%202005.pdf.

28. Martin Holland, "'Imagined' Interregionalism: Europe's Relations with the African, Caribbean and Pacific States (ACP)," in Heiner Hänggi et al. (eds.), *Interregionalism and International Relations* (Abingdon and New York: Routledge, 2006), 254–271. The website http://www.epawatch.net monitored the EU-ACP free trade negotiations between 2002 and 2007.

7

De-integration in Eurasia

—•(0)•—

Commonwealth of Independent States (CIS)

Basic Facts

On 8 December 1991, the then presidents of Russia, Belarus, and Ukraine met in the Belovezhskaya Pushcha Natural Reserve, fifty kilometers north of Brest, and signed the Agreement Establishing the Commonwealth of Independent States (CIS). They announced that the CIS (in Russian: SNG, Sodruzhestvo Nezavisimykh Gosudarstv) would be open to all former republics of the Soviet Union and other nations sharing the goals outlined in their agreement. The dissolution of the Soviet Union had accelerated since Estonia's unilateral declaration of sovereignty in November 1988. The failed coup d'état against Mikhail Gorbachev, the president of the Soviet Union, in August 1991 had been the most dramatic event in the process unleashed by his policies of glasnost and perestroika in the mid 1980s.

Gorbachev wanted to reform the Soviet Union in order to revitalize communism. He failed on both scores. Yet until the last moment, he maintained his claim to be in control of a process that had long ago begun to devour him. Gorbachev called the founding of the Commonwealth of Independent States an illegal and dangerous anti-constitutional coup. A coup it was indeed. Its intent was to replace the centralized Soviet system that had been built up since the Russian Revolution of 1917 and the subsequent inclusion of satellite states under the umbrella of the Soviet Union with a new form of cooperative federalism. The allusion to the British Commonwealth, which emerged from the ashes of the British colonial empire, was no coincidence. The Commonwealth of Independent States, for all intents and purposes, was outlined as a new beginning of Russian power and the Russian relationship with its closest and nearest partners and allies.

On 21 December 1991, the leaders of eleven of the fifteen republics of the Soviet Union met in Almaty, Kazakhstan, and signed the Alma Ata Declaration.[1]

De facto they were endorsing the initial CIS agreement of 8 December. For the Soviet Union, the signature of the majority of the leaders of its republics under the CIS agreement in fact meant termination. On 26 December 1991, Mikhail Gorbachev formally announced the end of the Soviet Union and hence his presidency over the biggest communist empire in world history—and one of the greatest failures in the modern history of mankind.

On 6 September 1991 the Soviet government had already recognized the independence of Estonia, Latvia, and Lithuania. Together with Georgia, the three Baltic republics—reestablished after a tragic century for their people—refused to join the Commonwealth of Independent States. They wanted to be recognized as sovereign states and favored an unquestionably westward strategy, bringing them "back to Europe." This motto was often heard in Central and Eastern Europe after the recognition of the first free trade union in the communist world, Solidarnosc, on 10 November 1980, and it was expressed with even greater commitment after the fall of the Berlin Wall on 9 November 1989. It was balm to the soul of Estonians, Latvians, Lithuanians, and Georgians who felt betrayed by history and wanted to be rehabilitated as independent and Western countries. No post-Soviet regional arrangement that included Russia could be to their liking.

Nevertheless, in December 1993 Georgia joined the Commonwealth of Independent States under rather dubious domestic political circumstances, following a chaotic civil war with Russian military intervention. The CIS was both a new promise and a disguised variation of the old threat of Russian dominance over its "near abroad." Geopolitical continuity replaced ideological hegemony. In February 2006, Georgia left the CIS Council of Defense Ministers. On 12 August 2008, following a spate of conventional warfare with Russia over Ossetia and Abkhazia between 7 and 12 August 2008, Georgia withdrew its membership from the CIS, a move that became effective on 18 August 2009. Ukraine declared on 19 August 2008 that it had never ratified the CIS Statute and considered itself a participating country, but not a member state of the CIS.

Turkmenistan had already announced its withdrawal from effective membership in the CIS on 26 August 2005. The oil- and gas-rich Central Asian country instead became an associate member. Rumor had it that Turkmenistan's authoritarian, self-declared Life President Turkmenbashy (Saparmurat Niyazov) was afraid that Russia would not come to his help if a democratic movement arose in Ashgabat as had been the case during the previous two years in Georgia, Ukraine, and, albeit with limited success, Belarus. While the Western partners of Russia were increasingly critical of neo-authoritarian and centralizing tendencies in the Russian Federation, it seemed paradoxical that one of Russia's closest allies was worried about the opposite. More than anything else, this constellation indicated the convoluted political culture and strategic ambitions in the territories and societies of the former Soviet Union. Fifteen years had not been enough to replace the system of communist hegemony with anything resembling

Western-style pluralism and cooperative multilateralism. The CIS, in essence, remained an instrument for managing an unfinished transition from the termination of the Soviet Union to regulated de-integration with unclear geopolitical consequences and regime outcome.

Yet it would be insufficient to characterize the CIS as the permanent and inevitable consequence of "getting it wrong."[2] Any judgment of the CIS depends on the perspective and expectations applied. Turning the CIS into a disguised Soviet Union in new clothes might have been a desire of the old Soviet *nomenklatura* or parts of it. But in light of the complete failure of the Soviet Union—to be morally convincing as a social model, to be economically successful according to the permanent promises of the state-planned communist economy, and to be culturally legitimate as a token of freedom—this was completely unrealistic. The idea of a "commonwealth" as a shared provider of affluence was certainly driven more by a promise than by a realistic analysis of the state of the Soviet economy at the time of the breakup of the Soviet empire. However, the CIS was able to manage the transition from empire to state-building in Eurasia in a reasonably peaceful manner.

The CIS became an unintended instrument in effecting the enormous geopolitical transformation that followed the dissolution of the Soviet Union. It was more successful in what it prevented from happening than in what it was able to positively achieve. In light of the enormous potential for destruction that could have been unleashed in the aftermath of the breakup of the Soviet Union, this was probably no small achievement. No alternative to the Soviet Union could have immediately "got it right." No blueprint existed to transform a hegemonic totalitarian empire with a failed state-run, planned, and centralized economy into a pluralistic, lively rule of law–based region with a successful market economy and full respect for cultural and national diversity and the recognition of human and minority rights. At the time of the breakdown of the Soviet Union, the dangers stemming from the possible proliferation, let alone the use, of atomic weapons, or the outbreak of other forms of violence in the aftermath of the regime changes in the Soviet Union and the claims to national independence were real and horrendous. Compared with the possible escalations and alternatives, the founding of the Commonwealth of Independent States was probably one of the greatest feats of the Soviet Union and those political actors who, in its terminal phase, brought the CIS about. It was with the Russian-Georgian war of 2008 that the CIS finally lost its reputation as the frame for the peaceful management of post-Soviet conflicts among its member states.

As of 2005, the death knell of the CIS was already heard. "Even Russia, which has been the organization's driving force since its inception 14 years ago," wrote *The Manila Times*, "now seems increasingly resigned to seeing the 12-member CIS sink into irrelevance."[3] Indeed, the message had spread across the world. Three faithful Kremlin allies had been toppled by peaceful democratic revolutions between 2003 and 2005: Shevardnadze in Georgia after local election fraud, Kuchma in Ukraine after dramatic weeks of power struggle, and Akayev in Kyrgyzstan after long weeks of demonstrations against the authoritarian tendency of his rule. As these leaders were considered close to the Kremlin, their replacement undermined Russian authority in other CIS countries. It seemed as if the neo-authoritarianism of Russian President Vladimir Putin was provoking the type of counter reactions in other CIS countries that would eventually undermine the very rationale of CIS cooperation and integration. It would have been difficult for Russia to maintain hegemonic supremacy in a non-democratic CIS. Then again, in an ironic twist, it could become the most laudable and interesting challenge ahead of the Commonwealth of Independent States to manage this transformation and yet maintain—or even rediscover—the value of regional cooperation based on equality and democratic freedoms. When in 2005 a somewhat nebulous Community of Democratic Choice was created by Georgia, Ukraine, Moldova, Poland, Slovenia, Macedonia, Estonia, Lithuania, Latvia, and Romania, it seemed as if this US-sponsored initiative could turn into an antechamber for NATO membership. This would be another blow to the CIS's future.

When Armenia, Azerbaijan, Belarus, Turkmenistan, Kazakhstan, Kyrgyzstan, Russia, Moldova, Tajikistan, Ukraine, and Uzbekistan formed the Commonwealth of Independent States in 1991, they were driven by geopolitical and economic considerations based on the common history under the totalitarian Soviet regime. Managing the shift away from a centralized state planned economy and managing the inevitable demise of the Soviet empire as a strategic pillar of world order were enormous challenges. The creation of the CIS was an attempt to manage these changes "from above." It did not occur to the leaders during this transitional period that the ultimate delegitimization of their regimes was rooted in the undemocratic nature of the regimes they represented. Unlike the countries of Central Europe, the republics of the Soviet Union were primarily concerned with national freedom and left political freedom and democratic rights to later decisions. Their struggle against Soviet imperialism was equivalent to the anti-colonial struggle in many former European colonies. In analogy to their postcolonial history, the issue of national self-determination was given the highest priority, often at the expense of democratic, popular self-determination.

But inevitably, the claim to democratic freedoms had to follow. In its absence, the CIS had started as an instrument of geopolitical transition. It then became a forum and a mirror of the claim to democratic transition. It was rather successful in managing the geopolitical transition, at least up to the point of an infant constellation ready for new allegiances and global partnerships. As for its democratic quality, the CIS was inevitably confronted with this dimension of the postcommunist transformation process—and seemed to fail in transforming itself from an instrument of imperial decline into a tool of propagation of democratic regionalism. The CIS, *The Manila Times* quoted Russian President Vladimir Putin as stating in April 2005 was only created "to allow a civilized divorce" and it "never had economic super-tasks."[4] Reluctance to embrace the prospect of democratic regionalism seemed to be the limit of the CIS rationale and the horizon of most of its partners. Over time, this might turn out to be a pity and a short-sighted loss. Nevertheless, for the time being it was acceptable to laud the Commonwealth of Independent States as a regional approach to the last decolonization process of the twentieth century.

The structures of the CIS were created immediately upon its inception. The CIS headquarters was established in Minsk and chaired by an executive secretary. To date, the position has always been filled by someone from either Russia or Belarus. In 2006, former Russian Interior Minister Vladimir Rushailo became the executive secretary of the CIS. The CIS was granted coordinating powers in matters of trade, finances, lawmaking, and security. The fight against cross-border crime and support for democratization became the declared goals of CIS. For 2005, the CIS envisaged realization of a full-fledged economic union. This goal was not achieved. A symbolic expression of the desire to peacefully dissolve the former Soviet empire was the formation of a CIS team to compete in the 1992 Olympic Games in Barcelona and Albertville. These remain the only occasions on which CIS athletes have competed as a unified team.

A more serious step—and for many members of the old Soviet *nomenklatura*, the heart of the CIS—was the signing of the CIS Collective Security Treaty on 15 May 1992 in Tashkent.[5] Armenia, Kazakhstan, Tajikistan, Uzbekistan, Kyrgyzstan, Azerbaijan, Georgia, and Belarus followed Russia's invitation to join the collective security arrangement. The main normative principle of the security treaty was the collective renunciation of the use of force as an instrument of conflict resolution among CIS member states. The signatory states forfeited their right to join any other military alliance. Acts of aggression against one CIS member state were to be considered acts of aggression against all of them. In 1993, also Azerbaijan, Georgia and Belarus joined the CIS Collective Security Treaty, colloquially called the Tashkent Treaty. The CIS Collective Security Treaty came into effect on 20 April 1994.

On 2 April 1999, the presidents of Armenia, Belarus, Kazakhstan, Kyrgyzstan, Russia, and Tajikistan signed a protocol renewing the CIS Collective Security Treaty for another period of five years. At this point, Azerbaijan, Georgia, and Uzbekistan refused to sign the protocol and declared their wishes to withdraw from the CIS Collective Security Treaty. On 7 October 2002, the six remaining signatory states restructured the CIS Collective Security Treaty and renamed their ambition the Collective Security Treaty Organization (CSTO). They signed a charter to this effect in Chisinau and appointed Nikolai Bordyuzha secretary general of the new organization. In 2006, Uzbekistan rejoined the CSTO.

The officially designated language for the whole Commonwealth of Independent States is Russian, which is an official state language anyway in Belarus,

Kazakhstan, Kyrgyzstan, and of course Russia. To this day, the CIS budget completely lacks transparency. Its basic regulation is outlined in the Charter of the Commonwealth of Independent States, which was adopted in 1993 (Articles 38–40). Budgetary statistics and figures about budgetary sources and allocation are not available.

The Commonwealth of Independent States features the following organs:

- The CIS Council of Heads of State and Government
- The CIS Council of Foreign Ministers
- The CIS Council of Defense Ministers
- The CIS Inter-Parliamentary Assembly with semi-annual sessions in Saint Petersburg since 1992 as a consultative body based on parliamentary delegations from national parliaments, maintaining nine permanent commissions (legal; economic; social policy/human rights; ecology/natural resources; defense/security; culture, science, education, information; foreign policy; state-building and local government; budget control)
- The CIS Executive Committee, located in Minsk and replacing the original Executive Secretariat
- The CIS Economic Court, mandated to deal with disputes arising from matters related to the implementation of economic obligations under the CIS provisions, based on a statute of its own and located in Minsk
- The CIS Council of Border Troop Commanders
- The CIS Council of Collective Security
- The CIS Interstate Bank
- The CIS Interstate Statistical Committee.

The Charter of the Commonwealth of Independent States originated in the Almaty Declaration of 21 December 1991 and was finally adopted in Minsk on 22 January 1993. It states that "the Commonwealth is not a state and does not hold supranational powers" and that "member states are independent and equal subjects of international law" (Article 1). The purpose of the CIS is defined as providing "universal and balanced economic and social development of member states under the framework of a common economic space, interstate cooperation and integration" (Article 2). The charter is explicit about the protection of human rights, the desire for arms reduction, and coordinated security. It speaks of peace, democratization, and the well-being of all the people of the CIS. In Article 9 it explicitly grants the right to withdraw from the Commonwealth of Independent States.[6]

The most comprehensive approach to economic cooperation and integration was taken on 23 February 2003 when Russia, Ukraine, Belarus, and Kazakhstan agreed in principle to establish the CIS Common Economic Space. The idea was to create a supranational commission on trade and tariffs, based in Kiev and starting with a secretary general from Kazakhstan. Eventually the Common Economic Space might lead to a single currency, while its membership would remain open to other interested countries. On 19 September 2003, the Agreement on the Creation of Common Economic Space was signed by the presidents of the four countries "for the purpose of creating conditions for a stable and effective development of the Parties' economies and increasing the living standards of their peoples" (Article 1).[7]

The Ukrainian presidential election in December 2004 dampened the Ukraine's readiness and enthusiasm for any form of CIS integration. Instead, the Ukraine began to hope for eventual EU (and NATO) membership. As of 2005, it looked as if the concept of a Common Economic Space might merge with the Eurasian Economic Community, another shadow organization grown out of the CIS Customs Union, formally created on 10 October 2000, and headquartered in Moscow. Russia, Belarus, Kazakhstan, Tajikistan, and Kyrgyzstan made new strides to link the Eurasian Economic Community with the idea of the Common Economic Space. In 2006, they were joined by Uzbekistan, Moldova, Armenia, and Ukraine, all of which maintain observer status in the Eurasian Economic Community. The idea of economic cooperation, or even integration, remains burdened by the shock of economic decline that followed the demise of the Soviet Union. By 2006, only resource-rich Kazakhstan, Turkmenistan, Azerbaijan, and Uzbekistan had surpassed their original GDP of 1990. All other former Soviet republics remained poorer than they were in 1990.

Struggle for Motives

The Commonwealth of Independent States was never a construction of choice. It came about as a consequence of the failure to reform the Soviet Union, and as an instrument for managing the dissolution of the Soviet empire. It also came about as a tool to peacefully redesign the geopolitical landscape in Eurasia. In sum, it was an attempt to develop a strategy for a peaceful reorganization of means of cooperation and integration among the independent, sovereign nations that emerged from the ashes of the Soviet Union. Whether or not this objective was feasible would largely depend on the character of the domestic regimes in the CIS member states.

Russia and its closest allies tried to base their relationship and common interests on a new platform. The Soviet Union had been discredited when it finally proved to be an instrument of Russian hegemony over the other republics in the union. Nominally, these republics had continued to exist throughout the history of the Soviet Union, but de facto they had become victims of Soviet centralism up to a point where their ethnic identity faced serious challenges. The claim to national identity and independence was strongest in the republics with a memory of former independence and genuine cultural identity. Estonia,

Latvia, and Lithuania were most ambitious to regain national sovereignty and guarantee their ethnic survival by returning to the European family of nations. The Caucasus republics Georgia, Armenia, and Azerbaijan were ambivalent in their orientation. The ethnic minorities in the Caucasus felt that the geopolitical revision could be turned into a way of gaining independence from what they considered Russian colonialism. The outbreak of war in Chechnya became most notorious and blurred the original claim of revisionism. Yet it indicated that the reintegration of the former Soviet Union would not be a simple option even under the most federal and voluntary structure.

Many representatives of the old *nomenklatura* in Russia maintained their initial hope of using the CIS as an instrument for reactivating and reinforcing Russian hegemony by other means. They understood the neighboring republics as Russia's natural "near abroad" and sphere of influence. In arguing with those who favored Russian isolation and retreat from world politics, they maintained the desire to recalibrate Russian power and its projection by counterbalancing what they saw as the expansion of NATO-led Western intrusion into their sphere of natural interests.[8] While they were ready to recognize cultural diversity, in fact they insisted on strong Russian identity and authenticity, and were deeply convinced of Russia's rightful natural leadership in the Commonwealth of Independent States.

As a consequence, the original motives for creating the CIS were not only mixed, but were also genuinely contradictory and mutually exclusive: either the CIS would become another variant of the Soviet Union, that is to say, an expression of Russian hegemony without the communist rationale for it, or the CIS would become a voluntary mechanism for mutual benefit among independent countries based on the coherent and unobstructed recognition of the right to national self-determination. In the first case, Russia would provoke more secession, potentially even from within the Russian Federation. In the second case, Russia and its partners in the CIS would have to go beyond formal structures of regional cooperation and need to discover democratic regionalism as the main precondition for the long-term sustainability of the CIS. In 1991, none of these ultimate alternatives were resolved. In fact, hardly any of their implications were properly reflected.

In the years following the founding of the CIS, the "former Soviet republics," as they were often labeled, became increasingly occupied with their genuine state-building. In some cases, even the task of nation-building remained pertinent. Coinciding with this challenge was their overwhelming struggle with the consequences of the collapse of the communist planned economy. This task was soon labeled "transformation to market economy." Often, privatization took place in a sociological vacuum. The conditions for the formation of a bourgeois society were largely absent. Under the best of circumstances, intuitive remnants of bourgeois attitudes were present in the former Soviet Union. Several generations of communist modes of production and distribution had put their lasting mark on the notion of and the attitude toward labor, work, capital, and private property. It was misleading to assume that a communist economy could be replaced almost overnight by a market economy based on private property protected by law and recognized in its social legitimacy. The unpredictable legal situation during the initial period of transition provided an unattractive environment for substantial private investment, which largely had to be foreign in nature. The preconditions for a sustainable market economy—among them the rule of law, respect for private property, labor and acquisitive forms of work, and the infrastructure to provide an attractive environment—were absent when the Soviet Union was dissolved. It would take years to establish these factors in a sustainable manner, if they could be established at all.[9]

One of the fields in which the CIS tried to build up a strong reputation was in monitoring elections and thus create for itself a claim to progress in the democratic process. In October 2002, the CIS adopted the Convention on the Standards of Democratic Elections, Electoral Rights, and Freedoms in the Member States of the Commonwealth of Independent States and launched the CIS Election Monitoring Organization. In 2005, the CIS was put to the test four times:

- Its monitoring mission supervised the parliamentary election in Uzbekistan, calling it "legitimate, free and transparent," while the Monitoring Mission of the Organization of Security and Cooperation in Europe (OSCE), to which most post-Soviet republics belong, qualified the elections as having fallen "significantly short of OSCE commitments and other international standards for democratic elections."
- Moldovan authorities refused to invite CIS election observers for the country's parliamentary election. Russia criticized this behavior of the government in Chisinau as overly "pro-Western." The OSCE found the elections "generally in compliance" with most commitments of the OSCE and the Council of Europe.
- The Tajikistan parliamentary elections were declared "legal, free and transparent" by the CIS while the OSCE criticized the country's failure to comply with international standards.
- The Kyrgyzstan parliamentary elections were considered well-organized, fair and free, while the OSCE reported that they had fallen short of international standards.[10]

The most contested political dispute had already taken place in late 2004: the presidential election in Ukraine had to be repeated amidst strong protest against fraud. The subsequent "orange revolution" brought the pro-Western opposition into power. The dramatic development was recognized by the OSCE and its election observer mission and criticized by the CIS election observer mission.[11] In early 2005, the Ukraine suspended its further participation in the CIS Election Monitoring Organization. Since then, election monitoring has not been recognized as the expression of a credible CIS contribution to the democratization process in former Soviet republics.

For the time being, the dissolution of the Soviet Union was easier than the creation of anything new, constructive, and lasting from this process of constructive destruction. The dissolution of the Soviet empire as a geopolitical measure had immediate implications for state-building in Eurasia. Comparable with the history of decolonization in Africa, Asia, and Latin America, the domestic agenda following the state-building process was not the immediate priority. The postcolonial experience in Africa, Asia, and Latin America was echoed in Eurasia after the demise of the Soviet Union. It was coupled with the quest for a new regional arrangement.

Sometimes, the model of the European Union was mentioned as an intrinsic motive for the creation of the Commonwealth of Independent States. This might have been flattering for the European integration experience. It might even be possible, at a later stage in the development process of the post-Soviet states, post-totalitarian societies, and post-communist economies united in the CIS. But in truth, the main and unifying motive for the establishment of the CIS was the peaceful management of the Soviet Union. Given that the Soviet Union had prevented its republics from being democratic, sovereign, and capable of dealing with the new agenda of the age of globalization, it could not possibly be both the perpetrator and the cure for its deeds. In this perspective, the actors and actions of the founding fathers of the CIS were equivalent to the decolonization efforts in the mid twentieth century of the French, British, Dutch, Belgian, Spanish and Portuguese representatives. They were products of the countries and empires they represented and buried. They could initiate a new era in the former colonies and in the relation between the colonial center and its peripheries. But they were hardly able to also set the framework for a new geopolitical relationship between the constituent parts, introduce a successful normative renewal in the name of democratic pluralism, and generate the conditions for a successful socioeconomic revival beneficial to all partners. After all, the centers of Western European colonialism were geographically distant from their colonies. In the case of the Soviet empire, geographical proximity between center and peripheries, that is to say, the fate of neighborhood, would survive the Soviet Union. This made the management of its demise at once easier and more difficult, frustrating and promising.

Attempts to organize functional association, cooperation, and even integration were a logical consequence of the interconnected Soviet economies. It was a natural interest for Russian minorities in many former Soviet republics to maintain socioeconomic and cultural ties and to link their new status as a minority with their "mother culture." It genuinely served the competencies and ambitions of the former Soviet *nomenklatura* to go ahead with their lives under less tainted conditions. Whether or not it might generate sociocultural support and a form of civil society ready and willing to uphold the idea of the Commonwealth of Independent States beyond its original purpose as an agency for imperial divorce remained to be seen. While the European Union was struggling with the discrepancy between emerging institutional rigidities and loose social identity, the CIS did the same but from almost opposite circumstances: rigid structures had to be loosened, while a new social identity was to be formed by decoupling from the old one that had shaped the Soviet sphere of interest from Brest to Vladivostok in a very similar, too homogenous, and mortally sterile manner. This was a stronger motive and a greater spur to action than anybody who started the CIS journey on 21 December 1991 could have imagined. No textbook for its subsequent navigation was available anywhere in the world.

During the late days of the Soviet Union, some analysts argue, the economic interdependence among the republics of the Soviet Union was higher than the degree of integration in the European Community. In 1989, the trade exchange among Soviet Union republics was 20 percent measured against their GDP and 80 percent measured against their respective exports. The corresponding figures for the European Community were 16 percent and 60 percent.[12] Soviet centralization was the engine of the interdependencies in the Soviet Union. Often, the production was split among several republics to make all of them dependent upon Russia. The demise of the Soviet Union was anticipated by the breakdown of internal markets and schemes of production. It was followed by monetary de-integration and ambivalent forms of privatization.

Initially, intra-regional trade among CIS republics decreased. In 1994 it was not more than one third of the volume of 1989/1990. In 1993, the monetary systems of Russia and Belarus reunited. Between 1992 and 1994 Russia lent $5.6 billion to its CIS partners, but it did not really help to reactivate economic integration. In 1995, 60 percent of imports in the former Soviet republics came from third countries. Iran became the destination of 80 percent of Azerbaijan's exports, and even in the case of Belarus, 30 percent of its exports went to Poland and Germany. Yet most CIS countries remained dependent upon Russia's supply of oil and gas. While it was Russia's main aim "to keep the organism of the centralized Soviet-type industry from immediate collapse,"[13] the deintegrating factors accelerated: migration, technological decline, lack of investment, political risks, the mixed record of privatization leading to new monopolies.

In 1993, eleven post-Soviet republics signed the Treaty on Economic Union. Ukraine preferred to be an associate member. The goal was to move from a free trade zone through a customs and payment union to an economic and monetary union. In reality, hardly anything happened. In 1996, Russia, Kazakhstan, Belarus, and Kyrgyzstan moved forward by signing a Treaty on Deepening Integration in the Economic and Humanitarian Spheres, stating their readiness to immediately create a single customs territory. While analysts criticized the stagnating implementation, political leaders painted a positive picture. By the end of

1996, Kazakhstan's President Nursultan Nazarbaev announced that trade among the signatory states had increased by 50 percent. Nobody was able to properly prove the figure.[14]

A new beginning for economic integration was undertaken in 2003 with the signing of the outline for the CIS Common Economic Space to be established between Russia, Kazakhstan, Belarus, and Ukraine. Moldova had rejected it from the very beginning due to lack of clarity about the CIS perspective. At the CIS summit of 27 August 2005, in Kazan, the presidents of Russia, Belarus, Ukraine, and Kazakhstan took stock. Ukraine, under its new, pro-Western President Victor Yushenko, wanted to accept only a free trade zone and opposed any supranationality in the CIS context. Russia, Belarus, and Kazakhstan wanted to implement a common economic space with the ultimate aim of a common currency. Russia's President Putin tried to downplay the conflict by stating that the Common Economic Space was to begin with a common external tariff, only later to be followed by common fees for transit and a common electricity grid.[15] To date the CIS Common Economic Space remains a declaratory project at best.

The Primacy of Security after the Economic Bankruptcy

The original goal of Russia after the end of the Soviet Union was focused on matters of security and defense. In so far as the Soviet Union was more successful in military matters than in socioeconomic matters, the driving force of Russian planners after the dissolution of the Soviet Union was the ambition to maintain the unity of the Soviet armed forces. Respect and power projection depended on the continuous presence of a strong and unified army, regardless of the crisis of the state and the failure in the economy. Immediately following the establishment of the Commonwealth of Independent States in December 1991, Russia pushed for the CIS Agreement on Unified Armed Forces, which was signed on 20 March 1992. It was designed to ensure continuous Russian domination of the unified armed forces of the CIS. The initial agreement was followed by the CIS Treaty on Collective Security, signed on 15 May 1992 by most CIS member states. The ultimate and rather undisguised Russian motive was to transform the emerging new geopolitical landscape of Central Asia into a Russian-led security system.

On the theoretical level, it was unclear whether the Russian-led security system would be one of collective security or an outright defense alliance. Events in several former Soviet republics overtook the Russian desire to guarantee security and peace through the continuous domination of its former satellites. In so far as such an effort would have restricted the freedom inherent in any true alliance, it was not feasible in the face of the outbreak of civil war in Tajikistan and in the Caucasus. Moreover, Russia itself undermined its plans by resorting to a bilateral military agreement with Turkmenistan in 1993 intended to neutralize growing

Iranian influence there. Bilateral military agreements with trans-Caucasian countries in 1993/1994 secured Russia's presence in Georgia, Armenia, and Azerbaijan against a perceived increase of Turkish influence in the Caucasus and in the Turkic regions of Central Asia. Things fell apart, the center could not hold: by 15 June 1993, the CIS Council of Defense Ministers was recommending the dissolution of the CIS Joint Command. On 24 September 1993 the CIS heads of state decided accordingly and replaced the CIS Joint Command with the looser CIS Council of Defense Ministers, whose tasks were purely coordinating. For the next decade or so, the CIS security structures, including the Collective Security Treaty Organization formed in 2002, were not in a position to do more than organize some common military drills and gain observer status at the United Nations General Assembly.

The main challenge to the CIS security ambition followed the outbreak of civil war and the need for peacekeeping in Tajikistan and in the Caucasus. The Treaty of Tashkent made no reference to peacekeeping, even though it was signed during the Tajik civil war. The violent disputes and territorial conflicts in Tajikistan and in the Caucasus cast a shadow over the claim of a peaceful dissolution of the Soviet Union. They compelled Russia to refocus the goals of its post-Soviet security architecture. CIS peacekeeping efforts were initiated as the most pragmatic means to reestablish Russian primacy and control over its unruly allies. The effects were altogether ambivalent.

The Agreement on Groups of Military Observers and Collective Peacekeeping Forces of 20 March 1992 had paved the way for possible CIS peacekeeping operations, should they be requested by conflicting parties. The CIS Council of Heads of State would have to decide the scope of action and define the mandate. The agreement made clear that CIS peacekeeping operations could only start after a stable cease-fire was reached. The subsequent Agreement on Collective Peacekeeping Forces and Joint Measures on Their Material and Technical Supply[16] of 24 September 1993 reflected in more detail the Tajik civil war that had broken out in 1992. It created a CIS peace mission for the period from 24 September 1993 through 30 June 1995, under Russian leadership. The use of coercive force was allowed without the prior authorization of the CIS council. Russia dominated the force that went into Tajikistan: 50 percent of its soldiers were Russian, 15 percent Kazakhs, 15 percent Uzbeks, 10 percent Kyrgyzs, and 10 percent Tajiks. Russian Border Forces were also deployed along the Tajik borders to control the infiltration of Muslim rebels. In the end, Russia deployed around 25,000 soldiers in Tajikistan, which aroused new suspicion about its readiness to recognize and respect the sovereignty of its former republics and CIS partners.

Critics argue that the CIS Tajik peacekeeping experience was used as a pretext for the CIS "intervention" in the Georgian province in Abkhazia in October 1994. To this day, the intervention in Abkhazia persists. After the cease-fire Abkhazia in May 1994, the United Nations sent a peacekeeping mission to monitor the area. A separate additional CIS force was accepted in Abkhazia. Since 1994, this additional peacekeeping mission has been designated a CIS operation. But for all intents and purposes it must be considered a Russian operation aimed at supporting the pro-Russian forces in the separatist Georgian province. After the cease-fire was brokered in Abkhazia in May 1994, Georgia and Abkhazia jointly appealed to the CIS council. Russia collected the approval of other CIS member states and informed the United Nations. It was Russia's then President Boris Yeltsin who finally decided on the peacekeeping operation. No CIS body was officially involved in the decision when the CIS peacekeepers began their operation in the rebellious province of Abkhazia. In fact, this was a purely Russian operation; soldiers from other CIS member states were not involved. Since Abkhazia's presidential elections in 2004/2005, the future of the region was over-shadowed by Russian interests and internal rival factions. A truly collective CIS peacekeeping effort has never evolved in Abkhazia or elsewhere in the CIS. Instead, the peacekeeping idea developed into an instrument for projecting Russian strategic interests. This approach has never resolved the underlying causes nor ameliorated the breadth of effects of any of the protracted violent conflicts in the post-Soviet republics.

It is not surprising that several CIS countries looked for truly collective security arrangements without Russian dominance. As early as 1993, Kazakhstan's President Nasarbaev proposed a Eurasian Union with supranational competencies outside the Tashkent Treaty system. This Eurasian Union should include a Eurasian citizenship and be mandated to resolve ethnic conflicts. Russia could never agree to this proposal. Instead, Russia continues to promote security in Eurasia under the umbrella of the Treaty of Tashkent. Various declarations and decisions have been made to this effect by the Council of CIS Defense Ministers, including a Convention on Common Defense and a Project for the Development of Integration within CIS. None, however, have had lasting and visible success. The same holds true for the structure of border troops. They were never unified under a CIS command but remained loosely coordinated under the Council of Commanders of Border Troops, thus preventing outright Russian dominance. This command is based on the Treaty on Common Defense of CIS Borders of May 1995 by Armenia, Belarus, Kazakhstan, Tajikistan, Russia, and Kyrgyzstan.

The suspicion among other CIS member republics about Russia's true intentions is a consequence of Russia's behavior in Chechnya. The conflict in Chechnya that broke out in 1993/1994 has cost the lives of more than 100,000 people. Even after the controversial election that took place in November 2005—the first in eight years—any solution to the Chechnya conflict seemed far away. The victory of the United Russia Party only indicated that the controversy between Russian hegemony and Chechnyan claims for independence continued. The other CIS republics were clearly watching with suspicion and concern about this development in Russia, which clearly had more than domestic Russian consequences. Russia's CIS partner countries were translating Chechnya into a matter of trusting Russia or not.

The enormous mistrust among CIS member states escalated in the summer of 2008. On the eve of the opening of the Olympic Games in Beijing, Russia invaded Georgia. For the first time since 1991, two CIS member states were engaging in warfare. Between 7 and 12 August 2008, the hope for peace in the CIS turned into disillusionment over the nature of the Russian political system and leadership. The original fear of post-Soviet dominance by a neo-authoritarian Russia was vindicated by a visible aggression. Along with truth, trust, and hope, the remaining reputation of the CIS fell victim to Russia's neo-nationalism and power politics. Georgia's immediate withdrawal from the CIS on the day Russia announced a cease-fire in Ossetia was only logical. Ukraine followed suit by declaring itself a participating country of CIS instead of a member state.

Transformation of Motives and Causes

The Commonwealth of Independent States has undergone several metamorphoses as far as the motives, causes, and objectives of its existence are concerned. Liberating the new republics that emerged from the demise of the Soviet Union was the first and immediate driving force. Reorganizing the geopolitical space of the former Soviet Union was the next attempt. Contributing to state-building through the provision of security followed. Redesigning the framework for economic cooperation and integration seemed to be most plausible, yet attempts to this end were thwarted by the limits of trust and political will. Generating new legitimacy through democracy-building clashed with Russian strategic ambitions and the domestic return of tamed or blatant authoritarianism. All in all in the formulation of motives, causes, and objectives of collaboration under the roof of the CIS, the negative driving forces turned out to be stronger than the positive ones. The pattern of dissolution and de-integration prevailed over the ambition to reintegrate the former Soviet space.[17]

In the process of advancing from managing the Soviet decline to safeguarding national independence, the CIS started a cautious recalibration of the potential of functional cooperation and reintegration based on equal sovereignty among the constituent republics. The Russian interest in maintaining security hegemony over its CIS partners had to confront its limits once peacekeeping operations became necessary. Crisis management helped Russia to reemerge with a limited projection of its geopolitical power. But Russia failed to translate its relative strength into a new and lasting collective security alliance. The disastrous failure of centralized economic planning impeded the search for sufficient support for the rationale of reconceptualized economic integration as an expression of an honest win-win situation, and the project to transform the CIS into a viable and comprehensive economic union did not succeed. Thus the primacy of de-integration and the quest for a geopolitical reorganization of Eurasia dominated the path chosen by the CIS over all the other possible push and pull factors combined. The CIS remained driven by the failures of the Soviet Union and by external considerations beyond its power and management capacity. It never became a community of trust.

This explains the European Union's reluctance to commit itself to biregional cooperation efforts with the CIS. As long as democratic regionalism had no chance of becoming the basis of sustainable cooperation and integration in Eurasia, the European Union preferred to maintain bilateral relations with Russia and, through a differentiated set of instruments, with the other republics or subregions of the CIS. After the European Community and the Soviet Union signed a trade and cooperation agreement on 18 December 1989, the course was set to support the transformation effort in the Commonwealth of Independent States, once it began to exist. As of 1991, the EU granted technical assistance to all CIS countries under the Technical Assistance for the CIS (TACIS) program. During the 1990s €4.2 billion went toward reconstructing public enterprises; promoting privatization; modernizing agriculture, infrastructure, the energy sector, telecommunications, and transportation; enhancing nuclear safety; protecting the environment; and reforming public administration, social services, and education. The TACIS program continued during the first decade of the twenty-first century, with €3.1 billion spent on its aims in the period from 2000 to 2006. New priorities included the development of subregions within the CIS republics and conditionality measures relating to the state of human rights in CIS republics.

The EU's relationship with Russia remained a mixed bag of hope and frustration, promise and sober realism. The EU-Russia Cooperation and Partnership Agreement was signed in 1994 and came into force on 1 December 1997. Unless replaced by a new arrangement, it was to be prolonged on a yearly basis. This was relevant because the idea to replace the original cooperation agreement after ten years failed in 2007, when EU-Russia relations soured, becoming more tense. The EU was increasingly critical of Russia's domestic political system. During past years, the European Union had supported the development of a market economy, the rule of law, and the democratic reform process. EU support programs such as TACIS were matched with a political dialogue between the leadership of the EU and Russia. After several years of experience, the EU was confronted with two main limits of its efforts: first, Russia did not want to be treated as a developing country, although its overall situation had declined to that level. And second, Russia was not ready to accept political conditionality regarding, for instance, its actions in the Chechnya conflict. Russia was highly sensitive to any external activity that could undermine its claim to be an autonomous world power. Reasonable predictability of Russia's relationship with the West coincided with increasing authoritarianism and lack of transparency inside Russia.

Gradually, the European Union embarked on a new strategic approach to its relations with the CIS. In May 2004, based on an EU strategy paper, the concept of the European Neighborhood Policy was introduced.[18] By 2007, as part of its overall recalibration of neighborhood relations, the TACIS program was replaced by a new European Neighborhood and Partnership Instrument (ENPI). The new, more focused and policy-driven approach introduces enhanced elements of specific cooperation with each individual partner country. The EU is not pursuing a coherent policy toward the CIS as such. Rather, it has begun to "discover" Central Asia on the one hand and the Southern Caucasus on the other as targets of a genuine projection of future policy strategies. While the European Union developed a Central Asian Strategy in 2007, it did not explicitly develop EU policy vis-à-vis the Commonwealth of Independent States. For the European Union, the CIS had lost is attraction as a pole of biregional relations. Instead, bilateral policies with Russia were coupled with an enhanced neighborhood engagement vis-à-vis Ukraine, Moldova, Georgia, Armenia, and Azerbaijan.

As far as Russia is concerned, since 2005 the EU has promoted four EU-Russia common spaces: Common Economic Space; Common Space of Freedom, Security and Justice; Common Space on External Security; and Common Space on Research, Education and Culture. This "space-building," as difficult as it proved to be, was a reflection of ambivalence. The EU was ambiguous in its long-term strategy toward Russia: should Russia become a privileged bilateral partner, or the center of the CIS as a genuine integration scheme, or something in between—and in what order? This uncertainty in its strategy toward Russia was echoed in the EU attitude toward the CIS and its respective subregions. The EU's growing energy dependency on Russia reduced the scope of strategic action while also forcing the EU to intensify the search for a common energy policy.

The Central Asian republics of the CIS, in turn, were losing interest in the EU. This happened despite the growing importance of their geopolitical role, for instance in the stabilization of Iraq and Afghanistan. While US policies were emphasizing the geopolitical role of Central Asia and therefore increasingly promoting NATO membership for Ukraine and Georgia, the European Union receded to the management of its own immediate, still fuzzy, border areas. The EU was trapped, for it did not seem to have an alternative that left room for options beyond the concepts of biregionalism and neighborhood policy. In particular, the EU could not promote regionalism in the CIS as long as its internal preconditions were weak or even absent, democratic trust being the basis for the formulation of common objectives in the first place.

The domestic situation in Russia looked increasingly dismal as far as the democratic prospects of its ongoing transformation were concerned. The CIS had failed to become "a tool of post-Soviet sociocultural transformation."[19] Instead of searching for a new cultural model as the basis for economic or even political integration, the constituent parts of the CIS were drifting apart and starting to connect with new partners beyond the former Soviet peripheries. Ukraine struggled to emancipate itself from a post-Soviet trend of authoritarian monopolist capitalism and establish a pluralistic democratic political culture that would enable it to join NATO and gradually connect with the European Union. Georgia and, to a lesser degree, Moldova, followed the same strategy.

Azerbaijan and the Central Asian republics were torn between modernization and Westernization, rediscovery of Islamic, Turkic, or both traces in their identity, and their proximity to China and Western Asia while increasingly alienating themselves from Western notions of democracy. Armenia and Belarus remained the closest allies of Russia, obviously not a voluntary choice but rather the reflection of the absence of truly liberating political emancipation and of their neglect by the European Union in the case of Belarus, and by Turkey in the case of Armenia. The lack of democratic emancipation in Armenia and Belarus was the genuine fault of their domestic elites, but in both countries it was also a consequence of their Western neighbors' disregard.

Under these conditions, several fundamental preconditions for positive regionalism remained missing in the sphere of the CIS. In particular, the voluntary will to seriously work together, mechanisms for the creation of a common law and its implementation, and most importantly, the sense of purpose and direction have to be mentioned. The communicative integration in the Soviet Union was strong, mainly based on the use of the Russian language. This advantage did not turn into a basis for a new normative integration after the demise of the Soviet Union. Loose intergovernmentalism in order to manage the de-integration of the Soviet empire was the best possible option the CIS could realize. It did not embark on new supranational mechanisms. The prevailing high degree of suspicion about Russia's will to hegemony could not be balanced by rational insights into the advantages of functional cooperation and integration. The CIS began as a regional scheme to peacefully dissolve a forced region. It could not reinvent itself as the engine to maintain this region under conditions of democratic regionalism. The lack of democratic freedom helped cause the downfall of the Soviet Union, and the weakness of democratic freedom obstructed the evolution of the Commonwealth of Independent States. Finally, even the rationale of peacekeeping disappeared from the CIS.

The CIS may only survive as a selective forum for sectoral cooperation. It is hard to imagine that it might become an engine for democratic region-building. Increasingly, the politics of oil and gas defines the geopolitical and geo-economic position of the Central Asian and Caucasian republics of the CIS. This constellation may theoretically serve as a unifying force. In practice, all CIS member states with oil and gas reserves tend to utilize them to strengthen their own independence and enhance their prospective economic well-being. The Baku-Tiflis-Ceyhan pipeline, operating since 2005, has contributed to the de-integration of the CIS region by circumnavigating Russia as a monopolist state of transit for all

Caspian Sea oil. Since 2006 the Deniz gas pipeline, which connects the largest natural gas field in Azerbaijan with Georgia and Turkey, has the same purpose, function, and effect. Oil and gas in the CIS are disintegrating factors, not integrating resources.

The role of Russian minorities across the CIS could be categorized similarly. When the Soviet Union collapsed, 25 million Russians were living outside Russia. They constitute different degrees of minorities, from 6 percent in Georgia and 8 percent in Uzbekistan to 21 percent in Kyrgyzstan and 37 percent in Kazakhstan. Under Russian pressure, Turkmenistan and Tajikistan accepted dual citizenship in 1994, thus recognizing the rights of their Russian minorities. But on the whole, the existence of Russian minorities in other CIS member states has rather had an opposite effect: instead of contributing to a reinvigoration of a communicative sphere in the CIS, they instigated a stronger interest in the fate of ethnic minorities inside Russia. Twenty-one of the eighty-eight federal subjects in today's Russia are considered ethnic republics: Adygea, Altai, Bashkortostan, Buryatia, Chechnya, Dagestan, Ingushetia, Kabardino-Balkaria, Kalmykia, Karachay-Cherkessia, Karelia, Komi, Mari El, Mordovia, Sakha, North Ossetia, Tatarstan, Tuva, Udmurtia, Khakassia, and Chuvashia have returned at least to the registers of sophisticated books on Russia, if not to the agenda of geopolitical realities of the twenty-first century.

Democratic regionalism could work in the CIS only if there were a fresh start in several of its key member states. Only such a second beginning could provide a lasting rationale for any Eurasian regional integration project. But a second series of postcommunist, or rather, post–postcommunist-authoritarian transformations seems unlikely across the CIS. Some of its member states have succeeded in democratizing. As a consequence, Ukraine, Georgia, and Kyrgyzstan have increasingly turned away from the centrality of CIS regionalism in search of outlets for their respective national ambitions beyond the CIS. In the eyes of their non-CIS neighbors, they provoke mixed reactions. They could end up finding themselves in a dually peripheral constellation: neither properly integrated in the CIS nor properly wanted in the alternative regional schemes outside their CIS neighborhood. In the cases of Ukraine and Georgia, the geostrategic alternative is NATO and EU membership. In the case of Kyrgyzstan, the prospect might be the status of a loyal satellite of China or Southwest Asia.

Whatever their prospects, one fact seems clear: the Commonwealth of Independent States needs to completely overhaul its rationale and opt for a comprehensive concept of democratic regionalism if it is ever to have a sustainable and legitimate future. Its past was better than many critics might conclude. The peaceful dissolution of the Soviet empire was an act of wisdom and cautious statesmanship. The outbreak of the first war between two CIS member states in the summer of 2008 marked the end of this period of hope, thaw, and cooperation. Even before the August 2008 warfare between Russia and Georgia, the

2008 CIS summit had underlined, once again, the trend toward drifting apart, with Kazakhstan's leader Nursultan Nasarbaev remaining the most active ideological engine of CIS regionalism. At the CIS summit, Russian leaders Putin and Medvedev blew the trumpet of rhetorical regionalism, but in reality they were focused on the fact that whereas 53 percent of all Russian trade happens with the European Union, only 2.3 percent of Russian direct investments flow into CIS partner countries. In spite of the 1,600 integration documents formulated since the creation of the Commonwealth of Independent States in 1991, its transformation from a grouping of negative security regionalism to one of positive democratic regionalism does not seem likely.

Notes

1. Commonwealth of Independent States (CIS), *The Alma-Ata Declaration* (21.12.1991), in Zbigniew Brzezinski and Paine Sullivan (eds.), *Russia and the Commonwealth of Independent States: Documents, Data, and Analysis* (Armonk, NY: M.E. Sharpe, 1997), 47–48.
2. Thus the compelling title of a study on the first decade of the CIS by Martha Brill Olcott et.al., *Getting it Wrong: Regional Cooperation and the Commonwealth of Independent States* (Washington, D.C.: Carnegie Endowment for International Peace, 1999).
3. Marielle Eudes, "Experts Hear Death Bells Ringing for Russia's CIS," *The Manila Times*, 4 April 2005.
4. Ibid.
5. Commonwealth of Independent States (CIS), *CIS Treaty on Collective Security* (15.05.1992), in Brzezinski and Sullivan, *Russia and the Commonwealth of Independent States*, 539–540.
6. Commonwealth of Independent States (CIS), *Charter of the Commonwealth of Independent States* (22.1.1993), in Brzezinski and Sullivan, *Russia and the Commonwealth of Independent States*, 506–511; see also Mark H. McCormack and William E. Butler (eds.), *The Law of Treaties in Russia and the Commonwealth of Independent Nations: Texts and Commentary* (Cambridge: Cambridge University Press, 2002).
7. Eurasian Economic Community (EAEC), *Agreement on the Creation of Common Economic Space (CES)* (19.09.2003), translation author, for the original document in Russian see http://archive.kremlin.ru/text/docs/2003/09/52478.shtml.
8. See Alexander A. Pikayev, "The Russian Debate on Policy Toward the 'Near Abroad,'" in Lena Jonson and Clive Archer (eds.), *Peacekeeping and the Role of Russia in Eurasia* (Boulder: Westview Press, 1996), 51–66.
9. See Tomasz Mickiewicz, *Economic Transition in Central Europe and the Commonwealth of Independent States* (Basingstoke: Palgrave Macmillan, 2005).
10. See http://en.wikipedia.org/wiki/Commonwealth_of_Independent_States.
11. See Geert-Hinrich Ahrens, *Die Präsidentschaftswahlen in der Ukraine: Die schwierige Mission der OSCE/ODIHR-Wahlbeobachter*, ZEI Discussion Paper C 151 (Bonn: Center for European Integration Studies, 2005).
12. See Marina Strezhneva, *Social Culture and Regional Governance: Comparison of the European Union and Post-Soviet Experiences* (Commack: Nova Science Publishers, 1999), 167.
13. Ibid., 170.
14. Ibid., 174; see also Lev Freinkman et al., *Trade Performance and Regional Integration of the CIS Countries* (Washington, D.C.: The World Bank, 2004); Stephen D. Shenfield, *Transborder and*

Interregional Cooperation between Russia and the Commonwealth of Independent States (Armonk, NY: M.E. Sharpe, 2005).

15. See *Frankfurter Allgemeine Zeitung*, no. 200, 29 August 2005, 5.

16. Commonwealth of Independent States (CIS), *Agreement on Collective Peacemaking Forces and Joint Measures on Their Material and Technical Supply* (24.09.1993), *Military News Bulletin* 10 (1993): 1–2.

17. See Jörg Stadelbauer, "Die GUS zwischen Integration und Fragmentierung: Zehn Jahre GUS—eine Zwangsgemeinschaft von Erben," *Praxis Geographie* 32, no. 1 (2002): 4–9.

18. See Andreas Marchetti, *The European Neighborhood Policy: Foreign Policy at the EU's Periphery*, ZEI Discussion Paper C 158 (Bonn: Center for European Integration Studies, 2006).

19. Strezhneva, *Social Culture and Regional Governance*, 155; see also Mikhail Molchanov, "Regionalism and Globalization in the Post-Soviet Space," *Studies in Post-Communism* 9 (2005): 1–28, online at: http://www.stfx.ca/pinstitutes/cpcs/studies-in-post-communism/Molchanov2005.pdf.

8

NON-INTEGRATION IN REGIONS
WITH GEOPOLITICAL TENSION

The Northeast Asian Paradox: Success without Stability

The Region's Constellation

Northeast Asia is a paradoxical region. Its economic dynamism provides global stability, but its geopolitical conflicts generate global uncertainty. No other region in the world is vacillating between a truly twenty-first–century aspiration to define, master, and promote globalization based on technological achievements, and nineteenth-century geopolitical parameters coupled with an irritating set of "leftovers" from twentieth-century regime controversies over totalitarian rule and strategic antagonisms defined by the Cold War era. While substantial energy has been spent to develop recommendations for viable mechanisms of regional integration in Northeast Asia—including the valuable distinction between economic regionalism, political regionalism, and security regionalism[1]—much less attention has been given to an honest analysis of the obstacles it faces.

For the time being, Northeast Asia has remained outside the global trend of regional integration formation, along with the Broader Middle East. These two regions are light years apart as far as their sociopolitical, cultural, and economic realities are concerned. Yet they share the same dearth of noticeable and thorough efforts to establish forms and goals of regional integration: the two are united in the obvious inability to bring the countries of the respective region together under the umbrella of a scheme of increasingly shared destiny and interest, commonality, and joint outlook on the world at large. Northeast Asia dominates the world's headlines with the impressive results of its economic dynamics. Japan, China, and South Korea generated 4 percent of the world's GDP in 1960. By 2005, together with Taiwan, they accounted for more than 20 percent of the world's GDP. Combined with the GDP of the ASEAN member states, their GDP matches that of the EU or the US. As for foreign-exchange reserves—Japan with 19 percent, China with 11 percent, Taiwan with 6.8 percent, South Korea with 5.1 percent, and Hong Kong with 4.8 percent of the global total—Northeast Asia is home to the five largest holders of foreign-exchange reserves in the world.

In the end, economic successes alone will not overcome the inherent competitive, if not confrontational, character of the geopolitical constellation of the region. Economic cooperation is no panacea for resolving political contradictions and overcoming mistrust if it cannot be transcended into a meaningful political and sociocultural concept. It will finally be up to the countries of Northeast Asia themselves to decide which type of order they want to live under. Neither a shared identity nor a shared consciousness of the common merits of supranational order-building can be found in Northeast Asia yet. A sense of belonging toward the region, however, is growing. For the time being, Northeast Asia can be characterized by "regionalization without regionalism."[2]

Usually, the geopolitical panorama of Northeast Asia is defined by evident political facts: the prevailing partition of the Korean peninsula; the danger of a North Korean atomic bomb; geopolitical tension between Japan and China over the primacy in Asia; conflicts over islands in the region that are symbolic of larger geopolitical rivalries (between China and Taiwan, China and Vietnam, Korea and Japan, Japan and Russia); the future role of the United States as an Asian power and US-China relations; the prospects for Russian-Chinese relations, particularly regarding the exploitation of Siberian natural resources. Europe is by and large absent from these debates, yet the European integration experience is regularly invoked as a model that might be emulated in order to overcome the geopolitical impasses Northeast Asia faces.

Three fundamental obstacles to achieving regional integration can be identified in Northeast Asia beyond the usual short-term reflection on the matter. When the lens of studying Northeast Asia is extended to take into account the historical legacy of the region, these three structural obstacles to regional integration in Northeast Asia become evident:

- Ambivalence between self-induced action and external dependencies, including the relationship between Northeast Asian nations and Western powers and the attitude of Northeast Asian nations vis-à-vis key notions of state philosophy emanating from the West.
- The ongoing relevance in Northeast Asian politics of categories of big power politics and balance-of-power strategies, including a traditional view of the relationship between war, national ambition, and politics.
- The prevalent presence of structures and mentalities shaped by World War II and its aftermath, including continuous contradictions between regimes and governance methods and an obsession with territorial disputes and alliance loyalties based on zero-sum assumptions.

Northeast Asia encountered the modern Western world as an intruding force in the nineteenth century. Missionaries, gunboats, merchants with dubious practices—the first modern encounters of China, Japan, and Korea with Western powers were not at all amicable.[3] Russia's advance into Siberia added to the perception of an expansionist, if not aggressive, outside world. Too often, the external forces were experienced as a curse and not an asset. Northeast Asian nationalism is deeply rooted in anti-Western traditions. Being what is here termed a modernization nationalism, it has always been focused on ways to meet the pressure from the West by improving and strengthening Northeast Asian cultures, people, and countries. No matter what internal quarrels may simmer among the people and countries of the region, overall skepticism of all external powers was and still is a constant historical factor in the self-perception and development of Northeast Asia. The undisputed cultural centrality that China claimed for its position in the world ("Middle Kingdom") was never really challenged by Japanese and Korean self-perceptions, notwithstanding their own ambivalent, if not hostile, attitude toward the Chinese during much of their mutual history. Interactions and struggles in the region were considered a matter of internal civilizational disputes, whereas encounters with the Western powers, Russia included, were of an altogether different nature. In contrasting them, since the second half of the nineteenth century Northeast Asians countries have felt their technological weakness while at the same time reassessing their cultural authenticity.

European encounters with Northeast Asia during the nineteenth century were not much different from the first presence of Americans and Russians in the region. In 1853, US Commodore Matthew Perry arrived with his battleships at Edo Bay and forced the Japanese emperor to open trade with the US after more than two centuries of seclusion. The Japanese shogun accepted the trade concessions US President Fillmore asked for: Shimoda and Hakodate were opened for US commerce.[4] Less known abroad, but leaving no small imprint on the national psyche, was the foreign effort to seek trade and to protect the growing Catholic community in Korea during the second half of the nineteenth century.[5] After nine French priests had been killed, and with anti-Catholic persecutions still under way in Korea, the American merchant ship *General Sherman* sailed up the Taedong River to Pyongyang, which its captain had confused with Seoul at the Han River. The ship was burned and its crew killed in August 1866.

In September 1866, the French Asiatic Squadron entered Korean waters with seven warships and prepared to attack Seoul. They failed to do so because of the Korean defense. In 1871, US Commander John Rodgers invaded Korea with five warships, attacking the fortifications on Kanghwa Island and returning to China only after fierce battles with the Koreans. In 1882, the US arranged peacefully for the opening of Korea through a Treaty of Armistice and Commerce signed at Chemulp'o, today's Incheon. This beginning of the Hermit Kingdom's opening to the West was followed by similar treaties with England and Russia in 1883 and

France in 1886. Russian ways to enter Northeast Asia were no less radical and belligerent than those of the Western powers. Since the Russians had entered Siberia and reached the Amur River and the Pacific Ocean in the seventeenth century, they had tried to gain access to Japan and Korea. After China had ceded the region around Vladivostok to Russia as part of the overall external humiliation of China through unequal treaties, Russia began to project its interests into Korea and, through the construction of the Trans-Siberian Railway, into Manchuria, clashing with the Japanese up until Russia lost an outright war against Japan in 1905.[6]

As for China's enforced opening to the West, the unequal treaties are legion. The Treaty of Nanking (1842) ended the First Opium War, forced China to cede Hong Kong to the British Empire, and opened Canton, Amoy, Foochow, Ningpo, and Shanghai as treaty ports for Western ships. The Treaty of Aigun (1858), signed by imperial Russia and the Qing Empire, established their border at the Amur River and thus the modern borders of Russia in the Far East. The Treaty of Tientsin (1858) between the Qing Empire, France, Russia, and the United States opened eleven more Chinese ports to foreigners, permitting foreign legations in Beijing, allowing Christian missionary activities, and legalizing the import of opium. The Treaty of Shimonoseki (1895) between China and Japan ended the Sino-Japanese War and with it Chinese suzerainty over Korea. Taiwan, in turn, came under Japanese rule. The Convention of Beijing (1860) between the British Empire and the Qing Empire forced China to cede the Kowloon Peninsula and Hong Kong "in perpetuity" to the British Empire and parts of Outer Manchuria to Russia. The Treaty of 1901 between China on the one hand, and the US, the UK, Japan, Russia, France, the German Empire, Italy, the Austro-Hungarian Empire, Belgium, Spain, and the Netherlands on the other hand, was signed after China's defeat in the Boxer Rebellion by the Eight Power Expeditionary Force. The Twenty-One Demands (1915), finally, secured temporary Japanese hegemony over China under the pretext of Japan's declaration of war against the German Empire in 1914.[7]

A belligerent pursuit of interests, the inclination to dominate, and a certain Western attitude of humiliation left no positive image of the outside world among many people in nineteenth-century Northeast Asia. Of course, Northeast Asian relations with Europeans and with Americans in the nineteenth century also included elements of mutual respect and cooperation. But all in all, the West was perceived as inclined to domination while one's own society was recognized as weak and still lacking modernization. The Meiji Restoration in Japan (1867/1868) and the dethronement of the Chinese emperor (1911) were similar symptoms of the same commonly shared desire to pursue an aggressive policy of self-induced modernization in order to protect one's own tradition and society from Western dominance.

As the West began to colonize the world, Northeast Asian nations started a period of self-colonization and self-improvement that subsequently triggered aggressive modernization, nationalism, and bilateral struggles for dominance in the region. The latter element was most notable in the relationship between China and Japan, which became an imperial power itself and in that behavior resembled Western powers more than it did its Northeast Asian neighbors: Taiwan became a Japanese colony in 1895, Korea in 1910. In contrast, Russia's role in Northeast Asia was more than just an external threat. For instance, Korea sought Russian assistance against the increasing Japanese intrusion after the Japanese defeat of China in 1895. The same, of course, became true of the US protection of Japan and South Korea after World War II and throughout the Cold War: the United States, formerly an imperial power in Northeast Asia, now became the embodiment of liberty.

Cultural pride and self-protection went hand in hand with the emergence of a distinct Northeast Asian modernization nationalism. Western technological devices as well as Western concepts of modern statehood were adopted whenever they helped to strengthen and protect the peoples of Northeast Asia from domination by Western powers. This became a genuine feature of the relationship between Northeast Asia and the West, unlike the relationship between Western powers and other regions of the world. This structure of encounter and the reaction to it, however, did not include recognition of any of the external powers as a well-respected and widely recognized "Asian power." To this day, neither Russia nor the United States nor Europe or any of its leading countries is recognized as a "natural Asian power" in Northeast Asia. As for Russia, efforts to develop a triangular regional project with Chinese, North Korean, and Russian participation indicate the potential.[8] But belying these plans is the factual depopulation of Russia's Far East, noticeable since the end of the Soviet Union. Some scholars have estimated the Russians' numbers in the Far East to have dropped to 7.2 million, warning that over 100 million Chinese in Northeastern China might seek "relief from overcrowding."[9]

Like the US, Russia maintains strategic interests and advanced positions in Northeast Asia to this day. Neither has become a fully respected Asian power. It is indicative that the promotion of a cultural sphere of communication in Northeast Asia by the Korean president in 2004 made no reference to Russia, which after all is an immediate neighbor of Korea, let alone to the US, continuously the provider of security and stability in South Korea and in Japan with more than 100,000 soldiers deployed in Northeast Asia. A sense of gratitude toward the Americans is disappearing even in places where, following the outbreak of the Cold War, freedom was absolutely dependent on their protection. While the US role in supporting or even providing liberty in Northeast Asia is not forgotten, it is also recalled that the US participated in gunboat politics and enforced policies of open doors in the second half of the nineteenth century across the region.

At the time, the US was no different from European imperial powers and their practices in Northeast Asia. Disputes over the US-led "War on Terror" have reinforced a sense of silent drifting apart between the US and new generations during the early years of the twenty-first century, even in Japan and South Korea, traditionally the most loyal countries of the region.

Big Power Politics and Disputes over Interpretations of History

Northeast Asia is beginning to reflect on cultural commonality, but it does so with the explicit exclusion of those external powers that have been key actors in the geopolitics of Northeast Asia for most of the last two centuries.[10] Although in reality the US has been an Asian power at least since World War II, it is facing various efforts of selective exclusion from the formation of regional Northeast Asian arrangements, notably from a possible ASEAN enlargement. The trend to limit US strategic influence in Northeast Asia coincides with an interesting reversion of the cultural and geopolitical reassessment of China and its global role: no longer considering itself the "Middle Kingdom," China has begun to awaken impressively, after a long century of internal turmoil, in full recognition of its role as an Asian, that is to say a Northeast Asian, country.

China's claim to universalism seems to be transcending into a new Chinese sense of regionalism. Due to the continuously high growth rates of its economy since the beginning of reforms under Deng Xiaoping in 1978, China has risen from thirteenth place among world trading nations to the first five ranks with the US, Canada, the EU, and Japan. China accounts for around one fifth of the growth in world trade during the early years of the twenty-first century. While 75 percent of all investment in China is of foreign origin, in 2002 China surpassed the US as the world's leading destination for foreign direct investment, "absorbing nearly $53 billion."[11] By 2010, China is projected to receive $100 billion in foreign direct investment. Politically, it is obvious that China has opted for a "selective support of regional initiatives,"[12] and as far as international and multinational forums are concerned, China has "moved from virtual isolation from international organizations to membership numbers approaching about 80 percent of those of the major industrialized states, and around 160 percent of the world average."[13] China's genuine revisionism since the early 1980s has not been revolutionary, but rather inclusive, thus stabilizing global order-building. It might be telling for things to come that China does this as an Asian country and no longer under the claim of autarkic Chinese universalism.

Some premodern concepts of politics prevail in Northeast Asia as part of its legacy of encountering external powers as forces of subjugation: the primacy of national sovereignty aspiration; the syndrome of balance-of-power equations; in the Chinese (as in the US) case, the continuous relevance of war as a category of conflict resolution, and in the South Korean case the realistic fear of a continuation of exactly such a pattern of behavior on the side of North Korea; a zero-sum mentality regarding the status, influence, and power of any of the regional or external actors, and as its consequence the assumption that regional cooperation must not curtail autonomous freedom to act and that regional integration might undermine the latter while distinctively devaluing national sovereignty as the prime source of national political autonomy and pride. External actors are inevitable partners in the pursuit of the globalization-related goals of the countries of Northeast Asia (i.e., modernization and mastery of globalization in order to strengthen the nation and its role in the region and the world), but they remain suspect as far as the scope of national action and autonomy of the region as a whole are concerned. Among themselves, however, the Northeast Asian nations tend to pursue policies of competition in the economic sphere with astuteness, as if traditional national rivalries have been transferred from the sphere of politics to that of the economy. By and large, competitive economic structures and ambitions make one wonder whether or not cooperative, let alone integrative, political approaches could ever be accommodated in such an environment.

The logic of big power politics prevails in Northeast Asia. Big power politics is based on the autonomous pursuit of power as the prime category of interstate relations and is intended to maximize one's own power at the expense of the other countries in the region. The attitude of big power politics can also be exercised by small countries because it is defined by the prevalence of a zero-sum mentality: my neighbor's gain is my own inevitable loss. In this context, a balance-of-power strategy is defined as the effort to gain power equilibrium or a freeze of power struggles in a specific region. Under the conditions of the prevailing attitude of big power politics, strategies of balance of power are the best possible approach to tame this attitude. However, such strategies cannot reverse the logic of weakness, unraveling, and destruction that is inherent in balance-of-power relations. Northeast Asia's countries have adopted the logic of big power politics from Western models that by now are long outdated in the West.

In Northeast Asia, however, big power politics and strategies of balance of power have been internalized as the only guarantee to national sovereignty and a respectable regional and international status. Big power politics has become a reflex in Northeast Asia's struggle for independence and national sovereignty. It has been reinforced and overlapped by the experience with the Cold War antagonisms pertinent to Northeast Asia: between the United States and the Soviet Union, the United States and the People's Republic of China, and the People's Republic of China and the Soviet Union. All have left their mark on the mindset and mentality of policy actors and public opinion in Northeast Asia. Most of Northeast Asia's indigenous conflicts of the second half of the twentieth century were a function of the Cold War paradigm.

Northeast Asia's geopolitical constellation has evolved from a conundrum of colonial and decolonizing (that is to say nationalistic) elements, ideological rivalries and Cold War parameters, and, finally, internal power ambitions and struggles for hegemony. Northeast Asia's big power mentality coincides with a traditional notion of warfare as a means of politics. Neither China nor the US has abandoned the idea that war can serve a means to resolve conflicts. Divided Korea continuously lives in the shadow of war, and the presence of US soldiers across the country is indicative of the fact that World War II will not end as long as the Korean armistice is executed in Pammunjon with an almost archaic precision. The Cairo Declaration of 1 December 1943, which states that "in due course Korea shall become free and independent,"[14] is still an unfulfilled promise to half of the Korean peninsula. The Korean War (1950–1953) can be considered a prolongation of World War II in Northeast Asia, for to this day it has not been overcome in its geopolitical consequences. North Korea continues to play with the effects of the threat of warfare looming over a region that it might be able to (relatively) hold hostage with nuclear arms.

Japan, in turn, has renounced warfare, but has not properly recognized its own role as perpetrator in bringing about much of today's geopolitical constellation of Northeast Asia (including the rise of communism in China and both communism and nationalism in Korea with the subsequent division of the Korean peninsula). Instead, Japan prefers to be perceived as a victim of World War II (atomic bombs over Hiroshima and Nagasaki) and strives for renewed global recognition in the shadow of the US-China rivalry. Japan's culture of shame still clashes with its neighbors' expectation of an expression of Japanese guilt about its past actions. This controversy about historical memories has limited Japan's ambition to join the UN Security Council. On a more realistic note, China—already a permanent member of the Security Council with veto power—does not intend to revoke or curtail its own plan to also become the leading Northeast Asian economic power. China, therefore, uses means of controlled provocation against Japan in order to define the limits of Japan's scope of action on the global stage. All of these attitudes stem from the logic of big power politics and are not conducive to a climate of reality-transforming integration.

What holds true for the geopolitical constellation of Northeast Asia is only reinforced by the region's geo-economic development: The highly dynamic economies of Northeast Asia are by and large structured along the limiting principle of competition and hardly along the mutually advantageous principle of complementarity. While this guarantees national focus in each country and impressive success in global markets, it does not automatically support interconnectedness and the ability to share one's potential for the sake of higher means of cooperative gains. Although indications might point to inherent trends of business-to-business cooperation across national boundaries and loyalties, Northeast Asia still has to prove the advantage of comprehensive patterns of complementarity in the name of regionalism, with economic and political implications.

Bitter disputes in interpreting history and historical justice resurge in Northeast Asia with almost predictable repetition. These disputes indicate an ongoing mistrust that is rooted not only in today's claims of status and power, but also in historical differences, disputes, and contradictions that have characterized the emergence of modern Northeast Asia. Most notable among a set of legacies of mistrust is the one stemming from regime antagonism prevailing in Northeast Asia to this day. Japan's critics perceive this country as disguising the prolongation of imperial attitudes that did not vanish from the Japanese political culture with the US-imposed democratic development after 1945. Yet nobody can deny the strength of modern Japan, which accounts for 67 percent of Northeast Asia's GDP.[15] South Korea considers itself the authentic moral leader in pursuit of democratic values, having struggled for them against external colonial imposition and internal military rule. By now, it has also become the tenth largest economy in the world.

The People's Republic of China prevails as a communist country with a one-party system and a long record of human rights abuses, despite its impressive economic modernization. North Korea, under China's protective umbrella and neutralizing control, is the modern version of a hermit kingdom and in fact has evolved to become the most secluded totalitarian state in the world, with a pronounced Orwellian character and horrifying practices of brainwashing. Its GDP in 2000 amounted to $17 billion, "a tiny fraction of South Korea's $455 billion."[16] Taiwan considers itself the "right China" because of its democratic record. Yet Taiwan is increasingly drawn back toward mainland China because of its magnetic modernization attraction: Taiwanese capital ranks second as source of foreign direct investment in the People's Republic of China. By now, one million Taiwanese are living in mainland China, 300,000 in Shanghai alone, and more than half of Taiwan's top hundred companies have investments in the People's Republic. Communist ideology and fear of violent Chinese annexation seem increasingly to be overtaken by a sense of national unity, recalling a long cultural and a rather shorter political tradition of unity (only from 1683 until 1895 was Taiwan under Chinese rule, being a prefecture of Fujian).

Russia, finally, has been so absorbed by its internal political and socioeconomic turmoil since the fall of the Soviet Union that it hardly has been able to project any promising image, let alone a model for any of the Northeast Asian countries. The proclamation of a Sino-Russian Treaty of Friendship in 2001, "representing to all appearances the best relationship between these two territorially imposing neighbors in nearly fifty years,"[17] cannot reverse the decline of Russia's Far East, although China has become the biggest customer of Russian weaponry, largely produced in the country's Far East. The People's Republic of China began to purchase Russian weaponry in 1990 after the US and the EU imposed an arms sale boycott against China following the Tiananmen Square massacre. Between 2000 and 2005, the Chinese arms purchase from Russia alone was expected to be worth \$5–6 billion.[18] Yet Russia's overall decline and crisis of political culture have prevented it from maintaining its power projection in Northeast Asia. In fact, Russia has even pushed Mongolia closer to Northeast Asia. Mongolia considers itself a successful model of postcommunist democratic transformation redirecting its cultural focus toward China and curtailing its ties with Russia.

Six-Party Talks and Multilateral Perspectives for Collective Security

Against this background, the prospects do not look too bright for immediate structures of regional integration in Northeast Asia comparable with the European ambition to pool sovereignty, law, and governance. In the first place, Northeast Asian countries and actors have to clarify topical and methodological confusion. Not every invocation of the term "regionalism" means "region-building." Northeast Asia is blessed with a wide array of proposals for free trade agreements (FTAs) and preferential trade agreements (PTAs).[19] It sometimes seems as if the prospect of free trade agreements has become a mania, not hampered by the obvious absence of political trust among many of the people and countries in the region. Nothing is wrong with viable free trade agreements, but they alone do not constitute a structure of regional integration. They might be considered a preintegration scheme; certainly they comply with the logic and aspiration of the World Trade Organization. Region-building can begin with a free trade agreement, and a free trade agreement does not preclude the development of more comprehensive schemes of political and legal forms of integration. But there can be no doubt that free trade agreements per se are expressions of regional cooperation, not of regional integration.

Without external input, region-building in Northeast Asia is barely conceivable in the first decade of the twenty-first century. But there are three components in the region that might evolve over time into a new and comprehensive order for Northeast Asia, if not for the whole of East Asia.

(1) Asia-Pacific Economic Cooperation (APEC) has become a loose scheme framing the vast region in the broadest possible way. The common strife of economic modernization and development has brought together all littoral states of the Pacific Ocean. Annual summit meetings of the heads of state gain public attention, but all other activities of APEC are rather peripheral and lack the potential for a quantum leap in regional integration. The cooperative structure of APEC allows for the broadest possible inclusion of membership with a set of contradictions almost reminiscent of the United Nations. APEC, the official webpage operating from the APEC Secretariat in Singapore states, "is the only intergovernmental grouping in the world operating on the basis of non-binding commitments, open dialogue and equal respect for the views of all participants."[20] APEC has no treaty obligations, and decisions are made by consensus among its twenty-one member states.

APEC was founded in 1989 in order "to enhance economic growth and prosperity for the region and to strengthen the Asia-Pacific community."[21] The reduction of tariffs and other trade barriers across the Asia-Pacific region has been the main objective of APEC activities, "creating efficient domestic economies and dramatically increasing exports."[22] It is hard to recognize APEC as an institution, yet scholars from the region consider it "a central organ for Asian regionalism."[23] For the time being, APEC vacillates between a consultative and a negotiation body. Yet in the long run, APEC might evolve into a loose, almost informal net of ties across the Asia-Pacific that uses its economic primacy as the starting point in order to formulate some sort of Asian-Pacific identity. In developing these features, APEC could play a role somewhat comparable to that of the Council of Europe. Most likely, APEC will continue to lack political power while it continues to perpetuate itself far from the center stage as seen by any of its members or any focused strategic objective beyond the growth of the economies in the region.

(2) ASEAN Plus Three has been described as "the most important change in Asia-Pacific regionalism" since the economic and financial crisis of 1997, its nature lauded as "an Asia-only regional economic cooperation."[24] ASEAN Plus Three has become the formula for increasing approximation of China, Japan, and South Korea toward the original ASEAN community, established in 1967. ASEAN is the Asian structure most comparable to a viable regional integration scheme, representing its member nations' collective will "to bind themselves together in friendship and cooperation and, through joint efforts and sacrifices, secure for their peoples and for posterity the blessings of peace, freedom, and prosperity."[25] Yet in spite of four decades of successful economic history, in spite of its original success in taming and stopping communist expansion in Southeast Asia, and in spite of its enlargement to include the former communist countries Vietnam, Laos, and Cambodia, as well as the controversial state of Myanmar, governed by authoritarian military rule, ASEAN has not been able to consistently implement structures or mechanisms of a supranational character comparable to those of European integration. While this might turn out to be advantageous in order to fully incorporate China, Japan, and South Korea as ASEAN members at some point, the absence of supranational elements will most certainly redefine the original character of ASEAN and shift its center of power toward Northeast Asia, should its three leading economies join ASEAN one day. This current absence means the absence of law-abiding mechanisms that generate predictable legal behavior.

Looking to its annual summit meetings, optimists consider ASEAN Plus Three the beginning of an East Asian Community, and at least the framework for an eventual East Asian Free Trade Area. China has "discovered" ASEAN Plus Three as a valuable forum for projecting its interest in economic cooperation and matching it with broader strategic considerations shared by Japan and

Korea. Taiwan is doubly marginalized, as it is neither a member of ASEAN nor considered a partner of the ASEAN Plus Three constellation. This feeling of exclusion is shared by the US, which has warned the original ASEAN member states not to go too far in their cooperation with China.

ASEAN's fear of being dominated by China is balanced by fascination with the recent rise of China. Since 1999, ASEAN and the representatives of China, Japan, and South Korea have intensified their contacts and cooperation. ASEAN maintains a wide set of bodies and a broad array of activities, yet it lacks the definite political commitment and decision-making mechanisms that would constitute a regional integration system similar to the European experience. Should ASEAN over time embrace China, Japan, and South Korea as full members, Southeast and Northeast Asia would move under one umbrella representing East Asia as a whole. This trend could turn ASEAN from an economic block into a strategic asset, certainly in accordance with long-term Chinese interests in the region and vis-à-vis the United States. But the implications of this development could also provoke skepticism in Japan and fears in some of the smaller ASEAN countries because of likely Chinese dominance. It is, however, not inconceivable that such a development might evolve within a decade or so, underlining the primacy of the economy in current East Asian order-building.

An interesting component evolving from the original ASEAN has been the development of its ASEAN Regional Forum, established in 1994 and broadening the economic cooperation into the sphere of security and strategy. It should be noted that ASEAN and ASEAN Plus Three have been identified as conceivable formats for the evolution of an East Asian currency system.26 So far, however, the emergence of conceptual structures has not been matched with a genuine political will among the main governments involved. While the potential of an East Asian currency system—and eventually of an East Asian monetary union—cannot be denied, its implementation will clearly remain a function of Chinese-Japanese strategic considerations. These considerations, in turn, are a function of the overall Northeast Asian strategic landscape and development. By its nature, emphasis on the strategic perspectives for Northeast Asia strengthens the role and influence of the US. While APEC, although not of a strategic nature, has been US-sponsored and ASEAN and ASEAN Plus Three are "Asian-only" without US participation, the strategic future of Northeast Asia is inconceivable without a strong role played by the US. World War II, after all, is not completely over in Northeast Asia.

(3) Confronted with the imminent danger of a North Korean nuclear bomb, the US, China, Japan, Russia, South Korea, and North Korea came together in the first semi-formal multilateral security arrangement in Northeast Asia during several rounds of talks in 2003 and 2004. US-sponsored Six-Party Talks originally focused on the North Korean nuclear issue, one of the consequences of an overlap of World War II legacies, Cold War parameters, and

struggle for anti-Western national autonomy and primacy of national sovereignty in Northeast Asia. The temporary withdrawal of North Korea from the Six-Party Talks in 2004 did not make them obsolete. It proved to be transient. South Korea has continuously expressed a particular interest in maintaining the format of the Six-Party Talks and in stretching its content beyond the nuclear issue to cover all other matters of security and cooperation in Northeast Asia.

The format of the Six-Party Talks might indeed serve as inspiration for the gradual evolution of a Northeast Asian security system. At best, it could evolve into a mechanism comparable to the Conference on Security and Cooperation in Europe (CSCE), one of the key engines in helping to overcome the Cold War and the continental division in Europe. As the Cold War is still alive in Northeast Asia as far as the partition of the Korean peninsula and the prevalence of the outlandish political and socioeconomic system in North Korea are concerned, improvement in regional security cooperation can only be welcomed. As a key member of the Six-Party Talks format, the continuous role of the United States as an Asian power would be guaranteed. Obvious is the absence of the European Union in the strategic discourse about the Northeast Asian security architecture. Given Europe's enormous economic interest in the stable development of Northeast Asia, this is astonishing; it reflects the limited global projection of the EU's ambition for a comprehensive foreign and security policy, but also the limited interest of the United States and, most likely, also of China, in including another external actor into the security conundrum of Northeast Asia. While the EU is a preferential partner of ASEAN and has successfully established an EU-Asian consultancy mechanism on economic and financial issues, the absence of the EU in the strategic discourse about the future of Northeast Asia is deplorable as far as Europe's global interests are concerned.[27]

It seems to be an iron law that economic competition in Northeast Asia reinforces the region's fascination with big power politics, primacy of national sovereignty, and skepticism of regional integration. It cannot be excluded categorically that, over time, the primacy of the economy in Northeast Asia will alter the role of politics. Should this occur, Northeast Asia would have to redefine the relationship between politics and the economy, thus becoming the first postmodern region in which depoliticized trading states would transform their mutual political relations from big power primacy to cooperative and integrative regionalism by way of economic means alone. With the recognition of the principle of "one country, two systems" in Hong Kong (since 1997) and in Macau (since 1999), the Chinese leadership in Beijing has demonstrated its potential for a certain flexibility and creativity in the pursuit of national goals. For the time being, it is hardly imaginable (but should not be ruled out entirely) that such an approach could also succeed unchallenged as far as the future of Taiwan is concerned.

In any case, the evolution of relations between the People's Republic of China and Taiwan remains the central test case to dispel skepticism about the dissolution of big power politics in Northeast Asia. While both mainland China and Taiwan (and Taiwan's political parties) struggle over how to apply the principle of "one China," they are even more bitterly divided over the legacy of ideological rifts whose divisive power has begun to dissipate. The first-ever visit of a Taiwanese Kuomintang leader, Lien Chan, to mainland China in early 2005 was indicative of the potential path of reconciliation. Before meeting the Secretary General of China's Communist Party and Head of State Hu Jintao in Beijing, Lien Chan paid respect to Sun Yat Sen's tomb in Nanking. To this day, Sun Yat Sen is revered by nationalists and communists alike as the founder of the anti-feudal, anti-imperial Chinese Republic. After their talks, Hu invoked the imminent, great reawakening of the Chinese nation.

Whether or not republicanism and a shared sense of material prosperity as the road to reinvigorate China's global strength might ultimately suffice to overcome the ideological barriers and territorial splits of the Cold War remains to be seen. The transformation of the People's Republic of China from a rigid, Maoist-Marxist country to a trading state under a patriotic, or perhaps increasingly nationalistic, one-party rule, indicates the enormous Chinese potential for pragmatism. Western notions of politics are probably much too burdened with the legacies and scars of ideology to believe in the primacy of economic materialism. But in China, Confucian ethics and neo-patriotism might disprove the universal applicability of Western notions of politics.

The approximation and eventual reconciliation of mainland China and Taiwan might indeed follow a genuine East Asian logic of relations between business and politics, power and culture. As long as good-weather periods prevail, the competitive character of Northeast Asian economies might not trouble any of the regional actors. However, irritations or outright symptoms of crisis in either of the countries could. The sensitivity of the People's Republic of China to a possible Taiwanese declaration of independence—which Beijing declared a possible justification for military intervention across the Taiwan Strait as recently as April 2005—is indicative. The unpredictable future of the divided Korean peninsula and the unpredictable social evolution in China are further matters of concern for Northeast Asia. They cannot be easily accommodated with the image of an evolving cultural community of cooperation.

Estimates regarding the prospects of China's enormous modernization vary. While some Chinese analysts suggest that China might catch up with the US's "comprehensive national power" (CNP) in 2020, others see China "reaching only 61 percent of America's and achieving a rank seventh in the world, even below that of South Korea, at 65 percent of America's CNP."[28] More pessimistic Chinese projections stop at only 50 percent, if not 40 percent, of US CNP.[29] With an average growth rate of 10 percent per year during most of the period between 1990 and 2005, China stands above all other economies in the world. Trade as a percentage of its GDP has doubled once every decade since the late 1970s, from 5.2 percent in 1970 to 44 percent in 2001 (compared with 18 percent for Japan, 19 percent for the US, and 20 percent for India). China has thus become the sixth largest trading country in the world, after the US, Germany, Japan, France, and the United Kingdom. Compared to a per capita income of $40,000 in Japan and $10,000 in South Korea, China's average per capita income of around $1,000 still ranks it as a poor country. But the trend toward successful market-based modernization is as impressive as the size of the Chinese population, which guarantees a continuous expansion of the country's economy. As long as China's economy is booming, social tension, internal migration, and the urban-rural divide are of secondary concern and might be accommodated. But what would happen in the event of a slowdown and crisis in China? The Chinese government has already struggled to tame the sometimes overheated economic boom while recognizing the dangerous urban-rural divide with 100 to 150 million surplus rural workers roaming between low-paid city jobs and rural unemployment.

While China is threatening its own success through the excesses of an overly booming modernization, the threat issuing from North Korea stems from failed modernization. As long as North Korea is a stable and sovereign state, it poses a potential threat to South Korea and a permanent tragedy to its own people. Neither of these factors is likely to unravel the socioeconomic and security web of Northeast Asia. But what might happen in case of an implosion of the system and a breakdown of order in inter-Korean relations?[30] South Korean contingency plans for mass refugee movements and plans to absorb millions of North Koreans or to enable them to lead a sustainable life in their own home are currently merely theoretical calculations in view of the secluded character of the regime in Pyongyang and the limited external influence that can be exerted on its actions. While Russia is pursuing a policy of restrained neutrality vis-à-vis North Korea, China and the US see North Korea also as a function of their overall geopolitical relationship and its inherent struggle over primacy in Asian affairs. This makes South Korea the weakest factor in this equation. As long as the situation is stable and does not change fundamentally, the North Koreans suffer most. Should the situation alter exponentially—no matter in which direction—South Korea's impressive rise and stability and the overall Northeast Asian geopolitical and geo-economic landscape might suffer too. In light of this prospect, it seems as if Northeast Asia is held hostage to North Korea's unpredictability, which is the consequence of a combination of nationalist rivalries, ideological contradictions,

Cold War paradigms, and the post–Cold War constructivist search for order. Northeast Asia's strategic limbo is also a consequence of the unresolved structure of the long-term relationship between the US and China.

A Role for the European Union?

It would be a matter of frustration for the European Union if any multilateral system in Northeast Asia were to be established without its participation. "With the end of the Cold War and the continuing economic development of eastern Asia," Francis Fukuyama wrote, "power relationships are changing in ways that have unlocked nationalist passions and rivalries. The potential for misunderstanding and conflict among South Korea, Japan, and China will be significant in the coming years—but it can be mitigated if multiple avenues of discussion exist between the states."[31] The plea for multilateralism in Northeast Asia by one of the leading conservative American academics should be read as both challenge and encouragement for the European Union to contemplate and focus its own strategic interests in the region. But where is the EU, as Americans begin to discuss Northeast Asian multilateralism, the idea dearest to many Europeans?

Fukuyama suggests turning the multilateral security framework that has emerged in Northeast Asia under the label of Six-Party Talks into a Five-Power Forum—that is to say, a forum composed of US, Chinese, Japanese, South Korean, and Russian representatives without North Korean participation. He expects that such a Five-Power Forum would clearly become an "institutional innovation."[32] Fukuyama did not mention participation by the EU in this potential Northeast Asian security forum. While in the Middle East the EU is an active and recognized partner of the Middle East Quartet (the EU, US, UN, and Russia) promoting a road map for the resolution of the conflict between Israel and the Palestinians, strategic considerations for the future of Northeast Asia are evolving in the seemingly natural absence of a possible role for the European Union.

Only the EU itself is to be criticized for this EU underperformance. It is up to the EU to project its ideas and concepts for global order, including the future place of Northeast Asia. "A secure Europe in a better world," as the EU's Security Strategy is titled—without discussing Northeast Asia in any relevant manner—will require such a broadening of the EU's foreign policy horizon.[33] The sooner this happens, the better for the interests of Europe.

In recognition of the difficulties and obstacles involved in regional integration in Northeast Asia, the EU could offer experience-based ideas that might be fruitful for the long-term evolution of region-building there. While Fukuyama propounds "security first" and most Asian analysts favor "economy first," the EU must conceptualize its Northeast Asian strategy as one of "law first." The promotion of norm-based interaction would contribute to turning suspicion and distrust in Northeast Asia into mutually advantageous and predictable patterns under common legal frames. It is not difficult to identify critical areas of modern life in which the enhancement of legal norms and predictable patterns of norm-based behavior could be a win-win situation for all Northeast Asian countries and societies. These include the future development of telecommunication technologies and related regulatory matters, the evolution of medical research, environmental protection and sea safety, and finally, the issue of commercial law and the terms of conduct for production, services, and labor in Northeast Asia. This list might be lengthened, but it constitutes a beginning beyond the traditional neglect of the perspective of a common regional legal *acquis* and the traditional dominance of zero-sum mentalities in Northeast Asia.

Against this background, it should be in the interests of the European Union to project itself as an "Asian power" by contributing to a reassessment of the usefulness of regional integration in Northeast Asia through cooperative advice, and by offering to participate in any emerging multilateral security scheme in Northeast Asia. For the time being, the EU still limits its Asian policies to bilateral relations largely of an economic nature. This is neither specific nor substantial enough to ultimately deal with the leading countries of this vast continent, the Northeast Asian powers China, Japan, and South Korea included. The value of a regular Asia-Europe Meeting (ASEM) remains limited as long as it does not turn from consultative diplomacy to cooperative regionalism. Such a shift would require a transformation of the EU's strategy in dealing with its ASEAN Plus Three partners. The EU would need a long-term strategy based on the primacy of multilateralism and integration and with a focus on the EU's possible contributions to the emulation of relevant institutional and conceptual processes in Northeast Asia.

The process of the Asia-Europe Meeting (ASEM) began in 1996. Summit meetings of heads of state and government of all EU member states and countries of ASEAN Plus Three take place every two years. They are characterized by informality, multidimensionality, and emphasis on equal partnership.[34] Following the respective enlargements in ASEAN and in the EU, the Hanoi summit in October 2004 brought thirty-nine partners together for the first time. Annual ministerial meetings contribute to interactions and consultations on a variety of international and biregional issues between the two regions. The European Union, however, has not been able to introduce the conceptual development of regional order-building in East Asia into the ASEM agenda yet. Before doing so, the EU would be well advised to formulate a comprehensive strategy that preferably includes the elements of a consultative exchange of thoughts and elaboration of the instruments at hand to enable the EU's foreign and security policy to impact a possible follow-up to any general strategic discussion. The EU simply needs a policy strategy for Northeast Asia. It would probably even be more meaningful if the EU developed a comprehensive policy strategy for East Asia that went beyond the quality of a shallow diplomatic communiqué. Such a strategy should emphasize EU interests, goals, and means with particular reference to the advantages of regional order-building in Northeast Asia with EU contribution and participation.

The sixth ASEM summit was held on 10 and 11 September 2006 in Helsinki, the EU capital physically closest to Northeast Asia. The summit reconfirmed the importance of the multilateral international system, discussed energy security and climate change, and emphasized intercultural dialogue and the need to resume WTO negotiations. It would have been much more spectacular had the EU suggested launching a comprehensive and joint study of the potential for regional-order building and law-based economic and political integration in ASEAN Plus Three as part of the evolution of a process that could lead to a biregional association agreement with the EU. But even if such a topic had made it on the ASEM summit agenda, it would have remained a largely academic exercise. The EU experience in building a region has not found appropriate resonance in East Asia yet. ASEM therefore, so it seems, cannot reach "beyond the triadic political economy."[35]

Building on its experience and strategic role, the EU should become more proactive in contributing to the Six-Party Talks on the North Korean nuclear issue. Restarted in July 2005 after one year of suspension and lauded for their breakthrough concerning the North Korean nuclear program in early 2007, the Six-Party Talks might gradually turn into a regional security grouping. In spite of the enormous European interest in economic cooperation with the region, the European Union has not explicitly projected a political interest in participating in the development of a North Asian security grouping. One visit by the EU's High Representative for Foreign and Security Policy and the EU Commissioner for Foreign Affairs to Pyongyang in May 2001, a series of political dialogues at the level of high civil servants, and €393 million in humanitarian aid between 1995 and 2005, which includes €115 million in support of the Korean Peninsula Energy Development Organization—all of this could be understood as the basis for a more political involvement in the next phase of multilateral activities regarding the Korean Peninsula. Over time, if EU representatives are not included in any meaningful institutionalized form of multilateral mechanism regarding the security of Northeast Asia, the EU will not be able to justify its financial input into alleviation of the Korean crisis. That is, EU taxpayers will not allow such generosity to happen a second time.

The EU should have learned this lesson from its experience with financial support of the Palestinian Authority in the Middle East. For a long time, it seemed as if the EU was only welcome in the Middle East as a financial donor, while political matters were considered in its absence. Criticism in the EU about this semi-servile participation in Middle East politics grew and, in the end, only the EU's inclusion in the Middle East Quartet justified its enormous financial contribution to the Middle East peace process. This analogy should be kept in mind in the context of any emerging security structure for and in Northeast Asia. The EU must project its political will to be recognized as one of the facilitating and mediating powers in Northeast Asia. Otherwise, its claim to be a global partner will lose credibility, its financial contributions will face increased criticism by EU taxpayers, and the overall EU interests in Northeast Asia will be undermined.

As for leadership in Northeast Asian integration-building, the European Union should identify the normative preconditions necessary to proceed with realistic developments. It should therefore identify South Korea and Japan as potentially the first architects for the promotion of a Northeast Asian political integration mechanism. South Korea and Japan are the only solidly democratic countries in the region. They are the leading economies as far as the level of modernization and human development is concerned. They are OECD members and have demonstrated cooperation even in such fields as jointly organizing the World Soccer Tournament in 2002. Yet the political relationship between both countries is still overshadowed by Korean suffering under Japanese colonial rule and the subsequent war that led to the division of the Korean people and their homeland. Instead of continuously speculating about a possible Korean reunification, it would probably be more appropriate to contemplate the potential of South Korean and Japanese efforts to launch the first steps of a Northeast Asian integration scheme that recalls the experience and ambition of the European Coal and Steel Community.

The 2005 controversy between Japan and South Korea over Dokdo, a tiny island between Korea and Japan, could have been used as a catalyst. The struggle over Dokdo was not over its territory or over historical arguments of right or wrong. It was primarily about the natural resources surrounding the island, and about pride and power in Northeast Asia. Why could Dokdo not be identified as an appropriate object to trigger a process of law-based integration among Northeast Asia's leading democracies? Here is an issue that could serve to establish a common supranational authority with a limited purpose over a specified matter. As this was, by and large, the definition and intention of the architects of the European Coal and Steel Community, one might wonder if and where a "Korean Jean Monnet" could appear. He or she would have to propose a joint authority over Dokdo and the related resources between South Korea and Japan. South Korea, Japan's past victim, would have to go a long way indeed to accept such a visionary proposal. But no other country in Northeast Asia is better placed to generate the moral authority to impress its neighbor and the world with such a proposal. Japan, meanwhile, would need to prove its democratic maturity by embracing such an initiative, should it ever be presented by South Korea. At first sight, this idea might sound like a strange dream, and so it is at the moment. But when studied in a broader perspective and with long-term considerations, there hardly seems a better opportunity for the two leading democratic trading states in Northeast Asia to begin an exceptional historical journey. They alone can bridge the waters that divide their shores through agreement on the common authority over an island that is too small to be recognized by the world for its damaging potential in its own region.

As for China, the EU must become more normative if its wants to be recognized as a global leader. In 2006, the EU contributed €100 million for measures to support China's integration into the international community and the global economy. With annual investments of €3 billion and a trade volume amounting to an annual sum of €150 billion, the EU has every reason to promote China's inclusion in the international economy. This inclusion has gone already an impressively long way since the beginning of reforms in China in 1978. But the dilemma persists between treating China as just another ordinary partner and holding to reservations about China's human rights record. The issue of lifting the weapons embargo against China—imposed after the massacre of thousands of young dissidents at Tiananmen Square on 4 June 1989—continues as a point of dispute between the EU and China. The EU has also had to address certain discrepancies emanating from China's WTO membership: the difficulty of acquiring licenses for banks, insurance companies, and telecommunication companies and issues of product piracy are matters of continuous complaint in Europe. The EU's readiness to recognize China as a market economy will not be strengthened if such Chinese actions continue.

As for human rights, the EU would need to insist that China sign the International Covenant on Political and Civil Rights. The EU must insist on China's recognition of international norms, including freedom of religion. Only China's clear commitment to freedom of religion, including the right of the Roman Catholic Church to choose its own bishops in China, would be true proof of China's recognition of international human rights. Such a commitment is needed to defuse fears of a return of Chinese nationalism and exceptionalism that is relativistic about universal norms. The full recognition of all international human rights norms would be a necessary revision of China's traditional universalism. Chinese recognition of the UN Covenant on Political and Civil Rights would not only affect China's relations with the Western democracies; most importantly, it would facilitate the dialogue about human rights and rule of law in China itself. Such a dialogue is particularly needed as far as freedom of religion is concerned. For the time being, it is more than regrettable that freedom of religion remains a highly limited right in China.

In dealing with its Northeast Asian partners, the EU will certainly encounter continuous and strong resistance to its multilateral and post-sovereigntist integration approach. In Northeast Asia, the EU continues to be confronted with countries that combine self-confidence with traditional concepts about the primacy of big power politics and a limited recognition of the political character and global strategic role of the European Union. Nevertheless, if the European Union wants to be taken seriously as a global player, it has to conceptualize an authentic policy strategy toward Northeast Asia that goes beyond the reflexes and instincts of a trading state.

The Broader Middle East Paradox: Stability without Success

Democratic Transformation as External Strategy

Geography is primarily politics: no region in the world can make this claim with more conviction than the Broader Middle East. This area between Marrakech and the fringes of Afghanistan, which in diplomatic and academic parlance has borne the name used here since the G8 summit of 2004, has undergone the most extraordinary transformations and conversions of labels. Since the ancient days of Mesopotamia through the Persian, Greek, and Roman civilizations, the region has been the pivotal center of religious and cultural, as well as ecological, economic, social, and political developments. The source of the most remarkable religious and cultural trends, innovations, and transformations, the cradle of the three great religions of monotheism, the fountain of ceaseless inspiration and contestation, this part of the world includes too much history to digest in a lifetime, too much recollection to come to terms with, too many conflicting identities to reconcile with the best of intentions, too many interpretations of the relationship between centrality and periphery, not to immediately inspire or provoke a counterargument. It has been called the Orient and the Fertile Crescent, the Near East and the Middle East. It has biblical and prebiblical roots unparalleled in any other corner of the world. And it has seen a degree of conflicts unmatched by all global standards. In the twenty-first century, it has become the quintessential example of a region without regionalism, the quintessential example of region-ness without regional integration.

No other area in the world projects such a strong sense of region-ness across the globe. Everybody seems to know about it, although most citizens of the earth have not had the chance to visit any of the famous places in the Broader Middle East. Yet they seem to belong to mankind as a whole. At the same time—or because of this collective property—the territories of the Broader Middle East have been more contested than any other pieces of land on the surface of the earth. Cultural memory, religious sanctuaries, limited ecological resources, and small size have made the heart of the Broader Middle East the space of the longest-lasting conflicts in the world. Politics and identity are strongly related and have many times been translated into territoriality. Reinterpretations of their meaning were fortified by the subjective righteousness of endless streams of claims in all directions, from all possible sources. The Broader Middle East—and more specifically the core of the Middle East, the area called Palestine—is the embodiment of human hope for salvation, of human quarrels over identity in religion and politics, and of human suffering in the name of conflicting claims.

The Broader Middle East is too complex to qualify for an easy approach to region-building. It is so vexed a region that it seems almost impossible to embark on the mundane effort to constitute a regional architecture that could tame the forces and memories of the area. Broadening the concept of the Middle East, it was hoped, would dilute the intensity of the inherent tension and dynamics. For the time being, the paradox of the politics of geography in the Middle East and its surroundings has been confirmed: stability prevails, albeit at a high price, and without success for the people in the region. The Broader Middle East follows its own logic and irrationality: it is the antithesis of order-building, and it does everything to support this rather mystical, if not outright demagogical, argument. It is an argument that claims no solution as the best and only possible solution for the intricacies of the Middle East and its broader neighborhood. One could also read the region by a reverse logic: because none of the principal actors is ultimately interested in a transformation of the status quo, they all have learned to live with the flaws of the status quo as if these flaws were the only possible form of normality.

The label "Broader Middle East" is the last in a long series of changing mental maps. Mental maps are drawn with the intention of relating geography and politics, physical realities and cultural interests. The term Broader Middle East was introduced by the US presidential administration in April 2004. In preparation for a meeting of the Group of 8(G8)—the leading eight industrial countries of the world—in Sea Island, Georgia, in June 2004, the US administration was circulating a working paper in which the term Greater Middle East was replaced by the term Broader Middle East. "Greater Middle East" had been used to classify the region of trouble and uncertainty following the terrorist attacks on the United States on 11 September 2001 (9/11). Introduced in a landmark policy paper written by Ronald D. Asmus and Kenneth Pollack, the term Greater Middle East was meant to describe the belt of instability, uncertainty, underdevelopment, lack of freedom, and potential Islamic fanaticism between Marrakech and Bangladesh.

The Greater Middle East was defined as the prime new strategic challenge for Western democracies in decades to come.[36] The paper called for a comprehensive Western strategy to deal with this zone of the world as the area of the most urgent and pressing challenges to long-term Western security and stability. Asmus and Pollack argued in favor of a revitalized transatlantic relationship to cope with the wide spectrum of issues related to the unpredictable tensions in the Greater Middle East. They wanted the United States and the European Union to reconceptualize a common long-term strategy driven by the promotion of freedom, pluralism, and democracy in the region. Their paper was widely discussed, and additional perspectives were added. Thus the term Greater Middle East made it into the public policy vocabulary. In light of the quarrels between the Bush administration and some of its European allies on how to deal with the dictatorship of Saddam Hussein in Iraq, the term Greater Middle East came to be criticized as alluding to neo-imperial Western claims of hegemony over that region. For largely cosmetic reasons, the Bush administration suggested changing the term, hoping that the term Broader Middle East indicated a broader and more inclusive approach.

The strategic outlook was identical: to stabilize and renew the Broader Middle East through democratic reform processes. Since 9/11, the lack of democratic openness and pluralism in the Arab world has become a leitmotiv of Western reflection on the future of the Arab world. The factual absence of civil society and a very limited role for the private economy in most Arab countries have added to the suspicion and concern. The Broader Middle East Initiative was intended to start a long-term process of transformation and, if necessary, regime change. The Bush administration tried to engage both its European and Japanese partners, along with moderate governments in the Arab world, in supporting its initiative. In the US, the strategy for transforming the Arab world had gained widespread consensus since the terrorist attacks of 9/11.[37] As for the potential Arab partners, the situation was more complicated. Ultimately, the Broader Middle East Initiative was implying regime change, while the primary interest of the regimes the US wanted to engage was to stay in power. The Broader Middle East Initiative, as agreed upon at the 2004 G8 summit, is based on manifold actions summarized under three distinct pillars:

- Supporting democracy and good governance.
- Creating a knowledge-based society.
- Developing and strengthening the economic potential.

Overshadowed by continuing insecurity in Iraq, the Broader Middle East Initiative lost its central place in the effort to stabilize the region. At least so far, the geopolitical reconceptualization of the Broader Middle East has not helped to support regional integration. One could also argue the other way around and suggest that exactly because of the absence of regional integration, geopolitical considerations dominate: external strategic interests and ambitions are stronger than regional designs. While the Arab states are involved in several mechanisms of regional cooperation, none of them has been able to present itself as the overarching shield for the future design of the region. Economic cooperation has been limited, for instance, to the Maghreb region or to the Persian Gulf. Political cooperation has been too grand and limitless, as in the case of the Arab League. None of these schemes has been able to portray a genuine and focused objective. Torn between localism and Arab cultural or even religious universalism, the efforts of Arab cooperation have not been able to reverse the relationship between objects and subjects in the region. In light of the ongoing conflict in Iraq, the

Broader Middle East Initiative and its enthusiastic commitment to democracy in the region have lost a certain momentum.

Since the existence of Israel, born in 1948 out of the ashes of the Holocaust in Europe, the Broader Middle East has been defined by the antagonism between Arab conceptualizations of the region that do not provide a place for Israel, and idealistic visions trying to redefine the region as one of peaceful coexistence between Jews, Muslims, and Christians. The Euro-Mediterranean Partnership launched by the European Union in 1995 has been the only scheme so far that includes all Arab countries around the Mediterranean and Israel. The Euro-Mediterranean Partnership (renamed Union for the Mediterranean in July 2008) is primarily a function of Europe's foreign policy projection. It was not born as a genuine design for the Broader Middle East, in spite of overlapping features. It is not inclusive as far as the Arab world is concerned. It has been highly asymmetric because of the economic, political, and organizational gaps that exist between the European Union and its partners on the southern rim of the Mediterranean. More than anything else, the Euro-Mediterranean Partnership underlines the absence of genuine and intrinsic regionalism in the Broader Middle East.

The combined GDP of all twenty-two member states of the Arab League is less than the GDP of Spain. Some 40 percent of adult Arabs—that is to say, around 65 million people—are illiterate, two thirds of them woman. The Arab labor market faces the entry of 50 million young people around 2010, 146 million by 2020. Estimates assume an unemployment rate of 25 percent for 2010. One third of all Arabs live on less than two dollars per day. Only 1.6 percent of the Arab population has access to the Internet. A desire to emigrate is expressed by 51 percent of young Arabs. In order to improve living standards in Arab countries substantially, the GDP growth rate would have to double from 3 to 6 percent annually. In reality, the average growth rates in Arab countries are around 1.3 percent annually. These are some of the dire facts describing the socioeconomic challenge in the Arab world. As far as Israel is concerned, only one figure will suffice to describe the contrast: with 7 million citizens, Israel has about one thirtieth of the population of all Arab countries in the Southern Mediterranean plus Iran, but Israel's GDP is one third of that of all these countries (Morocco, Algeria, Tunisia, Libya, Egypt, Lebanon, Jordan, Syria, Iran) together.[38]

The Arab Human Development Reports, prepared by Arab social scientists on behalf of the United Nations Development Programme, have been lauded as the most self-critical analysis of the Arab world's development deficits ever published. The reports have been highly sensitive to the development processes in the Arab world (2002), the status of Arab knowledge and education systems (2003), and the level of freedom in the Arab world (2004).[39] While the Arab world includes 7.5 percent of the world population, it generates only 2.5 percent of the global domestic economic product. While the world economy in 2002 benefited from $651 billion in foreign direct investment, the Arab countries were able to attract only $4.6 billion of this total amount. While the population growth in the Arab world, at 2.5 percent per year on average, is higher than population growth in most regions of the world, the average economic growth of 1.3 percent per year on average is lower than in all other developing regions except sub-Saharan Africa. But of all the deficits in the Arab worlds, the lack of political freedom is the most essential factor, as it impacts all spheres of life. Transforming the Arab world requires comprehensive actions in many fields. The Arab Human Development Reports reject the notion of cultural determinants for the current stage of freedom, democracy, and development in the Arab World: "Undoubtedly, the real flaw behind the failure of democracy in several Arab countries is not cultural in origin. It lies in the convergence of political, social and economic structures that have suppressed or eliminated organized social and political actors capable of turning the crisis of authoritarian and totalitarian regimes to their advantage."[40]

The Broader Middle East Initiative adopted at the G8 summit in June 2004 is a Western strategy: It is aimed at transforming the Arab world toward democracy and modernization that are compatible with Islamic traditions and Western interests. It will remain difficult to nurture a sense of ownership toward this approach across the Arab world. Despite the rhetoric of partnership, the Broader Middle East Initiative is driven by the assessment prevalent in the US since the terror attacks of 11 September 2001: that the Arab world poses the biggest strategic threat to Western security since the end of the Cold War. The initiative thus is built on Western perceptions of the region and is not intrinsically rooted in the region itself. This externalization of the region and its future has been an evident dilemma ever since the beginning of the Euro-Mediterranean Partnership in 1995 as well: regardless of the invocation of a Mediterranean "form of mind,"[41] the relationship between the European Union and its Southern Mediterranean Partners has remained asymmetric.

Both the US and EU initiatives reflect Western concerns about the unpredictability of developments in the Broader Middle East. Although motivated by different experiences and based on different geographical proximity to the area, the US and the EU strategies have one common feature: both were offered to the Broader Middle East mainly out of fear. They do not generate a genuine sense of region-ness or community-building under a local regional scheme in the Broader Middle East or on the southern shores of the Mediterranean. The idea of translating the experience of the system-opening character of the Conference on Security and Cooperation in Europe into a mechanism of stability, confidence-building, and transformation of relations into a form of regulated interdependence has not gained too much ground. The experience with the management of the final stages of the Cold War and the East-West-conflict is, at best, partially adaptable to the much more complex and genuine asymmetric relationship between Europe and its North African and Arab neighbors.[42]

Both Western-inspired initiatives are infused with goodwill regarding the establishment of a comprehensive partnership with the Arab countries. But in the end, their main driving force is a certain combination of fear and hope in the perception of the future potential of the Arab world. The Arab world, understood as a source of trouble, is meant to be transformed into a region of hope. The US and EU approaches differ in methods and instruments. The watershed of the terrorist attacks of 9/11 had an enormous impact on US foreign policy formulation, and still more on the American psyche. But the European Union cannot claim to have been any different in its principle approach and original attitude: the Arab world is perceived as a threat that has to be transformed into a partner. This legitimate foreign policy approach has many motives and functions, but it can hardly be considered instrumental to any substantial reflection about a regional architecture in the Broader Middle East. The external drive makes the absence of a genuine internal quest for region-building loom even larger over the Broader Middle East.[43]

Among the obstacles to a speedy implementation of an agenda of change favoring democracy, market economy, and global integration in the Broader Middle East, the following feature as the most serious and difficult to overcome:

- Globalization has been largely considered a unifying factor, but in many places, countries, and societies in the Broader Middle East, this has not been the experience. Rather, globalization has been experienced more as a pressure that crowds together the differences and tensions that follow from contrasting views of the world.
- International cooperation has been widely hailed as a vehicle for improving mutual understanding and enhancing respect for difference and authenticity. But for many places, people, and societies in the Broader Middle East, cooperation is understood as a cover for the imposition of Western values, sentiments, expressions of life, and experiences.
- Islamic terrorism has become a tactical expression of asymmetric warfare. It has added a new dimension of suspicion, fear, and strategic uncertainty to the relationship between the Western world and the Arab world. The absence of a resolution to the original Middle East conflict that reconciles Israel's right of existence with a democratic Palestinian state has sharpened the spiral of violence and demonstrated the limits of cooperative transformation of the broader region.
- The regime change in Iraq, triggered by the US-led invasion in 2003, toppled one of the most cruel and aggressive regimes in the Broader Middle East. The legacy of Saddam Hussein is horrendous. Yet the American use of violence has not helped to root the spirit of democracy, combined with sympathy for the US, as the embodiment of human freedom. To the contrary, the US-led invasion, and more so its aftermath of failed efforts to bring about peace, stability, and democracy in Iraq, has undermined much of the previously held goodwill toward Western values and notions of democratic politics.

- Democracy has been identified in the Western world as an inevitable precondition for peace and rule of law and as an irreplaceable precondition for solid and deep regional integration. The absence of both peace and rule of law in many Arab countries and other countries of the Broader Middle East, including Iran, has preempted any reasonable reflection about the potential for regional integration and regional community-building in the Broader Middle East.
- Israel has been torn in identity disputes about the relationship between its Jewish and its democratic character. Although democracy is more firmly rooted in Israel than in any other country of the Broader Middle East, the militarization of Israeli politics has turned out to be a continuous impediment to serious efforts to initiate trust-based measures to pool resources, not to mention sovereignty entitlements, with Israel's Arab neighbors.

Against this background, it seems rather unlikely that region-building could be helpful in resolving any of the fundamental differences dominating the Broader Middle East. Territorial controversies, regime differences, and economic asymmetries contribute to a set of identity conflicts that seem almost insurmountable. With the concept of the Broader Middle East, a new proposal for a mental map has been introduced into the region. But it has not been able to resolve any of the fundamental issues mentioned above. Reconciliation between Israel and the Arabs, between democracy and identity, between poverty and affluence—to name but the most burning and vexing issues—seems quite distant from the promises usually attributed to region-building.

One could, however, turn the logic of mistrust upside down. Following the French-German example in Europe, one could suggest that reconciliation between Israel and its main Arab neighbors might become exactly the type of engine the Broader Middle East would need to lay the foundation for long-term comprehensive region-building. Israeli-Arab reconciliation remains a dream for some of the most visionary minds, but part of the European experience might be of relevance in this context. Collective security arrangements cannot create stability or transform interstate relations if they are as contested as they are in the Middle East. Only a genuine transformation of relations between the main contending countries can create a new regional reality. Such a transformation, however, depends upon conditions that seem far from being realistically met in the Middle East or in the Broader Middle East.

Politics of Geography

The Broader Middle East abides under a strange paradox: the lack of success in recent decades had not triggered an uncontrollable desire for change. To the contrary, it has reinforced the desire for stability and the fear that any change could undermine stability. The region is grappling with external pressure, but it has not fully realized the opportunity for genuine internal change and modernization. At the heart of the paradoxical dilemma of the Broader Middle East lies the relationship between stability and success. In the Middle East this relationship is one of non-success as the prize for stability. As long as this attitude prevails, the Broader Middle East will continue to struggle with the inevitable eruptions of modernization and their counter reactions. It will simply remain an object of external strategies and interests. Only if the Broader Middle East genuinely internalizes the advantage and opportunity of change and transformation will it break the cycle of frustration and fear, external pressure and internal violence, foreign influence and domestic oppression.

The Broader Middle East has undergone many tremendous transformations as far as its perception is concerned. In the West, meanwhile, the mental map about this area has changed very often, according to shifting Western interests and image projections. In its modern history, the Broader Middle East has never had the opportunity—some say, the desire—to define itself in terms of region-ness, identity, and aspiration. Thus, what geographers label "Southwest Asia" has been redefined by outsiders more than by the indigenous people themselves. Northern Africa has been added to the geographic area traditionally defined as Southwest Asia in order to define the borders of the Broader Middle East as the most recent geopolitical delimitation of geography.

In 1916, the core of Southwest Asia, the ancient land of Mesopotamia, was labeled the Fertile Crescent. This area is more or less identical with the imperial borders drawn by the Sykes-Picot Agreement, "reserving areas" for France and Great Britain in the era of imperialism following the fall of the Ottoman Empire and the demise of its projection of power into Southwest Asia. The region of fertile land between the northern littoral of the Persian Gulf, Mesopotamia, Western Iran, and Southern Anatolia, and along the eastern shores of the Mediterranean up to the Sinai Peninsula, was understood to be the Fertile Crescent. When one of the Hashemites, the residing emir of Mecca, thought about the area he sincerely wanted to rule once the Ottomans had left, he had the same territories in mind. In the end, the Hashemites "only" got Transjordan and Iraq. In Syria, they were expelled by the French (1920) and across Saudi Arabia by Ibn Saud (1925).

The centrality of the region called the Fertile Crescent is evident throughout ancient history. Zion, the Phoenicians, Assyria, Babylon, Nebuchadnezzar—the Fertile Crescent is a crucial site in all their history. Southwest Asia, this "palimpsest of mental maps,"[44] has always inspired fantasy, archaeology, and cultural studies. It has never had a chance to conceptualize itself as a region. With the label "Orient," the region was designed as an expression of political geography with enormous impact on the evolution of Christianity and Roman history. In biblical geography, east corresponds with the orient. According to the Book of Genesis, the seat of paradise was located in the area of Mesopotamia and Persia.

The star announcing the birth of Jesus came from the east, as did the magi who adored the child in the manger in Bethlehem. The list of countries affected by the Holy Spirit—as mentioned in the Acts of the Apostles—reads from east to west. In the third century AD, the Roman Emperor Diocletian established a large administrative area called Diocesis Orientis. It included Libya, Egypt, Palestine, Phoenicia, Syria, Arabia, Mesopotamia, Osroene, Cyprus, Cilicia, and Isauria. Excluding the areas that belong to modern Turkey—as a member of NATO and a candidate for EU membership rather than a part of the "West"—the Diocesis Orientis corresponds largely to the Broader Middle East as conceived in the initiative of 2004.

For the Arabs, the East was the "Mashriq," the superior area of the rising sun. Arab historiographer Ibn Khallikan wrote in the thirteenth century that after the great flood—equivalent to the Old Testament flood survived by Noah and the inhabitants of his ark—the earth had the shape of a bird with its head in the east. Between the thirteenth and the seventeenth centuries, the Christian power in the Orient was shrinking. The year 1291 saw the fall of Acre, 1375 that of Armenia, 1453 of Constantinople, 1461 of Trebizond, 1523 of Rhodes, and 1669 of Crete. The Ottomans took control over large parts of the Orient. In the West, the Roman-Christian Orient became the Levant, an expression related to the primacy of commercial relations between Venice and Genoa and the Muslim ports of the eastern Mediterranean.

In Europe, the Orient was typically viewed with a mixture of fascination and horror. An obsession with the desert or romantic ideas about the origin of all civilizations became part of this perception of the East.[45] In terms of its political relevance in Europe and the US, in the nineteenth century the Orient was divided between the Ottoman Empire as the Near East and China as the Far East. For the influential strategist Alfred Thayer Mahan, it was imperative for Great Britain to balance Russian advances into Central Asia with British control of the region around the Persian Gulf. Mahan introduced the term "Middle East" in his work on the influence of sea power, but it was popularized by Valentine Chirol, a journalist writing in the *London Times* about the "Middle Eastern question." His articles were turned into a book in 1903 with the main thesis that, as India needed a security belt around its subcontinent, the Middle East would serve as an abstract space bordering India in the West. Mahan outlined the strategic implications for Great Britain: "The Middle East," he wrote in 1890, "if I may adopt a term which I have not seen, will some day need its Malta, as well as its Gibraltar . . . The British Navy should have the facility to concentrate in force, if occasion arise, about Aden, India, and the Gulf."[46]

Winston Churchill, then secretary of state for colonies, created a Middle East Department in the British Colonial Office in 1921, charged with supervising Iraq, Palestine, Transjordan, and Aden. In 1920, the Royal Geographical Association's Permanent Commission on Geographical Names proposed use of the term "Middle East" after the dissolution of the Ottoman Empire for the regions between the Bosporus and India. It also insisted that the term "Near East" should not be applied to the Balkan region. The efforts to reconceptualize the mental maps of imperial politics in the aftermath of the breakdown of the Ottoman Empire were made at the same time that cultural studies "discovered" the meaning of individual cultures and civilizations. German protestant theologian Ernst Troeltsch talked about "Kulturkreise." The orientalist Carl Heinrich Becker argued that the Western world and West Asian Islam should not be regarded as two different civilizations because both were molded by Hellenism. The Jewish historian Hans Kohn, in turn, propagated the idea of a common Mediterranean cultural space stretching from Gibraltar to Persia and Central Arabia.

In political reality, the dissolution of the Ottoman Empire brought smaller units, artificial and fledgling nation-states, territorial disputes, and conflicting nationalisms to the Broader Middle East. The dissolution of colonialism transpired parallel to the new fixture of terminology and perception. In 1939, the British army established a Middle East Command, the first regime under this nomenclature stretching from Malta to Eritrea and to Persia. After the end of World War II, decolonization and the rise of the Cold War overlapped. British and American efforts to establish an integrated Middle East Defense Structure directed against the expansionism of the Soviet Union failed. Amidst these transformations, a strong new and lasting fact was established: on 29 November 1947, the United Nations decided on the partition of Palestine, and on 14 May 1948, the state of Israel was founded. This was immediately followed by the outbreak of the first war between Israel and the Arabs as Egypt, Saudi Arabia, Jordan, Lebanon, Syria, and Iraq united to attack their new neighbor. The Middle East had found its central conflict for decades to come. Conflicting territorial claims lay at its root and were always to accompany it. Cooperation, let alone integration of any sort, was ruled out by definition.

Arab Efforts at Region-Building

In the absence of cultural homogeneity, pan-Arab nationalism grew as an alternative source and path of region-building. But because pan-Arabism's limited efforts to integrate the Arab countries were only based on ideological nationalism, the struggle against the existence of Israel was usually more focused than the efforts to integrate the Arab nations. Authoritarian nationalism such as that promoted under Egypt's charismatic President Gamal Abdel Nasser could not succeed in terms of either socioeconomic development or the Arab dream of cultural and ideological unity. Israel remained the thorn in the side of the Arab world.

In 1945, the Arab League was founded as one of the very first expressions of regional actor–ness in the world. Ideologically inspired by pan-Arab nationalism, the Arab League went through ambivalent stages. Its member states' unity against the existence of Israel was always stronger than any form of cooperation and integration among themselves. Meanwhile, the dilemma between national sovereignty and regional collaboration was ever present. In 1950, for example, the Arab League member states signed a defense pact that Jordan and Iraq refused to join. Instead, Iraq entered the Baghdad Pact (CENTO) in 1955, hoping to get a better deal in a security arrangement that included Great Britain and had the support of NATO and thus the US. The new Iraqi regime's withdrawal from CENTO in 1959 did not enhance efforts for an Arab security community either. The Arab League also launched an Arab Common Market in the mid 1960s, but it never succeeded. Intra-Arab trade was always limited and never reached more than 6 percent of the total trade of the Arab League countries. The development of a political "Arab consciousness" always encountered its limits in the dominance of national sovereignty and outright nationalism in key Arab states.

Among the most interesting expressions of symbolic politics in the Arab League was the establishment of an Arab Parliament on 27 December 2005. Initially with eighty-eight members—four from the parliaments or advisory councils of each Arab League member state—this parliament was the first-ever effort to democratize the activities of the Arab League. Paradoxically, the Arab Parliament includes representatives from Saudi Arabia and the United Arab Emirates, two countries without any elected representation. Since in most Arab countries the agenda of change associated with the US-inspired Broader Middle East Initiative is perceived with hesitation, if not rejection, the announcement of an Arab Parliament came as a pleasant surprise. Critically speaking, it might well be misused to substitute for national changes inside Arab League member states. For the time being, the Arab Parliament has no binding legislative authority. It can give its opinion only on matters referred to it by the Arab League Council. The parliament is based in Damascus and is meant to hold two meetings per year. Its first speaker, elected for the year 2006, was Muhammad Jassim al-Saqr, a moderate Kuwaiti who chaired his country's foreign relations committee.

The Arab League Parliament might serve the role of a consultative parliament in the period of early constitutionalism. It will be measured not only by the quality of its work, but by its degree of independent judgment and measurable influence. It will also be interesting to follow the impact of the Arab Parliament on the agenda of democratic change and transformation toward freedom and pluralism in the individual member states of the Arab League.

The Arab Maghreb Union, established in 1989, is Maghreb Arab countries' response to accelerating European integration. Its aim is a customs union along the lines of the European Community. When Algeria, Libya, Mauritania, Morocco, and Tunisia founded the Arab Maghreb Union, their joint GDP was equivalent to 1.5 percent of the EC's total. But the real difference was the absence of a clearly defined objective with plausible steps and criteria to be followed. Furthermore, the Arab Maghreb Union was not based on democratic governance.

It was an echo of Europe, not a genuine Arab construction. At the time of its creation, 65 percent of trade by the member states of the Arab Maghreb Union was with Europe, while intra-Maghreb trade was limited to 2.3 percent. Whereas Morocco and Tunisia had successfully completed structural adjustment programs as requested by the International Monetary Fund, Algeria had declined to do so. The most evident feature of the economies of the Arab Maghreb Union member states was their lack of complementarity: they were all largely focused on agricultural products and raw materials. All these factors made the Arab Maghreb Union from its beginning a structure of reactive regionalism, not an expression of community-building–oriented regionalism. Economic integration in the Arab world has largely been a rhetorical exercise.[47]

For the time being, this also holds true for the concept of the Greater Arab Free Trade Area (GAFTA). GAFTA was initiated in 1997 by Bahrain, Iraq, Egypt, Kuwait, Lebanon, Morocco, Oman, Qatar, Saudi Arabia, Sudan, Tunisia, the United Arab Emirates, and Yemen. In 2005 GAFTA was adopted as a pact by the Arab League. Its objective is most laudable, namely "to stimulate intra-Arab trade, encourage Arab and foreign investments and increase competition in domestic markets."[48] The hope to encourage non–oil-based intra-regional trade accompanies the evolution of GAFTA. Precise criteria and time frames are missing, however, so an early implementation of the overall GAFTA objectives cannot be expected. In the absence of valid transnational or supranational mechanisms for a functioning regional economic system of cooperation and integration, it is difficult to imagine how intra-regional trade can flourish. According to WTO figures, intra-regional trade among Arab countries in the Middle East has remained as low as 7 percent on average during the past decade.

The most advanced instrument of regional integration among Arab states is the Gulf Cooperation Council. But there are no indications that the Gulf Cooperation Council could possibly grow into an instrument of regional cooperation for and among all Arab states. The main reason lies in the inter-Arab "stalemate" between oil-rich and oil-poor countries.[49] The GCC remains, at least so far, confined to the conservative monarchies of the Persian Gulf. This is its strength and weakness. But even if the GCC broadened its membership to other Arab states—even if it eventually stretched toward Morocco in the west and Iraq in the Northeast—it would not be able to overcome the immanent limit of Arab efforts to conceptualize regional integration thus far: its focus, purpose, and objective remain linked to the identity among Arab states. In religious, linguistic, and cultural terms, the Arab countries prefer to remain among themselves. To conceptualize region-ness in purely geographical terms would require them to resolve the question of the membership of Israel and Iran in any possible regional scheme. As long as this is ruled out on principle, "Middle East regionalization seems to be an illusion with no real basis."[50] In fact, it tends to be conceptualized around and against one or two of the biggest actors in the region. To talk of regionalism, if it is understood and conceptualized as a mechanism of deterrence and purposeful prevention of inclusive regionalism, seems to be a contradiction in terms. At least it sheds light on the most delicate of all issues concerning region-ness in the Broader Middle East, whether it is labeled or qualified.

Arab regional integration efforts have remained marginal, overlapping, and needful of clear focus and objective.[51] They have all defined the region without the existence of Israel as part of it. They have refrained from addressing the issues of governance, democracy, and rule of law, including supranational rule of law. They have been ideology-driven. But at the same time, they have always been confronted with the dilemma between the quest for Arab unity and claims to national identity. Arab unity is largely a political term, based on common ethnicity, language, culture. The Arab nation is religiously diverse, as Christian minorities exist in most Arab countries. Since the expulsion of Jews from most Arab countries, hardly any Jews can be found in Arab states, except for small minorities in Morocco and in non-Arab Islamic countries like Turkey and Iran. Whether or not there is one Arab nation remains a matter of dispute in light of the diversity of Arab nation-states. They might be states without real nations, yet states they are; thus do they prevent Arab unity from happening. The Broader Middle East contributes no more than 4 percent to the world economy. Except for the role of oil and gas in the Gulf states, the Arab contribution to the world economy is peripheral. Under these conditions, it is difficult to imagine how Arab region-ness or efforts of region-building can be anything but weak.[52]

With, Without, or Against Israel?

Both Israel and Iran are excluded from Arab reflections on region-building. The ideological, national, and cultural arguments are well known. Yet most dramatic are the economic implications. All economies in the region have their main trading partners outside their own home region. The flip side of this fact is their mutual competition for external investment. They are also competing over collaboration related to sharing modern technologies. This lack of intra-regional cooperation has made all countries in the Broader Middle East more dependent upon external developments. It has also made them more vulnerable as a consequence. Cultural and ideological purity simply does not pay out.

Israel is more successful than any other country in the Broader Middle East region. Judged by its technological base, its education system, the structure of its economy, and the per capita income of its citizens, Israel is a country of the first world. To talk about Israel's membership in the OECD is not as far-fetched as it might seem. Occasionally, NATO membership or even the eligibility of EU membership is discussed. While NATO membership is more realistic than EU membership, Israel clearly is a first-world country amidst Third World neighbors. Even under the most optimistic of circumstances, its cooperation with Arab neighbors would always be asymmetric. Yet it is worth reflecting on its potential, notwithstanding the vexing political and security matters that prevent any peaceful neighborhood-ness from happening at this point in time. It is also worth recalling that relations between Israel and the Palestinians have not only and always been defined by enmity and tension.

During the 1970s, for instance, the Gaza Strip and the West Bank experienced enormous economic growth. Following the Camp David Agreement of 17 September 1978 and the subsequent Israel-Egypt Peace Treaty of March 1979—the first factual attempt to anchor Israel in its region—Palestinians went increasingly to Israel as guest workers. Before the outbreak of the first Intifada in 1987 and the first Iraq war in 1990, around 35 percent of the Palestinian workforce was commuting into the Israeli heartland. The first Intifada ended with the Oslo Agreement in 1993 and the establishment of the Palestinian Authority. Much of this hopeful development was interrupted and destroyed by the outbreak of the second Intifada following failed negotiations between Israel, the Palestinian Authority, and the US at Camp David in July 2000. In February 2005, a cease-fire between Israel and the Palestinian Authority was signed in Sharm el Sheikh, but the hope for peace based on a two-state solution diminished more and more. By 2006, unemployment in the Gaza Strip and in the West Bank figured between 70 and 80 percent. The election of a Hamas government in the Palestinian territories in January 2006 was a reflection of these depressing socioeconomic conditions.

The value-added relationship that existed between Israelis and Palestinians before the outbreak of the Intifada was by and large promising. The capital- and technology-based Israeli economy was in need of cheap Palestinian labor, including labor-intensive manufacturing and agricultural work. Any effort to reverse the trend of suspicion, hatred, destruction, and violence would have to start again at where hopeful trends in the relations between Israel, the Palestinians, and Jordan once stood, when Simon Peres outlined his vision for a "New Middle East" in 1992.[53]

The most promising ideas for regional cooperation in the Middle East have been designed to transform the relationship between Israel and Jordan. Both countries, after all, are the consequence of the 1947 partition plan of the United Nations and were confronted with the failed creation of a Palestinian state in its immediate aftermath. Jordan, with one tenth of Israel's GDP and three quarters of Israel's population, has a huge import dependency and a huge trade deficit, and is highly dependent upon food imports. Palestinians make up 50 percent of Jordanian's population. The outbreak of violence in the 1970s ("Black September") and bread riots in 1989 indicate the potential for dramatic eruptions in the Hashemite Kingdom. The Jordanian-Israeli Peace Agreement of 26 October 1994—the second peace agreement between Israel and an Arab country after the Camp David Agreement with Egypt of 1979—was not only the second attempt to anchor Israel in its region. It was also a far-sighted effort to transform the Israeli-Palestinian conflict through diplomatic and socioeconomic means without resolving the territorial disputes and without hoping for the creation of an overarching regional security system.

Between the Israeli-Egyptian peace accord and the Jordanian-Israeli peace accord, Israel was able to garner a strong and impressive peace dividend. Israel's GDP increased by 40 percent, while its military budget was reduced from 15 percent of the country's expenditures in 1982 to 8.2 percent in 1993. The Jordanian-Israeli Peace Agreement was coupled with the perspective of improved and, factually, renewed relations between the Palestinians and both Israel and Jordan. The Jordanian-Palestinian Economic Agreement of 7 January 1984 paved the way for the reopening of Jordanian banks in the West Bank for the first time since the Israeli occupation in 1967. Even more spectacular was the establishment of a joint Israeli-Palestinian-Jordanian water commission in 1995. Article 6 of the Jordanian-Israeli peace accord had defined water as an essential element in creating a new, peaceful, and prosperous Middle East.

In his search for a Middle East equivalent of the role that coal and steel played in the transformation of Europe after World War II, Prince Hassan bin Talal has suggested making use of water and energy. Both resources are needed more than ever in the Middle East. Both are scarce and their locations contested. It requires a sophisticated degree of imagination to contemplate putting water and energy in the Middle East under a common supranational authority composed of representatives of Israel, Jordan, and a Palestinian state. Prince Hassan's vision of a "full-fledged Conference for Security and Cooperation for the Middle East"[54] is probably the only realistic option, should the Middle East overcome its current spiral of mistrust and parochialism, hatred and violence. In order to do this, it will need—as the European experience shows—farsighted and courageous leaders. Visionary ideas will never turn into realistic and manageable programs by themselves. Such a shift will not come about by natural osmosis either. It will require political decisions and hence political leadership. No commodity is scarcer in the Middle East than courageous leadership. One should not, however, forget how long it took Europe to turn around and organize the continent on the basis of peace, partnership, and mutual respect.

It is not too difficult to imagine water as a catalyst to transform the Middle East. The Jordan River basin connects Jordan, Israel, Syria, and Lebanon through three rivers: the Hasbami River, originating in Syria with parts of its outflow in Lebanon; Dan and Banyias, beginning in the Golan Heights (occupied by Israel since 1967, annexed in 1981) and flowing into the Jordan River in northern Israel; and the Yarmouk River, originating in Syria, bordering Jordan, Syria, the Golan Heights, and hence also Israel, and then flowing eastward into Jordan. The Jordan River basin is "constantly overused"[55] and has become increasingly saline, with negative effects on its ecological system.

Israel has used its occupation of the West Bank to change the parameters of water distribution in the Middle East. Before 1967, one third of the water consumed by Israel originated as groundwater in the West Bank. Because West Bank aquifers extend over Israeli territory, Israel has been able to drill for this groundwater from inside its original borders. Today, 25 percent of all Israeli water comes from the West Bank. Of the replenishable water resources of the West Bank, 80 percent is used by Israel or by Jewish settlers in the West Bank. The Palestinians receive only 20 percent of the West Bank water, and even this amount is subject to harsh Israeli restrictions. Israel effectively controls the development and utilization of subsurface water across the West Bank. Water per unit is also more expensive for Palestinians than it is for Israelis. Palestinian wells may not exceed a depth of 140 meters, while Israeli wells can go as deep as 800 meters.[56] While Israel has developed sophisticated water-saving irrigation schemes, the agricultural production and productivity in the Palestinian territories is extremely underdeveloped. The conditions in the Gaza Strip are particularly poor.

In 1953, a US-sponsored plan ("Johnston United Water Plan") was the first effort to achieve an equitable distribution of water in the Middle East. Ever since, the issue has been present. Satisfactory results have not yet been found. The Jordanian-Israeli Peace Agreement of 26 October 1994 makes explicit reference to the water issue: "The Parties recognize that their water resources are not sufficient to meet their needs . . . Cooperation in water-related subjects would be to the benefit of both Parties, and will help alleviate their water shortages" (Article 6, 3–4).[57] An interim agreement of 28 September 1995 between Israel and the PLO recognized the importance and urgency of the water issue. Resolving it, however, was left for final status negotiations between Israel and the Palestinians.

Energy and its related technologies might serve as the second pillar on which to build a Middle East equivalent to the European Coal and Steel Community. The worldwide demand for liquefied natural gas and for oil will increase enormously during the next decades, and the Broader Middle East contains 40 percent of global oil reserves and 45 percent of global gas reserves. The energy divide between the energy-rich and energy-poor countries of the region could not be more intensive. The technology divide between Israel and practically all Arab countries—the energy-rich as well as the energy-poor—is similarly startling. Conceptualizing the future use of energy in favor of a comprehensive development scheme for the region and conceptualizing a future strategy to promote sophisticated energy-related technologies aimed at mutual gains and benefits—including technologies related to renewable energy resources—could lend consequential perspective to the Broader Middle East in general and to the conflict-ridden Middle East in particular.

Such perspective is only conceivable as part of a comprehensive scheme to reconceptualize the relations between countries and nations, people and societies, interests and values in the Broader Middle East. It would require a multi-pillar approach with multidimensional action plans. Moreover, it would require patience over the long haul, and optimism about the primacy of peace and the mutual advantage of cooperation. It would require no less than a complete reversion of the current trend and structure of the conflict that has dominated the Middle East for the last sixty years. Foremost, it would require a redefinition of the relationship between territory and identity, the main ingredients in the success or failure of any form of cooperation across borders drawn by culture and history.

Iran

It is highly speculative to anticipate developments related to the Iranian nuclear program. But it can be assumed with some confidence that Iran will be the focus of trepidation for many years to come. While the country's economy is suffering from isolation after three decades under an Islamic regime, and while the Iranian society is paradoxically as diverse as the country's regime is ultimately totalitarian, the geopolitical implication of Iran's nuclear ambitions is unpredictable. It is not surprising that the Iranian plan to produce enriched uranium that can be used to fabricate an atomic bomb has met with hectic global diplomacy and deep concern about the possible escalation of a new and highly dangerous military conflict in the Middle East. The situation has been further aggravated since 2005, when Iran's President Mahmoud Ahmadinejad declared the aim to wipe Israel off the map of the world.

Iran will remain a crucial factor in power relations in the Broader Middle East—and presumably beyond. Any regional architecture will have to include Iran if it is to be stable and viable. For two decades, the United States practiced a policy of double containment against Iraq and Iran. In the end, it ended in deadlock. The violent regime change 2003 in Iraq was seen by the Bush administration as the ultimate insurance policy against the unpredictable rise of radical adventurism by Saddam Hussein's regime. In fact, one could argue critically that the regime change in Iraq was akin to an American act of self-liberation from the self-imposed containment policy against Iraq that had gone nowhere. How the US, and the world community as a whole, will deal with Iran—the region's other long-standing target of a US policy of containment—once the country possibly acquires nuclear bombs, is an open question at the time of writing. Yet one conclusion can be drawn already. What has been true with regard to Israel is also applicable to Iran, despite the two countries seeming to be light years apart: any strategy that intends to exclude them from being anchored in their region will at best remain unsuccessful. Under the worst circumstances, such a strategy guarantees permanent conflict.

Building an inclusive regional strategy requires, of course, that all actors comply with international norms shared in their region. This is true for Israel and Iran alike. Iran must comply with international norms if it wants to be integrated in its region. Self-imposed exclusion has been an option for Iran since the Islamic revolution of 1979, but it cannot possibly be the perspective for another generation, given the socioeconomic and demographic developments in the Islamic Republic of Iran.[58]

Differences in religion and identity, politics and territoriality, geopolitical interests and links, economic resources and the sociocultural agenda, could not be bigger than they are between Iran and Israel, but they are similarly vast between Iran and most other Arab states. Yet the logic of globalization has also reached the shores of the Broader Middle East. It is conceivable that counter reactions to a gradual yet comprehensive opening of the whole region will be more radical, and if inevitable even more violent, than all rational arguments in favor of peaceful coexistence. The overarching question is about the precondition and function of regional cooperation and integration. Can it trigger substantial transformations in matters of identity, governance, and principled beliefs, or can it only be the consequence of related changes in the architecture and mechanics of the region's conflicts? In other words, to what degree is regional cooperation and integration cause or effect of conflict transformation? These abstract questions relating to theories of regionalism have essentially practical meaning for the evolution of the Broader Middle East. The weight of these questions, however, does not make it easier to expect early and simple solutions.

Region-ness Without Regionalism

Among geopolitical tensions of the highest possible order, regime and governance differences of magnitude, and seemingly insurmountable discrepancies in identities and principled beliefs, it is difficult to imagine stability and cooperation in the Broader Middle East. Before any reasonable perspective of inclusive cooperation, let alone integration, can be conceived, an impossibly tall agenda of transformations would have to be implemented:

- Transformation of the character of territorial disputes, and moreover of the relationship between territory and identity.
- Transformations of the ways and means of conflict resolution, including the threat of violence.
- Transformation of the nature and identity of regimes and governance methods.
- Transformation of the perception of resources, their usefulness, limits, and common purpose.
- Transformation from a zero-sum mentality to one of recognized mutual gains.
- Transformation of the mutual perception driven by hate and fear.
- Transformation in the relationship between internal changes and the role of external actors.

The Broader Middle East is the embodiment of region-ness without regionalism. A collective security system, imposed from the outside and guaranteed by outsiders, will not work. It may create short-term pacification, but it cannot contribute to long-term structural transformations of the nature indicated. Trust will not grow out of external strategies and imposed solutions. Neither can trust grow from above if the structures of society and politics are closed, introspective, and non-pluralistic. The prospects for a comprehensive and inclusive regionalization of the Broader Middle East are bleak. Turning the wheel of history, in this region of the most vexing geopolitical and domestic conflicts and tensions, seems implausible and perhaps impossible. Yet over time, retaining the same old parameters of interstate relations and intra-societal confrontations will come at a cost. The price will be the growing marginalization and inevitable impoverishment of a world region that feels as if it were the center of the world only because the rest of the world is watching—with fear, despair, and sometimes disgust. The Broader Middle East will have to learn to make politics in its region less intense, dramatic, and potentially violent. It will need to develop incentives for political actors and community leaders to refrain from inflating the importance of their convictions as though the fate of their community and the future of its principled belief depended only upon the degree of their politicians' radicalism. This is no easier than squaring the circle. But only if the Broader Middle East becomes less relevant for stability, peace, and the progress of the world can it learn to live with all countries, nations, and groups in the region.

A Role for the European Union?

Under the given circumstances of the Broader Middle East, the possible role of the European Union is extremely limited, yet necessary. In its Security Strategy of 2003, the EU underlined that the "resolution of the Arab/Israeli conflict is a strategic priority for Europe."[59] It is central to dealing with other problems and sources of instability stemming from the region. As a member of the Middle East Quartet along with the United Nations, the United States, and Russia, the European Union was involved in the strategic design of a roadmap—presented on 30 April 2003—intended to lead to a peaceful two-state solution in the Middle East. The US initiated the Quartet. Its Performance-Based Roadmap to a Permanent Two-State Solution to the Israeli-Palestinian Conflict[60] has been lauded and declared dead in equal measure. However, there is no alternative to this roadmap. And there is no alternative to European-American cooperation, no matter how long the process of confidence-building, peaceful coexistence, and eventually, reconciliation may last in the Middle East.

The European Union is articulating its own approach and pursuing its own focus and agenda. Since 1995, the European Union has actively promoted enhanced cooperation with all littoral states of the Mediterranean, including Israel, through the Euro-Mediterranean Partnership (renamed Union for the Mediterranean in 2008). In 2003, the EU launched its new Neighborhood Policy with the presentation of a Wider Europe Neighborhood Concept, an initiative aimed at promoting peace, stability, democracy, education, and market economy at the peripheries of the European Union. The EU understands its Neighborhood Policy as complementary to the Union for the Mediterranean. Since 2007, the European Neighborhood Policy has gained more structure, substance, and differentiation due to its European Neighborhood Policy Instrument, a tailor-made financial tool. The EU's proximity to the Broader Middle East makes EU engagement across the region imperative. The slow evolution of a coherent approach has not helped the EU gain credibility. On the other hand, the European Union is appreciated for its cautious, multidimensional, and rather balanced approach to the agenda of transformation and reform in the Broader Middle East. The weight and leverage of the European Union depend, however, on the EU's ability to connect with US involvement in the Broader Middle East. But even if the US and EU work together, substantial transformation in the area of one of the longest-standing conflicts in the world will not take place if the countries and political actors involved in the region fail to acquire a stronger sense of ownership in the process of change toward freedom and cooperation.

After the latest military escalation in the summer of 2006, the European Union grew into a strategic role in the Middle East. At the request of the United Nations, the European Union participated in the expanded UN peacekeeping force UNIFIL (United Nations Interim Force in Lebanon). Almost half of its 15,000 soldiers came from EU member states. In the absence of a single European army, individual EU member states had to provide contingents and were responsible for negotiating the mandate of the peacekeepers. Yet together with the EU Border Assistance Mission in Rafah at the Palestinian-Egyptian border and with the EU Police Mission in the Palestinian Territories (EUPOL COPPS), they were perceived as an EU peacekeeping force. Both these mission operations were in place in early 2006. The presence of European police officers and soldiers in the Middle East had become the strongest indication for a strategic role of the European Union in the Middle East. Traditionally, the EU had been perceived as a donor to the region; now it began to gain political and security responsibility in the region.

This also gave the EU leverage with the United States. During the annual summit meeting held in Dromoland (Ireland) on 26 June 2004, the EU and the US had agreed on the need for local ownership in all Middle East countries. Reconciling American and European attitudes and approaches on the future evolution of the Broader Middle East and the agenda for freedom and democracy was helpful and finally was considered necessary by both sides. Yet it does not by any means substitute for the primacy of the region and all its actors. No rhetoric or declaration in the world can transcend the daunting fact that has been at the source of the conflicts in the Broader Middle East and will remain the single most important engine of any viable solution. Until this happens, any agenda of cooperation and integration remains an alien construction in the Broader Middle East, an extraordinary region without regionalism.

Notes

1. See Christopher M. Dent, "Northeast Asia: A Region in Search of Regionalism?" in Christopher M. Dent and David W.F. Huang (eds.), *Northeast Asian Regionalism: Learning from the European Experience* (London: Routledge, 2002), 1–15.
2. Samuel S. Kim, "Northeast Asia in the Local-Regional-Global Nexus," in Samuel S. Kim (ed.), *The International Relations of Northeast Asia* (Lanham: Rowman and Littlefield, 2004), 13.
3. See David B. Abernethy, *The Dynamics of Global Dominance: European Overseas Empires, 1415–1980* (New Haven: Yale University Press, 2000).
4. See Edwin O. Reischauer, *Japan: The Story of a Nation*, 3rd ed. (Tokyo: Tuttle, 1982), 107–136; Albert M. Craig, *Japan: Tradition and Transformation*, 3rd ed. (Tokyo: Tuttle, 1981), 116–144.
5. See Andrew C. Nahm, *Introduction to Korean History and Culture*, 9th ed. (Elizabeth, NJ, and Seoul: Hollym, 2004), 141–175.
6. See John J. Stephan, *The Russian Far East: A History* (Stanford: Stanford University Press, 1994).
7. See John King Fairbank, *Trade and Diplomacy on the China Coast: The Opening of Treaty Ports, 1842–1854* (Stanford: Stanford University Press, 1969).
8. Called the "Tumen River Area Development Programme," it has more theoretical potential than practical promise; see its homepage online under http://www.tumenprogramme.org.
9. Gilbert Rozman, "Russian Foreign Policy in Northeast Asia," in Kim, *The International Relations of Northeast Asia*, 215.
10. An international conference in 2004 under the auspices of the Korean president's project for the formation of a Northeast Asian Cultural Community for Peace and Prosperity brought together representatives from China, Japan, and Korea, but no thought was spent on the Northeast Asian role of either the US or Russia. For the proceedings of the conference see Korean Research Council for Humanities and Social Sciences (ed.), *The Policy Study Session for the Formation of the Northeast Asian Cultural Community for Peace and Prosperity: Proceedings of the International Conference* (Seoul: Korean Research Council for Humanities and Social Sciences, 2004).
11. Thomas G. Moore, "China's International Relations: The Economic Dimension," in Kim, *The International Relations of Northeast Asia*, 106.
12. Ibid., 129.
13. Alastair Iain Johnston, "China's International Relations: The Political and Security Dimension," in Kim, *The International Relations of Northeast Asia*, 67.
14. Cited in Nahm, *Introduction to Korean History and Culture*, 213. See this book also for an account of the path that led from Japanese colonial rule to Soviet occupation and the subsequent partition under an American plan to limit Soviet influence on the Korean peninsula: 213–256.
15. Thomas Berger, "Japan's International Relations: The Political and Security Dimensions," in Kim, *The International Relations of Northeast Asia*, 135.
16. C.S. Eliot Kang, "North Korea's International Relations: The Successful Failure?" in Kim, *The International Relations of Northeast Asia*, 287.
17. Lowell Dittmer, "The Emerging Northeast Asian Regional Order," in Kim, *The International Relations of Northeast Asia*, 336.
18. Ibid., 339.
19. See Motoshige Itoh, "Economic Integration in East Asia: A Japanese Viewpoint," in Woosik Moon and Bernadette Andreosso-O'Callaghan (eds.), *Regional Integration: Europe and Asia Compared* (Aldershot: Ashgate, 2005), 78–93.

20. For details see the organization's homepage online at http://www.apecsec.org.sg/apec/about_apec.html.

21. Ibid. APEC members include Australia, Brunei, Canada, Chile, the People's Republic of China, Hong Kong, Indonesia, Japan, the Republic of Korea, Malaysia, Mexico, New Zealand, Papua New Guinea, Peru, the Philippines, Russia, Singapore, Taiwan (officially labeled "Chinese Taipei"), Thailand, the United States, and Vietnam.

22. Ibid.

23. Hyun-Seok Yu, "Asian Regionalism: A Post-Crisis Perspective," in Moon and Andreosso-O'Callaghan, Regional Integration, 30.

24. Ibid., 38.

25. For details see its homepage online at http://www.aseansec.org/64.htm.

26. See Woosik Moon et al., "Monetary Cooperation in East Asia," in Moon and Andreosso-O'Callaghan, Regional Integration, 134–152.

27. On EU-ASEAN relations see Karen Smith, European Union Foreign Policy in a Changing World (Oxford: Polity, 2003), 69–96.

28. Kim, "Northeast Asia in the Local-Regional-Global Nexus," 25. "Comprehensive national power" ("zonghe guoli") is a term used by Chinese social scientists to cover a whole set of indicators used to assess the overall performance and position of their country.

29. See Johnston, "China's International Relations," 77.

30. According to a 2004 opinion poll, 20 percent of South Koreans would be ready to support North Korea in case of a military conflict on the peninsula. While the GDP of South Korea is thirty times bigger than that of North Korea, the development gap ought to be leveled, according to the South Korean government, before a confederative development might bring the two Korean states together. See Peter Sturm, "Das Unbekannte planen," Frankfurter Allgemeine Zeitung, no. 26, 1 February 2005, 10.

31. Francis Fukuyama, "Re-Envisioning Asia," Foreign Affairs 84, no. 1 (2005): 75–87, 80–81.

32. Ibid., 83.

33. European Union, A Secure Europe in a Better World: European Security Strategy, adopted by the Heads of State and Government at the European Council in Brussels on 12 December 2003 (Paris: European Union Institute for Security Studies, 2004).

34. For details see European Commission (EC), "The Asia-Europe Meeting (ASEM)," online at: http://ec.europa.eu/external_relations/asem/index_en.html. So far, ASEM summits have been held in Bangkok (1996), London (1998), Seoul (2000), Copenhagen (2002), Vietnam (2004), and Helsinki (2006).

35. See Christopher M. Dent, "The Asia-Europe Meeting (ASEM) Process: Beyond the Triadic Political Economy?" in Heiner Hänggi et al. (eds.), Interregionalism and International Relations (Abingdon and New York: Routledge, 2006), 113–127.

36. Ronald D. Asmus and Kenneth M. Pollack, "The New Transatlantic Project," Policy Review 115 (2002): 3–18, online at: http://www.hoover.org/publications/policyreview/3459216.html.

37. For a critical analysis see Mohssen Massarat, "Demokratisierung des Greater Middle East," Aus Politik und Zeitgeschichte 45 (2005): 30–37; Serban Filip Cioculescu, "Thinking Globally, Acting Locally: The Greater Middle East Initiative and the International Community," Romanian Journal of International Affairs 10, nos. 1–2, (2005): 187–213.

38. See Bernard Hoekman and Patrick Messerlin, "Initial Conditions and Incentives for Arab Economic Integration: Can the European Community's Success Be Emulated?" in Ahmed Galal and Bernard Hoekman (eds.), Arab Economic Integration: Between Hope and Reality (Cairo: Egyptian Center for Economic Studies and Washington, D.C.: Brookings Institution Press, 2003), 116.

39. United Nations Development Programme (ed.), Arab Human Development Report 2002: Creating Opportunities for Future Generations (New York: UNDP Bureau for Arab States, 2003); United Nations Development Programme (ed.), Arab Human Development Report 2003: Building a Knowledge

Society (New York: UNDP Bureau for Arab States, 2004); United Nations Development Programme (ed.), *Arab Human Development Report, 2004: Toward Freedom in the Arab World* (New York: UNDP Bureau for Arab States, 2005).

40. United Nations Development Programme, *Arab Human Development Report, 2004*, 11.

41. Thus the former President of Malta, Guido de Marco, "The Future of Euro-Mediterranean Relations: The Vision of Malta," in: Jacobs, Andreas (ed.), *Euro-Mediterranean Co-operation: Enlarging and widening the perspective*, ZEI Discussion Paper C131 (Bonn: Center for European Integration Studies, 2005), 8–15; see also Stephen Calleya, *Is the Barcelona Process Working?* ZEI Discussion Paper C 75 (Bonn: Center for European Integration Studies, 2000); Felix Mayer (ed.), *Managing Asymmetric Interdependencies within the Euro-Mediterranean Partnership*, ZEI Discussion Paper C 101 (Bonn: Center for European Integration Studies, 2002); Andreas Marchetti (ed.), *Ten Years Euro-Mediterranean Partnership: Defining European Interests for the Next Decade*, ZEI Discussion Paper C 154 (Bonn: Center for European Integration Studies, 2005).

42. See Andreas Marchetti (ed.), *The CSCE as a Model to Transform Western Relations with the Greater Middle East*, ZEI Discussion Paper C 137 (Bonn: Center for European Integration Studies, 2004).

43. See Robert Looney, "The Broader Middle East Initiative: Requirements for Success in the Gulf," *Strategic Insights* 8 (2004), online at: http://www.nps.edu/Academics/centers/ccc/publications/OnlineJournal/2004/aug/looneyAug04.html.

44. Thomas Scheffler, "'Fertile Crescent,' 'Orient,' 'Middle East': The Changing Mental Maps of Southwest Asia," *European Review of History* 10, no. 2 (2003): 253–272, 258.

45. Scheffler recalls the early twentieth-century works of Ewald Banse about the desert Orient as a continent of culture and Georg Friedrich Wilhelm Hegel's assessment in the nineteenth century that the emptiness of the desert is related to the rigidity of Islam. He also recalls that the Arab historian Ibn Khaldun in the thirteenth century put nomads at the center of his analysis of the rise and fall of Muslim civilizations.

46. Alfred Thayer Mahan, "The Persian Gulf in International Relations," *National Review* (1902): 27–28.

47. See Bezen Balamir Coskun, *Region and Region Building in the Middle East: Problems and Prospects*, UNU-CRIS Occasional Paper O-2006/1 (Bruges: UNU-CRIS, 2006), online at: http://www.cris.unu.edu/fileadmin/workingpapers/20060117093527.O-2006-1.pdf.

48. Ibid., 10.

49. Ibid., 9.

50. Helena Lindholm Schulz and Michael Schulz, "The Middle East: Regional Instability and Fragmentation," in Mary Farrell et al. (eds.), *Global Politics of Regionalism: Theory and Practice* (London: Pluto Press, 2005), 187.

51. See Hassan Hakimian and Jeffrey B. Nugent (eds.), *Trade Policy and Economic Integration in the Middle East and North Africa: Economic Boundaries in Flux* (London and New York: Routledge Curzon, 2004).

52. See Marianna Laanatza et al., "Regionalization in the Middle East?" in Michael Schulz et. al. (eds.), *Regionalization in a Globalizing World: A Comparative Perspective on Forms, Actors and Processes* (London: Zed Books, 2001), 42–60.

53. Shimon Peres, *The New Middle East* (New York: Holt, 1993); see also Helena Lindholm Schulz and Michael Schulz, "Israel, Palestine and Jordan: Triangle of Peace or Conflict?" in Björn Hettne, Andras Inotai, and Osvaldo Sunkel (eds.), *The New Regionalism and the Future of Security and Development. The New Regionalism Series: vol. 4* (London: Macmillan, 2000), 144–175; Helena Lindholm Schulz and Michael Schulz, "Regional Integration—Israel, Jordan and the Palestinian Entity: In Whose Interest?" in Hettne et al., *The New Regionalism and the Future of Security and Development*, 221–241.

54. Prince Hassan bin Talal, *Continuity, Innovation and Change: Selected Essays* (Amman: Majlis El Hassan, 2001), 51–58.

55. Lindholm Schulz and Schulz, "Israel, Palestine and Jordan," 164; see also Scheffler, "'Fertile Crescent,' 'Orient,' 'Middle East,'" 272.
56. According to Lindholm Schulz and Schulz, "Israel, Palestine and Jordan," 165.
57. Cited ibid., 167.
58. See Timothy Garton Ash, "Soldiers of the Hidden Imam," *The New York Review of Books* 52, no. 17 (2005), online at: http://www.nybooks.com/articles/article-preview?article_id=18390.
59. European Union, *A Secure Europe In A Better World: European Security Strategy, adopted by the Heads of State and Government at the European Council in Brussels on 12. December 2003* (Paris: The European Institute for Security Studies, 2004), 13.
60. United States Department of State, *A Performance-Based Roadmap to a Permanent Two-State Solution to the Israeli-Palestinian Conflict* (30.04.2003), online at: http://www.state.gov/r/pa/prs/ps/2003/20062.htm.

Part III

CONTEXT AND IMPLICATION

9

THE EUROPEAN UNION IN THE GLOBAL PROLIFERATION OF REGIONAL INTEGRATION

━━━⊶⟨⊙⟩⊷━━━

Interpreting the European Union in World Affairs

The European Union is a work in progress. Most of the literature dealing with the European Union concentrates on the developments inside the EU. Likewise, the main focus of political and other actors within the European Union is on the internal evolution of EU governance and policy matters. This is natural, as the internal development of the European Union is their prime responsibility and center of reflection. But it does not devote sufficient reflection to the global role of Europe and the perception of the EU around the world. The perception of the EU, its global impact, and its worldwide effects is an altogether under-researched field in the academic literature about European integration. Moreover, it has neither conceptually nor empirically attracted enough attention to understand, analyze, and contextualize the role of the European Union in the global proliferation of regional integration.

Europe's place in the world is usually seen through two different academic mirrors. On the one hand, there is a very prolific and valuable body of literature about the historic role Europe has played in world affairs. The great discoveries and the age of colonial expansion, the development of the international state system, and the breakdown of the claim to imperial dominance by several European countries, have found enormous interest. The history of the two world wars has largely been written as a European history with global ramifications or as a European history with an Asia-Pacific subchapter. The thirty years' war between 1914 and 1945 is understood as a watershed separating Europe from being the dominating continent in the world to a Europe that became the object of world politics, a contested pawn in the power play between the United States and the Soviet Union. Some historians prefer to see 1917 as the decisive turning point in European history, with the beginning of US participation in the Great War that began in 1914 and the success of the Bolshevik Revolution in Russia, which turned Russia from a participating European power into a Eurasian nemesis of Europe.

Europe came out of the ashes of its second thirty years' war as a shattered community of nations. The division of the continent, grave doubts about the viability of democratic rule, deep moral depression in the wake of the Holocaust that became synonymous with Germany's rule of terror, and a declining colonialism around the world made any optimistic scenario about the future of Europe difficult. The United States clearly had become the leading power of the free world, while the Soviet Union represented expansionist communism. Europe's only chance was to begin anew in two fundamental spheres: stabilizing democratic rule in its Western half, West Germany included, and redesigning the European state system on the basis of a completely new model: regional integration. This revision of Europe's state system and renaissance of Europe's democracies required an unknown degree of trust and a moral investment in the former enemy, Germany. The best argument came from outside Europe: the pressure of Soviet expansionism made cooperation and swift changes among Western European countries possible. The pressure of the United States made integration and the inclusion of West Germany and its new democracy imperative. Weakened and exhausted European states were pushed to finally implement what were already century-old, noble European ideas.

The link between the secular process of decolonization and the emerging cautious hope in the concept of European integration has not often been studied in great detail.[1] The return of Europe (as European Union) as a global actor remains heavily debated and often contested inside Europe. Outside Europe, perceptions of this trend are ambivalent, ranging between skepticism owed to a belief that Europe adapts too slowly to global challenges, and support for Europe doing exactly this in order to constitute a new and balancing role in world affairs. One link in this chain of recalibrating the relationship between Europe and "the rest of the world" concerns the global proliferation of regional integration. Region-building is often considered an effort to emulate the European Union. Three standard reactions can be found in the literature dealing with the related phenomena, facts and trends:

- Disbelief in the ability to universalize European integration experience. In the absence of European experiences and the European degree of development, region-building is often considered impossible in other regions of the world. Reference to European integration is dismissed as shallow political rhetoric.
- Rejection of the relevance of region-building outside Europe measured against the dominating parameters of power and the state actors representing them. The leading roles of the US, Europe, and Japan, and increasingly China, in the world

economy leave little space dedicated to studies in the spirit of realism that genuinely appreciate region-building efforts in peripheral areas of the world.

- Underestimation of the genuine actor-ness of smaller, peripheral, poorer, or otherwise neglected areas in the global order. Remoteness from geopolitical conflict or
marginalization in terms of economic power often leads to the neglect of areas outside the northern hemisphere. In turn, studies focusing explicitly on the southern
hemisphere are often disconnected from the dominant "northern" discourses, often
a leftover of east-west coordinates.

Against this background, the perception of the global relevance of Europe
is predominantly driven by the mirroring position of each individual analyst in
the political sciences. There is no objectivity in these matters. Where you stand
determines how you look at Europe:

The transatlantic lens is the most common one. It regards Europe as the
main ally and partner of the United States. Some understand this relationship
as indispensable while others are inclined to write obituaries. Some focus on the
economic interdependencies while others demand a new mental framework to
prepare the transatlantic partners for a new global role. The global proliferation
of region-building has not really made it into the standard textbooks on transatlantic relations.

The developmental lens assesses Europe in its role of state-building, governance, and development strategies in what used to be called the Third World.
Although this term has lost its monopoly as an analytical category in defining
the role of the two thirds of mankind living outside Europe and North America,
the focus on development matters usually provides a genuine approach to the
perception of Europe and its role. Regional area studies or more microscopic
policy studies are, by and large, in line with the overall approach according to
which Europe's former colonial role has been replaced by a contributing, albeit in
general insufficient, role in the development of poorer countries.

The integrationist lens is enamored, and at times bedeviled, with region-building in Europe. It claims to produce universally applicable categories of analysis
but usually is reluctant to engage and link with empirical work in non-European
region-building schemes.

In view of these admittedly stereotypical generalizations, the body of analysis
of the global role of Europe and Europe's place in contemporary world history can
be divided into two camps. In the context of this study they have to be generalized, although a growing body of research stresses differentiated approaches and
arguments. Optimistic observers may hold that the European Union has been
involved in internally realizing a new dream that will have a transforming quality
for the world at large.[2] The EU as normative power is terminating the dominance
of power politics and the quest for hegemony. In promoting soft-power, focused
multilateralism, the EU is increasingly becoming attractive to other parts of the

world. Consequently, it is not surprising that the EU model of region-building is in the process of spreading globally. One area with limited application is Asia, where cultures and political systems are focused in a philosophy of "knowing the way" and remain apprehensive about institution-based decision-making. The other region with limited understanding and application is North America, with the hegemonic superpower the United States and its genuine state-centered bilateralism, which has not substantially altered with the project of continental economic cooperation with Canada and Mexico.

Skeptics, on the other hand, may point to the fact that Europe's global relevance is steadily sinking. Its share in the world's population has declined from one quarter in 1900 to one eighth in 2000 and will only be one fifteenth in 2050. The EU population is aging, one third being older than sixty-five in 2050. For five centuries Europe was a continent of emigration, but since the 1960s it has turned into a continent of immigration, with difficult consequences for social cohesion and identity formation. The European economy remains strong: the EU receives more than half of the world's stock of foreign direct investment, and it sends more than two thirds of global foreign direct investment around the world. But productivity has slowed, structural unemployment figures are constantly high, and the European education system has lost its attraction compared with the United States. "The most important lesson of Europe," writes a sober European critique, "is that there are so few good grounds for believing that Europe is the future of other regions."[3]

In other parts of the world, the appreciation of European integration seems to be stronger than in Europe itself, or in the United States for that matter. This is astonishing, given the colonial heritage of Europe and its image as hegemon over much of the world for many centuries. Obviously, Europe's perception has gone through a fundamental transition, almost a transfiguration. The breakdown of the global presence of European colonial powers was followed by a new beginning inside Europe. Peace, democracy, and affluence became the expressions of a new Europe that has overcome much of its traditional political theory of autarkic-state power and sovereignty. Europe as an incarnation of affluence through integration became attractive to many Third World areas, while the United States became the strategic power and the cultural pole of attraction. Often, the US was perceived as almost too powerful and affluent to even be contemplated as a viable partner. Europe, on the other hand, positioned itself with new modesty as the humble successor of its own glorious yet vanished past. For a long time, the notion of Europe as a civilian power was standard in academic discourses, often in very repetitive ways. In the meantime, new realities have led to more differentiated questions among academics about the European Union as a hybrid of civilian power and "soft imperialism."[4] Assessing the role of Europe as a civilian power is now usually done by adding a question mark behind the once iconic term.[5] Jan Zielonka, in a courageous polemic, even talked of "Europe as Empire" by describing the nature of the enlarged European Union (although primarily referring to the internal structure of the EU, which is compared with medieval polycentric political orders).[6]

The nature of European integration did not develop without obvious contradictions both inside Europe and in Europe's interplay with the main political, ideational, and cultural trends in much of the southern hemisphere. The first wave of relations between Europe and its former colonies was largely defined by anger and disgust over Europe's colonial arrogance and claim to dominance. The second wave of relations with Europe was framed by the expectation of European aid coming from an economically reborn giant. This wave of perception did not coincide on the ideational level: while community-building and integration in Europe were defined by democratic governance and the pooling of sovereignty, the southern hemisphere was largely pursuing the idolization of the nation-state, national sovereignty, and the primacy of the collective over individual interests and claims to rights. In hindsight, it is not surprising that the first period of region-building in the southern hemisphere failed, or at least underperformed, as long as the matter of domestic governance was not a concern among the actors involved in region-building there. Development regionalism was intended to be the answer to democratic regionalism in Europe. One could not succeed at the expense of the other. For a long time security regionalism was a variant of Cold War logic, and thus it did achieve certain objectives (the founding of ASEAN is one example). But security building since the Cold War has required the penetration of the principle of non-interference into domestic affairs if it wants to succeed. Democratic regionalism has—at least so far—never been fully embraced in non-European integration schemes.

Yet democratic peace, followed by rule of law–based regionalization, might be the most critical European experience and the most important precondition for any successful region-building. Had West Germany not embraced democratic governance, readiness to reconcile with its former enemy would hardly have been possible in post–World War II France, or in any other Western European state for that matter. Without democratic governance, none of the Central and Eastern European countries that have joined the EU since the fall of communism in 1989 would have been admitted to the European Union, no matter their doubtless cultural affinity with Western Europe. Democratic governance might not be an end in itself, as it requires additional tools and purposes to gain lasting legitimacy. Yet democratic governance in the constituent parts of a regional integration scheme is the single most important prerequisite for building trust among the actors as well as a mutual recognition that goes beyond calculated pragmatism. Democratic governance does not guarantee integrational success, or even the insight into its necessity and value. But only democratic governance can generate democratic regionalism—that is to say, region-building based on mutually shared democratic values, beliefs, and behavioral patterns.

The third wave of Europe's postcolonial encounter with the regions of the southern hemisphere was framed by the rising awareness of the success of European integration across the world. True, the economic experience of European integration cannot be applied elsewhere without preconditions, and the democracy gap between the European Union and a great number of countries across the globe remains enormous. Yet a new dimension of encounter between the European Union and other regions of the world has begun. It is by and large a two-way street: while other countries in region-building schemes have discovered the European Union as a laboratory that might contain useful elements for their own objectives, or even as a model that might be emulated with the hope of speedy economic progress and lasting security, the EU itself has begun to advertise regional integration as a tool for peace, stability, security, and development across the globe. Indeed, the European Union has almost become self-serving in applauding itself and portraying the expectations of others. In promoting its normative goals across the globe—the EU's homepage provides information on the work of its more than 120 EU delegations worldwide—it serves the purpose of "taking both the idea and reality of European Union to a world hungry for its presence."[7]

The meaning, scope, and effect of Europe's new *mission civilisatrice* are ambiguous. The EU's concrete expectations, as well as the expectations toward the EU, depend on contingent constellations. "Europe" is more than a catchword framing a whole world or a concrete idea. The meaning and scope of European integration is even more conceptually diverse. Yet it is a remarkable indicator of the EU's global presence that it is by now party to over fifty multilateral treaties concluded under its auspices. The broad agenda of European integration and of Europe's relations with other parts of the world cannot simply be reduced to the understanding that the promotion of region-building is the core principled belief of the EU in its interactions with other areas of the world. But nor can it be denied that the EU is developing a policy of promoting regional integration as an institutional concept. Since the first statement of the European Union in this regard, published in 1995, the EU has tried to enhance the coherence and visibility of its policy of promoting region-building. In supporting agreements with other regional groupings across the globe, the EU, as its first deliberation on the matter made clear, intends to contribute to the "reinforcement of regional identity and of the regional institutions."[8]

This claim is not easy to implement. The EU will be required to clarify the objectives of the respective efforts, to harmonize the appropriate tools, and most importantly, to develop some form of basic coherence about the original principles. Regional identity in Europe is a recurrent matter in search of clarification. There is no fixed and formalized definition of regional identity once and for all. To measure the reinforcement of regional identity is therefore a difficult task. It can be one with colliding content: while Europe has become the world's most secularized continent, cultural and religious identity has reverberated in other regions of the world—not leaving Europe unaffected. But Europe's insistence on the normative primacy of post-Westphalian concepts of sovereignty, enforcement of human rights, and rational, enlightenment-based rejection of religion from the public sphere, do not find unchallenged enthusiasm across all regions of the world. Such deliberations and experiences might even backfire in a Europe that thinks itself so very postmodern and sophisticated.

More research would be helpful to better understand the real effects of the EU policy in promoting regional integration. Such advanced on-site research would need to look into more details related to actors and structures alike. Which dimensions of the European integration experience may serve as models in other parts of the world? Which actors do in fact look to Europe, and with what objective? Can any causal links between EU institutions, norms, and policies be measured in their effect on region-building policies elsewhere?

For the time being, more plausible than describing the EU as a comprehensive and coherent model for regional integration is the assumption that the European Union can contribute to the reinforcement of regional institutions that need to grow on their own. Political institutions, in fact, have spread across the world in rather similar and interchangeable ways. With the global proliferation of the single state, procedures and structures of organizing public life in any given country have become coherent. The degree of success or failure is a different matter, as are the quality of democratic participation and other normative aspects of politics. But the main state institutions representing the sovereignty of the single state have become universal and identical, except in some failed states or in aspirants like the Palestinian state. This universalization of the single state has led to the assumption that regional integration schemes ought also to be interchangeable and rather similar, if not in performance then at least in structure. Most non-European integration efforts have been described as the consequence of "reactionary regionalism,"[9] meaning reactive region-building in response to, and presumably in line with, the EU example. In reality, they often only mimic European integration institutions. Preconditions, circumstances, and objectives remain a contingent experience in any region-building effort across the world.

The European Union actively contributes to region-building elsewhere in the world. This normative policy is often incoherent and may be debatable on principle, but it is a declared policy objective of the European Union. As "external federator"[10] the EU is not only setting integration benchmarks elsewhere: in many ways, the EU is providing a model for institutional evolution elsewhere. The European Union is increasingly developing a policy of biregional relations, labeled "inter-regionalism" in their theoretical reflection. It still may lack consistency and coherence, but it introduces a new dimension into global affairs. In promoting agreements between regional groupings, the EU is encouraging the existing regional groupings elsewhere to focus their activities and to enhance their objectives. The EU is also encouraging other regional groupings to see the EU as their preferred regional (and if possible, political) partner. Moreover, the EU actively promotes the very initiation of region-building as a precondition for structured and enhanced relations with the EU. Although this policy of inter-regionalism is only embryonic at best, its purpose and potential have already found scholarly attention.[11]

The policy of inter-regionalism is particularly noteworthy vis-à-vis those former European colonies that have maintained special relations with the European Union and its predecessors since the establishment of the Yaoundé Agreement and the different Lomé Conventions. The start of a proactive European policy in promoting region-building is related to the timely coincidence of the beginning of European integration and the dissolution of several European colonial empires during the 1950s and 1960s. Europe's promotion of regional integration began vis-à-vis its former colonies in Africa, the Caribbean, and the Pacific. Stretching this policy to other EU partner regions in Latin America, and increasingly in Asia, has become an element of social engineering. Conceptually the EU has reached neither cohesion nor undisputed success in these efforts. The tools used by the European Union to promote region-building as an element of world order include:

- Supporting existing efforts of regional integration.
- Advancing or even creating regional groupings by classifying partners.
- Connecting with existing and developing regional architectures.

The European Union has come a long way. Since the days of European discovery and colonialism, it has taken until the end of the twentieth century for the European Union to symbolize a completely different Europe: a Europe institutionally unified on the basis of democratic rule, market economy, and the common pursuit of defined interests; a Europe representing common values and norms as benchmarks for its internal governance and as guidelines for the pursuit of its external relations; a Europe that struggles with a long list of internal idiosyncrasies yet is envied and appreciated across the globe. Sometimes it seems that the farther the observer is away from Europe, the more Europe is perceived as a unified "one." But whatever the perception, it is interesting to see the emerging coherence of a global European approach to the promotion of region-building. It is the corresponding policy to the global proliferation of regional integration that was identified in the earlier chapters of this study.

Toward Biregional Relations with the ACP Countries

Thematically, a clear line of continuity and change can be identified in the European relationship with most countries of Africa, the Caribbean, and the Pacific. It is defined by the following agreements between them and Europe:

- 1963 Yaoundé Convention I
- 1969 Yaoundé Convention II
- 1975 Lomé Convention I, stretching the Yaoundé group to former colonies in the Pacific and in the Caribbean Basin
- 1980 Lomé Convention II
- 1985 Lomé Convention III
- 1990 Lomé Convention IV
- 1995 Lomé Convention V
- 2000 Cotonou Agreement.

With the Cotonou Agreement, the European Union changed its main policy objective from a development strategy to one of promoting free trade and the encouragement of regional groupings among the partner areas. This followed internal policy strategy revisions in the European Commission in 1999. Between 2002 and 2008, Economic Partnership Agreements were negotiated with several ACP subregions in order to comply with WTO standards in the economic relationship with the EU partner caucuses in Africa, the Pacific, and the Caribbean basin.[12] These negotiations were controversial because of their neoliberal approach to free trade. But they were also ambivalent as to their ability to actively promote deeper and sustainable regional integration in the ACP subregions.

As a result of its growing experience in integration, the European Union became increasingly confident in its ability to promote region-building elsewhere. The external objective of launching integration as tool to achieving peace, development, stability, and prosperity led to the assessment of integration as a possible export product. Although the "exportability" of European integration must be limited because of context differences, agenda contingency, and political asymmetries, the promotion of regional integration was increasingly suggested as a strategy for overcoming regional tensions. The WTO mantra—that liberalized trade fosters economic growth and development—does not necessarily require regional integration. Historic evidence suggests that peace and stability might be strengthened through economic development and the effects of an economy of scale. But whether or not economies of scale work more effectively under the framework of regional integration is a matter of ongoing debate in academia. The question of whether or not regional integration requires interplay between economic and political integration has remained even more controversial. In reality, however, political actors across the world have embarked on region-building efforts. They have done so and continue to do so, quite often in the absence of clearly defined objectives, under conditions of changing tools and goals, through the experience of crises, and driven more by unintended consequences than the logic of an aseptic blueprint.

Yet the European Union has begun to proactively suggest universalizable insights into the process of regional integration. For the negotiation of EPAs with its ACP partner regions, the European Commission developed a "toolbox" for the promotion of region-building. Published on 27 January 2003, the "toolbox," as part of an increasingly comprehensive strategy of promoting region-building, includes five main policy areas that the EU has identified as central to the evolution of sustainable region-building:

- Trade in goods
- Trade in services
- Trade-related rules
- Enforcement mechanisms
- Regional cooperation in "a wider sense," including macroeconomic matters, the issue of currency union, and the scope of political institutions.[13]

The basis for EC trade negotiations is Article 133 of the Treaty of Maastricht. The EU's shift from development to trade policy in its relations with developing countries in Africa, the Caribbean Basin, and the Pacific reflects an upgrading from the development agenda under post- and late-colonial conditions to reciprocal trade relations under the umbrella of the WTO. This policy development raises the global profile of the EU, which increased its share in world trade from 7 percent in 1970 to 25 percent in 2000. It also echoes growing foreign policy interests of the European Union in the projection of stability across the globe.

The EEC's original Treaties of Rome did not explicitly mention the development issue, yet they initiated the common trade policy of the EU (thus named since 1993). Thanks to the Single European Act of 1987, the powers of the European Parliament were increased as the parliament gained veto powers over agreements with third parties. The Treaty of Maastricht (signed in 1991, in force since 1993) formally constitutionalized the EU's development aid policy and specified EU objectives beyond the sphere of the economy. The Treaty of Maastricht explicitly mentions human rights, governance, and human development goals as criteria for receiving EU development aid. The activities of the European Development Fund, founded in 1957, were adjusted accordingly. The European Development Fund remained the main financial instrument during the period of all five Lomé Conventions. Of all the development aid provided by these Conventions, 77 percent was granted to Africa, 18 percent to the countries in the Caribbean Basin, and 5 percent to the Pacific island countries.[14] Given that the overall amount of contributions under the Lomé Convention was only a fourth of the combined national aid programs of EU member states, its effect as an expression of a common European interest must be put into perspective.

The Cotonou Agreement introduced a change in policy priorities. Preferential trade agreements had to be replaced by reciprocal partnerships, according to WTO rules. The European Union made use of this enforced transformation of its relations with the ACP subregions: several Economic Partnership Agreement negotiations aimed to promote free trade and regional integration at the same time. On 27 September 2002, the EU-ACP negotiations on EPAs began. After one year of initial negotiations at an all-ACP level, several ACP subgroupings entered into biregional negotiations:

- In October 2003, regional negotiations began with CEMAC and with ECOWAS.
- In February 2004, regional negotiations began with COMESA.
- In May 2004, regional negotiations began with CARIFORUM, established in 1992 as a combination of fourteen CARICOM countries, including Suriname, Haiti, and the Dominican Republic.
- In July 2004, regional negotiations began with SADC.
- In September 2004, regional negotiations began with most member states of the Pacific Islands Forum (excluding Australia and New Zealand).

It was confusing that the EU claimed to support regional integration but did not always negotiate with existing regional groupings. While in some cases not all grouping members were participating, in other cases further countries were added to the subregional negotiations. This in itself was a paradox that the EU could not properly explain. If EPA negotiations were genuinely to promote regional integration, it would be most logical to begin with existing structures and recognize their full membership. The EU partners in the several EPA negotiations reflected ACP traditions rather than maturing regional groupings. Yet the EU insisted that the process of EPA negotiations would eventually foster region-ness and the role of regional institutions. Critics argued that the issue of overlapping membership, and the subsequent need for rationalizing resources aimed at promoting region-building, should "receive greater attention" from both the EU and their various regional partners in Africa, the Caribbean, and the Pacific.[15] The EU argued that the EPA negotiations were intended to contribute to "regulatory convergence"[16] between the regions. While critics argue that the enormous development gap between the EU and its partners could not generate a solid economic relationship, others claimed that North-South free trade arrangements could be beneficial for both sides because the EU remains the largest trading partner for many of its partner countries, especially in Africa. The EU itself argued that biregional EPAs would contribute to internal development, regional integration, and the gradual inclusion of the developing regions of Africa, the Caribbean, and the Pacific in the world economy. The Economic Partnership Agreements are especially meant to facilitate intra-regional trade in the various ACP subregions.

Traditionally, the European Union focuses on the promotion of intra-regional trade. Its increase is reiterated like a mantra for the resolution of most regional problems anywhere in the world. But from the genuine European integration experience—and the absence of it in the late nineteenth and early twentieth centuries—it must be evident to EU strategists that increased intra-regional trade alone does not necessarily prevent the outbreak of conflicts and war-fare. It is consequential that the European Union's strategy for the promotion of EPAs and the gradual emergence of intra-regional relations with regional groupings in Africa, the Caribbean, and the Pacific includes a political element and a democracy clause in particular. As early as 1996, an EU green paper emphasized that with the end of the Cold War, the relationship between the EU and the ACP countries was meant to shift toward more political openness, including emphasis on the democratization process in African countries and elsewhere.[17]

The EPA negotiations were used by the European Union to emphasize the need for democratic governance as tool for development success and as an inherent precondition for meaningful region-building. The EU insisted on conditionality while asymmetry was evident in the negotiations between the strong and democratically rooted EU and the weak and emerging democracies and economies of Africa, the Caribbean, and the Pacific. For the EU, the extension of the Cotonou Agreement into a new set of biregional agreements was more than an experiment in enlarging the scope of its global action. The EU was confronted with a set of criticisms ranging from the charge of lacking geographical coherence to the charge of pursuing a neocolonial agenda of in-voluntary interference in the sovereignty of independent states. Critics argued that deeper regional integration in Africa, the Caribbean, and the Pacific may happen even without EPAs. Should deeper regional integration fail, it could hardly be revived by the mechanisms of an EPA. Eventually, by the end of 2007 a full Economic Partnership Agreement was concluded only with CARI-FORUM countries, including goods liberalization and other features such as sanitary and phytosanitary measures and matters of intellectual properties. The other negotiations led to several interim EPAs still aiming to be upgraded eventually to full Economic Partnership Agreements.[18] No matter the ongoing controversies, the EPA negotiation processes have added a new element to the emerging phenomenon of biregional relations.

In Search of Biregional Partners in Asia and Latin America

Biregional relations among regional groupings have never been before part of the global order. Bilateral interstate relations or alliances, regional orga-nizations, and supranationally integrated organizations were the institutions that defined world order and world politics. Biregional relations depend upon two functional regional groupings agreeing to voluntarily cooperate and be-gin to integrate some of their functions. Such a process is new, undecided in its outcome, and unsettled in its goals. The European Union is increasingly growing into the role of an institution that actively promotes the expansion of biregional cooperation.[19] However, the emerging biregional schemes between the EU and its traditional partners in Africa, the Caribbean, and the Pacific are extremely asymmetric.

Asia

EU relations with Asia's regional groupings have grown steadily, yet inconsistently. The idea of biregional cooperation between Europe and an Asian partner region was first launched in a follow-up to the Euro-Arab dialogue, a diplomatic venture active between 1973 and 1979. After Israel and Egypt concluded their peace agreement at Camp David, the Euro-Arab dialogue came to an end when Egypt was expelled from the Arab League. In 1981, the Gulf Cooperation Council (GCC) was founded, but it had fewer natural ties with Europe due to its geographic location. In 1988, then German Foreign Minister Hans-Dietrich Genscher suggested a cooperation agreement between the European Community and the Gulf Cooperation Council as a new element of interaction. In 1991, the EU decided that the GCC had to establish a customs union before the European Union was willing to negotiate a free trade agreement. After this customs union—a first important step toward economic integration—was achieved in 2003, the issue of biregional cooperation returned to the agenda of EU-Gulf relations.

EU relations with the GCC overlap with the Euro-Mediterranean Dialogue (Barcelona Process, now renamed Union for the Mediterranean). This has often blurred the focus of the EU. Both the Barcelona Process and the more recent European Neighborhood Policy have caused a certain indecisiveness regarding EU priorities and strategies across its borders.[20] The Union for the Mediterranean, initially proposed by French President Sarkozy in 2007 and formalized by the EU and all its partners of the Barcelona Process in 2008, was no less incoherent. At best, the Union for the Mediterranean may serve as a reinforcing element in the pursuit of authentic Arab regional integration-building. For geopolitical reasons, at the moment it is absolutely unimaginable that the North African Arab countries and Israel might be the engine of such a process. Envisaging such a role for the Arab states in the Gulf region would again leave open the connection with Northern Africa and the place for Israel in the whole region-building venture.

The European Neighborhood Policy does not overcome the typical idiosyncrasies of EU policy making. In a rare strategy, the EU intends to pursue special relations with the countries in its immediate neighborhood. It is not clear whether this approach is truly driven by the offer of cooperation—as has been argued by the EU—or rather by a sophisticated form of deterrence—as is feared by some of the EU's neighbors. The EU has not embarked on the project of supporting region-building on either its eastern borders or its immediate southern borders. As we have seen, the nature of geopolitical considerations in both regions makes region-building difficult. But the idea of projecting the EU as both a bridge and a river to its immediate eastern neighbors—Belarus, Ukraine, and Moldova—and to its immediate southern neighbors—who all participate in the Barcelona Process—has been illogical and mutually exclusive. By consequence, the European Neighborhood Policy remains controversial, ambivalent, and incoherent for both the EU and its partners.

To embark on intensive biregional relations with the Gulf Cooperation Council may very well be the right long-term strategy in EU relations with the Gulf region. An urgent priority should be to intensify the political and security dialogue between the EU and the GCC, as well as initiate a substantial energy dialogue and a governance dialogue. At this point, the idea of inter-regionalism must, however, meet its limit: the EU would either have to accept the largely undemocratic and at best democratizing character of the member state regimes of the GCC, or it would have to forfeit the ambition of turning biregional relations into an expression of globalized democratic regionalism. The GCC is clearly an expression of security regionalism but not of democratic regionalism. This may not be an obstacle to constructive integration inside the GCC as long as regime symmetry holds the Gulf monarchies together. But the possible inclusion of Yemen already poses governance and regime issues for the GCC. The same matter will be brought up if the EU tries to engage in a full-fledged biregional relationship with the GCC. Security regionalism and democratic regionalism might not be incompatible concepts after all, and they both provide common ground for the pursuit of mutual interests. But security regionalism and democratic regionalism are not fully complementary and will likely bring about critical disputes and hence limits on their potential for cooperation.

The South Asian Association of Regional Cooperation (SAARC) poses the same dilemma for the European Union. While SAARC has developed as an expression of security regionalism, the regime differences and political disputes among its member states have prevented it from aspiring to become an expression of democratic regionalism. The inherent limit of region-building in view of this fact impacts the potential for biregional cooperation with the EU. Although the European Union is the largest trading partner for India, Pakistan, and Bangladesh and an important trading partner for Nepal, Sri Lanka, and the Maldives, relations between the EU and SAARC have never passed the barriers defined by the Memorandum of Understanding of Cooperation signed in 1996 as a minimalist expression of biregional cooperation. De facto, the EU "has virtually ignored" SAARC.[21]

The EU relations with ASEAN and ASEM, in turn, have developed much more extensively. But this development has not clarified the objectives and the basis of this relationship.[22] Due to another initiative of then German Foreign Minister Hans-Dietrich Genscher, the European Community and ASEAN held their first ministerial meeting in November 1978; in 2007, the seventeenth of these regular meetings was held. The EC and ASEAN concluded a Cooperation Agreement in 1980 that constituted the regular political dialogue on the ministerial level. This political dimension of cooperation was hampered by problems stemming from regime differences between Europe's democratic regionalism and the non-democratic nature of some of ASEAN's member states. In 1991, following the outbreak of violence in Dili, Portugal blocked the revision of the EC-ASEAN Cooperation Agreement, condemning the undemocratic nature of the regime in Indonesia. Only after the change of the Indonesian government in 1999 did the European Union agree to relaunch the EU-ASEAN relationship at its full level. Two years earlier, another governance dispute had escalated: n 1997, the European Union imposed sanctions against Myanmar (Burma) on account of its state of human rights. Consequently, the political dialogue between the EU and ASEAN was temporarily suspended.

When biregional cooperation based on the norms of democratic regionalism could not be implemented immediately or without contradictions, the EU itself became inconsistent in its strategy. Besides maintaining the proclaimed special relationship with ASEAN, the EU was also eager to establish a corresponding relationship with the economic regionalism expressed in the APEC process since its inauguration in 1994. The geopolitical and geo-economic dimension of this interest underlined the ambivalence in the EU's perception of the role and future of ASEAN as the core of region-building in Southeast Asia. It also left the European Union with a completely new experience: reaction to a loose form of economic regionalism with its own approach to loose economic regionalism. In 1996, the process of Asia-Europe Meetings (ASEM) began—at the initiative of Singapore's then Prime Minister Goh Chok Tong—as an additional new biregional effort between the EU and ASEAN Plus Three (China, Japan, South Korea). Regular summit meetings between the heads of state and government of the EU and the ASEAN Plus Three partners have developed into the backbone of ASEM. This summitry (1996 Bangkok, 1998 London, 2000 Seoul, 2002 Copenhagen, 2004 Hanoi, 2006 Helsinki, 2008 Beijing) has taken on many of the original functions of the political dialogue between the EU and ASEAN.[23]

The EU Asia Strategy of 2001 tried to clarify some of the confusing, overlapping, and contradicting objectives and approaches of the EU's unsettled biregional relationship with Southeast and East Asia. The strategy was clear on the overall goal to strengthen the European Union's political and economic presence in the region. But it had to give in to confusing irresolution about the character, objectives, and finality of the respective Southeast and East Asian regional developments. A certain institutionalization of EU-ASEAN and EU-ASEAN Plus Three relations includes representatives of civil society. This rather rare feature of biregional activities is represented by the work of the Asia-Europe Foundation based in Singapore. Nevertheless, EU biregional relations with ASEAN and with ASEAN Plus Three remain somewhat un-settled. Economic regionalism has not created coherent structures, nor has security regionalism remained the dominant feature. Most of all, democratic regionalism is not on the agenda or in the structure of this multifaceted biregional relationship. It continues to alternate between strict economic regionalism and its inherent interests on the one hand, and on the other the effort to deepen biregional cooperation through civil society interactions, which would only become successful if translated into the political agenda of democratic regionalism. Given the regime and governance realities in Southeast and East Asia, it is unlikely that democratic regionalism and its logic will become the dominating feature of biregional relations with the European Union in the foreseeable future.

Latin America

The diverse development of regional integration efforts in Latin America is echoed in the region's relations with the European integration project.[24] During the 1960s and 1970s, the European Economic Community pursued only bilateral contacts with Latin America. Biregional activity began in Central America in relation to the peacekeeping effort in that region. In 1984, the European Community and the Central American foreign ministers met for the first time in San José, Costa Rica, to discuss the prospect for peace and stability in the region torn by civil war. At the peak of the Cold War, the European Community came in from the fringes. While it did not play any reasonable role in the Cold War management of Europe or between the two superpowers, it began to project its security potential and its philosophy of peace-building through region-building to Central America.

In November 1993, the European Union signed a Framework Cooperation Agreement with the Central American states that had established the Central American Integration System (SICA) only two years earlier in 1991. Between 1995 and 2001, the EU provided €134 million per year to SICA in support of regional integration. The location of the original meeting of 1984 had become the nomenclature for the San José Process, a regular format for the political dialogue between the EU and SICA. In December 2003, the EU and SICA upgraded their relations by signing a Political Dialogue and Cooperation Agreement, leading to the EU Regional Strategy for Central America for the period 2002–2006. At the EU–Latin American summit in May 2006, the EU and SICA took a step forward in their effort to establish biregional relations: they agreed to begin negotiations aimed at establishing a biregional association agreement.

This decision put EU-SICA relations on an equal footing with the state of EU-MERCOSUR relations. Following the conclusion of an Inter-regional Framework Cooperation Agreement on 12 December 1995, the EU and MERCOSUR had begun negotiations on an Inter-regional Association Agreement in 2000. Immediately after MERCOSUR was founded in 1991, the EU began providing technical assistance to MERCOSUR framed by an Inter-Institutional Cooperation Agreement between the EU Commission and the MERCOSUR Secretariat.[25]

By the mid 1990s, MERCOSUR had achieved internal free trade for about 85 percent of all its products and a customs union encompassing 90 percent of imported goods. It had become the fourth largest economic region in the world after the EU, the United States, and Japan. It did not seem to be ready yet for a currency union, although the matter had been brought up in the meantime, following the European example and its underlying logic.[26] The European Union was providing the MERCOSUR Secretariat with technical assistance, including support for MERCOSUR summit meetings and training courses for customs officers to facilitate the implementation of a MERCOSUR customs union. Pushed by an ambitious business lobby on both sides, EU exports to MERCOSUR—95 percent being industrial goods—increased by 375 percent during the 1990s. As for EU imports from MERCOSUR, slightly more than 50 percent are agricultural and slightly less than 50 percent are industrial goods. Harmonizing standards and establishing the parameters for a regulatory regionalism are among the main interests of the European Union.[27]

The EU-MERCOSUR relationship was fueled by competition of both of them with the United States following President Clinton's 1994 initiative to establish the Free Trade Area of the Americas (FTAA) by 2005. In 2004, both projects, the full implementation of the FTAA and the completion of the EU-MERCOSUR Association Agreement, were in gridlock. After thirteen rounds of negotiations, the EU-MERCOSUR plan was put on hold. The 2006 EU-Latin America summit in Vienna reaffirmed in shallow diplomatic terms the willingness of both sides to conclude the Association Agreement in due course. New negotiations have not materialized yet.

The same EU-Latin American summit also did not agree to start negotiating an Association Agreement with the Andean Community of Nations (CAN). Only days before the summit, Venezuela had declared that it was to leave CAN. Bolivia's membership was also questioned by the new President of Bolivia, Evo Morales. In 1993, the EU had concluded a Regional Framework Cooperation Agreement with CAN. It would have been in accordance with the efforts undertaken between the EU and MERCOSUR, and with the ambitious plan to repeat this effort in the EU-SICA relationship, to also bring the EU-CAN relationship toward a more viable level of biregional relations.[28] In 2004, both sides had agreed that the perspective of an EU-CAN Association Agreement was dependent upon progress in real integration in CAN. A comprehensive evaluation and assessment process was launched, as it was in SICA. Eventually, before the end of 2006, the EU eventually gave the go-ahead for the beginning of biregional association negotiations with both CAN and SICA.

Inter-regionalism as a New Dimension of Global Governance?

Like region-building, biregional relations and their theoretical reflection as inter-regionalism are policy-driven. Yet they transform the original structure, scope, and reality of the participating states. Region-building tends to occur in two directions: microregionalism is about cross-border cooperation among certain countries that share complementary resources and potential; macro regionalism is about treaty-based and law-driven interstate and intersocietal cooperation and integration. These vertical dimensions of multilevel governance might be complemented by the horizontal dimension of biregional cooperation and inter-regionalism. The related empirical phenomena of biregional relations are less researched than multilevel governance dimensions originating in vertical region-building.[29] There is only rudimentary knowledge so far about the effects or potential effects of inter-regionalism on the international order and on interstate relations in general. It remains worth considering whether or not biregional relations might produce some sort of multilevel horizontal and vertical global governance.

A word of caution is appropriate: "It is much too premature to speak of inter-regionalism as a form of transnational, not to speak of global, governance. At present one can only identify emerging cooperative networks based upon some kind of regional organization, but in a context that often is highly hierarchical."[30] Biregional relations, much like interstate relations, are driven by genuine ideals, contingent interests, and objectives. They raise questions related to one's own self and to the perception of the other. Analytically, inter-regionalism can be:

- A cognitive tool that potentially enables a region to be defined or redefined.
- A functional strategy instrument meant to manage relations between regions.

The evolution of biregional relations requires the existence of reasonably complementary regions. They require a counterpart region or at least a second region with the predictable objective of projecting a certain actor-ness. Inter-regionalism hence requires actors, tools, and goals.

Biregional relations are, at best, an embryonic element of international relations. Yet it can no longer be denied that "regions have acted themselves into significance."[31] Region-building has become a global phenomenon. There is evidence from all over the world that the idea of pooling comparative advantages in a region, elements of identity and mutual recognition, and the desire to respond to and shape globalization has gained global attraction. Even those regions that do not (yet) engage in formal region-building or can claim to already represent a homogenized and coherent region (the United States of America) have begun to study the rationale of region-building and the effect it potentially, or already de facto, has for them.

With its global presence, the nation-state has acquired the main functions of domestic as well as international sovereignty. The autonomous state is both a goal and a fact that has spread worldwide. Autonomous statehood has been an objective of emancipation. It began with the evolution of the European nation-state. In Europe, the original evolution of autonomous statehood occurred in response to and rejection of a homogenous European order held together by the binding glue of the Catholic Church. With the Age of Reformation, the age of national statehood dawned in Europe. The claims for religious liberty and political identity came together, often elegantly superimposed on the aspirations of regional or local nobility. In some cases, the representatives of regional or local nobility wanted to overcome the primacy of a distant emperor; other cases they were the engine behind the quest for centralized statehood. In the end, Europe evolved as the post-Reformation, postmedieval puzzle of nation-states.

The domestic structures of the European nation-states continued to differ. Monarchies came to stand beside republics. Rule of law began to evolve, only gradually giving way to democratic governance based on the full protection of human rights. State sovereignty hence was followed by popular sovereignty. The limits of both dimensions of sovereignty were felt after more than a century of almost autistic pride in the primacy of sovereignty. The self-destruction of Europe in the first half of the twentieth century had originated in the perversion of sovereignty: racist nationalism and totalitarian dictatorship marked the internal and external end to the unchallenged primacy of sovereignty. They also defined the end of autarkic state policies and the beginning of European integration. Academic debate to this day asks whether European integration was nourished and driven by a genuine quest for a unified Europe or by the desire to reinvigorate the nation-state. But regardless of the intention, the result has transformed the nation-state and Europe alike, and the result has brought about a multilevel system of democratic order.

Outside Europe, the rise of the autonomous state since the end of Spanish rule in Latin America—and in a way even since the days of North American independence in the late eighteenth century—echoed the stages of European state formation. The primacy of state independence stood at the beginning, often at the expense of the pursuit of real popular sovereignty and its grounding in human rights. The struggle for the rule of law had to follow, in many places as an internal series of conflicts. Democratic governance came last and has found declaratory consensus on a global scale only since the Millennium Declaration of the United Nations. The differences between democratic models prevail in today's world, and a good number of countries still must be considered undemocratic, authoritarian, or neototalitarian.

Yet the two stages in the evolution of statehood as they were known in European history have by and large become global realities.[32] Interestingly, the global movement from state sovereignty to a gradual recognition of popular sovereignty and democratic rule coincided with the worldwide evolution of regionalism. Region-building—and even more so inter-regionalism—does not evolve by itself. It requires the actor-ness of a region, at least in an embryonic state, and it requires driving forces, as both push and pull factors. By definition, inter-regionalism can only evolve by hybridization because region-building itself as a young concept is reasonably mixed. Compared with several centuries in the history of the notion of sovereignty, the evolution of regions as economic, political, and even cultural actors is a new phenomenon that in most regions of the world has been emerging in earnest only since the end of the Cold War in 1989/1990.

At the root of the global proliferation of region-building lie two different concepts of politics that are not necessarily free of contradiction:

• A redefinition of sovereignty beyond the classical "Westphalian" understanding of sovereignty as the embodiment of autonomous statehood.
• A recognition of the limits of autonomous statehood and of mutual welfare gains through cooperation and integration.

The recognition of the limits of autonomous statehood might lead to two different reactions: it might instigate new parochialism and politics of fear, or it might coincide with the gradual awareness of strengthened welfare gains through the medium of cooperation and the instruments of integration. Cooperation and the pooling of sovereignty is not a matter of absolute gains in power, mutual benefits, welfare, and security. It is rather an evolving process subject to crises, backlashes, and detours. It is a process with relational gains and losses and a multidimensional understanding of causes, effects, and new causes of gains and losses. Autonomous statehood is the end of a process that often turned into a static reality. Region-building is the beginning of a process whose final outcome cannot be imagined.

The academic reflection about region-building is rather differentiated, learned, and sophisticated. But surprisingly, the most under-researched aspect is the link between external and internal components of sovereignty and its consequences for region-building and inter-regionalism. Region-building, regionalism, and integration are largely considered economic matters, at best supported by political means. The genuine political nature of integration and region-building is often underestimated or even questioned. More surprising, however, is the lack of recognition of the nature and role of political regimes in the process of integration, region-building, and regionalism. While much has been written about security regionalism and development regionalism, the very term "democratic regional-ism" does not appear in any major study on the subject. But it is democratic regionalism that is at the heart of understanding the limits as well as the dynamics and potential of region-building.

Only democratic regimes—such is the main conclusion of this study—can develop the degree of trust necessary to nurture processes that can lead to real integration and region-building beyond the superficial use of most evident mutual interests. Regime symmetry might not supersede cultural affinity as a pull factor toward the emergence of a region as actor. But cultural affinity alone will not incite solid and sustainable regional developments in any serious sense if the regimes by which neighborly states are governed are antagonistic. Poland was no less European under the rule of communism, but it was unimaginable that Poland could join the European Union before it had become a democratic country with respect for the rule of law and human rights. Political values are pivotal for the success of region-building. Without shared political values, all region-ness remains hollow or falls short of developing structures of trust that are aimed at shared destiny. What is true of peace is also true of region-building: democratic rule of law is the essential precondition to make it work.

EU: Doctrine or Pragmatic Strategy?

Efforts of the European Union to project its experience with integration beyond the shores of the continent have grown gradually. What began as an intuitive encouragement of other countries and societies in order to build regional peace and regain trust in a region has turned increasingly into an intentional global strategy of norm-setting and process-promotion. As a consequence of Europe's own normative and enlightened self-interest in the promotion of regional integration and in echoing Europe's desire for a more proactive and recognized global role, the EU has begun to develop a strategy of promoting regional integration and community-building among many of its partners around the world. The European Union likes to be perceived as a normative power. The promotion of region-building as an act of transformed power-politics driven by antagonistic autonomous state practices attributes to this self-perception and claim. It is not surprising that the limits of this universal European claim are met wherever geo-political conditions are not conducive (or not yet conducive) to region-building. It is even less surprising that the whole issue of the global proliferation of region-building and the role of the European Union in supporting this process have not become a serious transatlantic matter for the dialogue between the European Union and its most important partner, the United States.

In a way, the US represents "old Europe" with its primacy on state sovereignty. One can argue that the US as such is the most elaborate and integrated region.

The economic cooperation with Canada and Mexico under the framework of NAFTA (North American Free Trade Agreement) is driven by economic self-interest and selective cooperation. It is not a scheme for region-building. The European sympathy, at times almost a European obsession, with the value of regional integration and region-building as an act of economic and political community-building has never been properly understood in the US, nor has Europe ever properly explained it to the US. It is telling that, so far, the European Union is not engaged in a treaty-based relationship with either the US or NAFTA. The shared democratic values in the transatlantic community have not been translated into any biregional activity beyond political summitry. Democratic coherence alone is no guarantee for inter-regionalism.

On the other hand, governance differences do not necessarily exclude inter-regional cooperation. Relations between the European Union and the Gulf Cooperation Council, but also those between the European Union and the African Union, are based on shared interests even in the absence of governance symmetry between the two regions. While the transatlantic community flourishes without formalized inter-regional processes, the EU-GCC and the EU-AU relationships remain limited because of political hindrances. On principle, the European Union is projecting itself globally as the normative power. "The EU is particularly active," as a paper of the European Commission about the EU as a "world player" stated in 2004, "in promoting the human aspects of international relations, such as solidarity, human rights and democracy."[33] However, this self-serving claim has not translated into a coherent strategy or consistent policy.

The EU also needs to address the possible constraints on its policy objectives imposed by competing world-order interests of other international players. While the EU and the US share common political values, their geopolitical interests may differ. As for China, both values and interests may differ. China's policies in other regions of the world are largely driven by Chinese economic interests without political conditionality. This may undermine the projection of EU norms, policies, and institutions of regional integration. More research would be helpful to better understand where, how, and why democratic region-building can be undermined by the diverging global policies of the key actors in today's world.

The global presence of the European Union still is selective and incoherent. Sometimes it operates region-by-region, as in the cases of MERCOSUR, SICA, or GCC; sometimes bilaterally, as in the cases of the US, Russia, China, South Africa, or India; sometimes in asymmetric ways, as in the cases of ASEM or the Union for the Mediterranean, where even the definition of region-ness is ambivalent as it includes the EU as a partner, a bridge, and an actor.

The presence of the European Union in the emerging inter-regionalism has begun to strengthen the sense of actor-ness on the side of the EU's partners. Most of them do not simply emulate the European Union out of fascination with the

European integration experience or as a means to hopefully overcome daunting realities in their own region. Most developed regional groupings in the world—as this study shows—have been supported one way or the other by the European Union in focusing and advancing their genuine region-building. The European Union is always keen to emphasize that region-building is not only about the economy, despite the importance of development regionalism. The meaning of region-building as a strategy of peace-building and an insurance policy for maintaining stability in a region has been recognized in several regions due to positive empirical evidence. The European Union has continuously recommended itself as a model for conflict resolution.

But it would remain a futile exercise to promote region-building as a means to conflict resolution without emphasizing the preconditions for sustainable security regionalism. A solid socioeconomic development is certainly one of these preconditions. But the European integration experience also points to the democratic rule of law and the protection of human rights as the indispensable basis for creating trust and building up confidence among former enemy countries. Without democracy across its member states, the European Union would never have been able to build itself. Its internal democracy was and is the cornerstone of Europe's democratic regionalism. The strong national roots of democracy, the rule of law, and human rights in the EU's member states constitute democratic regionalism even in the absence of complete democracy, transparency, and accountability on the EU level. It has been said that the European Union might not be able to join itself if it were to apply for EU membership. But surely no European country would ever have been able become an EU member without democratic rule at home.

The promotion of region-building and the pursuit of inter-regional relations by the European Union are not automatically linked to the promotion and advancement of democracy. But there can be no doubt that region-building and inter-regionalism will remain limited if the constituent actors of these processes are not democratic. Embedded democratic regionalism is the quintessential precondition for region-building that goes beyond opportunism and selective pragmatism. This does not mean that other interests are irrelevant or their pursuit inappropriate. In fact, the European Union faces criticism that its plea for region-building and its efforts to advance biregional relations are ultimately expressions of self-interest rather than reflections of universal normative goals.[34]

Such criticism seems too absolute, static, and non-historic. It does not take into account the long way Europe had to go in the process of its internal reconciliation while at the same time creating new conditions in its relations with former colonies. In fact, it is apparent that region-building has become a means to strengthen the identity and pride of postcolonial areas and promote their worldwide recognition. This does not exclude the pursuit of self-interests by the European Union. Like other actors in the world system, the European Union legitimately pursues its interests. Internally, the EU is often criticized for not doing this in a sufficiently coherent and rigid way. While externally, the EU might be considered too big a player in economically poorer regions and in regions with weak security, the EU is taken less seriously, sometimes to the point of benign neglect, in regions with similar or stronger clout and world power, notably the United States.

The only solution for the European Union lies in its ability to establish as much consistency as possibly between its internal claims and its external actions. The real antagonism does not exist between "normative" and "realist" approaches of the European Union. Instead, the real gap in credibility and performance lies in the inconsistency of many of its actions. As a work in progress, the EU is quintessentially an unfinished project. In order to act in line with its potential and its limits, the policy objectives of the European Union ought to be coherent and the tools appropriate to its means. The European Union would not be in a bad position if it could emulate the role (and the image) of the United States after 1945, when the US was widely perceived across Europe as pursuing a policy of enlightened self-interest.

The promotion of regional integration, biregional cooperation, and eventually inter-regionalism is not an end in itself. For the European Union, these processes are considered to be means conducive to development, security, stability, and a more balanced and sustained world order.[35] The EU policies toward the African, Caribbean, and Pacific countries reflect a trend. The same can be said regarding the Latin American regional integration schemes. As for the Asian regional groupings, EU policies cannot be more consistent than the consistency (or lack thereof) in the region-building of these regional groupings. The EU has not been able to turn the geopolitical wheel in regions where there is no region-building yet, largely because of its limits in transforming the internal governance asymmetries and the geopolitical tensions stemming from this antagonism. As for the post-Soviet space in Eurasia, the EU has been able to support the processes of managing the decline of the Soviet Empire. But the EU must insist that any internal renewal needs to originate in the voluntary and democratic aspiration of the region's independent countries. As for the United States and North America at large, the European Union needs to project its own interests, norms, and actions in a clearer and more prolific way in order to be taken seriously. In doing so, it must address the suspicion that the EU's normative policy of promoting regional integration and inter-regionalism is not much more than a disguised form of anti-Americanism.

In Search of Global Presence

In 2001, Belgian Prime Minister Guy Verhofstadt proposed to replace the G8 grouping of leading industrialized countries by a G8 based on more regional representation: "We need to create a forum where the leading continental partnerships can all speak on an equal footing: the European Union, the African Union, the Common Market of the South (MERCOSUR), the Association of Southeast Asian Nations (ASEAN), the North American Free Trade Agreement (NAFTA), etc."[36] Aside from the fact that "etc." does not resolve the matter of defining the eight relevant regions, and aside from the obvious provocation of not including the United States as a single country in his list, the Belgian Prime Minister failed to explain how to achieve his idea.

It cannot be denied that the global presence of the European Union has been steadily growing. Article 300 of the EC Treaty endowed the European Community with the legal personality to conclude legal treaties in foreign trade matters. To be more precise, it conferred powers on the European Commission to conclude international agreements with legally binding effect. In 1974, the European Community gained observer status in the United Nations with the right to address the UN General Assembly. During the 1970s, the European Community became a full member of the International Commodities Agreement (ICA), and during the 1990s, much more meaningfully, a full member of the World Trade Organization (WTO) and of the UN's Food and Agricultural Organization (FAO). The EU's voting rights in the WTO and FAO are organized in such a way that the EU has as many votes as its member states would have if they were counted separately and then added together. In spite of recurrent proposals, the EU has not been able—so far—to acquire a seat on the Security Council of the United Nations.

The increasing global presence of the European Union is evident. Whenever the EU member states agree to a common and single international representation, they put benefits of collective performance above individual gains and other considerations related to usual state behavior. Realist theories assume that international relations are about power, gains, market interests, and recognition. Realist theory also accepts that material interdependencies make cooperation increasingly inevitable. As for the role and power of the biggest and most influential actors in the world arena under such circumstances, the term "cooperative hegemony" was coined.[37] It indicates that countries try to increase and maximize their power through means of cooperation. As intra-regionalism is—at least potentially—a two-way street, such a win-win situation for all participating partner regions might in reality be more complex than is generally insinuated by political theory.

The European Union's motives in promoting regional integration, biregional cooperation, and if possible inter-regionalism are manifold. Altruistic motives (quest for stability, peace, and development) match with self-interest (market access, norm export, stabilizing regions for the potential export of trouble, and projection of the EU's power and reputation). The tools used by the European Union are still in the process of being developed. The declared objectives are not always coherent, and the conditions for a successful proliferation of European integration experience elsewhere in the world are most often incompatible with the European integration history and its engines. The European Union is, all in all, trying to apply the following instruments in its policies of promoting regional integration:

- Economic assistance for cross-border projects and support of the institutions of regional groupings.
- Cooperation agreements with more upgraded and larger projects of the same nature.
- Region-to-region political dialogues that include regular political and strategic exchanges among the leaders of the respective groupings.
- Conditionality as an instrument to guide economic and policy decisions among EU partner regions through persuasion and benign coercion.[38]

The European Union is obviously in the process of standardizing its approach to biregional cooperation. Yet the level of conditionality, among other things, differs:

- The GCC was called upon to create a customs union before engaging in negotiations for a biregional association agreement.
- ASEAN and ASEAN Plus Three were exempt from harsh political conditionality in spite of the mixed record on democracy and human rights in the region.
- The Cotonou Agreement insists that the African, Caribbean, and Pacific countries strengthen their respective region-building.

Framework agreements for biregional cooperation have been concluded with the most advanced partners among the leading regional groupings in the world. They are based on the same principles: promotion of trade liberalization, improvement of investment conditions, cooperation on macro-economic matters, and political dialogue including matters of good governance. The next step would entail the upgrading of a cooperation agreement into a biregional association agreement. The negotiations with MERCOSUR and SICA are the most advanced in this regard, while the EPAs with African, Caribbean, and Pacific countries are part of EU officials' never-ending project of enhancing the vocabulary of "Euro-speak."

Whenever possible, the European Union prefers region-to-region relations. In some cases it has insisted that a region be considered a preferential partner only if it presents itself as a region to the EU (i.e., the Pacific Islands Forum). In other cases the EU has been overly enthusiastic and proactive in pursuing region-to-region cooperation, only to reach its limits because of the limits of its partners (MERCOSUR, ASEAN). Again in other cases, the European Union has been hesitant to engage in deeper biregional cooperation, basically because of uncertainty about the status and prospects of a regional partner (GCC, SAARC, ECOWAS).

It should not be forgotten that the EU's biregional relations are a rather recent phenomenon. Judgment of their quality, scope, and effect must therefore remain open. Practically all existing agreements have been concluded over a short period spanning less than one generation:

- With ASEAN in 1980.
- With the Andean Community of Nations (CAN) in 1983.
- With the Central American Integration System (SICA) in 1985.
- With the Gulf Cooperation Council in 1988.
- With MERCOSUR in 1991.
- With the ACP countries under the Cotonou Agreement in 2000.

Some region-to-region relations have reached pre-association status, while others are frozen at the level of cooperation and some involve no more than political declarations and repetitiously expressed ambitions. The format of the relations of the European Union with the leading regional groupings around the world varies in density, mandate, objective, and relevance. But the global ambition of the European Union is evident from taking a comprehensive look around the world. The global proliferation of region-building has become an undeniable phenomenon. Whether this trend will lead to stable, effective, and lasting groupings largely depends upon the groups' individual ability to grow into serious expressions of democratic region-building. Only then will the global proliferation of region-building achieve its legitimizing breakthrough as a new reality in political theory and international relations.

Whether or not regional integration facilitates global order-building is a normative question and a matter of principled belief, but also an empirical matter. Inside the European Union, the majority assessment regards European integration as compatible with the positioning of Europe in the era of globalization. More divisive is the relationship between European integration and transatlantic relations. In reality, the two have proven to be compatible, often complementing each other, while both suffer if one of the two is not in good shape. One of the biggest noticeable differences between the United States and the European Union relates to the global proliferation of region-building. Regional integration is almost a universal value for the European Union. The United States, however, favors economic regions and open markets such as those represented by APEC, NAFTA, or FTAA. The individual participation of countries has priority, and integrationist ideas are largely absent. Neither the institutionalization of cooperation nor deeper forms of integration within the preferred free trade areas are a matter of explicit US interest. The US prefers to adhere to the necessary minimum of institutionalized regulatory measures, purely acceptable for purposes of supporting free trade. As seen from the European Union's perspective, the United States often acts like "old Europe," the last nation-state of an autarkic type. As for Europe, such a state concept has vanished to a large extent in Europe and is about to transform in most other parts of the world. Yet as much as the United States needs multilateralism, the European Union needs the United States as its indispensable partner for the management of world affairs.

For the European Union, meeting the future of world-order building through the lens of the proliferation of region-building implicitly means meeting Europe's past. The fall from global supremacy at the end of the colonial and imperial era was topped by Europe's internal self-destruction. After half a century of internal reconciliation, Europe has recovered and gained a new identity. Europeans as citizens might be missing, but Europe as an organized and institutionally viable composition is solid and vivid. Whether or not one welcomes the development, the EU has become the embodiment of the new Europe and the expression of its political identity in the twenty-first century. Outside Europe, the quest for a global presence and role of the EU has visibly grown. Its internal European preconditions are idiosyncratic and wayward and oscillate between ambition and performance. In its traditional neighborhood, the European Union is perceived as a mixed bag of hope and frustration coupled with lack of clarity about its ultimate goal and the degree to which the implementation of expectations can be assumed. The same holds true for the perception of the European Union among many elites in the United States.

Outside the traditional parameters of the Cold War and the post–Cold War order, Europe and the European Union have a good reputation. European integration is emulated in many regions that have gone through the valley of tears associated with Europe's colonial presence in the past. Today Europe is the voluntary model, a laboratory consulted for inspiration. The global proliferation of regional integration indicates nothing less than the return of Europe as a subject to the world stage. It is an indirect, transformed Europe that returns, almost in disguise and through the transposition of its contemporary political form as European Union.

Notes

1. See, for example, Marie-Thérèse Bitsch and Gérard Bossuat (eds.), *De l'Idée d'Eurafrique à la Convention de Lomé I* (Brussels: Bruylant, 2005).

2. See, for example, Jeremy Rifkind, *The European Dream: How Europe's Vision of the Future is Quietly Eclipsing the American Dream* (Cambridge: Polity Press, 2004), especially 358–385.

3. Andrew Hurrell, "The Regional Dimension in International Relations Theory," in Mary Farrell et al. (eds.), *Global Politics of Regionalism: Theory and Practice* (London: Pluto Press, 2005), 40.

4. See Björn Hettne and Fredrik Söderbaum, "Civilian Power or Soft Imperialism? The European Union as a Global Actor and the Role of Interregionalism," *European Foreign Affairs Review* 10, no. 4 (2005): 535–552.

5. See Mario Telò, *Europe, A Civilian Power? European Union, Global Governance, World Power* (New York: Palgrave Macmillan, 2006).

6. Jan Zielonka, *Europe as Empire: The Nature of the Enlarged European Union* (Oxford: Oxford University Press, 2006).

7. European Commission (EC), *Taking Europe to the World: 50 Years of European Commission's External Service* (2004), 59, online at: http://www.ec.Europa.eu/external_relations/library/publications/07_50_years_broch_en.pdf.

8. European Commission (EC), *Communication on European Community Support for Regional Economic Integration Efforts among Developing Countries*, COM (95) 219 final (16 June 1995), 18, online at: http://aei.pitt.edu/4328/01/001212_1.pdf.

9. Mark Beeson, *ASEAN Plus Three and the Rise of Reactionary Regionalism*, online at: http://espace.library.uq.edu.au/eserv/UQ:10998/mbasean03.pdf.

10. Jürgen Rüland, *ASEAN and the European Union: A Bumpy Interregional Relationship*, ZEI Discussion Paper C 95 (Bonn: Center for European Integration Studies, 2001), 8.

11. See Heiner Hänggi et al. (eds.), *Interregionalism and International Relations* (Abingdon and New York: Routledge, 2006).

12. For details see European Commission (EC), *The Cotonou Agreement*, online at: http://ec.europa.eu/development/icenter/repository/agr01_en.pdf.

13. European Commission (EC), *Africa, Caribbean, Pacific: EPA Negotiations: Toolbox*, online at: http://ec.europa.eu/trade/creating-opportunities/bilateral-relations/regions/africa-caribbean-pacific/index_en.htm, 2003.

14. See Martin Holland, *The European Union and the Third World* (Houndmills: Palgrave, 2002), 153.

15. Tesfaye Dinka and Walter Kennes, *Africa's Regional Integration Arrangements: History and Challenges*, ECDPM Discussion Paper No. 74 (Maastricht: European Centre for Development Policy, 2007), 24; see also Brigid Gavin, *Regional Integration and EPAs Timing and Safeguards*, UNU-CRIS Occasional Paper O-2003/4 (Bruges: United Nations University—CRIS, 2003), online at: http://www.cris.unu.edu/fileadmin/workingpapers/brigid%20ACP%20Engl%20final.pdf; Philippe de Lombaerde, *Supporting Regional Integration: The Roadmap of Indicators and Tools*, UNU-CRIS Occasional Paper, O-2003/3 (Bruges: United Nations University—CRIS, 2003), online at: http://www.cris.unu.edu/fileadmin/workingpapers/philippe%20ACP%20Engl%20final.pdf; Fernanda Faria, *Crisis Management in Sub-Saharan Africa: The Role of the European Union*, ISS Occasional Paper no. 51 (Paris: The European Union Institute for Security Studies, 2004), online at: http://www.iss.europa.eu/uploads/media/occ51.pdf; Mary Farrell, "A Triumph of Realism over Idealism? Cooperation between the European Union and Africa," *Journal of European Integration* 27, no. 3 (2005): 263–283.

16. Sanoussi Bilal, *Can the EU be a model of regional integration? Risks and challenges for developing countries*, Paper presented at the CODESRIA-Global Studies Network (GSN), Second International Conference on 'Globalisation: Overcoming Exclusion, Strengthening Inclusion' (Dakar, Senegal, 29–31 August 2005), online at: http://www.ecdpm.org/Web_ECDPM/Web/Content/Download.nsf/0/52D667FD6C95057DC125719D004B65F6/$FILE/Bilal%20-1%20of%20RI%20Draft%20for%20comments.pdf; see also John Ravenhill, "Back to the Nest? Europe's Relations with the African, Caribbean, and Pacific Group of Countries," in Vinod K. Aggarwal and Edward A. Fogarty (eds.), *EU Trade Strategies: Between Regionalism and Globalism* (Houndmills: Palgrave Macmillan, 2004), 118–147.

17. See European Commission (EC), *Green Paper on Relations between the European Union and the ACP Countries on the Eve of the 21st Century: Challenges and Options for a New Partnership*, COM (96) 570 (1996), iii, online at: http://aei.pitt.edu/1206/01/ACP_21st_gp_COM_96_570.pdf.

18. For further details see European Commission (EC), *EPA Flash News*, online at: http://ec.europa.eu/trade/creating-opportunities/bilateral-relations/regions/africa-caribbean-pacific/index_en.htm.

19. See Vinod K. Aggarwal and Edward A. Fogarty, "Explaining Trends in EU Interregionalism," in Aggarwal and Fogarty, *EU Trade Strategies*, 207–240.

20. See Beverly Crawford, "Why the Euro-Med Partnership? European Union Strategies in the Mediterranean Region," in Aggarwal and Fogarty, *EU Trade Strategies*, 93–117; Giacomo Luciani and

Felix Neugart (eds.), *The EU and the GCC: A New Partnership*. (Munich/Gütersloh: Bertelsmann Group for Policy Research, Center for Applied Policy Research/Bertelsmann Foundation, 2005); Andreas Marchetti (ed.), *Ten Years Euro-Mediterranean Partnership: Defining European Interests for the Next Decade*, ZEI Discussion Paper C 154 (Bonn: Center for European Integration Studies, 2005); Andreas Marchetti, *The European Neighborhood Policy: Foreign Policy at the EU's Periphery*, ZEI Discussion Paper C 158 (Bonn: Center for European Integration Studies, 2006).

21. Karen Smith, *European Union Foreign Policy in a Changing World* (Oxford: Polity Press, 2003), 78.

22. See Chin-Peng Chu, "Regionalism and Regional Integration in the Asia-Pacific and the European Union," in Christopher M. Dent and David W.F. Huang (eds.), *Northeast Asian Regionalism: Learning from the European Experience* (London: Routledge Curzon, 2002), 34–64; Julie Gilson, "New Interregionalism? The EU and East Asia," *Journal of European Integration* 27, no. 3 (2005): 307–326.

23. See Julie Gilson, *Asia Meets Europe: Interregionalism and the Asia-Europe Meeting* (Cheltenham: Edward Elgar, 2002).

24. See Hazel Smith, "Actually Existing Foreign Policy—Or Not? The EU in Latin and Central America," in John Peterson and Helen Sjursen (eds.), *A Common Foreign Policy for Europe? Competing Visions of the CFSP* (London and New York: Routledge, 1998), 152–168.

25. See Helio Jaguaribe and Alvaro Vasconcelos (eds.), *The European Union, Mercosul and the New World Order* (London: Frank Cass, 2003); Miriam Gomes Saraiva, *The European Union as an International Actor and the Mercosur Countries*, EUI Working Paper RSCAS No. 2004/14 (Florence: Robert Schuman Centre for Advanced Studies, 2004), online at: http://cadmus.iue.it/dspace/bitstream/1814/2756/1/04_14.pdf; Sebastian Santander, "The European Partnership with Mercosur: A Relationship Based on Strategic and Neo-Liberal Principles," *Journal of European Integration* 27, no. 3 (2005): 285–306.

26. See Philip Arestis and Luiz Fernando de Paula (eds.), *Monetary Union in South America: Lessons from EMU* (Cheltenham: Edward Elgar, 2003).

27. See Santander, "The European Partnership with Mercosur," 295–296; Robert Devlin and Ziga Vodusek, *Trade Related Capacity Building: An Overview in the Context of Latin American Trade Policy and the MERCOSUR-EU Association Agreement* (Buenos Aires: Institute for the Integration of Latin America and the Caribbean, 2005).

28. See Luis Xavier Grisanti, *El Nuevo Interregionalismo Transatlántico: La Asociación Estratégica Unión Europea—América Latina* (Buenos Aires: Institute for the Integration of Latin America and the Caribbean, 2004).

29. See Jürgen Rüland, "Interregionalism. An Unfinished Agenda," in Hänggi et al., *Interregionalism and International Relations*, 295–315.

30. Björn Hettne, "The New Regionalism Revisited," in Fredrik Söderbaum and Timothy M. Shaw (eds.), *Theories of New Regionalism: A Palgrave Reader* (Houndmills: Palgrave Macmillan, 2003), 40.

31. Gilson, "New Interregionalism?" 322.

32. See Ludger Kühnhardt, *Stufen der Souveränität: Selbstbestimmung und Staatsverständnis in der "Dritten Welt"* (Bonn: Bouvier, 1992).

33. European Commission (EC), *A World Player: The European Union's External Relations* (2004), 23, online at: http://www.ec.Europa.eu/publications/booklets/move/47/en.pdf.

34. See Farrell, "Triumph of Realism over Idealism," 263–283.

35. See Fredrik Söderbaum and Luk van Langenhove, "The EU as a Global Actor and the Role of Interregionalism," *Journal of European Integration* 27, no. 3 (2005): 249–262, 250. It is interesting to note that the European Union is also encouraging semi–region-building processes with limited objectives and scope, such as the Council of Baltic Sea States, the Barents Euro-Atlantic Council, the Black Sea Economic Cooperation, the Stability Pact for Southeastern Europe, and the Euro-Mediterranean Process. This does not help to resolve the confusion between authentic region-building in the global order and subregion-building efforts with limited actor capability, largely

defined by contingent security considerations stemming from European neighbor-ness with huge areas of geopolitical, economic, and sociopolitical transformations.

36. Guy Verhofstadt, "The Paradox of Anti-Globalisation," *The Guardian*, 28 September 2001, online at: http://www.guardian.co.uk/world/2001/sep/28/globalisation.

37. Thomas Pedersen, "Cooperative Hegemony: Power, Ideas and Institutions in Regional Integration," *Review of International Studies* 28, no. 4 (2002): 677–696; see also Robert Keohane, *International Institutions and State Power: Essays in International Relations Theory* (Boulder: Westview Press, 1989); Mary Farrell, *The EU and Inter-Regional Cooperation: In Search of Global Presence?* UNU-CRIS e-Working Paper W-2004/9 (Bruges: United Nations University-CRIS, 2004), online at: http://www.cris.unu.edu/fileadmin/workingpapers/WP%20Farrell.pdf.

38. Smith, European Union Foreign Policy in a Changing World, 86–90.

10

DEMOCRATIC GOVERNANCE, REGIONAL GROUPINGS, AND WORLD ORDER

———◦◉◦———

A Set of Remarks

In spite of backlashes and shortcomings, region-building continues across the world. Often, a confusing overlap of terminology blurs a clear-cut analysis of strength and weaknesses of the respective processes. Yet based on a cross-continental empirical study of the main region-building processes, one can identify the most obvious reasons that explain the underlying dynamics and inherent causes of continuous regionalization, regionalism, and region-building:

- Intuitive commonalities. Common features of identity due to geographic proximity, overarching cultural patterns, and shared historical memories are at the root of region-ness. Turning these markers of identification into region-building strategies has generated a wide array of possible (and plausible) approaches and characteristics. Several of these trends have led to a sort of intuitive region-ness, and sometimes these intuitive approaches have been transformed into material commonalities, or at least into the willingness to achieve them.
- Integration norms as features of hope. No matter the diverse strategies of region-building, the underlying assumption that integration norms represent a gateway to improved stability, enhanced security, and maximized affluence and welfare is a common feature. Integration and region-building can be understood as strategies of empowerment. The main focus can be on one's own community, society, or state. It need not be rooted in altruistic and idealistic notions of region-ness in order to make sense and activate political momentum. Whatever the root causes of region-building and the relationship among internal expectations, external pressures, and institutional composition, integration strategies promise added value and gains.
- Pressure of globalization. The idea of acquiring welfare and/or security gains through region-building dominates the existing regional groupings. Globalization and its

assumed effects tend to be a common push factor. The globalization concept and its link to integration efforts are divided into two different discourses and assumptions. In some cases the argument prevails that region-building is similar to globalization in one region. Here region-building is understood as a proactive way of shaping globalization in one's own region and as a means of maximizing the opportunities of globalization. In other cases, region-building is understood as the necessary response to both globalization and the fear of increasing marginalization. It is seen as the ultimate chance to overcome or avoid peripheral negligence and irrelevance in economic and global affairs.

- The attraction of the European model. Europeans are full of self-doubts about the limits of their integration process. They focus on the deficits of the European Union and struggle with ways and means to inject a sufficient degree of dynamics into their integration project. After more than five decades of successful integration, the European Union has lost some of its earlier charisma and dynamism. Outside Europe, however, the European integration experience is widely perceived as an exceptional success story and a fascinating laboratory that ought to be used for the sake of repeating the success in welfare and security gains.

- Ambivalence about US primacy. Region-building is not necessarily a means of limiting American power. Nor is it anti-American by nature. Although this is a fearful perception sometimes expressed in the US—and nurtured by some actors of regionalism who indeed aim to reduce American influence—region-building is inherently ambivalent about its links with the primacy of the US in world affairs. The main rational reason for this ambivalence lies in the procedural character of all regional groupings in the world. None of them can claim to have already achieved a final status and hence uphold certainty about its role in future world order–building.

The main trend in the academic literature dealing with matters of region-building is apologetic and contingent. It tries to explain how a certain regional grouping has come about and in which direction it is heading. It often is overly critical about the factual performance of the particular regional grouping. Much of the literature concentrates on one or two regional groupings but misses the larger global picture. The theoretical approaches to region-building and integration normally take the dominant theories of international relations as their starting point. Others look at regional groupings through the lens of the European integration experience. It is rare to find fresh thinking that links a global empirical approach with an integrated theoretical assessment, trying to combine the most sustainable theoretical findings of international relations, comparative government, and political theory. Such an approach, however, seems to be the most promising if one is to gain optimal insights into the nature and course of region-building as it unfolds in the twenty-first century.

It would also be useful and enlightening to better understand the main obstacles to regional integration and architecture-building. Before embarking on the rather artificial enterprise of conceptualizing the mode of measuring integration success,[1] it would be helpful to know why certain regional integration processes have not succeeded, or at least, have not achieved the expected results. Approaching region-building from its limits rather than from its hopes and promises might bring more than realism into the discourse: it could also lead to realistic examination of the current trends of regional integration and the potential of region-building and regionalism in the shaping of world order.

Among the structural obstacles to region-building, the following belong among the empirical findings of this study:

- Highly asymmetric realities in different regions (as far as size, population, and economic and political power disparities, but likewise leadership attitudes, degree of political will, and principled belief patterns are concerned);
- Historical animosities and externally driven hard-power choices that undermine the concept of regionalism as a normative illusion;
- Excessively different extra-regional orientations of the key countries in a region that preempt the potential for cooperation and pooling of resources;
- The artificial application of integration modes elsewhere (most notably, the European integration experience qualifies as a static model of emulation), leading to an unsuccessful sequencing of integration patterns that fail to take into account the necessary fulfillment of preconditions and contingent circumstances.

Among the most widespread domestic impediments to successful region-building are the following:

- Conflicting regime structures limiting the degree of trust necessary for a sustainable and expanding process of sharing interests and pooling resources;
- Missing political will or insufficient strategic focus among the political actors in a region, which can turn integration rhetoric from a shared opportunity into a collective obstacle;
- The fact that national calculations of gains and pains—that is, of costs and benefits of regional integration—can differ in spite of general rhetorical consensus about the value of common action toward deeper integration;
- Unequal degrees of internal shocks and the consequences of weak state capacity leading to the primacy and dominance of domestic political bargaining at the expense of the regional search for consensus and compromise;
- Insufficiency of human resources or other capacity-related constellations that would otherwise be beneficial to integration progress and the evolution of a regional grouping;
- The lack of domestic integration engines and the absence of mutually reinforcing yet balancing partners in two or more countries of a region;

• A grossly inward-oriented or autarkic orientation of economic protectionism or political myopia, which can lastingly undermine the integration potential of a region.

Among the most noticeable external obstacles to successful deeper regional integration, the following phenomena most often occur:

• The primacy of hard-power politics and geopolitical dependencies limits the necessary scope of action among one or more states in a regional grouping.
• The peripheral status of a region nurtures the sense of a "loser syndrome" instead of encouraging more energetic actions toward achieving improved region-ness.
• The lack of decisiveness between different and potentially conflicting aims impedes the formulation and focused implementation of integration goals.
• Different orientations and dependencies of a region or some of its main states vis-à-vis the United States undermine the ability to develop a regional grouping outside the shadow of the region's relationship with the dominant global power.

The main trends in region-building are certainly subject to interpretation and controversy. Yet certain generalizing conclusions that can be drawn from the global overview in this study will help to better contextualize the overall direction of regionalism in the contemporary world.

An almost universal trend seems to mobilize people, societies, countries, and regions—organized or unorganized—wherever possible globalization gains are concerned. Free trade as an instrument in advancing the development of regionalism is controversial. Critics of globalization are reluctant to accept the thesis that regional integration will support welfare gains through free trade. And those who question the idea of global trade as a suitable instrument to enhance collective welfare gains remain altogether doubtful about the side effects of region-building. Those, however, who consider free trade as the precondition to the successful use of the opportunities of globalization are inclined to see region-building as a stepping stone to the fulfillment of globalization promises. The argument has not been resolved between those who express a reluctant acceptance of the comprehensive creation of common markets and those who are afraid that welfare gains through the externalization of local costs will be outweighed by the painful negative effects of imported consequences of the creation of more integrated markets.

The hesitant, albeit unavoidable, realization of the relevance of law as a mediating and stabilizing factor in the pursuit of regional economic integration can be noticed worldwide. In many regional groupings community law is accepted as arbitration law for mediating trade disputes, but the political impact of community law and the theoretical recognition of the possible primacy of supranational law are still controversial. The logical link between community law and its effects on communitarian mechanisms and procedures of politics under the framework of an integration scheme are still debated and controversial. Yet the tendency to establish parliamentary assemblies in many regional groupings indicates a trend: economic cooperation and integration cannot evolve without a common legal base. The more this legal base develops, the more inevitable is the need to be rooted in common political structures. The more these common political structures are contemplated, the more the question of accountability and transparency becomes unavoidable. In the history of the national political arena, political integration and economic integration were mutually reinforcing. They opened the path to rule of law, which in turn was a necessary precondition for the evolution of broad-based democracy and the protection of human rights. It has become, however, an increasing and almost global trend to couple economic and political integration with the contemporaneous establishment of some form of a community legal body.

Hope that security regionalism will have pacifying effects is as widely shared as hope that development regionalism will lead to welfare gains. But the assessment of the desired outcomes' genuine root causes and preconditions is flawed and weak. Most underestimated (and under-researched) is the link between democratic governance and regional integration. This study emphasizes the instrumental character of democratic regionalism as a precondition and sustaining effect of region-building based on regime symmetry between the member states of a regional grouping. The political nature of integration—its causes and effects—remains controversial and often, more importantly, inexplicit. The opening of the political side of integration among the leading regional groupings in the world tends to follow a similar pattern. It often begins with the invocation of the institutional side of political integration (i.e., the establishment of parliamentary assemblies) or the formalistic expression of democracy (establishment of a common citizenship). But these processes normally have not happened in parallel with the attribution of competencies or judiciable mandates to these institutions or structures.

As for the notion of sovereignty, the invocation of its traditional role in epitomizing the claim to autonomous political and legal decision-making powers corresponds with an eerie sense of its de facto limits. Deepening of integration usually goes hand in hand with strong rhetorical commitments to the unalterable value of sovereignty. The transforming effects of integration practice, and the consequences of multilevel cooperation or even integration for the concept of governance and the notion of sovereignty, are often flatly denied. Yet the evolution of what might be called "intermestic" realities—the fluid interplay between domestic and international or supranational structures, processes, and effects—cannot be overlooked if one is to take empirical accounts seriously.

The links between region-ness, identity formation, and the political norms and objectives of regional integration are mostly unclear and often left out of any serious definition. Regional awareness is growing as a consequence of formal integration and certainly of de facto cooperation. Even in the absence of clearly defined goals of regional integration, the intuitive regional commonality serves as a pull factor for recognizing common sensitivity and community-building aspirations.

The Dominant Theoretical Approaches

Theoretical reflections about regional integration depend upon the historical context and move with their target. In 1975, Ernst B. Haas, who had introduced the understanding of functional-sectoral integration as the theoretical key to the European integration originating in the Treaties of Rome, and who in 1961 was the first to compare European integration and worldwide integration trends, was again looking at regional integration outside Europe. Amidst a crisis of European integration versus obvious formalism without solid integration effects in non-European integration efforts, Haas was unequivocal in his judgment. Regionalism theory, he flatly concluded, was "obsolete in Western Europe and obsolescent in the rest of the world."[2] International relations theory, he maintained, was enough of an analytical instrument to grasp the meaning of regional trends. Domestic governance would pursue its genuine life on the national level while regionalism would not be an in-between the vertical and horizontal levels of governance. Certain core notions of the relationship between geography, society, notions of political structures, and modes of power remained without consensual precision and often got blurred, he argued.

Given the quantum leaps in European integration and new waves of region-building efforts across the globe, a different light has been shed on the question of obsolescence. Region-building has not vanished as a constructivist political undertaking and as a source of academic reflection. To the contrary, it is on the rise. The most simple clarification regards the terminology: "region" stands for a geographical relationship echoed in mutual and multifaceted interdependence; "regionalism" alludes to the formation of groupings based in regions and in the notion of common gains through shared interests and common procedures and institutions; "region-building and integration," finally, means a genuine regional approach to creating and optimizing gains through common, and if possible single, efforts.

The causes for assessing the most recent waves of region-building are as manifold as the answers given to the question why these waves of region-building have not stopped but rather expanded. Four causes, and their often idiosyncratic interactions, are certainly essential to getting to the heart of the matter of a new trend in global order building:

1. After the end of the Cold War and the replacement of its explanatory monopoly by globalization as the new dominating paradigm, the limits of autonomous

state power and the possible welfare gains of resource accumulation and pooled sovereignty started to be discussed in a new context.

2.   With the increasing differentiation among developing countries, a static notion of a coherent Third World gave room to more focused area studies, reinstalling continents as geographical realities and discovering regions in their genuine character as cultural, economic, social, and political entities.

3.   The democratization following the end of communism did not become a universal success, but it redirected the global discourse about power and governance toward an appreciation of democracy, rule of law, and human rights as the indispensable base for security and welfare.

4.   The impressive achievements in European integration since the 1980s helped to transform the image of Europe in many regions that used to be colonies of European powers. Europe's experience in conflict resolution, and the nexus between Europe's integration history and the evolution of exceptional degrees of mass affluence in Europe, became two important explanatory variables for assessing the meaning and usefulness of regional integration efforts in other parts of the world.

Following a new beginning in region-building, yet often too much tied to its imminent expressions and events, a new batch of academic literature appeared, offering theoretical explanations about the cause and trend of regionalism.[3] Democratic governance and interstate capacities of trust form the basis of successful region-building. In the theoretical literature, though, these preconditions of region-building are surprisingly under-estimated. At best they appear in the negative, as in Louise Fawcett's assessment that "it remains difficult to refute the argument that regionalism so far enjoyed the greatest success among liberal, like-minded states."[4] The notion of democratic regionalism, as discussed in this study, will need to be incorporated into the nomenclature of regional integration theory.

Theories of regional integration originated in the context of the European integration process. In the meantime, their focus has mostly shifted from understanding European integration as an object of international relations theories to European integration as a phenomenon best analyzed by methods of comparative politics.[5] In this shift, however, neither the role of the EU in international affairs nor, as yet, comparative regional integration studies have been at the center of academic interest. The traditional European approach to integration theory has generated a broad set of features, concepts, and arguments. Some of the best-known theoretical arguments have grown into catchwords floating around much of the relevant scholarly literature and have been echoed in the literature on comparative regional integration:

  • Integration as a process of amalgamated security communities (Karl Deutsch).
  • Functional integration theories (Ernst B. Haas) expanded by neofunctional attributes (Philippe Schmitter).

- Intergovernmentalism as liberal institutionalism based on economic interests (Andrew Moravscik).
- Constructivism as a means to attribute to regions what we think of them (Jeffrey Checkel) or to assume that anarchy is what states make of it (Alexander Wendt).
- Game theory with its often-cited prisoner's dilemma in search of an optimal rational outcome (John Forbes Nash, Jr.).

Finn Laursen has linked a fine overview of these main trends in integration theory to a set of still-urgent critical questions in the assessment of integration processes beyond the European origin of its theory.[6] Based on the empirical findings of this study, one may extend his contribution about the character of non-European experiences in community-oriented region-building by posing the following questions:

1. Why have so many attempts to integration failed? This question is of relative applicability if integration is understood as a process that does not follow speedy and deterministic path dependencies but gives credit to crises, detours, unintended consequences, and a whole array of possible variations on the original integration objective.

2. How do we explain why outsiders seek to become insiders? This question reduces integration to the enlargement imperative, which is a relevant category but cannot replace the issue of deepening the integration processes.

3. Why do countries resist the temptation to defect? This is a question of the presumably spectacular resort of withdrawal from a regional grouping. Cases of membership withdrawal have occurred in various settings. Most interesting fact to note is that no withdrawal from any regional grouping has ever led to the dissolution of the grouping as such.

4. Why do members of a regional integration scheme accept distributional inequalities? This question implies that regional integration can only work if it generates and preserves equal living conditions. This has obviously not been the case, yet the leading integration schemes in the world continue to exist. The anticipated gains of membership in a regional grouping are obviously not only related to immediate economic effects. Long-term matters (reciprocal reliability, mutual recognition, strengthened political relevance) are as relevant for maintaining membership in a regional grouping as short-term economic gains.

5. Why can the sequencings of the integration process differ and yet not derail the process of region-building? The non-identical processes in sequencing, and regarding expectations, effects, and cost benefits of integration, are an expression of the plurality of historical, political, sociological, and economic conditions. They simply represent freedom.

A genuinely universal theory of region-building is yet to be developed. Andrew Hurrell has contributed two valuable theoretical reflections to the understanding of the global trend of region-building. In 1995, his main emphasis was on clarifying the nomenclature applied to phenomena of regional integration.[7] He distinguished:

- Regionalization as the expression of growth in integration within a region based on autonomous economic processes and an increasing flow of interacting people;
- Regional awareness and regional identity formation as a cognitive phenomenon changing with the self-perception of a region and its perception from the outside;
- State-promoted regional integration as a largely economic process with a limited role for the state, mainly involved in deregulating trade barriers before regulating common external tariffs in order to improve the competitive position of the region's economy;
- Regional cohesion as expressed in regional policies and the increasing pursuit of common regional policy interests.

On the basis of these clarifications, Hurrell contextualized region-building in its role in world politics and in world order. He did so by distinguishing three theoretical approaches.

1. Systemic theories such as neorealism deal with region-building processes on the basis of their recognition of the primacy of the unitary state. They describe external challenges as the main push factor for region-building and do not distinguish between economic and political aspects of regionalism. Hurrell argued that the security dependency of Western Europe on the United States after World War II was the key to beginning the European integration process, as it was in the context of the creation of ASEAN. Originally, regionalism was a function of the Cold War. After its demise in 1990, institutionalized regionalism became an attractive instrument "as a means of tying down or constraining the potentially disruptive effects of unequal power."[8] Hurrell might be too focused on the geopolitical constellation that shaped the world order after 1945 when he reduces the driving forces of region-building primarily to the external constellation of geopolitics. Intrinsic European motives (or Southeast Asian motives, for that matter) cannot be denied and should not be neglected. After all, European leaders implemented region-building against the current of centuries of nationalist rivalry and conflict. No geopolitical pressure would have been sufficient if the notion of region-building as a purposeful rupture with century-old patterns of state politics had not found support and consensus among them.

   The neorealistic primacy of autonomous state decision-making does not explain the complete process of region-building, particularly between big and small countries. But to raise one example, why would India want or even need the Maldives to join the South Asian Association for Regional Cooperation? Hurrell assumes that economic factors change politics but doubts that reverse patterns are possible. As much as he convincingly argues that "globalization may act as stimulus to regionalism,"[9] it is astonishing to frequently encounter not only his suspicion of politics but his underestimation of it. After all, the worst phenomena in history were dependent upon politics—wars and the establishment of totalitarian rule included. Positive and peaceful transformations of secular importance were also initiated by political events—from the Franco-German reconciliation after World War II to the creation of regional integration schemes across the world, as this study has amply shown. External pressure has often been a powerful engine, but without the deliberate political action of national leaders, no region-building process anywhere in the world would have started.

2. Hurrell's second argument deals with the links between regionalism and interdependence. Neofunctional theories and neoliberal institutionalism explain why states begin to interact as a consequence of the interdependence already rising among the respective societies. Integration, intended to resolve common problems and deficits, creates new problems. Hurrell argued that problems caused by state politics require even more, and stronger, common management by the states involved.[10] It is somewhat excessive to insinuate that regionalism is the answer to problems generated by those who try to resolve them through regionalism. At best, this is an unhistorical argument. Structurally it might have some meaning, but this is totally distorted when taken out of its historic-genetic context. It is empirically very rare to find examples of political actors who created problems for their own state or their neighboring states before embarking on a path toward region-building in order to reverse the initial disasters they were responsible for. Such a perception of the state and political actors reduces both of them to static, almost fatal concepts. Of course, it is conceivable and has often happened that political actors decided to use the power of state politics to overcome a false path of politics pursued by their own predecessors. But the personal responsibility for the failure of state policies and for a radical revision of these failures is almost always split between two completely different actors. It might not make sense to forge them into one anonymous bloc as if history were an interplay of dark forces. States are not abstract and ahistorical rational "individuals" in egoistic pursuit of unchanging interests.

3. Constructivist theories, Hurrell states in introducing his third argument, recognize the meaning of shared memories and common experiences as well as a regional sense of belonging. But they cannot, any more than can neofunctionalist and other theories based on assumptions of politics as a matter of social engineering, sufficiently explain and incorporate the role of the individual actor. Here is where Hurrell grounds his tour de force of theoretical understanding of regionalism in "domestic level theories."[11] Region-building, he contends, must be echoed in compatible values and, notably, a convergence of democratic rule.

In a 2005 follow-up to his first essay, Hurrell conceded the danger that theories of regionalism remain Euro-focused and therefore potentially impede the genuine study of comparative regionalism from a global perspective. Hurrell prefers to think in generalized theoretical terms but unfortunately up to the extreme point that he questions the possibility that any lesson could be learned from the European integration experience. As much as it makes sense to connect the evolution of regionalism to the overall development of the global system, it is not sufficient to conceptualize region-building purely from a bird's eye view. European integration experience is not per se a superior guiding star for integration efforts elsewhere. But it has become part of the historical legacy that other integration approaches build on. The European integration experience is part of the historical tradition of non-European region-building because those non-European processes of region-building are also a belated reaction to the global proliferation of the autonomous and independent state, which also originated in Europe. Hence, the development of non-European region-building stands in consequence of the initial impact of European order concepts.

Ten years after his first cautious assessment of the potentially encouraging role of globalization on region-building, Hurrell introduced a set of rational arguments to underline the inherent logic of his claim. In 2005 he described regionalism as a means to balance the process of global capitalism, to better manage globalization on a regional level against the pressure of domestic bargains, to improve the negotiating position of poor countries in their quest for entry into the global economy, and to facilitate a new bargain between market liberalization and social protection.[12] What Hurrell has labeled the "normative pull of the regionalist idea"[13] is no self-explicatory belief turned process. It requires conditions conducive to the implementation of an idea that will not unfold before the time is right. But whenever it is implemented, it will be done through the means and decisions of real-life people. Here begins the political dimension, rooted in history and its evolutionary character.

Adding to Hurrell's theoretical reflection are contributions that try to link political and psychological factors in the effort to explain the driving forces of region-building. "Positioning theory," for instance, has been introduced to further dissect region-building experiences. This approach combines constructivist and psychological approaches and can be understood as "an ontology for the study of meaning."[14]

To give meaning to region-building is certainly impossible without studying the principled beliefs that shape and inspire the political actors in a region. Their normative choices and political aspirations frame actions or try to prevent them from happening. But to put region-building in a broader context, it is necessary to apply a generic approach. With a historical sense of timing and with a spatial sense for the overall constellation and its link to the individual sequencing of region-building, one might be in the position to better assess the overall theoretical constellation of region-building. The key ingredients to be considered are circumstances and spatial matters, identity and culture, the power of resources and the human capacity in a region, the role of ideas and the legal meaning of norms, and, finally and most importantly, the relationship between economic and political conditions. Region-building is not a natural, given process. Nor is it predetermined by path dependencies. What has worked in one region might not work in another. The priorities chosen in one region might not be feasible, in fact, might not even be available, in another region. Region-building is about regions and not about universally applicable functional norms. Yet region-building is a man-made process and thus constructivist. It is engineered and as such open to comparison with other region-building experiences. In fact, emulating other experiences and *e negativo* learning from the failures and deficits of one's own region is a logical part of the process of region-building.

Each region builds its own narrative. Region-building gains legitimacy only if it is rooted in the memories of a region, in the experiences of common success and mutual struggle with failure. Region-building cannot work without the will to a common future, the application of common interests, even the faith in a common destiny. Meanwhile, understanding the processes of region-building at the theoretical level requires that a combination of genuine factors be taken into account and addressed accordingly.

Preconditions

Among the first preconditions for regional integration is the normative recognition of region-ness by political (and economic) actors in a given geographical space, coupled with the intention to develop a new balance and bargain of cost-benefits of their respective state autonomy and understanding of sovereignty.

Europe was the point of reference for the global dissemination of the primacy of sovereignty in political theory and the proliferation of autonomous statehood as the dominating political feature of today's world. Europe's successful transformation through the integration process framed by the European Union has become a new point of reference for the evolution of statehood, the meaning of regional cooperation and the relationship between public life and regional gains in many parts of the world.

Regions, continents, and subcontinents, along with a new appreciation of "proximity" and "neighborhood-ness," have returned to the global public discourse as a consequence of the completion of the cycle of postcolonialism with its fixation on center-periphery relations between "the West and the rest"; the end of the Cold War with its bipolar structure and mindset; the emerging agenda of globalization, which requires a new assessment of the costs and benefits of autonomy and interdependence and their effect on security, development, and social evolution; the diverse reactions to US primacy in world affairs, which, paradoxically, increase the quest for local and regional identity formation and have helped to reevaluate the role of Europe in the southern hemisphere; the end of "Third-World-ism" as an ideology and rhetorical alternative to "Westernization," which has given way to a differentiated development in many regions of the southern hemisphere; a new understanding of the link between modernization and identity; and, subsequently, a new appreciation of Europe's contribution to the new world order through the successful means of conflict resolution and welfare accumulation promoted by the European Union.

Engines

At the root of the global dynamics of regional integration lies the transformation of ideas about regionalism into instruments of region-building. Usually, the quest for development and affluence along with peace, security, and stability coincides with the recognition of the limits of autonomous statehood. Among the paradoxes of region-building is the hope that weak or weakened states will be in a position to build strong regions, while strong states will be ready and willing to share their perceived strength with their region, including smaller and weaker states. Doing so requires a reassessment of "weak" and "strong," "small" and "big" under the conditions of globalization and its inherent transformation of the perception of time, space, and size.

The European integration experience as a laboratory and mirror for a state's own efforts in region-building cannot be reduced to the technical and institutional aspects of the European Union and the crude economic figures defining the European Single Market. Any emulation of the European Union has to take issue with the democratization of the notion of sovereignty that has evolved in Europe through a long and often daunting process, accompanied by bitter conflict and severe crises. The reevaluation of political bargains over costs and benefits of state autonomy versus pooled sovereignty and shared resources makes it imperative to go beyond a technical analysis of porous autonomy and permeated state sovereignty. It has to ultimately address the role of democratic governance and the potential primacy of community law and joint legislation. In the European context, community law and the evolving parliamentarization of EU politics served both as precondition and engine of European integration, and in the end were, and remain, cause and effect of integration legitimacy and the gradual, albeit slow, emergence of a political identity of the European Union.

Integration and region-building as a tool for developing mutually beneficial cost-benefit structures require the experience of success and the patience of a long process coupled with detours and stalemates. The inevitable inertia can only be overcome through new engines of integration, be they events (including crises), political actors (including former adversaries), external pressure (including peripheral negligence or exposure to the power of globalization), or internal norm-reflections (including the readiness of a given country's elites to compromise with neighbors of different size and power). Successful community-building can only advance if the idea of a region as the interpretation of identity, uniqueness, and comparative advantage over other loyalties finds room to grow into a consensual public narrative.

Causes and Effects

As for the main internal effects of integration, it must always be stated that no universal blueprint is available to cope with detours, unintended consequences, redefinitions of priorities, tools, objectives, and the almost always recurring limits to integration. Across the globe, integration and region-building processes have always strengthened the original objectives. Transformation of the original objectives and continuous alterations in the form and function of a regional grouping are among the most frequently recurring features of regional integration. States that have started integration projects have always changed during the process of region-building, even as the process itself has also changed, many times and in unrecognizable degrees when compared to its initial start.

It is unavoidable in the course of an integration process that the issues of non-interference and democratic transparency, the primacy of community law, and the transforming effects of collective bargaining will be encountered. Bringing matters of democratic governance, rule of law, and sovereignty into a region-building process makes it compulsory to reconnect this project and the executing elites with the claim rights of the people who are at the core of any constituent state of the regional grouping. In the end, the main focus might no longer be on some artificial form of region-building and its finality but may shift to multilevel governance and its degree of democratic participation and transparency, as the European experience indicates.

As for external push and pull factors, the role of the World Trade Organization is certainly more relevant than that of the United Nations or any existing regional political grouping such as the Organization of American States or the Council of Europe. While external pull factors are dominated by trade and economic matters, the pull factors impacting the causes and effects of integration are a combination of economic, political, and societal factors. Claiming regional recognition and strength involves all social, economic, and political

forces available in a region. These features are common to all regional groupings, no matter how elaborate or strong they might appear. The initial ambition of regional integration might not be to alter the overall world order.
Globalization might even be perceived as a pull factor that makes regional
integration mandatory. But in the end, regional integration also impacts the
world order. States are not monolithic and holistic; nor are regional groupings
or, for that matter, the world order as such. World order, by nature of its evolving history, is porous, permeable, and open to change and transformation.

Stages of Region-Building

Some of the academic literature on regionalism introduces a distinction between "old" and "new" regionalism. The underlying assumption maintains that
regions are primarily the product of trade strategies: "old" regionalism was about
inward-looking, protectionist region-building; "new" regionalism is about economic liberalization and free global trade. Distinguishing between "old" and
"new" regionalism, as Björn Hettne has done, implies a static primacy of economics over any other possible factor in region-building. This static approach
does not cover the whole complexity and diversity of region-building as we
have presented it in this study. It is not very convincing to reduce the relationship between region-building and its initiating factors to one variable. It
would be more appropriate—as the findings of this study would indicate—to
understand region-building and its initiating factors as a two-sided chessboard.
On the one hand, there is the toolbox of region-building that might be used
in stages or simultaneously, in reverse order or with the parallelism of a double
or triple action. No approach to region-building is prohibited by any theory of
integration. A myriad of possible priorities in region-building have been experienced across the globe. On the other side of the chessboard lies the whole set
of elements that potentially or de facto initiate region-building: its engines, objects and subjects, economic factors, sociological and cultural factors, political
and institutional aspects, legal considerations, and external push and pull factors. It is only the invariable combination of all factors and actors that makes
the process of region-building work.

Alluding only to "old" and "new" regionalism in the economic sense is static
and potentially phlegmatic. It is self-limiting in its analytical capacity and will
most likely overlook many dynamic aspects and constellations inherent in region-building. Only a thorough and comprehensive historical overview, as this
study suggests, can provide the diversity and interconnectedness of the manifold
facets of region-building. Yet the distinction between "old" and "new" regionalism has gained some ground in academic literature. According to these academic publications, the main features of "old" and "new" regionalism are:[15]

Old Regionalism	New Regionalism
• Created from above and emerged as a function of the Cold War.	• Related to the multipolar world and emerging voluntarily from below.
• Inward-looking and protectionist.	• Open, compatible with the interdependent world economy.
• Specific with regard to its objectives.	• Multidimensional, driven by societal pressure.
• Concerned with relations with neighbors and driven by endogenous push factors.	• Formal part of a global structural transformation and driven by exogenous push factors.
• Creating formal regions.	• Creating "real" regions.

This schematic presentation clarifies some of the traces of region-building. But it does not facilitate a better understanding of the complete inherent dynamic of regional integration. It allots only one dimension to the comparison of region-building, providing, albeit in a limited and overly schematic way, a horizontal understanding of differences in the formation of region-building. But it completely excludes the vertical dimension—that is, the dimension of genuinely sequencing region-building that recognizes the European integration experience as one of the initiating and orienting components for non-European regional groupings.

Björn Hettne proposed a "staircase of region-ness"[16] as a way of understanding the sequencing of region-building. He distinguished between globalization as inherently driven by economic factors and regionalization as inherently driven by politics. This is certainly a debatable argument, one that dies not take into consideration the interplay between the two. To the extent that international and domestic developments interrelate—as expressed by the term "intermestic"—economic and political processes intermingle. One might talk of "politonomics," a term not yet invented or included in the staircase of region-ness, whose steps read as follows:

1. Regional space. Rooted in territory, regions are geographical givens, even if their inhabitants and member states do not appreciate this fact.
2. Regional complex. Among individuals and political units in a given region, the "ever-widening translocal relations between human groups"[17] can be identified.
3. Regional society. Following a certain degree of density of interactions, a formal region of organized life will emerge.
4. Regional community. Building on the notion of pluralistic security communities (Karl Deutsch), the development of a transnational society is the next step in the staircase.
5. Regional institutionalized polity. This level of region-ness corresponds with what Deutsch called "amalgamated security communities"[18].

Social scientists observably have a penchant for toying with the notion of a post-Westphalian order and even contrasting it with a neo-Westphalian order, differentiations between the two resembling the hair-splitting work of late medieval scholastic theologians. None of this truly captures the inherent spirit and dynamics of region-building as the product of a combination of the global proliferation of regional integration initiatives and the inherently local development of political forms and contents. Region-building is not just about "a compromise between Westphalian and post-Westphalian logic; between territorialism and supra-territorialism."[19] In essence, it is about the evolution of a new relationship between territory and politics in both its external and internal dimension.

Economic theories of regional integration claim to be more transparent and focused in their analysis. Traditionally, based on Jacob Viner's theory of customs union, they advanced the argument that regional integration is a tool to enable free trade. Under the conditions of revived region-building since the end of the Cold War, they claim that regional integration is a tool for intensifying interrelatedness through the promotion of foreign direct investment and services. But they also recognize that regional integration can generate regional security, as has been proven by ECOWAS and ASEAN.[20] More recent theories recognize that developing countries have become the main actors of regionalism. Through speedier integration they intend to gain a bigger local market, faster global market integration, stronger bargaining power in the WTO, a better framework to attract foreign direct investment, and improved use of complementary resources and production factors.[21] In light of globalization as the new defining paradigm of international economic trends, theoretical considerations about the meaning of region-building are struggling with the very rationale for regionalism. Traditionally, regional integration agreements were meant to generate economic growth and foster trade. This was the Viner argument.

In the age of globalization, it is less clear whether or not this still can be considered the main driving force for region-building. The fixation of economists led one of them to wonder why regionalism is necessary any more at all. Regional integration, he concluded, is no more than a "response of nervous nation-states to the new world (dis)order that is fitfully emerging."[22] The primacy of economic theory will come to a logical end if it responds to other facts and features of social life in such a superficial way. States are not psychiatric patients, and they might not be rational agents either. But to reduce the role of the state and of politics, of identity and political recognition, merely to the sphere of psychology is intellectually insufficient. Political ideas might be limited in their scope and shallow in their normative outreach, but they exist, and they include the idea of region-building as a normative answer to the limits of sovereign statehood and the wish to empower a region. Political actors might be superficial and short of legitimacy and vision. But they likewise exist and shape an important arena of public life across the globe. Economic theory that fails to account for these dimensions in its analysis of regional integration is leaving the analysis myopic at best.

Since Robert Mundell's groundbreaking article on "optimal currency areas," economists have refined his argument.[23] Social scientists sometimes deplore the absence of a similar theory of "optimal integration area" for political union. The fact of the matter is that there is no fact of this matter: political processes are open to contingent change. As the freedom to fail is the inherent nature of all history, it must also be the guiding experience for the study of political integration and region-building. In 1960, Walt W. Rostow gained academic fame with his theory of stages of economic growth. He argued that the traditional society will develop preconditions for "take-off." The "take-off" period will lead to economic maturity, which in turn opens onto the age of high mass production.[24] It is rather doubtful to suggest similar stages of regional integration. It seems to be more in the nature of region-building that the first and second stages change constantly, while the outcome of the third stage differs (potentially or even categorically) from the original expectation associated with it. This is no argument in favor of sheer historical coincidence, but it is a cautious reminder not to fall into the trap of deterministic notions of history either. Region-building is as much about building regions as it is about trial and error in doing so.

Based on the empirical evidence collected and analyzed in this study, it is fair to say that region-building signifies the return of the political. Region-building is a deliberative political decision dependent on preconditions, driven by intrinsic motives and external pressure, and subject to inherent transformations of the process and its agents. It depends upon the available resources and the ability to focus objectives. No region-building process is without obstacles, and practically all of them have undergone periods of crises.

The empirical evidence does not necessarily support a linear sequence of stages. Rather, it seems correct to recall that stages of region-building can overlap, unravel in contingent sequences, and are subject to contradiction, backlash, and detour. Based on a global study of region-building, it would be appropriate to include the following stages on a list that is potentially growing and yet cannot necessarily claim universal applicability or causal sequencing:

- Intuitive commonality among potential members of a regional grouping must exist in order to embark on the rational and often complex process of identifying possible gains of togetherness and weighing them against a cautious calculation of dominant obstacles and costs of region-ness.
- Searching for the tools of region-building is a more important and realistic aim than hammering down iron objectives with a claim to finality. Regional integration efforts have always demonstrated the ability to overcome obstacles as well as build on existing experience and success. However, they have never been able to turn a grand design into an immediate and contradiction-free operation.

- All regional groupings aim at achieving a level of sustainability and a critical momentum that make the overall effort irreversible. No regional grouping studied in this analysis has ever been limited in its time of existence. In spite of all difficulties and inherent obstacles, regional groupings tend to claim a permanency that can otherwise only be found in the constituent states of these groupings. None of the existing states in the world or any of the leading regional groupings was founded with a foreseen limited life expectancy.

- All regional groupings grant priority to the economy and recognize the integrating power of markets. Yet they have practically never excluded the possibility of going beyond the pure and simple creation of a market. Much as the establishment of a common market is not feasible without political decisions and interventions, no regional grouping has ever explicitly or implicitly excluded also engaging in political cooperation and, potentially, integration.

- Without exception, all regional groupings have struggled with crises, obstacles, and periods of stagnation. More remarkable than this fact has been their ability to revitalize the process of integration, often under new and different circumstances or with a new focus and objective. The dissolution of the East African Community was a rare exception; in the long run this decision was revised and the East African Community was reborn three decades after its initial demise.

- Regional integration is torn by a structural dilemma: the sphere of politics is—or pretends to be—the key enabling factor and guarantor of region-building, while the economy and its success in bringing a region closer as a market is the focus and necessary nucleus of lasting integration-building effects. Political aspects can impede their own goals—mostly without recognizing it—if the regime constellation in a region changes or if political actors conclude that the integration-led transformation of the region is to the detriment of their own power ambitions.

- All regional integration schemes have experienced the transformation of their factors and actors. The objects of integration have changed as much as the subjects of region-building. Whether or not formal political decisions initiate such developments or explicitly try to prevent them, integration, once started, unfolds its own dynamic and inescapable consequences. Bureaucratic procedures, political structures, and sometimes constitutional provisions have been affected by consequences of integration that were unforeseen when the process of region-building started.

- All regional groupings are confronted with internal resistance and resentment toward "too much integration." Countries, people, or social groups can have various reasons to object to "too much integration." But pretending that integration ought to go ahead without strengthening the political dimension of transforming the static notion of state sovereignty is usually futile. In fact, pretending that the integration process is not aimed at changing the parameters of sovereignty might even serve pro-integration governments as a tactical shield neutralizing domestic opposition to "too much integration." It is obvious that all processes of region-building and community-building take a long time and lack immediate and conflict-free results. But in reality, each step in any integration process adds to the regional memory and thus contributes to the transformation of the regional body politic, if only in microscopic ways.

- Region-building has a transforming effect on actors (institutions), memory (purpose), and objectives (priorities). The catalytic effect of crises and phases of stagnation has been evident in the European context and cannot be denied in non-European integration processes. The transformation of politics and society, of the economy and national identity, is a slow process that is idiosyncratic and not without conflict. But whenever the option of regional integration in chosen, the transforming effects of the regional idea begin to take root. Only serious reflection on the transforming effects of regional integration makes the beginning of a region-building process feasible. The absence of this reasoning explains the absence of any regional integration scheme in certain areas of the world that suffer from massive geopolitical conflicts and pervasive lack of the trust among people and regimes that is necessary to seriously start the assessment of integration gains.

- Regional integration is about objectives in motion. No law of nature or politics has ever generated eternally fixed and formulated objectives for region-building. All empirical experience indicates that normative objectives and instrumental objectives can be combined. Absolute and relational objectives are not necessarily mutually exclusive. Even overlapping objectives and detours by default are possible scenarios in the region-building process. There simply is no objective sequencing or prioritizing, in spite of certain insights into the logical precondition of a common market. Nor is there any path dependency in the case of security regionalism. Meanwhile, democratic regionalism follows the procedures of rule of law, accountability, participation, and transparency. Democratic regionalism is about normative decisions in the realm of governance, and not primarily about functional decisions in the realm of a common market.

In summary, the main insights in the nature and evolution of region-building relate to a bundle of push and pull factors. Regional integration, much like global order–building, is dependent upon an overlap of various domestic and intrinsic variables with exogenous and endogenous factors. The political will to regional integration must be rooted in pluralistic domestic norms, but it must also be compatible with external constellations and norms. Region-building depends on and generates "intermestic" structures and realities.

The main domestic push factors are related to the establishment of a common market, to a participatory political system, and to the augmentation of national benefits. Among the main domestic pull factors are normative pressure (benchmarking, comparative rule of law), fear of negative trends (marginalization), and expectation of positive trends (avoiding costs of non-integration, benefits of pooling resources).

The endogenous push factors include the benefits from joining a regional grouping, the positive effect of sharing interests with other countries, and the expectation of being able to shape the region and thus to enhance one's own autonomy. Among the exogenous pull factors are considerations of hard politics (the geopolitical agenda), external political or economic pressure, and exogenous incentives (EU offers of cooperation).

American Primacy and World Order-Building

A widely spread stereotype sees economic integration defined by globalization and the dominating international role of the United States of America, while in fact the US isembedded in local variants of community-building and political considerations (including norms, institutional issues, matters of security, policy objectives, and bargaining) that echo the European integration experience and hence go beyond a purely economic calculus. This potentially endless and cyclical discourse raises an inevitable question: How does the United States relate to the global proliferation of regional groupings? The broader question, taking also into account the EU's quest for a stronger global presence, might be phrased as follows: Does the global proliferation of regional groupings constitute a new dimension of a multiregional set of global governance?

It is evident that the United States does not belong to a comprehensive regional architecture with explicit institutional and political dimensions. Rather, the US favors economic regional arrangements with loose legal and political components. Instead of promoting deep integration, the US values minimalist regulatory (or interventionist) mechanisms.[25] In a broader perspective, and seen through a geopolitical and historical lens, one could argue that the United States has been favorable to, if not instrumental in, initiating, conceptualizing, and organizing regions as part of its Cold War rise to primacy. Peter Katzenstein argues that the strongest regions in the world were organized by America's empire, and that Japan and Germany each served as "a regional supporter state"[26] for the US encouragement of regions. Although this understanding of a region and of region-building is extremely loose, it does not coincide with the finding of this study, according to which Northeast Asia might have emerged as an economic region but instead continues to be a geopolitical space of tension, thus preempting the development of trust-based political institutionalism. In the case of Germany, it is true that over decades West Germany has been both a loyal strategic supporter of the US and a committed advocate of region-building in Europe. But the European Union has never relied on Germany only, nor was it ever shaped by Germany alone. Since unification Germany has continued to promote European integration, but it cannot define Europe's interests alone—which it never had done at any point during the Cold War, either.[27] On the other hand, whenever transatlantic relations became strenuous, European integration suffered. This supports the argument for an intrinsic interdependence between transatlantic relations and European integration, but it cannot fully explain the links between the European Union and the United States.

The United States, Katzenstein argues, is both an actor and a system in the world order. With 250,000 soldiers present in 153 countries, the global presence of United States power goes beyond that of any other country or regional grouping in the world. Most other regions and countries relate themselves to the United States. For better or worse, societies and individuals around the world have principled beliefs about the US, recognize US popular culture and lifestyle as a model for themselves, or see many facets of contemporary life through forms and processes originating in the US. Katzenstein argues that around the world, the United States is surrounded not by antagonistic regional blocs but by "porous regions."[28] He defines porousness as the inevitable consequence of a constellation in which states rush to regionalize, while in fact they are primarily forced to do so by globalization. His is clearly an America-centric approach to regionalism. He underestimates the genuine political and cultural dimension of regional integration. Region-building is as much about identity, recognition, and community-building as it is about shares in the global economy.

It is important and plausible to allude to the Cold War role of the United States in shaping regions as geopolitical units, including Europe through NATO. But it is not sufficient to explain the inner dynamics in the evolution of regions where there is no obvious geopolitical relevance or economic power. It is crucial to reassess the dialectical relationship in the triangle formed by the US, Europe, and "the rest of the world." Not all aspects of regionalism fit into the scheme constituted by US-Europe relations and the Cold War logic. But quite a few regional groupings, as this study has shown, develop a genuine and intrinsic logic of community-building without resorting to any role or relevance for the United States and its geopolitical worldview.

The United States, this child (or cousin) of Europe, rescued Europe from itself by forcing it to cooperate under the protection of a US security umbrella. A successful Europe then began struggling to emancipate itself from US preeminence while at the same time it earned recognition as a model of a non-hegemonic polity for its own former colonies. Academic theories that do not allude to the role of norms, ideas, and the shaping of governance structures overlook an important aspect of the region-building evolution. Even more so, they miss the dialectical subtleties of community-building if they underestimate or deny the history of imperialism, emancipation, and balanced freedom as an integral engine in the formation of regional groupings.

The current degree of community-building and regional integration certainly does not provide sufficient arguments to assume that regionalism is about to shape the format and the functions of a kind of world government. One might argue that the global dissemination of regional structures "might form part of a networked governance model."[29] But it is overly premature to assume that regional groupings will primarily shape the world order and its norms. The European Union, to some extent, is demonstrating both its potential (e.g., its role on the issue of climate change) and its limits (e.g., the absence of an EU seat on the UN Security Council). Although the United Nations system stimulates regional perspectives and encourages regional responsibilities in the management of global affairs, the United Nations has no authority or capacity to properly define, conceptualize, and implement concepts of region-building.

The academic literature on international relations is trying to conceptualize the multifaceted dimensions of regionalism. Often, these approaches lack empirical breadth and depth as they are confined to the study of one or two regional groupings, look at the world primarily through an American lens, or are heavy-handed because of an overly theoretical approach. The most consensual aspects of the role of regionalism in world order-building found in academic literature can be summarized as follows:

- Regionalism is a tool to contain globalization and globalism.
- Regionalism is a means to contain the global primacy of the US.
- Regionalism and regional groupings are instruments to tame the "pathological anarchism" that constitutes world politics.
- Regionalism in its enhanced stage is a medium to facilitate "positive globalism."
- Regionalism promotes positive norms embedded in its genuine domestic order.[30]

These insights indicate that regionalism could be divided into positive and negative regionalism, the former trying to achieve positive objectives and the latter trying to prevent certain trends. This seems a plausible distinction, yet it does not explain the intricacies of the relationship among regionalism, globalization, and the American primacy in world order. These interactions are not only understandable as functions of positive or negative norms or goals. In their interconnectedness they are also subject to push and pull factors.

It is impossible to define a genuine and universal contribution of regional integration to the transformation of world order. But regional groupings contribute to the piecemeal change of global politics, and they have norm-defining effects. The creation of regional architectures is certainly an ambivalent exercise. Organizing one region always means to distinguish this region from others. In some cases this has problematic effects, not the least in the immediate neighborhood of a regional grouping. A state's rejection from membership in a regional grouping can be as delicate a situation as the deepening of a regional grouping that is perceived as an effort to gain strength and a certain power projection vis-à-vis a neighboring region. Overlapping loyalties might challenge regional cohesion. But most delicate is a time when regime dissonances translate into open or subtle disputes about regional leadership and priorities in region-building.

Regional architectures must resort to intuitive or obvious regional identities and the awareness of region-ness. But region-ness alone cannot guarantee the success of region-building if the political norms among potential partner countries differ too fundamentally. Negative power relations among countries of a region might not be transformed through formal membership in a regional grouping. Usually, the insight into the usefulness or even inevitability of cooperation with neighboring countries stems from the rather painful experience of failing in the autonomous pursuit of national goals. This need not always be triggered by a violent and dramatic event. But it is highly plausible that regional cooperation, if induced alone on the basis of positive goals and intentions, could reach its limits early on. The experience of individual or collective failure, interesting enough, is a stronger indicator for regional success—if this region-ness is ultimately acceptable to conflicting neighbors and potential partners.

One of the most ambivalent—at times even controversial—aspects of region-building is its objectives. Empirical evidence shows that region-building tends to contingently change its objectives as well as the instruments it applies. Often the objectives of region-building are left unclear or ambiguous. This can be done purposefully in order not to provoke resistance among the constituent members of a regional grouping. They might accept pragmatic and gradual, incremental advancements in region-building even when they cannot reach a consensus if challenged to define their ultimate objectives. Integration objectives can also change in the process of surmounting an integration crisis and deadlock. Finally, it is possible for integration objectives to remain obscure, unfolding only as the process of region-building unfolds. But there cannot be any doubt that all regional groupings are embarking on long-term processes to generate new realities based on norms, ideas, and experience. Two types of new realities can be discerned: negative and positive integration.

Negative integration is a process that tends to overcome existing obstacles to cooperation and the peaceful transformation of interstate and intersocietal realities. Its main goal is the dissuasion of factors that generate conflict and hardened relations across borders. These can be strategic, economic, ideological, or political conflicts. Such conflicts might inherently be responsible for the lack of understanding cooperation as a win-win situation across borders and societies. Not all conflicts are bound to escalate, but they might do so, in relative or in absolute terms. This can lead to trade conflicts and protectionism, ideological dispute and acts of aggression, political ruptures and hardened or even violent international relations. In order to tame these conflicts that originate in the non-cooperative nature of interstate and intersocietal relations, measures of integration might be helpful. These measures would not intend to achieve positively defined objectives. Instead, they would be promoted in order to overcome the agenda and logic of conflict. Such efforts of negative integration, aimed at excluding conflict, need not be installed with the intention of long-term institutionalization. They can be temporary and thus reversible. Dissolving trade barriers, assuaging ideological splits, and reducing political, including territorial, quarrels could be normative goals that do not require the application of a lasting logic of integration. But temporary measures for overcoming non-cooperative and non-integrative regional realities can turn into more temporary ones. They can also generate effects of institutional or policy spillover.

Positive integration is a process that tends to implement concrete measures for binding countries and societies together. Unlike negative integration, positive integration has the potential to achieve community-building. One of the unintended consequences of negative integration might be that a process is launched during which community-building is supported. Measures intended to achieve positive integration can fail, be reversed, and be achieved only partially. But positive integration requires the clear definition of norms of integration, legal provisions, and political institutions to implement a broad set of integration tools and ensure the multidimensional application of these tools in order to generate sustainable integration. Positive integration requires proactive region-building. This in turn inevitably requires the assessment of the preconditions necessary to move ahead in the targeted process. The most obvious of these preconditions include the readiness of state actors to enact transnational bargains; the willingness of political actors in the constituent countries of a regional grouping to accept their partners' interference in the autonomy of decision-making and subsequently to share sovereignty, no matter how cautiously delineated; the recognition of a regional responsibility and regional opportunities for resolving problems and tackling common causes; the maintenance of domestic pluralism in order to cope with the implications of regional cooperation and integration; and, first and foremost, the development and acceptance of a sense of belonging to an intuitive community that starts to bind memories, decision-making, and destiny together.

Regional integration transforms underlying and well-established notions of politics and statehood. It usually does not begin with a clear understanding of its ultimate effects. But all empirical evidence assessed in this study shows that regional integration processes impact not only the image and actions of a region, but also the realities and structures of its constituent members. Although many of these effects are not subject to calculated planning and cannot be anticipated in all their possible implications, regional integration must be understood as the process of transforming the relationship between geography, identity, and politics. The tools of regional integration may differ, as may the paths chosen. But regional integration can become a contribution to commonly negotiated interests in order to overcome the limits of single state-ness, regardless of its contingent nature in different parts of the world.

Regional groupings could intend to build up a certain veto power against the United States, especially in the context of global trade negotiations. They might also consider their existence as a way of taming "the forces of globalization."

But all in all, as empirical evidence shows, regional groupings tend to be most successful if they manage to project themselves as a complementary partner of the US in dealing with the contemporary agenda. They are perceived as successful if they can contribute to the resolution of regional problems and the management of global trends. Whenever regional groupings are capable and ready to anticipate certain features of globalization in their respective region—such as policies of openness, competitiveness, and enhanced interaction—they tend also to be strongest in adding to the shape of globalization as such. Globalization is not an abstract process that overcomes regions, states, and societies like a natural disaster. It therefore encourages proactive participation as it unfolds. The regional groupings that best understand the relationship and dynamics between strengthened regional identity and proactive contribution to globalization will most likely experience the most fruitful effects.

Yet there seems to remain a paradox in region-building. Regional groupings are most visible if framed negatively, yet they are most effective if they can project themselves as constructive stepping stones in world order–building. Regional groupings gain the status of being "sustainable" and "irreversible" only if they have successfully transformed the region—and themselves with it. Regional groupings are not made to immediately create a new world order. As much as space is a political concept that is developing, changing, broadening, shrinking, and sometimes re-designed, other political concepts such as sovereignty, statehood, and democracy have become subject to consistent change. Eternally static notions of political theory hardly exist. The history of political ideas and empirical evidence provides many telling examples of relational and hence dynamic interpretations of political notions and their applied realities, including the idea and fact of region-building.

It would be misleading to assume that only regions are dynamic whereas states are static. For a long time, it was almost the other way around. The modern state as an autonomous provider of territorial protection of its citizens, endowed with the monopoly of power, has been superimposed upon geographical regions, partly in the struggle to overcome the limits and effects of open space, partly because statehood was exported from Europe and adapted across the world at the end of European-led colonial rule. With the region-building during the second half of the twentieth century and into the twenty-first century, regions return as additional norm-setting, organizing principles and expressions of social, economic, and political life. Worldwide, they have become a claim to social recognition and political identity.

The return of the region does not necessarily and certainly not immediately redefine power relations in terms of world order–building. This holds true for vertical relations between regions and for horizontal relations between notions of "soft" and of "hard" power. But the return of the regions certainly broadens the notions and interpretations of international politics and comparative governance. Vertically, the return of regions recognizes the permeability of state-centeredness while regional groupings cannot and do not intend to become "new states" in the Westphalian sense of this word. Regional groupings rather constitute a new sense and fact of mental interdependence and mutually beneficial transnational, intrastate, and suprasocietal bargaining that can be of a lasting nature only if a regional identity based on the rule of law and the primacy of pluralistic and mutually recognized political processes can be shaped. Horizontally, the return of regions transforms and adds to matters of identity, political culture, and norms of politics. The tools of regional integration have the most immediate and visible effect in the sphere of the economy. Yet neither the goal of a common market nor that of a common currency can be achieved without ultimate and genuine political decisions. The process of region-building contributes to the debate about the relationship between economic factors and political actors. It suggests the operational dominance of the economy in shaping a region as a market, but it also recognizes the ultimate power of politics in the process of decision-making (or decision-preventing) in shaping a region as community.

The emergence of regions as actors in world politics may also imply increasing competition to influence region-building processes. In the years ahead, more research ought to be conducted about competing aspects of EU, US, and Chinese policies toward emerging regional groupings. While the EU claims it acts as a normative global partner, the effects of EU policies, norms, and institutions are under-researched. They may coincide with US policies of promoting democracy but may collide with US geopolitical interests. They may be complemented by Chinese economic activities but may be undermined by China's neutrality about democratic norms and standards elsewhere. More attention will have to be paid to these aspects of the emerging world order.

For the European Union, one of the main preconditions for a stable and peaceful world order—whatever else ought to be said about its content, norms, and objectives—is democratic, accountable local governance. Regional groupings can indeed serve as intermediaries between world order and good governance on the local and state level. Regional groupings do not do this simply to remake the Westphalian paradigm with its emphasis on the primacy of rigid, holistic notions of statehood on the regional level. Nor do they play this role to re-create the Hobbesian paradigm of power as a means to tame power on the regional level. But whenever regional groupings are lasting and successful in balancing economic, political, and sociological notions of public life, gains and costs, and multilevel bargaining methods, they unintentionally transform and subsequently might even want to proactively change the configuration of the Westphalian and the Hobbesian paradigms. With a new set of regionally pooled interests, resources, objectives, bargaining methods, and ultimately, identity-shaping memories, regional groupings broaden the sphere of politics in the age of globalization. Region-building has become a new global reality.

Notes

1. See Philippe de Lombaerde (ed.), *Assessment and Measurement of Regional Integration* (London and New York: Routledge, 2006); Philippe de Lombaerde, Antoni Estevadeordal and Kati Suominen (eds.), *Governing Regional Integration for Development: Monitoring Experiences, Methods and Prospects* (Aldershot: Ashgate, 2008).
2. Ernst B. Haas, *The Obsolescence of Regional Integration Theory*, Working Paper (Berkeley: Institute of International Studies, 1975), 1.
3. See Louise Fawcett and Andrew Hurrell (eds.), *Regionalism in World Politics: Regional Organization and International Order* (New York: Oxford University Press, 1995); Finn Laursen (ed.), *Comparative Regional Integration: Theoretical Perspectives* (Aldershot: Ashgate, 2003); Peter J. Katzenstein, *A World of Regions: Asia and Europe in the American Imperium* (Ithaca: Cornell University Press, 2005); Mary Farrell et al. (eds.), *Global Politics of Regionalism: Theory and Practice* (London: Pluto Press, 2005).
4. Louise Fawcett, "Regionalism in Historical Perspective," in Fawcett and Hurrell, *Regionalism in World Politics*, 28.
5. From a huge body of recent theoretical literature on European integration see inter alia: Ben Rosamond, *Theories of European Integration* (Houndmills: Palgrave, 2000); Jeffrey T. Checkel, "Social Construction and European Integration," in Thomas Christiansen et al. (eds.), *The Social Construction of Europe* (London: Sage Publications, 2001), 50–64; Liesbet Hooghe and Gary Marks, *Multi-Level Governance and European Integration* (Lanham: Rowman and Littlefield, 2001); Brent F. Nelsen and Alexander Stubb (eds.), *The European Union: Readings on the Theory and Practice of European Integration* (Houndmills: Palgrave, 2003); Marc Pollack, *The Engines of European Integration: Delegation, Agency and Agenda Setting in the European Union* (Oxford: Oxford University Press, 2003); Antje Wiener and Thomas Diez, *European Integration Theory* (Oxford: Oxford University Press, 2004); Daniel R. Kelemen, *The Rules of Federalism: Institutions and Regulatory Politics in the EU and Beyond* (Cambridge, MA: Harvard University Press, 2004); Derek Beach, *The Dynamics of European Integration: Why and When EU Institutions Matter* (Houndmills: Palgrave Macmillan, 2005); Michelle Cini and Angela K. Bowne (eds.), *European Union Studies* (Houndmills: Palgrave Macmillan, 2006).
6. Finn Laursen, "Theoretical Perspectives on Comparative Regional Integration," in Laursen, *Comparative Regional Integration*, 3–28.
7. Andrew Hurrell, "Regionalism in Theoretical Perspective," in Fawcett and Hurrell (eds.), *Regionalism in World Politics*, 37–75.
8. Ibid., 51.
9. Ibid., 56.
10. Ibid., 58–63.
11. Ibid., 66.
12. Ibid., 42–46.
13. Ibid., 52.
14. Nikki Slocum and Luk van Langenhove, *The Meaning of Regional Integration: Introducing Positioning Theory to Regional Integration Studies*, UNU-CRIS e-Working Paper, W-2003/5 (Bruges: United Nations University, 2003), 12, online at: http://www.cris.unu.edu/fileadmin/workingpapers/Nikki%20and%20Luk%20WP.pdf; see also Farrell et al., *Global Politics of Regionalism*.

15. See Björn Hettne, "The New Regionalism Revisited," in Fredrik Söderbaum and Timothy M. Shaw (eds.), *Theories of New Regionalism: A Palgrave Reader* (Houndmills: Palgrave Macmillan, 2003), 22–42.
16. Ibid., 28.
17. Ibid., 28.
18. See Karl Deutsch et al., *Political Community and the North Atlantic Area: International Organization in the Light of the Historical Experience* (Princeton, NJ: Princeton University Press, 1957).
19. Hettne, "The New Regionalism Revisited," 40.
20. See Luk van Langenhove et al., *From Multilateralism to Multiregionalism: What Role for Regional Integration in Global Governance?* UNU-CRIS Occasional Paper O-2004/5 (Bruges: United Nations University—CRIS, 2004), online at: http://www.cris.unu.edu/fileadmin/workingpapers/Eur-Parliament%20OP.pdf; also Heiner Hänggi et al. (eds.), *Interregionalism and International Relations* (Abingdon and New York: Routledge, 2006).
21. See Barry Buzan, "The Logic of Regional Security in the Post-Cold War World," in Björn Hettne, et al. (eds.), *The New Regionalism and the Future of Security and Development* (London: Macmillan, 2000), 9.
22. Percy S. Mistry, "Regional Integration and Economic Development," in Hettne et al., *The New Regionalism and the Future of Security and Development*, 40.
23. Robert Mundell, "A Theory of Optimal Currency Areas," *American Economic Review* (1963): 657–665; see now Ludo Cuyvers et al., "Regional Monetary Cooperation and Integration" in Farrell et al., *Global Politics of Regionalism*, 120–136.
24. Walt W. Rostow, *The Stages of Economic Growth: A Non-Communist Manifesto* (Cambridge: Cambridge University Press, 1960).
25. See Heinz G. Preusse, *The New American Regionalism* (Cheltenham: Edward Elgar, 2004).
26. See Katzenstein, *A World of Regions*, 237.
27. See Timothy Garton Ash, *In Europe's Name: Germany and the Divided Continent* (New York: Random House, 1993).
28. Katzenstein, *A World of Regions*, 13.
29. Fawcett, "Regionalism in Historical Perspective," 24.
30. See Richard Falk, "Regionalism and World Order: The Changing Global Setting," in Söderbaum and Shaw, *Theories of New Regionalism*, 63–80.

PERSPECTIVES FOR
DEMOCRATIC REGION-BUILDING

Democracy, Trust, Loyalty

The study of region-building tends to be heavily focused on the building process and on the elaboration of hair-splitting definitions of region, region-ness, and regionalism. The study of regional integration has developed into a subdiscipline of international relations but often falls short of including the perspectives, methods, and questions arising from the fields of comparative governance and political theory. An approach combining these three fields makes the most sense, helping to enhance our knowledge and analytical competence in assessing region-building. Region-building will succeed only if it is lastingly recognized by its constituent parts. These are the member states of each regional arrangement—and their citizens. Traditionally, region-building has been an elite-driven project, and not only in Europe. In line with the European integration experience, non-European regional groupings have been invented, shaped, and transformed by political elites. Governments matter and so do states, but to take this as a natural given without asking about the context that frames the role of governments is confounding and intellectually insufficient. Region-building can lead to elucidating analytical assessments, but only if all its constituent factors are included in the reflection on regional integration.[1] So far this inclusion is deficient, which is why the concept of democratic region-building does not figure prominently in the methodology of regionalism or in the literature about its effects, causes, and expressions.

Democratic region-building means regional integration based on democratic governance among the member states of a regional grouping. It is insufficient to define a regional grouping through its economic parameters alone. As important as they are, the empirical results of this study show that political categories such as legitimacy and trust, accountability, and predictability are just as relevant to the pursuit of successful and lasting regional groupings. There simply cannot be community-building in a region that lacks the inherent trust needed for each social relation. Countries with highly antagonistic political systems and ideational compositions might be capable of limited cooperation in functional matters relating to their survival or strength. But there is little chance—and no empirical evidence supporting the conclusion—that countries with antagonistic ideational structures will be ready and willing to bind parts of their sovereignty, future, and destiny together. It takes symmetric regimes to create mutually reinforcing interests. This is the prime lesson of the success of European integration after World War II. European integration did not succeed simply because France and Germany were changing the parameters of their geopolitics. European integration succeeded because France and Germany began to embark on a common path laid out by trust and a certain benefit of the doubt in the ability and willingness of each partner to change traditional patterns of behavior and prevailing mistrust. France and Germany succeeded because both countries were democracies.

Democratic region-building has to grow from within a region. It cannot be induced from outside. Even the most sophisticated mechanisms of conditionality in the pursuit of intra-regional or intra-state relations will not turn the wheel of governance if domestic conditions do not make democratic governance a priority in the struggle for change and a priority in the lasting stability of a country. Democratic region-building is both a goal and a precondition for successful regional integration.

Democracy can only grow when there is trust among peoples, especially between them and those representing the political authorities. This minimalist definition is the bottom line for any realistic democratic theory. A sophisticated variety of concepts of democratic theory has evolved in the history of political philosophy, but in the end, trust and loyalty are the main test cases and benchmarks for assessing the viability and longevity of a regime and political system. Some regimes might label themselves democratic but in fact are not. Others are proud to be monarchical in nature but can be democratic at heart. The test case for the connection between people and rulers is the degree of confidence in political institutions, loyalty in their decision-making, and recognition of the consequences of these decisions. What holds true in the national context is no less relevant in the vertical relation between the different mechanisms of multilevel governance.

Region-building cannot grow without trust. It can even mean trust against mistrust. Regionalism can be encouraged and driven by the idea of overcoming mistrust through trust-based cooperation. But in any case, trust is at the root of regional integration. Regional schemes of cooperation and partial integration can be developed even if the constituent member states of the given regional grouping are governed by different regimes. These regimes might be antagonistic, and yet region-ness can be the overriding impulse for coming together. But as

the cooperation in South Asia demonstrates, there is a clear limit to cooperation or even potential integration among countries with antagonistic political
regimes. Rational interests in security and even in development matters might
spur a reasonable set of functional forms of cooperation, but translating them
into an integration scheme by which the participating countries prepare to pool
sovereignty and their future destiny seems to be more than unlikely. In fact, there
is no empirical evidence for such a mode of behavior.

The countries of Central and Eastern Europe have always belonged to the European cultural heritage. Yet their membership in the European Union was not
suggested by even the most liberal Europeans as long as they were ruled by communist, one-party dictatorships and belonged to a geopolitical system that was
the adversary of the Western world. Nor were Spain, Portugal, and Greece able
to become members of the then European Community while they were ruled by
authoritarian regimes. Only regime change made these countries' membership
in the European integration process possible. The European Union finally made
explicit reference to regime criteria for EU membership when it began to contemplate the membership of Turkey. Only democratic member states are in the
position to generate and uphold democratic regionalism.

Membership in regional groupings outside Europe has rarely been conditional
on the domestic political system. There have been limited forms of unspoken
veto, such as the rejection of Yemen's membership in the GCC (which, of course,
is the antithesis of democratic regionalism). Haiti has been suspended from the
CARICOM. ASEAN, under Western pressure, encouraged Myanmar (Burma)
not to take up its rotating presidency. The ASEAN Plus Three relationship can
hardly be extended to full membership of China, Korea, and Japan as long as
regime differences, coupled with geopolitical differences, dominate the region.
States have unilaterally withdrawn from regional groupings for political reasons,
as with Venezuela's withdrawal from CAN. In this case, the withdrawing country opposed the overall political and economic approach of its partners, rather
than the other way around. In general, regional integration in the non-European context has never been influenced by the primacy of democratic criteria for
membership.

Unlike in Europe, most non-European regional groupings were driven early
on by the ambition to be geographically comprehensive. They wanted to demonstrate regional coherence and unity more than they wanted to give testimony
to a common normative stand on governance matters. The two main reasons for
this attitude are rooted in their respective histories. First, these regional groupings were initiated in reaction to Western colonial dominance, postcolonial
weakness, and a new quest for regional identity and autonomy. Geographical
unity and inclusiveness were a function of their desire to project identity, ambition, and counter-power. Second, in moving from negative integration to positive integration, the failure to address the question of regime cohesion did not

seem to be all too important. For some time, regional integration can even work without addressing the regime issue. Up to a certain point, security regionalism and development regionalism can advance if they are based on reciprocal functional interests. These functional interests may not touch on normative aspects of the respective regimes, challenge their legitimacy, or transform their identity, no matter how gradual or cautious it may be. But once their consequences transgress the limits of normative differences between the member states of a regional grouping, they reach the limits of functional region-building.

Regional integration is most often perceived through the lens of region-ness and matters of regionalization. Theoretical efforts to assess, define, or shape regional integration usually take this as their point of departure. Consensus has developed about the watershed of the end of the Cold War for rediscovery of the meaning of the regions of the world.[2] However, analysts often look at region-building as a functional, almost mechanical process.[3] Sometimes, the efforts to conceptualize regionalism begin by defining the topical challenges and opportunities before any form or process of regional integration is discussed. Most obvious is the analysis of economic integration, sometimes referring to the potential of monetary union.[4] Some analysts focus on the link between socioeconomic challenges, such as food security in developing countries, and integration opportunities.[5] Seldom, however, does the assessment of regional integration genuinely take into account the limits and obstacles to integration. Reflections on regional asymmetries as an obstacle to inter-regionalism have only begun to emerge.[6]

Almost unnoticed in the academic discourse are considerations related to the role, relevance, and impact of the regime character of constituent parts of any regional grouping. The literature dealing with European integration has become obsessed with the notion of a democratic deficit, an argument that assumes that the structures and processes of the European Union are insufficiently transparent, inclusive, accountable, and representative. The democratic quality of EU proceedings, according to a stereotypical joke, would not qualify the European Union for EU membership if it were to apply for it. But none of the relevant literature doubts the democratic quality in the political life of the individual European Union member states. In fact, their democratic credentials are often overly praised in contrast to the genuine democracy on the EU level.

As for non-European integration schemes, almost the opposite experience is the norm. Most non-European integration groupings were rather inclusive at the start, in geographical terms, but they explicitly excluded matters that could be relevant to the regime character of the participating countries, including any clarification of matters regarding the pooling of sovereignty. By and large, the protagonists of European integration efforts have avoided the issue of the finality of the EU, so the matter of sovereignty remains contested in Europe. But a huge academic literature dealing with both questions, and continuous political debates on the political finality and the future of sovereignty under conditions of European integration, indicate awareness that the issues concerned are unavoidable.

Among non-European integration groupings, the opposite is the norm: governance matters have been introduced as an expression of last resort, and the notion of sovereignty has remained, at least formally, a virtual taboo. According to practically all documents on regional integration outside Europe, it is the goal of integration to preserve national sovereignty. It is almost explicitly and apodictically prohibited to limit it, notwithstanding a rather different constellation in the reality of constituent states and regional groupings. As for governance, the matter has been introduced only very late into the region-building process. There remains strong reluctance to accept regime symmetry as a relevant precondition for successful regional integration. In reality, however, the opposite is true: regional integration can only be successful and lasting if it is based on symmetrical regime conditions and reasonable symmetric governance structures among the constituent member states of a regional grouping. Democratic regionalism is not only a goal and a precondition but also a tool to successful region-building.

It is an experience of region-building that a region's constituent parts (that is, its member states) will change in the course of the region-building process. This dimension, which has been discovered only lately in the context of European integration, is no less relevant than the process of creating the higher structures of a regional grouping. The logic of region-building requires this transformation of its constituent parts, although it goes often hand in hand with resistance to "too much integration," as has been the European experience.

Democratic regionalism is the result of trust among member states of a regional grouping and the precondition for loyalty in the project of regional integration. The normative underpinning of both security and development regionalism, democratic regionalism is also the logical continuation of security and development regionalism if such schemes are to become sustainable and genuinely effective.[7] No regional grouping can honestly embark on the path toward a common political identity of a region without recognizing the importance of shared political values and the readiness to join together for a common future. Any rhetoric invoking regional integration that cannot resort to such normative foundations will remain limited and blunt. Only democratic regionalism can assure the inner cohesion and strength in a regional grouping that will help to project its power and credibility beyond the region.

Assessing the Future

It would be fascinating to encounter the future before it has in fact happened. Nobody would have been able to predict the path of European regional integration for the next five decades when it began in 1957. Nobody is in a position to project the evolution of the non-European groupings discussed in this study over the next five decades. Circumstances will invariably change, the inner cohesion, rationale, and path of regional integration will transform, and the approach to assessing and judging region-building will undergo its own hermeneutical meta-morphosis. Most exciting about the future is that it happens anyway.

In the early stages of the twenty-first century, regional integration has put its mark on the agenda of international relations, matters of governance, and issues relating to the key parameters of political theory. The procedural character of all politics will guarantee slow evolutions coupled with the usual daunting back-lashes, provocative bumps in the road, and rough debates over perspective and content in interpreting the outcome and implication of region-building. So far, nothing seems to be new.

What is without precedent, however, is the global proliferation of regional integration as an idea, a concrete issue, and a matter on the agenda across global deliberations. It is not regional integration itself that is debated or at stake; rather, its degree of global proliferation implies consequences that have no precedent. Most probably they will have a dimension that cannot be denied any longer as a constituent fact of international order and politics. The primacy of the United States might be affected over time by the implications of region-building. The US seems to act as one of the last staunch supporters of traditional concepts of autonomous state sovereignty. Nobody is questioning the democratic character or even the ideal of the US governance model. But the foreign policy conduct of the US around the turn of the twenty-first century has often resembled that of nineteenth-century European states, which at the time were proud and almost autistic about their sovereignty, power, and honor. The global dissemination of region-building will continue to confront the US with the interest some have in taming its overarching power.

Since the US is irreplaceable in managing world affairs, this ambition can be useful only if it is not pursued in a confrontational style, with elusive self-decep-tions about the ability to control or even replace the US. It must be done in a moderate, balanced way as far as the reshaping of world order is concerned. Find-ing a balance between bilateral, multilateral, and inter-regional interactions will remain a continual point on the policy-making agenda throughout the twenty-first century. In geopolitical matters, regional groupings will most likely continue to play a limited role, with the exception of the European Union. In geo-eco-nomic terms, the role of regional groupings will grow, probably even sharply. In political terms, the relevance of regional groupings in their contribution to world order and the evolution of global notions of politics, statehood, sovereignty, and integration will ultimately depend on the degree of democratic regionalism they can represent.

Non-European regional groupings will encounter frustration and crisis as much as progress and achievements. They will see transformations and reconfigurations as they have done in the past. Globalization and cross-border activities will impact regionalization and regional integration as much as any leadership action plan.[8] The representatives of non-European regional groupings will be well advised to address obstacles to regional integration just as honestly as they hold to their idealism about region-building. Their approach to regional integration is affecting, albeit gradually, the most widely spread notions of autonomous statehood and the sanctification of sovereignty that still prevails in many parts of the world. Yet new interpretations of statehood and recognition of the value of pooled sovereignty will only come about as a consequence of success in region-building and its legitimacy among the people involved.

In the end, region-building is about people's life chances and not just about abstract political concepts. For instance, it is no surprise to encounter academic studies dealing with the relationship between regional integration and food security in developing countries.[9] Regional integration is about the environmental security of human living and development conditions. Just as the definition of security has broadened since the end of the Cold War, so has the definition of the environment: no longer confined to a narrow sense, it now relates to the social, economic, political, and cultural environment as much as to the natural environment. Region-building can therefore be understood as a contribution to a more human, more sustainable, and less vulnerable environment.

More than 60 percent of world trade benefits already from some form of regional preference. In 2002 there existed 243 regional trade agreements, of which 30 to 40 percent were concluded among developing countries. The agreements are defined by a growing complexity, and many countries of the world belong to various schemes. Regional trade agreements are not only about the facilitation of regional trade but must be understood as a contribution to more sustainable security, community-building, good governance based on transparency, and a less vulnerable environment. They are in line with the United Nations' ambition to create a more secure and less vulnerable environment for human development.

Regional trade agreements can enhance the bargaining power of a region. They may generate welfare gains inside the region, depending upon an optimal use of market forces, integration mechanisms, accumulation of growth, effects of investment, reduction of transaction costs, and decreases in regulatory barriers. Regulatory coordination may lead to deeper integration and a broadening of the agenda as it requires legal provisions that may enhance the role of supranational legal structures. Regional public goods include environment management issues, management of water resources and natural reserves, health control, and construction of cross-border transportation networks as well as power grids and data transmission devices. Law enforcement is a high-priority activity in generating regional public goods. Sustainable conditions for region-building and the generation of regional public goods depend primarily on the fulfillment of supply and demand conditions beyond the sphere of economic logic. Without a favorable political environment, no regional public goods can emerge. Neither can joint regional law enforcement or regional legislation take place. Region-building, in the end, when understood as more than a regional preferential trade agreement, is a distinctively political project.

It seems to be productive to extend the study of regional integration into two fields. First, the evolution of criteria to measure the political effect of region-building warrants attention. Economic research has developed a scheme that tries to design the path of economic integration (preferential trade, free trade, customs union, common market, economic and possibly political union). But no law of nature suggests that the economic sequencing is universally applicable. Regional groupings have begun with security regionalism or even with political regionalism. The degree of success or failure is a different matter. Here, it is only necessary to point out the limited universality of economic path dependency in regional integration. It would therefore be instructive to broaden the scope of analysis and include political conditions for region-building. Second, there is a need to assess obstacles to region-building and to systematically reflect on failures in regional integration (lessons learned). Studies in regional integration tend to focus on normative objectives and their implementation. They are quick to criticize a regional grouping for having failed to implement its goals. But they are less refined in assessing the reasons for failure, detours, and obstacles in region-building. Enhancing our knowledge about these factors would undoubtedly help to put the current global trend of disseminating regional integration into a broader and more helpful perspective.

Among the insights of regional integration research is the experience that grand designs hardly work. Rare indeed is the success of a regional agenda with too many objectives intended to be achieved in a too short period of time. National obstacles, different interests and conflicting objectives, and shortages of human resources and administrative capacities are common impediments to speedy region-building. The understanding of the possible meaning and use of regional integration may conflict with long-standing experiences of national economic and political autarky. The weaker a state and its economy, the stronger the sense of the protective value of sovereignty may be. Only a sober cost-benefit analysis of regional integration can turn the wheel. Overlapping assessments among neighboring countries definitively facilitate increased acceptance of regional cooperation and integration as a means to strengthen one's own community and country by sharing the benefits of cooperation and integration with one's neighbors.

Regionalism that is defined solely by economic objectives and criteria has failed whenever protectionist interests of the acting states prevailed over the push toward open and cooperative region-building. Protectionism in economic terms is equivalent to the desire for autonomous autarky in political decision-making. Such an attitude or policy norm may succeed for a while and is certainly an attractive option to temporarily enhance domestic support for a certain regime. But this can not lead to region-building, let alone community-building.

The will to cooperate alone is not enough to reverse the trend of failure and limitation in regional development. Cooperative security failed in the interwar period in Europe because of deficits in trust among the major countries of the European state system. It also failed because of enormous differences in governance structures and regime constellations. Trust-building and regime asymmetries are potentially incompatible. Countries with antagonistic regimes and governance structures may define a limited sphere of pragmatic common interests, largely driven by the mutual interest of survival or common external threats beyond human management capacities (such as disaster control). But it is difficult to imagine the development of a common agenda of objectives aimed at building a region among antagonistic regimes.

Policy-driven integration can fail if the necessary decisions are not timed right. It can also fail if the agenda is overloaded. It can fail if external conditions have too strong and negative an effect. And it can fail if internal conditions within member states of a regional grouping change in ways not anticipated. The failure to achieve a European Defense Community in 1954 is an example of how political rhetoric can lead to wrong perceptions of the quality, substance, and perspective of a regional grouping. The founding documents of a regional grouping ought to be taken seriously, and respect for the actors behind the application of a certain document requires such an attitude. Yet no regional grouping's documents are infallible texts that may never be altered. Documents of regional integration are guiding "stars" for the pragmatic work within a regional grouping. They are by no means a magical tool that is able to transcend the obstacles any regional grouping can encounter. On the other hand, it is evident that excessive rhetoric enshrined in a document of a regional grouping might prove unhelpful to the proper implementation of goals, no matter how noble they are. If political rhetoric is not embedded in an emerging order of law, rhetoric will not turn into reality. The pompous promulgations of the Organization of African Unity never became the guiding path for a change in the reality of the African continent. When Africa started a new initiative with the founding of the African Union, the continent was as divided as it had been when the OAU was founded four decades earlier.

Each integration approach is unique. This is evident because each region is exceptional in its composition, potential, challenges, and ambition. Yet across the globe, regions as geographically (and often culturally) defined units are linked to the concept of integration as a tool and objective of public policy. Each regional grouping is multilayered. None of them follows a deterministic path-dependency. But the generic character of regional integration encourages comparative research aimed at better understanding the engines of integration, the obstacles to region-building, and the federators of regional integration. All empirical evidence points to links between the European experience of region-building and integration efforts elsewhere. This relationship might be dialectical, and European integration may at best be understood as a distant mirror. Still, the role of European integration as a laboratory that might be emulated—at least in a structural sense—is all-pervasive. Other regions in the world are a product of Europe's withdrawal from global colonial hegemony. They might even be continuous projections of the desire of European powers to divide the world in order to better rule it. Yet non-European regional groupings are reconnected with Europe as a point of reference for the evolution and formation of their genuine region-building.

Democratic Region-Building

European integration is often accompanied by rather critical and skeptical analysis. The deficits of the European Union—its structure, performance, and ambition—are the object of manifold academic studies. The political discourse on the future of the European Union is often rather unfocused, potentially parochial, and mostly technical, and the larger vision of European integration is often blurred by daily business in the multifaceted web of EU institutions and actors. The EU undergoes continuous soul-searching about its identity and goal with a rather skeptical oeuvre in the academic sphere.[10] The academic reflections on the state of European integration are all too often driven by self-doubt, skepticism, and harsh criticism of the incoherent, non-comprehensive, and myopic tendencies attributed to the actors and institutions of the EU. This is not the place to discuss the academic approaches to EU integration. They are certainly full of thoughtful insights, but they are frequently prone to exaggeration and myopia. The highly critical literature about EU integration does not take into consideration the perception of European integration in the wider world. Whatever the level of difficulties, shortcomings, and failures may be inside the EU, outside Europe the EU is perceived as a model and a pillar of hope for the management of public affairs.

It would be highly speculative to project the current trend of regional integration in the world onto the further path of the twenty-first century. But two conclusions from the experience with European integration can and must be drawn in light of the many regional groupings that have emerged and stabilized their existence across the globe. First, European integration would have been unthinkable, had the commitment to region-building been anything but an objective of democratic states. Its result is democratic region-building—that is, region-building based on democratic countries and increasingly aimed at installing democratic structures and mechanisms of transparency and accountability on the level of the European Union. Without democracy in its member states, no regional grouping will be able to achieve levels of density and integration approaching those in the European Union. Without democratic member states, no regional grouping will generate the necessary degree of trust and mutually reinforcing legitimacy that is essential to turning a regional grouping into a form of community-building.

The second conclusion drawn from the European integration experience is that it has been and remains a rather young process, given the long history of the European continent and its efforts at order-building. The European Union of the year 2007 was unfathomable in the year 1957, and it is impossible to project the evolution of the EU into the year 2057. By the same token, it is impossible to predict the further evolution and outcome of regional integration elsewhere in the world. Moreover, it would be overly unfair to render judgment on non-European regional integration, given the short period of time it has sincerely and objectively had to grow. No serious scholar would have dared to present a final, ultimate judgment on the state and future of European integration in, for example, the year 1967. Ten years after the signing of the Treaties of Rome and shortly after the crisis on voting rights in EU institutions that demonstrated the continuous primacy of the (French) nation-state, it would have been unimaginable to anticipate the introduction of a directly elected European parliament, a common currency, and a common European peacekeeping force in the Middle East. Recognizing that these and other achievements of European integration have taken place against all odds, it is wise not to preempt or preclude any development in non-European region-building over the next five decades.

Without domestic democratic structures, regional integration will always encounter the limits of trust among its member states. Without domestic democratic governance, regional integration will always encounter legitimacy problems and limits to reliable, sustainable, verifiable depths of integration on the regional level. Democratic region-building is a precondition, goal, and tool for successful regional integration.

In light of this central conclusion of our study, the main question that has guided our research has shifted: the quest for clarity about definitions of region and integration has ceded way to the need for clarity about preconditions and sustainable conditions of democracy in the world. It has also shifted from empirical study of region-building efforts to a more systematic assessment of the driving forces, interpretative ambiguities, and output discrepancies between democratic countries in the world. Region-building is a function of democracy-building. Region-building is also a subquestion of the search for global order. It is about security, development, stability, peace, and affluence. But most importantly, region-building is ultimately about participation and recognition. It is about the readiness of people and countries to bind their destiny together. To do so, they must share a minimum of features of identity, of values and visions. They must be ready to turn perceptions of one another's past into elements of a common memory. They must be prepared to define the tools and goals of common actions and institutions. And they must be capable and willing to relate to other regions and actors in world affairs as a group speaking with one voice.

The future of democratic governance is ultimately a cultural matter dependent on the cultural and political choices of societies around the world. Democracy is not a fixed and rigid concept, once and for all available as a blueprint ready for global dissemination. Like region-building, democracy is a work in progress. Democratic rule is a means to balance the desire for freedom and the need for authority. Democracy introduces order and rule, while at the same time it limits their effects. It hinges on realistic options of human beings and their social life. Yet its flourishing is also dependent upon cultural context. It would be misleading to assume that democracy is merely a matter of technical procedures of governance. These procedures are important, and technical skills and competencies are required to conduct political work under democratic conditions. But democracy would remain lifeless or become a soulless activity if it were not related to a specific notion of society and its development.

Democratic governance and regional integration are linked, and they conceptually reinforce each other. No democratic regime in the world is forced to join a regional grouping. But a regional grouping must consist of democratic regimes if it is to be successful over time. These inescapable insights into the nature and reality of region-building in the world of the twenty-first century may be modified, but the main trend is obvious.

Democratic region-building could become a pattern of order-building in the world of this twenty-first century. This would imply a rather substantial revision of the key parameters of the political theory of statehood. The autarkic, sovereign nation-state claimed recognition and obedience for the last two centuries. It has grown into the dominant political form across the world, even as its limits have become obvious. The sovereign autarkic nation-state, potentially the forum for open, at times even aggressive nationalism, has come under pressure because of systemic failures. In a world of permeable borders and unprecedented cross-border activities, the effort to maintain the traditional concept of sovereignty and to reproduce the concept of the primacy of the nation-state in all corners of the world has become a costly exercise that is not always successful. This concept may still be confronted by contrasting interests among key global actors. More important than the different approaches that the EU and the US take toward region-building could be the competing effects of the global projection of rising world powers such as China and, in a way, India. They are focused primarily on economic interests, and China in particular is not supportive of democratic region-building as understood by the EU. The new dimensions of global competition for raw materials and markets, political loyalties, and security interests could hamper or even undermine policies that promote democratic region-building.

Regional integration has become a tool recognized worldwide for maximizing welfare gains and security in the age of globalization. While the role of politics faces challenges under the conditions of the primacy of market forces, identity continues to matter more than ever. Identity tends to focus on that what is near and dear. It must be "felt" in order to be embraced by people in their genuine habitat. Regional integration is rather an abstract concept that suggests an improvement of life chances for exponentially numerous people in a region. The quest for identity and the promise of region-building are almost contradictory ends of the same stream of thought—which probably best explains why they relate to each other and mutually need each other. Region-building is the geopolitical and geo-economic expression of this quest for identity.

Based on the findings of this study, it would be inappropriate to position regional economic integration against regional political integration. They relate to each other and often are mutually dependent. Region-building is a process that requires political choices and actions, which inevitably are influenced by market developments and the effects of globalization. By the same token, the political choices and actions related to regional integration are intended to define the path and frame the effects of market forces and globalization patterns. Region-building might not necessarily facilitate the definition of regional identity, but by its very nature it is an expression of regional identity formation and a contribution to its evolution. Regional integration combines the recognition of diversity with the quest for unity. The specific expression of this combination and the scope and intensity of the "ingredients" it needs to function are a matter of trial and error, achievement and adjustment.

Region-building is a response to the rigid state-based ideologies of past centuries. It is also a perspective for the scattered world that has emerged around the turn of the twenty-first century. It leaves room for multiple variants and almost endless combinations, different sequencing and diverse factors facilitating or impeding region-building. Whenever region-building has become rooted, it is an indication of a transformed reality. This transformed reality in the realm of a region will continue to be transformed as it continues to transform its constituent parts. Compared to the petrified fixation on state sovereignty and national autarky, regional integration is a dynamic, innovative, humane concept. It considers the human, cultural, economic, and political diversity in the world. It shows its actors' commitment to the value of solidarity. Region-building aims to find a balance between the formulation of common interests and the pursuit of genuine identity of its constituent states and people. It is an inventive and peace-oriented form of managing resources, development goals, and security concerns. At the same time region-building is a new and promising expression of the pursuit of identity and commonality in a world that is shifting between atomized particularities and standardized globalization. It gives local, yet common answers to global, yet highly differentiated problems of economic and political management.

Region-building empowers its constituent parts, transforming them into larger spheres of action where stronger instruments can be forged and better conditions framed to deal with the challenges of an ever renewing world.

Notes

1. See Philippe de Lombaerde, *Supporting Regional Integration: The Roadmap of Indicators and Tools*, UNU-CRIS Occasional Papers, O-2003/3 (Bruges: United Nations University–CRIS, 2003), online at: http://www.cris.unu.edu/fileadmin/workingpapers/philippe%20ACP%20Engl%20final.pdf; Walter Mattli, "The Vertical and Horizontal Dimensions of Regional Integration," in Finn Laursen (ed.), *Comparative Regional Integration: Theoretical Perspectives* (Aldershot: Ashgate, 2003), 273–282.
2. See for one of the first groundbreaking efforts Stephen Calleya (ed.), *Regionalism in the Post–Cold War World* (Aldershot: Ashgate, 2000).
3. See Rasul Shams, *Regional Integration in Developing Countries: Some Lessons Based on Case Studies* (Hamburg: Hamburger Weltwirtschafts-Archiv, 2003), online at: http://ageconsearch.umn.edu/bitstream/26272/1/dp030251.pdf; Fernando Quevedo and Luis Villela, *Regional Integration* (Washington, D.C.: Inter-American Development Bank, 2003), online at: http://idbdocs.iadb.org/wsdocs/getdocument.aspx?docnum=353028.
4. See Ludo Cuyvers et al., "Regional Monetary Cooperation and Integration," in Mary Farrell et al. (eds.), *Global Politics of Regionalism: Theory and Practice* (London: Pluto Press, 2005), 120–136.
5. See Alan Matthews, *Regional Integration and Food Security in Developing Countries* (Rome: Food and Agriculture Organization of the United Nations, 2003), online at: http://www.fao.org//docrep/004/y4793e/y4793e00.htm.
6. See Paolo Giordano et al., *El Tratamiento de las Asimetrías en los Acuerdos de Integración Regional* (Buenos Aires: Institute for the Integration of Latin America and the Caribbean, 2004), online at: http://www.iadb.org/intal/aplicaciones/uploads/publicaciones/e_INTALITD_DD_26_2004_GiordanoMoreiraQuevedo.pdf.
7. See on security and development considerations Barry Buzan, "The Logic of Regional Security in the Post–Cold War World," in Björn Hettne et al. (eds.), *The New Regionalism and the Future of Security and Development. The New Regionalism Series: vol. 4* (London: Macmillan, 2000), 1–25; Percy S. Mistry, "Regional Integration and Economic Development," in Hettne et al., *The New Regionalism*, 26–49.
8. See for interesting perspectives Markus Perkmann and Sum Ngai-Ling (eds.), *Globalization, Regionalization and Cross-Border Regions* (Basingstoke and New York: Palgrave Macmillan, 2002).
9. See Matthews, *Regional Integration and Food Security*.
10. Among the more stimulating recent contributions see Jan Zielonka, *Europe as Empire: The Nature of the Enlarged European Union* (Oxford: Oxford University Press, 2006).

BIBLIOGRAPHY

Abernethy, David B. *The Dynamics of Global Dominance: European Overseas Empires, 1415–1980.* New Haven: Yale University Press, 2000.

Acharya, Amitav. *The Quest for Identity: International Relations of South East Asia.* Oxford: Oxford University Press, 2000.

Adelmann, Martin. *Regionale Kooperation im südlichen Afrika.* Freiburg: Arnold-Bergstraesser-Institut, 2003.

Adibe, Clement E. "Muddling Through: An Analysis of the ECOWAS Experience in Conflict Management in West Africa." In Liisa Laakso (ed.), *Regional Integration for Conflict Prevention and Peace Building in Africa: Europe, SADC and ECOWAS.* Helsinki: University of Helsinki, 2002: 103–169.

Adler, Emanuel, and Michael Barnett. *Security Communities.* Cambridge: Cambridge University Press, 1998.

Adotevi, Stanislas. "Cultural Dimensions of Economic and Political Integration in Africa." In Réal Lavergne (ed.), *Regional Integration and Cooperation in West Africa: A Multidimensional Perspective.* Trenton and Asmara: Africa World Press, 1997: 65–76.

African Union (AU). *Charter of the Organization of African Unity (OAU)* (25.05.1963). Online at: http://www.africa-union.org/root/au/Documents/Treaties/text/OAU_Charter_1963.pdf.

African Union (AU). *Treaty Establishing the African Economic Community* (03.06.1991). Online at: http://www.africa-union.org/root/au/Documents/Treaties/Text/AEC_Treaty_1991.pdf.

African Union (AU). *The Constitutive Act* (11.07.2000). Online at: http://www.africa-union.org/root/au/AboutAU/Constitutive_Act_en.htm.

African Union (AU). *The New Partnership For Africa's Development (NEPAD)* (25.10.2001). Online at: http://www.nepad.org/2005/files/documents/inbrief.pdf.

African Union (AU). *Solemn Declaration on a Common African Defence and Security Policy* (28.02.2004). Online at: http://www.africa-union.org/root/AU/Documents/Treaties/text/Non%20Aggression%20Common%20Defence%20Pact.pdf.

African Union (AU). *Consolidated Report: Consultative Meetings of Accra and Lusaka.* CAMEI/Consol Report (I), 27–28 March 2006. Ouagadougou: 2006. Online at: http://www.iss.co.za/dynamic/administration/file_manager/file_links/CAMEIREPMAR06.PDF?link_id=4057&slink_id=8497&link_type=12&slink_type=13&tmpl_id=3.

African Union (AU). *Rationalization of the Regional Economic Communities (REGs): Review of the Abuja Treaty and Adoption of Minimum Integration Programme.* Addis Ababa: African Union Commission, 2007.

Aggarwal, Vinod K., and Edward A. Fogarty. "The Limits of Interregionalism: The EU and North America." *Journal of European Integration* 27, no. 3 (2005): 327–346.

Aggarwal, Vinod K., and Edward A. Fogarty (eds.). *EU Trade Strategies: Between Regionalism and Globalism.* Houndmills: Palgrave Macmillan, 2004.

Agubuzu, Lawrence O.C. *From the OAU to AU: The Challenges of African Unity and Development in the Twentieth Century.* Lagos: Nigerian Institute of International Affairs, 2004.

Ahrens, Geert-Hinrich. *Die Präsidentschaftswahlen in der Ukraine: Die schwierige Mission der OSCE/ODIHR-Wahlbeobachter.* ZEI Discussion Paper C 151. Bonn: Center for European Integration Studies, 2005.

Al-Alkim, Hassan Hamdan. *The GCC States in an Unstable World: Foreign Policy Dilemmas of Small States.* London: Saqi Books, 1994: 69.

Andean Community (CAN). *Andean Subregional Integration Agreement (Cartagena Agreement)* (26.05.1969). Online at: http://www.comunidadandina.org/ingles/normativa/ande_trie1.htm.

Andean Community (CAN). *Treaty Creating the Court of Justice of the Cartagena Agreement* (10.03.1996). Online at: http://www.comunidadandina.org/ingles/treaties/trea/ande_trie2.htm.

Andean Community (CAN). *Trujillo Act* (10.03.1996). Online at: http://www.un.org/documents/ga/docs/51/plenary/a51–87.htm.

Andean Community (CAN). *Additional Protocol on the Treaty Establishing the Andean Parliament* (23.04.1997). Online at: http://www.comunidadandina.org/ingles/normativa/ande_trie5.htm.

Andean Community (CAN). *Sucre Protocol* (25.06.1997). Online at: http://www.comunidadandina.org/ingles/normativa/ande_trie4.htm.

Andean Community (CAN). *Presidential Summit: Declaration about Democracy and Integration* (07.08.1998). Online at: http://www.comunidadandina.org/ingles/documentos/documents/Preistate-08–07–98.htm.

Andean Community (CAN). *Additional Protocol to the Cartagena Agreement (Andean Community Commitment to Democracy* (27.10.1998). Online at: http://www.comunidadandina.org/ingles/normativa/democracy.htm.

Andean Community (CAN). *Presidential Summit: Quirama Declaration* (28.06.2003). Online at: http://www.comunidadandina.org/ingles/documentos/documents/Quirama.htm.

Arestis, Philip, and Luiz Fernando de Paula (eds.). *Monetary Union in South America: Lessons from EMU.* Cheltenham and Northampton: Edward Elgar, 2003.

Asian Development Bank—Commonwealth Secretariat. *Toward A New Pacific Regionalism: Joint Report to the Pacific Islands Forum Secretariat.* Manila: Asian Development Bank, 2005.

Asmus, Ronald D., and Kenneth M. Pollack. "The New Transatlantic Project." *Policy Review* 115 (2002): 3–18. Online at: http://www.hoover.org/publications/policyreview/3459216.html.

Association of Southeast Asian Nations (ASEAN). *The ASEAN Declaration (Bangkok Declaration)* (08.08.1967). Online at: http://www.aseansec.org/1629.htm.

Association of Southeast Asian Nations (ASEAN). *Declaration of ASEAN Concord* (24.02.1976). Online at: http://www.aseansec.org/1649.htm.

Association of Southeast Asian Nations (ASEAN). *Treaty of Amity and Cooperation in Southeast Asia* (24.02.1976). Online at: http://www.aseansec.org/1654.htm.

Association of Southeast Asian Nations (ASEAN). *Declaration of ASEAN Concord II* (07.10.2003). Online at: http://www.aseansec.org/15160.htm.

Association of Southeast Asian Nations (ASEAN). *Kuala Lumpur Declaration on the Establishment of the ASEAN Charter* (12.12.2005). Online at: http://www.aseansec.org/18031.htm.

Association of Southeast Asian Nations (ASEAN). *Chairman's Statement of the First East Asian Summit.* Kuala Lumpur (14.12.2005), online at: http://www.aseansec.org/18104.htm.

Association of Southeast Asian Nations (ASEAN). *Charter of the Association of Southeast Asian Nations* (20.11.2007). Online at: http://www.aseansec.org/21069.pdf.

Axline, Andrew W. "Free Trade in the Americas and Sub-Regional Integration in Central America and the Caribbean." *Canadian Journal of Development Studies* 21, no. 1 (2000): 31–53.

Babarinde, Olufemi, and Gerrit Faber. "From Lomé to Cotonou: Business as Usual?" *European Foreign Affairs Review* 9, no. 1 (2004): 27–47.

Bach, Daniel. "Institutional Crisis and the Search for New Models." In Réal Lavergne (ed.), *Regional Integration and Cooperation in West Africa: A Multidimensional Perspective.* Trenton and Asmara: Africa World Press, 1997: 77–101.

Bach, Daniel. "The Global Politics of Regionalism: Africa." In Mary Farrell et al. (eds.), *Global Politics of Regionalism: Theory and Practice.* London: Pluto Press, 2005: 171–186.

Balassa, Bela A. *The Theory of Economic Integration.* London: Allen and Unwin, 1962.

Bandara, Jayatilleke S., and Wusheng Yu. "How Desirable is the South Asian Free Trade Area? A Quantitative Economic Assessment." *World Economy* 26, no. 9 (2003): 1293–1323.

Bayoumi, Tamin, et al. *On Regional Monetary Arrangements for ASEAN.* London: Centre for Economic Policy Research 2000.

Beach, Derek. *The Dynamics of European Integration: Why and When EU Institutions Matter.* Houndmills: Palgrave Macmillan, 2005.

Beeson, Mark. *ASEAN Plus Three and the Rise of Reactionary Regionalism.* Online at: http://espace.library.uq.edu.au/eserv/UQ:10998/mbasean03.pdf.

Berger, Thomas. "Japan's International Relations: The Political and Security Dimensions." In Samuel S. Kim (ed.), *The International Relations of Northeast Asia.* Lanham: Rowman and Littlefield, 2004: 135–170.

Bhargava, Kant K. *EU-SAARC: Comparisons and Prospects for Cooperation.* ZEI Discussion Paper C 15. Bonn: Center for European Integration Studies, 1998.

Bilal, Sanoussi. *Can the EU be a model of regional integration? Risks and challenges for developing countries.* Paper presented at the CODESRIA-Global Studies Network (GSN), Second International Conference on 'Globalisation: Overcoming Exclusion, Strengthening Inclusion'. Dakar, 29–31 August 2005. Online at: http://www.ecdpm.org/bilal.

Bitsch, Marie-Thérèse, and Gérard Bossuat (eds.). *De l'Idée d'Eurafrique à la Convention de Lomé I.* Brussels: Bruylant, 2005.

Boas, Morten (ed.). *New Regionalism in the New Millenium.* New York: Palgrave Macmillan, 2003.

Brzezinski, Zbigniew, and Paine Sullivan (eds.), *Russia and the Commonwealth of Independent States: Documents, Data, and Analysis.* Armonk, NY: M.E. Sharpe, 1997.

Bulmer-Thomas, Victor (ed.). *Regional Integration in Latin America and the Caribbean.* London: University of London Institute of Latin American Studies, 2001.

Bundu, Abbas. "ECOWAS and the Future of Regional Integration in West Africa." In Réal Lavergne (ed.), *Regional Integration and Cooperation in West Africa: A Multidimensional Perspective.* Trenton and Asmara: Africa World Press, 1997: 29–48.

Butler, William E. *The Law of Treaties in Russia and the Commonwealth of Independent States: Text and Commentary.* Cambridge: Cambridge University Press, 2002.

Buzan, Barry. "The Logic of Regional Security in the Post–Cold War World." In Björn Hettne et al. (eds.), *The New Regionalism and the Future of Security and Development (The New Regionalism Series: vol. 4).* London: Macmillan, 2000: 1–25.

Buzan, Barry, and Ole Waever (eds.). *Regions and Powers: The Structure of International Security.* Cambridge and New York: Cambridge University Press, 2003.

Calleya, Stephen. *Is the Barcelona Process Working?* ZEI Discussion Paper C 75. Bonn: Center for European Integration Studies, 2000.

Calleya, Stephen (ed.). *Regionalism in the Post–Cold War World*. Aldershot: Ashgate, 2000.

Cantori, Louis J., and Steven L. Spiegel. *The International Politics of Regions: A Comparative Approach.* Englewood Cliffs, NJ: Prentice-Hall, 1970.

Cárdenas, Miguel E., and Christian Arnold. *La Experiencia de la Unión Europea y sus Anécdotas para la Comunidad Andina de Naciones (CAN).* ZEI Discussion Paper C 145. Bonn: Center for European Integration Studies, 2005.

Caribbean Community Secretariat (CARICOM). *Treaty Establishing the Caribbean Community* (04.07.1973). Online at: http://www.caricom.org/jsp/community/original_treaty-text.pdf.

Caribbean Community Secretariat (CARICOM). *The Revised Treaty of Chaguaramas Establishing the Caribbean Community including the CARICOM Single Market and Economy* (05.07.2001). Online at: http://www.caricom.org/jsp/community/revised_treaty-text.pdf.

Caribbean Community Secretariat (CARICOM). *The Rose Hall Declaration on Regional Governance and Integrated Development* (04.07.2003). Online at: http://www.caricomlaw.org/docs/rosehall-declaration.htm.

Caribbean Free Trade Association Secretariat (CARIFTA), *From CARIFTA to Caribbean Community.* Georgetown: CARIFTA, 1972.

Carrión, Fernando (ed.). *Procesos de Decentralisación en la Comunidad Andina.* Quito: FLACSO, 2003.

Casella, Alessandra. "On Markets and Clubs: Economic and Political Integration of Regions with Unequal Productivity." *American Economic Review* 82, no. 2 (1992): 115–121.

Central American Court of Justice (CACJ). *Convention on the Statute of the Central American Court of Justice* (10.12.1992). United Nations Treaty Series, vol. 1821, no. I-31191. New York: United Nations, 1994: 292–303. Online at: http://untreaty.un.org/unts/60001_120000/29/32/00057577.pdf.

Central American Economic Integration Secretariat (SIECA). *General Treaty on Central American Economic Integration* (13.12.1960). Online at: http://www.sieca.org.gt/site/VisorDocs.aspx?IDDOC=CacheING/17990000000005/17990000000005.swf.

Central American Integration System (SICA). *Tegucigalpa Protocol to the Charter of the Organization of Central American States* (13.12.1991). Online at: http://www.sica.int/busqueda/centro%20de%20documentaci%C3%B3n.aspx?IdItem=372&IdCat=8&IdEnt=1.

Central American Integration System (SICA). *Framework Treaty on Democratic Security in Central America* (15.12.1995). Online at: http://untreaty.un.org/unts/120001_144071/22/9/00018606.pdf.

Chabal, Patrick. "The Quest for Good Governance in Africa: Is NEPAD the Answer?" *International Affairs* 78, no. 3 (2002): 447–462.

Chambas, Mohammed Ibn. *The ECOWAS Agenda : Promoting Good Governance, Peace, Stability and Sustainable Development.* Lagos: Nigerian Institute of International Affairs, 2005.

Chamorro Marin, Edgar. *La Perspectiva Economica de la Integración Centroamericana.* Guatemala City: SIECA, 2005.

Chanona, Alejandro. *Is there a Comparative Perspective between the European Union and NAFTA?* UNU-CRIS e-Occasional Papers, O-2003/5. Bruges: United Nations University-CRIS, 2003. Online at: http://www.cris.unu.edu/fileadmin/workingpapers/Alejandro%20Chanona%20OP1.pdf.

Checkel, Jeffrey T. "Social Construction and European Integration." In Thomas Christiansen et al. (eds.), *The Social Construction of Europe.* London: Sage Publications, 2001: 50–64.

Cheru, Fantu. *African Renaissance: Roadmaps to the Challenge of Globalization.* London and New York: Zed Books, 2002.

Christie, John. "History and Development of the Gulf Cooperation Council: A Brief Overview." In John A. Sandwick (ed.), *The Gulf Cooperation Council: Moderation and Stability in an Interdependent World.* Boulder: Westview Press, 1987: 7–19.

Chin, Kin Wah. "ASEAN's Engagement with the EU and the US in the 21st Century: Political and Strategic Dimension." In K.S. Nathan (ed.), *The European Union, United States and ASEAN: Challenges and Prospects for Cooperative Engagement in the 21st Century*. London: ASEAN Academic Press, 2002: 69–98.

Chu, Chin-Peng. "Regionalism and Regional Integration in the Asia-Pacific and the European Union: Theoretical Discussion and Developmental Experience." In Christopher M. Dent and David W.F. Huang (eds.), *Learning from the European Experience*. London: Routledge, 2002: 34–64.

Cini, Michelle, and Angela K. Bowne (eds.). *European Union Studies*. Houndmills: Palgrave Macmillan, 2006.

Cioculescu, Serban Filip. "Thinking Globally, Acting Locally: The Greater Middle East Initiative and the International Community." *Romanian Journal of International Affairs* 10, nos. 1–2 (2005): 187–213.

Clapham, Christopher, et al.(eds.). *Regional Integration in Southern Africa: Comparative International Perspectives*. Johannesburg: South African Institute of International Affairs, 2001.

Clegg, Peter. "From Insiders to Outsiders: Caribbean Banana Interests in the New International Trading Framework." In Stephen J. H. Dearden (ed.), *The European Union and the Commonwealth Caribbean*. Aldershot: Ashgate, 2002: 79–113.

Common Market for Eastern and Southern Africa. *The COMESA Treaty* (08.12.1994). Online at: http://about.comesa.int/attachments/comesa_treaty_en.pdf.

Common Market of the South (MERCOSUR). *The Protocol of Olivos* (18.02.2002). Online at: http://www.sice.oas.org/Trade/MRCSR/olivos/polivos_p.asp.

Common Market of the South (MERCOSUR). *Constitutive Protocol of the Parliament of the MERCOSUR* (09.12.2005). Translation author, for the original document in Spanish see http://www.mercosursocialsolidario.org/images/stories/oficial/documentos/protocolo_constitutivo_mercosur.pdf.

Commonwealth of Independent States (CIS). *The Alma-Ata Declaration* (21.12.1991). In Zbigniew Brzezinski and Paine Sullivan (eds.), *Russia and the Commonwealth of Independent States: Documents, Data, and Analysis*. Armonk, NY: M.E. Sharpe, 1997: 47–48.

Commonwealth of Independent States (CIS). *Agreement on Collective Peacekeeping Forces and Joint Measures on their Material and Technical Supply* (24.09.1993). *Military News Bulletin*, no.10: 1–2.

Commonwealth of Independent States (CIS). *Charter of the Commonwealth of Independent States* (22.01.1993). In Zbigniew Brzezinski and Paine Sullivan (eds.), *Russia and the Commonwealth of Independent States: Documents, Data, and Analysis*. Armonk, NY: M.E. Sharpe, 1997: 506–511.

Commonwealth of Independent States (CIS). *CIS Treaty on Collective Security* (15.05.1992). In Zbigniew Brzezinski and Paine Sullivan (eds.), *Russia and the Commonwealth of Independent States: Documents, Data, and Analysis*. Armonk, NY: M.E. Sharpe, 1997; 539–540.

Cooper, Scott, and Brock Taylor. "Power and Regionalism: Explaining Regional Cooperation in the Persian Gulf." In Finn Laursen (ed.), *Comparative Regional Integration: Theoretical Perspectives*. Aldershot: Ashgate, 2003: 105–124.

Cooperation Council for the Arab States of the Gulf (GCC). *The Cooperation Council—Charter* (25.05.1981). Online at: http://www.gccsg.org/eng/index.php?action=Sec-Show&ID=1.

Cooperation Council for the Arab States of the Gulf (GCC). *The Unified Economic Agreement between the Countries of the Gulf Cooperation Council* (11.11.1981). Online at: http://www.worldtradelaw.net/fta/agreements/gccfta.pdf.

Cooperation Council for the Arab States of the Gulf (GCC). *The Economic Agreement between the Countries of the Gulf Cooperation Council (Revised)* (31.12.2001). Online at: http://library.gcc-sg.org/English/Books/econagree2004.htm.

Coskun, Bezen Balamir. *Region and Region Building in the Middle East: Problems and Prospects*. UNU-CRIS Occasional Papers O-2006/1. Bruges: United Nations University-CRIS, 2006. Online at: http://www.cris.unu.edu/fileadmin/workingpapers/20060117093527.O-2006–1.pdf.

Craig, Albert M. *Japan: Tradition and Transformation*. 3rd ed. Tokyo: Tuttle, 1981.

Crawford, Beverly. "Why the Euro-Med Partnership? European Union Strategies in the Mediterranean Region." In Vinod K. Aggarwal and Edward A. Fogarty (eds.), *EU Trade Strategies: Between Regionalism and Globalism*. Houndmills: Palgrave Macmillan, 2004: 93–117.

Crawley, Andrew. *MERCOSUR in Search of a New Agenda: Rapporteur's Report*. Buenos Aires: Institute for the Integration of Latin America and the Caribbean, 2004. Online at: http://idbdocs.iadb.org/wsdocs/getdocument.aspx?docnum=548062.

Creamer, Germán. "Open Regionalism in the Andean Community: A Trade Flow Analysis." *World Trade Review 2*, no. 1 (2003): 101–118.

Crocombe, Ron. *The South Pacific*. Suva: University of the South Pacific, 2001.

Cuyvers, Ludo, et al. "Regional Monetary Cooperation and Integration." In Mary Farrell, et al. (eds.), *Global Politics of Regionalism: Theory and Practice*. London: Pluto Press, 2005: 120–136.

Da Motta Veiga, Pedro. *Mercosur: In Search of a New Agenda. Mercosur's Institutionalization Agenda: The Challenges of a Project in Crisis*. INTAL Working Paper, SITI, 06E. Buenos Aires: Institute for the Integration of Latin America and the Caribbean, 2004. Online at: http://www.iadb.org/intal/aplicaciones/uploads/publicaciones/i_IECI_WP_06e_daMottaVeiga.pdf.

De Blij, Harm J., and Peter O. Muller (eds.). *Geography: Realms, Regions and Concepts*. Hoboken, NJ: Wiley Text Books, 2001.

De la Ossa, Alvaro. *Der zentralamerikanische Integrationsprozess: Ende einer Entwicklungsalternative*. IBERO-Analysen 6. 2000. Berlin: Ibero-Amerikanisches Institut Stiftung Preußischer Kulturbesitz. Online at: http://www.iai.spk-berlin.de/fileadmin/dokumentenbibliothek/Ibero-Analysen/Ibero-Analysen%20Heft%206.pdf.

De Lombaerde, Philippe. *Supporting Regional Integration: The Roadmap of Indicators and Tools*. UNU-CRIS Occasional Papers, O-2003/3. Bruges: United Nations University-CRIS, 2003. Online at: http://www.cris.unu.edu/fileadmin/workingpapers/philippe%20ACP%20Engl%20final.pdf.

De Lombaerde, Philippe (ed.). *Assessment and Measurement of Regional Integration*. London and New York: Routledge, 2006.

De Lombaerde, Philippe, Antoni Estevadeordal and Kati Suominen (eds.). *Governing Regional Integration for Development: Monitoring Experiences, Methods and Prospects*. Aldershot: Ashgate, 2008.

De Lombaerde, Philippe, and Liliana Lizarazo. *La problématique de l'intégration Monétaire en Amérique Latine et dans les Caraibes*. UNU-CRIS Occasional Papers, O-2004/13. Bruges: United Nations University-CRIS, 2004. Online at: http://www.cris.unu.edu/fileadmin/workingpapers/OP%20De%20Lombaerde%20LizarazoProbl%E9matiqueIntMonAL2003.pdf.

De Lombaerde, Philippe, Kochi Shigeru and José Briceño Ruiz (eds.). *Del regionalismo latinoamericano a la integración interregional*. Madrid: Fundación Carolina, 2008.

De Lombaerde, Philippe, and Luk van Langenhove. *Indicators of Regional Integration: Conceptual and Methodological Issues*. UNU-CRIS Occasional Papers, O-2004/15. Bruges: United Nations University-CRIS, 2004. Online at: http://www.cris.unu.edu/fileadmin/workingpapers/OP%20IndicatorsPDL-LVL-2004.pdf.

De Marco, Guido. "The Future of Euro-Mediterranean Relations: The Vision of Malta," in: Jacobs, Andreas (ed.), *Euro-Mediterranean Co-operation: Enlarging and widening the perspective*. ZEI Discussion Paper C131. Bonn: Center for European Integration Studies, 2005: 8–15.

De Waal, Alex. "What's New in the New Partnership for Africa's Development?" *International Affairs 78*, no. 3 (2002): 463–475.

Dearden, Stephen J.H. (ed.). *The European Union and the Commonwealth Caribbean*. Aldershot: Ashgate, 2002.

Demmelhuber, Thomas. *The Euro-Mediterranean Space as an Imagined (Geo-) Political, Economic and Cultural Entity*. ZEI Discussion Paper C 170. Bonn: Center for European Integration Studies, 2006.

Dennis, Peter M., and M. Leann Brown. "The ECOWAS: From Regional Economic Organization to Regional Peacekeeper." In Finn Laursen (ed.), *Comparative Regional Integration: Theoretical Perspectives*. Aldershot: Ashgate, 2003: 229–249.

Dent, Christopher M. "Northeast Asia: A Region in Search of Regionalism?" In Christopher M. Dent and David W.F. Huang (eds.), *Northeast Asian Regionalism: Learning from the European Experience*. London: Routledge, 2002: 1–15.

Dent, Christopher M. "The Asia-Europe Meetring (ASEM) Process: Beyond the Triadic Political Economy?" In Heiner Hänggi et al. (eds.), *Interregionalism and International Relations*. Abingdon and New York: Routledge, 2006: 113–127.

Dent, Christopher M., and David W.F. Huang (eds.). *Northeast Asian Regionalism: Learning from the European Experience*. London: Routledge, 2002.

Deutsch, Karl, et al. *Political Community and the North Atlantic Area: International Organization in the Light of the Historical Experience*. Princeton, NJ: Princeton University Press, 1957.

Devlin, Robert, and Antoni Estevadeordal. *What's New in the New Regionalism in the Americas?* INTAL/ITD Working Paper 2. Buenos Aires: Institute for the Integration of Latin America and the Caribbean, 2001. Online at: http://idbdocs.iadb.org/wsdocs/getdocument.aspx?docnum=776254.

Devlin, Robert, and Ricardo Ffrench-Davis. *Toward an Evaluation of Regional Integration in Latin América in the 1990s*. INTAL/ITD Working Paper 2. Buenos Aires: Institute for the Integration of Latin America and the Caribbean, 1998. Online at: http://idbdocs.iadb.org/wsdocs/getdocument.aspx?docnum=417959.

Devlin, Robert, and Ziga Vodusek. *Trade Related Capacity Building: An Overview in the Context of Latin American Trade Policy and the MERCOSUR-EU Association Agreement*. Buenos Aires: Institute for the Integration of Latin America and the Caribbean, 2005. Online at: http://idbdocs.iadb.org/wsdocs/getdocument.aspx?docnum=548075.

Diehl, Paul F., and Joseph Lepgold (eds.). *Regional Conflict Management*. Lanham: Rowman and Littlefield, 2003.

Dinan, Desmond. *Europe Recast: A History of European Union*. Boulder: Lynn Rieffer, 2004.

Dinka, Tesfaye, and Walter Kennes. *Africa's Regional Integration Arrangements: History and Challenges*. ECDPM Discussion Paper No. 74. Maastricht: European Centre for Development Policy Management, 2007.

Dittmer, Lowell. "The Emerging Northeast Asian Order." In Samuel Kim (ed.), *The International Relations of Northeast Asia*. Lanham: Rowman and Littlefield, 2004: 331–362.

Duina, Francesco. *The Social Construction of Free Trade: The European Union, NAFTA and Mercosur*. Princeton: Princeton University Press, 2006.

Durham, William. *Scarcity and Survival in Central America: Ecological Origins of the Soccer War*. Stanford: Stanford University Press, 1979.

Economic and Monetary Community of Central Africa (CEMAC). *Traité instituant la Communauté Economique et Monétaire de l'Afrique Centrale(CEMAC)* (16.03.1994). Online at: http://www.izf.net/affiche_oscar.php?num_page=2389.

Economic Commission for Africa (ed.). *Assessing Regional Integration in Africa*. Addis Ababa: Economic Commission for Africa, 2004. Online at: http://www.uneca.org/aria1.

Economic Commission for Latin America and the Caribbean (ed.). *Latin America and the Caribbean in the World Economy 2002–2003*. Santiago de Chile: United Nations Publications, 2004.

Economic Community of West African States (ECOWAS). *Treaty of the Economic Community of West African States (ECOWAS)* (28.05.1975). Online at: http://www.unhcr.org/cgi-bin/texis/vtx/refworld/rwmain?docid=49217f4c2&page=search.

Economic Community of West African States (ECOWAS). *Treaty of ECOWAS (Revised)* (24.07.1993). Online at: http://www.comm.ecowas.int/sec/index.php?id=treaty&lang=en.

Erling, Alvestad. *The ASEAN Regional Forum: A Catalyst for Change?* Oslo: University of Oslo, 2001.

Eudes, Marielle. "Experts Hear Death Bells Ringing for Russia's CIS." *The Manila Times*, 4 April 2005.

Eurasian Economic Community (EAEC). *Agreement on the Creation of Common Economic Space (CES)* (19.09.2003). Translation author, for the original document in Russian see http://archive.kremlin.ru/text/docs/2003/09/52478.shtml.

European Commission (EC). *Communication on European Community Support for Regional Economic Integration Efforts among Developing Countries.* COM (95) 219 final. (1995). Online at: http://aei. pitt.edu/4328/01/001212_1.pdf.

European Commission (EC). *Green Paper on Relations between the European Union and the ACP Countries on the Eve of the 21st Century: Challenges and Options for a New Partnership.* COM (96) 570 (1996). Online at: http://aei.pitt.edu/1206/01/ACP_21st_gp_COM_96_570.pdf.

European Commission (EC). *The Cotonou Agreement.* Brussels: European Commission (2000/2005). Online at: http://ec.europa.eu/development/icenter/repository/agr01_en.pdf.

European Commission (EC). *Africa, Caribbean, Pacific: EPA Negotiations (Toolbox)* (2003). Online at: http://ec.europa.eu/trade/creating-opportunities/bilateral-relations/regions/africa-caribbean-pacific/index_en.htm, 2003.

European Commission (EC). *A New Partnership with South East Asia* (2003). Online at: http://www.ec.Europa.eu/external_relations/library/publications/09_sea_en.pdf.

European Commission (EC). *EPA Flash News.* Online at: http://ec.europa.eu/trade/creating-opportunities/bilateral-relations/regions/africa-caribbean-pacific/index_en.htm.

European Commission (EC). *Taking Europe to the World: 50 Years of the European Commission's External Service* (2004). Online at: http://ec.europa.eu/external_relations/delegations/docs/50_years_brochure_en.pdf

European Commission (EC). *A World Player—The European Union's External Relations* (2004). Online at: http://www.ec.Europa.eu/publications/booklets/move/47/en.pdf.

European Commission (EC). *The EU & South Asian Association of Regional Co-Operation (SAARC).* Online at: http://www.ec.Europa.eu/comm/external_relations/saarc/intro/index.htm.

European Commission (EC). *The Asia-Europe Meeting (ASEM).* Online at: http://ec.europa.eu/external_relations/asem/index_en.html.

European Union (EU). *A Secure Europe in a Better World: European Security Strategy,* (European Council 12 December 2003). Online at: http://www.consilium.europa.eu/uedocs/cmsUpload/78367.pdf.

Fairbank, John King. *Trade and Diplomacy on the China Coast: The Opening of Treaty Ports, 1842–1854.* Stanford: Stanford University Press, 1969.

Falk, Richard. "Regionalism and World Order: The Changing Global Setting." In Fredrik Söderbaum and Timothy Shaw (eds.), *Theories of New Regionalism: A Palgrave Reader.* London: Palgrave Macmillan, 2003: 63–80.

Faria, Fernanda. *Crisis Management in Sub-Saharan Africa: The Role of the European Union.* ISS Occasional Paper no. 51. Paris: The European Union Institute for Security Studies, 2004. Online at: http://www.iss.europa.eu/uploads/media/occ51.pdf.

Farrell, Mary. *The EU and Inter-Regional Cooperation: In Search of Global Presence?* UNU-CRIS e-Working Papers, W-2004/9. Bruges: United Nations University- CRIS, 2004. Online at: http://www.cris.unu.edu/fileadmin/workingpapers/WP%20Farrell.pdf.

Farrell, Mary. "A Triumph of Realism over Idealism? Cooperation between the European Union and Africa." *Journal of European Integration* 27, no. 3 (2005): 263–283.

Farrell, Mary, et al. (eds.). *Global Politics of Regionalism: Theory and Practice.* London: Pluto Press, 2005.

Fasano, Ugo, and Andrea Schaechter (eds.). *Monetary Union Among the Member Countries of the Gulf Cooperation Council.* Washington, D.C.: International Monetary Fund, 2003.

Fawcett, Louise. "Regionalism in Historical Perspective." In Louise Fawcett and Andrew Hurrell (eds.), *Regionalism in World Politics: Regional Organization and International Order.* New York: Oxford University Press, 1995: 9–36.

Fawcett, Louise, and Andrew Hurrell (eds.). *Regionalism in World Politics: Regional Organization and International Order.* New York: Oxford University Press, 1995.

Ferdowsi, Mir A. (ed.). *Vom Enthusiasmus zur Ernüchterung? Die Entwicklungspolitik der Europäischen Union.* Munich: Forschungsstelle Dritte Welt, 1999.

Ferdowsi, Mir A. (ed.), *Afrika—Ein verlorener Kontinent?* Munich: Wilhelm Fink, 2004.

Ferguson, Niall. *Colossus: The Price of America's Empire.* New York: Penguin Press, 2004.

Fernando, P.D. *Has the South Asian Association for Regional Co-operation (SAARC) Achieved a Substantial Progress?* Colombo: Konrad-Adenauer-Foundation, 2001.

Fisher, C.A. "Southeast Asia: The Balkans of the Orient? A Study in Continuity and Change." *Geography* 47 (1962): 347–367.

Fisher, L. M., and Naison Ngoma. *The SADC Organ: Challenges in the New Millennium.* Institute for Security Studies Occasional Paper 114, 2005. Online at: http://www.iss.co.za/index.php?link_id=3&slink_id=388&link_type=12&slink_type=12&tmpl_id=3.

Fort, Bertrand, and Douglas Webber (ed.). *Regional Integration in East Asia and Europe: Convergence or Divergence?* London and New York: Routledge, 2006.

Francis, David J. *The Politics of Economic Regionalism: Sierra Leone in ECOWAS.* Aldershot: Ashgate, 2001.

Francis, David J. *Uniting Africa: Building Regional Peace and Security Systems.* Ashgate: Aldershot, 2006.

Frankfurter Allgemeine Zeitung, no. 200 (29 August 2005): 5.

Freeman, Nick J. "ASEAN Enlargement and Foreign Direct Investment." In Carolyn L.Gates and Mya Than (eds.). *ASEAN Enlargement: Impacts and Implications.* Singapore: Institute of Southeast Asian Studies, 2001: 80–101.

Freinkman, Lev, et al. *Trade Performance and Regional Integration of the CIS Countries.* Washington, D.C.: The World Bank, 2004.

Fukuyama, Francis. "Re-Envisioning Asia." *Foreign Affairs* 84, no. 1 (2005): 75–87.

Galal, Ahmed, and Bernard Hoekman (eds.). *Arab Economic Integration: Between Hope and Reality.* Cairo: Egyptian Center for Economic Studies/Washington D.C.: Brookings Institution Press, 2003.

Gallep, Bernd. "Der zentralamerikanische Integrationsprozess: Probleme und Scheinprobleme." *KAS-Auslandsinformationen* 10 (2005): 30–81.

Gambari, Ibrahim A. *Political and Comparative Dimensions of Regional Integration: The Case of ECOWAS.* Atlantic Highlands, NJ and London: Humanities Press International, 1991.

Garrón Bozo, Rodrigo Javier. *Derecho Comunitario: Principes, Fuentes y Sistema Jurisdiccional de la Comunidad Andina de Naciones y la Union Europea.* La Paz: Edicion Cima, 2004.

Garton Ash, Timothy. *In Europe's Name: Germany and the Divided Continent.* New York: Random House, 1993.

Garton Ash, Timothy. *Free World: Why a Crisis of the West Reveals the Opportunity of our Time.* London: Allen Lane, 2004.

Garton Ash, Timothy. "Soldiers of the Hidden Imam." *The New York Review of Books* 52, no. 17 (2005). Online at: http://www.nybooks.com/articles/18390.

Gates, Carolyn L., and Mya Than (eds.). *ASEAN Enlargement: Impacts and Implications.* Singapore: Institute of Southeast Asian Studies, 2001.

Gavin, Brigid. *Regional Integration and EPAs Timing and Safeguard.* UNU-CRIS Occasional Papers, O-2003/4. Bruges: United Nations University-CRIS, 2003. Online at: http://www.cris.unu.edu/fileadmin/workingpapers/brigid%20ACP%20Engl%20final.pdf.

Genge, Manelisi, et al., *African Union and a Pan-African Parliament.* Pretoria: Africa Institute of South Africa, 2000.

Giambiagi, Fabio. "Why does Monetary Union make Sense in the Long Run?" In Philip Arestis and Luiz Fernando de Paula (eds.). *Monetary Union in South America: Lessons from EMU.* Cheltenham and Northampton: Edward Elgar, 2003: 59–81.

Gibert, Marie V. *Monitoring a Region in Crisis: The European Union in West Africa.* Chaillot Paper No. 96. Paris: European Union Institute for Security Studies, 2007.

Gilson, Julie. *Asia Meets Europe: Interregionalism and the Asia-Europe Meeting.* Cheltenham: Edward Elgar, 2002.

Gilson, Julie. "New Interregionalism? The EU and East Asia." *Journal of European Integration* 27, no. 3 (2005): 307–326.

Giordano, Paolo. *The External Dimension of the Mercosur: Prospects for North-South Integration with the European Union*. London: Royal Institute for International Affairs, 2002. Online at: http://www.iadb.org/intal/aplicaciones/uploads/publicaciones/i_INTALITDSTA_OP_19_2003_Giordano.pdf.

Giordano, Paolo, et al. *El Tratamiento de las Asimetrías en los Acuerdos de Integración Regional*. Buenos Aires: Institute for the Integration of Latin America and the Caribbean, 2004. Online at: http://www.iadb.org/intal/aplicaciones/uploads/publicaciones/e_INTALITD_DD_26_2004_Giordano-MoreiraQuevedo.pdf.

Gomes Saraiva, Miriam. *The European Union as an International Actor and the Mercosur Countries*. EUI Working Paper RSCAS No. 2004/14. Florence: Robert Schuman Centre for Advanced Studies, 2004. Online at: http://cadmus.iue.it/dspace/bitstream/1814/2756/1/04_14.pdf.

Gonsalves, Eric, and Nancy Jetly (eds.). *The Dynamics of South Asia: Regional Cooperation and SAARC*. New Delhi: Sage Publications, 1999.

Gordon, Philip H., and Jeremy Shapiro. *Allies at War: America, Europe and the Crisis over Iraq*. New York: MacGraw-Hill, 2004.

Gottschalk, Keith, and Siegmar Schmidt. "The African Union and the New Partnership for Africa's Development: Strong Institutions for Weak States?" *International Politics and Society*, no. 4 (2004): 138–158.

Grisanti, Luis Xavier. *El Nuevo Interregionalismo Transatlántico: La Asociación Estratégica Unión Europea—América Latina*. Buenos Aires: Institute for the Integration of Latin America and the Caribbean, 2004.

Grudz, Steven, "Peace, Security and the African Peer Review Mechanism: Are the Tools up to the Task?" *African Security Review* 16, no. 3 (2007): 54–66.

Grugel, Jean, and Anthony J. Payne. "Regionalist Responses in the Caribbean Basin." In Björn Hettne et al. (eds.), *National Perspectives on the New Regionalism in the South (The New Regionalism Series: vol. 3)*. London: Macmillan, 2000: 198–220.

Guira, Jorge. *MERCOSUR: Trade and Investment amid Financial Crisis*. London and New York: Kluwer Law International, 2003.

Haas, Ernst B. *The Uniting of Europe: Political, Social and Economic Force, 1950–1957*. Stanford: Stanford University Press, 1958.

Haas, Ernst B. "International Integration: The European and the Universal Process." *International Organization* 15, no.3 (1961): 366–392.

Haas, Ernst B. *Beyond the Nation-State: Functionalism and International Organization*. Stanford: Stanford University Press, 1964.

Haas, Ernst B. "The Obsolescence of Regional Integration Theory." Working Paper. Berkeley: Institute of International Studies, 1975.

Haas, Michael. *The Pacific Way: Regional Cooperation in the South Pacific*. New York and Westview, CT: Praeger, 1989.

Hadjimichael, Michael J., and Michel Galy. *The CFA Franc Zone and the EMU*. Washington, D.C.: International Monetary Fund, 1997.

Hakimian, Hassan, and Jeffrey B. Nugent. *Trade Policy and Economic Integration in the Middle East and North Africa: Economic Boundaries in Flux*. New York: Routledge Curzon, 2004.

Hall, Kenneth O. *Re-Inventing CARICOM: The Road to a New Integration*. Kingston: Ian Randle, 2003.

Hallberg, Anna. *Regional Integration in Latin America: The MERCOSUR Experience*. Stockholm: Latinamerika-institutet, 2000.

Hamilton, Daniel S., and Joseph P. Quinlan. *Partners in Prosperity: The Changing Geography of the Transatlantic Economy*. Washington, D.C.: Center for Transatlantic Relations, Johns Hopkins University-SAIS, 2004.

Hamilton, Daniel S., and Joseph P. Quinlan. *The Transatlantic Economy 2005: Annual Survey of Jobs, Trade and Investment in between the United States and Europe.* Washington, D.C.: Center for Transatlantic Relations, Johns Hopkins University-SAIS, 2006.

Hänggi, Heiner, et al. (eds.). *Interregionalism and International Relations.* Abingdon and New York: Routledge, 2006.

Hanna, Daniel. *A New Fiscal Framework for GCC Countries Ahead of Monetary Union.* International Economic Programme Briefing Paper 06/02. London: Chatham House, 2006.

Harvie, Charles and Tran Van Hoa (eds.), *New Asian Regionalism: Responses to Globalisation and Crises.* Basingstoke: Macmillan, 2003.

Hassan bin Talal, Prince. *Continuity, Innovation and Change: Selected Essays.* Amman, Jordan: Majlis El Hassan, 2001

Hentz, James J., and Morten Boas (eds.). *New and Critical Security and Regionalism: Beyond the Nation-State.* Aldershot: Ashgate, 2003.

Herrera Cáceres, Hector Roberto. *Imperio del Derecho y Desarrollo de los Pueblos.* Tegucigalpa: Litografía Lopez, 2003.

Hettmann, Jens-U., and Fatima Kyari Mohammed. *Opportunities and Challenges of Parliamentary Oversight of the Security Sector in West Africa: The Regional Level.* Bonn: Friedrich-Ebert-Stiftung, 2005. Online at: http://www.fes.de/in_afrika/documents/SB_ECOWAS_Parl_1_1105_001 .pdf.

Hettne, Björn. "Security Regionalism in Europe and South Asia." In James J. Hentz and Morten Boas (eds.), *New and Critical Security and Regionalism: Beyond the Nation-State.* Aldershot: Ashgate, 2003: 149–166.

Hettne, Björn. "The New Regionalism Revisited." In Fredrik Söderbaum and Timothy M. Shaw (eds.), *Theories of New Regionalism: A Palgrave Reader.* Houndmills: Palgrave Macmillan, 2003: 22–42.

Hettne, Björn, Andras Inotai, and Osvaldo Sunkel (eds.). *The New Regionalism Series,* vols. 1–5. London: Macmillan Press, 1999–2001.

Hettne, Björn, and Fredrik Söderbaum. "Civilian Power or Soft Imperialism? The European Union as a Global Actor and the Role of Interregionalism." *European Foreign Affairs Review* 10, no. 4 (2005): 535–552.

Hoa, Tran Van, and Charles Harvie (eds.). *New Asian Regionalism: Responses to Globalisation and Crises.* Basingstoke: Macmillan, 2003.

Hoekman, Bernard, and Patrick Messerlin. "Initial Conditions and Incentives for Arab Economic Integration: Can the European Community's Success Be Emulated?" In Ahmed Galal, and Bernard Hoekman (eds.), *Arab Economic Integration: Between Hope and Reality.* Cairo: Egyptian Center for Economic Studies/Washington D.C.: Brookings Institution Press, 2003: 102–147.

Hofmeier, Rolf. "Regionale Kooperation und Integration." In Mir A. Ferdowsi (ed.), *Afrika: Ein verlorener Kontinent?* Munich: Wilhelm Fink, 2004: 213–244.

Holland, Martin. *The European Union and the Third World.* Houndmills: Palgrave, 2002.

Holland, Martin. "'Imagined' Interregionalism: Europe's Relations with the African, Caribbean and Pacific States (ACP)." In Heiner Hänggi et al. (eds.), *Interregionalism and International Relations.* Abingdon and New York: Routledge, 2006: 254–271.

Hooghe, Liesbet, and Gary Marks. *Multi-Level Governance and European Integration.* Lanham: Rowman and Littlefield, 2001.

Hossain, Masud. *Regional Conflict Transformation: A Reinterpretation of South Asian Association for Regional Co-operation (SAARC).* Helsinki: Institute of Development Studies, 2002.

Howe, K.R., et al. (eds). *Tides of History: The Pacific Islands in the Twentieth Century.* Honolulu: University of Hawaii Press, 1994.

Huntington, Samuel P. *The Clash of Civilizations and the Remaking of World Order.* New York: Simon and Schuster, 1993.

Hurrell, Andrew. "Regionalism in Theoretical Perspective." In Louise Fawcett and Andrew Hurrell (eds.), *Regionalism in World Politics: Regional Organization and International Order.* Oxford: Oxford University Press, 1995: 37–75.

Hurrell, Andrew. "The Regional Dimension in International Relations Theory." In Mary Farrell et al. (eds.), *Global Politics of Regionalism: Theory and Practice.* London: Pluto Press, 2005: 38–53.

Hurt, Stephen R. "Co-operation and Coercion? The Cotonou Agreement between the European Union and ACP States and the End of the Lomé Convention." *Third World Quarterly* 24, no. 1 (2003): 161–176.

Irving, Jacqueline. "Varied Impact on Africa Expected from New European Currency." *Africa Recovery* 12, no. 4 (1999). Online at: http://www.un.org/ecosocdev/geninfo/afrec/vol12no4/euro.htm.

Ishmael, Len. *The OECS Model of Integration in the Context of Caribbean Regionalism.* Castries: Organization of Eastern Caribbean States, 2006.

Itam, Samuel, et al. *Developments and Challenges in the Caribbean Region.* Washington, D.C.: International Monetary Fund, 2000.

Itoh, Motoshige. "Economic Integration in East Asia: A Japanese Viewpoint." In Woosik Moon and Bernadette Andreosso-O'Callaghan (eds.), *Regional Integration: Europe and Asia Compared.* Aldershot: Ashgate, 2005: 78–93.

Jacobs, Andreas (ed.). *Euro-Mediterranean Co-operation: Enlarging and widening the perspective.* ZEI Discussion Paper C131. Bonn: Center for European Integration Studies, 2005.

Jaguaribe, Helio, and Alvaro Vasconcelos (eds.). *The European Union, Mercosul and the New World Order.* London: Frank Cass, 2003.

Janowski, Cordula. *Globalization, Regional Integration and the EU: Pleading for a Broader Perspective.* ZEI Discussion Paper C 162. Bonn: Center for European Integration Studies, 2006.

Jessen, Anneke, and Ennio Rodríguez. *The Caribbean Community: Facing the Challenges of Regional and Global Integration.* Buenos Aires: Institute for the Integration of Latin America and the Caribbean, 1999.

Jessen, Anneke, and Christopher Vignoles. *CARICOM Report No. 2.* Buenos Aires: Institute for the Integration of Latin America and the Caribbean, 2005.

Johnston, Alastair Iain. "China's International Relations: The Political and Security Dimension." In Samuel S. Kim (ed.), *The International Relations of Northeast Asia.* Lanham: Rowman and Littlefield, 2004: 65–100.

Jonson, Lena, and Clive Archer (eds.). *Peacekeeping and the Role of Russia in Eurasia.* Boulder and Oxford: Westview Press, 1996.

Jorgensen, Bent D. "South Asia: An Anxious Journey toward Regionalization?" In Michael Schulz et al. (eds.), *Regionalization in a Globalizing World: A Comparative Perspective on Forms, Actors and Processes.* London: Zed Books, 2001: 125–146.

Kambudzi, Admore Mupoki. "Portrayal of a Possible Path to a Single Government for Africa." In Murithi, Timothy (ed.), *Towards a Union Government for Africa.* Thswane (Pretoria): Institute for Security Studies, 2008: 13–27.

Kang, Eliot C.S. "North Korea's International Relations: The Successful Failure?" In Samuel S. Kim (ed.), *The International Relations of Northeast Asia.* Lanham: Rowman and Littlefield, 2004: 281–300.

Katzenstein, Peter. "Regionalism in Comparative Perspective." *Cooperation and Conflict* 31, no. 2 (1996): 123–159.

Katzenstein, Peter. *A World of Regions: Asia and Europe in the American Imperium.* Ithaca: Cornell University Press, 2005.

Kelemen, Daniel R. *The Rules of Federalism: Institutions and Regulatory Politics in the EU and Beyond.* Cambridge, MA: Harvard University Press, 2004.

Kelsey, Jane. *A People's Guide to PACER: The Implications for the Pacific Islands of the Pacific Agreement on Closer Economic relations (PACER).* Suva: Pacific Network on Globalisation, 2004.

Keohane, Robert. *After Hegemony*. Princeton: Princeton University Press, 1984.

Keohane, Robert. *International Institutions and State Power: Essays in International Relations Theory*. Boulder: Westview Press, 1989.

Khandelwal, Padamja. *COMESA and SADC: Prospects and Challenges for Regional Trade Integration*. IMF Working Paper 04/227. Washington, D.C.: International Monetary Fund, 2004.

Kim, Samuel S. (ed.). *The International Relations of Northeast Asia*. Lanham: Rowman and Littlefield, 2004.

Koesler, Ariane. *The Southern African Development Community and its Relations to the European Union: Deepening Integration in Southern Africa?* ZEI Discussion Paper C 169. Bonn: Center for European Integration Studies, 2007.

Koesler, Ariane, and Martin Zimmek (eds.). *Global Voices on Regional Integration*. ZEI Discussion Paper C 176. Bonn: Center for European Integration Studies, 2007.

Kose, M. Ayhan, and Alessandro Rebucci. "How Might CAFTA Change Macroeconomic Fluctuations in Central America? Lessons from NAFTA." *Journal of Asian Economics* 16, no. 1 (2005): 77–104.

Krause, Alexandra. "The European Union's Africa Policy: The Commission as Policy Entrepreneur in the CFSP." *European Foreign Affairs Review* 8, no. 1 (2003): 221–237.

Kühnhardt, Ludger. *Stufen der Souveränität: Selbstbestimmung und Staatsverständnis in der "Dritten Welt."* Bonn: Bouvier, 1992.

Kühnhardt, Ludger. *Europäische Union und föderale Idee: Europapolitik in der Umbruchzeit*. Munich: C.H. Beck, 1993.

Kühnhardt, Ludger. *Contrasting Transatlantic Interpretations: The EU and the US toward a Common Global Role*. Stockholm: Swedish Institute for European Policy Studies, 2003.

Kühnhardt, Ludger. *African Regional Integration and the Role of the European Union*. ZEI Discussion Paper C 184. Bonn: Center for European Integration Studies, 2008.

Kühnhardt, Ludger. *European Union—The Second Founding: The Changing Rationale of European Integration*. Baden-Baden: Nomos, 2008.

Kühnhardt, Ludger (ed.). *Crises in European Integration. Challenges and Responses, 1945–2005*. Oxford and New York: Berghahn Books, 2009.

Kuroda, Haruhiko. "ASEAN Economic Outlook and Policy Issues." 2008. Online at: http://www.adb.org/Documents/Speeches/2008/ms2008018.asp

Laakso, Liisa (ed.). *Regional Integration for Conflict Prevention and Peace Building in Africa: Europe, SADC and ECOWAS*. Helsinki: University of Helsinki, 2002.

Laanatza, Marianne, et al. "Regionalization in the Middle East." In Michael Schulz et al. (eds.), *Regionalization in a Globalizing World: A Comparative Perspective on Forms, Actors and Processes*. London: Zed Books, 2001: 42–60.

Lal, Brij, and Kate Fortune (eds.). *The Pacific Islands: An Encyclopedia*. Honolulu: University of Hawaii Press, 2000.

Lamy, Pascal. "The Challenge of Integrating Africa into the World Economy." In Christopher Clapham et al. (eds.), *Regional Integration in Southern Africa: Comparative International Perspectives*. Johannesburg: South African Institute of International Affairs, 2001: 13–17.

Lauer, Rene. *Las Políticas Sociales en la Integración Regional: Estudio Comparativa de la Unión Europea y la Comunidad Andina de Naciones*. Quito: Universidad Andina Simón Bolívar, 2001.

Laurent, Edwin. *Understanding International Trade: The Trading System from the Perspective of the Eastern Caribbean*. Castries: Organization of Eastern Caribbean States, 2006.

Laursen, Finn (ed.). *Comparative Regional Integration: Theoretical Perspectives*. Aldershot: Ashgate, 2003.

Lavakare, P.J. "Science and Technology in SAARC: Aspiration, Achievements and Hopes." In Gonsalves, Eric, and Nancy Jetly (eds.), *The Dynamics of South Asia: Regional Cooperation and SAARC*. New Delhi: Sage Publications, 1999: 157–170.

Lavergne, Réal (ed.). *Regional Integration and Cooperation in West Africa: A Multidimensional Perspective*. Trenton and Asmara: Africa World Press, 1997.

Lecoutre, Delphine. *Vers Un Gouvernement de l'Union Africaine? Maximalistes vs. Gradualistes*. IIS Paper 147. Thswane (Pretoria): Institute for Security Studies, 2007.

Lecoutre, Delphine. "Reflections on the 2007 Grand Debate on a Union Government for Africa." In Timothy Murithi (ed.), *Towards a Union Government for Africa*. Thswane/Pretoria: Institute for Security Studies, 2007: 45–59.

Lindberg, Leon. *The Political Dynamics of European Economic Integration*. Stanford: Stanford University Press, 1963.

Lindholm Schulz, Helena, and Michael Schulz. "Israel, Palestine and Jordan: Triangle of Peace of Conflict?" In Björn Hettne et al. (eds.), *The New Regionalism and the Future of Security and Development (The New Regionalism Series: vol. 4)*. London: Macmillan, 2000: 144–175.

Lindholm Schulz, Helena, and Michael Schulz. "Regional Integration—Israel, Jordan and the Palestinian Entity: In Whose Interest?" In Björn Hettne et al. (eds.), *National Perspectives on the New Regionalism in the South (The New Regionalism Series: vol. 3)*. London: Macmillan, 2000: 221–241.

Lindholm Schulz, Helena, and Michael Schulz. "The Middle East: Regional Instability and Fragmentation." In Mary Farrell et al. (eds.), *Global Politics of Regionalism: Theory and Practice*. London: Pluto Press, 2005: 187–201.

Looney, Robert. "The Broader Middle East Initiative: Requirements for Success in the Gulf." *Strategic Insights* 8 (2004). Online at: http://www.nps.edu/Academics/centers/ccc/publications/OnlineJournal/2004/aug/looneyAug04.html.

Low, Linda. *ASEAN Economic Co-operation and Challenges*. Singapore: Institute of Southeast Asian Studies, 2004.

Luciani, Giacomo, and Felix Neugart (eds.). *The EU and the GCC: A New Partnership*. Munich/Gütersloh: Bertelsmann Group for Policy Research, Center for Applied Policy Research/Bertelsmann Foundation, 2005.

Magone, José. *Challenging the Monroe Doctrine? The Relations between the European Union and Mercosur*. Hull: University of Hull, 2002. Online at: http://www.psa.ac.uk/journals/pdf/5/2002/magone.pdf.

Mahan, Alfred Thayer. "The Persian Gulf in International Relations." *National Review* (1902).

Mair, Stefan. "Die regionale Integration und Kooperation in Afrika südlich der Sahara." *Aus Politik und Zeitgeschichte* 52, nos.13–14 (2002): 15–23. Online at: http://www.bpb.de/files/NDVA5B.pdf.

Malamud, Andrés. "Presidentialism and Mercosur: A Hidden Cause for a Successful Experience." In Finn Laursen (ed.), *Comparative Regional Integration: Theoretical Perspectives*. Aldershot: Ashgate, 2003: 53–73.

Marchetti, Andreas. *The European Neighbourhood Policy: Foreign Policy at the EU's Periphery*. ZEI Discussion Paper C 158. Bonn: Center for European Integration Studies, 2006.

Marchetti, Andreas (ed.). *The CSCE as a Model to Transform Western Relations with the Greater Middle East*. ZEI Discussion Paper C 137. Bonn: Center for European Integration Studies, 2004.

Marchetti, Andreas (ed.). *Ten Years Euro-Mediterranean Partnership: Defining European Interests for the Next Decade*. ZEI Discussion Paper C 154. Bonn: Center for European Integration Studies, 2005.

Markwald, Ricardo Andrés, "Mercosul: Beyond 2000." In Helio Jaguaribe and Alvaro Vasconcelos (eds.), *The European Union, Mercosul and the New World Order*. London: Frank Cass, 2003: 70–101.

Massarrat, Mohssen. "Demokratisierung des Greater Middle East." *Aus Politik und Zeitgeschichte* 45 (2005): 30–37.

Masson, Paul, and Catherine Pattillo. "A Single Currency for Africa?" *Finance and Development* 12 (2004): 8–15.

Masson, Paul, and Catherine Pattillo. *The Monetary Geography of Africa*. Washington, D.C.: Brookings Institution Press, 2005.

Matthews, Alan. *Regional Integration and Food Security in Developing Countries.* Rome: Food and Agriculture Organization of the United Nations, 2003. Online at: http://www.fao.org//docrep/004/ y4793e/y4793e00.htm.

Mattli, Walter. *The Logic of Regional Integration: Europe and Beyond.* Cambridge and New York: Cambridge University Press, 1999.

Mattli, Walter. "The Vertical and Horizontal Dimensions of Regional Integration." In Finn Laursen (ed.), *Comparative Regional Integration: Theoretical Perspectives.* Aldershot: Ashgate, 2003: 273–282.

Mayer, Felix (ed.). *Managing Asymmetric Interdependencies within the Euro-Mediterranean Partnership.* ZEI Discussion Paper 101. Bonn: Center for European Integration Studies, 2002.

Mbeki, Thabo. *African Renaissance, South Africa and the World.* Speech at the United Nations University, 9 April 1998. Online at: http://www.unu.edu/unupress/mbeki.html.

McCormack, Mark H., and William E. Butler (eds.). *The Laws of Treaties in Russia and the Commonwealth of Independent States: Texts and Comments.* Cambridge: Cambridge University Press, 2002.

McDougall, Derek. "Humanitarian Intervention and Peacekeeping as Issues for Asia-Pacific Security." In James J. Hentz and Morten Boas (eds.), *New and Critical Security and Regionalism: Beyond the Nation-State.* Aldershot: Ashgate, 2003: 33–53.

Mehrotra, L.L. "SAARC and the Information Revolution". In Eric Gonsalves, and Nancy Jetly (eds.), *The Dynamics of South Asia: Regional Cooperation and SAARC.* New Delhi: Sage Publications, 1999: 131–135.

Melber, Henning. *The New African Initiative and the African Union. A Preliminary Assessment and Documentation.* Current African Issues no. 25, Uppsala: Nordiska Afrikainstitutet, 2001. Online at: http://www.nai.uu.se/publications/download.html/91–7106–486–9.pdf?id=24670.

Mickiewicz, Tomasz. *Economic Transition in Central Europe and the Commonwealth of Independent States.* Basingstoke: Palgrave Macmillan, 2005.

Minkner-Bünjer, Mechthild. "Zentralamerikas 'China(alb)träume': Herausforderungen und Zukunftsaussichten." *Brennpunkt Lateinamerika* 17 (2005): 197–208.

Mistry, Percy S. "Regional Integration and Economic Development." In Björn Hettne et al. (eds.), *The New Regionalism and the Future of Security and Development (The New Regionalism Series: vol. 4).* London: Macmillan, 2000: 26–49.

Mitrany, David. *A Working Peace System: An Argument for the Functional Development of International Organization.* London: Royal Institute International Relations, 1943.

Molchanov, Mikhail. "Regionalism and Globalization in the Post-Soviet Space." *Studies in Post-Communism* 9 (2005): 1–28. Online at: http://www.stfx.ca/pinstitutes/cpcs/studies-in-post-communism/Molchanov2005.pdf.

Moon, Woosik et al. "Monetary Cooperation in East Asia." In Woosik Moon and Bernadette Andreosso-O'Callaghan (eds.), *Regional Integration: Europe and Asia Compared.* Aldershot: Ashgate, 2005: 134–152.

Moon, Woosik, and Bernadette Andreosso-O'Callaghan (eds.). *Regional Integration: Europe and Asia Compared.* Aldershot: Ashgate, 2005.

Moore, Thomas G. "China's International Relations: The Economic Dimension." In Samuel S. Kim (ed.), *The International Relations of Northeast Asia.* Lanham: Rowman and Littlefield, 2004: 101–134.

Moravscik, Andrew. *The Choice for Europe: Social Purpose and State Power from Messina to Maastricht.* Ithaca: Cornell University Press, 1998.

Moreau, Françoise, "The Cotonou Agreement: New Orientations." *The Courier* 9 (2000): 6–10.

Mundell, Robert. "A Theory of Optimal Currency Areas." *American Economic Review* (September 1963): 657–665.

Muni, S.D. "India in SAARC: A Reluctant Policy Maker." In Björn Hettne et al. (eds.), *National Perspectives on the New Regionalism in the South (The New Regionalism Series: vol. 3).* London: Macmillan Press, 2000: 108–131.

Murithi, Timothy. *Institutionalising Pan-Africanism: Transforming African Union Values and Principles into Policy and Practice*. ISS Paper 143. Thswane (Pretoria): Institute for Security Studies, 2007.

Murithi, Timothy (ed.). *Towards a Union Government for Africa*. Thswane (Pretoria): Institute for Security Studies, 2008.

Murray, Philomena. "Toward a Research Agenda on the European Union as a Model of Regional Integration." *Asia-Pacific Journal of EU Studies* 2, no. 1 (2004): 33–51.

Murthy, Radhakrishna K. "The Pace, Patterns and Problems of Urbanization in the SAARC Countries." In K.C. Reddy and T. Nirmala Devi (eds.), *Regional Cooperation in South Asia: New Dimensions*. New Delhi: Kanishka Publishers, 2002: 106–139.

Mutschler, Claudia. "Comparative International Experiences: Latin America." In Christopher Clapham, et al. (eds.), *Regional Integration in Southern Africa: Comparative International Perspectives*. Johannesburg: The South African Institute of International Affairs, 2001: 137–165.

Mutume, Gumisai. "Pan African Parliament Now a Reality: 'A Sign of Democratic Maturity'." *African Recovery* 18, no. 1 (2004). Online at: http://www.un.org/ecosocdev/geninfo/afrec/vol18no1/181africa.htm.

Nahm, Andrew C. *Introduction to Korean History and Culture*. 9th ed. Elizabeth, NJ, and Seoul: Hollym, 2004.

Nakleh, Emile A. *The Gulf Cooperation Council: Policies, Problems and Prospects*. New York/Westport/London: Praeger, 1986.

Nathan, K.S. (ed.). *The European Union, United States and Asean: Challenges and Prospects for Cooperative Engagement in the 21st Century*. London: ASEAN Academic Press, 2002.

Nathan, Laurie. "'Organ Failure': A Review of the SADC Organ on Politics, Defence and Security." In Liisa Laakso (ed.), *Regional Integration for Conflict Prevention and Peace Building in Africa: Europe, SADC and ECOWAS*. Helsinki: University of Helsinki, 2002: 62–102.

Nelsen, Brent F., and Alexander Stubb (eds.). *The European Union: Readings on the Theory and Practice of European Integration*. Houndmills: Palgrave, 2003.

Nicholls, Shelton, et al. "Open Regionalism and Institutional Developments among the Smaller Integration Schemes of CARICOM, the Andean Community and the Central America Common Market." In Victor Bulmer-Thomas (ed.), *Regional Integration in Latin America and the Caribbean: The Political Economy of Open Regionalism*. London: University of London, Institute of Latin American Studies, 2001: 141–164.

Nicolaidis, Kalypso, and Robert Howse (eds.). *The Federal Vision: Legitimacy and Levels of Governance in the United States and in the European Union*. New York: Oxford University Press, 2001.

Nivet, Bastien. *Security by proxy? The EU and (sub-)regional organisations: the case of ECOWAS*. Paris: European Union Institute for Security Studies, 2006.

Organization of African Unity (OAU). *A New African Initiative merger of the Millennium Partnership for the African Recovery Programme (MAP) and Omega Plan* (11.07.2001). In Henning Melber, *The New African Initiative and the African Union. A Preliminary Assessment and Documentation*. Current African Issues no. 25. Uppsala: Nordiska Afrikainstitutet, 2001: App. 1. Online at: http://www.polity.org.za/html/govdocs/misc/mapomega.html?rebookmark=1 and http://www.nai.uu.se/publications/download.html/91-7106-486-9.pdf?id=24670.

Odén, Bertil. "The Southern Africa Region and the Regional Hegemon." In Björn Hettne et al. (eds.), *National Perspectives on the New Regionalism in the South (The New Regionalism Series: vol. 4)*. London: Macmillan, 2000: 242–264.

Odén, Bertil. "Regionalization in Southern Africa: The Role of the Dominant." In Michael Schulz et al. (eds.), *Regionalization in a Globalizing World: A Comparative Perspective on Forms, Actors and Processes*. London: Zed Books 2001: 82–99.

Öjendal, Joakim. "Regional Hydropolitics in Mainland South East Asia: A New Deal in a New Era?" In Björn Hettne, Andras Inotai and Osvaldo Sunkel (eds.), *The New Regionalism and the Future of Security and Development (The New Regionalism Series: vol. 4)*. London: Macmillan, 2000: 176–209.

Öjendal, Joakim. "South East Asia at a Constant Crossroads: An Ambiguous 'New Region.'" In Michael Schulz et al. (eds.), *Regionalization in a Globalizing World: A Comparative Perspective on Forms, Actors and Processes.* London: Zed Books, 2001: 147–172.

Olcott, Martha Brill, et al. *Getting It Wrong: Regional Cooperation and the Commonwealth of Independent States.* Washington, D.C.: Carnegie Endowment for International Peace, 1999.

Olukoshi, Adebayo. *West Africa's Political Economy in the Next Millennium: Retrospect and Prospect.* CODESRIA Monograph Series 2/2001. Dakar: Council for the Development of Social Science Research in Africa, 2001. Online at: http://www.codesria.org/Links/Publications/monographs/Adebayo_Olukoshi.pdf.

Pacific Islands Forum (PIF). *Agreement Establishing the Pacific Islands Forum Secretariat* (30.10.2000). Online at: http://www.forumsec.org/userfiles/file/2000%20Secretariat%20Agreement(1).pdf.

Pacific Islands Forum (PIF). *Pacific Agreement on Closer Economic Relations (PACER)* (18.08.2001). Online at: http://www.forumsec.org.fj/_resources/article/files/PACER%20-%20endorse%20&%20sign(18–8-01).pdf.

Pacific Islands Forum (PIF). *Pacific Island Countries Trade Agreement (PICTA)* (18.08.2001). Online at: http://www.forumsec.org.fj/_resources/article/files/PICTA%20-%20endorse%20&%20sign(18–8-01).pdf.

Pacific Islands Forum (PIF). *The Pacific Plan* (28.10.2005). Online at: http://www.forumsec.org.fj/org/_resources/main/files/Pacific%20Plan%20at%20Oct202005%20text.pdf.

Pacific Islands Forum (PIF). *Agreement Establishing the Pacific Islands Forum* (08.11.2005). Online at: http://www.forumsec.org/_resources/article/files/Forum%20Agreement%202005.pdf.

Papageorgiou, Giannis F. *The Regional Integration Process of Central America.* The Federalist Debate: Papers for Federalists in Europe and the World, No. 3. Torino: The Einstein Center for International Studies, 2001.

Payne, Anthony, and Paul Sutton. *Charting Caribbean Developments.* Gainesville: University Press of Florida, 2001.

Pedersen, Thomas. "Cooperative Hegemony: Power, Ideas and Institutions in Regional Integration." *Review of International Studies* 28, no. 4 (2002): 677–696.

Pena, Celina, and Ricardo Rozemberg. *Mercosur: A Different Approach to Institutional Development.* FOCAL Policy Paper 6, 2005. Online at: http://www.focal.ca/pdf/mercosur.pdf.

Peña, Felix. *Civil Society, Transparency and Legitimacy in Integration Processes and Trade Negotiations: Mercosur's Experience and Lessons for the Negotiations with the European Union.* Chaire Mercosur de Sciences Po Discussion Paper 1, 2003. Online at: http://www.felixpena.com.ar/index.php?contenido=wpapers&wpagno=documentos/2003-09-eng.

Peña, Felix, and Ramón Torrent (eds.). *Hacia Una Nueva Etapa en las Relaciones Unión Europea-América Latina: Un Diagnóstico Inicial.* Barcelona: Universidad de Barcelona, Observatorio de Relaciones Unión Europea-América Latina, 2005.

Pennetta, Piero. *Le Organizzazioni Internazionali dei Paesi in Via di Svipullo: Le Organizzazioni Economiche Regionali Africane.* Bari: Cacucci Editore, 1998.

Peres, Shimon. *The New Middle East.* New York: Holt, 1993.

Perkmann, Markus, and Ngai-Ling Sum (eds.). *Globalization, Regionalization and Cross-Border Regions.* Basingstoke and New York: Palgrave Macmillan, 2002.

Peterson, Erik R. *The Gulf Cooperation Council: Search for Unity in a Dynamic Region.* Boulder: Westview Press, 1988.

Peterson, John E. and Helen Sjursen (eds.). *A Common Foreign Policy for Europe? Competing Visions of the CFSP.* London and New York: Routledge, 1998.

Pinheiro Guimares, Samuel. "The International Political Role of MERCOSUL II." In Helio Jaguaribe and Alvaro Vasconcelos (eds.), *The European Union, Mercosul and the New World Order.* London: Frank Cass, 2003: 102–138.

Pikayev, Alexander A. "The Russian Debate on Policy Toward the 'Near Abroad'." In Lena Jonson, and Clive Archer (eds.), *Peacekeeping and the Role of Russia in Eurasia.* Boulder and Oxford: Westview Press, 1996: 51–66.

Plummer, Michael G. "The EU and ASEAN: Real Integration and Lessons in Financial Cooperation." *The World Economy* 25, no. 10 (2002): 1469–1500.

Pollack, Marc. *The Engines of European Integration: Delegation, Agency and Agenda Setting in the European Union.* Oxford: Oxford University Press, 2003.

Pollard, Duke (ed.). *The CARICOM System: Basic Instruments.* Kingston: The Caribbean Law Publishing Company, 2003.

Pöttering, Hans-Gert, and Ludger Kühnhardt. "EU-US: Plädoyer für einen Atlantischen Vertrag." *Integration* 26, no. 3 (2003): 244–250.

Preusse, Heinz G. *The New American Regionalism.* Cheltenham: Edward Elgar, 2004.

Quevedo, Fernando, and Luis Villela. *Regional Integration.* Washington, D.C.: Inter-American Development Bank, 2003. Online at: http://idbdocs.iadb.org/wsdocs/getdocument.aspx?docnum=353028.

Rabi, Uzi. "The Dynamics of Gulf Cooperation Council (GCC): The Ceaseless Quest for Regional Security in a Changing Region." *Orient* 45, no. 2 (2004): 281–295.

Rao, Venkata R. "Strategic Implications of Forced Migration in SAARC Countries: The Need for Pan South Asian Approach." In K.C. Reddy and T. Nirmala Devi (eds.), *Regional Cooperation in South Asia: New Dimensions.* New Delhi: Kanishka Publishers, 2002: 140–146.

Ravenhill, John. "Back to the Nest? Europe's Relations with the African, Carribbean, and Pacific Group of Countries." In Vinod K. Aggarwal and Edward A. Fogarty (eds.), *EU Trade Strategies: Between Regionalism and Globalism.* Houndmills: Palgrave Macmillan, 2004: 118–147.

Reddy, K.C., and T. Nirmala Devi (eds.). *Regional Cooperation in South Asia: New Dimensions.* New Delhi: Kanishka Publishers, 2002.

Reid, T.R. *The United States of Europe: The New Superpower and the End of the American Supremacy.* New York: Penguin Press, 2004.

Reischauer, Edwin O. *Japan: The Story of a Nation.* 3rd ed. Tokyo: Tuttle, 1982.

Rifkind, Jeremy. *The European Dream: How Europe's Vision of the Future is Quietly Eclipsing the American Dream.* Cambridge: Polity Press, 2004.

Robles, Alfredo C., Jr. "The Association of Southeast Asian Nations (ASEAN) and the European Union: Limited Interregionalism." In Heiner Hänggi et al. (eds.), *Interregionalism and International Relations.* Abingdon and New York: Routledge, 2006: 97–112.

Rodlauer, Markus, and Alfred Schipke (eds.). *Central America: Global Integration and Regional Cooperation.* Occasional Paper No. 243. Washington, D.C.: International Monetary Fund, 2005.

Rolfe, Jim. "New Zealand and the South Pacific." *Revue Juridique Polynesienne* 1 (2001): 157–169.

Rolfe, Jim. "Peacekeeping the Pacific Way in Bougainville." *International Peacekeeping* 8, no. 4 (2001): 38–55.

Rolfe, Jim (ed.). *The Asia-Pacific: A Region in Transition.* Honolulu: Asia-Pacific Center for Security, 2004.

Rosamond, Ben. *Theories of European Integration.* Houndmills: Palgrave, 2000.

Rostow, Walt W. *The Stages of Economic Growth: A Non-Communist Manifesto.* Cambridge: Cambridge University Press, 1960.

Rozman, Gilbert. "Russian Foreign Policy in Northeast Asia." In Samuel S. Kim (ed.), *The International Relations of Northeast Asia.* Lanham: Rowman and Littlefield, 2004: 201–224.

Rubio Ríos, Arnoldo (ed.). *Estudios Europeos y Integración Regional.* San Juan: Universidad Nacional, 2005.

Ruggie, John Gerard (ed.). *Multilateralism Matters: The Theory and Praxis of an International Form.* New York: Columbia University Press, 1993.

Ruiz Díaz Labrano, Roberto. *Mercosur, Integracion y Derecho.* Buenos Aires: Ciudadargentina, 1998.

Rüland, Jürgen. *ASEAN and the European Union: A Bumpy Interregional Relationship.* ZEI Discussion Paper C 95. Bonn: Center for European Integration Studies, 2001.

Rüland, Jürgen. "Interregionalism. An Unfinished Agenda." In Heiner Hänggi et al. (eds.), *Interregionalism and International Relations*. Abingdon and New York: Routledge, 2006.

Rule, Steven P. "Option for the Composition of a Pan-African Parliament." In Manelisi Genge et al., *African Union and a Pan-African Parliament*. Pretoria: Africa Institute of South Africa, 2000: 30–37.

Russett, Bruce M. *International Regions and the International System: A Study in Political Ecology*. Chicago: RandMcNally, 1968.

Sabur, A.K.M. Abdus, and Mohammad Humayun Kabir. *Conflict Management and Sub-Regional Cooperation in ASEAN: Relevance for SAARC*. Dhaka: Academic Press, 2000.

Sánchez, Rafael. "Rebuilding the Central American Bloc in the 1990s: An Intergovernmentalist Approach to Integration." In Finn Laursen (ed.), *Comparative Regional Integration: Theoretical Perspectives*. Aldershot: Ashgate, 2003: 31–52.

Santander, Sebastian. "The European Partnership with Mercosur: A Relationship based on Strategic and Neo-Liberal Principles." *Journal of European Integration* 27, no. 3 (2005): 285–306.

Sandwick, John A. (ed.). *The Gulf Cooperation Council: Moderation and Stability in an Interdependent World*. Boulder: Westview Press, 1987.

Sauer, Carl Ortwin. "The Morphology in Landscape." *University of California Publications in Geography* 2 (1925): 19–54.

Sbragia, Alberta. "European Union and NAFTA." In Mario Telò (ed.), *European Union and New Regionalism: Regional Actors and Global Governance in a Post-Hegemonic Era*. Aldershot: Ashgate, 2001: 97–109.

Scheffler, Thomas. "'Fertile Crescent,' 'Orient,' 'Middle East': The Changing Mental Maps of Southwest Asia." *European Review of History* 10, no. 2 (2003): 253–272.

Schmidt, Axel. "Die ASEAN-Charter: Die Quadratur des Kreises oder der Scheideweg der Region?" *FES-Kurzberichte aus der internationalen Entwicklungszusammenarbeit* 11 (2005): 1–4. Online at: http:// library.fes.de/pdf-files/iez/03175.pdf.

Schmidt, Siegmar. "Aktuelle Aspekte der EU-Entwicklungspolitik: Aufbruch zu neuen Ufern?" *Aus Politik und Zeitgeschichte* 19–20 (2002): 29–38.

Schulz, Michael, et al. (eds.). *Regionalization in a Globalizing World: A Comparative Perspective on Forms, Actors and Processes*. London: Zed Books, 2001.

Shams, Rasul. *Regional Integration in Developing Countries: Some Lessons Based on Case Studies*. Hamburg: Hamburger Weltwirtschafts-Archiv, 2003. Online at: http://ageconsearch.umn.edu/bitstream/26272/1/dp030251.pdf.

Shenfield, Stephen D. (ed.). *Transborder and Interregional Cooperation Between Russia and the Commonwealth of Independent States*. Armonk, NY: M.E. Sharpe, 2005.

Shibuya, Eric. "The Problems and Potential of the Pacific Islands Forum." In Jim Rolfe (ed.), *The Asia-Pacific: A Region in Transition*. Honolulu: Asia-Pacific Center for Security Studies, 2004: 102–115. Online at: http://www.apcss.org/Publications/Edited%20Volumes/RegionalFinal%20chapters/Chapter7Shibuya.pdf.

Slocum, Nikki, and Luk van Langenhove. "*The Meaning of Regional Integration: Introducing Positioning Theory in Regional Integration Studies*. UNU-CRIS e-Working paper, W-2003/5. Bruges: United Nations University-CRIS, 2003: 12. Online at: http://www.cris.unu.edu/fileadmin/workingpapers/Nikki%20and%20Luk%20WP.pdf.

Smith, Hazel. "Actually Existing Foreign Policy—Or Not? The EU in Latin and Central America." In John Petersen and Helene Sjursen (eds.), *A Common Foreign Policy for Europe? Competing Visions of the CFSP*. London and New York: Routledge, 1998: 152–168.

Smith, Karen. *European Union Foreign Policy in a Changing World*. Oxford: Polity Press, 2003.

Smith, Rosaleen, et al. "Big Brother? Australia's Image in the South Pacific." *Australian Journal of International Affairs* 51, no. 1 (1997): 37–52.

Söderbaum, Fredrik. "The Role of the Regional Factor in West Africa." In Björn Hettne et al. (eds.), *The New Regionalism and the Future of Security and Development (The New Regionalism Series: vol. 4)*. London: Macmillan, 2000: 121–143.

Söderbaum, Fredrik. "Turbulent Regionalization in West Africa." In Michael Schulz et al. (eds.), *Regionalization in a Globalizing World: A Comparative Perspective on Forms, Actors and Processes*. London: Zed Books, 2001: 61–81.

Söderbaum, Fredrik. *The Political Economy of Regionalism: The Case of Southern Africa*. Basingstoke: Palgrave Macmillan, 2004.

Söderbaum, Fredrik, and Timothy M. Shaw (eds.). *Theories of New Regionalism: A Palgrave Reader*. Houndmills and New York: Palgrave Macmillan, 2003.

Söderbaum, Fredrik, and Ian Taylor (eds.). *Regionalism and Uneven Development in Southern Africa: The Case of the Maputo Development Corridor*. Aldershot: Ashgate, 2003.

Söderbaum, Fredrik, and Luk van Langenhove. "The EU as a Global Actor and the Role of Inter-regionalism." *Journal of European Integration* 27, no. 3 (2005): 249–262.

Solidum, Estrella D. *The Politics of ASEAN: An Instrument on Southeast Asian Regionalism*. Singapore: Eastern University Press, 2003.

South Asian Association for Regional Cooperation (SAARC). *Charter of the South Asian Association for Regional Cooperation* (08.12.1985). Online at: http://www.saarc-sec.org/data/docs/charter.pdf.

South Asian Association for Regional Cooperation (SAARC). *Regional Convention on Suppression of Terrorism* (04.11.1987). Online at: http://treaties.un.org/doc/db/Terrorism/Conv18-english.pdf.

South Asian Association for Regional Cooperation (SAARC). *Agreement on SAARC Preferential Trading Arrangement (SAPTA)* (11.04.1993). Online at: http://www.saarc-sec.org/data/agenda/economic/sapta/sapta.pdf.

South Asian Association for Regional Cooperation (SAARC). *Social Charter* (04.01.2004). Online at: http://www.saarc-sec.org/main.php?id=13.

South Asian Association for Regional Cooperation (SAARC). *Agreement on South Asian Free Trade Area (SAFTA)* (06.01.2004). Online at: http://www.saarc-sec.org/data/agenda/economic/safta/SAFTA%20AGREEMENT.pdf.

South Asian Association for Regional Cooperation (SAARC). *Additional Protocol to the Regional Convention on Suppression of Terrorism* (06.01.2004). Online at: http://www.satp.org/satporgtp/southasia/documents/papers/SAARC_pak.htm.

South Asian Association for Regional Cooperation (SAARC). *Agreement for Establishment of SAARC Arbitration Council* (13.11.2005). Online at: http://www.slmfa.gov.lk/saarc/images/agreements/saarc_arbitration_council%20_2005.pdf.

South Asian Association for Regional Cooperation (SAARC). Thirteenth SAARC Summit. *Dhaka Declaration* (13.11.2005). Online at: http://www.saarc-sec.org/main.php?id=159&t=7.1.

Southern African Development Community (SADC). *Consolidated Text of the Treaty of the Southern African Development Community* (17.08.1992). Online at: http://www.sadc.int/index/browse/page/120.

Southern African Development Community (SADC). *Protocol on Politics, Defence and Security Co-operation* (14.08.2001). Online at: http://www.sadc.int/index/browse/page/157.

Southern African Development Community (SADC). *Principles and Guidelines Governing Democratic Elections* (19.08.2004). Online at: http://www.sadc.int.

Southern Common Market (MERCOSUR). *Southern Common Market (MERCOSUR) Agreement* (26.03.1991). Online at: http://www.worldtradelaw.net/fta/agreements/mercosurfta.pdf.

Southern Common Market (MERCOSUR). *Protocol of Ouro Preto* (17.12.1994). Online at: http://www.sice.oas.org/Trade/MRCSR/Ourop/ourop_e.asp.

Stadelbauer, Jörg. "Die GUS zwischen Integration und Fragmentierung: Zehn Jahre GUS—eine Zwangsgemeinschaft von Erben." *Praxis Geographie* 32, no. 1 (2002): 4–9.

Stephan, John J. *The Russian Far East: A History*. Stanford: Stanford University Press, 1994.

Strezhneva, Marina. *Social Culture and Regional Governance: Comparison of the European Union and Post-Soviet Experiences*. Commack: Nova Science Publishers, 1999.

Sturm, Michael, and Siegfried Nikolaus. *Regional Monetary Integration in the Member States of the Gulf Cooperation Council*. Frankfurt: European Central Bank, 2003.

Sturm, Peter. "Das Unbekannte planen." *Frankfurter Allgemeine Zeitung*, no. 26, 1 February 2005.

Sturman, Kathryn. *New Growth on Deep Rocks? Prospects for an African Union Government*. IIS Paper 146. Thswane (Pretoria): Institute for Security Studies, 2007.

Swatuk, Larry A. "Power and Water: The Coming Order of Southern Africa." In Björn Hettne et al. (eds.), *The New Regionalism and the Future of Security and Development (The New Regionalism Series: vol. 4)*. London: Macmillan, 2000: 210–247.

Syed, M.H. *SAARC Challenges Ahead*. New Delhi: Kilaso Books, 2003.

Taccone, Juan José, and Uziel Nogueira (eds.). *Central American Report No. 2*. Buenos Aires: Institute for the Integration of Latin America and the Caribbean, 2004. Online at: http://www.iadb.org/intal/aplicaciones/uploads/publicaciones/i-Central_American_Report_2.pdf.

Tan, Gerald. *ASEAN Economic Development and Cooperation*. Singapore: Eastern Universities Press, 2003.

Tavares, Rodrigo. *The State of the Art of Regionalism: The Past, Present and Future of a Discipline*. UNU-CRIS e-working paper, W-2004/10. Bruges: United Nations University-CRIS, 2004. Online at: http://www.cris.unu.edu/fileadmin/workingpapers/WProdrigo%20tavares.pdf.

Telò, Mario (ed.). *European Union and New Regionalism: Regional Actors and Global Governance in a Post-Hegemonic Era*. Aldershot: Ashgate, 2001.

Telò, Mario. *Europe, A Civilian Power? European Union, Global Governance, World Power*. New York: Palgrave Macmillan, 2006.

Than, Mya and George Abonyi. "The Greater Mekong Sugregion: Co-Operation in Infrastructure and Finance." In Carolyn L. Gates and Mya Than (eds.), *ASEAN Enlargement: Impacts and Implications*. Singapore: Institute of Southeast Asian Studies, 2001: 128–163.

The Economist. "The Carribbean: Living and Dying on History and Artificial Economic Sweeteners."(24 September 2005): 61–62.

The Economist. 29 October 2005: 63.

Thompson, William R. "The Regional Subsystem: A Conceptual Explication and a Propositional Inventory." *International Studies Quarterly* 17, no. 1 (1973): 89–117.

Thongpakde, Nattapong. "Impact and Implications of ASEAN Enlargement on Trade." In Carolyn L. Gates and Mya Than (eds.), *ASEAN Enlargement: Impacts and Implications*. Singapore: Institute of Southeast Asian Studies, 2001: 45–79.

Tripp, Charles."Regional Organization in the Arab Middle East." In Louise Fawcett and Andrew Hurrell (eds.), *Regionalism in World Politics: Regional Organization and International Order*. Oxford: Oxford University Press, 1995: 283–308.

Turck, Mary. *South American Community of Nations*. Minneapolis: Resource Center of the Americas, 2005.

Ulate Chacón, Enrique. "Naturaleza Jurídica de las Comunidades Europeas y la Comunidad Centroamericana." In Arnoldo Rubio Ríos (ed.), *Estudios Europeos y Integración Regional*. San Juan: Universidad Nacional, 2005.

United Nations Development Programme (ed.). *Arab Human Development Report 2002: Creating Opportunities for Future Generations*. New York: UNDP Bureau for Arab States, 2003.

United Nations Development Programme (ed.). *Arab Human Development Report 2003: Building a Knowledge Society*. New York: UNDP Bureau for Arab States, 2004.

United Nations Development Programme (ed.). *Arab Human Development Report 2004: Toward Freedom in the Arab World*. New York: UNDP Bureau for Arab States, 2005.

United Nations Development Programme (ed.). *Human Development Report 2006, Beyond Scarcity: Power, Poverty and the Global Water Crisis*. New York: United Nations Development Programme, 2006.

United States Department of State. *A Performance-Based Roadmap to a Permanent Two-State Solution to the Israeli-Palestinian Conflict* (30.03.2003). Online at: http://www.state.gov/r/pa/prs/ps/2003/20062.htm.

Upreti, B.C. (ed.). *SAARC: Dynamics of Regional Cooperation in South Asia*, 2 vols. New Delhi: Kalinga Publications, 2000.

Van Langenhove, Luk. *Theorising Regionhood*. UNU-CRIS e-working papers, W-2003/1. Bruges: United Nations University-CRIS, 2003. Online at: http://www.cris.unu.edu/fileadmin/working-papers/paper%20regionhood.pdf.

Van Langenhove, Luk, et al. *From Multilateralism to Multiregionalism: What Role for Regional Integration in Global Governance?* UNU-CRIS Occasional Papers, O- 2004/5. Bruges: United Nations University-CRIS, 2004. Online at: http://www.cris.unu.edu/fileadmin/workingpapers/EurParliament%20OP.pdf.

Verhofstadt, Guy. "The Paradox of Anti-Globalisation." *The Guardian*, 28 September 2001. Online at: http://www.guardian.co.uk/world/2001/sep/28/globalisation.

Viner, Jacob. *The Customs Union Issue*. New York: Carnegie Endowment for International Peace, 1950.

Waltz, Kenneth. *Theory of International Politics*. Reading, MA: Addison-Wesley, 1979.

Weiland, Heribert. "The European Union and Southern Africa: Interregionalism between Vision and Reality." In Heiner Hänggi et al. (eds.), *Interregionalism and International Relations*. Abingdon and New York: Routledge, 2006: 185–198.

Wendt, Alexander. *Social Theory of International Politics*. Cambridge and New York: Cambridge University Press, 1999.

West African Economic and Monetary Union (UEMOA). *Traité de l'union économique et monétaire Ouest Africaine (UEMOA)* (10.01.1994). Online at: http://www.banque-france.fr/fr/Eurosys/telechar/zonefr/uemoa001.pdf.

Wiener, Antje, and Thomas Diez. *European Integration Theory*. Oxford: Oxford University Press, 2004.

Williams, Paul D. "From Non-Intervention to Non-Indifference: The Origins and Development of the African Union's Security Culture." *African Affairs* 106 (2007): 253–279.

Wolters, O.W. *History, Culture and Religion in Southeast Asian Perspectives*. Ithaca: Cornell University Press, 2000.

World Bank (ed.). *World Development Report 2006*. Online at: http://econ.worldbank.org/external/default/main?pagePK=64165259&theSitePK=469372&piPK=64165421&menuPK=64166093&entityID=000112742_20050920110826.

Yu, Hyun-Seok. "Asian Regionalism: A Post-Crisis Perspective." In Woosik Moon and Bernadette Andreosso-O'Callaghan (eds.), *Regional Integration: Europe and Asia Compared*. Aldershot: Ashgate, 2005: 28–48.

Zielonka, Jan. *Europe as Empire: The Nature of the Enlarged European Union*. Oxford: Oxford University Press, 2006.

Zimmek, Martin. *Integrationsprozesse in Lateinamerika: Aktuelle Herausforderungen in Mittelamerika und der Andenregion*. ZEI Discussion Paper C 153. Bonn: Center for European Integration Studies, 2005.

Internet resources, last date of access: November 2009.

INDEX

ABOUT THE AUTHOR

DR. LUDGER KÜHNHARDT has been Professor of Political Science and Director of the Center for European Integration Studies (ZEI) at the University of Bonn since 1997. After studying history, philosophy, and political science at Bonn, Geneva, Tokyo, and Harvard, and defending his dissertation (1983) and *Habilitation* thesis (1986) at the University of Bonn, he worked as a speechwriter for then German Federal President Richard von Weizsäcker from 1987 to 1989. He was Professor of Political Science at the University of Freiburg between 1991 and 1997, where he also served as Dean of his faculty. He has been Visiting Professor at the College of Europe, the University of Cape Town, the University of Jena, Dartmouth College, Stanford University, Seoul National University, and St Antony's College Oxford. He currently is Visiting Professor at the Catholic University of Milan (since 1997), the Diplomatic Academy Vienna (since 2002), and the Mediterranean Academy of Diplomatic Studies, Malta (since 2007). He has also worked as a Public Policy Fellow at the Woodrow Wilson International Center for Scholars in Washington, D.C. Kühnhardt has widespread experience in academic and political consultancy work. His books include *Die Flüchtlingsfrage als Weltordnungsproblem* (1984); *Die Universalität der Menschenrechte* (1987); *Stufen der Souveränität* (1992); *Europäische Union und föderale Idee* (1993); *Revolutionszeiten: Das Umbruchjahr 1989 im geschichtlichen Zusammenhang* (1994, also in Turkish); *Von der ewigen Suche nach Frieden* (1996); *Zukunftsdenker: Bewährte Ideen des politischen Denkens für das dritte Jahrtausend* (1999); *Atlantik-Brücke: Fünfzig Jahre deutsch-amerikanische Partnerschaft* (2002); *Constituting Europe: Identity, Institution-Building and the Search for a Global Role* (2003); *Erweiterung und Vertiefung* (2005); *European Union—The Second Founding: The Changing Rationale of European Integration* (2008; 2nd revised edition 2010); and *Crises in European Integration. Challenges and Responses, 1945–2005* (2009).